The Red Wings Book

THE MOST COMPLETE DETROIT RED WINGS FACT BOOK EVER PUBLISHED

HOCKEY
·OFFICIAL PROGRAM AND GUIDE·
OLYMPIA
GRAND RIVER AVE. AT McGRAW, DETROIT, MICH.

THE RED WINGS BOOK

1997

The most complete Detroit Red Wings fact book ever published

ANDREW PODNIEKS

ECW PRESS

CANADIAN CATALOGUING IN PUBLICATION DATA

Podnieks, Andrew

The Red Wings Book : the most complete
Detroit Red Wings fact book ever published

ISBN 1-55022-283-X

1. Detroit Red Wings (Hockey team). I. Title.

GV848.D4P62 1996 796.962′64′0977434 C96-990051-1

Design and imaging by ECW Type & Art, Oakville, Ontario.
Printed and bound by Webcom, Scarborough, Ontario.

Distributed by General Distribution Services,
30 Lesmill Road, Don Mills, Ontario M3B 2T6.
(416) 445-3333, (800) 387-0172 (Canada), FAX (416) 445-5967.

Published by ECW PRESS,
2120 Queen Street East, Suite 200
Toronto, Ontario M4E 1E2.

TABLE OF CONTENTS

The Red Wings Book

THE BIRTH OF THE RED WINGS

Detroit was granted an NHL franchise on September 25, 1926. The team was bought by local businessmen who took the Victoria Cougars of the Western Canadian Hockey League and moved them, with the nickname, to the Motor City and established the Detroit Hockey Club Incorporated. For the 1926–27 season, the Cougars played out of the Windsor Arena (more often referred to as the Border Cities Arena) on the Canadian side of the Detroit River. The Arena had been built the previous year for that city's Ontario Hockey Association team and was the largest in the OHA loop with a seating capacity of 6,000. Many of those fans came by boat from Detroit, and the following year, when the NHL arrived, the Arena's seating was increased to 9,000.

The Cougars weren't supposed to play many games in Windsor, but construction delays of their own stadium forced them to play out of the Border Cities Arena for the entirety of their inaugural season. Faithful Detroit fans had to buy their tickets in Detroit, pay an amusement tax at the time of purchase, and then pay a "War Tax" on the Canadian side when travelling to the games!

The following season, the Cougars finally had a native home — the Olympia on Grand River Avenue. Designed by Charles Howard Crane, this stadium housed the largest indoor skating rink in the United States when it opened in 1927. Crane was better known in Detroit and across America for his theatres. He built the Capital (1922), the State (1925), and the United Artists Theatre (1928) before creating the grandest of them all, the 5,000 seat Fox Theatre (also 1928). He also designed the Orchestra Hall (1919) which served as the home to the Detroit Symphony until 1955.

The Olympia was constructed at a cost of $1,259,300 and was of importance primarily for its Romanesque design on the outside and its refrigeration system on the inside (the latter which operated thanks to 74,800 feet of piping used to carry the brine coolant needed to make ice). The entrance was also designed to accommodate 13 retail stores along Grand River and McGraw.

The Olympia was a momument to contruction and the modern age, but the hockey club wasn't very good yet. In 1930, in an attempt to change the team's fortunes, the nickname was changed to Falcons. This had little effect on the team's ability to win, and coupled with the financial toll exacted by the Great Depression, the Club staggered under great losses. On April 28, 1932, the Union Guardian Trust Company filed a notice of default on the mortgage and on July 28, 1933 the Detroit Hockey Club was ordered to pay $776,770. Unable to do so, the mortgage was foreclosed on November 4 and the Trust Company took possession of the team and property. Later that month, however, James Norris, a grain broker from Chicago, bought the team and renamed it Red Wings after the Winged Wheelers, a team Norris played for in Montreal during his youth. Norris also imported the wheel insignia which he saw as a natural representation of Detroit's place as the centre of the nation's automobile industry.

The Olympia remained unaltered until 1965 when the northeast part of the building was enlarged to allow for 1,800 additional seats. At this time, all 13,000 seats were replaced (at $23 each), a new piping system was installed, new boards were added and a new scoreclock was hoisted above centre ice (a few years later, private boxes were also installed). However, the decline of the neighbourhood, the ageing of the building, and the need to increase revenues soon made the old red barn obsolete. The Red Wings left the Olympia for the city's new sports palace — the Joe Louis Arena. The last game to be played was an old-timers vs. current Red Wings game (won by the youngsters 6–2) on February 21, 1980. The last goal ever scored at the Olympia was scored by Gordie Howe.

The Red Wings played their first home game at the Joe Louis on December 27, 1979 and the Norris family continued to own the club until June 1982 when Bruce Norris sold the Wings to current owner Mike Ilitch. Detroit has won more Stanley Cups than any other American team (seven), and the club, now in its 71st season, continues to thrive as a result of remarkable fan support.

OWNERSHIP — DETROIT RED WINGS HOCKEY CLUB

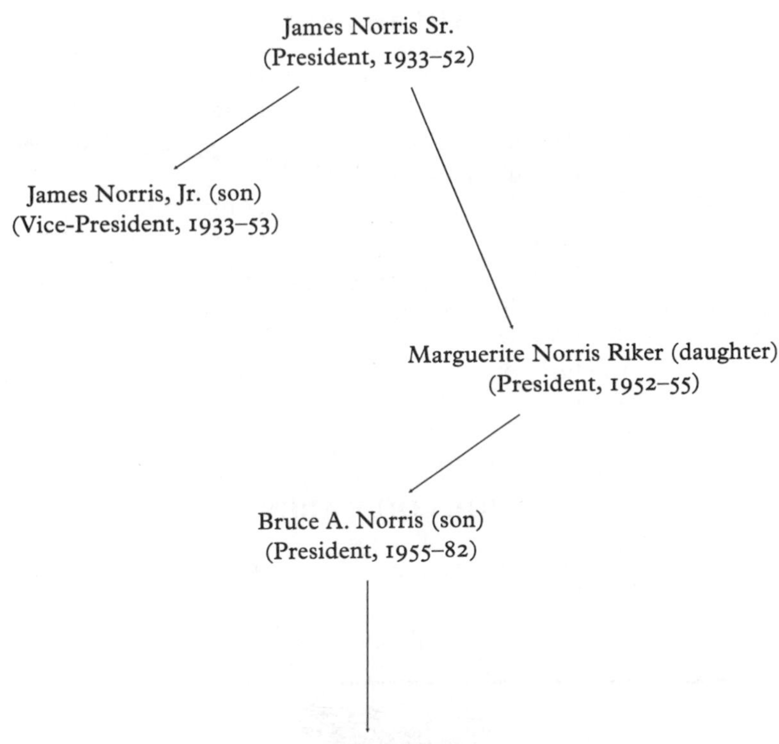

Mike Ilitch
(President, 1982–present)

SEATING CAPACITY

THE OLYMPIA

1947–48	11,900
1948–64	12,500 (14,500)
1964–65	13,000 (14,500)
1965–66	13,375 (16,375)
1966–69	13,192 (15,692)
1969–70	13,235 (15,400)
1970–71	13,500 (15,665)
1971–72	13,808 (15,808)
1972–78	14,200 (16,200)
1978–79	14,700 (16,700)

JOE LOUIS ARENA

1979–96	19,275

This is to certify that ____________________
was present at the opening hockey game in the

Joe Louis Sports Arena

on this the twenty-seventh day of December
nineteen hundred and seventy-nine
Detroit Red Wings vs. St. Louis Blues

Signed: Coleman A. Young — *Signed:* Ted Lindsay

Coleman A. Young, Mayor
City of Detroit

Ted Lindsay, General Manager
Detroit Hockey Club

PROGRAM PRICES

1926–27	10 cents
1927–44	15 cents
1946–60	25 cents
1960–63	35 cents
1964–66	50 cents
1968–71	75 cents
1971–72	$1.00
1982–83	$2.00
1992–93	$4.00
1993–present	$3.00

HOME OPENERS

WINDSOR ARENA

November 18, 1926	Boston	0–2

THE OLYMPIA

November 22, 1927	Ottawa	1–2
November 15, 1928	Rangers	0–2
November 14, 1929	Boston	2–5
November 13, 1930	Rangers	1–0
November 12, 1931	Americans	2–5
November 10, 1932	Chicago	3–1
November 12, 1933	Americans	5–2
November 11, 1934	Boston	2–4
November 10, 1935	Rangers	1–1 (OT)
November 8, 1936	Rangers	5–2
November 7, 1937	Rangers	0–3
November 6, 1938	Boston	1–4
November 5, 1939	Rangers	1–1 (OT)
November 3, 1940	Americans	4–2
November 2, 1941	Americans	3–3
November 1, 1942	Boston	3–0
October 31, 1943	Rangers	8–3
October 29, 1944	Boston	7–1
October 28, 1945	Boston	7–0
October 16, 1946	Toronto	3–3
October 15, 1947	Chicago	4–2
October 13, 1948	Chicago	3–1
October 12, 1949	Boston	2–1
October 11, 1950	Rangers	3–2
October 11, 1951	Boston	1–0
October 9, 1952	Rangers	5–3
October 8, 1953	Rangers	4–1
October 7, 1954	Toronto	2–1
October 6, 1955	Chicago	2–3
October 11, 1956	Chicago	3–1
October 10, 1957	Rangers	2–3
October 12, 1958	Rangers	3–0
October 11, 1959	Rangers	4–2
October 6, 1960	Chicago	2–4
October 12, 1961	Toronto	2–4
October 14, 1962	Canadiens	3–1
October 10, 1963	Chicago	5–3

October 15, 1964	Toronto	3–5
October 24, 1965	Toronto	3–0
October 22, 1966	Chicago	4–7
October 15, 1967	Rangers	3–2
October 13, 1968	Toronto	1–2
October 11, 1969	Toronto	3–2
October 10, 1970	California	5–3
October 9, 1971	Minnesota	2–4
October 7, 1972	Rangers	5–3
October 13, 1973	Boston	4–9
October 9, 1974	Chicago	2–1
October 8, 1975	St. Louis	1–1
October 7, 1976	Washington	3–3
October 13, 1977	Toronto	3–3
October 11, 1978	St. Louis	4–5

JOE LOUIS ARENA

October 20, 1979	Flyers	3–7
October 16, 1980	Islanders	4–6
October 15, 1981	St. Louis	6–3
October 8, 1982	Minnesota	3–3
October 8, 1983	New Jersey	3–6
October 13, 1984	New Jersey	4–1
October 10, 1985	Minnesota	5–6
October 11, 1986	Chicago	4–3
October 16, 1987	Toronto	3–2
October 14, 1988	St. Louis	8–8
October 12, 1989	Winnipeg	5–4
October 10, 1990	Calgary	6–5
October 10, 1991	Canadiens	1–4
October 15, 1992	Quebec	2–4
October 13, 1993	St. Louis	2–5
January 20, 1995*	Chicago	4–1
October 13, 1995	Edmonton	9–0
October 9, 1996	Edmonton	2–0

OVERALL RECORD: 37–25–9

* opener delayed by owners' lockout

GAMES-TO-DAYS RATIO

YEAR	GAMES	DAYS	AVERAGE
1926–27	44	129	2.93
1927–28	44	131	2.98
1928–29	44	120	2.73
1929–30	44	125	2.84
1930–31	44	130	2.95
1931–32	48	130	2.71
1932–33	48	130	2.71
1933–34	48	130	2.71
1934–35	48	127	2.65
1935–36	48	134	2.79
1936–37	48	136	2.83
1937–38	48	137	2.85
1938–39	48	134	2.79
1939–40	48	137	2.85
1940–41	48	136	2.83
1941–42	48	139	2.90
1942–43	50	138	2.76
1943–44	50	141	2.82
1944–45	50	141	2.82
1945–46	50	140	2.80
1946–47	60	158	2.63
1947–48	60	158	2.63
1948–49	60	158	2.63
1949–50	70	166	2.37
1950–51	70	166	2.37
1951–52	70	165	2.36
1952–53	70	165	2.36
1953–54	70	165	2.36
1954–55	70	165	2.36
1955–56	70	165	2.36
1956–57	70	165	2.36
1957–58	70	165	2.36
1958–59	70	163	2.33
1959–60	70	163	2.33
1960–61	70	166	2.37
1961–62	70	165	2.36
1962–63	70	165	2.36
1963–64	70	165	2.36
1964–65	70	165	2.36
1965–66	70	163	2.33
1966–67	70	166	2.37
1967–68	74	173	2.34
1968–69	76	171	2.25
1969–70	76	177	2.33
1970–71	78	177	2.27
1971–72	78	176	2.26
1972–73	78	177	2.27
1973–74	78	180	2.31
1974–75	80	180	2.25
1975–76	80	180	2.25
1976–77	80	179	2.29
1977–78	80	179	2.29
1978–79	80	180	2.25
1979–80	80	180	2.25
1980–81	80	178	2.23
1981–82	80	181	2.26
1982–83	80	180	2.25
1983–84	80	180	2.25
1984–85	80	179	2.24
1985–86	80	179	2.24
1986–87	80	179	2.24
1987–88	80	180	2.25
1988–89	80	179	2.24
1989–90	80	179	2.24
1990–91	80	179	2.24
1991–92	80	186	2.23
1992–93	84	179	2.13
1993–94	84	191	2.27
1994–95	48	104	2.17
1995–96	82	192	2.34
1996–97	82	190	2.32

TRAINERS

Honey Walker	1928–1958
Lefty Wilson	1958–1982
Jim Pengelly	1982–1985
Bert Godin	1985–1986
Mark Brennan	1986–1994
John Wharton	1994–present

Lefty Wilson

FEBRUARY 29 RECORDS

The Red Wings have played six Leap Year games in their history, with a record of 3–3.

1940	Detroit 1 at Toronto 3
1964	Detroit 1 at Boston 2
1968	Rangers 4 at Detroit 2
1972	Vancouver 2 at Detroit 8
1992	Detroit 3 at St. Louis 2
1996	Islanders 1 at Detroit 5

GAMES PLAYED CHRISTMAS DAY

December 25 games at the Olympia were a long-standing tradition in Detroit until the Players' Association won the right to holidays. The Red Wings played 38 games Christmas Day with a record of 14–18–6.

1926	Detroit 0 at Chicago 2
1930	Toronto 1 at Detroit 10
1932	Chicago 0 at Detroit 4
1933	Ottawa 6 at Detroit 3
1934	Chicago 2 at Detroit 1
1935	Chicago 2 at Detroit 0
1936	Chicago 1 at Detroit 1 (OT)
1937	Detroit 1 at Toronto 1 (OT)
1938	Canadiens 1 at Detroit 4
1939	Canadiens 1 at Detroit 3
1940	Toronto 2 at Detroit 3
1941	Americans 2 at Detroit 3 (OT)
1942	Rangers 3 at Detroit 1
1944	Toronto 4 at Detroit 6
1945	Toronto 3 at Detroit 6
1946	Toronto 2 at Detroit 1
1947	Rangers 2 at Detroit 0
1948	Detroit 1 at Toronto 2
1949	Canadiens 2 at Detroit 4
1950	Rangers 1 at Detroit 4
1951	Rangers 1 at Detroit 2
1952	Chicago 3 at Detroit 3
1954	Detroit 3 at Toronto 2
1955	Toronto 1 at Detroit 1
1956	Rangers 1 at Detroit 8
1957	Detroit 1 at Boston 4
1958	Toronto 2 at Detroit 0
1959	Rangers 5 at Detroit 2
1960	Chicago 3 at Detroit 0
1961	Rangers 6 at Detroit 4
1962	Toronto 1 at Detroit 2
1963	Rangers 3 at Detroit 4
1964	Canadiens 2 at Detroit 2
1965	Detroit 3 at Canadiens 4
1966	Canadiens 4 at Detroit 0
1967	Toronto 3 at Detroit 1
1968	Detroit 3 at Pittsburgh 6
1971	Detroit 3 at Toronto 5

RED WINGS DRAFT CHOICES

1963 Montreal, June 5

(2nd choice overall)

Round 1	2	Peter Mahovlich	St Michael's College School, Toronto (OHA)
Round 2	8	Bill Cosburn	Bick's Pickles, Toronto

1964 Montreal, June 11

(1st choice overall)

Round 1	1	Claude Gauthier	Rosemount (Quebec)
Round 2	7	Brian Watts	Toronto Midgets
Round 3	13	Ralph Buchanan	Montreal East Int.
Round 4	19	Renald LeClerc	Hamilton (Jr. B)

1965 Montreal, April 27

(3rd choice overall)

Round 1	3	George Forgie	Flin Flon Bombers (WCJHL)
Round 2	8	Bill Birdsell	Stettler

1966 Montreal, April 25

(6th choice overall)

Round 1	6	Steve Atkinson	Niagara Falls Flyers (OHA)
Round 2	12	Jim Whittaker	Oshawa Generals (OHA)
Round 3	18	Lee Carpenter	Hamilton Red Wings (OHA)
Round 4	24	Grant Cole	St. Mike's Buzzers (Jr. B)

1967 Montreal, June 7

(9th choice overall)

Round 1	9	Ron Barkwell	Flin Flon Bombers (WCJHL)
Round 2	17	Al Karlander	Michigan Tech (WCHA)

1968 Montreal, June 13

(11th choice overall)

Round 1	11	Steve Andrascik	Flin Flon Bombers (WJHL)
Round 2	17	Herb Boxer	Michigan Tech (WCHA)

1969 Montreal, June 12

(10th choice overall)

Pete Mahovlich, the Wings' first-ever draft choice in 1963.

Round 1	10	Jim Rutherford	Hamilton Red Wings (OHA)
Round 2	21	Ron Garwasiuk	Regina Pats (WJHL)
Round 3	33	Wayne Hawrysh	Flin Flon Bombers (WJHL)
Round 4	45	Warren Chernecki	Winnipeg Jets (WJHL)
Round 5	57	Warren Olds	University of Minnesota (WCHA)

1970 Montreal, June 11

(12th choice overall)

Round 1	12	Serge Lajeunesse	Montreal Jr. Canadiens (OHA)
Round 2	26	Bobby Guindon	Montreal Jr. Canadiens (OHA)
Round 3	40	Yvon Lambert	Drummondville Rangers (QMJHL)
Round 4	54	Tom Johnstone	Toronto Marlies (OHA)
Round 5	68	Tom Mellor	Boston College (HE)
Round 6	82	Bernie MacNeil	Espanola
Round 7	95	Ed Hays	University of Denver (WCHA)

1971 Montreal, June 10

(2nd choice overall)

Round 1	2	Marcel Dionne	St. Catharines Black Hawks (OHA)
Round 2	16	Henry Boucha	U.S. Nationals
Round 3	30	Ralph Hopiavuori	Toronto Marlies (OHA)
Round 4	44	George Hulme	St. Catharines Black Hawks (OHA)
Round 5	58	Earl Anderson	North Dakota University (WCHA)
Round 6	72	Charlie Shaw	Toronto Marlies (OHA)
Round 7	86	Jim Nahrgang	Michigan Tech (WCHA)
Round 8	100	Bobby Boyd	Michigan State University (CCHA)

1972 Montreal, June 8

(10th choice overall)

Round 1	10	traded to Rangers (Albert Blanchard) with Joe Zanussi on May 25, 1972 for Gary Doak and Rick Newell	
Round 2	26	Pierre Guite	St. Catharines Black Hawks (OHA)
Round 3	42	Bob Kreiger	University of Denver (WCHA)
Round 4	58	Dan Gruen	Thunder Bay Vulcans (OHA)
Round 5	74	Dennis Johnson	North Dakota University (WCHA)
Round 6	90	Bill Miller	Medicine Hat Tigers (WJHL)
Round 7	106	Glenn Seperich	Kitchener Rangers (OHA)
Round 8	122	Mike Ford	Brandon Wheat Kings (WJHL)
Round 9	138	George Kuzmicz	Cornell University (ECAC)
Round 10	150	Dave Arundel	University of Wisconsin (WCHA)

1973 Montreal, May 15

(11th choice overall)

Round 1	11	Terry Richardson	New Westminster Bruins (WCHL)
Round 2	27	traded to Pittsburgh (Colin Campbell)	
Round 3[1]	39	Nelson Pyatt	Oshawa Generals (OHA)

Round 3	43	Robbie Neale	Brandon Wheat Kings (WCHL)
Round 4	59	Mike Korney	Winnipeg Jets (WCHL)
Round 5	75	Blair Stewart	Winnipeg Jets (WCHL)
Round 6	91	Glenn Cickello	Hamilton Red Wings (OHA)
Round 7	107	Brian Middleton	University of Alberta (CIAU)
Round 8	118	Dennis Polonich	Flin Flon Bombers (WCHL)
Round 8	123	George Lyle	Michigan Tech (WCHA)
Round 9	135	Dennis O'Brien	Laurentian University (CIAU)
Round 9	138	Tom Newman	Kitchener Rangers (OHA)
Round 9	139	Ray Bibeau	Montreal-Red, White, and Blue (QMJHL)
Round 10	151	Kevin Neville	Toronto Marlies (OHA)
Round 10	154	Ken Gibb	North Dakota University (WCHA)
Round 10	155	Mitch Brandt	University of Denver (WCHA)

1. acquired with cash February 25, 1973 from Penguins for Andy Brown

1974 Montreal, May 28

(9th choice overall)

Round 1	9	Bill Lochead	Oshawa Generals (OHA)
Round 2	27	traded to Penguins (Jacques Cossette)	
Round 3	44	Dan Mandryk	Calgary Centennials (WCHL)
Round 3	45	Bill Evo	Peterborough Petes (OHA)
Round 4	63	Michel Bergeron	Sorel Black Hawks (QMJHL)
Round 5	81	John Taft	University of Wisconsin (WCHA)
Round 6	99	Don Dufek	University of Michigan (CCHA)
Round 7	117	Jack Carlson	Marquette Seniors (USHL)
Round 8	134	Greg Steele	Calgary Centennials (WCHL)
Round 9	151	Glenn McLeod	Sudbury Wolves (OHA)

1975 Montreal, June 3

(5th choice overall)

Round 1	5	Rick Lapointe	Victoria Cougars (WJHL)
Round 2	23	Jerry Rollins	Winnipeg Clubs (WJHL)
Round 3[1]	37	Alan Cameron	New Westminster Bruins (WCHL)
Round 3	41	traded to Minnesota (Alex Pirus)	
Round 3[2]	45	Blair Davidson	Flin Flon Bombers (WJHL)
Round 3[3]	50	Clark Hamilton	University of Notre Dame (CCHA)
Round 4	59	Mike Wirachowsky	Regina Pats (WCHL)
Round 5	77	Mike Wong	Montreal Juniors (QJHL)
Round 6	95	Mike Harazny	Regina Pats (WCHL)
Round 7	113	Jean-Luc Phaneuf	Montreal Juniors (QJHL)
Round 8	131	Steve Carlson	Johnstown Jets (NAHL)
Round 9	148	Gary Vaughan	Medicine Hat Tigers (WCHL)
Round 10	164	Jean Thibodeau	Shawinigan Dynamos (QJHL)
Round 10	176	Dave Hanson	Colorado College (WCHA)
Round 10	178	Robin Larson	University of Minnesota (WCHA)

1. acquired February 28, 1975 from Washington for Nelson Pyatt
2. acquired from St. Louis with Phil Roberto on December 30, 1974 for Red Berenson
3. acquired from Boston with Walt McKechnie on February 18, 1975 for Earl Anderson and Hank Nowak

1976 Montreal, June 1

(4th choice overall)

Round 1	4	Fred Williams	Saskatoon Blades (WCHL)
Round 2	22	Reed Larson	University of Minnesota (WCHA)
Round 2	31	aquired from Los Angeles with Terry Harper on June 23, 1975 (later traded to Minnesota — Jimmy Roberts) for Bart Crashley and the rights to Marcel Dionne	
Round 3	40	Fred Berry	New Westminster Bruins (WCHL)
Round 4	58	Kevin Schamehorn	New Westminster Bruins (WCHL)
Round 5	76	Dwight Schofield	London Knights (OHA)
Round 6	94	Tony Horvath	Sault Ste. Marie Greyhounds (OHA)
Round 7	111	Fernand Leblanc	Sherbrooke Castors (QJHL)
Round 7	120	Claude Legris	Sorel Black Hawks (QJHL)

1977 Montreal, June 14

(1st choice overall)

Round 1	1	Dale McCourt	St. Catharines Fincups (OHA)
Round 2	19	traded November 20, 1975 to Chicago (Jean Savard) for Jean-Paul LeBlanc	
Round 3	37	Rick Vask	Peterborough Petes (OHA)
Round 4	55	John Hilworth	Medicine Hat Tigers (WCHL)
Round 5	73	Jim Korn	Providence College (HE)
Round 6	91	Jim Baxter	Union College (Division II)
Round 7	109	Randy Wilson	Providence College (HE)
Round 7	125	Raymond Roy	Sherbrooke Castors (QMJHL)
Round 8	141	Kip Churchill	Union College (Division II)
Round 9	155	Lance Gatoni	University of Toronto Blues (OUAA)
Round 10	163	Robert Plumb	Kingston Canadians (OHA)
Round 10	170	Alain Belanger	Trois-Rivières Draveurs (QMJHL)
Round 10	175	Dean Willers	Union College (Division II)
Round 10	178	Roland Cloutier	Trois-Rivières Draveurs (QMJHL)
Round 11	181	Edward Hill	University of Vermont (ECAC)
Round 11	184	Valmore James	Quebec Remparts (QMJHL)
Round 11	185	Grant Morin	Calgary Centennials (WCHL)

1978 Montreal, June 15

(9th choice overall)

Round 1	9	Willie Huber	Hamilton Fincups (OHA)
Round 1[1]	12	Brent Peterson	Portland Winter Hawks (WCHL)
Round 2	28	Glenn Hicks	Flin Flon Bombers (WCHL)
Round 2[2]	31	Al Jensen	Hamilton Fincups (OHA)
Round 3	45	traded to Washington (Jay Johnston) with Walt McKechnie and a 2nd-round draft choice in 1979 (Errol Rausse) to Washington for the rights to Ron Low and a 3rd-round draft choice in 1979 (Borris Fistric) as compensation for Detroit signing restricted free agent Low	
Round 3[3]	53	Doug Derkson	New Westminster Bruins (WCHL)
Round 4	62	Bjorn Skaare	Ottawa 67's (OHA)
Round 5	78	Ted Nolan	Sault Ste. Marie Greyhounds (OHA)
Round 6	95	Sylvain Locas	Sherbrooke Castors (QMJHL)
Round 7	112	Wes George	Saskatoon Blades (WCHL)
Round 8	129	John Barrett	Windsor Spitfires (OHA)

Round 9	146	Jim Malazdrewicz	St. Boniface (MJHL)
Round 10	163	Geoff Shaw	Hamilton Fincups (OHA)
Round 10	178	Carl Van Harrewyn	New Westminster Bruins (WCHL)
Round 11	194	Ladislav Svozil	Czechoslovakia National Junior Team
Round 12	208	Tom Bailey	Kingston Canadians (OHA)
Round 13	219	Larry Lozinski	Flin Flon Bombers (WCHL)
Round 13	224	Randy Betty	New Westminster Bruins (WCHL)
Round 13	226	Brian Crawley	St. Lawrence University (ECAC)
Round 13	228	Doug Feasby	Toronto Marlies (OHA)

1. acquired with Errol Thompson, a 2nd-round draft choice in 1978 (Al Jensen), and a 1st-round draft choice in 1980 (Mike Blaisdell) on March 13, 1978 from Toronto for Dan Maloney and a 2nd-round draft choice in 1980 (Craig Muni)
2. acquired with Errol Thompson, a 1st-round draft choice in 1978 (Brent Peterson), and a 1st-round draft choice in 1980 (Mike Blaisdell) on March 13, 1978 from Toronto for Dan Maloney and a 2nd-round draft choice in 1980 (Craig Muni)
3. acquired from Los Angeles via Canadiens with the rights to Barry Long on January 9, 1978 for Danny Grant

1979 Montreal, August 9

(3rd choice overall)

Round 1	3	Mike Foligno	Sudbury Wolves (OHA)
Round 2	24	traded to Washington (Errol Rausse) with a 3rd- round draft choice in 1978 (Jay Johnston) and Walt McKechnie for the rights to Ron Low and a 3rd-round draft choice in 1979 (Borris Fistric) as compensation for Detroit signing restricted free agent Low	
Round 3	45	Jody Gage	Kitchener Rangers (OHA)
Round 3[1]	46	Boris Fistric	New Westminster Bruins (WHL)
Round 4	66	John Ogrodnick	New Westminster Bruins (WHL)
Round 5	87	Joe Paterson	London Knights (OHA)
Round 6	108	Carmine Cirella	Peterborough Petes (OHA)

1. acquired from Washington with the rights to Ron Low for Walt McKechnie, a 3rd-round draft choice in 1978 (Jay Johnston) and a 2nd-round rdaft choice in 1979 (Errol Rausse) as compensation for Detroit signing restricted free agent Low

1980 Montreal, June 11

(4th choice overall)

Round 1	4	traded to Los Angeles (Larry Murphy) with Andre St. Laurent and a 1st-round draft choice in 1981 (Doug Smith) on August 22, 1979 for Dale McCourt	
Round 1[1]	11	Mike Blaisdell	Regina Pats (WHL)
Round 2	25	traded to Toronto (Craig Muni) with Dan Maloney on March 13, 1978 for Errol Thompson, a 1st-round draft choice in 1978 (Brent Peterson), a 2nd-round draft choice in 1978 (Al Jensen), and a 1st-round draft choice in 1980 (Mike Blaisdell)	
Round 3	46	Mark Osborne	Niagara Falls Flyers (OHA)
Round 4	67	traded to Chicago (Carey Wilson) on December 2, 1977 for Dennis Hull	
Round 5	88	Mike Corrigan	Cornwall Royals (QMJHL)
Round 6	109	Wayne Crawford	Toronto Marlies (OHA)
Round 7	130	Mike Braun	Niagara Falls Flyers (OHA)
Round 8	151	John Beukeboom	Peterborough Petes (OHA)
Round 9	172	Dave Miles	Brantford Alexanders (OHA)
Round 10	193	Brian Rorabeck	Niagara Falls Flyers (OHA)

1. acquired with Errol Thompson, a 1st-round draft choice in 1978 (Brent Peterson), and a 2nd-round draft choice in 1978 (Al Jensen) on March 13, 1978 from Toronto for Dan Maloney and a 2nd-round draft choice in 1980 (Craig Muni)

1981 Montreal, June 10

(2nd choice overall)

Round 1	2	traded to Los Angeles (Doug Smith) with Andre St. Laurent and a 1st-round draft choice in 1980 (Larry Murphy) for Dale McCourt	
Round 2	23	Claude Loiselle	Windsor Spitfires (OHL)
Round 3	44	Corrado Micalef	Sherbrooke Beavers (QMJHL)
Round 4	65	traded to Philadelphia (David Michayluk)	
Round 5	86	Larry Trader	London Knights (OHL)
Round 6	107	Gerard Gallant	Sherbrooke Beavers (QMJHL)
Round 7	128	Greg Stefan	Oshawa Generals (OHL)
Round 8	149	Rick Zombo	Austin (USHL)
Round 9	170	Don Leblanc	Moncton (Tier II)
Round 10	191	Robert Nordmark	Sweden

1982 Montreal, June 9

(2nd choice overall)

Round 1	2	traded to Minnesota (Brian Bellows) on August 21, 1981 for Don Murdoch, Greg Smith, and a 1st-round draft choice in 1982 (Murray Craven)	
Round 1[1]	17	Murray Craven	Medicine Hat Tigers (WCJHL)
Round 2	23	Yves Courteau	Laval Voisins (QMJHL)
Round 3	44	Carmine Vani	Kingston Canadians (OHL)
Round 4[2]	66	Craig Coxe	St. Albert (Tier II)
Round 5	86	Brad Shaw	Ottawa 67's (OHL)
Round 6	107	Claude Vilgrain	Laval Voisins (QMJHL)
Round 7	128	Greg Hudas	Redford Royals A (GLHL)
Round 8	149	Pat Lahey	Windsor Spitfires (OHL)
Round 9	170	Gary Cullen	Cornell University (ECAC)
Round 10	191	Brent Meckling	Calgary Canucks (Tier II)
Round 11	212	Mike Stern	Oshawa Generals (OHL)
Round 12	233	Shaun Reagan	Brantford Alexanders (OHL)

1. acquired from Minnesota with Don Murdoch and Greg Smith for a 1st-round draft choice in 1982 (Brian Bellows)
2. acquired from Toronto with a 5th-round draft choice in 1983 (Joey Kocur) on March 8, 1982 for Jim Korn

1983 Montreal, June 8

(4th choice overall)

Round 1	4	Steve Yzerman	Peterborough Petes (OHL)
Round 2	25	Lane Lambert	Saskatoon Blades (WHL)
Round 3	46	Bob Probert	Brantford Alexanders (OHL)
Round 4	66	traded to Calgary with Gary McAdam on November 10, 1981 for Eric Vail	
Round 4	68	David Korol	Winnipeg Warriors (WHL)
Round 5	86	Petr Klima	Czech National Junior Team
Round 5[1]	88	Joey Kocur	Saskatoon Blades (WHL)
Round 6	106	Chris Pusey	Brantford Alexanders (OHL)
Round 6	126	Bob Pierson	London Knights (OHL)
Round 7	146	Craig Butz	Kelowna Wings (WHL)

Round 8	166	Dave Sikorski	Cornwall Royals (OHL)
Round 9	186	Stu Grimson	Regina Pats (WHL)
Round 10	206	Jeff Frank	Regina Pats (WHL)
Round 11	226	Charles Chiatto	Cranbrook High School (Michigan)

1. acquired from Toronto with a 4th-round draft choice in 1982 (Craig Coxe) on March 8, 1982 for Jim Korn

1984 Montreal, June 9

(7th choice overall)

Round 1	7	Shawn Burr	Kitchener Rangers (OHL)
Round 2	28	Doug Houda	Calgary Wranglers (WHL)
Round 3	49	Milan Chalupa	Czechoslovakian Army team
Round 4	70	traded November 17, 1983 to Los Angeles (later traded to Islanders — Doug Wieck)	
Round 5	91	Mats Lundstrom	Skelleflea (Swedish Elite League)
Round 6	112	Randy Hansch	Victoria Cougars (WHL)
Round 7	133	Stefan Larsson	Vastra Frolunda (Swedish Elite League)
Round 8	152	Lars Karlsson	Farjestad (Swedish Junior Team)
Round 8	154	Urban Nordin	MoDo (Swedish Junior League)
Round 9	175	Bill Shibicky	Michigan State University (CCHA)
Round 10	195	Jay Rose	New Prep High School (Massachusetts)
Round 11	216	Tim Kaise	Guelph Platers (OHL)
Round 12	236	Tom Nickolau	Guelph Platers (OHL)

1. acquired from Hartford for rights to Brad Shaw

1985 Toronto, June 15

(8th choice overall)

Round 1	8	Brent Fedyk	Regina Pats (WHL)
Round 2	29	Jeff Sharples	Kelowna Wings (WHL)
Round 3	50	Steve Chiasson	Guelph Platers (OHL)
Round 4	71	Mark Gowans	Windsor Compuware Spitfires (OHL)
Round 5	92	Chris Luongo	Detroit Falcons (GLHL)
Round 6	113	Randy McKay	Michigan Tech University (WCHA)
Round 7	134	Thomas Bjur	AIK Stockholm Junior Team (Swedish Junior League)
Round 8	155	Mike Luckraft	Burnsville High School (Minnesota)
Round 9	176	Rob Schenna	St. John's High School (Massachusetts)
Round 10	197	Eerik Hamalainen	Lukko (Finnish Elite League)
Round 11	218	Bo Svanberg	Farjestad (Swedish Junior League)
Round 12	239	Mikael Lindman	AIK Stockholm Junior Team (Swedish Junior League)

1986 Montreal, June 21

(1st choice overall)

Round 1	1	Joe Murphy	Michigan State University (CCHA)
Round 2	22	Adam Graves	Windsor Spitfires (OHL)
Round 3	43	Derek Mayer	University of Denver (WCHA)
Round 4	64	Tim Cheveldae	Saskatoon Blades (WHL)

Round 5	85	Johan Garpenlov	Nacka/Djurgarden (Swedish Division One)
Round 6	106	Jay Stark	Portland Winter Hawks (WHL)
Round 7	127	Per Djoos	Mora (Swedish League)
Round 8	148	Dean Morton	Oshawa Generals (OHL)
Round 9	169	Marc Potvin	Stratford (Ontario Junior B)
Round 10	190	Scott King	Richmond & Vernon, B.C. (Junior B)
Round 11	211	Tom Bissett	Michigan Tech University (WCHA)
Round 12	232	Peter Ekroth	Sodertalje (Swedish Elite League)

1987 Detroit, June 13

(11th choice overall)

Round 1	11	Yves Racine	Longueuil (QMJHL)
Round 2	32	Gord Kruppke	Prince Albert Raiders (WHL)
Round 2[1]	41	Bob Wilkie	Swift Current Broncos (WHL)
Round 3[2]	52	Dennis Holland	Portland Winter Hawks (WHL)
Round 3	53	traded to New Jersey (later sent to Sabres — Andrew MacVicar) with Chris Cichoki on March 9, 1987 for Mel Bridgman	
Round 4	74	Mark Reimer	Saskatoon Blades (WHL)
Round 5	95	Radomir Brazda	Pardubice (Czech League)
Round 6	116	Sean Clifford	Ohio State (CCHA)
Round 7	137	Mike Gober	Laval Titans (QMJHL)
Round 8	158	Kevin Scott	Vernon (BCJHL)
Round 9	179	Mikko Haapakoski	Karpat (Finnish League)
Round 10	200	Darin Bannister	Illinois-Chicago (CCHA)
Round 11	221	Craig Quinlan	Hill Murray High School (Minnesota)
Round 12	242	Tomas Jansson	IK Talje (Swedish League)

1. acquired from Flyers on June 13, 1987 for Mark Laforest
2. acquired from Rangers with Glen Hanlon and a 3rd-round draft choice in 1988 (Guy Dupuis) on July 29, 1986 for Kelly Kisio, Jim Leavins, and Lane Lambert

1988 Montreal, June 11

(17th choice overall)

Round 1	17	Kory Kocur	Saskatoon Blades (WHL)
Round 2	38	Serge Anglehart	Drummondville Voltigeurs (QMJHL)
Round 3[1]	47	Guy Dupuis	Hull Olympics (QMJHL)
Round 3	59	Petr Hrbek	Sparta Praha (Czech)
Round 4	80	Sheldon Kennedy	Swift Current Broncos (WHL)
Round 5	101	traded to Winnipeg (Benôit Lebeau)	
Round 6	122	traded to Vancouver (Phil von Stefenelli) on November 21, 1986 for Doug Halward	
Round 7	143	Kelly Hurd	Michigan Tech University (WCHA)
Round 8	164	Brian McCormack	St. Paul's Vulcans (USHL)
Round 9	185	Jody Praznik	Colorado College (WCHA)
Round 10	206	Glenn Goodall	Seattle Breakers (WJHL)
Round 11	227	Darren Colbourne	Cornwall Royals (OHL)
Round 12	248	Donald Stone	Michigan University (CCHA)

1. acquired from Rangers with Glen Hanlon and a 3rd-round draft choice in 1987 (Dennis Holland) on July 29, 1986 for Kelly Kisio, Jim Leavins, and Lane Lambert

1989 Minnesota, June 17

(11th choice overall)

Round 1	11	Mike Sillinger	Regina Pats (WJHL)
Round 2	32	Bob Boughner	Sault Ste. Marie Greyhounds (OHL)
Round 3	53	Nicklas Lidstrom	Vasteras (Sweden)
Round 4	74	Sergei Fedorov	CSKA (Russia)
Round 5	95	Shawn McCosh	Niagara Falls Thunder (OHL)
Round 6	116	Dallas Drake	Northern Michigan University (WCHA)
Round 7	137	Scott Zygulski	Culver Academy (U.S. High School)
Round 8	158	Andy Suhy	Western Michigan (CCHA)
Round 9	179	Bob Jones	Sault Ste. Marie Greyhounds (OHL)
Round 10	200	Greg Bignell	Belleville Bulls (OHL)
Round 10[1]	204	Rick Judson	Illinois-Chicago (CCHA)
Round 11	221	Vladimir Konstantinov	CSKA, Russia
Round 12	242	Joseph Frederick	Madison (Junior A)
Round 12[2]	246	Jason Glickman	Hull Olympics (QMJHL)

1. acquired from Edmonton on January 3, 1989 for Miroslav Frycer
2. acquired from Edmonton on January 23, 1989 for Doug Halward

1990 Vancouver, June 16

(3rd choice overall)

Round 1	3	Keith Primeau	Niagara Falls Thunder (OHL)
Round 2	24	traded to Calgary (later sent to New Jersey-David Harlock) on June 15, 1990 for Brad McCrimmon	
Round 3	45	Viacheslav Kozlov	Khimik (Russia)
Round 4	66	Stewart Malgunas	Seattle Thunderbirds (WHL)
Round 5	87	Tony Burns	Duluth-Denfeld
Round 6	108	Claude Barthe	Victoriaville Tigers (QMJHL)
Round 7	129	Jason York	Kitchener Rangers (OHL)
Round 8	150	Wes McCauley	Michigan State (CCHA)
Round 9	171	Anthony Gruba	Hill-Murray
Round 10	192	Travis Tucker	Avon Old Farms
Round 11	213	Brett Larson	Duluth-Denfeld
Round 12	234	John Hendry	Lake Superior State (CCHA)

1991 Buffalo, June 22

(10th choice overall)

Round 1	10	Martin Lapointe	Laval Titans (QMJHL)
Round 2	32	Jamie Pushor	Lethbridge Hurricanes (WHL)
Round 3	54	Chris Osgood	Medicine Hat Tigers (WHL)
Round 4	76	Michael Knuble	Kalamazoo (Junior A)
Round 5	98	Dimitri Motkov	CSKA (Russia)
Round 6	120	traded to Toronto (Alexander Kuzminsky) on March 5, 1991 for Allan Bester	
Round 7	142	Igor Malykhin	CSKA, Russia
Round 8	164	traded to Toronto (Robb McIntyre) on February 4, 1991 for Brad Marsh	
Round 9	186	Jim Bermingham	Laval Titans (QMJHL)
Round 10	208	Jason Firth	Kitchener Rangers (OHL)

Round 11	230	Bart Turner	Michigan State (CCHA)
Round 12	252	Andrew Miller	Wexford (Junior B)

1992 Montreal, June 20

(22nd choice overall)

Round 1	22	Curtis Bowen	Ottawa 67s (OHL)
Round 2	46	Darren McCarty	Belleville Bulls (OHL)
Round 3	70	Sylvain Cloutier	Guelph Storm (OHL)
Round 4	94	traded to New Jersey (Scott McCabe) with Lee Norwood on November 27, 1990 for Paul Ysebaert	
Round 5	118	Mike Sullivan	Reading
Round 6	142	Jason MacDonald	Owen Sound Platers (OHL)
Round 7	166	Greg Scott	Niagara Falls Thunder (OHL)
Round 8[1]	183	Justin Krall	Omaha (Junior A)
Round 8[2]	189	C.J.Denomme	Kitchener Rangers (OHL)
Round 8	190	traded to Rangers (Colin Schmidt) December 26, 1991 for Greg Millen	
Round 9	214	Jeff Walker	Peterborough Petes (OHL)
Round 10	238	Daniel McGillis	Hawksbury (Tier II, Junior A)
Round 11	262	Ryan Bach	Notre Dame (Tier II, Junior A)

1. acquired from Los Angeles on August 15, 1990 for Shawn McCosh
2. acquired from San Jose via Vancouver with Bob McGill on March 9, 1992 for Johan Garpenlov

1993 Quebec City, June 26

(22nd choice overall)

Round 1	22	Anders Eriksson	MoDo (Sweden)
Round 2	48	Johnathon Coleman	Andover Academy
Round 3	74	Kevin Hilton	University of Michigan (CCHA)
Round 4[1]	88		
Round 4[2]	97	John Jakopin	St. Michael's, Toronto (Junior B)
Round 4	100	Benôit Larose	Laval Titans (QMJHL)
Round 5	126	Norm Maracle	Saskatoon Blades (WHL)
Round 6[3]	152	Tim Spitzig	Kitchener Rangers (OHL)
Round 7	178	Yuri Yeresko	CSKA (Russia)
Round 8	204	Vitezslav Skuta	Vitkovice (Czechoslovakia)
Round 9	230	Ryan Shanahan	Sudbury Wolves (OHL)
Round 10	256	James Kosecki	Berkshire High School
Round 11	282	Gordon Hunt	Detroit Compuware (Junior A)

1. acquired from Flyers (later sent to Boston — Charles Paquette) on October 1, 1992 for Brent Fedyk
2. acquired from Winnipeg (via Washington via Toronto)
3. traded to Hartford on March 22, 1993 for Steve Konroyd (selection later re-acquired by Detroit)

1994 Hartford, June 28–29

(23rd choice overall)

Round 1	23	Yan Golubovsky	CSKA (Russia)
Round 2	49	Mathieu Dandenault	Sherbrooke Fauçons (QMJHL)
Round 3	75	Sean Gillam	Spokane Chiefs (WHL)
Round 4	101	traded to Flyers (Sebastien Vallee) with Yves Racine on October 5, 1993 for Terry Carkner	

Round 5[1]	114	Frederic Deschenes	Granby Bisons (QMJHL)
Round 5	127	Doug Battaglia	Brockville (Jr. A)
Round 6	153	Pavel Agarkov	Soviet Wings (Russia)
Round 7	179	traded to Edmonton (Chris Wickenheiser) on August 30, 1993 for Peter Ing	
Round 8	205	Jason Ellio	Kimberley
Round 9	231	Jeff Mikesch	Michigan Tech (WCHA)
Round 10	257	Tomas Holmstrom	Boden (Sweden)
Round 11	283	Toivo Suursoo	Soviet Wings (Russia)

1. acquired from Flyers with Greg Johnson on June 20, 1993 for Jim Cummins and a 4th-round draft choice in 1993 (later sent to Boston — Charles Paquette)

1995 Edmonton, July 8

(26th choice overall)

Round 1	26	Maxim Kuznetsov	Moscow Dynamo (Russia)
Round 2	52	Philippe Audet	Granby Bisons (QMJHL)
Round 3	58[1]	Darryl Laplante	Moose Jaw Warriors (WHL)
Round 3	78	traded to New Jersey (David Gosselin) April 3, 1995 to New Jersey for Viacheslav Fetisov	
Round 4	104	Anatoly Ustugov	Yaroslavl (Russia)
Round 5	125[2]	Chad Wilchynski	Regina Pats (WHL)
Round 5	126[3]	David Arsenault	Drummondville Voltigeurs (QMJHL)
Round 5	130	traded to San Jose (Michal Bros)	
Round 6	156	Tyler Perry	Seattle Thunderbirds (WHL)
Round 7	182	Per Eklund	Djurgarden (Sweden)
Round 8	208	Andrei Samokvalov	UST-Kamenogorsk (Russia)
Round 9	234	David Engblom	Vallentuna (Sweden)

1. acquired May 25, 1994 from Winnipeg for Sheldon Kenedy
2. acquired January 17, 1994 from Boston for Vincent Riendeau
3. acquired from Flyers

1996 St. Louis, June 22

(26th choice overall)

Round 1	26	Jesse Wallin	Red Deer Rebels (WHL)
Round 2	52	Aren Miller	Spokane Chiefs (WHL)
Round 3	80	traded with Shawn Burr on August 17, 1995 to Tampa Bay for Marc Bergevin and Ben Hankinson (selection later traded to Boston — Jason Doyle)	
Round 4	108	Johan Forsander	Hv 71 (MHA Europe)
Round 5	135	Michael Podolka	Sault Ste. Marie Greyhounds (OHL)
Round 6[1]	144	Magnus Nilsson	Vita Hasten (Europe)
Round 6	162	Alexandre Jacques	Shawinigan Cataracts (QMJHL)
Round 7	189	Colin Beardsmore	North Bay Centennials (OHL)
Round 8	215	Craig Stahl	Tri-City Americans (WHL)
Round 9	241	Evgeniy Afanasiev	Detroit L. C. Midgets

1. acquired with Mark Ferner and Stu Grimson on April 4, 1995 from Anaheim for Mike Sillinger and Jason York

The 1997 Draft will be held June 21 in Pittsburgh.

ALL-TIME YEAR-BY-YEAR STANDINGS

The column immediately before the total points column indicates the teams' yearly penalty minutes. From 1917–21, when the schedule was divided in two, year-end penalty minutes are listed in the second half of the schedule. The Stanley Cup winner for each season is identified by bold type. After playoff scores, goalies who have registered a shutout will appear in square brackets (i.e., [Sawchuk] means Terry Sawchuk registered a shutout.)

* denotes overtime (for times and scores, please refer to the "overtime" section)

1917–1918

First Half Schedule							
Montreal Canadiens	14	10	4	81	47	N/A	20
Toronto Arenas	14	8	6	71	75		16
Ottawa Senators	14	5	9	67	79		10
Montreal Wanderers	6	1	5	17	35		2
Second Half Schedule							
Toronto Arenas	8	5	3	37	34	205	10
Ottawa Senators	8	4	4	35	35	142	8
Montreal Canadiens	8	3	5	34	37	167	6

- winner of first half played winner of second half in a two-game total goals series for a place in the Stanley Cup finals against the winner of the Pacific Coast Hockey League and the Western Canada Hockey League. If one team won both halves, it went to the best-of-five finals automatically.
- from 1917–1921 games were played until a winner decided
- minor penalties three minutes, majors five minutes, match penalties meant no substitute allowed for the rest of the game
- forward passing permitted in a newly-created neutral zone
- Montreal Arena burned down and Wanderers withdrew from the league. Toronto and Montreal each counted a win for defaulted games with the Wanderers.

1918–1919

First Half Schedule							
Montreal Canadiens	10	7	3	57	50	N/A	14
Ottawa Senators	10	5	5	39	39		10
Toronto Arenas	10	3	7	42	49		6
Second Half Schedule							
Ottawa Senators	8	7	1	32	14	215	14
Montreal Canadiens	8	3	5	31	28	257	6
Toronto Arenas	8	2	6	22	43	239	4

- Spanish influenza epidemic caused the cancellation of the Stanley Cup finals

1919–1920

First Half Schedule							
Ottawa Senators	12	9	3	59	23	N/A	18
Montreal Canadiens	12	8	4	62	51		16
Toronto St. Pats	12	5	7	52	62		10
Quebec Bulldogs	12	2	10	44	81		4
Second Half Schedule							
Ottawa Senators	12	10	2	62	41	237	20
Toronto St. Pats	12	7	5	67	44	219	14
Montreal Canadiens	12	5	7	67	62	221	10
Quebec Bulldogs	12	2	10	47	96	114	4

1920–1921

First Half Schedule							
Ottawa Senators	10	8	2	49	23	N/A	16
Toronto St. Pats	10	5	5	39	47		10
Montreal Canadiens	10	4	6	37	51		8
Hamilton Tigers	10	3	7	34	38		6
Second Half Schedule							
Toronto St. Pats	14	10	4	66	53	258	20
Montreal Canadiens	14	9	5	75	48	285	18
Ottawa Senators	14	6	8	48	52	177	12
Hamilton Tigers	14	3	11	58	94	154	6

1921–1922

Ottawa Senators	24	14	8	2	106	84	99	30
Toronto St. Pats	24	13	10	1	98	97	114	27
Montreal Canadiens	24	12	11	1	88	94	174	25
Hamilton Tigers	24	7	17	0	88	105	76	14

- overtime limited to 20 minutes
- minor penalties reduced from three to two minutes
- top two teams advance to playoffs; winner met the Canadian Hockey Association-Western Canadian Hockey League Champion for the Stanley Cup

1922–1923

Ottawa Senators	24	14	9	1	77	54	188	29
Montreal Canadiens	24	13	9	2	73	61	174	28
Toronto St. Pats	24	13	10	1	82	88	200	27
Hamilton Tigers	24	6	18	0	81	110	182	12

1923–1924

Ottawa Senators	24	16	8	0	74	54	154	32
Montreal Canadiens	24	13	11	0	59	48	146	26
Toronto St. Pats	24	10	14	0	59	85	178	20
Hamilton Tigers	24	9	15	0	63	68	81	18

- a player given a match penalty may be replaced after twenty minutes

1924–1925

Hamilton Tigers	30	19	10	1	90	60	332	39
Toronto St. Pats	30	19	11	0	90	84	245	38
Montreal Canadiens	30	17	11	2	93	56	371	36
Ottawa Senators	30	17	12	1	83	66	331	35
Montreal Maroons	30	9	19	2	45	65	268	20
Boston Bruins	30	6	24	0	49	119	264	12

- the top two teams (Hamilton and Toronto) were supposed to play for the NHL championship and the right to advance to the Stanley Cup Finals against the WCHL winners. However, the Tigers demanded more money for these extra games and the NHL simply disqualified them. Thus, the St. Pats played the Canadiens.
- Stanley Cup won by Victoria Cougars (PCHL)

1925–1926

Ottawa Senators	36	24	8	4	77	42	341	52
Montreal Maroons	36	20	11	5	91	73	554	45
Pittsburgh Pirates	36	19	16	1	82	70	264	39
Boston Bruins	36	17	15	4	92	85	279	38
New York Americans	36	12	20	4	68	89	361	28
Toronto St. Pats	36	12	21	3	92	114	325	27
Montreal Canadiens	36	11	24	1	79	108	458	23

1926–1927

American Division								
New York Rangers	44	25	13	6	95	72	385	56
Boston Bruins	44	21	20	3	97	89	521	45
Chicago Black Hawks	44	19	22	3	115	116	448	41
Pittsburgh Pirates	44	15	26	3	79	108	230	33
Detroit Cougars	44	12	28	4	76	105	409	28
Canadian Division								
Ottawa Senators	44	30	10	4	86	69	607	64
Montreal Canadiens	44	28	14	2	99	67	395	58
Montreal Maroons	44	20	20	4	71	68	716	44
New York Americans	44	17	25	2	82	91	349	36
Toronto St. Pats	44	15	24	5	79	94	546	35

- did not qualify for playoffs

1927–1928

American Division								
Boston Bruins	44	20	13	11	77	70	558	51
New York Rangers	44	19	16	9	94	79	462	47
Pittsburgh Pirates	44	19	17	8	67	76	395	46
Detroit Cougars	44	19	19	6	88	79	395	44
Chicago Black Hawks	44	7	34	3	68	134	375	17
Canadian Division								
Montreal Canadiens	44	26	11	7	116	48	496	59
Montreal Maroons	44	24	14	6	96	77	549	54
Ottawa Senators	44	20	14	10	78	57	483	50
Toronto Maple Leafs	44	18	18	8	89	88	436	44
New York Americans	44	11	27	6	63	128	563	28

- overtime limited to 10 minutes of sudden death
- forward passing now allowed in defending zone
- did not qualify for playoffs

1928–1929

American Division								
Boston Bruins	44	26	13	5	89	52	472	57
New York Rangers	44	21	13	10	72	65	384	52
Detroit Cougars	44	19	16	9	72	63	381	47
Pittsburgh Pirates	44	9	27	8	46	80	324	26
Chicago Black Hawks	44	7	29	8	33	85	363	22
Canadian Division								
Montreal Canadiens	44	22	7	15	71	43	465	59
New York Americans	44	19	13	12	53	53	486	50
Toronto Maple Leafs	44	21	18	5	85	69	541	47
Ottawa Senators	44	14	17	13	54	67	461	41
Montreal Maroons	44	15	20	9	67	65	638	39

- overtime set at 10 minutes without sudden death
- passing allowed into, but not in, the offensive zone
- the two division winners played a best-of-five series and the two second place teams and third place teams played two-game total goals series. Those two winners then played to see who would play the winner of the two division champions' series

Quarter-finals:	March 19	Toronto 3	Cougars 1 (at Detroit)
	March 21	Toronto 4	Cougars 1 (at Toronto)
	Toronto won 2–game total goals 7–2		

1929–1930

American Division								
Boston Bruins	44	38	5	1	179	98	449	77
Chicago Black Hawks	44	21	18	5	117	111	573	47
New York Rangers	44	17	17	10	136	143	445	44
Detroit Falcons	44	14	24	6	117	133	474	34
Pittsburgh Pirates	44	5	36	3	102	185	384	13

Canadian Division								
Montreal Maroons	44	23	16	5	141	114	651	51
Montreal Canadiens	44	21	14	9	142	114	600	51
Ottawa Senators	44	21	15	8	138	118	536	50
Toronto Maple Leafs	44	17	21	6	116	124	613	40
New York Americans	44	14	25	5	113	161	372	33

- forward passing allowed in all three zones, producing twice the number of goals
- did not qualify for playoffs

1930–1931

American Division								
Boston Bruins	44	28	10	6	143	90	403	62
Chicago Black Hawks	44	24	17	3	108	78	416	51
New York Rangers	44	19	16	9	106	87	514	47
Detroit Falcons	44	16	21	7	102	105	429	39
Philadelphia Quakers	44	4	36	4	76	184	477	12
Canadian Division								
Montreal Canadiens	44	26	10	8	129	89	602	60
Toronto Maple Leafs	44	22	13	9	118	99	540	53
Montreal Maroons	44	20	18	6	105	106	568	46
New York Americans	44	18	16	10	76	74	495	46
Ottawa Senators	44	10	30	4	91	142	486	24

- did not qualify for playoffs

1931–1932

American Division								
New York Rangers	48	23	17	8	134	112	511	54
Chicago Black Hawks	48	18	19	11	86	101	464	47
Detroit Falcons	48	18	20	10	95	108	415	46
Boston Bruins	48	15	21	12	122	117	373	42
Canadian Division								
Montreal Canadiens	48	25	16	7	128	111	450	57
Toronto Maple Leafs	48	23	18	7	155	127	625	53
Montreal Maroons	48	19	22	7	142	139	593	45
New York Americans	48	16	24	8	95	142	596	40

Quarter-finals:	March 27	Maroons 1	Detroit 1 (at Detroit)
	March 29	Maroons 2	Detroit 0 (at Montreal) [Walsh]
	Maroons won 2-game total goals 3–1		

1932–1933

American Division								
Boston Bruins	48	25	15	8	124	88	517	58
Detroit Falcons	48	25	15	8	111	93	462	58
New York Rangers	48	23	17	8	135	107	599	54
Chicago Black Hawks	48	16	20	12	88	101	401	44

Canadian Division								
Toronto Maple Leafs	48	24	18	6	119	111	622	54
Montreal Maroons	48	22	20	6	135	119	442	50
Montreal Canadiens	48	18	25	5	92	115	468	41
New York Americans	48	15	22	11	91	118	460	41
Ottawa Senators	48	11	27	10	88	131	398	32

Quarter-finals:

March 25	Detroit 2	Maroons 0 (at Montreal) [Roach]
March 28	Detroit 3	Maroons 2 (at Detroit)

Detroit won 2–game total goals 5–2

Semi-finals:

March 30	Rangers 2	Detroit 0 (at New York) [Aitkenhead]
April 2	Rangers 4	Detroit 3 (at Detroit)

Rangers won 2–game total goals 6–3

1933–1934

American Division								
Detroit Red Wings	48	24	14	10	113	98	368	58
Chicago Black Hawks	48	20	17	11	88	83	337	51
New York Rangers	48	21	19	8	120	113	401	50
Boston Bruins	48	18	25	5	111	130	385	41
Canadian Division								
Toronto Maple Leafs	48	26	13	9	174	119	529	61
Montreal Canadiens	48	22	20	6	99	101	308	50
Montreal Maroons	48	19	18	11	117	122	414	49
New York Americans	48	15	23	10	104	132	365	40
Ottawa Senators	48	13	29	6	115	143	344	32

Semi-finals:

March 22	Detroit 2	Toronto 1* (at Toronto)
March 24	Detroit 6	Toronto 3 (at Toronto)
March 26	Toronto 3	Detroit 1 (at Detroit)
March 28	Toronto 5	Detroit 1 (at Detroit)
March 30	Detroit 1	Toronto 0 (at Detroit) [Cude]

Detroit won best-of-five 3–2

Finals:

April 3	Chicago 2	Detroit 1* (at Detroit)
April 5	Chicago 4	Detroit 1 (at Detroit)
April 8	Detroit 5	Chicago 2 (at Chicago)
April 10	Chicago 1	Detroit 0* (at Chicago) [Gardiner]

Chicago won Stanley Cup best-of-five 3–1

1934–1935

American Division								
Boston Bruins	48	26	16	6	129	112	368	58
Chicago Black Hawks	48	26	17	5	118	88	375	57
New York Rangers	48	22	20	6	137	139	334	50
Detroit Red Wings	48	19	22	7	127	114	305	45

Canadian Division								
Toronto Maple Leafs	48	30	14	4	157	111	444	64
Montreal Maroons	48	24	19	5	123	92	380	53
Montreal Canadiens	48	19	23	6	110	145	314	44
New York Americans	48	12	27	9	100	142	250	33
St. Louis Eagles	48	11	31	6	86	144	385	28

• did not qualify for playoffs

1935–1936

American Division								
Detroit Red Wings	48	24	16	8	124	103	384	56
Boston Bruins	48	22	20	6	92	83	397	50
Chicago Black Hawks	48	21	19	8	93	92	411	50
New York Rangers	48	19	17	12	91	96	381	50
Canadian Division								
Montreal Maroons	48	22	16	10	114	106	504	54
Toronto Maple Leafs	48	23	19	6	126	106	579	52
New York Americans	48	16	25	7	109	122	392	39
Montreal Canadiens	48	11	26	11	82	123	317	33

Semi-finals:	March 24	Detroit 1	Maroons 0* (at Montreal) [N. Smith]
	March 26	Detroit 3	Maroons 0 (at Montreal) [N. Smith] (all goals in 3rd)
	March 29	Detroit 2	Maroons 1 (at Detroit)
	Detroit won best-of-five 3–0		
Finals:	April 5	Detroit 3	Toronto 1 (at Detroit)
	April 7	Detroit 9	Toronto 4 (at Detroit)
	April 9	Toronto 4	Detroit 3* (at Toronto) (Kelly (T) tied game at 19:18)
	April 11	Detroit 3	Toronto 2 (at Toronto)
	Detroit won Stanley Cup best-of-five 3–1		

1936–1937

American Division								
Detroit Red Wings	48	25	14	9	128	102	244	59
Boston Bruins	48	23	18	7	120	110	303	53
New York Rangers	48	19	20	9	117	106	312	47
Chicago Black Hawks	48	14	27	7	99	131	291	35
Canadian Division								
Montreal Canadiens	48	24	18	6	115	111	298	54
Montreal Maroons	48	22	17	9	126	110	379	53
Toronto Maple Leafs	48	22	21	5	119	115	371	49
New York Americans	48	15	29	4	122	161	481	34

Semi-finals:	March 23	Detroit 4	Canadiens 0 (at Detroit) [N. Smith]
	March 25	Detroit 5	Canadiens 1 (at Detroit)
	March 27	Canadiens 3	Detroit 1 (at Montreal)

	March 30	Canadiens 3	Detroit 1 (at Montreal)
	April 1	Detroit 2	Canadiens 1* (at Montreal)
	Detroit won best-of-five 3–2		
Finals:	April 6	Rangers 5	Detroit 1 (at New York)
	April 8	Detroit 4	Rangers 2 (at Detroit)
	April 11	Rangers 1	Detroit 0 (at Detroit) [Kerr]
	April 13	Detroit 1	Rangers 0 (at Detroit) [Robertson]
	April 15	Detroit 3	Rangers 0 (at Detroit) [Robertson]
	Detroit won Stanley Cup best-of-five 3–2		

1937–1938

American Division								
Boston Bruins	48	30	11	7	142	89	284	67
New York Rangers	48	27	15	6	149	96	435	60
Chicago Black Hawks	48	14	25	9	97	139	238	37
Detroit Red Wings	48	12	25	11	99	133	258	35
Canadian Division								
Toronto Maple Leafs	48	24	15	9	151	127	404	57
New York Americans	48	19	18	11	110	111	327	49
Montreal Canadiens	48	18	17	13	123	128	340	49
Montreal Maroons	48	12	30	6	101	149	470	30

- did not qualify for playoffs

1938–1939

Boston Bruins	48	36	10	2	156	76	251	74
New York Rangers	48	26	16	6	149	105	393	58
Toronto Maple Leafs	48	19	20	9	114	107	370	47
New York Americans	48	17	21	10	119	157	276	44
Detroit Red Wings	48	18	24	6	107	128	240	42
Montreal Canadiens	48	15	24	9	115	146	294	39
Chicago Black Hawks	48	12	28	8	91	132	367	32

- Only the last place team did not qualify for the playoffs with the new one-division, 7-team format. The first and second place team played a best-of-seven to advance to the finals. The second played third and fourth played fifth in best-of-three series, the two winners playing another best-of-three to advance to the Finals.

Quarter-finals:	March 21	Canadiens 2	Detroit 0 (at Montreal) [Bourque]
	March 23	Detroit 7	Canadiens 3 (at Detroit)
	March 26	Detroit 1	Canadiens 0* (at Detroit) [Thompson]
	Detroit won best-of-three 2–1		
Semi-finals:	March 28	Toronto 4	Detroit 1 (at Toronto)
	March 30	Detroit 3	Toronto 1 (at Detroit)
	April 1	Toronto 5	Detroit 4* (at Toronto)
	Toronto won best-of-three 2–1		

1939–1940

Boston Bruins	48	31	12	5	170	98	345	67
New York Rangers	48	27	11	10	136	77	520	64
Toronto Maple Leafs	48	25	17	6	134	110	485	56
Chicago Black Hawks	48	23	19	6	112	120	340	52
Detroit Red Wings	48	16	26	6	90	126	250	38
New York Americans	48	15	29	4	106	140	232	34
Montreal Canadiens	48	10	33	5	90	167	338	25

Quarter-finals:	March 19	Detroit 2	Americans 1* (at Detroit)
	March 22	Americans 5	Detroit 4 (at New York)
	March 24	Detroit 3	Americans 1 (at Detroit)
	Detroit won best-of-three 2–1		
Semi-finals:	March 26	Toronto 2	Detroit 1 (at Toronto)
	March 28	Toronto 3	Detroit 1 (at Detroit)
	Toronto won best-of-three 2–0		

1940–1941

Boston Bruins	48	27	8	13	168	102	246	67
Toronto Maple Leafs	48	28	14	6	145	99	306	62
Detroit Red Wings	48	21	16	11	112	102	337	53
New York Rangers	48	21	19	8	143	125	356	50
Chicago Black Hawks	48	16	25	7	112	139	335	39
Montreal Canadiens	48	16	26	6	121	147	435	38
New York Americans	48	8	29	11	99	186	231	27

Quarter-finals:	March 20	Detroit 2	Rangers 1* (at Detroit)
	March 23	Rangers 3	Detroit 1 (at New York)
	March 25	Detroit 3	Rangers 2 (at Detroit)
	Detroit won best-of-three 2–1		
Semi-finals:	March 27	Detroit 3	Chicago 1 (at Detroit)
	March 30	Detroit 2	Chicago 1* (at Chicago)
	Detroit won best-of-three 2–0		
Finals:	April 6	Boston 3	Detroit 2 (at Boston)
	April 8	Boston 2	Detroit 1 (at Boston)
	April 10	Boston 4	Detroit 2 (at Detroit)
	April 12	Boston 3	Detroit 1 (at Detroit)
	Boston won Stanley Cup best-of-seven 4–0		

1941–1942

New York Rangers	48	29	17	2	177	143	400	60
Toronto Maple Leafs	48	27	18	3	158	136	341	57
Boston Bruins	48	25	17	6	160	118	349	56
Chicago Black Hawks	48	22	23	3	145	155	365	47
Detroit Red Wings	48	19	25	4	140	147	440	42
Montreal Canadiens	48	18	27	3	134	173	504	39
Brooklyn Americans	48	16	29	3	133	175	425	35

Quarter-finals:	March 22	Detroit 2	Canadiens 1 (at Detroit)
	March 24	Canadiens 5	Detroit 0 (at Montreal) [Bibeault]
	March 26	Detroit 6	Canadiens 2 (at Detroit)
	Detroit won best-of-three 2–1		
Semi-finals:	March 29	Detroit 6	Boston 4 (at Boston)
	March 31	Detroit 3	Boston 1 (at Detroit)
	Detroit won best-of-three 2–0		
Finals:	April 4	Detroit 3	Toronto 2 (at Toronto)
	April 7	Detroit 4	Toronto 2 (at Toronto)
	April 9	Detroit 5	Toronto 2 (at Detroit)
	April 12	Toronto 4	Detroit 3 (at Detroit)
	April 14	Toronto 9	Detroit 3 (at Toronto)
	April 16	Toronto 3	Detroit 0 (at Detroit) [Broda]
	April 18	Toronto 3	Detroit 1 (at Toronto)
	Toronto won Stanley Cup best-of-seven 4–3		

1942–1943

Detroit Red Wings	50	25	14	11	169	124	371	61
Boston Bruins	50	24	17	9	195	176	364	57
Toronto Maple Leafs	50	22	19	9	198	159	431	53
Montreal Canadiens	50	19	19	12	181	191	318	50
Chicago Black Hawks	50	17	18	15	179	180	361	49
New York Rangers	50	11	31	8	161	253	352	30

- because of wartime restrictions on train schedules overtime was eliminated as of November 21, 1942
- the top four teams qualified for the playoffs in the six-team league, and both rounds were best-of-seven series

Semi-finals:	March 21	Detroit 4	Toronto 2 (at Detroit)
	March 23	Toronto 3	Detroit 2* (at Detroit)
	March 25	Detroit 4	Toronto 2 (at Toronto)
	March 27	Toronto 6	Detroit 3 (at Toronto)
	March 28	Detroit 4	Toronto 2 (at Detroit)
	March 30	Detroit 3	Toronto 2* (at Toronto)
	Detroit won best-of-seven 4–2		
Finals:	April 1	Detroit 6	Boston 2 (at Detroit)
	April 4	Detroit 4	Boston 3 (at Detroit)
	April 7	Detroit 4	Boston 0 (at Boston) [Mowers]
	April 8	Detroit 2	Boston 0 (at Boston) [Mowers]
	Detroit won Stanley Cup best-of-seven 4–0		

1943–1944

Montreal Canadiens	50	38	5	7	234	109	557	83
Detroit Red Wings	50	26	18	6	214	177	374	58
Toronto Maple Leafs	50	23	23	4	214	174	303	50
Chicago Black Hawks	50	22	23	5	178	187	240	49
Boston Bruins	50	19	26	5	223	268	207	43
New York Rangers	50	6	39	5	162	310	253	17

Semi-finals:	March 21	Chicago 2	Detroit 1 (at Detroit)
	March 23	Detroit 4	Chicago 1 (at Detroit)
	March 26	Chicago 2	Detroit 0 (at Chicago) [Karakas]
	March 28	Chicago 7	Detroit 1 (at Chicago)
	March 30	Chicago 5	Detroit 2 (at Detroit)
	Chicago won best-of-seven 4–1		

1944–1945

Montreal Canadiens	50	38	8	4	228	121	376	80
Detroit Red Wings	50	31	14	5	218	161	260	67
Toronto Maple Leafs	50	24	22	4	183	161	317	52
Boston Bruins	50	16	30	4	179	219	275	36
Chicago Black Hawks	50	13	30	7	141	194	245	33
New York Rangers	50	11	29	10	154	247	305	32

Semi-finals:	March 20	Boston 4	Detroit 3 (at Detroit)
	March 22	Boston 4	Detroit 2 (at Detroit)
	March 25	Detroit 3	Boston 2 (at Boston)
	March 27	Detroit 3	Boston 2 (at Boston)
	March 29	Detroit 3	Boston 2* (at Detroit)
	April 1	Boston 5	Detroit 3 (at Boston)
	April 3	Detroit 5	Boston 3 (at Detroit)
	Detroit won best-of-seven 4–3		
Finals:	April 6	Toronto 1	Detroit 0 (at Detroit) [McCool]
	April 8	Toronto 2	Detroit 0 (at Detroit) [McCool]
	April 12	Toronto 1	Detroit 0 (at Toronto) [McCool]
	April 14	Detroit 5	Toronto 3 (at Toronto)
	April 19	Detroit 2	Toronto 0 (at Detroit) [Lumley]
	April 21	Detroit 1	Toronto 0* (at Toronto) [Lumley]
	April 22	Toronto 2	Detroit 1 (at Detroit)
	Toronto won Stanley Cup best-of-seven 4–3		

1945–1946

Montreal Canadiens	50	28	17	5	172	134	337	61
Boston Bruins	50	24	18	8	167	156	273	56
Chicago Black Hawks	50	23	20	7	200	178	339	53
Detroit Red Wings	50	20	20	10	146	159	298	50
Toronto Maple Leafs	50	19	24	7	174	185	247	45
New York Rangers	50	13	28	9	144	191	285	35

Semi-finals:	March 19	Boston 3	Detroit 1 (at Boston)
	March 21	Detroit 3	Boston 0 (at Boston) [Lumley]
	March 24	Boston 5	Detroit 2 (at Detroit)
	March 26	Boston 4	Detroit 1 (at Detroit)
	March 28	Boston 4	Detroit 3* (at Boston)
	Boston won best-of-seven 4–1		

1946–1947

Montreal Canadiens	60	34	16	10	189	138	561	78
Toronto Maple Leafs	60	31	19	10	209	172	669	72
Boston Bruins	60	26	23	11	190	175	463	63
Detroit Red Wings	60	22	27	11	190	193	535	55
New York Rangers	60	22	32	6	167	186	426	50
Chicago Black Hawks	60	19	37	4	193	274	467	42

Semi-finals:	March 26	Toronto 3	Detroit 2* (at Toronto)
	March 29	Detroit 9	Toronto 1 (at Toronto)
	April 1	Toronto 4	Detroit 1 (at Detroit)
	April 3	Toronto 4	Detroit 1 (at Detroit)
	April 5	Toronto 6	Detroit 1 (at Toronto)
	Toronto won best-of-seven 4–1		

1947–1948

Toronto Maple Leafs	60	32	15	13	182	143	758	77
Detroit Red Wings	60	30	18	12	187	148	593	72
Boston Bruins	60	23	24	13	167	168	515	59
New York Rangers	60	21	26	13	176	201	480	55
Montreal Canadiens	60	20	29	11	147	169	724	51
Chicago Black Hawks	60	20	34	6	195	225	572	46

Semi-finals:	March 24	Detroit 2	Rangers 1 (at Detroit)
	March 26	Detroit 5	Rangers 2 (at Detroit)
	March 28	Rangers 3	Detroit 2 (at New York)
	March 30	Rangers 3	Detroit 1 (at New York)
	April 1	Detroit 3	Rangers 1 (at Detroit)
	April 4	Detroit 4	Rangers 2 (at New York)
	Detroit won best-of-seven 4–2		
Finals:	April 7	Toronto 5	Detroit 3 (at Toronto)
	April 10	Toronto 4	Detroit 2 (at Toronto)
	April 11	Toronto 2	Detroit 0 (at Detroit) [Broda]
	April 14	Toronto 7	Detroit 2 (at Detroit)
	Toronto won Stanley Cup best-of-seven 4–0		

1948–1949

Detroit Red Wings	60	34	19	7	195	145	621	75
Boston Bruins	60	29	23	8	178	163	434	66
Montreal Canadiens	60	28	23	9	152	126	782	65
Toronto Maple Leafs	60	22	25	13	147	161	706	57
Chicago Black Hawks	60	21	31	8	173	211	695	50
New York Rangers	60	18	31	11	133	172	413	47

Semi-finals:	March 22	Detroit 2	Canadiens 1* (at Detroit)
	March 24	Canadiens 4	Detroit 3* (at Detroit)
	March 26	Canadiens 3	Detroit 2 (at Montreal)

	March 29	Detroit 3	Canadiens 1 (at Montreal)
	March 31	Detroit 3	Canadiens 1 (at Detroit)
	April 2	Canadiens 3	Detroit 1 (at Montreal)
	April 5	Detroit 3	Canadiens 1 (at Detroit)
	Detroit won best-of-seven 4–3		
Finals:	April 8	Toronto 3	Detroit 2* (at Detroit)
	April 10	Toronto 3	Detroit 1 (at Detroit)
	April 13	Toronto 3	Detroit 1 (at Toronto)
	April 16	Toronto 3	Detroit 1 (at Toronto)
	Toronto won Stanley Cup best-of-seven 4–0		

1949–1950

Detroit Red Wings	70	37	19	14	229	164	736	88
Montreal Canadiens	70	29	22	19	172	150	736	77
Toronto Maple Leafs	70	31	27	12	176	173	804	74
New York Rangers	70	28	31	11	170	189	639	67
Boston Bruins	70	22	32	16	198	228	449	60
Chicago Black Hawks	70	22	38	10	203	244	620	54

Semi-finals:	March 28	Toronto 5	Detroit 0 (at Detroit) [Broda]
	March 30	Detroit 3	Toronto 1 (at Detroit)
	April 1	Toronto 2	Detroit 0 (at Toronto) [Broda]
	April 4	Detroit 2	Toronto 1* (at Toronto)
	April 6	Toronto 2	Detroit 0 (at Detroit) [Broda]
	April 8	Detroit 4	Toronto 0 (at Toronto) [Lumley]
	April 9	Detroit 1	Toronto 0* (at Detroit) [Lumley]
	Detroit won best-of-seven 4–3		
Finals:	April 11	Detroit 4	Rangers 1 (at Detroit)
	April 13	Rangers 3	Detroit 1 (at Toronto)†
	April 15	Detroit 4	Rangers 0 (at Toronto)† [Lumley]
	April 18	Rangers 4	Detroit 3* (at Detroit)
	April 20	Rangers 2	Detroit 1* (at Detroit)
	April 22	Detroit 5	Rangers 4 (at Detroit)
	April 23	Detroit 4	Rangers 3* (at Detroit)
	Detroit won Stanley Cup best-of-seven 4–3		

† played at Maple Leaf Gardens because Madison Square Garden was previously booked

1950–1951

Detroit Red Wings	70	44	13	13	236	139	566	101
Toronto Maple Leafs	70	41	16	13	212	138	823	95
Montreal Canadiens	70	25	30	15	173	184	835	65
Boston Bruins	70	22	30	18	178	197	656	62
New York Rangers	70	20	29	21	169	201	774	61
Chicago Black Hawks	70	13	47	10	171	280	615	36

Semi-finals:	March 27	Canadiens 3	Detroit 2* (at Detroit)
	March 29	Canadiens 1	Detroit 0* (at Detroit) [McNeil]
	March 31	Detroit 2	Canadiens 0 (at Montreal) [Sawchuk]

April 3	Detroit 4	Canadiens 1 (at Montreal)
April 5	Canadiens 5	Detroit 2 (at Detroit)
April 7	Canadiens 3	Detroit 2 (at Montreal)

Canadiens won best-of-seven 4–2

1951–1952

Detroit Red Wings	70	44	14	12	215	133	694	100
Montreal Canadiens	70	34	26	10	195	164	661	78
Toronto Maple Leafs	70	29	25	16	168	157	841	74
Boston Bruins	70	25	29	16	162	176	601	66
New York Rangers	70	23	34	13	192	219	532	59
Chicago Black Hawks	70	17	44	9	158	241	627	43

Semi-finals:

March 25	Detroit 3	Toronto 0 (at Detroit) [Sawchuk]
March 27	Detroit 1	Toronto 0 (at Detroit) [Sawchuk]
March 29	Detroit 6	Toronto 2 (at Toronto)
April 1	Detroit 3	Toronto 1 (at Toronto)

Detroit won best-of-seven 4–0

Finals:

April 10	Detroit 3	Canadiens 1 (at Montreal)
April 12	Detroit 2	Canadiens 1 (at Montreal)
April 13	Detroit 3	Canadiens 0 (at Detroit) [Sawchuk]
April 15	Detroit 3	Canadiens 0 (at Detroit) [Sawchuk]

Detroit won Stanley Cup best-of-seven 4–0

1952–1953

Detroit Red Wings	70	36	16	18	222	133	645	90
Montreal Canadiens	70	28	23	19	155	148	777	75
Boston Bruins	70	28	29	13	152	172	528	69
Chicago Black Hawks	70	27	28	15	169	175	736	69
Toronto Maple Leafs	70	27	30	13	156	167	812	67
New York Rangers	70	17	37	16	152	211	548	50

Semi-finals:

March 24	Detroit 7	Boston 0 (at Detroit) [Sawchuk]
March 26	Boston 5	Detroit 3 (at Detroit)
March 29	Boston 2	Detroit 1* (at Boston)
March 31	Boston 6	Detroit 2 (at Boston)
April 2	Detroit 6	Boston 4 (at Detroit)
April 5	Boston 4	Detroit 2 (at Boston)

Boston won best-of-seven 4–2

1953–1954

Detroit Red Wings	70	37	19	14	191	132	814	88
Montreal Canadiens	70	35	24	11	195	141	1064	81
Toronto Maple Leafs	70	32	24	14	152	131	1022	78
Boston Bruins	70	32	28	10	177	181	685	74
New York Rangers	70	29	31	10	161	182	717	68
Chicago Black Hawks	70	12	51	7	133	242	797	31

Semi-finals:	March 23	Detroit 5	Toronto 0 (at Detroit) [Sawchuk]
	March 25	Toronto 3	Detroit 1 (at Detroit)
	March 27	Detroit 3	Toronto 1 (at Toronto)
	March 30	Detroit 2	Toronto 1 (at Toronto)
	April 1	Detroit 4	Toronto 3* (at Detroit)
	Detroit won best-of-seven 4–1		
Finals:	April 4	Detroit 3	Canadiens 1 (at Detroit)
	April 6	Canadiens 3	Detroit 1 (at Detroit)
	April 8	Detroit 5	Canadiens 2 (at Montreal)
	April 10	Detroit 2	Canadiens 0 (at Montreal) [Sawchuk]
	April 11	Canadiens 1	Detroit 0* (at Detroit) [McNeil]
	April 13	Canadiens 4	Detroit 1 (at Montreal)
	April 16	Detroit 2	Canadiens 1* (at Detroit)
	Detroit won Stanley Cup best-of-seven 4–3		

1954–1955

Detroit Red Wings	70	42	17	11	204	134	827	95
Montreal Canadiens	70	41	18	11	228	157	890	93
Toronto Maple Leafs	70	24	24	22	147	135	990	70
Boston Bruins	70	23	26	21	169	188	863	67
New York Rangers	70	17	35	18	150	210	690	52
Chicago Black Hawks	70	13	40	17	161	235	733	43

Semi-finals:	March 22	Detroit 7	Toronto 4 (at Detroit)
	March 24	Detroit 2	Toronto 1 (at Detroit)
	March 26	Detroit 2	Toronto 1 (at Toronto)
	March 29	Detroit 3	Toronto 0 (at Toronto) [Sawchuk]
	Detroit won best-of-seven 4–0		
Finals:	April 3	Detroit 4	Canadiens 2 (at Detroit)
	April 5	Detroit 7	Canadiens 1 (at Detroit)
	April 7	Canadiens 4	Detroit 2 (at Montreal)
	April 9	Canadiens 5	Detroit 3 (at Montreal)
	April 10	Detroit 5	Canadiens 1 (at Detroit)
	April 12	Canadiens 6	Detroit 3 (at Montreal)
	April 14	Detroit 3	Canadiens 1 (at Detroit)
	Detroit won Stanley Cup best-of-seven 4–3		

1955–1956

Montreal Canadiens	70	45	15	10	222	131	977	100
Detroit Red Wings	70	30	24	16	183	148	794	76
New York Rangers	70	32	28	10	204	203	911	74
Toronto Maple Leafs	70	24	33	13	153	181	1051	61
Boston Bruins	70	23	34	13	147	185	929	59
Chicago Black Hawks	70	19	39	12	155	216	826	50

Semi-finals:	March 20	Detroit 3	Toronto 2 (at Detroit)
	March 22	Detroit 3	Toronto 1 (at Detroit)

	March 24	Detroit 5	Toronto 4* (at Toronto)
	March 27	Toronto 2	Detroit 0 (at Toronto) [Lumley]
	March 29	Detroit 3	Toronto 1 (at Detroit)
	Detroit won best-of-seven 4–1		
Finals:	March 31	Canadiens 6	Detroit 4 (at Montreal)
	April 3	Canadiens 5	Detroit 1 (at Montreal)
	April 5	Detroit 3	Canadiens 1 (at Detroit)
	April 8	Canadiens 3	Detroit 0 (at Detroit) [Plante]
	April 10	Canadiens 3	Detroit 1 (at Montreal)
	Canadiens won Stanley Cup best-of-seven 4–1		

1956–1957

Detroit Red Wings	70	38	20	12	198	157	656	88
Montreal Canadiens	70	35	23	12	210	155	870	82
Boston Bruins	70	34	24	12	195	174	978	80
New York Rangers	70	26	30	14	184	227	870	66
Toronto Maple Leafs	70	21	34	15	174	192	829	57
Chicago Black Hawks	70	16	39	15	169	225	809	47

• penalized player allowed to return after a power-play goal has been scored by the opposition

Semi-finals:	March 26	Boston 3	Detroit 1 (at Detroit)
	March 28	Detroit 3	Boston 1 (at Detroit)
	March 31	Boston 4	Detroit 3 (at Boston)
	April 2	Boston 2	Detroit 0 (at Boston) [Simmons]
	April 4	Boston 4	Detroit 3 (at Detroit)
	Boston won best-of-seven 4–1		

1957–1958

Montreal Canadiens	70	43	17	10	250	158	945	96
New York Rangers	70	32	25	13	195	188	781	77
Detroit Red Wings	70	29	29	12	176	207	758	70
Boston Bruins	70	27	28	15	199	194	849	69
Chicago Black Hawks	70	24	39	7	163	202	906	55
Toronto Maple Leafs	70	21	38	11	192	226	861	53

Semi-finals:	March 25	Canadiens 8	Detroit 1 (at Montreal)
	March 27	Canadiens 5	Detroit 1 (at Montreal)
	March 30	Canadiens 2	Detroit 1* (at Detroit)
	April 1	Canadiens 4	Detroit 3 (at Detroit)
	Canadiens won best-of-seven 4–0		

1958–1959

Montreal Canadiens	70	39	18	13	258	158	760	91
Boston Bruins	70	32	29	9	205	215	838	73
Chicago Black Hawks	70	28	29	13	197	208	921	69
Toronto Maple Leafs	70	27	32	11	189	201	846	65
New York Rangers	70	26	32	12	201	217	860	64
Detroit Red Wings	70	25	37	8	167	218	613	58

• did not qualify for playoffs

1959–1960

Montreal Canadiens	70	40	18	12	255	178	756	92
Toronto Maple Leafs	70	35	26	9	199	195	859	79
Chicago Black Hawks	70	28	29	13	191	180	970	69
Detroit Red Wings	70	26	29	15	186	197	538	67
Boston Bruins	70	28	34	8	220	241	932	64
New York Rangers	70	17	38	15	187	247	850	49

Semi-finals:	March 23	Detroit 2	Toronto 1 (at Toronto)
	March 26	Toronto 4	Detroit 2 (at Toronto)
	March 27	Toronto 5	Detroit 4* (at Detroit)
	March 29	Detroit 2	Toronto 1* (at Detroit)
	April 2	Toronto 5	Detroit 4 (at Toronto)
	April 3	Toronto 4	Detroit 2 (at Detroit)
	Toronto won best-of-seven 4–2		

1960–1961

Montreal Canadiens	70	41	19	10	254	188	811	92
Toronto Maple Leafs	70	39	19	12	234	176	844	90
Chicago Black Hawks	70	29	24	17	198	180	1022	75
Detroit Red Wings	70	25	29	16	195	215	655	66
New York Rangers	70	22	38	10	204	248	591	54
Boston Bruins	70	15	42	13	176	254	810	43

Semi-finals:	March 22	Toronto 3	Detroit 2* (at Toronto)
	March 25	Detroit 4	Toronto 2 (at Toronto)
	March 26	Detroit 2	Toronto 0 (at Detroit) [Sawchuk]
	March 28	Detroit 4	Toronto 1 (at Detroit)
	April 1	Detroit 3	Toronto 2 (at Toronto)
	Detroit won best-of-seven 4–1		
Finals:	April 6	Chicago 3	Detroit 2 (at Chicago)
	April 8	Detroit 3	Chicago 1 (at Detroit)
	April 10	Chicago 3	Detroit 1 (at Chicago)
	April 12	Detroit 2	Chicago 1 (at Detroit)
	April 14	Chicago 6	Detroit 3 (at Chicago)
	April 16	Chicago 5	Detroit 1 (at Detroit)
	Chicago won Stanley Cup best-of-seven 4–2		

1961–1962

Montreal Canadiens	70	42	14	14	259	166	818	98
Toronto Maple Leafs	70	37	22	11	232	180	762	85
Chicago Black Hawks	70	31	26	13	217	186	894	75
New York Rangers	70	26	32	12	195	207	668	64
Detroit Red Wings	70	23	33	14	184	219	684	60
Boston Bruins	70	15	47	8	177	306	712	38

- did not qualify for playoffs

1962–1963

Toronto Maple Leafs	70	35	23	12	221	180	816	82
Chicago Black Hawks	70	32	21	17	194	178	906	81
Montreal Canadiens	70	28	19	23	225	183	751	79
Detroit Red Wings	70	32	25	13	200	194	964	77
New York Rangers	70	22	36	12	211	233	657	56
Boston Bruins	70	14	39	17	198	281	636	45

Semi-finals:	March 26	Chicago 5	Detroit 4 (at Chicago)
	March 28	Chicago 5	Detroit 2 (at Chicago)
	March 31	Detroit 4	Chicago 2 (at Detroit)
	April 2	Detroit 4	Chicago 1 (at Detroit)
	April 4	Detroit 4	Chicago 2 (at Chicago)
	April 7	Detroit 7	Chicago 4 (at Detroit)
	Detroit won best-of-seven 4–2		
Finals:	April 9	Toronto 4	Detroit 2 (at Toronto)
	April 11	Toronto 4	Detroit 2 (at Toronto)
	April 14	Detroit 3	Toronto 2 (at Detroit)
	April 16	Toronto 4	Detroit 2 (at Detroit)
	April 18	Toronto 3	Detroit 1 (at Toronto)
	Toronto won Stanley Cup best-of-seven 4–1		

1963–1964

Montreal Canadiens	70	36	21	13	209	167	982	85
Chicago Black Hawks	70	36	22	12	218	169	1116	84
Toronto Maple Leafs	70	33	25	12	192	172	928	78
Detroit Red Wings	70	30	29	11	191	204	771	71
New York Rangers	70	22	38	10	186	242	715	54
Boston Bruins	70	18	40	12	170	212	858	48

Semi-finals:	March 26	Chicago 4	Detroit 1 (at Chicago)
	March 29	Detroit 5	Chicago 4 (at Chicago)
	March 31	Detroit 3	Chicago 0 (at Detroit) [Sawchuk]
	April 2	Chicago 3	Detroit 2* (at Detroit)
	April 5	Chicago 3	Detroit 2 (at Chicago)
	April 7	Detroit 7	Chicago 2 (at Detroit)
	April 9	Detroit 4	Chicago 2 (at Chicago)
	Detroit won best-of-seven 4–3		
Finals:	April 11	Toronto 3	Detroit 2 (at Toronto)
	April 14	Detroit 4	Toronto 3* (at Toronto)
	April 16	Detroit 4	Toronto 3 (at Detroit)
	April 18	Toronto 4	Detroit 2 (at Detroit)
	April 21	Detroit 2	Toronto 1 (at Toronto)
	April 23	Toronto 4	Detroit 3* (at Detroit)
	April 25	Toronto 4	Detroit 0 (at Toronto) [Bower]
	Toronto won Stanley Cup best-of-seven 4–3		

1964–1965

Detroit Red Wings	70	40	23	7	224	175	1121	87
Montreal Canadiens	70	36	23	11	211	185	1033	83
Chicago Black Hawks	70	34	28	8	224	176	1051	76
Toronto Maple Leafs	70	30	26	14	204	173	1068	74
New York Rangers	70	20	38	12	179	246	760	52
Boston Bruins	70	21	43	6	166	253	946	48

Semi-finals:	April 1	Detroit 4	Chicago 3 (at Detroit)
	April 4	Detroit 6	Chicago 3 (at Detroit)
	April 6	Chicago 5	Detroit 2 (at Chicago)
	April 8	Chicago 2	Detroit 1 (at Chicago)
	April 11	Detroit 4	Chicago 2 (at Detroit)
	April 13	Chicago 4	Detroit 0 (at Chicago) [Hall]
	April 15	Chicago 4	Detroit 2 (at Detroit)
	Chicago won best-of-seven 4–3		

1965–1966

Montreal Canadiens	70	41	21	8	239	173	884	90
Chicago Black Hawks	70	37	25	8	240	187	815	82
Toronto Maple Leafs	70	34	25	11	208	187	811	79
Detroit Red Wings	70	31	27	12	221	194	804	74
Boston Bruins	70	21	43	6	174	275	787	48
New York Rangers	70	18	41	11	195	261	894	47

Semi-finals:	April 7	Chicago 2	Detroit 1 (at Chicago)
	April 10	Detroit 7	Chicago 0 (at Chicago) [Crozier]
	April 12	Chicago 2	Detroit 1 (at Detroit)
	April 14	Detroit 5	Chicago 1 (at Detroit)
	April 17	Detroit 5	Chicago 3 (at Chicago)
	April 19	Detroit 3	Chicago 2 (at Detroit)
	Detroit won best-of-seven 4–2		
Finals:	April 24	Detroit 3	Canadiens 2 (at Montreal)
	April 26	Detroit 5	Canadiens 2 (at Montreal)
	April 28	Canadiens 4	Detroit 2 (at Detroit)
	May 1	Canadiens 2	Detroit 1 (at Detroit)
	May 3	Canadiens 5	Detroit 1 (at Montreal)
	May 5	Canadiens 3	Detroit 2* (at Detroit)
	Canadiens won Stanley Cup best-of-seven 4–2		

1966–1967

Chicago Black Hawks	70	41	17	12	264	170	757	94
Montreal Canadiens	70	32	25	13	202	188	879	77
Toronto Maple Leafs	70	32	27	11	204	211	736	75
New York Rangers	70	30	28	12	188	189	666	72
Detroit Red Wings	70	27	39	4	212	241	719	58
Boston Bruins	70	17	43	10	182	253	764	44

• did not qualify for playoffs

1967–1968

East Division								
Montreal Canadiens	74	42	22	10	236	167	700	94
New York Rangers	74	39	23	12	226	183	673	90
Boston Bruins	74	37	27	10	259	216	1043	84
Chicago Black Hawks	74	32	26	16	212	222	606	80
Toronto Maple Leafs	74	33	31	10	209	176	634	76
Detroit Red Wings	74	27	35	12	245	257	759	66
West Division								
Philadelphia Flyers	74	31	32	11	173	179	987	73
Los Angeles Kings	74	31	33	10	200	224	810	72
St. Louis Blues	74	27	31	16	177	191	792	70
Minnesota North Stars	74	27	32	15	191	226	738	69
Pittsburgh Penguins	74	27	34	13	195	216	554	67
Oakland Seals	74	15	42	17	153	219	787	47

- top four teams in each division qualified for the playoffs
- did not qualify for playoffs

1968–1969

East Division								
Montreal Canadiens	76	46	19	11	271	202	780	103
Boston Bruins	76	42	18	16	303	221	1297	100
New York Rangers	76	41	26	9	231	196	806	91
Toronto Maple Leafs	76	35	26	15	234	217	961	85
Detroit Red Wings	76	33	31	12	239	221	885	78
Chicago Black Hawks	76	34	33	9	280	246	842	77
West Division								
St. Louis Blues	76	37	25	14	204	157	838	88
Oakland Seals	76	29	36	11	219	251	811	69
Philadelphia Flyers	76	20	35	21	174	225	964	61
Los Angeles Kings	76	24	42	10	185	260	698	58
Pittsburgh Penguins	76	20	45	11	189	252	677	51
Minnesota North Stars	76	18	43	5	189	270	862	51

- did not qualify for playoffs

1969–1970

East Division								
Chicago Black Hawks	76	45	22	9	250	170	887	99
Boston Bruins	76	40	17	19	277	216	1184	99
Detroit Red Wings	76	40	21	15	246	199	899	95
New York Rangers	76	38	22	16	246	189	843	92
Montreal Canadiens	76	38	22	16	244	201	874	92
Toronto Maple Leafs	76	29	34	13	222	242	886	71
West Division								
St. Louis Blues	76	37	27	12	224	179	862	86
Pittsburgh Penguins	76	26	38	12	182	238	1034	64
Minnesota North Stars	76	19	35	22	224	257	988	60

Oakland Seals	76	22	40	14	169	243	835	58
Philadelphia Flyers	76	17	35	24	197	225	1107	58
Los Angeles Kings	76	14	52	10	168	290	967	38

Quarter-finals:	April 8	Chicago 4	Detroit 2 (at Chicago)
	April 9	Chicago 4	Detroit 2 (at Chicago)
	April 11	Chicago 4	Detroit 2 (at Detroit)
	April 12	Chicago 4	Detroit 2 (at Detroit))
	Chicago won best-of-seven 4–0		

1970–1971

East Division								
Boston Bruins	78	57	14	7	399	207	1146	121
New York Rangers	78	49	18	11	259	177	944	109
Montreal Canadiens	78	42	23	13	291	216	1261	97
Toronto Maple Leafs	78	37	33	8	248	211	1127	82
Buffalo Sabres	78	24	39	15	217	291	1178	63
Vancouver Canucks	78	24	46	8	229	296	1357	56
Detroit Red Wings	78	22	45	11	209	308	968	55
West Division								
Chicago Black Hawks	78	49	20	9	277	184	1268	107
St. Louis Blues	78	34	25	19	223	208	1068	87
Philadelphia Flyers	78	28	33	17	207	225	1052	73
Minnesota North Stars	78	28	34	16	191	223	894	72
Los Angeles Kings	78	25	40	13	239	303	767	63
Pittsburgh Penguins	78	21	37	20	221	240	1073	62
California Golden Seals	78	20	53	5	199	320	931	45

- did not qualify for playoffs

1971–1972

East Division								
Boston Bruins	78	54	13	11	330	204	1106	119
New York Rangers	78	48	17	13	317	192	1006	109
Montreal Canadiens	78	46	16	16	307	205	771	108
Toronto Maple Leafs	78	33	31	14	209	208	877	80
Detroit Red Wings	78	33	35	10	261	262	846	76
Buffalo Sabres	78	16	43	19	203	289	817	51
Vancouver Canucks	78	20	50	8	203	297	1084	48
West Division								
Chicago Black Hawks	78	46	17	15	256	166	836	107
Minnesota North Stars	78	37	29	12	212	191	845	86
St. Louis Blues	78	28	39	11	208	247	1138	67
Pittsburgh Penguins	78	26	38	14	220	258	970	66
Philadelphia Flyers	78	26	38	14	200	236	1219	66
California Golden Seals	78	21	39	18	216	288	1001	60
Los Angeles Kings	78	20	49	9	206	305	709	49

- did not qualify for playoffs

1972–1973

East Division

Montreal Canadiens	78	52	10	16	329	184	783	120
Boston Bruins	78	51	22	5	330	235	1097	107
New York Rangers	78	47	23	8	297	208	765	102
Buffalo Sabres	78	37	27	14	257	219	940	88
Detroit Red Wings	78	37	29	12	265	243	893	86
Toronto Maple Leafs	78	27	41	10	247	279	716	64
Vancouver Canucks	78	22	47	9	233	339	943	53
New York Islanders	78	12	60	6	170	347	881	30

West Division

Chicago Black Hawks	78	42	27	9	284	225	864	93
Philadelphia Flyers	78	37	30	11	296	256	1756	85
Minnesota North Stars	78	37	30	11	254	230	881	85
St. Louis Blues	78	32	34	12	233	251	1195	76
Pittsburgh Penguins	78	32	37	9	257	265	866	73
Los Angeles Kings	78	31	36	11	232	245	888	73
Atlanta Flames	78	25	38	15	191	239	852	65
California Golden Seals	78	16	46	16	213	323	840	48

• did not qualify for playoffs

1973–1974

East Division

Boston Bruins	78	52	17	9	349	221	968	113
Montreal Canadiens	78	45	24	9	293	240	761	99
New York Rangers	78	40	24	14	300	251	782	94
Toronto Maple Leafs	78	35	27	16	274	230	903	86
Buffalo Sabres	78	32	34	12	242	250	787	76
Detroit Red Wings	78	29	39	10	255	319	917	68
Vancouver Canucks	78	24	43	11	224	296	952	59
New York Islanders	78	19	41	18	182	247	1075	56

West Division

Philadelphia Flyers	78	50	16	12	273	164	1750	112
Chicago Black Hawks	78	41	14	23	272	164	877	105
Los Angeles Kings	78	33	33	12	233	231	1055	78
Atlanta Flames	78	30	34	14	214	238	841	74
Pittsburgh Penguins	78	28	41	9	242	273	950	65
St. Louis Blues	78	26	40	12	206	248	1147	64
Minnesota North Stars	78	23	38	17	235	275	821	63
California Golden Seals	78	13	55	10	195	342	651	36

• did not qualify for playoffs

1974–1975

PRINCE OF WALES CONFERENCE

Norris Division

Montreal Canadiens	80	47	14	19	374	225	1155	113
Los Angeles Kings	80	42	17	21	269	185	1185	105
Pittsburgh Penguins	80	37	28	15	326	289	1119	89

Detroit Red Wings	80	23	45	12	259	335	1078	58
Washington Capitals	80	8	67	5	181	446	1085	21
Adams Division								
Buffalo Sabres	80	49	16	15	354	240	1229	113
Boston Bruins	80	40	26	14	345	245	1153	94
Toronto Maple Leafs	80	31	33	16	280	309	1079	78
California Golden Seals	80	19	48	13	212	316	1101	51
CLARENCE CAMPBELL CONFERENCE								
Patrick Division								
Philadelphia Flyers	80	51	18	11	293	181	1969	113
New York Rangers	80	37	29	14	319	276	1053	88
New York Islanders	80	33	25	22	264	221	1118	88
Atlanta Flames	80	34	31	15	243	233	915	83
Smythe Division								
Vancouver Canucks	80	38	32	10	271	254	965	86
St. Louis Blues	80	35	31	14	269	267	1275	84
Chicago Black Hawks	80	37	35	8	268	241	1112	82
Minnesota North Stars	80	23	50	7	221	341	1106	53
Kansas City Scouts	80	15	54	11	184	328	744	41

- the top three teams in each division qualified for the playoffs. The four division champions received byes and all second and third place clubs were ranked 1–8 by points, #1 playing # 8, #2 and #7, etc. The first round was best-of-three, the subsequent rounds best-of-seven.
- did not qualify for playoffs

1975–1976

PRINCE OF WALES CONFERENCE

Norris Division

Montreal Canadiens	80	58	11	11	337	174	977	127
Los Angeles Kings	80	38	33	9	263	265	1022	85
Pittsburgh Penguins	80	35	33	12	339	303	1004	82
Detroit Red Wings	80	26	44	10	226	300	1922	62
Washington Capitals	80	11	59	10	224	394	951	32
Adams Division								
Boston Bruins	80	48	15	17	313	237	1195	113
Buffalo Sabres	80	46	21	13	339	240	943	105
Toronto Maple Leafs	80	34	31	15	294	276	1368	83
California Golden Seals	80	27	42	11	250	278	1058	65
CLARENCE CAMPBELL CONFERENCE								
Patrick Division								
Philadelphia Flyers	80	51	13	16	348	209	1980	118
New York Islanders	80	42	21	17	297	190	1277	101
Atlanta Flames	80	35	33	12	262	237	928	82
New York Rangers	80	29	42	9	262	333	911	67
Smythe Division								
Chicago Black Hawks	80	32	30	18	254	261	944	82
Vancouver Canucks	80	33	32	15	271	272	1122	81
St. Louis Blues	80	29	37	14	249	290	1274	72
Minnesota North Stars	80	20	53	7	195	303	1191	47
Kansas City Scouts	80	12	56	12	190	351	984	36

- did not qualify for playoffs

1976–1977

PRINCE OF WALES CONFERENCE

Norris Division

Montreal Canadiens	80	60	8	12	387	171	764	132
Los Angeles Kings	80	34	31	15	271	241	1186	83
Pittsburgh Penguins	80	34	33	13	240	252	669	81
Washington Capitals	80	24	42	14	221	307	1231	62
Detroit Red Wings	80	16	55	9	183	309	1332	41
Adams Division								
Boston Bruins	80	49	23	8	312	240	1065	106
Buffalo Sabres	80	48	24	8	301	220	848	104
Toronto Maple Leafs	80	33	32	15	301	285	1200	81
Cleveland Barons	80	25	42	13	240	292	1011	63
CLARENCE CAMPBELL CONFERENCE								
Patrick Division								
Philadelphia Flyers	80	48	16	16	323	213	1547	112
New York Islanders	80	47	21	12	288	193	1012	106
Atlanta Flames	80	34	34	12	264	265	889	80
New York Rangers	80	29	37	14	272	310	1164	72
Smythe Division								
St. Louis Blues	80	32	39	9	239	276	877	73
Minnesota North Stars	80	23	39	18	240	310	774	64
Chicago Black Hawks	80	26	43	11	240	298	1104	63
Vancouver Canucks	80	25	42	13	235	294	1078	63
Colorado Rockies	80	20	46	14	226	307	978	54

• did not qualify for playoffs

1977–1978

PRINCE OF WALES CONFERENCE

Norris Division

Montreal Canadiens	80	59	10	11	359	183	745	129
Detroit Red Wings	80	32	34	14	252	266	1534	78
Los Angeles Kings	80	31	34	15	243	245	903	77
Pittsburgh Penguins	80	25	37	18	254	321	1300	68
Washington Capitals	80	17	49	14	195	321	1332	48
Adams Division								
Boston Bruins	80	51	18	11	333	218	1237	113
Buffalo Sabres	80	44	19	17	288	215	800	105
Toronto Maple Leafs	80	41	29	10	271	237	1258	92
Cleveland Barons	80	22	45	13	230	325	1010	57
CLARENCE CAMPBELL CONFERENCE								
Patrick Division								
New York Islanders	80	48	17	15	334	210	938	111
Philadelphia Flyers	80	45	20	15	296	200	1668	105
Atlanta Flames	80	34	27	19	274	252	984	87
New York Rangers	80	30	37	13	279	280	1057	73
Smythe Division								
Chicago Black Hawks	80	32	29	19	230	220	1308	83
Colorado Rockies	80	19	40	21	257	305	818	59

Vancouver Canucks	80	20	43	17	239	320	962	57
St. Louis Blues	80	20	47	13	195	304	845	53
Minnesota North Stars	80	18	53	9	218	325	1096	45

• playoff format altered so that all 1st and 2nd place teams qualified and the next best four regardless of division.

1st round:	April 11	Detroit 5	Atlanta 3 (at Atlanta)
	April 13	Detroit 3	Atlanta 2 (at Detroit)
	Detroit won best-of-three 2–0		
Quarter-finals:	April 17	Canadiens 6	Detroit 2 (at Montreal)
	April 19	Detroit 4	Canadiens 2 (at Montreal)
	April 21	Canadiens 4	Detroit 2 (at Detroit)
	April 23	Canadiens 8	Detroit 0 (at Detroit) [K. Dryden]
	April 25	Canadiens 4	Detroit 2 (at Montreal)
	Canadiens won best-of-seven 4–1		

1978–1979

PRINCE OF WALES CONFERENCE

Norris Division								
Montreal Canadiens	80	52	17	11	337	204	803	115
Pittsburgh Penguins	80	36	31	13	281	279	1039	85
Los Angeles Kings	80	34	34	12	292	286	1134	80
Washington Capitals	80	24	41	15	273	338	1312	63
Detroit Red Wings	80	23	41	16	252	295	1359	62
Adams Division								
Boston Bruins	80	43	23	14	316	270	1222	100
Buffalo Sabres	80	36	28	16	280	263	1026	88
Toronto Maple Leafs	80	34	33	13	267	252	1440	81
Minnesota North Stars	80	28	40	12	257	289	1102	68
CLARENCE CAMPBELL CONFERENCE								
Patrick Division								
New York Islanders	80	51	15	14	358	214	1077	116
Philadelphia Flyers	80	40	25	15	281	248	1548	95
New York Rangers	80	40	29	11	316	292	1214	91
Atlanta Flames	80	41	31	8	327	280	1158	90
Smythe Division								
Chicago Black Hawks	80	29	36	15	244	277	1254	73
Vancouver Canucks	80	25	42	13	217	291	1134	63
St. Louis Blues	80	18	50	12	249	348	1055	48
Colorado Rockies	80	15	53	12	210	331	838	42

• did not qualify for playoffs

1979–1980

PRINCE OF WALES CONFERENCE

Norris Division								
Montreal Canadiens	80	47	20	13	328	240	874	107
Los Angeles Kings	80	30	36	14	290	313	1124	74
Pittsburgh Penguins	80	30	37	13	251	303	1038	73

Hartford Whalers	80	27	34	19	303	312	875	73
Detroit Red Wings	80	26	43	11	268	306	1114	63
Adams Division								
Buffalo Sabres	80	47	17	16	318	201	967	110
Boston Bruins	80	46	21	13	310	234	1460	105
Minnesota North Stars	80	36	28	16	311	253	1064	88
Toronto Maple Leafs	80	35	40	5	304	327	1158	75
Quebec Nordiques	80	25	44	11	248	313	1062	61
CLARENCE CAMPBELL CONFERENCE								
Patrick Division								
Philadelphia Flyers	80	48	12	20	327	254	1844	116
New York Islanders	80	39	28	13	281	247	1298	91
New York Rangers	80	38	32	10	308	284	1342	86
Atlanta Flames	80	35	32	13	282	269	1048	83
Washington Capitals	80	27	40	13	261	293	1198	67
Smythe Division								
Chicago Black Hawks	80	34	27	19	241	250	1325	87
St. Louis Blues	80	34	34	12	266	278	1037	80
Vancouver Canucks	80	27	37	16	256	281	1808	70
Edmonton Oilers	80	28	39	13	301	322	1528	69
Winnipeg Jets	80	20	49	11	214	314	1251	51
Colorado Rockies	80	19	48	13	234	308	1020	51

- top four teams in each division qualified for the playoffs
- did not qualify for playoffs

1980–1981

PRINCE OF WALES CONFERENCE								
Norris Division								
Montreal Canadiens	80	45	22	13	332	232	1398	103
Los Angeles Kings	80	43	24	13	337	290	1627	99
Pittsburgh Penguins	80	30	37	13	302	345	1807	73
Hartford Whalers	80	21	41	18	292	372	1584	60
Detroit Red Wings	80	19	43	18	252	339	1687	56
Adams Division								
Buffalo Sabres	80	39	20	21	327	250	1194	99
Boston Bruins	80	37	30	13	316	272	1836	87
Minnesota North Stars	80	35	28	17	291	263	1624	87
Quebec Nordiques	80	30	32	18	314	318	1524	78
Toronto Maple Leafs	80	28	37	15	322	367	1830	71
CLARENCE CAMPBELL CONFERENCE								
Patrick Division								
New York Islanders	80	48	18	14	355	260	1442	110
Philadelphia Flyers	80	41	24	15	313	249	2621	97
Calgary Flames	80	39	27	14	329	298	1450	92
New York Rangers	80	30	36	14	312	317	1981	74
Washington Capitals	80	26	36	18	286	317	1872	70
Smythe Division								
St. Louis Blues	80	45	18	17	352	281	1657	107
Chicago Black Hawks	80	31	33	16	304	315	1660	78

Vancouver Canucks	80	28	32	20	289	301	1892	76
Edmonton Oilers	80	29	35	16	328	327	1544	74
Colorado Rockies	80	22	45	13	258	344	1418	57
Winnipeg Jets	80	9	57	14	246	400	1191	32

• did not qualify for playoffs

1981–1982

CLARENCE CAMPBELL CONFERENCE

Norris Division

Minnesota North Stars	80	37	23	20	346	288	1358	94
Winnipeg Jets	80	33	33	14	319	332	1314	80
St. Louis Blues	80	32	40	8	315	349	1579	72
Chicago Black Hawks	80	30	38	12	332	363	1775	72
Toronto Maple Leafs	80	20	44	16	298	380	1888	56
Detroit Red Wings	80	21	47	12	270	351	1250	54

Smythe Division

Edmonton Oilers	80	48	17	15	417	295	1473	111
Vancouver Canucks	80	30	33	17	290	286	1840	77
Calgary Flames	80	29	34	17	334	345	1331	75
Los Angeles Kings	80	24	41	15	314	369	1730	63
Colorado Rockies	80	18	49	13	241	362	1138	49

PRINCE OF WALES CONFERENCE

Adams Division

Montreal Canadiens	80	46	17	17	360	223	1463	109
Boston Bruins	80	43	27	10	323	285	1266	96
Buffalo Sabres	80	39	26	15	307	273	1425	93
Quebec Nordiques	80	33	31	16	356	345	1757	82
Hartford Whalers	80	21	41	18	264	351	1493	60

Patrick Division

New York Islanders	80	54	16	10	385	250	1328	118
New York Rangers	80	39	27	14	316	306	1402	92
Philadelphia Flyers	80	38	31	11	325	313	2493	87
Pittsburgh Penguins	80	31	36	13	310	337	2212	75
Washington Capitals	80	26	41	13	319	338	1932	65

• did not qualify for playoffs

1982–1983

CLARENCE CAMPBELL CONFERENCE

Norris Division

Chicago Black Hawks	80	47	23	10	338	268	1185	104
Minnesota North Stars	80	40	24	16	321	290	1520	96
Toronto Maple Leafs	80	28	40	12	293	330	1481	68
St. Louis Blues	80	25	40	15	285	316	1281	65
Detroit Red Wings	80	21	44	15	263	344	1064	57

Smythe Division

Edmonton Oilers	80	47	21	12	424	315	1771	106
Calgary Flames	80	32	34	14	321	317	1146	78

Vancouver Canucks	80	30	35	15	303	309	1639	75
Winnipeg Jets	80	33	39	8	311	333	1089	74
Los Angeles Kings	80	27	41	12	308	365	1367	66
PRINCE OF WALES CONFERENCE								
Adams Division								
Boston Bruins	80	50	20	10	327	228	1202	110
Montreal Canadiens	80	42	24	14	350	286	1116	98
Buffalo Sabres	80	38	29	13	318	285	1031	89
Quebec Nordiques	80	34	34	12	343	336	1648	80
Hartford Whalers	80	19	54	7	261	403	1392	45
Patrick Division								
Philadelphia Flyers	80	49	23	8	326	240	1337	106
New York Islanders	80	42	26	12	302	226	1266	96
Washington Capitals	80	39	25	16	306	283	1329	94
New York Rangers	80	35	35	10	306	287	1100	80
New Jersey Devils	80	17	49	14	230	338	1270	48
Pittsburgh Penguins	80	18	53	9	257	394	1859	45

- did not qualify for playoffs

1983–1984

CLARENCE CAMPBELL CONFERENCE								
Norris Division								
Minnesota North Stars	80	39	31	10	345	344	1696	88
St. Louis Blues	80	32	41	7	293	316	1614	71
Detroit Red Wings	80	31	42	7	298	323	1546	69
Chicago Black Hawks	80	30	42	8	277	311	1358	68
Toronto Maple Leafs	80	26	45	9	303	387	1682	61
Smythe Division								
Edmonton Oilers	80	57	18	5	446	314	1577	119
Calgary Flames	80	34	32	14	311	314	1390	82
Vancouver Canucks	80	32	39	9	306	328	1474	73
Winnipeg Jets	80	31	38	11	340	374	1579	73
Los Angeles Kings	80	23	44	13	309	376	1265	59
PRINCE OF WALES CONFERENCE								
Adams Division								
Boston Bruins	80	49	25	6	336	261	1606	104
Buffalo Sabres	80	48	25	7	315	257	1190	103
Quebec Nordiques	80	42	28	10	360	278	1600	94
Montreal Canadiens	80	35	40	5	286	295	1371	75
Hartford Whalers	80	28	42	10	288	320	1184	66
Patrick Division								
New York Islanders	80	50	26	4	357	269	1157	104
Washington Capitals	80	48	27	5	308	226	1252	101
Philadelphia Flyers	80	44	26	10	350	290	1488	98
New York Rangers	80	42	29	9	314	304	1471	93
New Jersey Devils	80	17	56	7	231	350	1352	41
Pittsburgh Penguins	80	16	58	6	254	390	1695	38

- 5 minute sudden death overtime introduced

1st round:	April 4	St. Louis 3	Detroit 2 (at St. Louis)
	April 5	Detroit 5	St. Louis 3 (at St. Louis)
	April 7	St. Louis 4	Detroit 3* (at Detroit)
	April 8	St. Louis 3	Detroit 2* (at Detroit)
	St. Louis won best-of-five 3–1		

1984–1985

CLARENCE CAMPBELL CONFERENCE								
Norris Division								
St. Louis Blues	80	37	31	12	299	288	1301	86
Chicago Black Hawks	80	38	35	7	309	299	1432	83
Detroit Red Wings	80	27	41	12	313	357	1741	66
Minnesota North Stars	80	25	43	12	268	321	1735	62
Toronto Maple Leafs	80	20	52	8	253	358	1627	48
Smythe Division								
Edmonton Oilers	80	49	20	11	401	298	1567	109
Winnipeg Jets	80	43	27	10	358	332	1540	96
Calgary Flames	80	41	27	12	363	302	1400	94
Los Angeles Kings	80	34	32	14	339	326	1413	82
Vancouver Canucks	80	25	46	9	284	401	1451	59
PRINCE OF WALES CONFERENCE								
Adams Division								
Montreal Canadiens	80	41	27	12	309	262	1464	94
Quebec Nordiques	80	41	30	9	323	275	1643	91
Buffalo Sabres	80	38	28	14	290	237	1221	90
Boston Bruins	80	36	34	10	303	287	1825	82
Hartford Whalers	80	30	41	9	268	318	1606	69
Patrick Division								
Philadelphia Flyers	80	53	20	7	348	241	1540	113
Washington Capitals	80	46	25	9	322	240	1161	101
New York Islanders	80	40	34	6	345	312	1516	86
New York Rangers	80	26	44	10	295	345	1301	62
New Jersey Devils	80	22	48	10	264	346	1282	54
Pittsburgh Penguins	80	24	51	5	276	385	1493	53

1st round:	April 10	Chicago 9	Detroit 5 (at Chicago)
	April 11	Chicago 6	Detroit 1 (at Chicago)
	April 13	Chicago 8	Detroit 2 (at Detroit)
	Chicago won best-of-five 3–0		

1985–1986

CLARENCE CAMPBELL CONFERENCE								
Norris Division								
Chicago Black Hawks	80	39	33	8	351	349	1537	86
Minnesota North Stars	80	38	33	9	327	305	1672	85
St. Louis Blues	80	37	34	9	302	291	1478	83
Toronto Maple Leafs	80	25	48	7	311	386	1716	57
Detroit Red Wings	80	17	57	6	266	415	2393	40

Smythe Division								
Edmonton Oilers	80	56	17	7	426	310	1928	119
Calgary Flames	80	40	31	9	354	315	2297	89
Winnipeg Jets	80	26	47	7	295	372	1774	59
Vancouver Canucks	80	23	44	13	282	333	1813	59
Los Angeles Kings	80	23	49	8	284	389	2004	54
PRINCE OF WALES CONFERENCE								
Adams Division								
Quebec Nordiques	80	43	31	6	330	289	1847	92
Montreal Canadiens	80	40	33	7	330	280	1372	87
Boston Bruins	80	37	31	12	311	288	1919	86
Hartford Whalers	80	40	36	4	332	302	1759	84
Buffalo Sabres	80	37	37	6	296	291	1608	80
Patrick Division								
Philadelphia Flyers	80	53	23	4	335	241	2025	110
Washington Capitals	80	50	23	7	315	272	1418	107
New York Islanders	80	39	29	12	327	284	1343	90
New York Rangers	80	36	38	6	280	276	1496	78
Pittsburgh Penguins	80	34	38	8	313	305	1538	76
New Jersey Devils	80	28	49	3	300	374	1424	59

• did not qualify for playoffs

1986–1987

CLARENCE CAMPBELL CONFERENCE								
Norris Division								
St. Louis Blues	80	32	33	15	281	293	1972	79
Detroit Red Wings	80	34	36	10	260	274	2209	78
Chicago Blackhawks	80	29	37	14	290	310	1692	72
Toronto Maple Leafs	80	32	42	6	286	319	1827	70
Minnesota North Stars	80	30	40	10	296	314	1936	70
Smythe Division								
Edmonton Oilers	80	50	24	6	372	284	1721	106
Calgary Flames	80	46	31	3	318	289	2036	95
Winnipeg Jets	80	40	32	8	279	271	1537	88
Los Angeles Kings	80	31	41	8	318	341	2038	70
Vancouver Canucks	80	29	43	8	282	314	1917	66
PRINCE OF WALES CONFERENCE								
Adams Division								
Hartford Whalers	80	43	30	7	287	270	1496	93
Montreal Canadiens	80	41	29	10	277	241	1802	92
Boston Bruins	80	39	34	7	301	276	1870	85
Quebec Nordiques	80	31	39	10	267	276	1741	72
Buffalo Sabres	80	28	44	8	280	308	1810	64
Patrick Division								
Philadelphia Flyers	80	46	26	8	310	245	2082	100
Washington Capitals	80	38	32	10	285	278	1720	86
New York Islanders	80	35	33	12	279	281	1857	82
New York Rangers	80	34	38	8	307	323	1718	76
Pittsburgh Penguins	80	30	38	12	297	290	1693	72
New Jersey Devils	80	29	45	6	293	368	1735	64

1st round:	April 8	Detroit 3	Chicago 1 (at Detroit)
	April 9	Detroit 5	Chicago 1 (at Detroit)
	April 11	Detroit 4	Chicago 3* (at Chicago)
	April 12	Detroit 3	Chicago 1 (at Chicago)
	Detroit won best-of-seven 4–0		
Quarter-finals:	April 21	Toronto 4	Detroit 2 (at Detroit)
	April 23	Toronto 7	Detroit 2 (at Detroit)
	April 25	Detroit 4	Toronto 2 (at Toronto)
	April 27	Toronto 3	Detroit 2* (at Toronto)
	April 29	Detroit 3	Toronto 0 (at Detroit) [Hanlon]
	May 1	Detroit 4	Toronto 2 (at Toronto)
	May 3	Detroit 3	Toronto 0 (at Detroit) [Hanlon]
	Detroit won best-of-seven 4–3		
Semi-finals:	May 5	Detroit 3	Edmonton 1 (at Edmonton)
	May 7	Edmonton 4	Detroit 1 (at Edmonton)
	May 9	Edmonton 2	Detroit 1 (at Detroit)
	May 11	Edmonton 3	Detroit 2 (at Detroit)
	May 13	Edmonton 6	Detroit 3 (at Edmonton)
	Edmonton won best-of-seven 4–1		

1987–1988

CLARENCE CAMPBELL CONFERENCE								
Norris Division								
Detroit Red Wings	80	41	28	11	322	269	2391	93
St. Louis Blues	80	34	38	8	278	294	1919	76
Chicago Black Hawks	80	30	41	9	284	326	2228	69
Toronto Maple Leafs	80	21	49	10	273	345	1782	52
Minnesota North Stars	80	19	48	13	242	349	2313	51
Smythe Division								
Calgary Flames	80	48	23	9	397	305	2431	105
Edmonton Oilers	80	44	25	11	363	288	2173	99
Winnipeg Jets	80	33	36	11	292	310	2278	77
Los Angeles Kings	80	30	42	8	318	359	2124	68
Vancouver Canucks	80	25	46	9	272	320	2196	59
PRINCE OF WALES CONFERENCE								
Adams Division								
Montreal Canadiens	80	45	22	13	298	238	1830	103
Boston Bruins	80	44	30	6	300	251	2443	94
Buffalo Sabres	80	37	32	11	283	305	2277	85
Hartford Whalers	80	35	38	7	249	267	2046	77
Quebec Nordiques	80	32	43	5	271	306	2042	69
Patrick Division								
New York Islanders	80	39	31	10	308	267	1732	88
Washington Capitals	80	38	33	9	281	249	1680	85
Philadelphia Flyers	80	38	33	9	292	282	2194	85
New Jersey Devils	80	38	36	6	295	296	2315	82
New York Rangers	80	36	34	10	300	283	1775	82
Pittsburgh Penguins	80	36	35	9	319	316	2211	81

1st Round:	April 6	Toronto 6	Detroit 2 (at Detroit)
	April 7	Detroit 6	Toronto 2 (at Detroit)
	April 9	Detroit 6	Toronto 3 (at Toronto)
	April 10	Detroit 8	Toronto 0 (at Toronto) [Hanlon]
	April 12	Toronto 6	Detroit 5* (at Detroit)
	April 14	Detroit 5	Toronto 3 (at Toronto)
	Detroit won best-of-seven 4–2		
Quarter-finals:	April 19	Detroit 5	St. Louis 4 (at Detroit)
	April 21	Detroit 6	St. Louis 0 (at Detroit) [Stefan]
	April 23	St. Louis 6	Detroit 3 (at St. Louis)
	April 25	Detroit 3	St. Louis 1 (at St. Louis)
	April 27	Detroit 4	St. Louis 3 (at Detroit)
	Detroit won best-of-seven 4–1		
Semi-finals:	May 3	Edmonton 4	Detroit 1 (at Edmonton)
	May 5	Edmonton 5	Detroit 3 (at Edmonton)
	May 7	Detroit 5	Edmonton 2 (at Detroit)
	May 9	Edmonton 4	Detroit 3* (at Detroit)
	May 11	Edmonton 8	Detroit 4 (at Edmonton)
	Edmonton won best-of-seven 4–1		

1988–1989

CLARENCE CAMPBELL CONFERENCE

Norris Division								
Detroit Red Wings	80	34	34	12	313	316	2245	80
St. Louis Blues	80	33	35	12	275	285	1675	78
Minnesota North Stars	80	27	37	16	258	278	1972	70
Chicago Blackhawks	80	27	41	12	297	335	2496	66
Toronto Maple Leafs	80	28	46	6	259	342	1740	62
Smythe Division								
Calgary Flames	80	54	17	9	354	226	2444	117
Los Angeles Kings	80	42	31	7	376	335	2215	91
Edmonton Oilers	80	38	34	8	325	306	1931	84
Vancouver Canucks	80	33	39	8	251	253	1569	74
Winnipeg Jets	80	26	42	12	300	355	1843	64

PRINCE OF WALES CONFERENCE

Adams Division								
Montreal Canadiens	80	53	18	9	315	218	1537	115
Boston Bruins	80	37	29	14	289	256	1929	88
Buffalo Sabres	80	38	35	7	291	299	2034	83
Hartford Whalers	80	37	38	5	299	290	1672	79
Quebec Nordiques	80	27	46	7	269	342	2004	61
Patrick Division								
Washington Capitals	80	41	29	10	305	259	1836	92
Pittsburgh Penguins	80	40	33	7	347	349	2670	87
New York Rangers	80	37	35	8	310	307	1891	82
Philadelphia Flyers	80	36	36	8	307	285	2317	80
New Jersey Devils	80	27	41	12	281	325	2499	66
New York Islanders	80	28	47	5	265	325	1822	61

Preliminary round:	April 5	Detroit 3	Chicago 2 (at Detroit)
	April 6	Chicago 5	Detroit 4* (at Detroit)
	April 8	Chicago 4	Detroit 2 (at Chicago)
	April 9	Chicago 3	Detroit 2 (at Chicago)
	April 11	Detroit 6	Chicago 4 (at Detroit)
	April 13	Chicago 7	Detroit 1 (at Chicago)
	Chicago won best-of-seven 4–2		

1989–1990

CLARENCE CAMPBELL CONFERENCE

Norris Division

Chicago Blackhawks	80	41	33	6	316	294	2426	88
St. Louis Blues	80	37	34	9	295	279	1809	83
Toronto Maple Leafs	80	38	38	4	337	358	2419	80
Minnesota North Stars	80	36	40	4	284	291	2041	76
Detroit Red Wings	80	28	38	14	288	323	2140	70

Smythe Division

Calgary Flames	80	42	23	15	348	265	1751	99
Edmonton Oilers	80	38	28	14	315	283	2046	90
Winnipeg Jets	80	37	32	11	298	290	1639	85
Los Angeles Kings	80	34	39	7	338	337	1844	75
Vancouver Canucks	80	25	41	14	245	306	1644	64

PRINCE OF WALES CONFERENCE

Adams Division

Boston Bruins	80	46	25	9	289	232	1458	101
Buffalo Sabres	80	45	27	8	286	248	1449	98
Montreal Canadiens	80	41	28	11	288	234	1590	93
Hartford Whalers	80	38	33	9	275	268	2102	85
Quebec Nordiques	80	12	61	7	240	407	2104	31

Patrick Division

New York Rangers	80	36	31	13	279	267	2021	85
New Jersey Devils	80	37	34	9	295	288	1659	83
Washington Capitals	80	36	38	6	284	275	2204	78
New York Islanders	80	31	38	11	281	288	1777	73
Pittsburgh Penguins	80	32	40	8	318	359	2132	72
Philadelphia Flyers	80	30	39	11	290	297	2067	71

• did not qualify for playoffs

1990–1991

CLARENCE CAMPBELL CONFERENCE

Norris Division

Chicago Blackhawks	80	49	23	8	284	211	2412	106
St. Louis Blues	80	47	22	11	310	250	1987	105
Detroit Red Wings	80	34	38	8	273	298	1940	76
Minnesota North Stars	80	27	39	14	256	266	1964	68
Toronto Maple Leafs	80	23	46	11	241	318	1962	57

Smythe Division								
Los Angeles Kings	80	46	24	10	340	254	2228	102
Calgary Flames	80	46	26	8	344	263	2201	100
Edmonton Oilers	80	37	37	6	272	272	1823	80
Vancouver Canucks	80	28	43	9	243	315	2063	65
Winnipeg Jets	80	26	43	11	260	288	1675	63
PRINCE OF WALES CONFERENCE								
Adams Division								
Boston Bruins	80	44	24	12	299	264	1694	100
Montreal Canadiens	80	39	30	11	273	249	1425	89
Buffalo Sabres	80	31	30	19	292	278	1733	81
Hartford Whalers	80	31	38	11	238	276	2209	73
Quebec Nordiques	80	16	50	14	236	354	1741	46
Patrick Division								
Pittsburgh Penguins	80	41	33	6	342	305	1641	88
New York Rangers	80	36	31	13	297	265	1893	85
Washington Capitals	80	37	36	7	258	258	1839	81
New Jersey Devils	80	32	33	15	272	264	2024	79
Philadelphia Flyers	80	33	37	10	252	267	1945	76
New York Islanders	80	25	45	10	223	290	1723	60

Preliminary round:	April 4	Detroit 6	St. Louis 3 (at St. Louis)
	April 6	St. Louis 4	Detroit 2 (at St. Louis)
	April 8	Detroit 5	St. Louis 2 (at Detroit)
	April 10	Detroit 4	St. Louis 3 (at Detroit)
	April 12	St. Louis 6	Detroit 1 (at St. Louis)
	April 14	St. Louis 3	Detroit 0 (at Detroit) [Riendeau]
	April 16	St. Louis 3	Detroit 2 (at St. Louis)
	St. Louis won best-of-seven 4–3		

1991–1992

CLARENCE CAMPBELL CONFERENCE								
Norris Division								
Detroit Red Wings	80	43	25	12	320	256	2078	98
Chicago Blackhawks	80	36	29	15	257	236	2663	87
St. Louis Blues	80	36	33	11	279	266	2041	83
Minnesota North Stars	80	32	42	6	246	278	2169	70
Toronto Maple Leafs	80	30	43	7	234	294	1734	67
Smythe Division								
Vancouver Canucks	80	42	26	12	285	250	2075	96
Los Angeles Kings	80	35	31	14	287	296	2161	84
Edmonton Oilers	80	36	34	10	295	297	1907	82
Winnipeg Jets	80	33	32	15	251	244	1907	81
Calgary Flames	80	31	37	12	296	305	2643	74
San Jose Sharks	80	17	58	5	219	359	1894	39
PRINCE OF WALES CONFERENCE								
Adams Division								
Montreal Canadiens	80	41	28	11	267	207	1556	93
Boston Bruins	80	36	32	12	270	275	1752	84
Buffalo Sabres	80	31	37	12	289	299	2713	74

Hartford Whalers	80	26	41	13	247	283	1793	65
Quebec Nordiques	80	20	48	12	255	318	2044	52
Patrick Division								
New York Rangers	80	50	25	5	321	246	1805	105
Washington Capitals	80	45	27	8	330	275	1777	98
Pittsburgh Penguins	80	39	32	9	343	308	1907	87
New Jersey Devils	80	38	31	11	289	259	1611	87
New York Islanders	80	34	35	11	291	299	1713	79
Philadelphia Flyers	80	32	37	11	252	273	1838	75

- video replays used to help referees call goals

Preliminary round:	April 18	Minnesota 4	Detroit 3 (at Detroit)
	April 20	Minnesota 4	Detroit 2 (at Detroit)
	April 22	Detroit 5	Minnesota 4* (at Minnesota)
	April 24	Minnesota 5	Detroit 4 (at Minnesota)
	April 26	Detroit 3	Minnesota 0 (at Detroit) [Cheveldae]
	April 28	Detroit 1	Minnesota 0* (at Minnesota) [Cheveldae]
	April 30	Detroit 5	Minnesota 2 (at Detroit)
	Detroit won best-of-seven 4–3		
Quarter-finals:	May 2	Chicago 2	Detroit 1 (at Detroit)
	May 4	Chicago 3	Detroit 1 (at Detroit)
	May 6	Chicago 5	Detroit 4 (at Chicago)
	May 8	Chicago 1	Detroit 0 (at Chicago) [Belfour]
	Chicago won best-of-seven 4–0		

1992–1993

CLARENCE CAMPBELL CONFERENCE

Norris Division								
Chicago Blackhawks	84	47	25	12	279	230	2394	106
Detroit Red Wings	84	47	28	9	369	280	1832	103
Toronto Maple Leafs	84	44	29	11	288	241	1815	99
St. Louis Blues	84	37	36	11	282	278	1889	85
Minnesota North Stars	84	36	38	10	272	293	1885	82
Tampa Bay Lightning	84	23	54	7	245	332	1625	53
Smythe Division								
Vancouver Canucks	84	46	29	9	346	278	2326	101
Calgary Flames	84	43	30	11	322	282	1951	97
Los Angeles Kings	84	39	35	10	338	340	2247	88
Winnipeg Jets	84	40	37	7	322	320	1851	87
Edmonton Oilers	84	26	50	8	242	337	2027	60
San Jose Sharks	84	11	71	2	218	414	2134	24

PRINCE OF WALES CONFERENCE

Adams Division								
Boston Bruins	84	51	26	7	332	268	1552	109
Quebec Nordiques	84	47	27	10	351	300	1846	104
Montreal Canadiens	84	48	30	6	326	280	1788	102
Buffalo Sabres	84	38	36	10	335	297	1873	86
Hartford Whalers	84	26	52	6	284	369	2354	58
Ottawa Senators	84	10	70	4	202	395	1716	24

Patrick Division								
Pittsburgh Penguins	84	56	21	7	367	268	1776	119
Washington Capitals	84	43	34	7	325	286	1709	93
New York Islanders	84	40	37	7	335	297	1701	87
New Jersey Devils	84	40	37	7	308	299	1815	87
Philadelphia Flyers	84	36	37	11	319	319	1887	83
New York Rangers	84	34	39	11	304	308	1657	79

1st Round:	April 19	Detroit 6	Toronto 3 (at Detroit)
	April 21	Detroit 6	Toronto 2 (at Detroit)
	April 23	Toronto 4	Detroit 2 (at Toronto)
	April 25	Toronto 3	Detroit 2 (at Toronto)
	April 27	Toronto 5	Detroit 4* (at Detroit)
	April 29	Detroit 7	Toronto 3 (at Toronto)
	May 1	Toronto 4	Detroit 3* (at Detroit)
	Toronto won best-of-seven 4–3		

1993–1994

WESTERN CONFERENCE

Central Division								
Detroit Red Wings	84	46	30	8	356	275	1775	100
Toronto Maple Leafs	84	43	29	12	280	243	1877	98
Dallas Stars	84	42	29	13	286	265	1919	97
St. Louis Blues	84	40	33	11	270	283	1659	91
Chicago Blackhawks	84	39	36	9	254	240	2125	87
Winnipeg Jets	84	24	51	9	245	344	2143	57
Pacific Division								
Calgary Flames	84	42	29	13	302	256	1847	97
Vancouver Canucks	84	41	40	3	279	276	1923	85
San Jose Sharks	84	33	35	16	252	265	1343	82
Mighty Ducks of Anaheim	84	33	46	5	229	251	1507	71
Los Angeles Kings	84	27	45	12	294	322	2017	66
Edmonton Oilers	84	25	45	14	261	305	1858	64

EASTERN CONFERENCE

Northeast Division								
Pittsburgh Penguins	84	44	27	13	299	285	1624	101
Boston Bruins	84	42	29	13	289	252	1442	97
Montreal Canadiens	84	41	29	14	283	248	1524	96
Buffalo Sabres	84	43	32	9	282	218	1760	95
Quebec Nordiques	84	34	42	8	277	292	1625	76
Hartford Whalers	84	27	48	9	227	288	1809	63
Ottawa Senators	84	14	61	9	201	397	1710	37
Atlantic Division								
New York Rangers	84	52	24	8	299	231	1688	112
New Jersey Devils	84	47	25	12	306	220	1734	106
Washington Capitals	84	39	35	10	277	263	2007	88
New York Islanders	84	36	36	12	282	264	1787	84
Florida Panthers	84	33	34	17	233	233	1620	83
Philadelphia Flyers	84	35	39	10	294	314	1697	80
Tampa Bay Lightning	84	30	43	11	224	251	1579	71

- the top eight teams in each conference qualified for the playoffs

Preliminary round:	April 18	San Jose 5	Detroit 4 (at Detroit)
	April 20	Detroit 4	San Jose 0 (at Detroit) [Osgood]
	April 22	Detroit 3	San Jose 2 (at San Jose)
	April 23	San Jose 4	Detroit 3 (at San Jose)
	April 26	San Jose 6	Detroit 4 (at San Jose)
	April 28	Detroit 7	San Jose 1 (at Detroit)
	April 30	San Jose 3	Detroit 2 (at Detroit)
	San Jose won best-of-seven 4–3		

1994–1995

WESTERN CONFERENCE

Central Division								
Detroit Red Wings	48	33	11	4	180	117	932	70
St. Louis Blues	48	28	15	5	178	135	1077	61
Chicago Blackhawks	48	24	19	5	156	115	1123	53
Toronto Maple Leafs	48	21	19	8	135	146	744	50
Dallas Stars	48	17	23	8	136	135	1117	42
Winnipeg Jets	48	16	25	7	157	177	1141	39
Pacific Division								
Calgary Flames	48	24	17	7	163	135	1249	55
Vancouver Canucks	48	18	18	12	153	148	1093	48
San Jose Sharks	48	19	25	4	129	161	840	42
Los Angeles Kings	48	16	23	9	142	174	978	41
Edmonton Oilers	48	17	27	4	136	183	1183	38
Mighty Ducks of Anaheim	48	16	27	5	125	164	731	37

EASTERN CONFERENCE

Northeast Division								
Quebec Nordiques	48	30	13	5	185	134	770	65
Pittsburgh Penguins	48	29	16	3	181	158	1036	61
Boston Bruins	48	27	18	3	150	127	793	57
Buffalo Sabres	48	22	19	7	130	119	1022	51
Hartford Whalers	48	19	24	5	127	141	915	43
Montreal Canadiens	48	18	23	7	125	148	840	43
Ottawa Senators	48	9	34	5	116	174	749	23
Atlantic Division								
Philadelphia Flyers	48	28	16	4	150	132	741	60
New Jersey Devils	48	22	18	8	136	121	787	52
Washington Capitals	48	22	18	8	136	120	1144	52
New York Rangers	48	22	23	3	139	134	781	47
Florida Panthers	48	20	22	6	115	127	770	46
Tampa Bay Lightning	48	17	28	3	120	144	1040	37
New York Islanders	48	15	28	5	126	158	901	35

Preliminary round:	May 7	Detroit 4	Dallas 3 (at Detroit)
	May 9	Detroit 4	Dallas 1 (at Detroit)
	May 11	Detroit 5	Dallas 1 (at Dallas)
	May 14	Dallas 4	Detroit 1 (at Dallas)
	May 15	Detroit 3	Dallas 1 (at Detroit)
	Detroit won best-of-seven 4–1		

Quarter-finals:	May 21	Detroit 6	San Jose 0 (at Detroit) [Vernon]
	May 23	Detroit 6	San Jose 2 (at Detroit)
	May 25	Detroit 6	San Jose 2 (at San Jose)
	May 27	Detroit 6	San Jose 2 (at San Jose)
	Detroit won best-of-seven 4–0		
Semi-finals:	June 1	Detroit 2	Chicago 1* (at Detroit)
	June 4	Detroit 3	Chicago 2 (at Detroit)
	June 6	Detroit 4	Chicago 3* (at Chicago)
	June 8	Chicago 5	Detroit 2 (at Chicago)
	June 11	Detroit 2	Chicago 1* (at Detroit)
	Detroit won best-of-seven 4–1		
Finals:	June 17	New Jersey 2	Detroit 1 (at Detroit)
	June 20	New Jersey 4	Detroit 2 (at Detroit)
	June 22	New Jersey 5	Detroit 2 (at New Jersey)
	June 24	New Jersey 5	Detroit 2 (at New Jersey)
	New Jersey won Stanley Cup best-of-seven 4–0		

1995–1996

WESTERN CONFERENCE								
Central Division								
Detroit Red Wings	82	62	13	7	325	181	1551	131
Chicago Blackhawks	82	40	28	14	273	220	1880	94
Toronto Maple Leafs	82	34	36	12	247	252	1742	80
St. Louis Blues	82	32	34	16	219	248	1823	80
Winnipeg Jets	82	36	40	6	275	291	1622	78
Dallas Stars	82	26	42	14	227	280	1652	66
Pacific Division								
Colorado Avalanche	82	47	25	10	326	240	1536	104
Calgary Flames	82	34	37	11	241	240	1524	79
Vancouver Canucks	82	32	35	15	278	278	1546	79
Mighty Ducks of Anaheim	82	35	39	8	234	247	1707	78
Edmonton Oilers	82	30	44	8	240	304	1709	68
Los Angeles Kings	82	24	40	18	256	302	1460	66
San Jose Sharks	82	20	55	7	252	357	1480	47
EASTERN CONFERENCE								
Northeast Division								
Pittsburgh Penguins	82	49	29	4	362	284	1623	102
Boston Bruins	82	40	31	11	282	269	1039	91
Montreal Canadiens	82	40	32	10	265	248	1847	90
Hartford Whalers	82	34	39	9	237	259	1834	77
Buffalo Sabres	82	33	42	7	247	262	2195	73
Ottawa Senators	82	18	59	5	191	291	1553	41
Atlantic Division								
Philadelphia Flyers	82	45	24	13	282	208	1785	103
New York Rangers	82	41	27	14	272	237	1849	96
Florida Panthers	82	41	31	10	254	234	1494	92
Washington Capitals	82	39	32	11	234	204	1553	89

Tampa Bay Lightning	82	38	32	12	238	248	1628	88
New Jersey Devils	82	37	33	12	215	202	1486	86
New York Islanders	82	22	50	10	229	315	1669	54

Preliminary round:	April 17	Detroit 4	Winnipeg 1 (at Detroit)
	April 19	Detroit 4	Winnipeg 0 (at Detroit) [Osgood]
	April 21	Winnipeg 4	Detroit 1 (at Winnipeg)
	April 23	Detroit 6	Winnipeg 1 (at Winnipeg)
	April 26	Winnipeg 3	Detroit 1 (at Detroit)
	April 28	Detroit 4	Winnipeg 1 (at Winnipeg) (last game in the Winnipeg Arena)
	Detroit won best-of-seven 4–2		
Quarter-finals:	May 3	Detroit 3	St. Louis 2 (at Detroit)
	May 5	Detroit 8	St. Louis 3 (at Detroit)
	May 8	St. Louis 5	Detroit 4* (at St. Louis)
	May 10	St. Louis 1	Detroit 0 (at St. Louis) [Casey] (Gretzky 4:40 2nd)
	May 12	St. Louis 3	Detroit 2 (at Detroit)
	May 14	Detroit 4	St. Louis 2 (at St. Louis)
	May 16	Detroit 1	St. Louis 0* (at Detroit) [Osgood] (Yzerman 21:15 OT)
	Detroit won best-of-seven 4–3		
Semi-finals:	May 19	Colorado 3	Detroit 2* (at Detroit)
	May 21	Colorado 3	Detroit 0 (at Detroit) [Roy]
	May 23	Detroit 6	Colorado 4 (at Colorado)
	May 25	Colorado 4	Detroit 2 (at Colorado)
	May 27	Detroit 5	Colorado 2 (at Detroit)
	May 29	Colorado 4	Detroit 1 (at Colorado)
	Colorado won best-of-seven 4–2		

ALL-TIME TEAM-BY-TEAM YEAR-BY-YEAR RESULTS (from longest rivalry to most recent)

TORONTO MAPLE LEAFS
(70 seasons)

YEAR	GP	W	L	T	GF	GA	PTS
1926–27	4	1	2	1	9	8	3
1927–28	4	2	2	0	5	5	4
1928–29	4	2	2	0	7	8	4
1929–30	4	2	2	0	8	7	4
1930–31	4	2	1	1	15	6	5
1931–32	6	3	3	0	18	19	6
1932–33	6	2	3	1	11	12	5
1933–34	6	2	3	1	13	22	5
1934–35	6	3	2	1	10	7	7
1935–36	6	3	3	0	14	14	6
1936–37	6	3	2	1	17	14	7
1937–38	6	0	4	2	7	22	2
1938–39	8	3	4	1	10	21	7
1939–40	8	1	6	1	11	27	3
1940–41	8	3	5	0	13	19	6
1941–42	8	2	5	1	21	26	5
1942–43	10	5	4	1	28	27	11
1943–44	10	6	2	2	40	29	14
1944–45	10	8	1	1	44	24	17
1945–46	10	3	6	1	33	49	7
1946–47	12	2	8	2	32	47	6
1947–48	12	2	6	4	27	37	8
1948–49	12	7	3	2	35	22	16
1949–50	14	8	5	1	47	26	17
1950–51	14	7	3	4	33	25	18
1951–52	14	6	4	4	37	31	16
1952–53	14	7	4	3	40	28	17
1953–54	14	6	3	5	28	19	17
1954–55	14	7	4	3	27	15	17
1955–56	14	5	5	4	38	26	14
1956–57	14	10	2	2	39	23	22
1957–58	14	10	2	2	45	34	22
1958–59	14	6	7	1	36	38	13
1959–60	14	4	9	1	33	47	9
1960–61	14	2	7	5	30	45	9
1961–62	14	3	9	2	33	49	8
1962–63	14	7	6	1	37	37	15
1963–64	14	3	8	3	28	40	9
1964–65	14	7	6	1	35	39	15
1965–66	14	8	4	2	47	26	18

1966–67	14	6	6	2	45	44	14
1967–68	10	1	8	1	23	41	3
1968–69	8	3	4	1	19	24	7
1969–70	8	6	2	0	24	19	12
1970–71	6	1	4	1	14	33	3
1971–72	6	3	3	0	19	22	6
1972–73	6	4	2	0	25	14	8
1973–74	5	2	2	1	17	20	5
1974–75	5	1	3	1	15	16	3
1975–76	5	1	2	2	12	23	4
1976–77	5	1	3	1	8	23	3
1977–78	5	1	2	2	13	17	4
1978–79	4	2	2	0	10	13	4
1979–80	4	0	4	0	9	18	0
1980–81	4	3	1	0	18	14	6
1981–82	7	3	3	1	23	30	7
1982–83	8	4	4	0	26	31	8
1983–84	8	3	5	0	34	32	6
1984–85	8	5	3	0	37	34	10
1985–86	8	3	4	1	33	42	7
1986–87	8	2	5	1	16	26	5
1987–88	8	3	3	2	33	33	8
1988–89	8	5	3	0	41	26	10
1989–90	8	4	3	1	32	29	9
1990–91	8	5	2	1	32	25	11
1991–92	8	4	4	0	30	32	8
1992–93	7	3	3	1	27	19	7
1993–94	6	1	4	1	20	25	3
1994–95	4	3	1	0	13	7	6
1995–96	5	5	0	0	22	15	10
Totals	612	261	262	89	1731	1767	611

MONTREAL CANADIENS
(70 seasons)

1926–27	4	0	4	0	6	15	0
1927–28	4	2	2	0	5	8	4
1928–29	4	1	1	2	8	7	4
1929–30	4	1	3	0	8	13	2
1930–31	4	2	2	0	9	11	4
1931–32	6	2	3	1	11	14	5
1932–33	6	3	2	1	18	14	7
1933–34	6	2	3	1	13	13	5
1934–35	6	4	1	1	25	15	9
1935–36	6	4	0	2	15	7	10
1936–37	6	1	4	1	10	17	3
1937–38	6	3	2	1	18	10	7
1938–39	8	4	3	1	23	14	9

1939–40	8	5	3	0	22	19	10
1940–41	8	4	3	1	19	13	9
1941–42	8	5	3	0	30	16	10
1942–43	10	5	3	2	35	30	12
1943–44	10	0	9	1	17	46	1
1944–45	10	1	8	1	21	46	3
1945–46	10	6	3	1	23	19	13
1946–47	12	4	6	2	34	41	10
1947–48	12	7	2	3	35	24	17
1948–49	12	7	4	1	25	19	15
1949–50	14	5	3	6	32	30	16
1950–51	14	8	4	2	47	29	18
1951–52	14	9	2	3	48	26	21
1952–53	14	4	4	6	29	31	14
1953–54	14	6	6	2	27	27	14
1954–55	14	7	7	0	38	38	14
1955–56	14	4	8	2	26	35	10
1956–57	14	4	6	4	34	39	12
1957–58	14	3	7	4	24	50	10
1958–59	14	1	9	4	29	67	6
1959–60	14	2	7	5	29	38	9
1960–61	14	4	7	3	43	48	11
1961–62	14	3	8	3	36	54	9
1962–63	14	3	9	2	29	47	8
1963–64	14	5	7	2	39	55	12
1964–65	14	8	4	2	41	30	18
1965–66	14	4	7	3	34	45	11
1966–67	14	4	10	0	32	42	8
1967–68	10	3	6	1	31	40	7
1968–69	8	2	5	1	20	25	5
1969–70	8	4	2	2	26	21	10
1970–71	6	1	4	1	16	29	3
1971–72	6	3	3	0	20	27	6
1972–73	6	2	3	1	15	16	5
1973–74	5	2	3	0	20	26	4
1974–75	6	0	4	2	18	31	2
1975–76	6	0	5	1	9	31	1
1976–77	6	0	5	1	7	26	1
1977–78	6	1	4	1	12	25	3
1978–79	8	2	4	2	18	29	6
1979–80	4	0	3	1	10	20	1
1980–81	4	1	3	0	9	19	2
1981–82	3	1	2	0	9	12	2
1982–83	3	0	1	2	11	13	2
1983–84	3	0	3	0	4	12	0
1984–85	3	1	1	1	11	11	3
1985–86	3	0	3	0	7	21	0
1986–87	3	1	1	1	10	10	3
1987–88	3	1	2	0	12	14	2
1988–89	3	2	1	0	9	11	4
1989–90	3	0	1	2	9	11	2
1990–91	3	2	1	0	12	10	4

1991–92	3	0	3	0	5	12	0
1992–93	2	0	2	0	4	9	0
1993–94	2	1	1	0	10	8	2
1994–95	–	–	–	–	–	–	–
1995–96	2	2	0	0	14	3	4
Totals	550	189	265	96	1405	1684	474

CHICAGO BLACKHAWKS

(70 seasons)

1926–27	6	2	3	1	10	16	5
1927–28	6	3	2	1	15	7	7
1928–29	6	4	1	1	11	4	9
1929–30	6	3	2	1	12	13	7
1930–31	6	3	2	1	12	11	7
1931–32	8	4	3	1	18	15	9
1932–33	6	5	1	0	17	7	10
1933–34	6	4	1	1	13	9	9
1934–35	6	3	3	0	12	14	6
1935–36	8	4	3	1	17	16	9
1936–37	8	5	2	1	23	11	11
1937–38	8	4	3	1	21	16	9
1938–39	8	5	1	2	22	14	12
1939–40	8	0	6	2	10	20	2
1940–41	8	6	2	0	20	10	12
1941–42	8	5	3	0	30	19	10
1942–43	10	4	2	4	32	24	12
1943–44	10	5	5	0	32	34	10
1944–45	10	7	3	0	42	27	14
1945–46	10	4	3	3	41	40	11
1946–47	12	7	4	1	60	41	15
1947–48	12	10	2	0	61	29	20
1948–49	12	9	3	0	51	40	18
1949–50	14	9	3	2	56	39	20
1950–51	14	13	1	0	68	26	26
1951–52	14	12	2	0	50	24	24
1952–53	14	8	3	3	48	22	19
1953–54	14	11	2	1	58	27	23
1954–55	14	12	1	1	50	22	25
1955–56	14	8	2	4	44	24	20
1956–57	14	10	2	2	45	27	22
1957–58	14	7	7	0	36	35	14
1958–59	14	7	6	1	37	36	15
1959–60	14	8	4	2	36	30	18
1960–61	14	4	6	4	23	38	12
1961–62	14	3	7	4	29	43	10
1962–63	14	6	5	3	34	31	15
1963–64	14	6	5	3	47	48	15

1964–65	14	5	8	1	34	41	11
1965–66	14	1	11	2	27	51	4
1966–67	14	4	10	0	38	60	8
1967–68	10	3	4	3	31	38	9
1968–69	8	4	3	1	26	26	9
1969–70	8	4	4	0	22	24	8
1970–71	6	0	6	0	7	22	0
1971–72	6	0	5	1	11	23	1
1972–73	5	2	3	0	14	21	4
1973–74	5	0	4	1	14	27	1
1974–75	4	1	2	1	13	18	3
1975–76	4	2	1	1	13	8	5
1976–77	4	0	4	0	6	18	0
1977–78	4	1	3	0	6	12	2
1978–79	4	3	0	1	19	10	7
1979–80	4	1	3	0	8	13	2
1980–81	4	1	1	2	15	12	4
1981–82	7	3	3	1	32	30	7
1982–83	8	2	6	0	19	29	4
1983–84	8	4	4	0	32	27	8
1984–85	8	3	3	2	31	33	8
1985–86	8	2	6	0	36	45	4
1986–87	8	4	3	1	28	25	9
1987–88	8	5	3	0	40	28	10
1988–89	8	2	4	2	25	29	6
1989–90	8	3	4	1	31	32	7
1990–91	8	3	4	1	20	24	7
1991–92	8	5	1	2	27	20	12
1992–93	9	5	4	0	30	27	10
1993–94	6	4	2	0	17	15	8
1994–95	5	4	1	0	15	9	8
1995–96	6	5	0	1	26	12	11
Totals	629	316	236	77	1956	1718	709

NEW YORK RANGERS

(70 seasons)

1926–27	6	1	3	2	5	11	4
1927–28	6	2	3	1	8	11	5
1928–29	6	1	4	1	5	11	3
1929–30	6	2	1	3	19	17	7
1930–31	6	2	3	1	5	8	5
1931–32	8	3	3	2	18	19	8
1932–33	6	4	2	0	15	9	8
1933–34	6	3	3	0	15	10	6
1934–35	6	2	4	0	25	20	4
1935–36	8	4	1	3	24	18	11
1936–37	8	5	1	2	21	12	12

1937–38	8	1	6	1	14	29	3
1938–39	8	2	6	0	17	31	4
1939–40	8	2	3	3	9	13	7
1940–41	8	3	2	3	19	21	9
1941–42	8	1	7	0	18	36	2
1942–43	10	7	1	2	49	21	16
1943–44	10	8	1	1	67	26	17
1944–45	10	6	2	2	53	32	14
1945–46	10	4	4	2	25	25	10
1946–47	12	6	3	3	35	29	15
1947–48	12	5	4	3	35	29	13
1948–49	12	7	4	1	43	27	15
1949–50	14	7	5	2	44	33	16
1950–51	14	8	3	3	51	34	19
1951–52	14	9	3	2	45	29	20
1952–53	14	7	3	4	43	33	18
1953–54	14	6	5	3	36	30	15
1954–55	14	9	2	3	44	22	21
1955–56	14	5	6	3	40	38	13
1956–57	14	10	3	1	47	32	21
1957–58	14	4	5	5	34	40	13
1958–59	14	6	7	1	31	38	13
1959–60	14	4	4	6	42	39	14
1960–61	14	7	5	2	45	47	16
1961–62	14	6	5	3	39	43	15
1962–63	14	9	3	2	46	34	20
1963–64	14	6	6	2	39	37	14
1964–65	14	10	2	2	58	36	22
1965–66	14	7	3	4	49	37	18
1966–67	14	7	7	0	46	42	14
1967–68	10	3	5	2	21	29	8
1968–69	8	4	3	1	25	21	9
1969–70	8	2	4	2	23	30	6
1970–71	6	1	4	1	11	21	3
1971–72	6	1	4	1	15	20	3
1972–73	5	1	3	1	14	23	3
1973–74	6	2	3	1	23	24	5
1974–75	4	1	2	1	18	18	3
1975–76	4	1	3	0	12	17	2
1976–77	4	1	3	0	12	18	2
1977–78	4	1	2	1	12	15	3
1978–79	4	1	1	2	12	13	4
1979–80	4	1	3	0	12	12	2
1980–81	4	2	1	1	21	16	5
1981–82	3	1	2	0	9	12	2
1982–83	3	0	2	1	6	16	1
1983–84	3	0	3	0	10	18	0
1984–85	3	2	1	0	11	8	4
1985–86	3	0	3	0	8	20	0
1986–87	3	2	1	0	11	11	4
1987–88	3	1	1	1	14	12	3
1988–89	3	3	0	0	12	8	6

1989–90	3	0	2	1	7	13	1
1990–91	3	3	0	0	16	9	6
1991–92	3	1	1	1	13	14	3
1992–93	2	0	1	1	5	7	1
1993–94	2	2	0	0	12	7	4
1994–95	–	–	–	–	–	–	–
1995–96	2	1	1	0	3	2	2
Totals	556	246	207	103	1691	1543	595

BOSTON BRUINS

(70 seasons)

1926–27	6	1	5	0	8	19	2
1927–28	6	2	4	0	15	18	4
1928–29	6	1	4	1	7	13	3
1929–30	6	0	6	0	12	24	0
1930–31	6	1	4	1	14	22	3
1931–32	8	1	3	4	6	11	6
1932–33	6	3	2	1	9	15	7
1933–34	6	4	1	1	15	12	9
1934–35	6	0	5	1	10	17	1
1935–36	8	3	5	0	11	18	6
1936–37	8	7	1	0	28	18	14
1937–38	8	2	5	1	15	29	5
1938–39	8	1	7	0	8	25	2
1939–40	8	3	5	0	19	32	6
1940–41	8	0	3	5	14	23	5
1941–42	8	2	4	2	16	25	6
1942–43	10	4	4	2	25	22	10
1943–44	10	7	1	2	58	42	16
1944–45	10	9	0	1	58	32	19
1945–46	10	3	4	3	24	26	9
1946–47	12	3	6	3	29	35	9
1947–48	12	6	4	2	29	29	14
1948–49	12	4	5	3	41	37	11
1949–50	14	8	3	3	50	36	19
1950–51	14	8	2	4	37	25	20
1951–52	14	8	3	3	35	23	19
1952–53	14	10	2	2	62	19	22
1953–54	14	8	3	3	42	29	19
1954–55	14	7	3	4	45	37	18
1955–56	14	8	3	3	35	25	19
1956–57	14	4	7	3	33	36	11
1957–58	14	5	8	1	37	48	11
1958–59	14	5	8	1	34	39	11
1959–60	14	8	5	1	46	43	17
1960–61	14	8	4	2	54	37	18
1961–62	14	8	4	2	47	30	18

1962–63	14	7	2	5	54	45	19
1963–64	14	10	3	1	38	24	21
1964–65	14	10	3	1	56	29	21
1965–66	14	11	2	1	64	35	23
1966–67	14	6	6	2	51	53	14
1967–68	10	3	5	2	41	43	8
1968–69	8	2	3	3	26	28	7
1969–70	8	2	1	5	27	24	9
1970–71	6	1	5	0	18	36	2
1971–72	6	1	5	0	18	26	2
1972–73	5	2	3	0	16	26	4
1973–74	6	1	4	1	14	37	3
1974–75	5	1	4	0	21	31	2
1975–76	5	0	3	2	9	25	2
1976–77	5	1	4	0	14	27	2
1977–78	5	0	4	1	10	27	1
1978–79	4	1	3	0	18	18	2
1979–80	4	1	2	1	17	18	3
1980–81	4	0	2	2	14	19	2
1981–82	3	0	2	1	10	14	1
1982–83	3	0	3	0	4	17	0
1983–84	3	1	2	0	10	16	2
1984–85	3	0	3	0	7	13	0
1985–86	3	1	2	0	11	20	2
1986–87	3	2	0	1	11	8	5
1987–88	3	2	1	0	5	3	4
1988–89	3	2	0	1	15	11	5
1989–90	3	0	3	0	6	10	0
1990–91	3	1	2	0	10	14	2
1991–92	2	0	2	0	4	9	0
1992–93	2	2	0	0	13	5	4
1993–94	2	2	0	0	9	3	4
1994–95	–	–	–	–	–	–	–
1995–96	2	2	0	0	10	7	4
Totals	559	237	227	95	1679	1692	569

LOS ANGELES KINGS

(29 seasons)

1967–68	4	1	2	1	16	17	3
1968–69	6	4	2	0	27	17	8
1969–70	6	6	0	0	22	8	12
1970–71	6	1	2	3	19	21	5
1971–72	6	3	2	1	25	19	7
1972–73	5	2	2	1	20	18	5
1973–74	5	3	1	1	19	13	7
1974–75	6	0	5	1	12	27	1
1975–76	6	2	3	1	17	19	5

1976–77	6	0	5	1	15	24	1
1977–78	6	3	2	1	16	16	7
1978–79	8	1	5	2	25	39	4
1979–80	4	0	3	1	11	16	1
1980–81	4	1	3	0	12	25	2
1981–82	3	1	2	0	14	15	2
1982–83	3	0	1	2	10	13	2
1983–84	3	0	2	1	15	19	1
1984–85	3	1	2	0	14	19	2
1985–86	3	2	1	0	14	7	4
1986–87	3	0	3	0	8	15	0
1987–88	3	2	1	0	15	11	4
1988–89	3	0	3	0	9	22	0
1989–90	3	1	2	0	10	19	2
1990–91	3	1	2	0	9	14	2
1991–92	3	2	1	0	13	9	4
1992–93	4	1	2	1	17	23	3
1993–94	4	2	1	1	21	20	5
1994–95	4	1	2	1	13	15	3
1995–96	4	3	0	1	20	13	7
Totals	127	44	62	21	458	513	109

PHILADELPHIA FLYERS

(29 seasons)

1967–68	4	3	1	0	13	10	6
1968–69	6	3	1	2	23	12	8
1969–70	6	3	1	2	21	15	8
1970–71	6	3	2	1	15	13	7
1971–72	6	3	2	1	23	15	7
1972–73	5	3	1	1	22	15	7
1973–74	5	0	5	0	7	30	0
1974–75	4	1	2	1	13	19	3
1975–76	4	2	2	0	9	14	4
1976–77	4	1	3	0	8	15	2
1977–78	4	1	2	1	9	11	3
1978–79	4	0	2	2	9	12	2
1979–80	4	0	3	1	16	22	1
1980–81	4	1	3	0	11	19	2
1981–82	3	0	2	1	5	11	1
1982–83	3	0	3	0	10	22	0
1983–84	3	0	1	2	10	14	2
1984–85	3	0	2	1	7	11	1
1985–86	3	1	2	0	10	12	2
1986–87	3	1	2	0	11	10	2
1987–88	3	0	2	1	12	19	1
1988–89	3	2	1	0	16	12	4
1989–90	3	1	0	2	17	14	4

1990–91	3	2	1	0	8	9	4
1991–92	2	1	1	0	10	7	2
1992–93	3	2	0	1	16	11	5
1993–94	2	2	0	0	9	4	4
1994–95	–	–	–	–	–	–	–
1995–96	2	1	1	0	6	7	2
Totals	105	37	48	20	346	385	94

PITTSBURGH PENGUINS

(29 seasons)

1967–68	4	3	1	0	21	12	6
1968–69	6	4	2	0	20	14	8
1969–70	6	4	2	0	21	17	8
1970–71	6	1	3	2	13	30	4
1971–72	6	4	2	0	25	19	8
1972–73	5	2	0	3	9	7	7
1973–74	5	2	2	1	13	20	5
1974–75	6	2	4	0	15	24	4
1975–76	6	1	4	1	13	24	3
1976–77	6	2	4	0	17	19	4
1977–78	6	3	2	1	22	21	7
1978–79	8	3	5	0	31	29	6
1979–80	4	2	2	0	19	18	4
1980–81	4	1	2	1	11	13	3
1981–82	3	2	1	0	11	11	4
1982–83	3	2	0	1	17	11	5
1983–84	3	3	0	0	21	9	6
1984–85	3	1	1	1	10	10	3
1985–86	3	1	2	0	11	15	2
1986–87	3	2	1	0	6	5	4
1987–88	3	2	1	0	15	13	4
1988–89	3	0	2	1	13	19	1
1989–90	3	0	2	1	7	14	1
1990–91	3	0	3	0	5	16	0
1991–92	3	1	0	2	11	10	4
1992–93	2	1	1	0	14	9	2
1993–94	2	1	1	0	10	9	2
1994–95	–	–	–	–	–	–	–
1995–96	2	1	1	0	5	5	2
Totals	117	51	51	15	406	423	117

ST. LOUIS BLUES

(29 seasons)

1967–68	4	2	1	1	13	10	5
1968–69	6	0	4	2	9	16	2
1969–70	6	4	2	0	25	18	8
1970–71	6	0	5	1	6	15	1

1971–72	6	2	3	1	16	22	5
1972–73	5	2	3	0	15	17	4
1973–74	5	3	1	1	20	12	7
1974–75	4	0	3	1	10	14	1
1975–76	4	2	1	1	11	11	5
1976–77	4	0	3	1	9	17	1
1977–78	4	3	1	0	16	7	6
1978–79	4	1	3	0	12	16	2
1979–80	4	1	2	1	9	9	3
1980–81	4	0	4	0	8	18	0
1981–82	7	2	5	0	28	36	4
1982–83	8	1	5	2	19	29	4
1983–84	8	5	3	0	28	25	10
1984–85	8	1	6	1	28	43	3
1985–86	8	2	5	1	27	33	5
1986–87	8	3	4	1	21	22	7
1987–88	8	4	1	3	34	22	11
1988–89	8	3	3	2	33	31	8
1989–90	8	3	4	1	21	33	7
1990–91	8	2	6	0	24	37	4
1991–92	8	7	1	0	44	28	14
1992–93	7	3	3	1	30	21	7
1993–94	6	2	1	3	19	20	7
1994–95	5	2	2	1	15	15	5
1995–96	5	3	1	1	21	11	7
Totals	176	63	86	27	571	608	153

BUFFALO SABRES

(26 seasons)

1970–71	6	3	3	0	23	26	6
1971–72	6	4	0	2	24	15	10
1972–73	5	4	1	0	20	14	8
1973–74	6	1	5	0	12	22	2
1974–75	5	1	3	1	10	21	3
1975–76	5	1	4	0	10	21	2
1976–77	5	1	4	0	10	17	2
1977–78	5	2	2	1	20	16	5
1978–79	4	1	3	0	10	15	2
1979–80	4	1	3	0	8	18	2
1980–81	4	0	3	1	13	20	1
1981–82	3	0	3	0	5	12	0
1982–83	3	1	1	1	12	10	3
1983–84	3	1	1	1	9	9	3
1984–85	3	1	1	1	15	13	3
1985–86	3	1	1	1	7	9	3
1986–87	3	0	2	1	8	14	1
1987–88	3	2	1	0	11	8	4
1988–89	3	0	3	0	8	18	0
1989–90	3	1	2	0	14	14	2

1990–91	3	1	1	1	14	11	3
1991–92	3	2	0	1	16	9	5
1992–93	2	1	1	0	13	15	2
1993–94	2	1	1	0	8	7	2
1994–95	–	–	–	–	–	–	–
1995–96	2	1	1	0	5	4	2
Totals	94	32	50	12	305	358	76

MINNESOTA NORTH STARS
(26 seasons)
(moved to Dallas for 1993-94)

1967–68	4	2	2	0	13	9	4
1968–69	6	4	2	0	26	21	8
1969–70	6	1	1	4	15	12	6
1970–71	6	2	3	1	15	17	5
1971–72	6	2	4	0	14	18	4
1972–73	5	1	3	1	14	23	3
1973–74	5	2	1	2	19	17	6
1974–75	4	0	2	2	15	19	2
1975–76	4	3	1	0	16	7	6
1976–77	4	0	3	1	6	14	1
1977–78	4	4	0	0	14	7	8
1978–79	4	1	2	1	9	16	3
1979–80	4	2	1	1	18	17	5
1980–81	4	0	2	2	9	19	2
1981–82	7	1	6	0	26	35	2
1982–83	8	0	6	2	22	36	2
1983–84	8	2	6	0	26	40	4
1984–85	8	3	2	3	33	28	9
1985–86	8	1	6	1	28	52	3
1986–87	8	7	0	1	38	23	15
1987–88	8	4	3	1	30	26	9
1988–89	8	5	3	0	30	24	10
1989–90	8	4	4	0	27	25	8
1990–91	8	3	4	1	29	33	7
1991–92	8	3	4	1	29	27	7
1992–93	7	5	1	1	32	15	11
Totals	160	62	72	26	553	580	150

VANCOUVER CANUCKS
(26 seasons)

1970–71	6	4	2	0	26	22	8
1971–72	6	5	0	1	26	12	11
1972–73	6	3	0	3	28	12	9
1973–74	5	2	3	0	19	26	4
1974–75	4	1	3	0	10	18	2
1975–76	4	0	4	0	8	20	0

1976–77	4	3	1	0	16	14	6
1977–78	4	2	1	1	19	14	5
1978–79	4	1	3	0	14	15	2
1979–80	4	2	2	0	12	8	4
1980–81	4	1	2	1	9	12	3
1981–82	3	1	1	1	10	13	3
1982–83	3	1	1	1	13	12	3
1983–84	3	1	2	0	13	15	2
1984–85	3	2	1	0	19	13	4
1985–86	3	0	3	0	5	17	0
1986–87	3	2	1	0	14	15	4
1987–88	3	2	1	0	9	8	4
1988–89	3	0	0	3	7	7	3
1989–90	3	1	1	1	11	10	3
1990–91	3	1	2	0	11	11	2
1991–92	3	1	2	0	5	6	2
1992–93	3	2	0	1	15	8	5
1993–94	4	3	1	0	21	15	6
1994–95	4	4	0	0	16	7	8
1995–96	4	3	1	0	12	9	6
Totals	99	48	38	13	368	339	109

NEW YORK ISLANDERS
(24 seasons)

1972–73	5	4	1	0	19	6	8
1973–74	5	4	1	0	21	16	8
1974–75	4	2	2	0	11	14	4
1975–76	4	1	3	0	8	17	2
1976–77	4	2	2	0	11	13	4
1977–78	4	0	4	0	12	24	0
1978–79	4	0	3	1	7	15	1
1979–80	4	3	1	0	16	14	6
1980–81	4	0	4	0	9	20	0
1981–82	3	0	3	0	6	16	0
1982–83	3	2	0	1	10	6	5
1983–84	3	2	1	0	10	7	4
1984–85	3	1	2	0	11	17	2
1985–86	3	0	3	0	8	18	0
1986–87	3	1	2	0	11	10	2
1987–88	3	2	1	0	12	8	4
1988–89	3	3	0	0	17	13	6
1989–90	3	1	1	1	9	9	3
1990–91	3	2	0	1	12	6	5
1991–92	3	1	2	0	10	13	2
1992–93	2	1	1	0	5	5	2
1993–94	2	1	1	0	5	4	2
1994–95	–	–	–	–	–	–	–
1995–96	2	2	0	0	11	3	4
Totals	77	35	38	4	251	274	74

WASHINGTON CAPITALS

(22 seasons)

1974–75	6	5	1	0	33	20	10
1975–76	6	3	3	0	25	24	6
1976–77	6	0	3	3	10	20	3
1977–78	6	4	1	1	23	12	9
1978–79	8	3	2	3	25	25	9
1979–80	4	2	1	1	12	10	5
1980–81	4	1	2	1	14	20	3
1981–82	3	0	1	2	11	14	2
1982–83	3	1	2	0	12	17	2
1983–84	3	2	1	0	9	6	4
1984–85	3	1	2	0	6	11	2
1985–86	3	1	2	0	13	8	2
1986–87	3	0	2	1	6	13	1
1987–88	3	2	0	1	9	3	5
1988–89	3	1	1	1	10	10	3
1989–90	3	0	3	0	8	16	0
1990–91	3	0	3	0	7	11	0
1991–92	3	3	0	0	14	9	6
1992–93	3	1	2	0	10	13	2
1993–94	2	0	1	1	5	8	1
1994–95	–	–	–	–	–	–	–
1995–96	2	2	0	0	8	5	4
Totals	80	32	33	15	270	275	79

EDMONTON OILERS

(17 seasons)

1979–80	4	2	1	1	16	15	5
1980–81	4	1	2	1	12	16	3
1981–82	3	0	2	1	11	19	1
1982–83	3	1	2	0	16	19	2
1983–84	3	0	3	0	9	22	0
1984–85	3	0	3	0	14	19	0
1985–86	3	0	3	0	7	22	0
1986–87	3	0	3	0	9	15	0
1987–88	3	2	1	0	15	11	4
1988–89	3	2	1	0	18	16	4
1989–90	3	2	1	0	15	15	4
1990–91	3	1	1	1	12	11	3
1991–92	3	2	0	1	12	7	5
1992–93	3	2	0	1	12	7	5
1993–94	4	1	3	0	12	13	2
1994–95	4	3	1	0	15	10	6
1995–96	4	4	0	0	21	7	8
Totals	56	23	27	6	226	244	52

HARTFORD WHALERS

(17 seasons)

1979–80	4	1	2	1	13	16	3
1980–81	4	0	2	2	11	15	2
1981–82	3	0	2	1	5	13	1
1982–83	3	3	0	0	17	9	6
1983–84	3	1	1	1	14	11	3
1984–85	3	1	2	0	9	15	2
1985–86	3	1	2	0	10	14	2
1986–87	3	1	1	1	9	8	3
1987–88	3	1	2	0	6	6	2
1988–89	3	1	2	0	9	10	2
1989–90	3	0	2	1	6	10	1
1990–91	3	1	2	0	8	12	2
1991–92	2	2	0	0	12	5	4
1992–93	2	2	0	0	7	2	4
1993–94	3	2	1	0	12	7	4
1994–95	–	–	–	–	–	–	–
1995–96	2	2	0	0	7	4	4
Totals	47	19	21	7	155	157	45

WINNIPEG JETS

(17 seasons)

(moved to Phoenix for 1996–97)

1979–80	4	3	1	0	18	11	6
1980–81	4	3	0	1	19	15	7
1981–82	7	2	3	2	15	22	6
1982–83	3	0	3	0	5	20	0
1983–84	3	1	0	2	14	9	4
1984–85	3	0	2	1	10	16	1
1985–86	3	0	3	0	6	15	0
1986–87	3	1	1	1	8	8	3
1987–88	3	2	0	1	19	13	5
1988–89	3	2	0	1	14	7	5
1989–90	3	1	1	1	13	14	3
1990–91	3	3	0	0	14	4	6
1991–92	3	0	2	1	6	8	1
1992–93	3	1	2	0	9	12	2
1993–94	6	3	3	0	26	17	6
1994–95	5	3	1	1	25	14	7
1995–96	6	3	2	1	26	20	7
Totals	65	28	24	13	247	225	69

CALGARY FLAMES

(16 seasons)
(formerly Atlanta, 1972–80)

1980–81	4	1	2	1	12	22	3
1981–82	3	1	1	1	20	15	3
1982–83	3	1	2	0	13	14	2
1983–84	3	2	1	0	12	9	4
1984–85	3	1	2	0	13	17	2
1985–86	3	0	2	1	11	17	1
1986–87	3	2	1	0	14	15	4
1987–88	3	1	1	1	10	10	3
1988–89	3	0	3	0	5	15	0
1989–90	3	2	1	0	17	17	4
1990–91	3	1	1	1	10	16	3
1991–92	3	3	0	0	14	9	6
1992–93	4	1	2	1	15	13	3
1993–94	4	2	1	1	15	10	5
1994–95	4	1	3	0	9	10	2
1995–96	4	3	0	1	15	6	7
Totals	53	22	23	8	205	215	52

NEW YORK AMERICANS

(16 seasons)

1926–27	4	3	1	0	8	6	6
1927–28	4	2	0	2	12	8	6
1928–29	4	2	1	1	6	4	5
1929–30	4	1	3	0	8	11	2
1930–31	4	0	2	2	9	12	2
1931–32	6	2	2	2	9	11	6
1932–33	6	3	0	3	15	7	9
1933–34	6	3	0	3	14	9	9
1934–35	6	2	1	3	12	10	7
1935–36	6	4	1	1	20	11	9
1936–37	6	2	3	1	14	15	5
1937–38	6	2	2	2	14	11	6
1938–39	8	3	3	2	27	23	8
1939–40	8	5	3	0	20	15	10
1940–41	8	5	1	2	27	16	12
1941–42	8	4	3	1	25	25	9
Totals	94	43	26	25	240	194	111

QUEBEC NORDIQUES
(16 seasons)
(moved to Colorado for 1995–96)

1979–80	4	2	1	1	21	22	5
1980–81	4	0	3	1	7	12	1
1981–82	3	0	3	0	8	16	0
1982–83	3	1	1	1	13	13	3
1983–84	3	2	1	0	9	10	4
1984–85	3	2	1	0	13	12	4
1985–86	3	1	2	0	7	15	2
1986–87	3	2	1	0	10	11	4
1987–88	3	0	3	0	8	12	0
1988–89	3	1	2	0	14	13	2
1989–90	3	3	0	0	20	8	6
1990–91	3	2	1	0	14	10	4
1991–92	3	2	0	1	14	6	5
1992–93	2	1	1	0	8	6	2
1993–94	2	1	1	0	7	7	2
1994–95	–	–	–	–	–	–	–
Totals	45	20	21	4	173	173	44

NEW JERSEY DEVILS
(14 seasons)
(formerly Kansas City, 1974–76 and
Colorado, 1976–82)

1982–83	3	1	1	1	8	7	3
1983–84	3	1	2	0	9	13	2
1984–85	3	1	1	1	14	14	3
1985–86	3	0	2	1	7	13	1
1986–87	3	1	2	0	11	10	2
1987–88	3	3	0	0	13	9	6
1988–89	3	0	2	1	8	14	1
1989–90	3	1	1	1	8	10	3
1990–91	3	0	2	1	6	15	1
1991–92	3	1	1	1	12	8	3
1992–93	2	1	1	0	11	11	2
1993–94	2	1	1	0	6	10	2
1994–95	–	–	–	–	–	–	–
1995–96	2	1	1	0	5	5	2
Totals	36	12	17	7	118	139	31

MONTREAL MAROONS

(12 seasons)

1926–27	4	1	3	0	5	6	2
1927–28	4	3	1	0	10	4	6
1928–29	4	2	1	1	6	4	5
1929–30	4	1	2	1	14	20	3
1930–31	4	0	3	1	6	13	1
1931–32	6	3	3	0	15	19	6
1932–33	6	1	4	1	17	24	3
1933–34	6	2	1	3	13	9	7
1034–35	6	2	3	1	10	13	5
1935–36	6	2	3	1	23	19	5
1936–37	6	2	1	3	15	15	7
1937–38	6	0	3	3	10	16	3
Totals	62	19	28	15	144	162	53

OAKLAND (CALIFORNIA GOLDEN) SEALS

(9 seasons)

1967–68	4	3	0	1	22	8	7
1968–69	6	3	2	1	18	17	7
1969–70	6	4	2	0	20	11	8
1970–71	6	4	2	0	26	23	8
1971–72	6	2	2	2	25	24	6
1972–73	5	2	2	1	21	20	5
1973–74	5	4	1	0	28	15	8
1974–75	5	2	2	1	19	18	5
1975–76	5	1	3	1	14	17	3
Totals	48	25	16	7	193	153	57

ATLANTA FLAMES

(8 seasons)
(moved to Calgary for 1980–81)

1972–73	5	3	2	0	13	11	6
1973–74	5	1	3	1	9	14	3
1974–75	4	2	2	0	12	20	4
1975–76	4	3	1	0	20	9	6
1976–77	4	1	2	1	8	8	3
1977–78	4	2	1	1	14	11	5
1978–79	4	0	3	1	13	21	1
1979–80	4	1	2	1	12	13	3
Totals	34	13	16	5	101	107	31

OTTAWA SENATORS
(7 seasons)

1926–27	4	1	3	0	8	8	2
1927–28	4	0	3	1	4	11	1
1928–29	4	1	1	2	5	4	4
1929–30	4	0	3	1	12	16	1
1930–31	4	2	2	0	9	6	4
1931–32			did not compete				
1932–33	6	4	1	1	9	5	9
1933–34	6	4	2	0	17	14	8
Totals	32	12	15	5	64	64	29

COLORADO ROCKIES (6 seasons)
(formerly Kansas City, 1974–76;
moved to New Jersey for 1982–83)

1976–77	4	0	4	0	9	19	0
1977–78	4	2	1	1	18	16	5
1978–79	4	3	0	1	20	9	7
1979–80	4	1	3	0	11	16	2
1980–81	4	2	1	1	18	13	5
1981–82	3	3	0	0	12	5	6
Totals	23	11	9	3	88	78	25

SAN JOSE SHARKS
(5 seasons)

1991–92	3	2	0	1	19	8	5
1992–93	4	4	0	0	20	10	8
1993–94	4	3	1	0	21	12	6
1994–95	4	4	0	0	19	4	8
1995–96	4	3	1	0	17	12	6
Totals	19	16	2	1	96	46	33

OTTAWA SENATORS
(4 seasons)

1992–93	2	2	0	0	8	6	4
1993–94	2	1	1	0	12	6	2
1994–95	–	–	–	–	–	–	–
1995–96	2	1	1	0	5	4	2
Totals	6	4	2	0	25	16	8

PITTSBURGH PIRATES

(4 seasons)

1926–27	6	2	4	0	17	16	4
1927–28	6	3	2	1	14	7	7
1928–29	6	5	1	0	17	8	10
1929–30	6	4	2	0	24	12	8
Totals	24	14	9	1	72	43	29

TAMPA BAY LIGHTNING

(4 seasons)

1992–93	7	6	1	0	48	26	12
1993–94	3	2	1	0	11	8	4
1994–95	–	–	–	–	–	–	–
1995–96	2	2	0	0	5	2	4
Totals	12	10	2	0	64	36	20

MIGHTY DUCKS OF ANAHEIM

(3 seasons)

1993–94	4	3	0	1	22	12	7
1994–95	4	3	0	1	21	15	7
1995–96	4	3	0	1	18	6	7
Totals	12	9	0	3	61	33	21

DALLAS STARS

(3 seasons)

(formerly Minnesota, 1967–93)

1993–94	6	3	3	0	35	22	6
1994–95	5	5	0	0	19	11	10
1995–96	6	5	0	1	22	7	11
Totals	17	13	3	1	76	40	27

FLORIDA PANTHERS

(3 seasons)

1993–94	2	2	0	0	11	6	4
1994–95	–	–	–	–	–	–	–
1995–96	2	1	1	0	5	5	2
Totals	4	3	1	0	16	11	6

CLEVELAND BARONS
(2 seasons)

1976–77	5	3	2	0	17	17	6
1977–78	5	2	2	1	16	15	5
Totals	10	5	4	1	33	32	11

KANSAS CITY SCOUTS
(2 seasons)
(moved to Colorado for 1976–77,
then to New Jersey for 1982–83)

1974–75	4	3	1	0	14	7	6
1975–76	4	3	1	0	20	13	6
Totals	8	6	2	0	34	20	12

PHILADELPHIA QUAKERS
(one season)

1930–31	6	4	2	0	23	16	8

ST. LOUIS EAGLES
(one season)

1934–35	6	3	3	0	23	18	6

COLORADO AVALANCHE (one season)
(formerly Quebec, 1979–95)

1995–96	4	3	1	0	16	7	6

ALL-TIME TEAM-BY-TEAM YEAR-BY-YEAR PLAYOFF RECORDS

TORONTO MAPLE LEAFS
(23 series)

1929	2	0	2	0	2	7	0–1
1934	5	3	2	0	11	12	1–0
1936	4	3	1	0	18	11	1–0
1939	3	1	2	0	8	10	0–1
1940	2	0	2	0	2	5	0–1
1942	7	3	4	0	19	25	0–1
1943	6	4	2	0	20	17	1–0
1945	7	3	4	0	9	9	0–1
1947	5	1	4	0	14	18	0–1
1948	4	0	4	0	7	18	0–1
1949	4	0	4	0	5	12	0–1
1950	7	4	3	0	10	11	1–0
1952	4	4	0	0	13	3	1–0
1954	5	4	1	0	15	8	1–0
1955	4	4	0	0	14	6	1–0
1956	5	4	1	0	14	10	1–0
1960	6	2	4	0	16	20	0–1
1961	5	4	1	0	15	8	1–0
1963	5	1	4	0	10	17	0–1
1964	7	3	4	0	17	22	0–1
1987	7	4	3	0	20	18	1–0
1988	6	4	2	0	32	20	1–0
1993	7	3	4	0	30	24	0–1
Totals	117	59	58	0	321	311	11–12

CHICAGO BLACKHAWKS
(14 series)

1934	4	1	3	0	7	9	0–1
1941	2	2	0	0	5	2	1–0
1944	5	1	4	0	8	17	0–1
1961	6	2	4	0	12	20	0–1
1963	6	4	2	0	25	19	1–0
1964	7	4	3	0	24	18	1–0
1965	7	3	4	0	19	23	0–1
1966	6	4	2	0	22	10	1–0
1970	4	0	4	0	8	16	0–1

1985	3	0	3	0	8	23	0–1
1987	4	4	0	0	15	6	1–0
1989	6	2	4	0	18	25	0–1
1992	4	0	4	0	6	11	0–1
1995	5	4	1	0	13	12	1–0
Totals	69	31	38	0	190	211	6–8

MONTREAL CANADIENS
(11 series)

1937	5	3	2	0	13	8	1–0
1942	3	2	1	0	8	8	1–0
1949	7	4	3	0	17	14	1–0
1951	6	2	4	0	12	13	0–1
1952	4	4	0	0	11	2	1–0
1954	7	4	3	0	14	12	1–0
1955	7	4	3	0	27	20	1–0
1956	5	1	4	0	9	18	0–1
1958	4	0	4	0	6	19	0–1
1966	6	2	4	0	14	18	0–1
1978	5	1	4	0	10	24	0–1
Totals	59	27	32	0	141	156	6–5

BOSTON BRUINS
(7 series)

1941	4	0	4	0	6	12	0–1
1942	2	2	0	0	9	5	1–0
1943	4	4	0	0	16	5	1–0
1945	7	4	3	0	22	22	1–0
1946	5	2	3	0	10	16	0–1
1953	6	2	4	0	21	21	0–1
1957	5	1	4	0	10	14	0–1
Totals	33	15	18	0	94	95	3–4

NEW YORK RANGERS
(5 series)

1933	2	0	2	0	3	6	0–1
1937	5	3	2	0	9	8	1–0
1941	3	2	1	0	6	6	1–0
1948	6	4	2	0	17	12	1–0
1950	7	4	3	0	22	17	1–0
Totals	23	13	10	0	57	49	4–1

ST. LOUIS BLUES
(4 series)

1984	4	1	3	0	12	13	0–1
1988	5	4	1	0	21	14	1–0
1991	7	3	4	0	20	24	0–1
1996	7	4	3	0	22	16	1–0
Totals	23	12	11	0	75	67	2–2

MONTREAL MAROONS
(3 series)

1932	2	0	1	1	1	3	0–1
1933	2	2	0	0	5	2	1–0
1936	3	3	0	0	6	1	1–0
Totals	7	5	1	1	12	6	2–1

EDMONTON OILERS
(2 series)

1987	5	1	4	0	10	16	0–1
1988	5	1	4	0	16	23	0–1
Totals	10	2	8	0	26	39	0–2

SAN JOSE SHARKS
(2 series)

1994	7	3	4	0	27	21	0–1
1995	4	4	0	0	24	6	1–0
Totals	11	7	4	0	51	27	1–1

ATLANTA FLAMES
(one series)

1978	2	2	0	0	8	5	1–0

COLORADO AVALANCHE
(one series)

1996	6	2	4	0	16	20	0–1

DALLAS STARS
(one series)

1995	5	4	1	0	17	10	1–0

MINNESOTA NORTH STARS
(one series)

1992	7	4	3	0	23	19	1–0

NEW JERSEY DEVILS
(one series)

1995	4	0	4	0	7	16	0–1

NEW YORK AMERICANS
(one series)

1940	3	2	1	0	9	7	1–0

WINNIPEG JETS (one series)

1996	6	4	2	0	20	10	1–0

ALL NHL FRANCHISE HISTORIES AND ARENA NAMES

Mighty Ducks of Anaheim	1993–present	Anaheim Arena (Arrowhead Pond)
Atlanta Flames	1972–1980	The Omni
Boston Bruins	1924–1928	Boston Arena
	1928–1995	Boston Garden
	1995–present	Fleet Centre
Brooklyn Americans	1941–1942	Madison Square Garden
Buffalo Sabres	1970–1996	Memorial Auditorium (The Aud)
	1996–present	Marine Midland Bank Arena
Calgary Flames	1980–1983	Calgary Corral
	1983–1995	Olympic Saddledome
	1995–present	Canadian Airlines Saddledome
California Golden Seals	*see* Oakland Seals	
Chicago Blackhawks	1926–1932	Chicago Coliseum
	1932–1994	Chicago Stadium
	1994–present	The United Centre
Cleveland Barons	1976–1978	The Coliseum
Colorado Rockies	1976–1982	McNichols Sports Arena
Colorado Avalanche	1995–present	McNichols Sports Arena
Dallas Stars	1993–present	Reunion Arena
Detroit Cougars	1926–1927	Windsor Arena (Border Cities Arena)
	1927–1929	The Olympia
Detroit Falcons	1929–1933	The Olympia
Detroit Red Wings	1933–1979	The Olympia
	1979–present	Joe Louis Arena
Edmonton Oilers	1979–present	Northlands Coliseum
Florida Panthers	1993–present	Miami Arena
Hamilton Tigers	1920–1925	The Arena
Hartford Whalers	1979–1980	Springfield Civic Centre/ Hartford Civic Centre
	1980–present	Hartford Civic Centre
Kansas City Scouts	1974–1976	Kemper Arena
Los Angeles Kings	1967–1968	Long Beach Sports Arena/Sports Arena/ The Forum
	1968–present	The Forum (name changed in 1988 to Great Western Forum)
Minnesota North Stars	1967–1993	Met Centre (name changed in 1982 from Metropolitan Sports Centre)
Montreal Canadiens	1917–1918	Jubilee Arena
	1918–1919	Jubilee Arena/Montreal Arena
	1919–1924	Mount Royal Arena/The Forum
	1924–1996	The Forum (refurbished in 1968)
	1996–present	Molson Centre

Montreal Maroons	1924–1938	The Forum
Montreal Wanderers	1917–1918	Montreal Arena
New Jersey Devils	1982–present	Continental Airlines Arena (formerly Brendan Byrne Arena)
New York Islanders	1972–present	Nassau Veterans' Memorial Coliseum
New York Americans	1925–1941	Madison Square Garden
New York Rangers	1926–1968	Madison Square Garden
	1968–present	Madison Square Garden (newly built)
Oakland Seals	1967–1976	The Coliseum (San Fransisco)
Ottawa Senators	1918–1919	The Arena
	1919–1922	Dey's Arena
	1922–1931 & 1932–1934	The Auditorium
	1992–1996	Ottawa Civic Centre
	1996–present	Corel Centre (formerly The Palladium)
Philadelphia Flyers	1967–1996	The Spectrum
	1996–present	Core States Centre
Philadelphia Quakers	1930–1931	Philadelphia Arena
Phoenix Coyotes	1996–present	America West Arena
Pittsburgh Penguins	1967–present	Civic Arena
Pittsburgh Pirates	1925–1930	Duquesne Gardens
Quebec Bulldogs	1919–1920	*unavailable*
Quebec Nordiques	1979–1995	Le Colisée de Quebec
St. Louis Blues	1967–1994	St. Louis Arena (called The Checkerdome 1977–82)
	1994–present	Kiel Centre
St. Louis Eagles	1934–1935	St. Louis Arena
San Jose Sharks	1991–1993	Cow Palace
	1993–present	San Jose Arena
Tampa Bay Lightning	1992–1993	Expo Hall
	1993–1996	ThunderDome
	1996–present	Tampa Bay Ice Palace
Toronto Arenas	1917–1919	Arena Gardens (Mutual Street Arena)
Toronto Maple Leafs	1927–1931	Arena Gardens (Mutual Street Arena)
	1931–present	Maple Leaf Gardens
Toronto St. Pats	1919–1927	Arena Gardens
Vancouver Canucks	1970–1995	Pacific Coliseum
	1995–present	GM Place
Washington Capitals	1974–1993	Capital Centre
	1993–present	US Air Arena
Winnipeg Jets	1979–1995	Winnipeg Arena

0 - 0 GAMES

Detroit has been involved in 25 scoreless games since 1926 (goalies listed in brackets under their respective teams; shots from 1955–56, when the NHL began to keep such records).

1.	November 26, 1927	Detroit Cougars at Chicago Blackhawks (Harry Holmes) (Chuck Gardiner)
2.	February 23, 1928	Ottawa Senators at Detroit Cougars (Alex Connell) (Harry Holmes)
3.	February 26, 1928	New York Rangers at Detroit Cougars (Lorne Chabot) (Harry Holmes)
4.	February 23, 1929	Detroit Cougars at Chicago Blackhawks (Dolly Dolson) (Chuck Gardiner)
5.	January 7, 1932	Boston Bruins at Detroit Falcons (Cecil Thompson) (Alex Connell)
6.	February 18, 1932	Boston Bruins at Detroit Falcons (Cecil Thompson) (Alex Connell)
7.	December 30, 1934	New York Americans at Detroit Red Wings (Roy Worters) (John Ross Roach)
8.	January 26, 1935	Detroit Red Wings at Toronto Maple Leafs (John Ross Roach) (George Hainsworth)
9.	November 14, 1935	Chicago Blackhawks at Detroit Red Wings (Mike Karakas) (Norm Smith)
10.	November 28, 1935	Montreal Canadiens at Detroit Red Wings (Wilf Cude) (Norm Smith)
11.	February 28, 1937	Montreal Canadiens at Detroit Red Wings (Wilf Cude) (Norm Smith)
12.	December 17, 1939	New York Rangers at Detroit Red Wings (Dave Kerr) (Cecil Thompson)
13.	December 4, 1946	Detroit Red Wings at Chicago Blackhawks (Harry Lumley) (Paul Bibeault)
14.	March 17, 1948	Detroit Red Wings at Boston Bruins (Harry Lumley) (Frank Brimsek)
15.	October 23, 1948	Detroit Red Wings at Montreal Canadiens (Harry Lumley) (Bill Durnan)
16.	January 21, 1951	Toronto Maple Leafs at Detroit Red Wings (Al Rollins) (Terry Sawchuk)
17.	November 6, 1951	Detroit Red Wings at Boston Bruins (Terry Sawchuk) (Jim Henry)
18.	December 14, 1952	Montreal Canadiens at Detroit Red Wings (Al McNeil) (Terry Sawchuk)

19.	March 15, 1953	Detroit Red Wings at Chicago Blackhawks (Terry Sawchuk) (Al Rollins)
20.	January 3, 1954	Toronto Maple Leafs at Detroit Red Wings (Harry Lumley) (Terry Sawchuk)
21.	February 17, 1954	Detroit Red Wings at Toronto Maple Leafs (Terry Sawchuk) (Harry Lumley)
22.	October 22, 1955	Boston Bruins at Detroit Red Wings (Terry Sawchuk-31) (Glenn Hall-29)
23.	November 13, 1955	Detroit Red Wings at Boston Bruins (Glenn Hall) (Terry Sawchuk)
24.	October 13, 1962	Detroit Red Wings at Chicago Blackhawks (Terry Sawchuk-28) (Glenn Hall-23)
25.	November 7, 1976	Atlanta Flames at Detroit Red Wings (Phil Myre-26) (Ed Giacomin-23)

When You Can't Get to Olympia . . .
GET TO YOUR RADIO TO

FOLLOW THE "WINGS"
ON WKMH

FIRST SPORT SPOT
ON YOUR RADIO DIAL

1310 Kc.

All "Red Wing" Home Games Play by Play
By AL NAGLER . . Direct From Olympia

WKMH - 8:30 P.M.

GAMES WITH 10 GOALS BY ONE TEAM

(home team in bold)

FOR

January 23, 1944	**Detroit** 15 Rangers 0
November 5, 1942	**Detroit** 12 Rangers 5
February 3, 1944	**Detroit** 12 Rangers 2
October 29, 1981	**Detroit** 12 Calgary 4
December 4, 1987	**Detroit** 12 Chicago 0
December 13, 1934	Detroit 11 **St. Louis** 2
December 21, 1944	**Detroit** 11 Rangers 3
February 7, 1951	**Detroit** 11 Chicago 3
October 21, 1973	**Detroit** 11 California 2
February 27, 1985	**Detroit** 11 Vancouver 5
February 15, 1992	**Detroit** 11 San Jose 1
November 25, 1992	**Detroit** 11 St.Louis 6
December 2, 1995	Detroit 11 **Canadiens** 1
December 25, 1930	**Detroit** 10 Toronto 1
January 4, 1942	**Detroit** 10 Canadiens 0
March 16, 1944	**Detroit** 10 Boston 9
November 2, 1944	**Detroit** 10 Rangers 3
March 4, 1945	**Detroit** 10 Boston 4
March 16, 1947	Detroit 10 **Chicago** 6
December 29, 1948	**Detroit** 10 Boston 2
November 22, 1952	**Detroit** 10 Chicago 1
December 11, 1952	Detroit 10 **Boston** 1
March 2, 1953	**Detroit** 10 Boston 2
March 18, 1965	**Detroit** 10 Boston 3
December 2, 1965	**Detroit** 10 Boston 2
November 16, 1977	**Detroit** 10 St. Louis 1
November 5, 1981	**Detroit** 10 Los Angeles 2
November 25, 1987	**Detroit** 10 Winnipeg 8
November 7, 1991	**Detroit** 10 St. Louis 3
November 23, 1992	**Detroit** 10 Tampa Bay 5
November 27, 1993	**Detroit** 10 Dallas 4
January 6, 1994	Detroit 10 **San Jose** 3

AGAINST

January 2, 1971	**Toronto** 13 Detroit 0
February 2, 1974	**Flyers** 12 Detroit 2
March 14, 1986	**Edmonton** 12 Detroit 3
January 25, 1942	**Rangers** 11 Detroit 2
March 17, 1946	Toronto 11 **Detroit** 7
March 16, 1971	Boston 11 **Detroit** 4
January 20, 1981	**Los Angeles** 11 Detroit 4
February 23, 1988	Flyers 11 **Detroit** 6
February 13, 1940	**Boston** 10 Detroit 3
March 7, 1959	**Canadiens** 10 Detroit 2
December 5, 1964	**Toronto** 10 Detroit 2
March 29, 1967	**Rangers** 10 Detroit 5
October 23, 1974	**Atlanta** 10 Detroit 1
March 27, 1980	**Sabres** 10 Detroit 1
January 15, 1981	**Calgary** 10 Detroit 0
December 1, 1984	**St. Louis** 10 Detroit 5
October 17, 1985	**Minnesota** 10 Detroit 1
November 30, 1985	**Canadiens** 10 Detroit 1
December 11, 1985	Minnesota 10 **Detroit** 2
December 23, 1985	**Rangers** 10 Detroit 2
January 28, 1989	**Penguins** 10 Detroit 5
October 5, 1989	**Calgary** 10 Detroit 7
February 24, 1993	**Sabres** 10 Detroit 7
October 9, 1993	**Los Angeles** 10 Detroit 3

MOST GOALS
BOTH TEAMS
(16 or more)

19	March 16, 1944	**Detroit** 10 Boston 9
18	March 17, 1946	Toronto 11 **Detroit** 7
	November 25, 1987	**Detroit** 10 Winnipeg 8
17	November 5, 1942	**Detroit** 12 Rangers 5
	February 23, 1988	Flyers 11 **Detroit** 6
	October 5, 1989	**Calgary** 10 Detroit 7
	November 25, 1992	**Detroit** 11 St. Louis 6
	February 24, 1993	**Sabres** 10 Detroit 7
16	March 16, 1947	Detroit 10 **Chicago** 6
	October 29, 1981	**Detroit** 12 Calgary 4
	March 19, 1983	Edmonton 9 **Detroit** 7
	March 24, 1984	Detroit 7 **Los Angeles** 9
	February 27, 1985	**Detroit** 11 Vancouver 5
	October 24, 1988	St. Louis 8 **Detroit** 8

OLYMPIA'S NEXT

ALL-STAR

BOXING SHOW

Friday, March 10

WATCH NEWSPAPERS FOR ANNOUNCEMENT OF FIGHTERS

HIGHEST TIE SCORES

8–8	October 14, 1988 vs. St. Louis
7–7	November 26, 1980 vs. Washington
	December 27, 1989 at Toronto
6–6	December 7, 1943 at Boston
	January 11, 1959 vs. Toronto
	March 19, 1965 at Rangers
	January 25, 1979 at Los Angeles
	December 13, 1979 at Boston
	October 5, 1983 at Winnipeg
	February 1, 1984 vs. Hartford
	December 11, 1986 vs. Minnesota
	February 23, 1989 vs. Penguins
	February 11, 1993 at Los Angeles

PENALTY-FREE GAMES REGULAR SEASON

1.	March 10, 1927	Pirates 1 at Detroit 7
2.	February 26, 1935	Detroit 2 at Americans 3
3.	December 10, 1936	Canadiens 1 at Detroit 2
4.	January 5, 1937	Detroit 3 at Boston 2
5.	January 31, 1937	Detroit 2 at Boston 1
6.	March 2, 1937	Detroit 7 at Maroons 4
7.	March 11, 1937	Detroit 4 at Rangers 2
8.	February 3, 1938	Detroit 6 at Americans 1
9.	March 3, 1938	Detroit 3 at Rangers 4
10.	March 20, 1938	Rangers 3 at Detroit 4
11.	January 9, 1940	Detroit 1 at Boston 3
12.	March 5, 1940	Detroit 2 at Boston 7
13.	March 9, 1940	Detroit 0 at Canadiens 3
14.	January 25, 1944	Detroit 6 at Boston 3
15.	February 13, 1944	Detroit 4 at Boston 1
16.	March 19, 1944	Detroit 0 at Chicago 2
17.	November 6, 1946	Boston 3 at Detroit 3
18.	November 16, 1947	Detroit 3 at Boston 2
19.	February 7, 1951	Chicago 3 at Detroit 11
20.	March 19, 1960	Rangers 3 at Detroit 6
21.	January 14, 1962	Rangers 1 at Detroit 2

SHUTOUTS FOR AND AGAINST FOR ALL NHL SEASONS

Season	For–Against	Season	For–Against	Season	For–Against
1926–27	6–9	1950–51	11–5	1974–75	2–2
1927–28	11–9	1951–52	12–3	1975–76	6–7
1928–29	10–9	1952–53	10–8	1976–77	3–11
1929–30	2–5	1953–54	13–8	1977–78	2–5
1930–31	6–6	1954–55	12–5	1978–79	1–2
1931–32	6–6	1955–56	12–6	1979–80	5–1
1932–33	10–4	1956–57	4–5	1980–81	0–3
1933–34	5–4	1957–58	3–8	1981–82	0–1
1934–35	6–6	1958–59	6–10	1982–83	2–5
1935–36	6–5	1959–60	6–1	1983–84	3–1(2)
1936–37	6–4	1960–61	2–5	1984–85	0–1
1937–38	3–4	1961–62	8–6	1985–86	2–5
1938–39	4–9	1962–63	3–4	1986–87	2–2
1939–40	3–9	1963–64	7–2	1987–88	5–1
1940–41	4–4	1964–65	6–3	1988–89	1–0
1941–42	5–2	1965–66	7–2	1989–90	1–4
1942–43	6–0	1966–67	4–5	1990–91	2–4
1943–44	2–2	1967–68	1–3	1991–92	3–0
1944–45	1–0	1968–69	4–4	1992–93	4–2
1945–46	2–3	1969–70	2–6	1993–94	4–1
1946–47	3–3	1970–71	1–7(1)	1994–95	2–1
1947–48	7–4	1971–72	4–1	1995–96	9–0
1948–49	6–6	1972–73	7–5		
1949–50	8–4	1973–74	2–7	Total:	334–280

(1) Plante and Gamble shared a shutout for Toronto vs. Detroit on January 2, 1971
(2) Low and Resch shared a shutout for New Jersey vs. Detroit on December 4, 1983

BACK-TO-BACK-TO-BACK SHUTOUTS REGULAR SEASON

Dolly Dolson	February 21 & 24 & 26, 1929
Terry Sawchuk	November 20 & 21 & 25, 1954
Glenn Hall	December 11 & 15 & 18, 1955

BACK-TO-BACK SHUTOUTS — REGULAR SEASON

Harry Holmes	November 30 & December 4, 1926
Harry Holmes	November 26 & 27, 1927
Harry Holmes	February 23 & 26, 1928

Dolly Dolson	February 9 & 10, 1929
Bill Beveridge	January 2 & 5, 1930
John Ross Roach	January 17 & 22, 1933
John Ross Roach	December 30 & January 1, 1934–35
Norm Smith	January 14 & 17, 1937
Cecil Thompson	January 10 & 15, 1939
Harry Lumley	December 28 & 31, 1947
Harry Lumley	October 17 & 23, 1948
Harry Lumley	February 6 & 9, 1949
Harry Lumley	November 30 & December 1, 1949
Terry Sawchuk	December 6 & 9, 1950
Terry Sawchuk	March 11 & 15, 1951
Terry Sawchuk	January 17 & 19, 1952
Terry Sawchuk	November 26 & 28, 1953
Glenn Hall	December 31 & January 2, 1956–57
Glenn Hall	October 27 & 29, 1957
Glenn Hall	December 31 & January 1, 1960–61
Terry Sawchuk	October 28 & November 1, 1962
Terry Sawchuk	November 7 & 10, 1963
Roger Crozier	October 25 & 29, 1964
Roger Crozier	December 26 & 28, 1965
Roger Crozier	November 6 & 10, 1966
Roger Crozier	December 15 & 18, 1966
Roy Edwards	January 6 & 7, 1973
Jim Rutherford	December 31 & January 3, 1975–76
Tim Cheveldae	November 13 & 14, 1992
Chris Osgood	February 24 & 26, 1994

BACK-TO-BACK SHUTOUTS AGAINST

December 25 & 30, 1926
February 24 & March 1, 1927
February 23 & 26, 1928
November 26 & 29, 1936
February 12 & 15, 1950
December 5 & 6, 1953
November 11 & 13, 1954
November 12 & 13, 1955
February 22 & 25, 1967
January 29 & February 1, 1969
January 17 & 21, 1971
March 26 & 27, 1977
March 30 & April 1, 1978
December 28 & 31, 1990

ALL-TIME TEAM RECORDS

MOST CONSECUTIVE YEARS IN PLAYOFFS

20	1938–58
6	1990–present
4	1962–66

MOST CONSECUTIVE YEARS MISSING PLAYOFFS

7	1970–77
5	1978–83
3	1966–69

MOST WINS — SEASON (over .500 record)

62*	1995–96 (82 games)
47	1992–93 (84 games)
46	1993–94 (84 games)
44	1951–52 (70 games)
43	1991–92 (80 games)

* NHL record

FEWEST WINS — SEASON (under .500 record)

12	1926–27 (44 games)
	1937–38 (48 games)
14	1929–30 (44 games)
16	1930–31 (44 games)
	1976–77 (80 games)
17	1985–86 (80 games)
18	1931–32 (48 games)
	1938–39 (48 games)

BEST WIN PERCENTAGE — SEASON

.799	1995–96 (82 games)
.729	1994–95 (48 games)
.721	1950–51 (70 games)
.714	1951–52 (70 games)
.679	1954–55 (70 games)
.670	1944–45 (50 games)
.643	1952–53 (70 games)

WORST WIN PERCENTAGE — SEASON

.250	1985–86 (80 games)
.256	1976–77 (80 games)
.318	1926–27 (44 games)
.338	1981–82 (80 games)
.350	1980–81 (80 games)
.353	1970–71 (78 games)
.356	1982–83 (80 games)

FEWEST LOSSES — SEASON
(over .500 record)

11	1994–95 (48 games)
13	1995–96 (82 games)
	1950–51 (70 games)
14	1951–52 (70 games)
	1944–45 (50 games)
	1942–43 (50 games)
	1936–37 (48 games)
	1933–34 (48 games)
15	1932–33 (48 games)
16	1952–53 (70 games)
	1940–41 (48 games)
	1935–36 (48 games)
	1928–29 (44 games)

MOST LOSSES — SEASON
(under .500 record)

57	1985–86 (80 games)
55	1976–77 (80 games)
47	1981–82 (80 games)
45	1970–71 (78 games)
	1974–75 (80 games)
44	1982–83 (80 games)
	1975–76 (80 games)

MOST TIES — SEASON

18	1952–53 (70 games)
	1980–81 (80 games)
16	1955–56 (70 games)
	1960–61 (70 games)
	1978–79 (80 games)
15	1959–60 (70 games)
	1969–70 (76 games)

FEWEST TIES — SEASON

4	1966–67 (70 games)
	1941–42 (48 games)
	1994–95 (48 games)
	1926–27 (44 games)
5	1944–45 (50 games)
6	1985–86 (80 games)
	1943–44 (50 games)
	1939–40 (48 games)
	1938–39(48 games)
	1929–30 (44 games)
	1927–28 (44 games)

MOST POINTS — SEASON

131	1995–96 (82 games)
103	1992–93 (84 games)
101	1950–51 (70 games)
100	1951–52 (70 games)
	1993–94 (84 games)

FEWEST POINTS — SEASON
(under .500 record)

28	1926–27 (44 games)
34	1929–30 (44 games)
35	1937–38 (48 games)
39	1930–31 (44 games)
40	1985–86 (80 games)
41	1976–77 (80 games)
42	1941–42 (48 games)
	1938–39 (48 games)

MOST WINS HOME — SEASON (over .500 record)

36	1995–96 (41 dates)
26	1990–91 (40 dates)
25	1950–51 (35 dates)
	1954–55 (35 dates)
	1964–65 (35 dates)
	1971–72 (39 dates)
	1992–93 (42 dates)
24	1951–52 (35 dates)
	1953–54 (35 dates)
	1987–88 (40 dates)
	1991–92 (40 dates)

FEWEST WINS HOME — SEASON (under .500 record)

6	1926–27 (22 dates)
8	1937–38 (24 dates)
9	1927–28 (22 dates)
	1929–30 (22 dates)
12	1976–77 (40 dates)
13	1958–59 (35 dates)
14	1982–83 (40 dates)
	1979–80 (40 dates)

FEWEST LOSSES HOME — SEASON (over .500 record)

3	1995–96 (41 dates)
	1950–51 (35 dates)
	1932–33 (24 dates)
	1931–32 (24 dates)
4	1953–54 (35 dates)
	1942–43 (25 dates)
	1994–95 (24 dates)
5	1954–55 (35 dates)
	1952–53 (35 dates)
	1945–46 (25 dates)
	1944–45 (25 dates)
	1943–44 (25 dates)
	1940–41 (24 dates)
	1936–37 (24 dates)
	1935–36 (24 dates)
	1933–34 (24 dates)

MOST LOSSES HOME — SEASON (under .500 record)

26	1985–86 (40 dates)
22	1976–77 (40 dates)
21	1979–80 (40 dates)
20	1983–84 (40 dates)
19	1982–83 (40 dates)
	1981–82 (40 dates)
17	1958–59 (35 dates)
	1974–75 (40 dates)
	1978–79 (40 dates)
15	1926–27 (22 dates)
	1967–68 (37 dates)
	1970–71 (39 dates)
	1980–81 (40 dates)

MOST TIES HOME — SEASON

10	1952–53 (35 dates)
9	1980–81 (40 dates)
8	1955–56 (35 dates)
	1957–58 (35 dates)
	1975–76 (40 dates)
	1978–79 (40 dates)

FEWEST TIES HOME — SEASON

0*	1990–91 (40 dates)
1	1944–45 (25 dates)
	1926–27 (22 dates)
2	1995–96 (41 dates)
	1983–84 (40 dates)
	1943–44 (25 dates)
	1938–39 (24 dates)
	1992–93 (42 dates)
	1971–72 (39 dates)
	1966–67 (35 dates)
	1964–65 (35 dates)
	1963–64 (35 dates)
	1959–60 (35 dates)
	1948–49 (30 dates)
	1941–42 (24 dates)
	1939–40 (24 dates)
	1994–95 (24 dates)
	1929–30 (22 dates)
	1927–28 (22 dates)

* ties NHL record

MOST WINS ROAD — SEASON

26	1995–96 (41 dates)
23	1993–94 (42 dates)
22	1992–93 (42 dates)
20	1951–52 (35 dates)
	1969–70 (38 dates)
19	1991–92 (40 dates)
18	1949–50 (35 dates)

FEWEST WINS ROAD — SEASON (under .500 record)

3	1980–81 (40 dates)
	1931–32 (24 dates)
4	1976–77 (40 dates)
	1945–46 (25 dates)
	1938–39 (24 dates)
	1937–38 (24 dates)
5	1970–71 (39 dates)
	1941–42 (24 dates)
	1939–40 (24 dates)
	1929–30 (22 dates)

FEWEST LOSSES ROAD— SEASON (over .500 record)

7	1951–52 (35 dates)
	1994–95 (24 dates)
9	1947–48 (30 dates)
	1944–45 (25 dates)
	1936–37 (24 dates)
	1927–28 (22 dates)
10	1995–96 (41 dates)
	1969–70 (38 dates)
	1950–51 (35 dates)
	1949–50 (35 dates)
11	1952–53 (35 dates)

MOST LOSSES ROAD— SEASON (under .500 record)

33	1976–77 (40 dates)
31	1985–86 (40 dates)
30	1970–71 (39 dates)
29	1975–76 (40 dates)
28	1966–67 (35 dates)
	1981–82 (40 dates)
	1980–81 (40 dates)
	1974–75 (40 dates)

MOST TIES ROAD — SEASON

12	1959–60 (35 dates)
9	1960–61 (35 dates)
	1980–81 (40 dates)
8	1951–52 (35 dates)
	1952–53 (35 dates)
	1955–56 (35 dates)
	1963–64 (35 dates)
	1967–68 (37 dates)
	1969–70 (38 dates)
	1978–79 (40 dates)
	1982–83 (40 dates)
	1989–90 (40 dates)
	1990–91 (40 dates)
	1991–92 (40 dates)

FEWEST TIES ROAD — SEASON

1	1966–67 (35 dates)
	1994–95 (24 dates)
	1941–42 (24 dates)
2	1993–94 (42 dates)
	1985–86 (40 dates)
	1975–76 (40 dates)
	1934–35 (24 dates)
	1930–31 (22 dates)
3	1976–77 (40 dates)
	1939–40 (24 dates)
	1935–36 (24 dates)
	1929–30 (22 dates)
	1927–28 (22 dates)
	1926–27 (22 dates)

(minimum 70-game schedule)

MOST GOALS FOR — SEASON

369	1992–93 (84 games)
356	1993–94 (84 games)
325	1995–96 (82 games)
322	1987–88 (80 games)
320	1991–92 (80 games)

FEWEST GOALS FOR — SEASON

167	1958–59 (70 games)
176	1957–58 (70 games)
183	1976–77 (80 games)
	1955–56 (70 games)
184	1961–62 (70 games)
186	1959–60 (70 games)

FEWEST GOALS AGAINST SEASON

(minimum 70-game schedule)

132	1953–54 (70 games)
133	1951–52 (70 games)
	1952–53 (70 games)
134	1954–55 (70 games)
139	1950–51 (70 games)
148	1955–56 (70 games)
157	1956–57 (70 games)

MOST GOALS AGAINST SEASON

415	1985–86 (80 games)
357	1984–85 (80 games)
351	1981–82 (80 games)
344	1982–83 (80 games)
339	1980–81 (80 games)
335	1974–75 (80 games)

MOST CONSECUTIVE WINS

9 March 3–21, 1951
February 27–March 20, 1955

MOST CONSECUTIVE HOME WINS

14 January 21–March 25, 1965

MOST CONSECUTIVE ROAD WINS

7 March 25–April 14, 1995

LONGEST UNDEFEATED STREAK

15 November 27–December 28, 1952

LONGEST HOME UNDEFEATED STREAK

18 December 26–March 20, 1955

LONGEST ROAD UNDEFEATED STREAK

15 October 18–December 26, 1951

LONGEST LOSING STREAK

14 February 24–March 25, 1982

LONGEST HOME LOSING STREAK

7 February 20–March 25, 1982

LONGEST ROAD LOSING STREAK

14 October 19–December 21, 1966

LONGEST WINLESS STREAK

19 February 26–April 3, 1977

LONGEST HOME WINLESS STREAK

10 December 11, 1985–January 18, 1986

LONGEST ROAD WINLESS STREAK

26	December 15, 1976–April 3, 1977

MOST CONSECUTIVE TIES

4	January 25–February 1, 1934
	November 6–11, 1951
	February 14–22, 1973
	March 1–10, 1981
3	January 26–31, 1935
	November 10–19, 1935
	January 13–16, 1938
	January 25–28, 1950
	February 1–5, 1950
	December 14–20, 1952
	November 7–11, 1953
	December 20–23, 1956
	December 26–31, 1972

MOST CONSECUTIVE OVERTIME GAMES

4	November 10–21, 1935
	March 10–15, 1936
	December 13–19, 1940
3	December 17–27, 1927
	January 27–February 1, 1933
	January 26–31, 1935
	January 13–16, 1938
	December 18–25, 1941
	February 19–24, 1990

MOST CONSECUTIVE GAMES WITHOUT BEING SHUTOUT

143	November 25, 1987–October 7, 1989

MOST CONSECUTIVE GAMES WITHOUT RECORDING A SHUTOUT

217	February 3, 1980–December 4, 1982

LONGEST SHUTOUT SEQUENCE

209:32	November 14–27, 1954
206:48	February 19–March 2, 1929
203:10	December 10–22, 1955

LONGEST SHUTOUT SEQUENCE AGAINST

209:23	November 7–14, 1954
197:58	March 24–29, 1977
172:52	January 26–February 2, 1969
162:15	December 3–9, 1953

MOST GAMES ON CONSECUTIVE NIGHTS

The Red Wings have played games on three consecutive nights three times:

1953	October 16	Detroit 2 at Chicago 2
	October 17	Chicago 1 at Detroit 2
	October 18	Canadiens 0 at Detroit 4
1964	December 25	Canadiens 2 at Detroit 2
	December 26	Detroit 3 at Canadiens 6
	December 27	Rangers 1 at Detroit 3
1976	February 6	Islanders 3 at Detroit 6
	February 7	Rangers 5 at Detroit 4
	February 8	Detroit 0 at Boston 7

MOST CONSECUTIVE GAMES AGAINST ONE OPPONENT

3	vs. Chicago, December 30–January 6, 1928–29
	vs. Toronto, March 11–14, 1943
	vs. Chicago, December 16–23, 1945
	vs. Canadiens, February 3–10, 1945
	vs. Canadiens, February 18–22, 1954

MOST CONSECUTIVE ROAD GAMES AGAINST ONE OPPONENT

2	January 26 & 28, 1950 at Canadiens
	January 1 & 6, 1929 at Chicago

LONGEST HOME STAND

7 games	February 3–18, 1980
6 games	February 23–March 6, 1994

LONGEST ROAD TRIP

7 games	March 2–16, 1966
	November 16–29, 1967
	March 6–17, 1968
	November 7–24, 1971

YEARS RED WINGS LED THE LEAGUE

GOALS — INDIVIDUAL

1936–37	Larry Aurie (tied with one other)	23
1947–48	Ted Lindsay	33
1948–49	Sid Abel	28
1950–51	Gordie Howe	43
1951–52	Gordie Howe	47
1952–53	Gordie Howe	49
1956–57	Gordie Howe	44
1962–63	Gordie Howe	38
1964–65	Norm Ullman	42

ASSISTS — INDIVIDUAL

1946–47	Billy Taylor	46
1949–50	Ted Lindsay	55
1950–51	Gordie Howe (tied with one other)	43
1952–53	Gordie Howe	46
1953–54	Gordie Howe	48
1956–57	Ted Lindsay	55

POINTS — INDIVIDUAL

1949–50	Ted Lindsay	78
1950–51	Gordie Howe	86
1951–52	Gordie Howe	86
1952–53	Gordie Howe	95
1953–54	Gordie Howe	81
1956–57	Gordie Howe	89
1962–63	Gordie Howe	86

PENALTY MINUTES INDIVIDUAL

1930–31	Harvey Rockburn	118
1940–41	Jimmy Orlando	99*
1941–42	Jimmy Orlando	81*
1942–43	Jimmy Orlando	89*
1945–46	Jack Stewart	73
1962–63	Howie Young	273
1985–86	Joey Kocur	377
1987–88	Bob Probert	398

* match misconduct penalties not included

GOALS AGAINST AVERAGE — INDIVIDUAL

1936–37	Norm Smith	2.05
1942–43	Johnny Mowers	2.47
1951–52	Terry Sawchuk	1.90
1952–53	Terry Sawchuk	1.90
1954–55	Terry Sawchuk	1.94

PENALTY MINUTES — TEAM

1962–63	964
1964–65	1121
1985–86	2393
1986–87	2209

GOALS SCORED — TEAM

Season	Goals
1936–37	128
1948–49	195
1949–50	229
1950–51	236
1951–52	215
1952–53	222
1964–65	224 (tied)
1992–93	369
1993–94	356

GOALS AGAINST — TEAM

Season	Goals
1936–37	102
1942–43	124
1951–52	133
1952–53	133
1954–55	134
1995–96	181

Norm Ullman

RED WINGS ALL-TIME LEADERS
REGULAR SEASON

MOST SEASONS

Gordie Howe	25	Syd Howe	12
Alex Delvecchio	24	Sid Abel	12
Marcel Pronovost	15	Shawn Burr	11
Ebbie Goodfellow	14	Bruce MacGregor	11
Ted Lindsay	14	Herbie Lewis	11
Terry Sawchuk	14	Gary Bergman	11
Steve Yzerman	13	Mud Brûneteau	11
Norm Ullman	13	Jack Stewart	10
Red Kelly	13	Reed Larson	10
Warren Godfrey	12	Marty Pavelich	10
Nick Libett	12	Jim Rutherford	10
Larry Aurie	12		

MOST GAMES — CAREER

Gordie Howe	1687	Terry Sawchuk	734
Alex Delvecchio	1549	Reed Larson	708
Marcel Pronovost	983	Gary Bergman	699
Steve Yzerman	942	Bruce MacGregor	673
Norm Ullman	875	Shawn Burr	659
Ted Lindsay	862	Marty Pavelich	634
Nick Libett	861		
Red Kelly	846		

By Position

CENTRE

Alex Delvecchio	1549
Steve Yzerman	942
Norm Ullman	875
Red Kelly	846

LEFT WING

Ted Lindsay	862
Nick Libett	861
Shawn Burr	659
Marty Pavelich	634

RIGHT WING

Gordie Howe	1687
Bruce MacGregor	673
Larry Aurie	489

DEFENCE

Marcel Pronovost	983
Reed Larson	708
Gary Bergman	699
Jack Stewart	503

MOST POINTS — CAREER

Gordie Howe	1809
Alex Delvecchio	1281
Steve Yzerman	1255
Norm Ullman	758
Ted Lindsay	728
Reed Larson	570
John Ogrodnick	546
Sergei Fedorov	529
Red Kelly	472
Gerard Gallant	467
Nick Libett	467
Sid Abel	463
Syd Howe	435
Marcel Dionne	366
Shawn Burr	362
Dale McCourt	337
Bruce MacGregor	335
Ebbie Goodfellow	324
Herbie Lewis	309
Mickey Redmond	309
Gary Bergman	299

By Position

CENTRE

Alex Delvecchio	1281
Steve Yzerman	1255
Norm Ullman	758
Sergei Fedorov	529

LEFT WING

Ted Lindsay	728
John Ogrodnick	546
Gerard Gallant	467
Nick Libett	467

RIGHT WING

Gordie Howe	1809
Bruce MacGregor	335
Mickey Redmond	309
Mud Brûneteau	277

DEFENCE

Reed Larson	570
Gary Bergman	299
Marcel Pronovost	297
Paul Coffey	239

Gordie Howe

1,000TH POINT

Only five players have scored their 1,000th career point while playing for the Red Wings:

1.	GORDIE HOWE	November 17, 1960 vs. Toronto at The Olympia Earned an assist in his 938th NHL game
2.	ALEX DELVECCHIO	February 16, 1969 vs. Los Angeles at The Olympia Earned an assist in his 1,143rd NHL game
3.	STEVE YZERMAN	February 24, 1993 vs. Buffalo at Memorial Auditorium Earned an assist in his 737th NHL game
4.	DINO CICCARELLI	March 9, 1994 vs. Calgary at the Saddledome Scored a goal in his 957th NHL game
5.	PAUL COFFEY	December 13, 1995 vs. Chicago at the Joe Louis Arena Earned an assist in his 1105th NHL game

MOST GOALS — CAREER

Gordie Howe	786
Steve Yzerman	517
Alex Delvecchio	456
Ted Lindsay	335
Norm Ullman	324
John Ogrodnick	265
Nick Libett	217
Sergei Fedorov	212
Gerard Gallant	207
Syd Howe	188
Reed Larson	188
Sid Abel	184
Mickey Redmond	177
Red Kelly	162
Ray Sheppard	152

By Position

CENTRE

Steve Yzerman	517
Alex Delvecchio	456
Norm Ullman	324
Sergei Fedorov	212

LEFT WING

Ted Lindsay	335
John Ogrodnick	265
Nick Libett	217
Gerard Gallant	207

RIGHT WING

Gordie Howe	786
Mickey Redmond	177
Ray Sheppard	152

DEFENCE

Reed Larson	188
Marcel Pronovost	80
Willie Huber	68
Gary Bergman	62

500TH GOAL

Only three players have scored their 500th career goal while playing for the Red Wings:

1.	GORDIE HOWE	March 14, 1962 vs. Rangers at Madison Square Garden (Glenn Hall)
2.	DINO CICCARELLI	January 8, 1994 vs. Los Angeles at the Great Western Forum (Kelly Hrudey)
3.	STEVE YZERMAN	January 17, 1996 vs. Colorado at the Joe Louis Arena (Patrick Roy)

MOST ASSISTS — CAREER

Gordie Howe 1023
Alex Delvecchio 825
Steve Yzerman 738
Norm Ullman 434
Ted Lindsay 393
Reed Larson 382
Sergei Fedorov 317
Red Kelly 310
John Ogrodnick 281
Sid Abel 279
Gerard Gallant 260
Nick Libett 250
Syd Howe 247
Gary Bergman 237
Marcel Dionne 227
Marcel Pronovost 217
Shawn Burr 214

By Position

CENTRE
Alex Delvecchio 825
Steve Yzerman 738
Norm Ullman 434
Sergei Fedorov 317

LEFT WING
Ted Lindsay 393
John Ogrodnick 281
Gerard Gallant 260
Nick Libett 250

RIGHT WING
Gordie Howe 1023
Bruce MacGregor 184
Vaclav Nedomansky 139

DEFENCE
Reed Larson 382
Gary Bergman 237
Marcel Pronovost 217

1,000TH ASSIST

Two players have registered their 1,000th career assist while with the Red Wings:

1. Gordie Howe, October 29, 1970 vs. Boston at the Olympia
2. Paul Coffey, December 13, 1995 vs. Chicago at the Joe Louis Arena

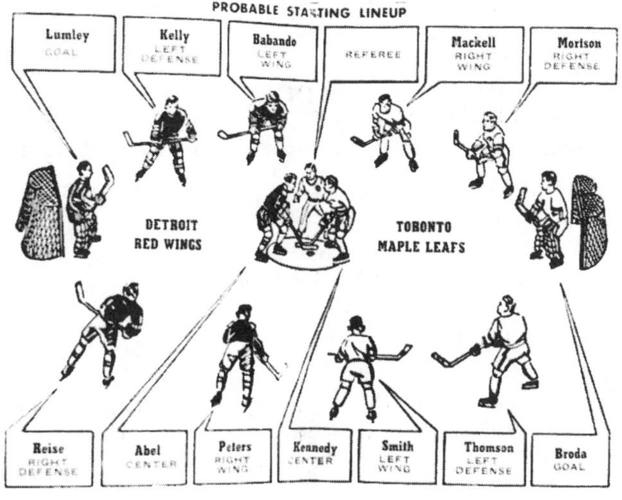

MOST PENALTY MINUTES — CAREER

Bob Probert	2090
Joey Kocur	1714
Gordie Howe	1643
Gerard Gallant	1600
Ted Lindsay	1423
Dennis Polonich	1242
Reed Larson	1127
Gary Bergman	1112
Bryan Watson	897
Steve Chiasson	886
Keith Primeau	781
Shawn Burr	765
Jack Stewart	696
Vladimir Konstantinov	687
Marcel Pronovost	687
Howie Young	660
Steve Yzerman	616
Willie Huber	612
Danny Gare	593

By Position

CENTRE

Dennis Polonich	1242
Keith Primeau	781
Steve Yzerman	616

LEFT WING

Bob Probert	2090
Gerard Gallant	1600
Ted Lindsay	1423
Shawn Burr	765

RIGHT WING

Joey Kocur	1714
Gordie Howe	1643
Danny Gare	593

DEFENCE

Reed Larson	1127
Gary Bergman	1112
Bryan Watson	897
Steve Chiasson	886

MOST POINTS — SEASON

Player	Points
Steve Yzerman ('88–'89)[1]	155
Steve Yzerman ('92–'93)[2]	137
Steve Yzerman ('89–'90)[3]	127
Marcel Dionne ('74–'75)[4]	121
Sergei Fedorov ('93–'94)[5]	120
Steve Yzerman ('90–'91)[6]	108
John Ogrodnick ('84–'85)[7]	105
Gordie Howe ('68–'69)[8]	103
Steve Yzerman ('91–'92)[9]	103
Steve Yzerman ('87–'88)[10]	102

100TH POINT

Ten times a Red Wing has scored 100 points in a season. Here are the dates for those occasions:

1. January 27, 1989 (goal) vs. Toronto at Joe Louis Arena
2. February 24, 1993 (assist) vs. Sabres at the Aud
3. February 19, 1990 (assist) vs. Canadiens at Joe Louis Arena
4. March 9, 1975 (assist) vs. Flyers at the Spectrum
5. March 1, 1994 (goal) vs. Calgary at Joe Louis Arena
6. March 10, 1991 (goal) vs. St. Louis at the Arena
7. March 22, 1985 (assist) vs. Rangers at Joe Louis Arena
8. March 30, 1969 (goal) vs. Chicago at the Stadium
9. April 14, 1992 (goal) vs. Minnesota at the Met Centre
10. February 27, 1988 (assist) vs. Quebec at the Colisée

By Position

CENTRE

Steve Yzerman ('88–'89) 155
Steve Yzerman ('92–'93) 137
Steve Yzerman ('89–'90) 127
Marcel Dionne ('74–'75) 121

LEFT WING

John Ogrodnick ('84–'85) 105
Gerard Gallant ('88–'89) 93
Ted Lindsay ('56–'57) 85

RIGHT WING

Gordie Howe ('68–'69) 103
Gordie Howe ('52–'53) 95
Mickey Redmond ('72–'73) 93
Ray Sheppard ('93–'94) 93

DEFENCE

Paul Coffey ('93–'94) 77
Reed Larson ('82–'83) 74
Paul Coffey ('95–'96) 74
Reed Larson ('78–'79) 67

MOST GOALS — SEASON

Steve Yzerman ('88–'89)[1] 65
Steve Yzerman ('89–'90)[2] 62
Steve Yzerman ('92–'93)[3] 58
Sergei Fedorov ('93–'94)[4] 56
John Ogrodnick ('84–'85)[5] 55
Mickey Redmond ('72–'73)[6] 52
Ray Sheppard ('93–'94)[7] 52
Steve Yzerman ('90–'91)[8] 51
Mickey Redmond ('73–'74)[9] 51
Danny Grant ('74–'75)[10] 50
Steve Yzerman ('87–'88)[11] 50
Gordie Howe ('52–'53) 49
Frank Mahovlich ('68–'69) 49
Gordie Howe ('51–'52) 47
Marcel Dionne ('74–'75) 47

50TH GOAL

On eleven occasions a Red Wing has scored 50 goals in a season. Here are the dates for those games (opposing goalie in brackets):

1. February 5, 1989 vs. Winnipeg (Pokey Reddick) at the Arena
2. February 24, 1990 vs. Islanders (Glen Healy) at Nassau Coliseum
3. March 10, 1993 vs. Edmonton (Bill Ranford) at Northlands Coliseum
4. March 15, 1994 vs. Vancouver (Kirk McLean) at Joe Louis Arena
5. March 13, 1985 vs. Edmonton (Grant Fuhr) at Northlands Coliseum
6. March 27, 1973 vs. Toronto (Ron Low) at Maple Leaf Gardens
7. March 29, 1994 vs. Hartford (Sean Burke) at Joe Louis Arena
8. March 30, 1991 vs. Rangers (Mike Richter) at Joe Louis Arena
9. March 23, 1974 vs. Rangers (Ed Giacomin) at the Olympia
10. April 2, 1975 vs. Washington (John Adams) at the Olympia
11. March 1, 1988 vs. Buffalo (Tom Barrasso) at Joe Louis Arena

By Position

CENTRE

Steve Yzerman ('88–'89)	65
Steve Yzerman ('89–'90)	62
Steve Yzerman ('92–'93)	58
Sergei Fedorov ('93–'94)	56

LEFT WING

John Ogrodnick ('84–'85)	55
Danny Grant ('74–'75)	50
Frank Mahovlich ('68–'69)	49

RIGHT WING

Mickey Redmond ('72–'73)	52
Ray Sheppard ('93–'94)	52
Mickey Redmond ('73–'74)	51
Gordie Howe ('52–'53)	49

DEFENCE

Reed Larson ('80–'81)	27
Reed Larson ('83–'84)	23
Reed Larson ('79–'80)	22
Reed Larson ('82–'83)	22

MOST ASSISTS — SEASON

Steve Yzerman ('88–'89)	90
Steve Yzerman ('92–'93)	79
Marcel Dionne ('74–'75)	74
Steve Yzerman ('89–'90)	65
Sergei Fedorov ('93–'94)	64
Paul Coffey ('93–'94)	63
Adam Oates ('88–'89)	62
Paul Coffey ('95–'96)	60
Gordie Howe ('68–'69)	59
Steve Yzerman ('84–'85)	59
Steve Yzerman ('86–'87)	59
Alex Delvecchio ('68–'69)	58
Steve Yzerman ('91–'92)	58
Steve Yzerman ('93–'94)	58
Steve Yzerman ('90–'91)	57
Walt McKechnie ('75–'76)	56
Dale McCourt ('80–'81)	56
Dino Ciccarelli ('92–'93)	56

By Position

CENTRE

Steve Yzerman ('88–'89)	90
Steve Yzerman ('92–'93)	79
Marcel Dionne ('74–'75)	74
Steve Yzerman ('89–'90)	65

LEFT WING

Ted Lindsay ('49–'50)	55
Ted Lindsay ('56–'57)	55
Gerard Gallant ('88–'89)	54
John Ogrodnick ('84–'85)	50

RIGHT WING

Gordie Howe ('68–'69)	59
Dino Ciccarelli ('92–'93)	56
Gordie Howe ('60–'61)	49
Gordie Howe ('53–'54 & '62–'63)	48

DEFENCE

Paul Coffey ('93–'94)	63
Paul Coffey ('95–'96)	60
Reed Larson ('82–'83)	52
Steve Chiasson ('92–'93)	50

MOST PENALTY MINUTES — SEASON

Bob Probert ('87–'88) 398
Joey Kocur ('85–'86) 377
Bryan Watson ('75–'76) 322
Bob Probert ('90–'91) 315
Dennis Polonich ('75–'76) 302
Bob Probert ('92–'93) 292
Joey Kocur ('86–'87) 276
Bob Probert ('91–'92) 276
Bob Probert ('93–'94) 275
Dennis Polonich ('76–'77) 274
Howie Young ('62–'63) 273
Joey Kocur ('89–'90) 268
Joey Kocur ('87–'88) 263
Dennis Polonich ('77–'78) 254
Gerard Gallant ('89–'90) 254
Joey Kocur ('90–'91) 253

By Position

CENTRE
Dennis Polonich ('75–'76) 302
Dennis Polonich ('76–'77) 274
Dennis Polonich ('77–'78) 254

LEFT WING
Bob Probert ('87–'88) 398
Bob Probert ('90–'91) 315
Bob Probert ('92–'93) 292
Bob Probert ('91–'92) 276

RIGHT WING
Joey Kocur ('85–'86) 377
Joey Kocur ('86–'87) 276
Joey Kocur ('89–'90) 268
Joey Kocur ('87–'88) 263

DEFENCE
Bryan Watson ('75–'76) 322
Howie Young ('62–'63) 273
Bryan Watson ('74–'75) 238

Have stick, will hit

Spotted in downtown Toronto yesterday, a man carrying a sign, "Will hit Claude Lemieux from behind for food."

ALL GOALIE RECORDS — REGULAR SEASON

MOST SHUTOUTS — CAREER

Player	Shutouts
Terry Sawchuk	85
Harry Lumley	26
Roger Crozier	20
Norm Smith	17
Glenn Hall	17
Harry Holmes	17
Dolly Dolson	16
John Mowers	15
John Ross Roach	15
Roy Edwards	12
Jim Rutherford	10
Tim Cheveldae	9
Chris Osgood	8
Glen Hanlon	7
Cecil Thompson	7

MOST SHUTOUTS — SEASON

Player	Shutouts
Terry Sawchuk ('51–'52)	12
Terry Sawchuk ('53–'54)	12
Terry Sawchuk ('54–'55)	12
Glenn Hall ('55–'56)	12
Harry Holmes ('27–'28)	11
Terry Sawchuk ('50–'51)	11
Dolly Dolson ('28–'29)	10
John Ross Roach ('32–'33)	10
Terry Sawchuk ('52–'53)	9
Harry Lumley ('47–'48)	7
Harry Lumley ('49–'50)	7
Roger Crozier ('65–'66)	7

MOST WINS — CAREER

Terry Sawchuk	351
Harry Lumley	163
Roger Crozier	131
Tim Cheveldae	128
Greg Stefan	115
Jim Rutherford	96
Roy Edwards	90
Norm Smith	76
Chris Osgood	76
Glenn Hall	74
John Mowers	65
Glen Hanlon	65
John Ross Roach	41
Dolly Dolson	35

MOST WINS — SEASON

Terry Sawchuk ('50–'51)	44
Terry Sawchuk ('51–'52)	44
Terry Sawchuk ('54–'55)	40
Roger Crozier ('64–'65)	40
Chris Osgood ('95–'96)	39
Glenn Hall ('56–'57)	38
Tim Cheveldae ('91–'92)	38
Terry Sawchuk ('53–'54)	35
Harry Lumley ('48–'49)	34
Harry Lumley ('49–'50)	33
Terry Sawchuk ('52–'53)	32
Harry Lumley ('47–'48)	30
Glenn Hall ('55–'56)	30

MOST LOSSES — CAREER

Terry Sawchuk	243
Jim Rutherford	165
Greg Stefan	127
Roger Crozier	123
Harry Lumley	105
Tim Cheveldae	93
Roy Edwards	80
Glen Hanlon	71
Norm Smith	71
John Mowers	61
Corrado Micalef	59
Rogie Vachon	57

MOST LOSSES — SEASON

Terry Sawchuk ('58–'59)	36
Jim Rutherford ('76–'77)	34
Roger Crozier ('66–'67)	30
Rogie Vachon ('79–'80)	30
Terry Sawchuk ('57–'58)	29
Jim Rutherford ('74–'75)	29
Harry Holmes ('26–'27)	27
Rogie Vachon ('78–'79)	27

BEST GOALS AGAINST AVERAGE — CAREER (minimum 100 games)

Glenn Hall	2.14
Norm Smith	2.25
Chris Osgood	2.43
Terry Sawchuk	2.45
John Mowers	2.56
Harry Lumley	2.75
Roger Crozier	2.93
Roy Edwards	2.94

BEST GOALS AGAINST AVERAGE — SEASON (minimum half a season played)

Dolly Dolson ('28–'29)	1.37
John Ross Roach ('32–'33)	1.88
Terry Sawchuk ('51–'52)	1.90
Terry Sawchuk ('52–'53)	1.90
Terry Sawchuk ('53–'54)	1.94
Terry Sawchuk ('54–'55)	1.96
Terry Sawchuk ('50–'51)	1.99
Norm Smith ('34–'35)	2.01
Norm Smith ('35–'36)	2.04
Norm Smith ('36–'37)	2.05
Glenn Hall ('55–'56)	2.11
Alex Connell ('31–'32)	2.12
John Mowers ('40–'41)	2.13
Chris Osgood ('95–'96)	2.17

MOST MINUTES PLAYED — CAREER

Terry Sawchuk	43,556
Harry Lumley	19,449
Jim Rutherford	18,122
Roger Crozier	17,483
Tim Cheveldae	15,025
Greg Stefan	16,333
Roy Edwards	12,262
Norm Smith	11,030
Glen Hanlon	9,830

MOST MINUTES PLAYED — SEASON

Tim Cheveldae ('91–'92)	4,236
Terry Sawchuk ('50–'51)	4,200
Terry Sawchuk ('51–'52)	4,200
Glenn Hall ('55–'56)	4,200
Glenn Hall ('56–'57)	4,200
Terry Sawchuk ('57–'58)	4,200
Roger Crozier ('64–'65)	4,167
Terry Sawchuk ('54–'55)	4,040
Terry Sawchuk ('58–'59)	4,020
Terry Sawchuk ('53–'54)	4,000

MOST ASSISTS — CAREER
(for all goalies)

Greg Stefan	15
Tim Cheveldae	9
Jim Rutherford	8
Corrado Micalef	5
Glen Hanlon	5
Al Smith	4
Rogie Vachon	4
Terry Sawchuk	2
Ed Mio	2
Hank Bassen	2
Andy Brown	1
Roy Edwards	1
Ed Giacomin	1
Gilles Gilbert	1
Mark Laforest	1
Ron Low	1
Jerry Lozinski	1
John Mowers	1
Terry Richardson	1

MOST ASSISTS — SEASON

Al Smith ('71–'72)	4
Greg Stefan ('86–'87)	4
Glen Hanlon ('90–'91)	4
Tim Cheveldae ('91–'92)	4
Tim Cheveldae ('92–'93)	4
Jim Rutherford ('73–'74)	3
Rogie Vachon ('79–'80)	3
Greg Stefan ('83–'84)	3
Corrado Micalef ('84–'85)	3
Glen Hanlon ('89–'90)	3

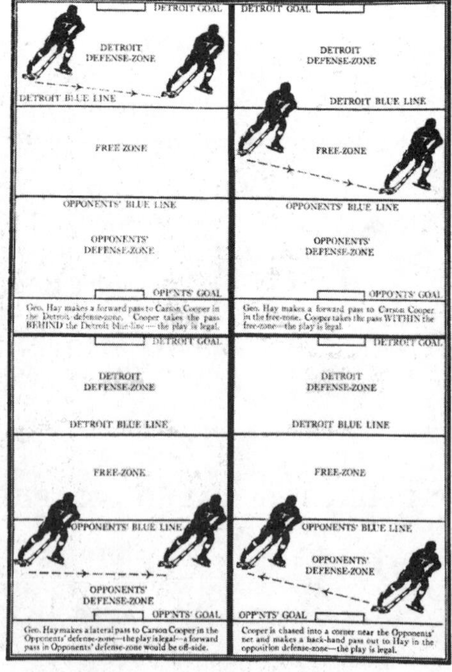

MOST ASSISTS — GAME & PERIOD

2	Jim Rutherford, 1st period February 18, 1979 vs. Pittsburgh

MOST PENALTY MINUTES — CAREER
(for all goalies)

Greg Stefan	200
Terry Sawchuk	116
Glen Hanlon	90
Corrado Micalef	43
Harry Lumley	40
Jim Rutherford	38
Mark Laforest	30
Hank Bassen	28
Ed Mio	25
Al Smith	23
Rogie Vachon	23
Gilles Gilbert	18
Glenn Hall	16
Roger Crozier	14
Tim Cheveldae	14
Roy Edwards	6
Terry Richardson	4
Ed Giacomin	4
Bill McKenzie	4
Andre St. Laurent	4
Joe Daly	2
Doug Grant	2
Pete McDuffe	2
Darren Eliot	2
Vincent Riendeau	2

MOST PENALTY MINUTES — SEASON

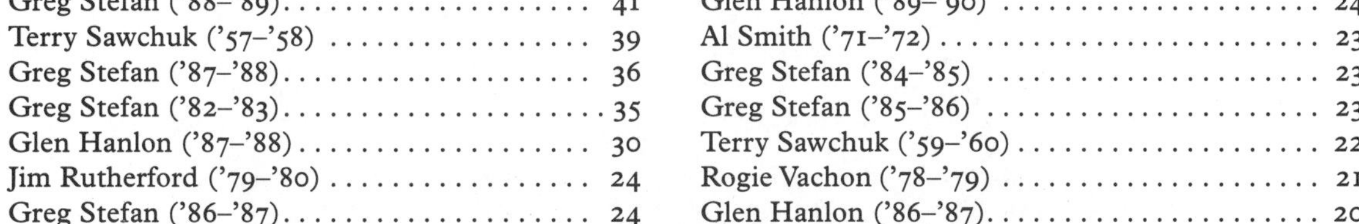

Greg Stefan ('88–'89)	41
Terry Sawchuk ('57–'58)	39
Greg Stefan ('87–'88)	36
Greg Stefan ('82–'83)	35
Glen Hanlon ('87–'88)	30
Jim Rutherford ('79–'80)	24
Greg Stefan ('86–'87)	24
Glen Hanlon ('89–'90)	24
Al Smith ('71–'72)	23
Greg Stefan ('84–'85)	23
Greg Stefan ('85–'86)	23
Terry Sawchuk ('59–'60)	22
Rogie Vachon ('78–'79)	21
Glen Hanlon ('86–'87)	20

Jim Rutherford

MOST POINTS — INDIVIDUAL — GAME

7	Carl Liscombe	November 5, 1942	(3 goals, 4 assists) Rangers 5 at Detroit 12
	Don Grosso	March 4, 1944	(1 goal, 6 assists) Chicago 2 at Detroit 6
	Billy Taylor	March 16, 1947	(7 assists) Detroit 10 at Chicago 6
6	Syd Howe	November 5, 1942	(2 goals, 4 assists) Rangers 5 at Detroit 12
	Gordie Howe	December 25, 1956	(3 goals, 3 assists) Rangers 1 at Detroit 8
	Norm Ullman	December 2, 1965	(3 goals, 3 assists) Boston 2 at Detroit 10
	Dale McCourt	November 5, 1981	(2 goals, 4 assists) Los Angeles 2 at Detroit 10
	Bob Probert	November 14, 1987	(2 goals, 4 assists) Detroit 6 at New Jersey 4
	Steve Yzerman	March 15, 1989	(2 goals, 4 assists) Detroit 8 at Edmonton 6
	Steve Yzerman	February 16, 1990	(2 goals, 4 assists) Flyers 6 at Detroit 9
	Dino Ciccarelli	April 5, 1994	(4 goals, 2 assists) Detroit 8 at Vancouver 3

MOST POINTS — INDIVIDUAL — PERIOD

4	Ebbie Goodfellow	1st period, January 26, 1930 (4 assists) Rangers 3 at Detroit 7
	Syd Howe	1st period, November 5, 1942 (2 goals, 2 assists) Rangers 5 at Detroit 12
	Carl Liscombe	3rd period, November 5, 1942 (2 goals, 2 assists) Rangers 5 at Detroit 12
	Murray Armstrong	3rd period, January 23, 1944 (1 goal, 3 assists) Rangers 0 at Detroit 15
	Joe Carveth	3rd period, January 23, 1944 (4 assists) Rangers 0 at Detroit 15
	Don Grosso	3rd period, January 23, 1944 (2 goals, 2 assists) Rangers 0 at Detroit 15
	Ted Lindsay	3rd period, March 9, 1949 (2 goals, 2 assists) Toronto 0 at Detroit 5
	Ted Lindsay	3rd period, March 16, 1949 (2 goals, 2 assists) Rangers 2 at Detroit 6

Dutch Reibel	2nd period, March 20, 1955 (1 goal, 3 assists) Canadiens 0 at Detroit 6
Gordie Howe	3rd period, December 25, 1956 (2 goals, 2 assists) Rangers 1 at Detroit 8
Gordie Howe	1st period, December 8, 1968 (2 goals, 2 assists) Detroit 5 at Rangers 2
Mickey Redmond	3rd period, October 21, 1973 (1 goal, 3 assists) California 2 at Detroit 11
Brent Ashton	2nd period, January 21, 1987 (2 goals, 2 assists) Islanders 5 at Detroit 8
Steve Yzerman	1st period, February 20, 1987 (2 goals, 2 assists) Quebec 3 at Detroit 6
Steve Yzerman	1st period, November 17, 1990 (3 goals, 1 assist) Detrit 8 at Toronto 4
Sergei Fedorov	2nd period, January 21, 1992 (1 goal, 3 assists) Flyers 3 at Detroit 7

MOST GOALS — INDIVIDUAL — PERIOD

3	Herb Lewis	3rd period, February 9, 1930 Pirates 1 at Detroit 8
	Carl Liscombe	1st period, March 13, 1938 Chicago 1 at Detroit 5
	Gus Giesebrecht	1st period, February 5, 1939 Americans 3 at Detroit 7
	Syd Howe	3rd period, December 25, 1939 Canadiens 1 at Detroit 3
	Mud Brûneteau	1st period, November 7, 1943 Boston 4 at Detroit 6
	Syd Howe	3rd period, January 23, 1944 Rangers 0 at Detroit 15
	Joe Carveth	2nd period, March 4, 1945 Boston 4 at Detroit 10
	Roy Conacher	1st period, March 16, 1947 Detroit 10 at Chicago 6
	Gerry Couture	3rd period, February 11, 1950 Detroit 9 at Boston 4
	Gordie Howe	3rd period, March 19, 1950 Toronto 0 at Detroit 5
	Gordie Howe	3rd period, March 17, 1951 Chicago 2 at Detroit 8
	Gordie Howe	2nd period, January 29, 1953 Detroit 5 at Chicago 2
	Ted Lindsay	2nd period, March 2, 1953 Boston 2 at Detroit 10

Gordie Howe	3rd period, March 3, 1955 Chicago 1 at Detroit 6
Jack McIntyre	2nd period, February 22, 1958 Boston 1 at Detroit 6
Norm Ullman	1st period, March 14, 1961 Rangers 2 at Detroit 5
Vic Stasiuk	3rd period, October 19, 1961 Boston 3 at Detroit 7
Paul Henderson	2nd period, October 27, 1966 Rangers 3 at Detroit 5
Norm Ullman	2nd period, February 8, 1967 Detroit 5 at Toronto 2
Frank Mahovlich	2nd period, November 19, 1969 Detroit 5 at Canadiens 5
Vaclav Nedomansky	2nd period, February 28, 1979 St. Louis 6 at Detroit 5
Vaclav Nedomansky	2nd period, October 17, 1979 Detroit 5 at Winnipeg 1
Reed Larson	2nd period, February 15, 1983 Penguins 3 at Detroit 7
John Ogrodnick	3rd period, December 4, 1984 Toronto 6 at Detroit 7
Ron Duguay	2nd period, March 15, 1985 Detroit 6 at Vancouver 5
Steve Yzerman	3rd period, March 30, 1985 Detroit 9 at Toronto 3
Danny Gare	1st period, October 30, 1985 Penguins 3 at Detroit 6
Shawn Burr	3rd period, November 13, 1986 Detroit 5 at Flyers 7
Steve Yzerman	2nd period, January 3, 1988 Detroit 4 at Winnipeg 4
Jimmy Carson	3rd period, December 27, 1989 Detroit 7 at Toronto 7
Steve Yzerman	1st period, November 17, 1990 Detroit 8 at Toronto 4
Jimmy Carson	1st period, February 15, 1992 San Jose 1 at Detroit 11

MOST ASSISTS — INDIVIDUAL — GAME

7*	Billy Taylor	March 16, 1947	Detroit 10 at Chicago 6
6	Don Grosso	March 4, 1944	Chicago 2 at Detroit 6
5	Jim McFadden	November 23, 1947	Detroit 9 at Chicago 3
	Gordie Howe	December 28, 1950	Canadiens 1 at Detroit 8
	Marcel Dionne	October 13, 1974	California 3 at Detroit 7
	Mark Osborne	February 7, 1982	St. Louis 5 at Detroit 8
4	Ebbie Goodfellow	January 26, 1930	Rangers 3 at Detroit 7
	Cooney Weiland	February 27, 1934	Rangers 1 at Detroit 5
	Ebbie Goodfellow	February 25, 1940	Americans 1 at Detroit 4
	Gus Giesebrecht	March 6, 1941	Detroit 6 at Americans 1
	Joe Carveth	January 23, 1944	Rangers 0 at Detroit 15
	Norm Ullman	November 18, 1956	Canadiens 3 at Detroit 8
	Gordie Howe	February 22, 1958	Boston 1 at Detroit 6
	Johnny Wilson	March 16, 1958	Detroit 6 at Boston 3
	Nick Mickoski	November 18, 1958	Boston 0 at Detroit 6
	Al Langlois	March 19, 1964	Rangers 3 at Detroit 9
	Alex Delvecchio	December 31, 1968	Minnesota 3 at Detroit 6
	Alex Delvecchio	February 6, 1969	Chicago 1 at Detroit 6
	Paul Popiel	February 16, 1969	Los Angeles 3 at Detroit 6
	Gordie Howe	January 3, 1970	Detroit 6 at Flyers 1
	Carl Brewer	January 24, 1970	Detroit 5 at St. Louis 2
	Marcel Dionne	March 21, 1972	Detroit 7 at Vancouver 5
	Gary Bergman	October 21, 1973	California 2 at Detroit 11
	Mickey Redmond	October 21, 1973	California 2 at Detroit 11
	Pierre Jarry	January 6, 1974	Minnesota 6 at Detroit 9
	Walt McKechnie	December 12, 1975	Detroit 5 at Washington 3
	Dale McCourt	November 5, 1981	Los Angeles 2 at Detroit 10
	Kelly Kisio	February 27, 1985	Vancouver 5 at Detroit 11
	Kelly Kisio	November 2, 1985	Detroit 5 at St. Louis 5
	Steve Yzerman	December 27, 1986	Detroit 5 at Toronto 5
	Bob Probert	November 14, 1987	Detroit 6 at New Jersey 4
	Gerard Gallant	November 12, 1988	Detroit 5 at Flyers 4
	Steve Yzerman	March 15, 1989	Detroit 8 at Edmonton 6
	Steve Yzerman	January 9, 1990	Minnesota 0 at Detroit 9
	Steve Chiasson	December 5, 1992	Detroit 9 at Tampa Bay 7
	Steve Yzerman	January 17, 1993	Detroit 7 at Flyers 4
	Paul Coffey	January 14, 1994	Dallas 3 at Detroit 9
	Steve Yzerman	April 5, 1994	Detroit 8 at Vancouver 3
	Steve Yzerman	April 13, 1994	Canadiens 0 at Detroit 9
	Paul Coffey	January 24, 1995	Vancouver 3 at Detroit 6
	Steve Yzerman	February 7, 1995	San Jose 0 at Detroit 6

MOST ASSISTS — INDIVIDUAL — PERIOD

4	Joe Carveth	3rd period, January 23, 1944 Chicago 2 at Detroit 8
3	Ebbie Goodfellow	1st period, January 26, 1930 Rangers 3 at Detroit 7
	Cooney Weiland	1st period, February 27, 1934 Rangers 1 at Detroit 5
	Ebbie Goodfellow	2nd period, February 28, 1935 Chicago 1 at Detroit 5
	Marty Barry	2nd period, March 19, 1936 Chicago 3 at Detroit 5
	Ebbie Goodfellow	1st period, February 25, 1940 Americans 1 at Detroit 4
	Mud Brûneteau	1st period, November 5, 1942 Rangers 5 at Detroit 12
	Murray Armstrong	3rd period, January 23, 1944 Rangers 0 at Detroit 15
	Don Grosso	3rd period, March 4, 1944 Chicago 2 at Detroit 6
	Carl Liscombe	2nd period, March 4, 1944 Chicago 2 at Detroit 6
	Harry Taylor	1st period, March 16, 1947 Detroit 10 at Chicago 6
	Jim McFadden	2nd period, November 23, 1947 Detroit 9 at Chicago 3
	Ted Lindsay	3rd period, March 9, 1949 Toronto 0 at Detroit 5
	Ted Lindsay	3rd period, March 19, 1950 Toronto 0 at Detroit 5
	Alex Delvecchio	2nd period, January 25, 1953 Canadiens 3 at Detroit 3
	Metro Prystai	2nd period, March 5, 1953 Rangers 1 at Detroit 7
	Alex Delvecchio	2nd period, November 28, 1953 Chicago 0 at Detroit 9
	Red Kelly	2nd period, January 30, 1955 Canadiens 1 at Detroit 7
	Red Kelly	2nd period, March 20, 1955 Canadiens 0 at Detroit 6
	Dutch Reibel	2nd period, March 20, 1955 Canadiens 0 at Detroit 6
	Dutch Reibel	2nd period, October 15, 1955 Detroit 4 at Chicago 1
	Norm Ullman	3rd period, December 23, 1956 Canadiens 3 at Detroit 3
	Ted Lindsay	3rd period, December 25, 1956 Rangers 1 at Detroit 8
	Gordie Howe	2nd period, February 22, 1958 Boston 1 at Detroit 6

Alex Delvecchio	3rd period, November 3, 1960 Boston 5 at Detroit 8
Al Langlois	1st period, March 19, 1964 Rangers 3 at Detroit 9
Norm Ullman	2nd period, December 3, 1964 Boston 2 at Detroit 4
Ron Murphy	2nd period, November 4, 1965 Boston 1 at Detroit 8
Alex Delvecchio	2nd period, February 6, 1969 Chicago 1 at Detroit 6
Mickey Redmond	1st period, December 11, 1971 Flyers 3 at Detroit 6
Alex Delvecchio	3rd period, December 29, 1971 Detroit 7 at Buffalo 3
Gary Bergman	3rd period, October 21, 1973 California 2 at Detroit 11
Mickey Redmond	3rd period, October 21, 1973 California 2 at Detroit 11
Bill Lochead	2nd period, February 4, 1976 Minnesota 0 at Detroit 5
John Ogrodnick	2nd period, January 25, 1983 Detroit 6 at Vancouver 2
Kelly Kisio	2nd period, February 27, 1985 Vancouver 5 at Detroit 11
Randy Ladouceur	3rd period, March 30, 1985 Detroit 9 at Toronto 3
Kelly Kisio	2nd period, November 21, 1985 Los Angeles 5 at Detroit 4
Steve Yzerman	3rd period, December 27, 1986 Detroit 5 at Toronto 5
Steve Yzerman	2nd period, January 21, 1987 Islanders 5 at Detroit 8
Adam Oates	1st period, March 5, 1987 Minnesota 3 at Detroit 9
Bob Probert	2nd period, November 14, 1987 Detroit 6 at New Jersey 4
Steve Yzerman	3rd period, December 18, 1987 Minnesota 3 at Detroit 8
Shawn Burr	3rd period, November 9, 1988 Detroit 6 at Minnesota 3
Gerard Gallant	1st period, November 12, 1988 Detroit 5 at Flyers 4
Steve Yzerman	1st period, January 15, 1989 Detroit 8 at Flyers 4
Joey Kocur	3rd period, December 31, 1989 New Jersey 4 at Detroit 6
Steve Yzerman	3rd period, December 31, 1989 New Jersey 4 at Detroit 6

	Steve Yzerman	1st period, January 9, 1990 Minnesota 0 at Detroit 9
	Gerard Gallant	3rd period, January 27, 1990 Detroit 8 at Quebec 6
	Sergei Fedorov	2nd period, January 21, 1992 Flyers 3 at Detroit 7
	Steve Chiasson	3rd period, December 5, 1992 Detroit 9 at Tampa Bay 7
	Paul Coffey	1st period, December 2, 1995 Detroit 11 at Canadiens 1
	Vyacheslav Kozlov	3rd period, February 13, 1996 Los Angeles 4 at Detroit 9

MOST POINTS — GAME — DEFENCEMAN

5	Reed Larson	February 27, 1985	(3 goals, 2 assists)

MOST GOALS — GAME — DEFENCEMAN

3	Flash Hollett	December 21, 1944 Rangers 3 at Detroit 11
	Reed Larson	January 3, 1981 Detroit 4 at Penguins 6
	Reed Larson	February 15, 1983 Penguins 3 at Detroit 7
	Reed Larson	February 27, 1985 Vancouver 5 at Detroit 11

MOST ASSISTS — GAME — DEFENCEMAN

4	Al Langlois	March 19, 1964 Rangers 3 at Detroit 9
	Paul Popiel	February 16, 1969 Los Angeles 3 at Detroit 6
	Carl Brewer	January 24, 1970 Detroit 5 at St. Louis 2
	Gary Bergman	October 21, 1973 California 2 at Detroit 11
	Steve Chiasson	December 5, 1992 Detroit 7 at Flyers 4
	Paul Coffey	January 14, 1994 Dallas 3 at Detroit 9
	Paul Coffey	January 24, 1995 Vancouver 3 at Detroit 6

MOST GOALS — TEAM — PERIOD

	Date	Game
8	January 23, 1944, 3rd period	Rangers 0 at Detroit 15
7	February 9, 1930, 3rd period	Pirates 1 at Detroit 8
	March 30, 1985, 3rd period	Detroit 9 at Toronto 3
	November 25, 1987, 3rd period	Winnipeg 8 at Detroit 10
6	January 5, 1933, 3rd period	Canadiens 1 at Detroit 6
	November 5, 1942, 3rd period	Rangers 5 at Detroit 12
	December 25, 1956, 3rd period	Rangers 1 at Detroit 8
	November 3, 1960, 3rd period	Boston 5 at Detroit 8
	October 21, 1973, 3rd period	California 2 at Detroit 11
	January 21, 1987, 2nd period	Islanders 5 at Detroit 8
	March 5, 1987, 1st period	Minnesota 3 at Detroit 9
	December 4, 1987, 1st period	Chicago 0 at Detroit 12

OVERTIME RECORDS — REGULAR SEASON

	GP	W	L	T
1926–27	8	1	3	4
1927–28	9	2	1	6
1928–29	12	2	1	9
1929–30	9	0	3	6
1930–31	11	2	2	7
1931–32	14	3	1	10
1932–33	9	0	1	8
1933–34	14	4	0	10
1934–35	13	2	4	7
1935–36	15	1	6	8
1936–37	10	1	0	9
1937–38	11	0	0	11
1938–39	6	0	0	6
1939–40	7	0	1	6
1940–41	16	3	2	11
1941–42	6	0	2	4
1942–43	1	0	0	1
Totals	171	21	27	123

	GP	W	L	T
1983–84	11	3	1	7
1984–85	14	0	2	12
1985–86	13	3	4	6
1986–87	17	2	5	10
1987–88	16	2	3	11
1988–89	15	2	1	12
1989–90	17	2	1	14
1990–91	12	2	2	8
1991–92	16	3	1	12
1992–93	11	2	0	9
1993–94	17	5	4	8
1994–95	4	0	0	4
1995–96	11	3	1	7
Totals	174	29	25	120

MOST OVERTIME GOALS — CAREER

Herbie Lewis 7
Steve Yzerman 5
Sergei Fedorov 5
John Sorrell 4
Ebbie Goodfellow 3

MOST GOALS IN OVERTIME — ONE GAME

2	Herbie Lewis	January 21, 1934	Toronto 2 at Detroit 4

FASTEST GOAL FROM START OF OVERTIME PERIOD

21 seconds	Bob Manno Quebec 3 at Detroit 4	October 29, 1983
26 seconds	Cooney Weiland Detroit 1 at Americans 1	January 25, 1934
28 seconds	Sheldon Kennedy Ottawa 4 at Detroit 5	December 31, 1992
29 seconds	Vyacheslav Kozlov Detroit 4 at New Jersey 3	November 20, 1993

Herbie Lewis

ROOKIE SEASON RECORDS

MOST POINTS

87 Steve Yzerman ('83–'84)
79 Sergei Fedorov ('90–'91)
72 Dale McCourt ('77–'78)
71 Mike Foligno ('79–'80)
60 Reed Larson ('77–'78)
60 Nicklas Lidstrom ('91–'92)
56 Petr Klima ('85–'86)

MOST GOALS

39 Steve Yzerman ('83–'84)
36 Mike Foligno ('79–'80)
33 Dale McCourt ('77–'78)
32 Petr Klima ('85–'86)
31 Sergei Fedorov ('90–'91)
28 Marcel Dionne ('71–'72)
26 Mark Osborne ('81–'82)
24 Jim McFadden ('47–'48)
22 Shawn Burr ('86–'87)
20 Lane Lambert ('83–'84)

MOST ASSISTS

49 Marcel Dionne ('71–'72)
49 Nicklas Lidstrom ('91–'92)
48 Steve Yzerman ('83–'84)
48 Sergei Fedorov ('90–'91)
41 Reed Larson ('77–'78)
41 Mark Osborne ('81–'82)
39 Dale McCourt ('77–'78)
35 Mike Foligno ('79–'80)
33 Dutch Reibel ('53–'54)
26 Dallas Drake ('92–'93)

MOST PENALTY MINUTES

302 Dennis Polonich ('75–'76)
186 Bob Probert ('85–'86)
181 Darren McCarty ('93–'94)
172 Vladimir Konstantinov ('91–'92)
148 Gerry Hart ('70–'71)
143 Daniel Shank ('89–'90)

THE MOST SUCCESSFUL RED WINGS DEBUTS IN THE NHL
(rookies who have registered a point in their first NHL game as a Red Wing)

Dutch Reibel	4 assists
Len Fontaine	1 goal, 2 assists
Chris Cichocki	2 goals
Nelson Debenedet	1 goal, 1 assist
Adam Oates	1 goal, 1 assist
Steve Yzerman	1 goal, 1 assist
Mike Foligno	2 assists
Viacheslav Kozlov	2 assists
Micah Aivazoff	1 goal
Michel Bergeron	1 goal
Henry Boucha	1 goal
Arnie Brown	1 goal
Connie Brown	1 goal
Mal Davis	1 goal
Sergei Fedorov	1 goal
Gerard Gallant	1 goal
Gus Giesebrecht	1 goal
Gordie Howe	1 goal
Larry Jeffrey	1 goal
Greg Johnson	1 goal
Petr Klima	1 goal
Claude Loiselle	1 goal
Pat Lundy	1 goal
Steve Martineau	1 goal
Dean Morton	1 goal*
Mark Osborne	1 goal
Billy Reay	1 goal
Bernie Ruelle	1 goal
Dwight Schofield	1 goal
Frank Sheppard	1 goal
Gary Shuchuk	1 goal
Ted Speers	1 goal
Tim Taylor	1 goal
Bob Wilkie	1 goal
Fred Williams	1 goal
Eddie Wiseman	1 goal
Frank Bathe	1 assist
Frank Bennett	1 assist
Thommie Bergman	1 assist
Marcel Bonin	1 assist
Brent Fedyk	1 assist
Tim Friday	1 assist
Jody Gage	1 assist
Lorry Gloeckner	1 assist
Ron Harris	1 assist
Chuck Holmes	1 assist
Lou Jankowski	1 assist
Bill Jennings	1 assist
Butch Keating	1 assist
Red Kelly	1 assist
Kelly Kisio	1 assist
Pete Mahovlich	1 assist
Pit Martin	1 assist
Doug McCaig	1 assist
Dale McCourt	1 assist
Bill McDougall	1 assist
Al McLeod	1 assist
Hank Monteith	1 assist
Ted Nolan	1 assist
John Ogrodnick	1 assist
Murray Oliver	1 assist
Clare Raglan	1 assist
Rollie Rossignol	1 assist
Cliff Simpson	1 assist
Ray Staszak	1 assist
Doug Volmar	1 assist
Murray Wing	1 assist

* scored in his first and only NHL game

RED WINGS GOALIE DEBUTS IN THE NHL

(chronological order)

NAME AND OPPONENT	DATE	MINUTES PLAYED	GOALS ALLOWED	AVG.	W/L/T/ND*
Herb Stuart vs. Boston	November 18, 1926	60	2	2.00	L
Dolly Dolson vs. Rangers	November 15, 1928	60	2	2.00	L
Jimmy Franks vs. Canadiens	March 27, 1937*	30	2	4.00	L
Harvey Teno vs. Canadiens	November 17, 1938	60	1	1.00	W
John Mowers vs. Americans	November 3, 1940	60	2	2.00	W
Joe Turner vs. Toronto	February 5, 1942	60	3	3.00	T
Harry Lumley vs. Rangers	December 19, 1943	60	6	6.00	L
Connie Dion vs. Canadiens	January 13, 1944	60	2	2.00	T
Red Almas vs. Toronto	March 23, 1947	60	5	5.00	L
Tom McGratton vs. Toronto	November 9, 1947	8	1	7.50	ND
Terry Sawchuk vs. Canadiens	January 8, 1949	60	4	4.00	L
Glenn Hall vs. Canadiens	December 27, 1952	60	2	2.00	T
Dave Gatherum vs. Toronto	October 11, 1953**	60	0	0.00	W
Gilles Boisvert vs. Canadiens	November 26, 1959	60	4	4.00	L
Dennis Riggin vs. Rangers	February 4, 1960	60	3	3.00	L
Harrison Gray vs. Canadiens	November 28, 1963	40	5	7.50	ND
Roger Crozier vs. Toronto	November 30, 1963	60	1	1.00	T
Carl Wetzel vs. Canadiens	December 26, 1964	31	4	7.74	L
George Gardner vs. Toronto	March 20, 1966	60	1	1.00	W
Roy Edwards vs. Penguins	November 9, 1967	60	1	1.00	W

Jim Rutherford vs. Sabres	October 23, 1970	60	4	4.00	L
Don McLeod vs. Toronto	November 28, 1970	20	3	9.00	ND
Gerry Gray vs. Flyers	March 4, 1971	60	2	2.00	T
Andy Brown vs. Rangers	February 20, 1972	60	4	4.00	L
Doug Grant vs. Rangers	October 10, 1973	60	4	4.00	L
Bill McKenzie vs. Los Angeles	December 18, 1973	60	4	4.00	T
Al Jensen vs. Canadiens	November 20, 1980	60	7	7.00	L
Larry Lozinski vs. Edmonton	December 27, 1980	60	4	4.00	T
Claude Legris vs. Colorado	March 24, 1981	20	0	0.00	ND
Corrado Micalef vs. Hartford	October 17, 1981	28	4	8.57	L
Greg Stefan vs. Chicago	March 24, 1982	60	6	6.00	L
Chris Pusey vs. Chicago	October 19, 1985	40	3	4.50	ND
Mark Laforest vs. Flyers	December 3, 1985	60	1	1.00	W
Scott King vs. New Jersey	January 28, 1991	45	2	2.67	ND
Chris Osgood vs. Toronto	October 15, 1993	32	4	7.50	L

* Franks is the only Red Wings goalie to make his NHL debut in a playoff game
** Gatherum is the only Red Wings goalie to register a shutout in his first NHL game

ALL-TIME POWER PLAY AND SHORT-HANDED GOALS — TEAM — REGULAR SEASON

(times of penalties were not kept before 1932–33)

	POWER PLAY		SHORT-HANDED			POWER PLAY		SHORT-HANDED	
	F	A	F	A		F	A	F	A
1932–33	26	10	6	2	1964–65	55	52	10	7
1933–34	28	17	2	5	1965–66	42	44	7	9
1934–35	30	17	5	1	1966–67	46	46	6	7
1935–36	21	16	2	4	1967–68	43	54	4	5
1936–37	3	7	1	1	1968–69	40	61	7	4
1937–38	5	11	1	7	1969–70	57	57	8	3
1938–39	14	11	5	8	1970–71	48	66	5	10
1939–40	16	9	2	3	1971–72	58	45	6	9
1940–41	10	9	1	1	1972–73	53	40	4	8
1941–42	11	10	1	2	1973–74	59	49	8	13
1942–43	30	16	4	2	1974–75	76	69	15	14
1943–44	13	16	2	0	1975–76	47	86	9	6
1944–45	23	10	2	1	1976–77	37	73	10	10
1945–46	26	23	2	3	1977–78	59	64	10	7
1946–47	38	24	2	7	1978–79	78	63	10	9
1947–48	25	23	7	2	1979–80	61	64	6	2
1948–49	37	33	6	3	1980–81	60	82	7	12
1949–50	53	30	2	6	1981–82	43	75	10	6
1950–51	39	19	2	6	1982–83	37	80	7	9
1951–52	46	27	5	5	1983–84	79	77	9	10
1952–53	52	27	3	3	1984–85	73	89	10	15
1953–54	53	36	3	2	1985–86	79	111	8	11
1954–55	47	38	7	1	1986–87	69	73	9	7
1955–56	51	29	5	3	1987–88	72	73	20	8
1956–57	48	30	4	2	1988–89	73	79	15	8
1957–58	36	52	7	7	1989–90	58	92	18	13
1958–59	41	32	7	9	1990–91	57	89	17	5
1959–60	30	24	5	4	1991–92	72	78	18	7
1960–61	37	36	5	4	1992–93	113	79	18	10
1961–62	38	37	3	6	1993–94	85	73	22	14
1962–63	49	36	5	7	1994–95	52	28	5	7
1963–64	42	36	2	5	1995–96	97	44	17	9

MOST POWER-PLAY GOALS — CAREER — INDIVIDUAL

Gordie Howe	207
Steve Yzerman	138
Alex Delvecchio	131
John Ogrodnick	79
Ted Lindsay	78
Norm Ullman	68
Reed Larson	67
Sergei Fedorov	62
Gerard Gallant	59
Mickey Redmond	55
Dino Ciccarelli	52
Ray Sheppard	51
Red Kelly	47
Sid Abel	43
Dale McCourt	41
Bob Probert	40

MOST POWER-PLAY GOALS — SEASON — INDIVIDUAL
(all players who have scored at least 10 in one season)

Goals	Player	Season
21	Mickey Redmond	(1973–74)
	Dino Ciccarelli	(1992–93)
19	Doug Grant	(1974–75)
	John Ogrodnick	(1983–84)
	Ray Sheppard	(1993–94)
17	Gerard Gallant	(1986–87)
	Steve Yzerman	(1988–89)
16	Parker MacDonald	(1962–63)
	Paul MacLean	(1988–89)
	Steve Yzerman	(1989–90)
	Steve Yzerman	(1995–96)
15	Gordie Howe	(1956–57)
	Mickey Redmond	(1972–73)
	Marcel Dionne	(1974–75)
	John Ogrodnick	(1984–85)
	John Ogrodnick	(1985–86)
	Bob Probert	(1987–88)
14	Gordie Howe	(1955–56)
	Ted Lindsay	(1955–56)
	Frank Mahovlich	(1969–70)
	Dale McCourt	(1978–79)
13	Gordie Howe	(1953–54)
	Gordie Howe	(1962–63)
	Vaclav Nedomansky	(1978–79)

	Ron Duguay	(1983–84)
	Steve Yzerman	(1983–84)
	Gerard Gallant	(1988–89)
	Jimmy Carson	(1992–93)
	Sergei Fedorov	(1992–93)
	Steve Yzerman	(1992–93)
	Sergei Fedorov	(1993–94)
	Dino Ciccarelli	(1995–96)
12	Gordie Howe	(1963–64)
	Gordie Howe	(1964–65)
	Garry Unger	(1969–70)
	Michel Bergeron	(1975–76)
	Ivan Boldirev	(1983–84)
	Gerard Gallant	(1989–90)
	Steve Yzerman	(1990–91)
	Dino Ciccarelli	(1993–94)
11	Gordie Howe	(1952–53)
	Gordie Howe	(1957–58)
	Gordie Howe	(1961–62)
	Gordie Howe	(1969–70)
	Vaclav Nedomansky	(1979–80)
	Dale McCourt	(1980–81)
	Ivan Boldirev	(1984–85)
	Ron Duguay	(1984–85)
	Reed Larson	(1985–86)
	Sergei Fedorov	(1990–91)
	Jimmy Carson	(1991–92)
	Ray Sheppard	(1991–92)
	Ray Sheppard	(1994–95)
	Sergei Fedorov	(1995–96)
10	John Sorrell	(1933–34)
	Sid Abel	(1949–50)
	Joe Carveth	(1949–50)
	Ron Murphy	(1964–65)
	Gordie Howe	(1967–68)
	Tim Ecclestone	(1971–72)
	Mickey Redmond	(1971–72)
	Marcel Dionne	(1972–73)
	Dale McCourt	(1977–78)
	Andre St. Laurent	(1977–78)
	Reed Larson	(1983–84)
	Gerard Gallant	(1987–88)
	Steve Yzerman	(1987–88)
	Jimmy Carson	(1989–90)
	Ray Sheppard	(1992–93)

MOST SHORT-HANDED GOALS — CAREER — INDIVIDUAL

Steve Yzerman	43
Gordie Howe	27
Sergei Fedorov	19
Shawn Burr	14
Alex Delvecchio	13
Red Kelly	11
Nick Libett	11
Marcel Dionne	10
John Ogrodnick	10
Ted Lindsay	9
Dale McCourt	9

MOST SHORT-HANDED GOALS — SEASON — INDIVIDUAL
(all players who have scored at least 4 in one season)

Goals	Player	Season
10	Marcel Dionne	(1974–75)
8	Steve Yzerman	(1991–92)
7	Steve Yzerman	(1989–90)
	Steve Yzerman	(1992–93)
6	Steve Yzerman	(1987–88)
	Steve Yzerman	(1990–91)
5	Petr Klima	(1987–88)
4	Gordie Howe	(1964–65)
	Alex Delvecchio	(1965–66)
	Gordie Howe	(1969–70)
	Shawn Burr	(1988–89)
	Marc Habscheid	(1990–91)
	Paul Ysebaert	(1991–92)
	Sergei Fedorov	(1992–93)
	Sergei Fedorov	(1993–94)

EMPTY NET GOALS
REGULAR SEASON

CAREER LEADERS

Steve Yzerman	16
Gordie Howe	12
Alex Delvecchio	8
Danny Gare	7
Norm Ullman	6
Nick Libett	5
Frank Mahovlich	5
Shawn Burr	4
Red Kelly	4
Walt McKechnie	4
Mickey Redmond	4
Ray Sheppard	4

TWO EMPTY NET GOALS — ONE GAME — ONE PLAYER

Danny Gare is the only Red Wing to score two empty net goals in a single game, October 26, 1984 vs. Buffalo Sabres. Gare scored at 19:16 and again at 19:45.
On only six other occasions have the Wings scored two empty net goals in one game:

1.	February 21, 1956	Boston 1 at Detroit 4 Gordie Howe 19:23 Alex Delvecchio 19:39
2.	October 22, 1959	Boston 1 at Detroit 4 Marcel Pronovost 19:02 Gordie Howe 19:35
3.	April 5, 1970	Detroit 5 at Rangers 9 Gordie Howe 17:29 Nick Libett 19:05
4.	December 23, 1976	Pittsburgh 2 at Detroit 5 Jim Nahrgang 19:00 Rick Wilson 19:43
5.	January 22, 1978	Washington 3 at Detroit 6 Greg Joly 19:31 Dale McCourt 19:50
6.	March 15, 1994	Vancouver 2 at Detroit 5 Sergei Fedorov 18:50 Ray Sheppard 19:12

THREE EMPTY NET GOALS IN ONE GAME

Only once have the Red Wings scored *three* empty net goals in the same game:

October 26, 1984	Buffalo 3 at Detroit 7
	Bob Manno 19:11 Danny Gare 19:16 Danny Gare 19:45

Mickey Redmond

REGULAR SEASON GOAL SCORING RECORDS — INDIVIDUAL — ONE GAME

Syd Howe

SIX GOALS

1944	February 3	Syd Howe vs. New York Rangers in 12-2 Detroit win at the Olympia

FOUR GOAL GAMES

1930	February 9	Herbie Lewis vs. Pittsburgh Pirates in 8–1 Detroit win at the Olympia
1930	December 25	Ebbie Goodfellow vs. Toronto Maple Leafs in 10–1 Detroit win at the Olympia
1933	November 12	Johnny Sorrell vs. New York Americans in 5–2 Detroit win at the Olympia
1941	March 6	Mud Brûneteau vs. New York Americans in 6–1 Detroit win at Madison Square Garden
1943	Novemebr 7	Mud Brûneteau vs. Boston Bruins in 6–4 Detroit win at the Olympia
1947	January 23	Pete Horeck vs. Chicago Blackhawks in 8–2 Detroit win at the Olympia
1947	March 16	Roy Conacher vs. Chicago Blackhawks in 10–6 Detroit win at the Stadium
1950	February 11	Gerry Couture vs. Boston Bruins in 9–4 Detroit win at the Garden
1953	March 2	Ted Lindsay vs. Boston Bruins in 10–2 Detroit win at the Olympia
1961	March 14	Norm Ullman vs. New York Rangers in 5–2 Detroit win at the Olympia
1966	October 27	Paul Henderson vs. New York Rangers in 5–3 Detroit win at the Olympia
1968	February 1	Floyd Smith vs. Los Angeles Kings in 8–6 Los Angeles win at the Olympia
1969	January 12	Frank Mahovlich vs. Oakland Seals in 5–1 Detroit win at the Olympia
1976	March 18	Michel Bergeron vs. St. Louis Blues in 6–3 Detroit win at the Olympia
1984	March 24	Ivan Boldirev vs. Los Angeles Kings in 9–7 Los Angeles win at the Forum
1990	January 31	Steve Yzerman vs. Edmonton Oilers 7–5 Detroit win at the Joe Louis Arena
1990	November 23	Johan Garpenlov vs. St. Louis Blues in 5–3 Detroit win at the Joe Louis Arena
1994	April 5	Dino Ciccarelli vs. Vancouver Canucks in 8–3 Detroit win at the Pacific Coliseum
1995	February 12	Sergei Fedorov vs. Los Angeles Kings in 4–4 tie at the Joe Louis Arena
1995	December 2	Vyacheslov Kozlov vs. Canadiens in 11–1 win at the Forum

HAT TRICKS

1927	March 10	Duke Keats vs. Pittsburgh Pirates 7–1 Detroit win at Windsor Arena
1928	January 3	Larry Aurie vs. New York Rangers in 4–2 Detroit win at Madison Square Garden
1928	March 6	George Hay vs. Chicago Blackhawks in 3–1 Detroit win at the Olympia
1929	November 28	Carson Cooper vs. Montreal Maroons in 7–6 Detroit win at the Forum
1930	December 21	Larry Aurie vs. New York Americans in 6–4 Americans win at Madison Square Garden
1932	November 15	Johnny Sorrell vs. New York Americans in 6–2 Detroit win at the Olympia
1934	December 13	Cooney Weiland vs. St. Louis Eagles 11–2 Detroit win at St. Louis Arena
1936	January 5	Marty Barry vs. Montreal Canadiens in 5–2 Detroit win at the Olympia
1936	March 22	Syd Howe vs. New York Americans in 7–2 Detroit win at the Olympia
1937	February 2	Larry Aurie vs. New York Rangers in 4–4 tie at Madison Square Garden
1937	February 7	Johnny Sorrell vs. Boston Bruins in 8–0 Detroit win at the Olympia
1937	February 21	Syd Howe vs. Chicago Blackhawks in 6–0 Detroit win at the Olympia
1937	March 2	Marty Barry vs. Montreal Maroons in 7–4 Detroit win at the Forum
1938	March 6	Herbie Lewis vs. Boston Bruins in 4–3 Detroit win at the Olympia
1938	March 13	Carl Liscombe vs. Chicago Blackhawks in 5–1 Detroit win at the Olympia
1939	February 5	Gus Geisebrecht vs. New York Americans in 7–3 Detroit win at the Olympia
1939	March 2	Syd Howe vs. New York Americans in 7–3 Detroit win at the Olympia
1939	December 25	Syd Howe vs. Montreal Canadiens in 3–1 Detroit win at the Olympia
1942	November 5	Carl Liscombe vs. New York Rangers in 12–5 Detroit win at the Olympia
1942	December 12	Syd Howe vs. Toronto Maple Leafs in 5–4 Toronto win at Maple Leaf Gardens
1943	January 24	Carl Liscombe vs. New York Rangers in 7–0 Detroit win at the Olympia
1943	November 21	Mud Brûneteau vs. Chicago Blackhawks in 5–2 Detroit win at the Olympia
1944	January 23	Syd Howe vs. New York Rangers in 15–0 Detroit win at the Olympia
1944	February 10	Joe Carveth vs. New York Rangers in 8–3 Detroit win at Madison Square Garden
1944	March 2	Adam Brown vs. New York Rangers in 6–5 Detroit win at the Olympia
1944	March 12	Mud Brûneteau vs. Toronto Maple Leafs in 4–1 Detroit win at the Olympia
1944	March 16	Carl Liscombe vs. Boston Bruins in 10–9 Detroit win at the Olympia
1944	November 2	Jud McAtee vs. New York Rangers in 10–3 Detroit win at the Olympia
1944	December 21	Flash Hollett vs. New York Rangers in 11–3 Detroit win at the Olympia
1945	March 4	Joe Carveth vs. Boston Bruins in 10–4 Detroit win at the Olympia
1945	October 28	Adam Brown vs. Boston Bruins in 7–0 Detroit win at the Olympia
1947	February 22	Roy Conacher vs. Montreal Canadiens in 7–3 Detroit win at the Olympia
1947	March 16	Ted Lindsay vs. Chicago Blackhawks in 10–6 Detroit win at the Stadium
1947	November 22	Jim McFadden vs. Chicago Blackhawks in 8–5 Detroit win at the Olympia
1948	November 28	Gerry Couture vs. Chicago Blackhawks in 9–6 Detroit win at the Stadium
1949	February 2	Ted Lindsay vs. Chicago Blackhawks in 6–4 Detroit win at the Olympia
1949	November 2	Sid Abel vs. Boston Bruins in 5–3 Detroit win at the Olympia
1950	February 11	Gordie Howe vs. Boston Bruins in 9–4 Detroit win at the Garden
1950	March 19	Gordie Howe vs. Toronto Maple Leafs in 5–0 Detroit win at the Olympia
1951	January 17	Gordie Howe vs. Chicago Blackhawks in 4–2 Detroit win at the Stadium
1951	January 23	Gordie Howe vs. Chicago Blackhawks in 8–2 Detroit win at the Stadium
1951	March 11	George Gee vs. Chicago Blackhawks in 7–0 Detroit win at the Stadium
1951	March 17	Gordie Howe vs. Chicago Blackhawks in 8–2 Detroit win at the Olympia
1951	December 31	Gordie Howe vs. Montreal Canadiens in 5–3 Canadiens win at the Olympia
1952	March 23	Gordie Howe vs. Montreal Canadiens in 7–2 Detroit win at the Olympia
1953	January 11	Gordie Howe vs. Toronto Maple Leafs in 5–2 Detroit win at the Olympia
1953	January 29	Gordie Howe vs. Chicago Blackhawks in in 5–2 Detroit win at the Stadium
1954	October 21	Red Kelly vs. Boston Bruins in 5–3 Detroit win at the Olympia
1955	January 9	Dutch Reibel vs. Chicago Blackhawks in 6–2 Detroit win at the St. Louis Arena
1955	March 3	Gordie Howe vs. Chicago Blackhawks in 6–1 Detroit win at the Olympia
1955	March 13	Dutch Reibel vs. Toronto Maple Leafs in 6–1 Detroit win at the Olympia
1955	March 20	Ted Lindsay vs. Montreal Canadiens in 6–0 Detroit win at the Olympia
1956	January 19	Gordie Howe vs. Boston Bruins in 4–2 Detroit win at the Olympia

1956	November 18	Ted Lindsay vs. Montreal Canadiens in 8–3 Detroit win at the Olympia
1956	December 25	Gordie Howe vs. New York Rangers in 8–1 Detroit win at the Olympia
1957	February 2	Lorne Ferguson vs. New York Rangers in 5–4 Detroit win at Madison Square Garden
1958	February 22	Jack McIntyre vs. Boston Bruins in 6–1 Detroit win at the Olympia
1958	October 18	Alex Delvecchio vs. Chicago Blackhawks in 3–1 Detroit win at the Stadium
1958	November 18	Johnny Wilson vs. Boston Bruins in 6–0 Detroit win at the Olympia
1960	January 21	Norm Ullman vs. Boston Bruins in 5–2 Detroit win at the Olympia
1961	January 4	Howie Glover vs. Toronto Maple Leafs in 6–4 Toronto win at Maple Leaf Gardens
1961	October 19	Vic Stasiuk vs. Boston Bruins in 7–3 Detroit win at the Olympia
1961	December 3	Norm Ullman vs. Toronto Maple Leafs in 3–1 Detroit win at the Olympia
1961	December 31	Gordie Howe vs. Toronto Maple Leafs in 4–2 Detroit win at the Olympia
1963	March 14	Norm Ullman vs. New York Rangers in 9–4 Detroit win at the Olympia
1964	March 8	Norm Ullman vs. Boston Bruins in 5–3 Detroit win at the Garden
1964	March 15	Floyd Smith vs. Chicago Blackhawks in 5–3 Detroit win at the Olympia
1965	February 28	Norm Ullman vs. Montreal Canadiens in 5–1 Detroit win at the Olympia
1965	March 19	Norm Ullman vs. New York Rangers in 6–6 tie at Madison Square Garden
1965	March 21	Gordie Howe vs. Chicago Blackhawks in 5–1 Detroit win at the Olympia
1965	March 25	Alex Delvecchio vs. New York Rangers in 7–4 Detroit win at the Olympia
1965	December 2	Norm Ullman vs. Boston Bruins in 10–2 Detroit win at the Olympia
1965	December 12	Gordie Howe vs. Boston Bruins in 5–3 Detroit win at the Garden
1965	December 19	Bruce MacGregor vs. Chicago Blackhawks in 5–4 Chicago win at the Stadium
1966	January 16	Norm Ullman vs. Toronto Maple Leafs in 4–0 Detroit win at the Olympia
1967	January 22	Dean Prentice vs. New York Rangers in 7–2 Detroit win at the Olympia
1967	February 8	Norm Ullman vs. Toronto Maple Leafs in 5–2 Detroit win at Maple Leafs Gardens
1967	December 17	Norm Ullman vs. Montreal Canadiens in 8–6 Detroit win at the Olympia
1968	March 16	Gordie Howe vs. St. Louis Blues in 6–3 Detroit win at the Arena
1968	October 31	Frank Mahovlich vs. Boston Bruins in 7–5 Detroit win at the Olympia
1968	December 15	Garry Unger vs. Minnesota North Stars in 5–2 Detroit win at the Olympia
1968	December 31	Frank Mahovlich vs. Minnesota North Stars in 6–3 Detroit win at the Olympia
1969	January 9	Pete Stemkowski vs. Los Angeles Kings in 5–0 Detroit win at the Olympia
1969	February 6	Gordie Howe vs. Chicago Blackhawks in 6–1 Detroit win at the Olympia
1969	February 9	Frank Mahovlich vs. Los Angeles Kings in 5–0 Detroit win at the Olympia
1969	February 16	Gordie Howe vs. Los Angeles Kings in 6–3 Detroit win at the Olympia
1969	November 2	Gordie Howe vs. Pittsburgh Penguins 4–3 Detroit win at the Olympia
1969	November 19	Frank Mahovlich vs. Montreal Canadiens in 5–5 tie at the Forum
1969	December 28	Garry Unger vs. Oakland Seals in 5–3 Detroit win at the Olympia
1970	January 3	Alex Delvecchio vs. Philadelphia Flyers in 6– 1 Detroit win at the Spectrum
1972	January 27	Nick Libett vs. Buffalo Sabres in 3–1 Detroit win at the Aud
1972	February 6	Mickey Redmond vs. California Golden Seals in 8–2 Detroit win at the Olympia
1972	March 19	Marcel Dionne vs. Montreal Canadiens in 7–6 Detroit win at the Olympia
1973	January 12	Mickey Redmond vs. Vancouver Canucks in 7–1 Detroit win at the Pacific Coliseum
1973	February 22	Marcel Dionne vs. Montreal Canadiens in 3–3 tie at the Olympia
1973	October 21	Guy Charron vs. California Golden Seals in 11–2 Detroit win at the Olympia
1973	November 11	Guy Charron vs. Toronto Maple Leafs in 5–4 Detroit win at the Olympia
1974	January 12	Red Berenson vs. Los Angeles Kings in 6–0 Detroit win at the Olympia
1974	February 24	Mickey Redmond vs. New York Islanders in 5–3 Detroit win at the Olympia
1974	March 20	Mickey Redmond vs. Montreal Canadiens in 7–6 Detroit win at the Forum
1974	October 19	Mickey Redmond vs. Washington Capitals in 6–4 Detroit win at the Olympia
1974	November 20	Marcel Dionne vs. New York Rangers in 5–4 Rangers win at the Olympia
1974	December 5	Marcel Dionne vs. Boston Bruins in 6–4 Detroit win at the Garden
1975	February 9	Phil Roberto vs. Toronto Maple Leafs in 5–3 Detroit win at the Olympia
1975	February 14	Danny Grant vs. Vancouver Canucks in 5–4 Vancouver win at the Pacific Coliseum
1975	March 22	Mickey Redmond vs. New York Rangers in 7–4 Detroit win at the Olympia
1975	December 12	Michel Bergeron vs. Washington Capitals in 5– 3 Detroit win at the Capital Centre
1976	November 19	Dan Maloney vs. Cleveland Barons in 5–2 Detroit win at the Olympia

1976	December 18	Dennis Hextall vs. Atlanta Flames in 6–3 Detroit win at the Olympia
1978	January 22	Dale McCourt vs. Washington Capitals in 6–3 Detroit win at the Olympia
1978	February 12	Paul Woods vs. Vancouver Canucks in 8–3 Detroit win at the Olympia
1978	February 16	Dale McCourt vs. Atlanta Flames in 5–3 Detroit win at the Olympia
1978	March 22	Dale McCourt vs. Atlanta Flames in 4–1 Detroit win at the Olympia
1978	October 28	Vaclav Nedomansky vs. Chicago Blackhawks in 7–2 Detroit win at the Olympia
1978	December 7	Errol Thompson vs. Boston Bruins in 6–5 Boston win at the Garden
1978	December 20	Dale McCourt vs. Vancouver Canucks in 7–2 Detroit win at the Olympia
1979	February 18	Dale McCourt vs. Pittsburgh Penguins in 6–2 Detroit win at the Olympia
1979	February 25	Vaclav Nedomansky and Andre St. Laurent vs. Colorado Rockies in 8–1 Detroit win at the Olympia
1979	February 28	Vaclav Nedomansky vs. St. Louis Blues in 6–5 St. Louis win at the Olympia
1979	October 17	Vaclav Nedomansky vs. Winnipeg Jets in 5–1 Detroit win at the Arena
1979	December 16	Errol Thompson vs. Chicago Blackhawks in 7–3 Chicago win at the Stadium
1980	January 27	Mike Foligno vs. Quebec Nordiques in 7–6 Detroit win at the Colisée
1980	January 31	Mike Foligno vs. Pittsburgh Penguins in 4–3 Detroit win at the Joe Louis Arena
1980	December 20	Dale McCourt vs. Colorado Rockies in 3–3 tie at McNichols Sports Arena
1981	January 3	Reed Larson vs. Pittsburgh Penguins in 6–4 Pittsburgh win at the Civic Arena
1981	February 19	Dale McCourt vs. New York Rangers in 7–3 Detroit win at the Joe Louis Arena
1981	October 29	Mike Foligno and John Ogrodnick vs. Calgary Flames in 12–4 Detroit win at the Joe Louis Arena
1981	November 5	John Ogrodnick vs. Los Angeles Kings in 10–2 Detroit win at the Joe Louis Arena
1981	December 1	Mark Osborne vs. St. Louis Blues in 7–5 St. Louis win at the Checkerdome
1982	December 12	John Ogrodnick vs. Calgary Flames in 7–3 Detroit win at the Corral
1983	February 15	Reed Larson vs. Pittsburgh Penguins in 7–3 Detroit win at the Joe Louis Arena
1983	February 20	Ivan Boldirev vs. Hartford Whalers in 7–2 Detroit win at the Civic Centre
1983	November 3	Ron Duguay vs. Chicago Blakhawks in 7–4 Detroit win at the Joe Louis Arena
1983	December 23	Steve Yzerman and John Ogrodnick vs. Toronto Maple Leafs in 9–2 Detroit win at the Joe Louis Arena
1984	February 19	Ivan Boldirev vs. Toronto Maple Leafs in 6–2 Detroit win at Maple Leaf Gardens
1984	December 4	John Ogrodnick vs. Toronto Maple Leafs in 7–6 Detroit win at the Joe Louis Arena
1984	December 28	Lane Lambert vs. Calgary Flames in 4–3 Detroit win at the Olympic Saddledome
1985	February 17	Ron Duguay vs. Chicago Blackhawks in 4–4 tie at the Stadium
1985	February 27	Danny Gare and Reed Larson vs. Vancouver Canucks in 11–5 win at the Joe Louis Arena
1985	March 1	Ron Duguay vs. Minnesota North Stars in 6–2 Detroit win at the Joe Louis Arena
1985	March 13	John Ogrodnick vs. Edmonton Oilers in 7–6 Edmonton win at the Northlands Coliseum
1985	March 15	Ron Duguay vs. Vancouver Canucks in 6–5 Detroit win at the Pacific Coliseum
1985	March 30	Steve Yzerman vs. Toronto Maple Leafs in 9–3 Detroit win at Maple Leaf Gardens
1985	October 30	Danny Gare vs. Pittsburgh Penguins in 6–3 Detroit win at the Joe Louis Arena
1985	December 7	Warren Young vs. St. Louis Blues in 5–4 St. Louis win at the Arena
1986	March 5	Petr Klima vs. Chicago Blackhawks in 8–3 Detroit win at the Stadium
1986	March 22	Petr Klima vs. Chicago Blackhawks in 8–4 Detroit win at the Joe Louis Arena
1986	November 13	Shawn Burr vs. Philadelphia Flyers in 7–5 Flyers win at the Spectrum
1987	March 2	Petr Klima vs. Boston Bruins in 4–3 Detroit win at the Garden
1987	December 4	Tim Higgins vs. Chicago Blackhawks in 12–0 Detroit win at the Joe Louis Arena
1987	December 18	Gerard Gallant vs. Minnesota North Stars in 8–3 Detroit win at the Joe Louis Arena
1987	December 31	Bob Probert vs. St. Louis Blues in 7–2 Detroit win at the Joe Louis Arena
1988	January 3	Steve Yzerman vs. Winnipeg Jets in 4–4 tie at the Arena
1988	February 6	Steve Yzerman vs. Montreal Canadiens in 5–4 Detroit win at the Forum
1988	February 12	Gerard Gallant vs. New Jersey Devils in 4–3 Detroit win at the Joe Louis Arena
1988	March 26	Gerard Gallant vs. New York Rangers in 4–4 tie at the Joe Louis Arena
1988	November 4	Steve Yzerman vs. Philadelphia Flyers in 4–3 Flyers win at the Joe Louis Arena
1988	November 12	Steve Yzerman vs. Philadelphia Flyers in 5–4 Detroit win at the Spectrum

1989	January 4	Gerard Gallant vs. St. Louis Blues in 4–2 Detroit win at the Joe Louis Arena
1989	February 21	Dave Barr vs. New York Islanders in 6–5 Detroit win at Nassau Coliseum
1989	December 15	Steve Yzerman vs. Chicago Blackhawks in 8–4 Detroit win at the Joe Louis Arena
1989	December 27	Jimmy Carson vs. Toronto Maple Leafs in 7–7 tie at Maple Leaf Gardens
1990	January 9	Shawn Burr vs. Minnesota North Stars in 9–0 Detroit win at the Joe Louis Arena
1990	February 14	Steve Yzerman vs. Los Angeles Kings in 6–5 Detroit win at the Joe Louis Arena
1990	November 17	Steve Yzerman vs. Toronto Maple Leafs in 8–4 Detroit win at Maple Leaf Gardens
1990	December 22	Steve Yzerman vs. Winnipeg Jets in 5–2 Detroit win at the Arena
1991	January 26	Steve Yzerman vs. St. Louis Blues in 5–4 St. Louis win at the Arena
1991	March 5	Jimmy Carson vs. Quebec Nordiques in 6–3 Detroit win at the Joe Louis Arena
1991	November 12	Ray Sheppard vs. Calgary Flames in 5–4 Detroit win at the Olympic Saddledome
1991	December 3	Steve Yzerman vs. Calgary Flames in 5–2 Detroit win at the Joe Louis Arena
1992	January 3	Paul Ysebaert vs. Toronto Maple Leafs in 6–4 Detroit win at the Joe Louis Arena
1992	January 29	Steve Yzerman vs. Buffalo Sabres in 4–4 tie at the Joe Louis Arena
1992	February 12	Kevin Miller vs. Buffalo Sabres in 9–4 Detroit win at Memorial Auditorium
1992	February 15	Jimmy Carson vs. San Jose Sharks in 11–1 win at the Joe Louis Arena
1992	April 14	Steve Yzerman vs, Minnesota North Stars in 7– 4 Detroit win at the Met Centre
1992	October 24	Steve Yzerman vs. St. Louis Blues in 6–1 win at the Arena
1992	November 13	Jimmy Carson vs. Pittsburgh Penguins in 8–0 win at the Joe Louis Arena
1993	January 26	Steve Yzerman vs. Calgary Flames in 9–1 win at the Olympic Saddledome
1993	February 14	Steve Yzerman vs. Chicago Blackhawks in 5–3 Detroit win at the Stadium
1993	October 18	Shawn Burr vs. Buffalo Sabres in 6–4 Detroit win at Memorial Auditorium
1994	January 6	Vyacheslav Kozlov and Ray Sheppard vs. San Jose Sharks in 10–3 Detroit win at the San Jose Arena
1994	January 29	Ray Sheppard vs. Winnipeg Jets in 7–1 Detroit win at the Joe Louis Arena
1994	March 1	Sergei Fedorov vs. Calgary Flames in 5–2 Detroit win at the Joe Louis Arena
1995	January 24	Ray Sheppard vs. Vancouver Canucks in 6–3 Detroit win at the Joe Louis Arena

CONSECUTIVE HAT TRICKS

Only once has a Red Wing ever scored hat tricks in two consecutive games. Vaclav Nedomansky scored three goals vs. Colorado on February 25, 1979 and again three nights later vs. the St. Louis Blues.

TWO RED WINGS HAT TRICKS IN ONE GAME

On six occasions two Red Wings have scored three goals in the same game:

1. March 16, 1947 . . . . Roy Conacher (4 goals) and Ted Lindsay
2. February 11, 1950 . . . . Gerry Couture (4 goals) and Gordie Howe
3. October 29, 1981 . . . . Mike Foligno and John Ogrodnick
4. December 23, 1983 . . . . Steve Yzerman and John Ogrodnick
5. February 27, 1985 . . . . Danny Gare and Reed Larson
6. January 6, 1994 . . . . Ray Sheppard and Vyacheslav Kozlov

MOST HAT TRICKS — CAREER

Gordie Howe	19
Steve Yzerman	18
Norm Ullman	11
Syd Howe	7
Dale McCourt	7
Mickey Redmond	6
John Ogrodnick	6
Ted Lindsay	5
Frank Mahovlich	5

MOST HAT TRICKS — SEASON

Frank Mahovlich ('68–'69)	4
Mud Brûneteau ('43–'44)	3
Gordie Howe ('50–'51)	3
Dale McCourt ('77–'78)	3
Vaclav Nedomansky ('78–'79)	3
Ron Duguay ('84–'85)	3
Gerard Gallant ('87–'88)	3
Steve Yzerman ('89–'90)	3
Steve Yzerman ('90–'91)	3
Steve Yzerman ('91–'92)	3
Steve Yzerman ('92–'93)	3

PENALTY SHOTS

The penalty shot was introduced in 1934. The shot was taken from inside a 10' circle located 38' from the goal. The goalie could not be off his line by more than one foot, but he clearly had the advantage.

Beginning with the 1938–39 season, the puck carrier could skate in on goal before shooting.

For the 1941–42 season, a "minor" and "major" penalty shot were introduced. A minor meant a shot was taken 28' from the goal; a major meant the player could skate in on goal (awarded when a player on a breakaway, with only the goalie to beat, was tripped).

A new rule for the '47–'48 season: if a stick is thrown by a player in his defending zone but the thrown stick is not considered to have prevented a goal, a penalty shot is awarded.

PENALTY SHOTS FOR

1934	November 15	Ebbie Goodfellow stopped by Percy Jackson (Rangers) in 8–2 Detroit win at the Olympia
1934	December 13	Ebbie Goodfellow beat Bill Beveridge (St. Louis Eagles) in 11–2 win at the St. Louis Arena
1934	December 21	Ebbie Goodfellow stopped by Alex Connell (Maroons) in 1–1 tie at the Olympia
1935	February 10	Ebbie Goodfellow stopped by Alex Connell (Maroons) in 2–1 Maroons win at the Olympia
1940	March 3	Mud Brûneteau beat Frank Brimsek (Bruins) in 6–3 Detroit win at the Boston Garden
1942	February 26	Sid Abel beat Jim Henry (Rangers) in 7–4 Rangers win at Madison Square Garden
1946	January 12	Carl Liscombe stopped by Frank McCool (Toronto) in 9–3 Toronto win at Maple Leaf Gardens
1953	March 5	Gordie Howe beat Gump Worsley (Rangers) in 7– 1 Detroit win at the Olympia
1961	December 31	Gordie Howe beat Johnny Bower (Leafs) in 4–2 Detroit win at the Olympia
1962	January 31	Bruce MacGregor stopped by Glenn Hall (Chicago) in 4–1 Blackhawks win at the Stadium
1962	February 4	Alex Delvecchio stopped by Bruce Gamble (Bruins) in 6–0 Detroit win at the Olympia
1963	November 20	Doug Barkley beat Glenn Hall (Chicago) in 5–2 Blackhawks win at the Stadium
1963	December 8	Claude Laforge beat Don Simmons (Leafs) in 5–3 Toronto win at the Olympia
1967	January 5	Norm Ullman beat Glenn Hall (Chicago) in 6–4 Detroit win at the Olympia
1972	February 19	Guy Charron stopped by Ed Dyck (Vancouver) in 8–2 Detroit win at the Olympia
1975	January 23	Pierre Jarry stopped by Roger Crozier (Buffalo) in 5–1 Sabres win at the Aud
1976	December 4	Dennis Polonich stopped by Rogie Vachon (Los Angeles) in 4–1 Kings win at the Forum
1976	December 12	Bill Lochead stopped by Gilles Gilbert (Boston) in 5–3 Detroit win at the Garden
1977	November 5	Reed Larson stopped by Gilles Meloche (Cleveland) in 5–3 Barons win at the Olympia
1978	March 5	Andre St. Laurent stopped by Gary Smith (Minnesota) in 4–3 Detroit win at the Olympia
1978	November 22	Dale McCourt stopped by Mario Lessard (Los Angeles) in 3–3 tie at the Forum
1980	January 30	Mike Foligno beat Paul Harrison (Leafs) in 6–4 Toronto win at Maple Leaf Gardens
1980	March 26	Mike Foligno stopped by Ron Low (Edmonton) in 5–2 Oilers win at the Joe Louis Arena
1984	January 9	Ron Dugay stopped by Grant Fuhr (Edmonton) in 7–3 Oilers win at the Joe Louis Arena
1984	February 1	Bob Crawford beat Ken Holland (Whalers) in 6–6 tie at the Joe Louis Arena
1985	February 7	Dwight Foster beat Rick Wamsley (St. Louis) in 5–5 tie at the Joe Louis Arena
1987	February 17	Petr Klima stopped by John Vanbiesbrouck (Rangers) in 6–2 New York win at Madison Square Garden
1987	March 5	Bob Probert beat Kari Takko (Minnesota) in 9– 3 Detroit win at the Joe Louis Arena
1987	March 25	Mel Bridgman beat Rollie Melanson (Los Angeles) in 6–1 Kings win at the Joe Louis Arena
1987	November 22	Steve Yzerman stopped by Doug Keans (Boston) in 1–0 Bruins win at the Joe Louis Arena
1988	October 28	Miroslav Frycer stopped by Don Beaupre (Minnesota) in 4–1 Detroit win at the Met Centre
1989	February 13	Steve Yzerman beat Bob Essensa (Winnipeg) in 2–2 tie at the Joe Louis Arena
1989	March 31	Petr Klima stopped by Jon Casey (Minnesota) in 5–1 North Stars win at the Joe Louis Arena
1989	November 3	Jimmy Carson stopped by Mike Liut (Hartford) in 4–3 Whalers win at the Joe Louis Arena
1990	November 29	Joey Kocur beat Jacques Cloutier (Chicago) in 5–1 Detroit win at the Stadium
1991	January 25	Brent Fedyk stopped by Vincent Riendeau (St. Louis) in 9–4 Blues win at the Joe Louis Arena
1991	October 10	Kevin Miller beat Patrick Roy (Canadiens) in 4–1 Montreal win at the Joe Louis Arena
1992	January 3	Steve Yzerman beat Grant Fuhr (Leafs) in 6– 4 Detroit win at the Joe Louis Arena
1992	January 29	Steve Yzerman beat Daren Puppa (Buffalo) in 4–4 tie at the Joe Louis Arena

1992	November 27	Paul Ysebaert beat Robb Stauber (Los Angeles) in 5–3 Kings win at the Joe Louis Arena
1993	March 18	Steve Yzerman stopped by Darcy Wakaluk (Minnesota) in 5–1 Detroit win at the Joe Louis Arena
1993	December 27	Sergei Fedorov beat Andy Moog (Dallas) in 6–0 Detroiit win at Reunion Arena
1994	March 22	Mark Howe stopped by Ed Belfour (Chicago) in 3–1 Detroit win at the Joe Louis Arena
1995	February 12	Sergei Fedorov stopped by Kelly Hrudey (Los Angeles) in 4–4 tie at the Joe Louis Arena
1995	March 22	Bob Errey stopped by Nikolai Khabibulin (Winnipeg) in 6–3 Detroit win at the Joe Louis Arena
1995	November 2	Steve Yzerman stopped by Blaine Lacher (Bruins) in 6–5 Detroit win at the Fleet Centre
1995	November 22	Igor Larionov beat Arturs Irbe (Sharks) in 5–2 Detroit win at the Joe Louis Arena

PENALTY SHOTS SCORING SUMMARY

PLAYER	GOALS	MISSES	SHOTS
Steve Yzerman	3	3	6
Gordie Howe	2	0	2
Sid Abel	1	0	1
Doug Barkley	1	0	1
Mel Bridgman	1	0	1
Mud Brûneteau	1	0	1
Bob Crawford	1	0	1
Dwight Foster	1	0	1
Joey Kocur	1	0	1
Claude Laforge	1	0	1
Igor Larionov	1	0	1
Kevin Miller	1	0	1
Bob Probert	1	0	1
Norm Ullman	1	0	1
Paul Ysebaert	1	0	1
Sergei Fedorov	1	1	2
Mike Foligno	1	1	2
Ebbie Goodfellow	1	3	4
Jimmy Carson	0	1	1
Guy Charron	0	1	1
Alex Delvecchio	0	1	1
Ron Dugay	0	1	1
Bob Errey	0	1	1
Brent Fedyk	0	1	1
Miroslav Frycer	0	1	1
Mark Howe	0	1	1
Pierre Jarry	0	1	1
Reed Larson	0	1	1
Carl Liscombe	0	1	1
Bill Lochead	0	1	1
Bruce MacGregor	0	1	1
Dale McCourt	0	1	1
Dennis Polonich	0	1	1
Andre St. Laurent	0	1	1
Petr Klima	0	2	2

PENALTY SHOTS AGAINST

1935	February 21	John Ross Roach stopped Earl Robinson (Maroons) in 3–1 Detroit win at the Olympia
1935	March 3	Norm Smith stopped Charley McVeigh (Americans) in 3–1 Detroit win at the Olympia
1935	March 9	Norm Smith stopped Armand Mondou (Canadiens) in 5–3 Detroit win at the Forum
1936	January 1	Paul Thompson (Chicago) beat Norm Smith in 4– 2 Detroit win at the Stadium
1939	January 22	Woody Dumart (Boston) beat Cecil Thompson in 5–0 Bruins win at the Olympia
1941	January 24	Charlie Conacher (Americans) beat Johnny Mowers in 3–2 Detroit win at the Olympia
1945	January 18	Fred Thurier (Rangers) beat Harry Lumley in 7–3 Detroit win at the Olympia
1945	January 21	Ray Getliffe (Canadiens) beat Harry Lumley in 6–3 Montreal win at the Olympia
1945	November 25	Alex Shibicky (Rangers) beat Harry Lumley in 4–1 New York win at the Olympia
1962	March 14	Andy Bathgate (Rangers) beat Hank Bassen in 3–2 New York win at Madison Square Garden
1963	November 27	Rod Gilbert (Rangers) beat Terry Sawchuk in 3–2 New York win at Madison Square Garden
1967	February 8	Roger Crozier stopped Pete Stemkowski (Toronto) in 5–2 Detroit win at Maple Leaf Gardens
1968	January 28	Roger Crozier stopped Wayne Connelly (Minnesota) in 2–1 North Stars win at the Met Centre
1968	March 9	Mike Walton (Toronto) beat Roger Crozier in 7–5 Leafs win at Maple Leaf Gardens
1968	October 20	Roger Crozier stopped Claude Provost (Canadiens) in 4–2 Montreal win at the Olympia
1969	December 6	Roger Crozier stopped Andre Boudrias (St. Louis) in 5–1 Detroit win at the St. Louis Arena
1973	January 10	Roy Edwards stopped Ron Schock (Pittsburgh) in 2–1 Detroit win at the Civic Arena
1973	January 28	Dennis DeJordy stopped Jacques Lemaire (Canadiens) in 4–2 Detroit win at the Forum
1974	March 7	Jim Rutherford stopped Bill Clement (Philadelphia) in 6–1 Flyers win at the Spectrum
1975	February 1	Lorne Henning (Islanders) beat Jim Rutherford in 4–1 New York win at the Olympia
1977	January 6	Ed Giacomin stopped Dean Talafous (Minnesota) in 7–2 North Stars win at the Olympia
1977	March 12	Jim Rutherford stopped Lanny McDonald (Toronto) in 6–0 Leaf win at Maple Leaf Gardens
1981	March 14	Bernie Federko (St. Louis) beat Larry Lozinski in 5–3 Blues win at the Checkerdome
1982	February 11	Thomas Gradin (Vancouver) beat Gilles Gilbert in 4–4 tie at the Joe Louis Arena
1982	February 11	Ivan Hlinka (Vancouver) beat Gilles Gilbert in 4–4 tie at the Joe Louis Arena
1982	December 8	Corrado Micalef stopped Clark Gillies (Islanders) in 2–0 Detroit win at the Joe Louis Arena
1983	December 10	Alain Lemieux (St. Louis) beat Greg Stefan in 8–3 Blues win at the Arena
1985	October 10	Bo Berglund (Minnesota) beat Corrado Micalef in 6–6 tie at the Joe Louis Arena
1985	December 15	Denis Savard (Chicago) beat Greg Stefan in 6–4 Blackhawks win at the Stadium
1986	February 16	Corrado Micalef stopped Pierre Larouche (Rangers) in 3–1 New York win at Madison Square Garden
1986	February 16	Corrado Micalef stopped Mike Ridley (Rangers) in 3–1 New York win at Madison Square Garden
1988	February 3	Glen Hanlon stopped Denis Savard (Chicago) in 6–4 Detroit win at the Stadium
1989	February 19	Glen Hanlon stopped Mike Foligno (Buffalo) in 8–4 Sabres win at the Aud
1990	February 19	Russ Courtnall (Canadiens) beat Tim Cheveldae in 5–5 tie at the Joe Louis Arena
1990	November 23	Tim Cheveldae stopped Rich Sutter (St. Louis) in 5–3 Detroit win at the Joe Louis Arena
1991	January 9	Tim Cheveldae stopped Ken Linseman (Edmonton) in 5–3 Detroit win at the Joe Louis Arena
1991	November 2	Tim Cheveldae stopped Wes Walz (Boston) in 4–1 Bruin win at the Garden
1994	March 4	Chirs Osgood stopped Peter Zezel (Toronto) in 6–5 Leafs win at the Joe Louis Arena
1995	April 1	Chris Osgood stopped Dave Gagner (Dallas) in 3–2 Detroit win at Reunion Arena
1996	April 7	Mike Vernon stopped Jim Cummins (Chicago) in 4–1 Detroit win at the United Centre

RED WINGS GOALIES' RECORD — PENALTY SHOTS

PLAYER	SAVES	ALLOWED	SHOTS
Roger Crozier	4	1	5
Tim Cheveldae	3	1	4
Corrado Micalef	3	1	4
Glen Hanlon	2	0	2
Chris Osgood	2	0	2
Jim Rutherford	2	1	3
Norm Smith	2	1	3
Dennis DeJordy	1	0	1
Roy Edwards	1	0	1
Ed Giacomin	1	0	1
John Ross Roach	1	0	1
Mike Vernon	1	0	1
Hank Bassen	0	1	1
Larry Lozinski	0	1	1
John Mowers	0	1	1
Terry Sawchuk	0	1	1
Cecil Thompson	0	1	1
Gilles Gilbert	0	2	2
Greg Stefan	0	2	2
Harry Lumley	0	3	3

SPEED RECORDS

FASTEST GOAL FROM START OF GAME AND PERIOD

6 seconds	Henry Boucha, 1st period, January 28, 1973
	Michel Bergeron, 3rd period, March 21, 1976
	Dan Maloney, 2nd period, January 11, 1978
8 seconds	Gordie Howe, 3rd period, March 6, 1966
	Gary McAdam, 2nd period, March 12, 1981
9 seconds	Norm Ullman, 3rd period, October 31, 1959
	Paul Henderson, 3rd period, January 15, 1966

FASTEST TWO GOALS FROM START OF GAME

37 seconds	December 4, 1987 vs. Chicago
	Tim Higgins (:24)
	Steve Yzerman (:37)

FASTEST THREE GOALS FROM START OF GAME

2:02	October 29, 1981
	Paul Woods (:20)
	Willie Huber (:46)
	John Ogrodnick (2:02)

FASTEST TWO GOALS

5 seconds	October 26, 1984, 3rd period vs. Buffalo
	Bob Manno (19:11)
	Danny Gare (19:16)
6 seconds	November 5, 1936, 3rd period vs. Toronto
	Syd Howe (11:13)
	Larry Aurie (11:19)
7 seconds	February 11, 1934, 3rd period vs. Ottawa
	Cooney Weiland (1:46)
	Eddie Wiseman (1:53)
	March 15, 1947, 1st period vs. Chicago
	Pat Lundy (10:29)
	Roy Conacher (10:36)
	December 26, 1970, 3rd period vs. Rangers
	Wayne Connelly (19:36)
	Hank Monteith (19:43)
	January 3, 1984, 3rd period vs. Hartford
	Kelly Kisio (16:20)
	Joe Paterson (16:27)

November 25, 1987, 3rd period vs. Winnipeg
Jeff Sharples (9:10)
Brent Ashton (9:17)

January 6, 1982, 2nd period vs. Buffalo
Greg Smith (2:06)
Mark Osborne (2:13)

March 26, 1983, 1st period vs. Minnesota
Walt McKechnie (2:58)
John Ogrodnick (3:05)

8 seconds — March 9, 1989, 3rd period vs. Rangers
Steve Chiasson (11:49)
Shawn Burr (11:57)

9 seconds — March 18, 1970, 3rd period vs. Minnesota
Garry Unger (6:13)
Nick Libett (6:22)

10 seconds — March 23, 1974, 3rd period vs. Rangers
Henry Boucha (15:11)
Mickey Redmond (15:21)

December 13, 1973, 2nd period vs. St. Louis
Pierre Jarry (5:59)
Guy Charron (6:09)

December 23, 1982, 2nd period vs. Pittsburgh
Mike Blaisdell (14:49)
Reg Leach (14:59)

FASTEST TWO GOALS — INDIVIDUAL

8 seconds — Don Grosso (19:42 and 19:50), March 19, 1942, 1st period.
Chicago 4 at Detroit 6

10 seconds — Ed Brûneteau (16:26 and 16:36), January 3, 1946, 3rd period.
Rangers 3 at Detroit 3

John Ogrodnick (12:30 and 12:40), March 12, 1980, 2nd period.
Hartford 4 at Detroit 4

12 seconds — Bill Hogaboam (10:18 and 10:30), March 30, 1975, 3rd period.
Detroit 8 at Washington 5

Mike Foligno (13:57 and 14:09, penalty shot), January 30, 1980, 3rd period.
Detroit 4 at Toronto 6

15 seconds — Red Kelly (4:39 and 4:54), December 6, 1958, 3rd period.
Detroit 4 at Chicago 3

FASTEST THREE GOALS

27 seconds — November 15, 1944, 3rd period vs. Toronto
Hal Jackson (11:48)
Steve Wojciechowski (12:02)
Don Grosso (12:15)

February 19, 1981, 3rd period vs. Rangers
Joe Paterson (9:27)
Dale McCourt (9:44)
Mike Foligno (9:54)

41 seconds	December 28, 1960, 3rd period vs. Rangers Murray Oliver (13:40) Howie Glover (13:53) Norm Ullman (14:21)
42 seconds	January 3, 1984, 3rd period vs. Hartford John Ogrodnick (15:45) Kelly Kisio (16:20) Joe Paterson (16:27)
44 seconds	December 4, 1987, 3rd period vs. Chicago Joey Kocur (15:46) Gerard Gallant (15:59) Petr Klima (16:30)
56 seconds	December 13, 1973, 3rd period vs. St. Louis Garnet Bailey (6:00) Red Berenson (6:37) Nelson Debenedet (6:56)
49 seconds	October 14, 1988, 2nd period vs. St. Louis Adam Oates (16:56) Steve Yzerman (17:27) Tim Higgins (17:45)

FASTEST THREE GOALS — INDIVIDUAL

1:52	Carl Liscombe (16:02, 17:31, 17:54), March 13, 1938, 1st period vs. Chicago
3:19	Norm Ullman (11:07, 13:33, 14:26), February 8, 1967, 2nd period vs. Toronto
4:21	Reed Larson (5:17, 5:52, 9:38), February 15, 1983, 2nd period vs. Pittsburgh
6:10	Gus Giesebrecht (11:43, 16:25, 17:53), February 5, 1939, 1st period vs. Americans
6:22	Mud Brûneteau (:28, 2:58, 6:50), November 7, 1943, 1st period vs. Boston

FASTEST THREE GOALS — BOTH TEAMS

26 seconds	February 8, 1991, 3rd period vs. Islanders Sergei Fedorov (1:59 Detroit) Pat Flatley (2:11 Islanders) Pat Flatley (2:25 Islanders) Islanders 4 at Detroit 8
29 seconds	February 19, 1984, 3rd period vs. Toronto Eddie Johnstone (14:06 Detroit) Gary Nylund (14:18 Toronto) Gary Leeman (14:35 Toronto) Detroit 6 at Toronto 2
39 seconds	December 8, 1977, 2nd period vs. Islanders Mike Bossy (5:59 Islanders) Reed Larson (6:26 Detroit) Bryan Trottier (6:38 Islanders) Detroit 4 at Boston 6
40 seconds	January 29, 1983, 1st period vs. Boston Keith Crowder (5:03 Boston) Ivan Boldirev (5:26 Detroit) Luc Dufour (5:43 Boston) Boston 7 at Detroit 3

41 seconds	March 19, 1983, 3rd period vs. Edmonton Ivan Boldirev (11:09 Detroit) Glenn Anderson (11:31 Edmonton) Murray Craven (11:50 Detroit) Edmonton 9 at Detroit 7
47 seconds	December 10, 1977, 2nd period vs. Islanders Clark Gillies (14:58 Islanders) Andre St. Laurent (15:27 Detroit) Larry Wright (15:45 Detroit) Detroit 4 at Islanders 7

FASTEST FOUR GOALS

2:25	November 7, 1991, 1st period vs. St. Louis Shawn Burr (13:20) Jimmy Carson (14:19) Niklas Lidstrom (15:00) Paul Ysebaert (15:45)
2:33	March 15, 1947, 1st period vs. Chicago Pat Lundy (10:29) Roy Conacher (10:36) Billy Taylor (11:38) Ted Lindsay (13:02)

FASTEST FOUR GOALS — BOTH TEAMS

1:10	February 9, 1993, 1st period vs. New Jersey Gerard Gallant (1:44 Detroit) Jim Hiller (2:14 Detroit) Stephane Richer (2:28 New Jersey) Paul MacLean (2:54 New Jersey) New Jersey 5 at Detroit 8
1:36	March 2, 1952, 2nd period vs. Rangers Gordie Howe (10:56 Detroit) Gordie Howe (11:15 Detroit) Reg Sinclair (11:42 Rangers) Jim Ross (12:32 Rangers) Detroit 6 at Rangers 4
1:41	April 6, 1974, 2nd period vs. Rangers Bill Fairbairn (1:54 Rangers) Mickey Redmond (2:28 Detroit) Pete Stemkowski (3:04 Rangers) Guy Charron (3:35 Detroit) Rangers 3 at Detroit 8

FASTEST FIVE GOALS

4:54	November 25, 1987, 3rd period vs. Winnipeg Gerard Gallant (4:23) Adam Oates (5:55) Mel Bridgman (6:37) Jeff Sharples (9:10) Brent Ashton (9:17) Winnipeg 8 at Detroit 10

FASTEST FIVE GOALS — BOTH TEAMS

2:21	February 9, 1993, 1st period vs. New Jersey Keith Primeau (:33 Detroit) Gerard Gallant (1:44 Detroit) Jim Hiller (2:14 Detroit) Stephane Richer (2:28 New Jersey) Paul MacLean (2:54 New Jersey) NewJersey 5 at Detroit 8
3:27	January 18, 1988, 1st period vs. Toronto Petr Klima (16:15 Detroit) Gary Leeman (17:04 Toronto) Al Secord (17:33 Toronto) Mark Osborne (19:01 Toronto) Petr Klima (19:42 Detroit) Toronto 3 at Detroit 4
4:06	March 1, 1977, 3rd period vs. Boston Wayne Cashman (:48 Boston) Gregg Sheppard (1:18 Boston) Stan Johnathan (2:22 Boston) Bryan Hextall (4:45 Detroit) Dave Forbes (4:54 Boston) Detroit 3 at Boston 8

FASTEST SIX GOALS — BOTH TEAMS

3:40	December 31, 1963, 3rd period vs. Toronto Floyd Smith (8:33 Detroit) Dave Keon (9:36 Toronto) Dick Duff (10:11 Toronto) Floyd Smith (10:56 Detroit) Frank Mahovlich (11:31 Toronto) Pit Martin (12:13 Detroit) Toronto 5 at Detroit 4

POWER-PLAY GOALS — REGULAR SEASON

MOST POWER-PLAY GOALS — TEAM — GAME

6	November 5, 1942
	November 22, 1952
5	November 15, 1934

MOST POWER-PLAY GOALS — TEAM — PERIOD

4	November 5, 1942
3	1st period, December 13, 1934
	2nd period, February 28, 1935
	1st period, February 25, 1940
	1st period, February 18, 1943

MOST POWER-PLAY GOALS — INDIVIDUAL — GAME

3	Ted Lindsay, March 20, 1955 vs. Canadiens
	Jimmy Carson, December 27, 1989 vs. Toronto

MOST POWER-PLAY GOALS — INDIVIDUAL — PERIOD

3	Jimmy Carson, 3rd period, December 27, 1989 vs. Toronto

FASTEST TWO POWER-PLAY GOALS — INDIVIDUAL

42 seconds	3rd period, March 6, 1949 Bud Poile (8:48 & 9:30)

FASTEST TWO POWER-PLAY GOALS — TEAM

13 seconds	November 15, 1944 Steve Wojciechowski (12:02) Don Grosso (12:15)
15 seconds	December 13, 1932, 3rd period Herbie Lewis (:55) Larry Aurie (1:10)
	February 27, 1934, 1st period vs. Rangers John Sorrell (10:27) Ebbie Goodfellow (10:42)
16 seconds	February 18, 1943, 1st period vs. Rangers Sid Abel (9:32) Mud Brûneteau (9:48)

FASTEST THREE POWER-PLAY GOALS — TEAM

27 seconds	November 15, 1944 Hal Jackson (11:48) Steve Wojciechowski (12:02) Don Grosso (12:15)
49 seconds	February 18, 1943, 1st period Mud Brûneteau (8:59) Sid Abel (9:32) Mud Brûneteau (9:48)
1:00	February 27, 1934, 1st period John Sorrell (9:42) John Sorrell (10:27) Ebbie Goodfellow (10:42)

SHORT-HANDED GOALS — REGULAR SEASON

MOST SHORT-HANDED GOALS — TEAM — GAME

3	January 9, 1990 vs. Minnesota Shawn Burr Shawn Burr Steve Yzerman
	April 14, 1992 vs. Minnesota Steve Yzerman Steve Yzerman Sergei Fedorov
	February 11, 1994 vs. Flyers Sergei Fedorov Vyacheslav Kozlov Steve Yzerman
	March 22, 1996 vs. Colorado Steve Yzerman Keith Primeau Viacheslav Fetisov

MOST SHORT-HANDED GOALS — INDIVIDUAL — GAME

2	Lorne Ferguson	February 2, 1957 vs. Rangers
	Shawn Burr	January 9, 1990 vs. Minnesota
	Steve Yzerman	April 14, 1992 vs. Minnesota
	Steve Yzerman	April 8, 1993 vs. Tampa Bay

MOST SHORT-HANDED GOALS — INDIVIDUAL — PERIOD

2	Shawn Burr	2nd period, January 9, 1990 vs. Minnesota
	Lorne Ferguson	1st period, February 2, 1957 vs. Rangers

FASTEST TWO SHORT-HANDED GOALS

14 seconds	December 28, 1958, 1st period Alex Delvecchio (9:06) Nick Mickoski (9:20)

IDENTIFICATION OF OFFICIALS AND THEIR SIGNALS

NHL REFEREES

1—FRANK UDVARI	6—ART CASTERTON
2—VERN BUFFEY	11—KEN MacLEOD
3—JOHN ASHLEY	12—BRUCE HOOD
4—ART SKOV	14—BOB SLOAN
5—BILL FRIDAY	15—DAVE SMITH

LINESMEN'S NUMBERS

7—MATT PAVELICH	16—BILL MORRISON
8—NEIL ARMSTRONG	17—BOB FRAMPTON
9—GEORGE HAYES	18—BILLY CLEMENTS
10—RON WICKS	19—WALT ATANAS

HOLDING

Clasping either wrist with the other hand well in front of the chest.

HOOKING

A series of tugging motions with both arms, as if pulling something toward the stomach.

INTERFERENCE

Crossed arms stationary in front of chest.

SLOW WHISTLE

Either arm, in which whistle is held, extended above head. If play returns to Neutral Zone without stoppage, arm is drawn down the instant the puck crosses the line.

TRIPPING

Extending right leg forward, clear of the ice, and striking it with right hand below the knee.

HIGH-STICKING

Holding both fists, clenched, one immediately above the other, at the height of the forehead.

SLASHING

A series of chopping motions with the edge of one hand across the opposite forearm.

CHARGING

Rotating clenched fists around one another in front of chest.

CROSS-CHECKING

A series of forward and backward motions with both fists clenched extending from the chest.

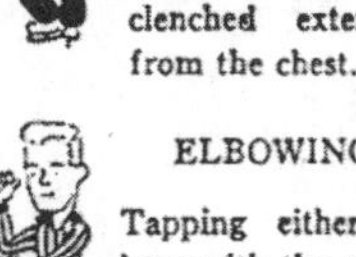

ELBOWING

Tapping either elbow with the opposite hand.

MISCONDUCT

Placing of both hands on hips several times and pointing to penalized player.

DELAYED CALLING OF PENALTY

Referee repeatedly points, with free hand (without whistle) to player to be penalized until play is stopped.

ICING

Arms folded across the chest.

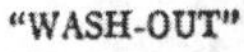

"WASH-OUT"

Both arms swung laterally across the body with palms down:

1. When used by the Referee it means goal disallowed.
2. When used by Linesmen it means there is no icing or no off-side.

PENALTY RECORDS
REGULAR SEASON

MOST PENALTY MINUTES — INDIVIDUAL — GAME

42	Joey Kocur	November 2, 1985 vs. St. Louis

MOST PENALTY MINUTES — INDIVIDUAL — PERIOD

37	Joey Kocur	November 2, 1985 vs. St. Louis

MOST PENALTIES — INDIVIDUAL — GAME

8	Dennis Polonich	March 24, 1976 vs. Washington
	Bob Probert	December 23, 1987 vs. Buffalo

MOST PENALTIES — INDIVIDUAL — PERIOD

6	Joey Kocur	November 2, 1985 vs. St. Louis

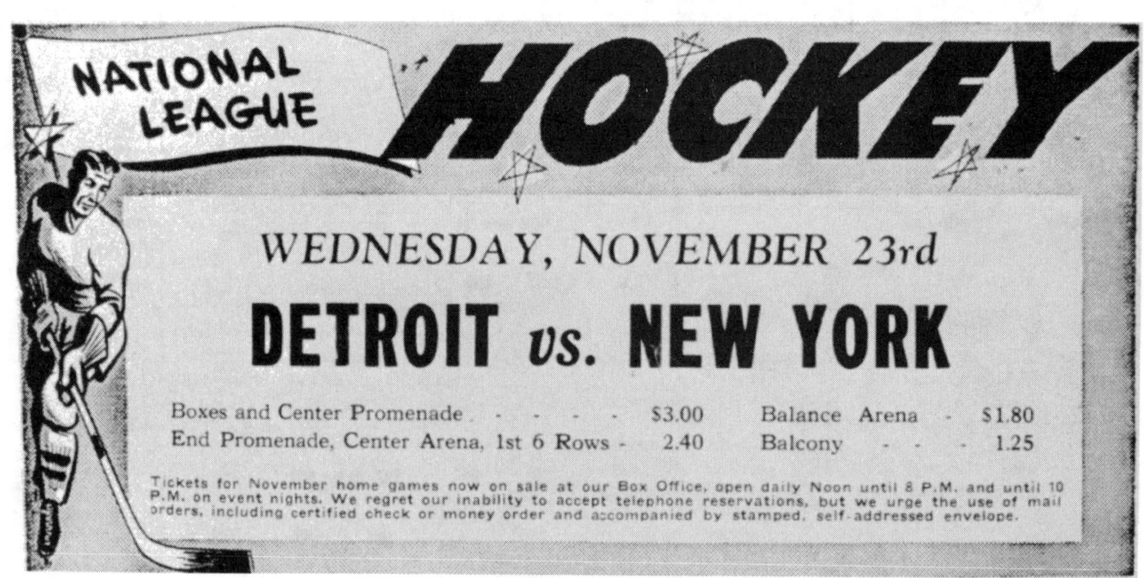

SPECIAL FEATURE

TERRANCE GORDON "TERRY" SAWCHUK

In Terry Sawchuk's 21 years in the NHL, he played 57,205 minutes, appeared in 971 games, allowed 2,401 goals, and recorded 103 shutouts. All of these numbers are NHL records for goaltenders.

He was the first player to win rookie of the year in three different pro leagues, the United States Hockey League in 1947–48, the American Hockey League in 1948–49, and the National Hockey League in 1950–51. He led the league in shutouts three times, won the Vezina four (three with Detroit, one — shared with Johnny Bower — in Toronto), and was a First All-Star three times (1950–53).

Although he died under "odd" circumstances in New York on May 31, 1970, aged 40, he will forever be remembered for his 103 shutouts, a record that will almost certainly never be broken (consider also his 106 playoff games and 12 playoff shutouts). Here is a complete breakdown of those games:

REGULAR SEASON

By Opponent:

	HOME	AWAY	TOTAL
Chicago Blackhawks	13	13	26
New York Rangers	11	9	20
Boston Bruins	14	4	18
Montreal Canadiens	11	6	17
Toronto Maple Leafs	12	3	15
Detroit Red Wings	3	1	4
Philadelphia Flyers	0	2	2
Pittsburgh Penguins	1	0	1
Total	65	38	103

CHRONOLOGICAL ORDER
(double space indicates season)

As a Detroit Red Wing:

1.	January 15, 1950	Detroit 1 at Rangers 0
2.	October 29, 1950	Boston 0 at Detroit 2
3.	November 12, 1950	Canadiens 0 at Detroit 4
4.	December 6, 1950	Detroit 9 at Rangers 0
5.	December 9, 1950	Rangers 0 at Detroit 5
6.	January 4, 1951	Chicago 0 at Detroit 1
7.	January 7, 1951	Boston 0 at Detroit 3
8.	January 21, 1951	Toronto 0 at Detroit 0
9.	March 7, 1951	Detroit 3 at Toronto 0
10.	March 11, 1951	Detroit 7 at Chicago 0

11.	March 15, 1951	Boston 0 at Detroit 4
12.	March 25, 1951	Canadiens 0 at Detroit 5
13.	October 11, 1951	Boston 0 at Detroit 1
14.	October 20, 1951	Canadiens 0 at Detroit 3
15.	November 6, 1951	Detroit 0 at Boston 0
16.	November 20, 1951	Detroit 2 at Boston 0
17.	December 8, 1951	Detroit 3 at Canadiens 0
18.	December 15, 1951	Chicago 0 at Detroit 3
19.	December 23, 1951	Canadiens 0 at Detroit 4
20.	January 17, 1952	Boston 0 at Detroit 5
21.	January 19, 1952	Detroit 4 at Canadiens 0
22.	January 27, 1952	Detroit 2 at Chicago 0
23.	February 10, 1952	Detroit 2 at Boston 0
24.	March 16, 1952	Detroit 4 at Chicago 0
25.	October 16, 1952	Chicago 0 at Detroit 7
26.	November 13, 1952	Boston 0 at Detroit 3
27.	December 6, 1952	Detroit 2 at Chicago 0
28.	December 14, 1952	Canadiens 0 at Detroit 0
29.	January 15, 1953	Detroit 4 at Boston 0
30.	January 31, 1953	Chicago 0 at Detroit 4
31.	March 7, 1953	Detroit 3 at Toronto 0
32.	March 11, 1953	Detroit 2 at Rangers 0
33,	March 15, 1953	Detroit 0 at Chicago 0
34.	October 18, 1953	Canadiens 0 at Detroit 4
35.	October 25, 1953	Toronto 0 at Detroit 2
36.	November 26, 1953	Toronto 0 at Detroit 2
37.	November 28, 1953	Chicago 0 at Detroit 9
38.	December 3, 1953	Rangers 0 at Detroit 4
39.	January 3, 1954	Toronto 0 at Detroit 0
40.	January 21, 1954	Detroit 1 at Canadiens 0
41.	January 24, 1954	Toronto 0 at Detroit 2
42.	February 4, 1954	Boston 0 at Detroit 5
43.	February 14, 1954	Detroit 5 at Chicago 0
44.	February 17, 1954	Detroit 0 at Toronto 0
45.	February 22, 1954	Canadiens 0 at Detroit 3
46.	October 9, 1954	Rangers 0 at Detroit 4
47.	October 30, 1954	Boston 0 at Detroit 4
48.	November 7, 1954	Rangers 1 at Detroit 0
49.	November 20, 1954	Chicago 0 at Detroit 5
50.	November 21, 1954	Detroit 1 at Chicago 0
51.	November 25, 1954	Toronto 0 at Detroit 2
52.	January 8, 1955	Chicago 0 at Detroit 1
53.	January 13, 1955	Boston 0 at Detroit 4
54.	January 16, 1955	Rangers 0 at Detroit 3
55.	January 23, 1955	Toronto 0 at Detroit 4
56.	February 20, 1955	Detroit 5 at Rangers 0
57.	March 20, 1955	Canadiens 0 at Detroit 6

As a Boston Bruin:

58.	October 12, 1955	Toronto 0 at Boston 2
59.	October 22, 1955	Boston 0 at Detroit 0
60.	October 29, 1955	Boston 1 at Rangers 0
61.	November 13, 1955	Detroit 0 at Boston 0
62.	December 4, 1955	Toronto 0 at Boston 5
63.	January 20, 1956	Boston 3 at Chicago 0
64.	February 19, 1956	Boston 3 at Rangers 0
65.	March 10, 1956	Boston 4 at Canadiens 0
66.	March 13, 1956	Detroit 0 at Boston 4
67.	October 27, 1956	Boston 1 at Canadiens 0
68.	November 29, 1956	Boston 2 at Chicago 0

As a Detroit Red Wing:

69.	October 30, 1957	Detroit 4 at Rangers 0
70.	November 16, 1957	Detroit 1 at Chicago 0
71.	December 22, 1957	Chicago 0 at Detroit 2
72.	October 12, 1958	Rangers 0 at Detroit 3
73.	November 18, 1958	Boston 0 at Detroit 6
74.	December 4, 1958	Boston 0 at Detroit 4
75.	February 12, 1959	Rangers 0 at Detroit 1
76.	March 17, 1959	Chicago 0 at Detroit 2
77.	October 14, 1959	Detroit 2 at Chicago 0
78.	October 18, 1959	Toronto 0 at Detroit 3
79.	November 14, 1959	Detroit 4 at Rangers 0
80.	December 9, 1959	Detroit 2 at Chicago 0
81.	March 8, 1960	Canadiens 0 at Detroit 3
82.	October 20, 1960	Boston 0 at Detroit 5
83.	November 27, 1960	Toronto 0 at Detroit 2
84.	November 2, 1961	Rangers 0 at Detroit 1
85.	November 12, 1961	Canadiens 0 at Detroit 3
86.	December 9, 1961	Chicago 0 at Detroit 3
87.	December 14, 1961	Boston 0 at Detroit 5
88.	January 24, 1962	Detroit 3 at Rangers 0
89.	October 13, 1962	Detroit 0 at Chicago 0
90.	October 28, 1962	Toronto 0 at Detroit 2
91.	November 1, 1962	Rangers 0 at Detroit 4
92.	October 13, 1963	Boston 0 at Detroit 3
93.	November 7, 1963	Rangers 0 at Detroit 1
94.	November 10, 1963	Canadiens 0 at Detroit 3
95.	January 18, 1964	Detroit 2 at Canadiens 0
96.	February 6, 1964	Chicago 0 at Detroit 4

As a Toronto Maple Leaf:

97. November 21, 1964 — Chicago 0 at Toronto 1

98. February 9, 1966 — Rangers 0 at Toronto 3

99. February 25, 1967 — Detroit 0 at Toronto 4
100. March 4, 1967 — Chicago 0 at Toronto 3

As a Los Angeles King:

101. January 28, 1968 — Los Angeles 2 at Flyers 0
102. March 14, 1968 — Los Angeles 0 at Flyers 0 (played at Quebec City)

As a New York Ranger:

103. February 1, 1970 — Penguins 0 at Rangers 6

PLAYOFFS

By Opponent:

	HOME	AWAY	TOTAL
Toronto Maple Leafs	4	1	5
Montreal Canadiens	2	2	4
Boston Bruins	1	0	1
Chicago Blackhawks	1	0	1
Minnesota North Stars	1	0	1
Totals	9	3	12

CHRONOLOGICAL ORDER

As a Detroit Red Wing:

1. March 31, 1951 — Detroit 2 at Canadiens 0

2. March 25, 1952 — Toronto 0 at Detroit 3
3. March 27, 1952 — Toronto 0 at Detroit 1
4. April 13, 1952 — Canadiens 0 at Detroit 3
5. April 15, 1952 — Canadiens 0 at Detroit 3

6. March 24, 1953 — Boston 0 at Detroit 7

7. March 23, 1954 — Toronto 0 at Detroit 5
8. April 10, 1954 — Detroit 2 at Canadiens 0

9. March 29, 1955 — Detroit 3 at Toronto 0
10. March 26, 1961 — Toronto 0 at Detroit 2

11. March 31, 1964 — Chicago 0 at Detroit 3

As a Los Angeles King:

12. April 6, 1968 — Minnesota 0 at Los Angeles 2

FAMOUS LINES

FRENCH CONNECTION
(so called because of their French names)
Fern Leblanc — Jean-Paul Leblanc — Roland Cloutier

HEM LINE
Billy **H**arris — Gerry **E**hman — Frank **M**ahovlich

HUM LINE
Paul **H**enderson — Norm **U**llman — Bruce **M**acGregor

LINIMENT LINE
(so called because of their frequent injuries)
Don Grosso — Eddie Wares — Sid Abel

NOTHING LINE
(so called because of their unglamorous style of play)
Gerry Melnyk — Val Fonteyne — Len Haley

PRODUCTION LINE (II)
Alex Delvecchio — Gordie Howe — Frank Mahovlich

GREAT "NAMELESS" LINES
Syd Howe — Mud Brûneteau — Carl Liscombe
Marty Barry — Larry Aurie — Herbie Lewis
Art Skov — Tony Leswick — Marty Pavelich
Parker MacDonald — Alex Delvecchio — Gordie Howe
John Ogrodnick — Steve Yzerman — Ron Duguay
Gerard Gallant — Steve Yzerman — Paul MacLean

PRODUCTION LINE
(originally called the Abel line — so called because of their great scoring abilities)
Gordie Howe — Sid Abel — Ted Lindsay

YOUNGEST TO PLAY FOR THE RED WINGS (under 19)

Harry Lumley	17, 1 month, 8 days
Hy Buller	17, 8 months, 22 days
Martin Lapointe	18, 23 days
Pit Martin	18, 1 month, 15 days
Shawn Burr	18, 3 months, 11 days
Gordie Howe	18, 6 months, 17 days
Claude Loiselle	18, 8 months, 9 days
Dave Amadio	18, 9 months, 22 days
Keith Primeau	18, 10 months, 12 days
Vic Lynn	18, 10 months, 20 days

Harry Lumley

OLDEST TO PLAY FOR THE RED WINGS (over 37)

Gordie Howe	43, 3 days
Doug Harvey	42, 24 days
Alex Delvecchio	41, 11 months, 0 days
Ron Moffatt	41+ (exact date of birth unknown)
Borje Salming	39, 11 months, 15 days
Mark Howe	39, 11 months, 5 days
Ted Lindsay	39, 7 months, 27 days
Jack Walker	39, 3 months, 24 days
Terry Sawchuk	39, 2 months, 20 days
Terry Harper	39, 2 months, 12 days
Vyacheslav Fetisov	38, 1 month, 9 days*
Harry Holmes	38, 11 months, 9 days
Bill Gadsby	38, 7 months, 24 days
Ed Giacomin	38, 6 months, 15 days
Vaclav Nedomansky	38, 17 days
Ted Harris	37, 6 months, 26 days
Reg Noble	37, 5 months, 11 days
Dino Ciccarelli	36, 3 months, 21 days

* still active

FEWEST GAMES PLAYED WITH THE RED WINGS

1 Gerry Abel
Claude Bourque
Jeff Brubaker
Craig Cameron
Dwight Carruthers
Lude Check
Bobby Crawford
Rene Drôlet
Harrison Gray
Galen Head
Rick Healey
Miroslav Ihnacak
Al Jensen
Earl Johnson
Brian Kilrea
Dick Kotanen
Real Lemieux
Dave Lucas
Ken Mann
Tom McGratton
Bill Mitchell
Alfie Moore
Dean Morton
Brian Murphy
Eddie Nicholson
Bert Peer
Nelson Podolsky
Chris Pusey
Dave Richardson
Jack Riley
Dave Rochefort
Pat Rupp
Steve Short
Bjorne Skaare
Bob Solinger
Frank Steele
Barry Sullivan
Joe Turner
Lefty Wilson
Murray Wing

2 Dave Amadio
Tom Bladon
Abbie Cox
Peter Dineen
Ken Doraty
Dave Gagner
Red Green
Doug Harvey
Red Kane
Scott King
Chris Kotsopoulos
Bill McDougall
Mike McMahon
John Rivers
Bernie Ruelle
Ted Taylor
Carl Wetzel
Ed Zeniuk
Rudy Zunich

These players never played a regular season game for the Red Wings but did play in the playoffs:

1. Bob Champoux (one game in 1964)
2. Gord Haidy (one game in 1950)
3. Doug McKay (one game in 1950)
4. Gilles Dube (2 games in 1954)
5. Steve Hrymnak (2 games in 1953)
6. Gerry Reid (2 games in 1949)
7. Gene Carrigan (4 games in 1934)
8. Earl Robertson (6 games in 1937)
9. Cliff Purpur (7 games in 1945)

BROTHERS AND SONS WITH THE RED WINGS

(b)=brother (f)=father (s)=son

ABEL	Sid (f)
	Gerry (s)
BROWN	Adam (f)
	Andy (s)
BRUNETEAU	Ed (b)
	Mud (b)
CONACHER	Charlie (b)
	Roy (b)
CULLEN	Barry (b)
	Ray (b)
DINEEN	Bill (f)
	Peter (s)
GLOVER	Fred (b)
	Howie (b)
HEXTALL	Bryan (b)
	Dennis (b)
HOWE	Gordie (f)
	Mark (s)
KILREA	Hec (b)
	Ken (b)
	Wally (b)
MAHOVLICH	Frank (b)
	Pete (b)
MCRAE	Basil (b)
	Chris (b)
MORRISON	Don (b)
	Rod (b)
PETERS	Jim (f)
	Jim Jr. (s)
POILE	Bud (b)
	Don (b)
ROCHE	Desse (b)
	Earl (b)
SHEPPARD	Frank (b)
	Johnny (b)
SIMON	Cully (b)
	Thain (b)
SMITH	Nakina (b)
	Winky (b)
WILSON	Johnny (b)
	Larry (b)

Cully Simon

Thain Simon

RED WINGS WHO INTERRUPTED THEIR NHL CAREERS TO FIGHT IN WORLD WAR II

Sid Abel	Royal Canadian Air Force
Murray Armstrong	Canadian Armed Forces
Dick Behling	United States Army
Adam Brown	Canadian Armed Forces
Gerry Brown	Canadian Armed Forces
Connie Brown	Canadian Armed Forces
Eddie Bush	Royal Canadian Air Force
Jim Conacher	Royal Canadian Air Force
Red Doran	Canadian Armed Forces
Les Douglas	Royal Canadian Air Force
Pat Egan	Canadian Armed Forces
Joe Fisher	Canadian Armed Forces
Gus Giesebrecht	Canadian Armed Forces
Art Herchenratter	Royal Canadian Air Force
John Holota	Canadian Armed Forces
Doug McCaig	Royal Canadian Air Force
Pat McCreavy	Royal Canadian Air Force
Red Morrison	Canadian Armed Forces
John Mowers	Royal Canadian Air Force
Cliff Simpson	Canadian Armed Forces
Jack Stewart	Royal Canadian Air Force
Joe Turner*	United States Army
Eddie Wares	Canadian Armed Forces
Harry Watson	Royal Canadian Air Force

* killed in action

RED WINGS ALL-STARS

These Red Wings have been selected to or competed for the All-Star team. The selection of all-stars began in 1930–31 and was intended simply to identify and honour the best players in the league (until the All-Star game became an annual event). Since 1969, the best players from the NHL have made up both teams. Numbers in brackets indicate first or second team selection; where no number is given, players were picked by the coach as the team's representative or to fill the roster. Because the game was played at the beginning of the season, players were chosen all-stars for one season (i.e., '38–'39), but did not play the game until the next ('39–'40). Underneath each season is listed the date, score, and venue for each All-Star Game.

1930–31	No Red Wings selected
1931–32	No Red Wings selected
1932–33	John Ross Roach, goal (1st)
1933–34	Larry Aurie, right wing
FEBRUARY 14, 1934	Herbie Lewis, left wing
MAPLE LEAF GARDENS	
TORONTO 7	
ALL-STARS 3	
1934–35	Cooney Weiland, centre (2nd)
1935–36	Ebbie Goodfellow, defence (2nd)
1936–37	Jack Adams, coach (1st)
NOVEMBER 3, 1937	Marty Barry, centre (1st)
MONTREAL FORUM	Ebbie Goodfellow, defence (1st)
ALL-STARS 6	Norm Smith, goal (1st)
CANADIENS 5	Larry Aurie, right wing (1st)
1937–38	No Red Wings selected
1938–39	Ebbie Goodfellow, defence
OCTOBER 29, 1939	Syd Howe, right wing
MONTREAL FORUM	
ALL-STARS 5	
CANADIENS 2	
1939–40	Ebbie Goodfellow, defence (1st)
1940–41	No Red Wings selected
1941–42	Sid Abel, left wing (2nd)
1942–43	Jack Adams, coach (1st)
	Johnny Mowers, goal (1st)
	Jack Stewart, defence (1st)
1943–44	No Red Wings selected
1944–45	Jack Adams, coach (2nd)
	Flash Hollett, defence (1st)
	Syd Howe, left wing (2nd)
1945–46	Jack Stewart, defence (2nd)

9
8
10
NORTHLAND

1946–47	Ted Lindsay, left wing
OCTOBER 13, 1947	Bill Quackenbush, defence (2nd)
MAPLE LEAF GARDENS	Jack Stewart, defence (2nd)
ALL-STARS 4	
TORONTO 3	
1947–48	Tommy Ivan, coach
NOVEMBER 3, 1948	Gordie Howe, right wing
CHICAGO STADIUM	Ted Lindsay, left wing (1st)
ALL-STARS 3	Bill Quackenbush, defence (1st)
TORONTO 1	Jack Stewart, defence (1st)
1948–49	Tommy Ivan, coach
OCTOBER 10, 1949	Sid Abel, centre (1st)
MAPLE LEAF GARDENS	Bill Quackenbush, defence (1st) (did not play)
ALL-STARS 3	Gordie Howe, right wing (2nd)
TORONTO 1	Ted Lindsay, left wing (2nd)
	Jack Stewart, defence (1st)
1949–50	Cup-winning Red Wing team vs. NHL All-Stars
OCTOBER 8, 1950	Sid Abel, centre (1st)
OLYMPIA STADIUM	Ted Lindsay, left wing (1st)
DETROIT 7	Leo Reise, defence (2nd)
ALL-STARS 1	Red Kelly, defence (2nd)
	Gordie Howe, right wing (2nd)

The All-Star format changed for the 1951 game. The First Team stars, supplemented by players from the four American clubs, played the Second Team stars, with added players from the two Canadian clubs. As a result, Sid Abel and Leo Reise played against their mates in the 1951 game!

1950–51	Gordie Howe, right wing (1st)
OCTOBER 9, 1951	Red Kelly, defence (1st)
1ST TEAM 2	Ted Lindsay, left wing (1st)
2ND TEAM 2	Terry Sawchuk, goal (1st)
	Sid Abel, centre (2nd)
	Leo Reise, defence (2nd)
1951–52	Tommy Ivan, coach
OCTOBER 5, 1952	Bob Goldham, defence
OLYMPIA STADIUM	Gordie Howe, right wing (1st)
1ST TEAM 1	Red Kelly, defence (1st)
2ND TEAM 1	Tony Leswick, left wing
	Ted Lindsay, left wing (1st)
	Marty Pavelich, left wing
	Terry Sawchuk, goal (1st)
	Reg Sinclair, right wing

The NHL reverted to its previous format, the Stanley Cup champions versus the rest of the league.

1952–53	Alex Delvecchio, centre (2nd)
OCTOBER 3, 1953	Gordie Howe, right wing (1st)
MONTREAL FORUM	Red Kelly, defence (1st)
ALL-STARS 3	Ted Lindsay, left wing (1st)
MONTREAL 1	Metro Prystai, centre
	Terry Sawchuk, goal (1st)

1953–54	Cup-winning Red Wings vs. NHL All-Stars
OCTOBER 2, 1954	Red Kelly, defence (1st)
OLYMPIA STADIUM	Gordie Howe, right wing (1st)
DETROIT 2	Ted Lindsay, left wing (1st)
ALL-STARS 2	Terry Sawchuk, goal (2nd)
1954–55	Cup-winning Red Wings vs. NHL All-Stars
OCTOBER 2, 1955	Red Kelly, defence (1st)
OLYMPIA STADIUM	Terry Sawchuk, goal (2nd)
DETROIT 3	Bob Goldham, defence (2nd)
ALL-STARS 1	
1955–56	Jimmy Skinner, coach
OCTOBER 9, 1956	Alex Delvecchio, centre
MONTREAL FORUM	Glenn Hall, goal (2nd)
ALL-STARS 1	Red Kelly, defence (2nd)
CANADIENS 1	Ted Lindsay, left wing (1st)
	Johnny Wilson, left wing
	Gordie Howe, right wing (2nd) (did not play)
1956–57	Alex Delvecchio, centre
OCTOBER 5, 1957	Glenn Hall, goal (1st)
MONTREAL FORUM	Gordie Howe, right wing (1st)
ALL-STARS 5	Red Kelly, defence (1st)
CANADIENS 3	Ted Lindsay, left wing (1st)
	Marcel Pronovost, defence
1957–58	Alex Delvecchio, centre
OCTOBER 4, 1958	Gordie Howe, right wing (1st)
MONTREAL FORUM	Red Kelly, defence
CANADIENS 6	Marcel Pronovost, defence (2nd)
ALL-STARS 3	
1958–59	Alex Delvecchio, centre (2nd)
OCTOBER 3, 1959	Gordie Howe, right wing (2nd)
MONTREAL FORUM	Marcel Pronovost, defence (2nd)
CANADIENS 6	Terry Sawchuk, goal (2nd)
ALL-STARS 1	
1959–60	Gordie Howe, right wing (1st)
OCTOBER 1, 1960	Marcel Pronovost, defence (1st)
MONTREAL FORUM	Norm Ullman, centre
ALL-STARS 2	
CANADIENS 1	
1960–61	Sid Abel, coach
OCTOBER 7, 1961	Alex Delvecchio, centre
CHICAGO STADIUM	Gordie Howe, right wing (2nd)
ALL-STARS 3	Marcel Pronovost, defence (1st)
CHICAGO 1	Norm Ullman, centre
1961–62	Alex Delvecchio, centre
OCTOBER 6, 1962	Gordie Howe, right wing (2nd)
MAPLE LEAF GARDENS	Norm Ullman, centre
TORONTO 4	
ALL-STARS 1	

1962–63	Sid Abel, coach
OCTOBER 5, 1963	Alex Delvecchio, centre
MAPLE LEAF GARDENS	Gordie Howe, right wing (1st)
TORONTO 3	Marcel Pronovost, defence
ALL-STARS 3	Terry Sawchuk, goal (2nd)
	Norm Ullman, centre
1963–64	Sid Abel, coach
OCTOBER 10, 1964	Alex Delvecchio, centre
MAPLE LEAFS GARDENS	Gordie Howe, right wing (2nd)
ALL-STARS 3	Norm Ullman, centre
TORONTO 2	
1964–65	Roger Crozier, goal (1st) (did not play)
OCTOBER 20, 1965	Alex Delvecchio, centre
MONTREAL FORUM	Bill Gadsby, defence (1st)
ALL-STARS 5	Gordie Howe, right wing (1st)
CANADIENS 2	Marcel Pronovost, defence
	Norm Ullman, centre (1st)

For the first time since the Ace Bailey Benefit, the All-Star game was played at mid-season. Thus, there was no game during the calendar year 1966.

1965–66	Gordie Howe, right wing (1st)
1966–67	Sid Abel, coach
JANUARY 18, 1967	Alex Delvecchio, centre
MONTREAL FORUM	Gordie Howe, right wing (2nd)
CANADIENS 3	Norm Ullman, centre (2nd)
ALL-STARS 0	
1967–68	Gordie Howe, right wing (1st)
JANUARY 16, 1968	Norm Ullman, centre
MAPLE LEAF GARDENS	
TORONTO 4	
ALL-STARS 3	

Starting with the '68–'69 season, the game matched All-Stars from one division against All-Stars from the other. As the game was played at mid-season, the All-Stars now played the same year as their selection to the Team.

1968–69	Gordie Howe, right wing (1st)
JANUARY 21, 1969	Frank Mahovlich, left wing (2nd)
MONTREAL FORUM	
EAST 3	
WEST 3	
1969–70	Carl Brewer, defence (2nd)
JANUARY 20, 1970	Gordie Howe, right wing (1st)
ST. LOUIS ARENA	Frank Mahovlich, left wing (2nd)
EAST 4	
WEST 4	
1970–71	Gordie Howe, right wing
JANUARY 19, 1971	
BOSTON GARDEN	
WEST 2	
EAST 1	

1971–72	Red Berenson, centre
JANUARY 25, 1972	
MET SPORTS CENTRE	
EAST 3	
WEST 2	
1972–73	Gary Bergman, defence
JANUARY 30, 1973	Mickey Redmond, right wing (1st) (did not play)
MADISON SQUARE GARDEN	
EAST 5	
WEST 4	
1973–74	Red Berenson, centre
JANUARY 29, 1974	Mickey Redmond, right wing (2nd)
CHICAGO STADIUM	
WEST 6	
EAST 4	
1974–75	Marcel Dionne, centre
JANUARY 21, 1975	
MONTREAL FORUM	
WALES 7	
CAMPBELL 1	
1975–76	Dan Maloney, left wing
JANUARY 20, 1976	
THE SPECTRUM	
WALES 7	
CAMPBELL 5	
1976–77	Nick Libett, left wing
JANUARY 25, 1977	
PACIFIC COLISEUM	
WALES 4	
CAMPBELL 3	
1977–78	Reed Larson, defence
JANUARY 24, 1978	
MEMORIAL AUDITORIUM	
WALES 3	
CAMPBELL 2 (OT)	
1978–79	NHL All-Stars vs. USSR National Team (Challenge Cup)
FEBRUARY 8, 10, 11, 1979	No Red Wings selected
MADISON SQUARE GARDEN	
NHL STARS 4, USSR 2	
USSR 5, NHL STARS 4	
USSR 6, NHL STARS 0	
1979–80	Reed Larson, defence
FEBRUARY 5, 1980	
JOE LOUIS ARENA	
WALES 6	
CAMPBELL 3	

1980–81
FEBRUARY 10, 1981
LOS ANGELES FORUM
CAMPBELL 4
WALES 1

Reed Larson, defence
John Ogrodnick, right wing

1981–82
FEBRUARY 9, 1982
THE CAPITAL CENTRE
WALES 4
CAMPBELL 2

John Ogrodnick, right wing

1982–83
FEBRUARY 8, 1983
NASSAU COLISEUM
CAMPBELL 9
WALES 3

Willie Huber, defence

1983–84
JANUARY 31, 1984
MEADOWLANDS ARENA
WALES 7
CAMPBELL 6

John Ogrodnick, right wing
Steve Yzerman, centre

1984–85
FEBRUARY 12, 1985
OLYMPIC SADDLEDOME
WALES 6
CAMPBELL 4

John Ogrodnick, left wing (1st)

1985–86
FEBRUARY 4, 1986
HARTFORD CIVIC CENTRE
WALES 4
CAMPBELL 3 (OT)

John Ogrodnick, left wing

1986–87
FEBRUARY 11 & 13, 1987
LE COLISÉE
NHL STARS 4, USSR 3
USSR 5, NHL STARS 3

NHL All-Stars vs. Soviet National Team (Rendez-vous '87)
No Red Wings selected

1987–88
FEBRUARY 9, 1988
ST. LOUIS ARENA
WALES 6
CAMPBELL 5

Bob Probert, left wing
Steve Yzerman, centre

1988–89
FEBRUARY 7, 1989
NORTHLANDS COLISEUM
CAMPBELL 9
WALES 5

Gerard Gallant, left wing (2nd) (did not play)
Steve Yzerman, centre

1989–90	Steve Yzerman, centre
JANUARY 21, 1990	
CIVIC ARENA	
WALES 12	
CAMPBELL 7	
1990–91	Steve Yzerman, centre
JANUARY 19, 1991	
CHICAGO STADIUM	
CAMPBELL 11	
WALES 5	
1991–92	Tim Cheveldae, goal
JANUARY 18, 1992	Sergei Fedorov, centre
THE SPECTRUM	Steve Yzerman, centre
CAMPBELL 10	
WALES 6	
1992–93	Steve Chiasson, defence
FEBRUARY 6, 1993	Paul Coffey, defence
MONTREAL FORUM	Steve Yzerman, centre
WALES 16	
CAMPBELL 6	
1993–94	Paul Coffey, defence
JANUARY 22, 1994	Sergei Fedorov, centre (1st)
MADISON SQUARE GARDEN	
EASTERN 9	
WESTERN 8	
1994–95	Owners' lockout — no game
JANUARY 21, 1995	
SAN JOSE ARENA	
1995–96	Chris Osgood, goal
JANUARY 20, 1996	Paul Coffey, defence
FLEET CENTRE	Sergei Fedorov, centre
EAST 5	
WEST 4	

The 1997 All-Star Game will be played January 18 in San Jose.

MOST VALUABLE PLAYER

(this honour began in 1962)

1965 . . . . Gordie Howe
1969 . . . . Frank Mahovlich

ALL-STAR RECORDS HELD BY RED WINGS

MOST GAMES — CAREER

23 . . . . Gordie Howe

MOST POINTS — CAREER

19 . . . . Gordie Howe (10 goals, 9 assists)
(tied with one other)

MOST PENALTY MINUTES — CAREER

27 . . . . Gordie Howe

MOST POWER-PLAY GOALS — CAREER

6 . . . . Gordie Howe

OLDEST PLAYER IN ALL-STAR GAME

Gordie Howe . . . . 51 years, 10 months, 5 days

FASTEST GOAL FROM START OF GAME

19 seconds . . . . Ted Lindsay (1950)

FASTEST GOAL FROM START OF PERIOD

19 seconds . . . . Ted Lindsay
(tied with one other)

ALL-TIME RED WINGS STATISTICS FOR ALL-STAR GAMES

COACHES

	G	W	L	T
Tommy Ivan	4	3	0	1
Sid Abel	4	2	1	1
Jimmy Skinner	3	1	0	2
Jack Adams	1	1	0	0

GOALIES
(ranked by average)
(sweater numbers precede name)

		G	Mins	GA	W–L–T	Avg.
1/24	Terry Sawchuk	7	358:25	13	2–1–3	1.17
1	Glenn Hall	3	149:30	4	2–0–0	1.61
32	Tim Cheveldae	1	20:00	2	0–0–0	6.00
31	Chris Osgood	1	20:00	2	0–0–0	6.00
1	Norm Smith	(selected to 1937 team but did not play)				

PLAYERS
(ranked by points, then goals, then games played)
(sweater numbers precede name)

		GA	G	A	P	PIM
9	Gordie Howe	22	10	8	18	33*
7	Ted Lindsay	11	5	5	10	8
15/8/10	Alex Delvecchio	13	3	3	6	0
10/6/7/19/18	Steve Yzerman	7	2	4	6	0
4/5	Red Kelly	9	1	5	6	5**
8/16	Norm Ullman	9	2	3	5	0
14/8	Earl Reibel	2	2	3	5	0
91	Sergei Fedorov	3	1	4	5	0
27/26/25	John Ogrodnick	5	2	2	4	0
77	Paul Coffey	3	2	2	4	0
15/10/11	Marty Pavelich	4	2	1	3	0
14/10	Metro Prystai	3	1	2	3	0
27	Frank Mahovlich	2	2	0	2	0
22/3/2/6/5	Marcel Pronovost	10	1	1	2	6
10	Jim Peters	1	1	1	2	2
17	Marty Barry	1	1	1	2	0
8	Dan Maloney	1	1	1	2	0
28	Reed Larson	3	1	0	1	0
21	Mickey Redmond	1	1	0	1	0
2/14	Bob Goldham	4	0	1	1	0
12	Sid Abel	3	0	1	1	2
5/11	Red Berenson	2	0	1	1	2
4	Bill Gadsby	1	0	1	1	2
5	Carl Brewer	1	0	1	1	0
24	Bob Probert	1	0	1	1	0
—	Jack Stewart	3	0	0	0	0
3/5	Ebbie Goodfellow	2	0	0	0	2
5/3	Leo Reise	2	0	0	0	0
15	Tony Leswick	2	0	0	0	0
17	Bill Dineen	2	0	0	0	2
10/15	Johnny Wilson	2	0	0	0	0
11	Bill Quackenbush	2	0	0	0	0
21	Norm Corcoran	1	0	0	0	4

The legend named Gordie Howe.

—	Larry Aurie	1	0	0	0	0
—	Herbie Lewis	1	0	0	0	0
8	Syd Howe	1	0	0	0	0
19	Steve Black	1	0	0	0	0
17	Joe Carveth	1	0	0	0	0
18	Doc Couture	1	0	0	0	2
21	Lee Fogolin	1	0	0	0	0
8	George Gee	1	0	0	0	0
16	Jim McFadden	1	0	0	0	0
3	Steve Chiasson	1	0	0	0	0
5	Nicklas Lidstrom	1	0	0	0	0
11	Gaye Stewart	1	0	0	0	2
18	Keith Allen	1	0	0	0	0
20	Marcel Bonin	1	0	0	0	6
19	Don Poile	1	0	0	0	0
12	Glen Skov	1	0	0	0	0
5	Benny Woit	1	0	0	0	2

20	John Bucyk	1	0	0	0	2
14	Real Chevrefils	1	0	0	0	0
1	Warren Godfrey	1	0	0	0	0
15	Larry Hillman	1	0	0	0	0
18	Gord Hollingworth	1	0	0	0	4
12	Ed Sandford	1	0	0	0	0
21	Reg Sinclair	1	0	0	0	0
19	Jerry Toppazzini	1	0	0	0	0
3	Gary Bergman	1	0	0	0	2
12	Marcel Dionne	1	0	0	0	0
14	Nick Libett	1	0	0	0	0
3	Willie Huber	1	0	0	0	0

* including a 5-minute fighting major with Gus Mortson in 1948
** including a 5-minute fighting major with Bert Olmstead in 1953

EMPTY NET GOALS

There have only been three empty net goals in the history of the All-Star Game, two of which have been scored by Red Wings (Mike Gartner got the other).

1. Alex Delvecchio, October 3, 1953
2. Dutch Reibel, October 2, 1955

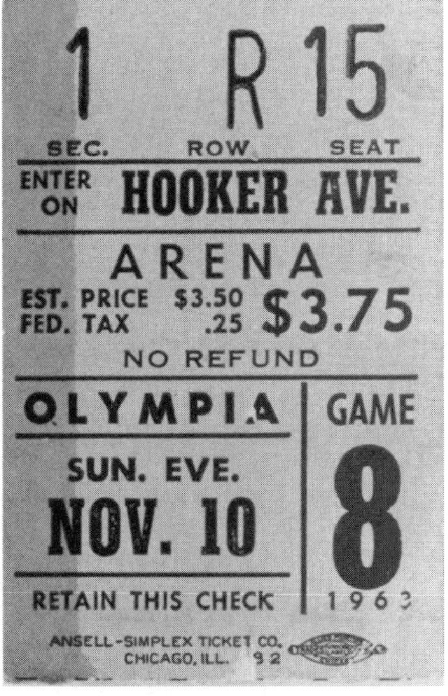

COMPLETE SEASONS PLAYED

(a complete list of those Red Wings who have played every game of a particular season)

1926–27
None

1927–28
Larry Aurie
Reg Noble
Johnny Sheppard

1928–29
Carson Cooper
Reg Noble

1929–30
Carson Cooper
Ebbie Goodfellow
Hal Hicks
Herb Lewis

1930–31
Ebbie Goodfellow
George Hay
Herb Lewis
Stan McCabe
Reg Noble

1931–32
Larry Aurie
Carson Cooper
Ebbie Goodfellow
Herb Lewis
Reg Noble
Alex Smith
John Sorrell

1932–33
Stu Evans
Herb Lewis
Doug Young

1933–34
Larry Aurie
Ebbie Goodfellow
Gord Pettinger
Doug Young

1934–35
Larry Aurie
Ebbie Goodfellow
Herb Lewis
Doug Young

1935–36
Scotty Bowman
Ebbie Goodfellow
Syd Howe
Pete Kelly
Hec Kilrea
Bucko McDonald
John Sorrell
Doug Young

1936–37
Marty Barry
Ebbie Goodfellow
Pete Kelly
Hec Kilrea
Wally Kilrea
Gord Pettinger
John Sorrell

1937–38
Marty Barry
Hec Kilrea
Doug Young

1938–39
Marty Barry
Ebbie Goodfellow
Syd Howe
Hec Kilrea

1939–40
Mud Brûneteau
Syd Howe
Jimmy Orlando
Jack Stewart

1940–41
Syd Howe
Jimmy Orlando

1941–42
Syd Howe
Sid Abel
Mud Brûneteau
Jimmy Orlando

1942–43
Mud Brûneteau
Don Grosso

Syd Howe
Carl Liscombe
Alex Motter
Harry Watson

1943–44
Adam Brown
Harold Jackson
Carl Liscombe

1944–45
Murray Armstrong
Joe Carveth
Flash Hollett
Harold Jackson
Bill Quackenbush

1945–46
None

1946–47
Sid Abel
Ed Brûneteau
Roy Conacher
Billy Taylor

1947–48
Sid Abel
Jim Conacher
Gordie Howe
Red Kelly
Ted Lindsay
Jim McFadden
Jack Stewart

1948–49
Sid Abel
Pete Horeck
Marty Pavelich
Bud Poile
Bill Quackenbush
Jack Stewart

1949–50
Gerry Couture
Gordie Howe
Sid Abel
Red Kelly
Jim Peters, Sr.
Leo Reise, Jr.

1950–51
George Gee
Gordie Howe
Red Kelly
Jim McFadden

1951–52
Gordie Howe
Tony Leswick
Ted Lindsay
Glen Skov

1952–53
Alex Delvecchio
Bob Goldham
Gordie Howe
Red Kelly
Tony Leswick
Ted Lindsay
Metro Prystai
Glen Skov
Johnny Wilson
Benny Woit

1953–54
Bill Dineen
Gordie Howe
Tony Leswick
Ted Lindsay
Metro Prystai
Glen Skov
Johnny Wilson
Benny Woit

1954–55
Red Kelly
Tony Leswick
Marty Pavelich
Marcel Pronovost
Dutch Reibel
Glen Skov
Johnny Wilson

1955–56
Alex Delvecchio
Gordie Howe
Red Kelly
Marty Pavelich

1956–57
Bill Dineen
Lorne Ferguson
Gordie Howe
Red Kelly
Ted Lindsay
Marcel Pronovost
Metro Prystai
Dutch Reibel

1957–58
Alex Delvecchio
Forbes Kennedy
Johnny Wilson

1958–59
Alex Delvecchio
Charlie Burns
Gordie Howe
Johnny Wilson

1959–60
Gary Aldcorn
Alex Delvecchio
Gordie Howe
Jim Morrison
Norm Ullman

1960–61
Alex Delvecchio
Al Johnson
Parker MacDonald
Gerry Melnyk
Marcel Pronovost
Norm Ullman

1961–62
Alex Delvecchio
Val Fonteyne
Bill Gadsby
Gordie Howe
Marcel Pronovost
Norm Ullman

1962–63
Doug Barkley
Alex Delvecchio
Alex Faulkner
Bill Gadsby
Gordie Howe
Norm Ullman

1963–64
Alex Delvecchio
Andre Pronovost

1964–65
Paul Henderson
Gordie Howe
Norm Ullman

1965–66
Andy Bathgate
Alex Delvecchio
Gordie Howe
Bruce MacGregor
Norm Ullman
Bryan Watson

1966–67
Gary Bergman
Alex Delvecchio
Bruce MacGregor

1967–68
Gary Bergman
Alex Delvecchio
Gordie Howe

1968–69
Bob Baun
Gary Bergman
Gordie Howe
Frank Mahovlich
Garry Unger

1969–70
Wayne Connelly
Gordie Howe
Nick Libett
Pete Stemkowski
Garry Unger

1970–71
Nick Libett
Tom Webster

1971–72
Red Berenson
Marcel Dionne
Mickey Redmond

1972–73
Red Berenson
Bill Collins
Tim Ecclestone
Nick Libett
Ron Stackhouse

1973–74
None

1974–75
Marcel Dionne
Danny Grant
Jean Hamel
Nick Libett

1975–76
Rick Lapointe
Nick Libett
Walt McKechnie

1976–77
Al Cameron
Nick Libett
Walt McKechnie

1977–78
Terry Harper
Nick Libett
Paul Woods

1978–79
Paul Woods

1979–80
Mike Foligno
Reed Larson
Barry Long
Pete Mahovlich
Dale McCourt

1980–81
Mike Foligno
Willie Huber
Dale McCourt
John Ogrodnick

1981–82
Mike Blaisdell
Reed Larson
John Ogrodnick
Mark Osborne

1982–83
Mike Blaisdell
Reed Larson
John Ogrodnick
Mark Osborne

1983–84
Ron Duguay
Brad Park
Steve Yzerman
1984–85
Ron Duguay
Randy Ladouceur
Steve Yzerman
1985–86
None
1986–87
Brent Ashton (played 81 games in an 80-game schedule with Quebec and Detroit)
Shawn Burr
Gerard Gallant
Steve Yzerman
1987–88
None
1988–89
Steve Yzerman
1989–90
None
1990–91
Steve Yzerman
1991–92
Jimmy Carson
Sergei Fedorov
Nicklas Lidstrom
Kevin Miller
1992–93
Nicklas Lidstrom
Steve Yzerman
1993–94
Nicklas Lidstrom
1994–95
Bob Rouse
1995–96
Vyacheslov Kozlov

GOALIES WHO HAVE PLAYED EVERY GAME IN A SEASON

1922–23 (24 games)
John Ross Roach
1927–28 (44 games)
Harry Holmes
1928–29 (44 games)
Dolly Dolson
1930–31 (44 games)
Dolly Dolson
1931–32 (48 games)
Alex Connell
1932–33 (48 games)
John Ross Roach
1935–36 (48 games)
Norm Smith
1936–37 (48 games)
Norm Smith
1940–41 (48 games)
John Mowers
1942–43 (50 games)
John Mowers
1945–46 (50 games)
Harry Lumley
1947–48 (60 games)
Harry Lumley
1948–49 (60 games)
Harry Lumley
1950–51 (70 games)
Terry Sawchuk
1951–52 (70 games)
Terry Sawchuk
1955–56 (70 games)
Glenn Hall
1956–57 (70 games)
Glenn Hall
1957–58 (70 games)
Terry Sawchuk
1964–65 (70 games)
Roger Crozier

MOST COMPLETE SEASONS

Gordie Howe	17
Alex Delvecchio	12
Ebbie Goodfellow	8
Red Kelly	7
Nick Libett	7
Syd Howe	6
Norm Ullman	6
Steve Yzerman	6

Red Kelly

THE RED WINGS' IRON MAN

Alex Delvecchio played 548 consecutive games for the Red Wings, from December 13, 1956 to November 11, 1964.

ALL-TIME RED WINGS COACHING REGISTER REGULAR SEASON

SID ABEL ("Boot Nose") *b.* Melville, Saskatchewan, February 22, 1918

1957–58	33	16	12	5
1958–59	70	25	37	8
1959–60	70	26	29	15
1960–61	70	25	29	16
1961–62	70	23	33	14
1962–63	70	32	25	13
1963–64	70	30	29	11
1964–65	70	40	23	7
1965–66	70	31	27	12
1966–67	70	27	39	4
1967–68	74	27	35	12
1969–70	74	38	21	15
Totals	811	340	339	132

- assumed coaching duties January 2, 1958 for an ailing Jimmy Skinner (recurring migraines)
- stepped down as coach after '67–'68 to concentrate on GM duties
- replaced Bill Gadsby on October 16, 1969
- hired Ned Harkness on May 22, 1970 as his replacement

JACK ADAMS ("Jolly Jack")
b. Fort William, Ontario, June 14, 1895
d. Detroit, May 1, 1968

1927–28	44	19	19	6
1928–29	44	19	16	9
1929–30	44	14	24	6
1930–31	44	16	21	7
1931–32	48	18	20	10
1932–33	48	25	15	8
1933–34	48	24	14	10
1934–35	48	19	22	7
1935–36	48	24	16	8
1936–37	48	25	14	9
1937–38	48	12	25	11
1938–39	48	18	24	6
1939–40	48	16	26	6
1940–41	48	21	16	11
1941–42	48	19	25	4
1942–43	50	25	14	11
1943–44	50	26	18	6
1944–45	50	31	14	5
1945–46	50	20	20	10
1946–47	60	22	27	11
Totals	964	413	390	161

- resigned in 1947 to concentrate on GM duties

DOUG BARKLEY *b.* Lethbridge, Alberta, January 6, 1937

1970–71	40	10	23	7
1971–72	11	3	8	0
1975–76	26	7	15	4
Totals	77	20	46	11

- hired January 8, 1971
- resigned immmediately after game October 31, 1971
- hired June 29, 1975
- fired December 4, 1975

SCOTTY BOWMAN *b.* Montreal, Quebec, September 18, 1933

1993–94	84	46	30	8
1994–95	48	33	11	4
1995–96	82	62	13	7
Totals	214	141	54	19

- signed June 15, 1993
- current Red Wings coach

Scotty Bowman

BILLY DEA *b.* Edmonton, Alberta, April 3, 1933

1975–76	45	17	22	6
1976–77	44	14	25	5
1981–82	11	1	10	0
Totals	100	32	57	11

- took over December 31, 1975
- fired January 18, 1977
- rehired March 10, 1982
- fired August 4, 1982

ALEX DELVECCHIO *b.* Fort William, Ontario, December 4, 1931

1973–74	67	27	31	9
1974–75	80	23	45	12
1975–76	9	3	6	0
Totals	156	53	82	21

- took over as coach November 7, 1973
- while General Manager, took over as coach December 4, 1975 after firing Doug Barkley until December 31 when he hired Billy Dea

JACQUES DEMERS *b.* Montreal, Quebec, August 25, 1944

1986–87	80	34	36	10
1987–88	80	41	28	11
1988–89	80	34	34	12
1989–90	80	28	38	14
Totals	320	137	136	47

- hired June 13, 1986
- fired July 13, 1990

ART DUNCAN *b.* Sault Ste. Marie, 1893 *d.* Aurora, Ontario, April 13, 1975

1926–27	33	10	21	2

BILL GADSBY *b.* Calgary, Alberta, August 8, 1927

1968–69	76	33	31	12
1969–70	2	2	0	0
Totals	78	35	31	12

- hired June 3, 1968
- fired October 16, 1969

TED GARVIN *b.* Sarnia, Ontario, August 30, 1920 *d.* Sarnia, Ontario, November 17, 1992

1973–74	11	2	8	1

- hired April 24, 1973
- fired the afternoon of November 7, 1973 and replaced by Alex Delvecchio. However, as the NHL did not allow playing coaches and Delvecchio hadn't yet retired as a player, Garvin coached the game that night. With 2:55 to go in the 3rd, he left the building and Tim Ecclestone, a Wing not dressed for that game, coached the remainder of the game. Officially, the loss went on Delvecchio's record even though he neither played nor coached that night!

NED HARKNESS *b.* Ottawa, Ontario, September 19, 1921

1970–71	38	12	22	4

- hired May 22, 1970
- promoted to General Manager January 8, 1971; replaced as coach by Doug Barkley

TOMMY IVAN *b.* Toronto, Ontario, January 31, 1911

1947–48	60	30	18	12
1948–49	60	34	19	7
1949–50	70	37	19	14
1950–51	70	44	13	13
1951–52	70	44	14	12
1952–53	70	36	16	18
1953–54	70	37	19	14
Totals	470	262	118	90

- replaced Jack Adams, who stepped down to concentrate on GM duties, in October 1947
- left Detroit in July 1954 to become GM in Chicago

GORDON "DUKE" KEATS *b.* Montreal, Quebec, March 1, 1895 *d.* Victoria, British Columbia, January 16, 1972

1926–27	11	2	7	2

BOBBY KROMM *b.* Calgary, Alberta, June 8, 1928

1977–78	80	32	34	14
1978–79	80	23	41	16
1979–80	71	23	36	11
Totals	231	79	111	41

- hired June 16, 1977
- fired March 21, 1980

TED LINDSAY *b.* Renfrew, Ontario, July 29, 1925

1980–81	20	3	14	3

- hired April 1980
- fired November 24, 1980

WAYNE MAXNER *b.* Halifax, Nova Scotia, September 27, 1942

1980–81	60	16	29	15
1981–82	69	18	39	12
Totals	129	34	68	27

- hired November 24, 1980
- fired March 10, 1982

BRYAN MURRAY *b.* Shawville, Quebec, December 5, 1942

1990–91	80	34	38	8
1991–92	80	43	25	12
1992–93	84	47	28	9
Totals	244	124	91	29

- hired July 13, 1990
- fired June 15, 1993

HARRY NEALE *b.* Sarnia, Ontario, March 9, 1937

1985–86	35	8	23	4

- hired June 24, 1985
- fired December 30, 1985

BRAD PARK *b.* Toronto, Ontario, July 6, 1948

1985–86	45	9	36	2

- hired December 30, 1985
- fired June 3, 1986

NICK POLANO *b.* Sudbury, Ontario, March 25, 1941

1982–83	80	21	44	15
1983–84	80	31	42	7
1984–85	80	27	41	12
Totals	240	79	127	34

- hired August 4, 1982
- promoted June 21, 1985 to Assistant GM/Player Development

MARCEL PRONOVOST *b.* Lac la Tortue, Quebec, June 15, 1930

1979–80	9	2	7	0

- replaced Bobby Kromm on March 21, 1980
- replaced by Ted Lindsay in April 1980

JIMMY SKINNER *b.* Selkirk, Manitoba, January 12, 1917

1954–55	70	42	17	11
1955–56	70	30	24	16
1956–57	70	38	20	12
1957–58	37	13	17	7
Totals	247	123	78	46

- appointed coach July 1954 after Tommy Ivan left to become GM in Chicago
- retired January 2, 1958 due to health problems (recurring migraines)

JOHNNY WILSON *b.* Kincardine, Ontario, June 14, 1929

1971–72	67	30	27	10
1972–73	78	37	29	12
Totals	145	67	56	22

- hired October 31, 1971
- fired April 13, 1973

LARRY WILSON *b.* Kincardine, Ontario, October 23, 1930 *d.* Queensbury, New York, August 12, 1979

1976–77	36	3	29	4

- hired January 18, 1977
- fired June 16, 1977

ALL-TIME REGULAR SEASON COACHING RECORDS

MOST SEASONS

Jack Adams	20
Sid Abel	12
Tommy Ivan	7
Jacques Demers	4
Jimmy Skinner	4

MOST GAMES

Jack Adams	964
Sid Abel	811
Tommy Ivan	470
Jacques Demers	320
Jimmy Skinner	247

MOST WINS

Jack Adams	413
Sid Abel	340
Tommy Ivan	262
Scotty Bowman	141
Jacques Demers	137

MOST LOSSES

Jack Adams	390
Sid Abel	339
Jacques Demers	136
Nick Polano	127
Tommy Ivan	118
Bobby Kromm	111

BEST WIN PERCENTAGE (minimum 100 games)

Scotty Bowman	750
Tommy Ivan	653
Jimmy Skinner	589
Bryan Murray	568
Johnny Wilson	538
Jack Adams	512
Jacques Demers	502
Sid Abel	501

GUIDE TO ALL HOCKEY CLUB REFERENCES

Here is a list of the hockey teams referred to in *The Red Wings Book*. The first term listed, in quotation marks, is used consistently throughout to denote the team. The second designation, after the = sign, fully identifies the club and its league. Following the team references is an explanatory list of all the league abbreviations used in referring to the teams.

"Adirondack" = Adirondack Red Wings (AHL)
"Alberta Oilers" = WHA (precursor to Edmonton Oilers, NHL)
"Anaheim" = Mighty Ducks of Anaheim (NHL)
"Atlanta" = Atlanta Flames (NHL, defunct)
"Atlanta (IHL)" = Atlanta
"Arenas" = Toronto Arenas (NHL)
"Baltimore" = Baltimore Clippers (AHL 1963–76) Skipjacks (AHL 1983–present)
"Bisons" = Buffalo Bisons (CPHL 1929/AHL 1941–70)
"Blueshirts" = Toronto Blueshirts (NHA)
"Boston" = Boston Bruins (NHL)
"Boston Tigers" = (Can-Am League)
"Brandon Wheat Kings" = WHL
"Brooklyn Americans" = NHL (defunct)
"Buffalo (IL)" = Buffalo Bisons (IL)
"Calgary" = Calgary Flames (NHL)
"Calgary (WHL)" = Calgary Stampeders (WHL)
"California" = California Seals (NHL, defunct)
"Canadiens" = Montreal Canadiens (NHL)
"Charlotte Checkers" = EHL/SHL
"Charlottetown (MMHL)" = MMHL
"Chicago" = Chicago Blackhawks (NHL)
"Chicoutimi" = Chicoutimi Saguenéens (QMJHL)
"Cincinnati" = Cincinnati Tigers (CHL)
"Cincinnati Stingers" = WHA
"Cleveland (AHL)" = Cleveland Barons (AHL)
"Cleveland (NHL)" = Cleveland Barons (NHL, defunct)
"Cleveland Crusaders" = WHA
"Colorado Avalanche" = NHL
"Colorado Rockies" = NHL (defunct)
"Dallas (CHL)" = Dallas Black Hawks
"Dallas Stars" = NHL
"Dentals" = University of Toronto Dentals (OHA)
"Denver (WHL)" = Denver Spurs
"Denver Grizzlies" = IHL
"Denver Rangers (IHL)" = IHL
"Detroit" = Detroit Red Wings (NHL)
"Detroit Cougars" = NHL (defunct)
"Detroit Falcons" (NHL, defunct)
"Detroit Olympics" = CPHL/IL
"Edmonton" = Edmonton Oilers (NHL)
"Edmonton (WHL)" = WHL
"Flin Flon (WHL)" = Flin Flon Bombers (WHL)
"Flint" = IHL
"Florida" = Florida Panthers (NHL)
"Flyers" = Philadelphia Flyers (NHL)
"Fort William Juniors"
"Fort Worth"
"Guelph Biltmores" = OHA
"Hamilton Tigers (OHA)" = OHA
"Hamilton Tigers (NHL)" = NHL (defunct)
"Hampton" = Hampton Gulls (SHL)
"Hartford" = Hartford Whalers (NHL)
"Hershey" = Hershey Bears (AHL)
"Hornets" = Pittsburgh Hornets (AHL)
"Hollywood Wolves" = PCHL
"Houston" = Houston (IHL)
"Houston Aeros" = WHA
"Islanders" = New York Islanders (NHL)
"Kansas City (CHL)" = Kansas City Red Wings (CHL)
"Kingston" = Kingston Canadians (OHL)
"Kitchener" = Kitchener Rangers (OHA/OHL)
"London Knights" = OHL/OHA
"London Lions" = English League
"London Panthers" = Can Pro League
"London Tecumsehs" = CPHL
"Los Angeles Kings" = NHL
"Los Angeles Monarchs" = PCHL
"Marlies" = Toronto Marlies (OHL/OHA)
"Melville Millionaires" = (Saskatchewan Junior League)
"Milwaukee (IHL)" = Milwaukee Admirals (IHL)
"Minnesota" = Minnesota North Stars (NHL, defunct)
"Minnesota Fighting Saints (WHA)" = WHA
"Maroons" = Montreal Maroons (NHL, defunct)
"Moncton" = Moncton Hawks (AHL)
"Muskegon" = Muskegon Lumberjacks (IHL)

"Niagara Falls Flyers" = OHA/OHL
"New Brunswick" = New Brunswick Hawks (AHL)
"New England Whalers" = WHA
"New Haven" = New Haven Eagles (AHL)
"New Jersey" = New Jersey Devils (NHL)
"New Westminster" = New Westminster Bruins (WJHL)
"New York Americans" = NHL (defunct)
"Newmarket" = Newmarket Saints (AHL)
"North Bay" = North Bay Centennials (OHL)
"Oakland" = Oakland Seals (NHL, defunct)
"Oklahoma" = Oklahoma City Blazers (CHL)
"Orillia Terriers" = OHA Sr. A team
"Oshawa (OHA)" = Oshawa Generals (OHA)
"Ottawa Senators" = NHL (current and defunct)
"Ottawa (QHL)" = Ottawa Senators (QHL)
"Penguins" = Pittsburgh Penguins (NHL)
"Peterborough" = Peterborough Petes (OHA/OHL)
"Phoenix (NHL)" = Phoenix Coyotes (NHL)
"Phoenix" = Phoenix Roadrunners (WHL/CHL/PHL)
"Pirates" = Pittsburgh Pirates (NHL, defunct)
"Port Arthur" = OHA
"Portland" = Portland Winter Hawks (WJHL)
"Providence" = Providence Reds (AHL)
"Quebec (AHL)" = Quebec Aces (AHL)
"Quebec Aces" = QHL
"Quebec Bulldogs" = NHL (defunct)
"Quebec" = NHL (defunct)
"Rangers" = New York Rangers (NHL)
"Rochester" = Rochester Americans (AHL)
"Sabres" = Buffalo Sabres (NHL)
"Saginaw" = Saginaw Gears (IHL)
"St. Catharines" = St. Catharines Saints (AHL)
"St. John (MMHL)" = MMHL
"St. John's" = St. John's Maple Leafs (AHL)
"St. Louis" = St. Louis Blues (NHL)
"St. Pats" = Toronto St. Patricks (now the Maple Leafs)
"Salt Lake" = Salt Lake Golden Eagles (WHL)
"San Francisco" = San Francisco Seals (WHL)
"San Jose" = San Jose Sharks (NHL)
"Sarnia" = Sarnia Sailors (OHA Senior A)
"St. Louis Eagles" = NHL (defunct)
"St. Mike's" = St. Mike's Jr. A, Toronto
"Saskatoon" = Saskatoon Sheiks (WCHL)
"Saskatoon (WCHL)" = Saskatoon Crescents (WCHL)
"Saskatoon (WJHL)" = Saskatoon Blades (WJHL)
"Sault Ste. Marie" = Sault Ste. Marie Greyhounds (OHA/OHL)
"Sault Ste. Marie (EPHL)" = Sault Ste. Marie Thunderbirds (EPHL)
"Seattle (PCHA)" = Seattle Metropolitans (PCHA)
"Shawinigan" = Shawinigan Cataracts (QHL/QMJHL)
"Spokane" = (WHL)
"Springfield" = Springfield Indians (AHL)
"Stratford Nationals" = Can Pro League
"Sudbury Frood Mines"
"Sudbury Tigers"
"Sudbury Wolves" = OHL
"Syracuse" = Syracuse Stars (IL/AHL)
"Tampa Bay" = Tampa Bay Lightning (NHL)
"Toronto Goodyears" = OHA
"Toronto Granites" = Senior OHA
"Toronto Millionaires" = Can Pro League
"Toronto Ravinas"
"Toronto Shamrocks"
"Toronto Toros" = WHA
"Tulsa" = Tulsa Oilers (AHA/USHL/CHL)
"Vancouver Blazers" = WHA
"Vancouver Canucks" = NHL
"Vancouver Millionaires" = PCHA
"Vancouver (WHL)" = Vancouver Canucks (WHL)
"Victoria (WHL)" = Victoria Cougars (WHL)
"Victoria Cougars" = PCHA
"Wanderers" = Montreal Wanderers (NHL, defunct)
"Washington" = Washington Capitals (NHL)
"Windsor Bulldogs" = CPHL
"Windsor Hornets"
"Windsor Spitfires" = OHA
"Winnipeg Jets" = (NHL, defunct)
"Winnipeg Monarchs" = WJHL
"Winnipeg Warriors" = WHL

REFERENCES TO HOCKEY LEAGUES

AHA = American Hockey Association
AHL = American Hockey League
BIHA = British Ice Hockey Association
CCHA = Central Collegiate Hockey Association
CHL = Central Hockey League
CIAU = Canadian Intercollegiate Athletic Union
CPHL = Canadian Professional Hockey League
ECAC = Eastern Collegiate Athletic Conference
EHL = Eastern Hockey League
GLHL = Great Lakes Hockey League
HE = Hockey East
IHL = International Hockey League
IL = International League
MJHL = Montreal Junior Hockey League
MMHL = Maritime Major Hockey League
NHA = National Hockey Association
NHL = National Hockey League
OHA = Ontario Hockey Association
OHL = Ontario Hockey League
PCHA = Pacific Coast Hockey Association
PCHL = Pacific Coast Hockey League
QHL = Quebec Hockey League
QMJHL = Quebec Major Junior Hockey League
SHL = Southern Hockey League
THL = Toronto Hockey League
USHL = United States Hockey League
WCHA = Western Collegiate Hockey Association
WCHL = Western Canada Hockey League
WHA = World Hockey Association
WHL = Western Hockey League
WJHL = Western Junior Hockey League

ALL-TIME RED WINGS PLAYER REGISTER

- Place of birth assumed to be Michigan unless otherwise noted.
- An "R" after the year indicates the player was a rookie and played his first NHL game in a Red Wings uniform; all rookies' first game dates are also listed.
- An "L" after the year indicates the player's last year in the NHL; all last career game dates are also listed.
- All current players include a photograph above his Red Wings statistics.
- Those players whose name appears in a box played their entire NHL careers with the Red Wings.
- Information on goalies is listed in the following order: games played/won-lost-tied record/minutes played/goals against/shutouts/goals against average.

GERRY ABEL #11 LEFT WING 6′2″ 168
b. Detroit, December 25, 1944

1966–67R/L	1	0	0	0	0

- signed August 1965
- first and only Red Wings game March 8, 1967

SID ABEL ("Boot"/"Boot Nose") #4 – 7 – 9 – 11 – 12 – 14 – 19 – 20 CENTRE 5′11″ 190
b. Melville, Saskatchewan, February 22, 1918

1938–39R	15	1	1	2	0
1939–40	24	1	5	6	4
1940–41	47	11	22	33	29
1941–42	48	18	31	49	45
1942–43	49	18	24	42	33
1945–46	7	0	2	2	0
1946–47	60	19	29	48	29
1947–48	60	14	30	44	69
1948–49	60	28	26	54	49
1949–50	70	34	35	69	46
1950–51	69	23	38	61	30
1951–52	62	17	36	53	32
Totals	571	184	279	463	366

- signed October 21, 1938
- first Red Wings game November 15, 1938
- played most of '38–'39 with Pittsburgh Hornets
- played much of '39–'40 with Indianapolis Capitals

- missed 1943–45 — Royal Canadian Air Force
- sold July 29, 1952 to Chicago to become Black Hawks coach

GENE ACHTYMICHUK ("Acky") #12 CENTRE 5′11″ 170 *b.* Lamont, Alberta, September 7, 1932

1958–59L	12	0	0	0	0

- claimed June 3, 1958 from Montreal at Intra-League Draft
- first and only Red Wings games December 10/13/14/25/28/31, January 3/4/7/10/15/17, 1958–59
- played in minors '59–'66

GREG ADAMS #20 LEFT WING 6′1″ 190 *b.* Duncan, British Columbia, May 31, 1960

1989–90L	28	3	7	10	16

- acquired December 4, 1989 with Robert Picard from Quebec for Tony McKegney
- last Red Wings game February 25, 1990
- retired after '89–'90

MICAH AIVAZOFF #27 CENTRE 6′ 195 *b.* Powell River, British Columbia, May 4, 1969

1993–94R	59	4	4	8	38

- signed as a free agent March 18, 1993
- first Red Wings game October 8, 1993
- claimed January 18, 1995 by Penguins in Waiver Draft

GARY ALDCORN #11 FORWARD 5′11″ 180 *b.* Shaunavon, Saskatchewan, March 7, 1935

1959–60	70	22	29	51	32
1960–61	49	2	6	8	16
Totals	119	24	35	59	48

- claimed June 10, 1959 from Toronto at Intra-League Draft
- traded January 1961 with Murray Oliver and Tom McCarthy to Boston for Vic Stasiuk and Leo Labine

COURTNEY "KEITH" ALLEN ("Bingo") #18 – 19 DEFENCE 5′11″ 190 *b.* Meota, Saskatchewan, August 21, 1923

1953–54R	10	0	4	4	2
1954–55L	18	0	0	0	6
Totals	28	0	4	4	8

- contract acquired from Syracuse in February 1954
- first Red Wings games March 4/6/7/11/13/14/16/18/20/21, 1954
- played most of '53–'54 with Sherbrooke Saints (QHL) and Syracuse Warriors (AHL)
- played most of '54–'55 with Edmonton Flyers (WHL)
- last Red Wings game December 25, 1955
- played '55–'56 with Brandon Regals (WHL) and '56–'57 with Seattle Americans (WHL)

RALPH "RED" ALMAS #17 – 1 GOALIE 5′9″ 160 *b.* Saskatoon, Saskatchewan, April 26, 1924

1946–47R	1	0–1–0	60	5	0	5.00
1952–53L	1	0–0–1	60	3	0	3.00
Totals	2	0–1–1	120	8	0	4.00

- turned pro with Indianapolis for '46–'47
- played March 23, 1947
- traded September 9, 1948 with Lloyd Doran, Tony Licari, Barry Sullivan, and Thain Simon to St. Louis Flyers for Joe Lund and Hec Highton
- acquired September 23, 1952 from Chicago with Steve Hrymnak and Greg Fielder for cash
- played December 25, 1952 when Sawchuk injured
- played '53–'54 with Bisons and Victoria, '54–'55 with Calgary (WHL), before retiring

DAVE AMADIO #19 DEFENCE 6′1″ 205 *b.* Glace Bay, Nova Scotia, April 23, 1939 *d.* Unknown

1957–58R	2	0	0	0	2

- contract sold to Springfield in 1961
- first and only Red Wings games February 15 & 16, 1958

DALE ANDERSON #18 DEFENCE 6′3″ 190 *b.* Regina, Saskatchewan, March 5, 1932

1956–57R/L	13	0	0	0	6

- first and only Red Wings games January 26/27/31, February 2 & 14, March 2/9/10/12/14/21/23/24, 1957

EARL ANDERSON #16 RIGHT WING 6′ 185
b. Roseau, Minnesota, February 24, 1951

1974–75R	45	7	3	10	12

- selected 58th overall at 1971 Entry Draft
- first Red Wings game October 9, 1974
- traded February 18, 1975 with Hank Nowak to Boston for Walt McKechnie and a 3rd-round draft choice in 1975 (Clark Hamilton)

RON ANDERSON ("Goings") #15 – 22
RIGHT WING 6′ 180 *b.* Red Deer, Alberta, July 29, 1945

1967–68R	18	2	0	2	13
1968–69	7	0	0	0	8
Totals	25	2	0	2	21

- first Red Wings game November 29, 1967
- played '65–'67 with Memphis; part of '67–'68 with Fort Worth
- played October 11/13/17/20/27/31, November 7, 1968
- traded November 12, 1968 to Los Angeles for Paul Popiel

TOM ANDERSON ("Cowboy") #9
LEFT WING 5′10″ 180 *b.* Edinburgh, Scotland, July 9, 1911 *d.* Unknown

1934–35R	27	5	2	7	16

- played '33–'34 with Detroit Olympics (IL)
- first Red Wings game November 11, 1934
- sold to Americans summer 1935

ALGER "AL" ARBOUR ("Radar") #2 – 5 – 18
DEFENCE 6′1″ 180
b. Sudbury, Ontario, November 1, 1932

1953–54R	36	0	1	1	18
1956–57	44	1	6	7	38
1957–58	69	1	6	7	104
Totals	149	2	13	15	160

- first Red Wings game October 8, 1953
- played parts of '52–'53 and '54–'57 with Edmonton, '53–'54 with Sherbrooke, '54–'55 with Quebec
- claimed June 1958 by Chicago at Intra-League Draft

JOHN ARBOUR ("Jack") #15 FORWARD
b. Wabushene, Ontario, March 7, 1899
d. Unknown

1926–27R	37	4	1	5	45

- first Cougars game November 27, 1926
- traded April 8, 1928 with $12,500 to Toronto for Sailor Herberts

MURRAY ARMSTRONG #3 CENTRE
5′10″ 170 *b.* Manor, Saskatchewan, January 1, 1916

1943–44	28	12	22	34	4
1944–45	50	15	24	39	31
1945–46L	40	8	18	26	4
Totals	118	35	64	99	39

- signed in 1943 with Detroit after being discharged from the Canadian Armed Forces
- last Red Wings game March 16, 1946
- played '46–'47 with Regina Pats; retired to coach the team

BRENT ASHTON #14 – 33 LEFT WING
6′1″ 210 *b.* Saskatoon, Saskatchewan, May 18, 1960

1986–87	81	40	35	75	39
1987–88	73	26	27	53	50
Totals	154	66	62	128	89

- aquired January 17, 1987 from Quebec with Gilbert Delorme and Mark Kumpel for John Ogrodnick, Basil McRae, and Doug Shedden
- traded June 13, 1988 to Winnipeg for Paul MacLean

OSCAR "OSSIE" ASMUNDSON #9
CENTRE 5′11″ 170 *b.* Red Deer, Alberta, November 17, 1908

1934–35	3	0	0	0	0

- played January 26/27/31, 1935
- sold February 6, 1935 to St. Louis

LARRY AURIE

PIERRE AUBRY #24 – 27 LEFT WING
5′10″ 175 *b.* Cap-de-la-Madeleine, Quebec, April 15, 1960

1983–84	14	4	1	5	8
1984–85L	25	2	2	4	33
Totals	39	6	3	9	41

- rights acquired February 29, 1984 from Quebec
- played most of '84–'87 with Adirondack
- last Red Wings game January 5, 1985

LARRY AURIE ("Little Dempsey"/"The Little Rag Man") #6 – 12 RIGHT WING 5′6″ 148
b. Sudbury, Ontario, February 8, 1905
d. Detroit, December 12, 1952

1927–28R	44	13	3	16	43
1928–29	35	1	1	2	26
1929–30	43	14	5	19	28
1930–31	41	12	6	18	23
1931–32	48	12	8	20	18
1932–33	45	12	11	23	25
1933–34	48	16	19	35	36
1934–35	48	17	29	46	24
1935–36	44	16	18	34	17
1936–37	45	23	20	43	20
1937–38	47	10	9	19	19
1938–39L	1	1	0	1	0
Totals	489	147	129	276	279

- played for Sudbury Juniors, then London (CanPro League) in '26–'27
- first Cougars game November 15, 1927
- retired after '37–'38, but when Coach Adams needed help, Aurie played January 10, 1939, scoring a goal!

PETE BABANDO #14 LEFT WING
5′9″ 187 *b.* Braeburn, Pennsylvania, May 10, 1925

1949–50	56	6	6	12	25

- acquired August 16, 1949 with Clare Martin, Lloyd Durham, and Jim Peters from Boston for Pete Horeck and Bill Quackenbush
- traded July 13, 1950 with Harry Lumley, Jack Stewart, and Don Morrison to Chicago for Jim Henry, Bob Goldham, Gaye Stewart, and Metro Prystai

GARNET "ACE" BAILEY #12 LEFT WING
5′11″ 192 *b.* Lloydminster, Saskatchewan, June 13, 1948

1972–73	13	2	11	13	16
1973–74	45	9	14	23	33
Totals	58	11	25	36	49

- acquired March 1, 1973 with future considerations (Murray Wing — June 4, 1973) from Boston for Gary Doak
- traded February 14, 1974 with Ted Harris and Bill Collins to St. Louis for Bryan Watson, Chris Evans, and Jean Hamel

BOB BAILEY #20 – 21 RIGHT WING 6′ 197
b. Kenora, Ontario, May 29, 1931

1957–58L	36	6	6	12	41

- bought September 22, 1956 from Toronto
- claimed June 5, 1957 by Chicago at Intra-League Draft
- acquired December 17, 1957 with Nick Mickoski, Jack McIntyre, and Hec Lalande from Chicago for Earl Reibel, Billy Reay, Lorne Ferguson, and Bill Dineen
- last Red Wings game March 23, 1958
- played '58–'59 with Cleveland

DOUG BALDWIN #18 DEFENCE 6′0 175
b. Winnipeg, Manitoba, November 2, 1922

1946–47	4	0	0	0	0

- acquired in 1946 with Ray Powell from Toronto for Gerry Brown
- played October 16/19/20/23, 1946

DOUG BARKLEY #5 DEFENCE 6′2″ 185
b. Lethbridge, Alberta, January 6, 1937

1962–63	70	3	24	27	78
1963–64	67	11	21	32	115

1964–65	67	5	20	25	122
1965–66L	43	5	15	20	65
Totals	247	24	80	104	380

- acquired June 5, 1962 from Chicago for Len Lunde and John McKenzie
- career ended January 30, 1966 when Doug Mohns' stick caught him in the eye

DAVE BARR #22 RIGHT WING 6′1″
b. Toronto, Ontario, November 30, 1960

1986–87	37	13	13	26	49
1987–88	51	14	26	40	58
1988–89	73	27	32	59	69
1989–90	62	10	25	35	45
1990–91	70	18	22	40	55
Totals	293	82	118	200	276

- acquired January 12, 1987 from Hartford for Randy Ladouceur
- lost September 9, 1991 with Randy McKay to New Jersey as equal compensation for Detroit's signing of Troy Crowder

JOHN BARRETT #2 – 3 DEFENCE 6′1″ 210
b. Ottawa, Ontario, July 1, 1958

1980–81R	56	3	10	13	60
1981–82	69	1	12	13	93
1982–83	79	4	10	14	74
1983–84	78	2	8	10	78
1984–85	71	6	19	25	117
1985–86	65	2	12	14	125
Totals	418	18	71	89	547

- selected 129th overall at 1978 Entry Draft
- first Red Wings game November 29, 1980
- traded March 10, 1986 with Greg Smith to Washington for Darren Veitch

MARTY BARRY #7 CENTRE 5′11″ 175
b. St. Gabriel, Quebec, December 8, 1904
d. Halifax, Nova Scotia, August 20, 1969

1936–37	48	17	27	44	6
1937–38	48	9	20	29	34
1938–39	48	13	28	41	4
Totals	144	39	75	114	44

- acquired in 1936 from Boston for Cooney Weiland
- sold to Canadiens after '38–'39

HENRY "HANK" BASSEN ("Red") #1 – 25 – 30
GOALIE 5′10″ 170 *b.* Calgary, Alberta, December 6, 1932

1960–61	35	13–13–8	2120	102	0	2.89
1961–62	27	9–12–6	1620	76	3	2.81
1962–63	17	6–5–5	980	53	0	3.24
1963–64	1	0–1–0	60	4	0	4.00
1965–66	11	3–4–0	406	17	0	2.51
1966–67	8	2–4–0	384	22	1	3.44
Totals	99	33–39–19	5570	274	4	2.95

- acquired July 1957 with Forbes Kennedy, Johnny Wilson, and William Preston from Chicago for Ted Lindsay and Glenn Hall
- played '57–'58 with Seattle; '58–'59 with Springfield; '59–'60 with Vancouver
- played part of '61–'62 with Sudbury and Edmonton, part of '62–'64 and all of '64–'65 with Pittsburgh, part of '63–'64 with Cincinnati
- played December 1, 1963
- played October 23, November 19/20/26, December 1/3, January 14, 1966–67
- traded September 7, 1967 to Penguins for Roy Edwards

FRANK BATHE #24 DEFENCE 6′1″ 190
b. Oshawa, Ontario, September 27, 1954

1974–75R	19	0	3	3	31
1975–76	7	0	1	1	9
Totals	26	0	4	4	40

- first Red Wings game February 8, 1975
- played part of '74–'75 with Virginia, '75–'76 with New Haven, Kalamazoo, and Port Huron
- played October 8/9/11/16/18/19/22, 1975
- signed October 6, 1977 by Flyers as a free agent

ANDY BATHGATE ("Handy Andy") #21
RIGHT WING 6′ 180
b. Winnipeg, Manitoba, August 28, 1932

1965–66	70	15	32	47	25
1966–67	60	8	23	31	24
Totals	130	23	55	78	49

- acquired May 20, 1965 with Billy Harris and Gary Jarrett from Toronto for Marcel Pronovost, Ed Joyal, Larry Jeffrey, Lowell MacDonald, and Aut Erickson
- lost June 6, 1967 to Penguins in Expansion Draft

BOB BAUN #4 DEFENCE 5′9″ 182 *b.* Lanigan, Saskatchewan, September 9, 1936

1968–69	76	4	16	20	121
1969–70	71	1	18	19	112
1970–71	11	0	3	3	24
Totals	158	5	37	42	257

- acquired May 27, 1968 with Ron Harris from Oakland for Gary Jarrett, Doug Roberts, Howie Young, and Chris Worthy
- lost on waivers November 3, 1970 to Sabres

SERGEI BAUTIN #29 DEFENCE 6′3″ 200 *b.* Rogachev, USSR, March 11, 1967

1993–94	1	0	0	0	0

- acquired March 8, 1994 with Bob Essensa from Winnipeg for Tim Cheveldae and Dallas Drake
- played April 14, 1994
- played part of '93–'95 with Adirondack

JOHN "RED" BEATTIE #11 LEFT WING 5′9″ 170 *b.* Ibstock, England, October 7, 1907

1937–38	11	1	2	3	0

- acquired December 19, 1937 from Boston for Gord Pettinger
- traded January 24, 1938 to Americans for Joe Lamb

DICK BEHLING #2 – 5 – 16 DEFENCE *b.* Kitchener, Ontario, March 16, 1916

1940–41R	3	0	0	0	0
1942–43L	2	1	0	1	2
Totals	5	1	0	1	2

- first Red Wings games January 24/26/30, 1941
- last Red Wings games December 6 & 17, 1942
- joined United States Army — never played in the NHL again

PETE BELLEFEUILLE ("The Fleeting Frenchman"/"French Pete") #3 – 12 – 15 RIGHT WING 5′8″ 155 *b.* 1901 *d.* Unknown

1926–27	18	6	0	6	14
1928–29	1	1	0	1	0
1929–30L	24	5	2	7	10
Totals	43	12	2	14	24

- acquired January 10, 1927 from Toronto for Slim Halderson
- played December 20, 1928
- last Cougars game January 26, 1930

FRANK BENNETT #15 FORWARD *b.* Toronto, Ontario, March 4, 1923

1943–44R/L	7	0	1	1	2

- first and only Red Wings games October 31, November 4/7/11/13/14/18, 1943

GORDON "RED" BERENSON ("The Red Baron") #7 CENTRE 6′ 195 *b.* Regina, Saskatchewan, December 8, 1939

1970–71	24	5	12	17	4
1971–72	78	28	41	69	16
1972–73	78	13	30	43	8
1973–74	76	24	42	66	28
1974–75	27	3	3	6	8
Totals	283	73	128	201	64

- acquired February 6, 1971 with Tim Ecclestone from St. Louis for Garry Unger and Wayne Connelly
- traded December 30, 1974 to St. Louis for Phil Roberto and a 3rd-round draft choice in 1975 (Blair Davidson)

MICHEL BERGERON #16 RIGHT WING 5′10″ 170 *b.* Chicoutimi, Quebec, November 11, 1954

1974–75R	25	10	7	17	10
1975–76	72	32	27	59	48
1976–77	74	21	12	33	98
1977–78	3	1	0	1	0
Totals	174	64	46	110	156

- selected 63rd overall at 1974 Entry Draft
- first Red Wings game February 8, 1975
- played October 13/15/18, 1977
- traded October 20, 1977 to the Islanders for Andre St. Laurent

MARC BERGEVIN #27 DEFENCE 6′ 197 *b.* Montreal, Quebec, August 11, 1965

1995–96	70	1	9	10	33

- acquired August 17, 1995 with Ben Hankinson from Tampa Bay for Shawn Burr and a 3rd-round draft choice in 1996 (Jason Doyle)
- currently with Red Wings

GARY BERGMAN #2 – 3 – 18 – 23 DEFENCE 5′11″ 185 *b.* Kenora, Ontario, October 7, 1938

1964–65R	58	4	7	11	85
1965–66	61	3	16	19	96
1966–67	70	5	30	35	129
1967–68	74	13	28	41	109
1968–69	76	7	30	37	80
1969–70	69	6	17	23	122
1970–71	68	8	25	33	149
1971–72	68	8	25	33	149
1972–73	68	3	28	31	71
1973–74	11	0	6	6	18
1974–75	76	5	25	30	104
Totals	699	62	237	299	1112

- claimed June 19, 1964 from Canadiens at Intra-League Draft
- first Red Wings game October 15, 1964
- traded November 6, 1973 to Minnesota for Ted Harris
- acquired October 1, 1974 from Minnesota for a 3rd-round draft choice in 1975 (Alex Pirus)
- traded August 22, 1975 with Bill McKenzie to Kansas City for Pete McDuffe and Glen Burdon

THOMMIE BERGMAN #4 DEFENCE 6′2″ 200 *b.* Munkfors, Sweden, December 10, 1947

1972–73R	75	9	12	21	70
1973–74	43	0	3	3	21
1974–75	18	0	1	1	27
1977–78	14	1	6	7	16
1978–79	68	10	17	27	64
1979–80	28	1	5	6	45
Totals	246	21	44	65	243

- signed from Vastra Frolunda team in Sweden after 1972 Olympics
- first Red Wings game October 7, 1972
- played part of '73–'74 with Virginia
- signed as a free agent March 16, 1978 from Winnipeg (WHA)
- played part of '79–'80 with Adirondack
- retired August 20, 1980 to coach in Sweden

FRED BERRY #29 CENTRE 5′9″ 175 *b.* Stoney Plains, Alberta March 26, 1956

1976–77R/L	3	0	0	0	0

- selected 40th overall at 1970 Entry Draft
- first and only Red Wings games January 4 & 6, March 1, 1977
- played with Kalamazoo, Kansas City, and Toledo '76–'79

PHIL BESLER #15 RIGHT WING *b.* Melville, Saskatchewan, December 9, 1913

1938–39L	5	0	1	1	2

- only Red Wings games January 28/29, February 5/9/12, 1939

PETE BESSONE #5 – 17 DEFENCE 5′10″ 200 *b.* New Bedford, Massachusetts, January 13, 1913

1937–38R/L	6	0	1	1	6

- signed January 14, 1938
- only Red Wings games January 15/16/20/23/27/29, 1938
- sold outright to Pittsburgh (AHL) on October 6, 1939

ALLAN BESTER #35 GOALIE 5′7″ 150 *b.* Hamilton, Ontario, March 26, 1964

1990–91	3	0–3–0	178	13	0	4.38
1991–92	1	0–0–0	31	2	0	3.87
Totals	4	0–3–0	209	15	0	4.31

- acquired March 5, 1991 from Toronto for a 6th-round draft choice in 1991 (Alexander Kuzminsky)
- played March 9/14/23, 1991
- played October 5, 1991
- lost September 9, 1993 as a free agent to Anaheim

BILL BEVERIDGE #1 GOALIE 5′8″ 170 *b.* Ottawa, Ontario, July 1, 1909 *d.* Ottawa, February 13, 1995

1929–30	39	14–20–5	2410	109	2	2.79

THOMAS "TIM" BISSETT #7 CENTRE 6′ 180
b. Seattle, Washington, March 13, 1966

1990–91R/L	5	0	0	0	0

- selected 211th overall at 1986 Entry Draft
- played most of '90–'91 with Adirondack
- first and only Red Wings games November 14/17/19, January 4 & 5, 1990–91
- played '91–'92 with Brynas (Sweden)

STEVE BLACK #19 LEFT WING 6′ 185
b. Fort William, Ontario, March 31, 1927

1949–50R	69	7	14	21	53
1950–51	5	0	0	0	2
Totals	74	7	14	21	55

- played '47–'49 with St. Louis (AHL)
- first Red Wings game October 12, 1949
- acquired September 1949 with Bill Brennan from St. Louis Flyers for Fern Gauthier, Cliff Simpson, Ed Nicholson, and future considerations
- traded December 10, 1950 with Lee Fogolin to Chicago for Bert Olmstead and Vic Stasiuk

TOM BLADON ("Bomber") #4
DEFENCE 6′1″ 195
b. Edmonton, Alberta, December 29, 1952

1980–81L	2	0	0	0	2

- signed as a free agent January 14, 1981
- played most of '80–'81 with Adirondack
- only Red Wings games March 4 & 8, 1981
- retired after '80–'81

MIKE BLAISDELL ("Blazer") #14 – 21
RIGHT WING 6′1″ 195 *b.* Moose Jaw, Saskatchewan, January 18, 1960

1980–81R	32	3	6	9	10
1981–82	80	23	32	55	48
1982–83	80	18	23	41	22
Totals	192	44	61	105	80

- selected 11th overall at 1980 Entry Draft
- first Red Wings game October 10, 1980
- played part of '80–'81 with Adirondack
- traded June 13, 1983 with Willie Huber and Mark Osborne to Rangers for Ron Duguay, Ed Mio, and Ed Johnstone

MIKE BLOOM #25 LEFT WING 6′3″ 205
b. Ottawa, Ontario, April 12, 1952

1974–75	13	4	8	12	10
1975–76	76	13	17	30	99
1976–77L	45	6	3	9	22
Totals	134	23	28	51	131

- acquired March 9, 1975 from Washington for Blair Stewart
- played part of '76–'77 with Rhode Island, '76–'78 with Kansas City
- last Red Wings game March 5, 1977

JOHN BLUM #33 DEFENCE 6′3″ 205
b. Detroit, October 8, 1959

1988–89L	6	0	0	0	8

- signed as a free agent August 12, 1988
- only Red Wings games December 30/31, January 7/9/14, February 3, 1988–89
- lost July 6, 1989 as a free agent to Boston

MARC BOILEAU #19 CENTRE 5′11″ 170
b. Pointe Claire, Quebec, September 3, 1932

1961–62R/L	54	5	6	11	8

- recalled from Hershey in November 1961
- first Red Wings game November 15, 1961
- last Red Wings game March 25, 1962

GILLES BOISVERT #1 GOALIE 5′8″ 152
b. Trois-Rivières, Quebec, February 15, 1933

1959–60R/L	3	0–3–0	180	9	0	3.00

- acquired June 3, 1955 from Boston with Ed Sandford, Real Chevrefils, Norm Corcoran, and Warren Godfrey for Marcel Bonin, Terry Sawchuk, Vic Stasiuk, and Lorne Davis
- played November 26/28/29, 1959
- career minor-leaguer; sold to Baltimore in August 1963

LEO BOIVIN #4 – 24 DEFENCE 5′7″ 190
b. Prescott, Ontario, August 2, 1932

1965–66	16	0	5	5	16
1966–67	69	4	17	21	55
Totals	85	4	22	26	71

- acquired February 18, 1966 with Dean Prentice from Boston for Gary Doak, Bill Lesuk, and Steve Atkinson
- claimed June 6, 1967 by Penguins in Expansion Draft

IVAN BOLDIREV ("Ike") #12 – 19 CENTRE 6′ 190 *b.* Zranjanin, Yugoslavia, August 15, 1949

1982–83	33	13	17	30	14
1983–84	75	35	48	83	20
1984–85L	75	19	30	49	16
Totals	183	67	95	162	50

- acquired January 17, 1983 from Vancouver Canucks for Mark Kirton
- last Red Wings game April 7, 1985
- contract bought out October 15, 1985; Boldirev retired

DAN BOLDUC #19 LEFT WING 5′9″ 180 *b.* Waterville, Maine, April 6, 1953

1978–79	56	16	13	29	14
1979–80L	44	6	5	11	19
Totals	100	22	18	40	33

- signed as a free agent August 24, 1978
- played much of '79–'82 with Adirondack
- last Red Wings game March 2, 1980
- lost September 1, 1982 as a free agent to Calgary

MARCEL BONIN #17 – 20 LEFT WING 5′9″ 175 *b.* Montreal, Quebec, September 12, 1932

1952–53R	37	4	9	13	14
1953–54	1	0	0	0	0
1954–55	69	16	20	36	53
Totals	107	20	29	49	67

- first Red Wings game December 27, 1952
- played October 10, 1953
- played part of '52–'53 with St. Louis, '53–'54 with Sherbrooke and Edmonton (WHL)
- traded June 3, 1955 to Boston with Terry Sawchuk, Vic Stasiuk, and Lorne Davis for Gilles Boisvert, Ed Sandford, Red Chevrefils, Norm Concoran, and Warren Godfrey

HENRY BOUCHA ("Chief") #12 – 16 CENTRE 6′ 185 *b.* Warroad, Minnesota, June 1, 1951

1971–72R	16	1	0	1	2
1972–73	73	14	14	28	82
1973–74	70	19	12	31	32
Totals	159	34	26	60	116

- selected 16th overall at 1971 Entry Draft
- first Red Wings game February 22, 1972
- played part of '72–'73 with Tidewater
- traded August 27, 1974 to Minnesota for Danny Grant

CLAUDE BOURQUE #1 GOALIE 5′6″ 140 *b.* Oxford, Nova Scotia, March 31, 1915

1939–40L	1	0–1–0	60	3	0	3.00

- loaned for one game from Canadiens
- only Red Wings game February 15, 1940

RALPH "SCOTTY" BOWMAN #3 – 11 – 16 DEFENCE 5′11″ 190 *b.* Winnipeg, Manitoba, June 20, 1911 *d.* Unknown

1934–35	13	1	3	4	21
1935–36	48	3	2	5	44
1936–37	37	0	1	1	24
1937–38	45	0	2	2	26
1938–39	43	2	3	5	26
1939–40L	11	0	2	2	4
Totals	197	6	13	19	145

- bought February 11, 1935 from St. Louis with Syd Howe for Ted Graham and $50,000
- last Red Wings games November 2/5/12/14/18/19/23/25/26/28, December 3, 1939
- released November 13, 1940

RICK BOWNESS #11 RIGHT WING 6′1″ 185 *b.* Moncton, New Brunswick, January 25, 1955

1977–78	61	8	11	19	76

- bought August 18, 1977 from Atlanta
- sold October 10, 1978 to St. Louis

IRWIN BOYD ("Yank") #16 RIGHT WING 5′10″ 152 *b.* Ardmore, Pennsylvania, November 13, 1908

1934–35	42	2	3	5	14

JOHN BRENNEMAN #21 LEFT WING 5′10″ 175 *b.* Fort Erie, Ontario, January 5, 1943

1967–68	9	0	2	2	0

- acquired October 19, 1967 from St. Louis for Craig Cameron, Larry Hornung, and Don Giesebrecht
- played October 14/15/18/19/22/26/28/29, November 4, 1967
- traded January 9, 1968 with Ted Hampson and Bert Marshall to Oakland for Kent Douglas

CARL BREWER #5 DEFENCE 5′10″ 180 *b.* Toronto, Ontario, October 21, 1938

1969–70	70	2	37	39	51

- acquired March 3, 1968 with Garry Unger and Pete Stemkowski from Toronto for Paul Henderson, Norm Ullman, and Floyd Smith
- traded February 18, 1971 to St. Louis for Mike Lowe, Ab McDonald, and Bob Wall

ARCHIBALD "ARCHIE" BRIDEN #4 FORWARD *b.* Unknown *d.* Unknown

1926–27R	42	5	2	7	36

- first Cougars game January 9, 1927

MEL BRIDGMAN #15 CENTRE 6′ 190 *b.* Trenton, Ontario, April 28, 1955

1986–87	13	2	2	4	19
1987–88	57	6	11	17	42
Totals	70	8	13	21	61

- acquired March 9, 1987 from New Jersey for Chris Cichocki and a 3rd-round draft choice in 1987 (later traded to Buffalo — Andrew MacVicar)
- released outright May 19, 1988

BERNIE BROPHY #11 FORWARD *b.* Collingwood, Ontario *d.* Unknown

1928–29	37	2	4	6	23
1929–30L	15	2	0	2	2
Totals	52	4	4	8	25

- last Cougars game January 2, 1930

ADAM BROWN #11 – 16 LEFT WING 5′10″ 175 *b.* Johnstone, Scotland, February 4, 1920 *d.* Hamilton, Ontario, August 9, 1960

1941–42R	28	6	9	15	15
1943–44	50	24	18	42	56
1945–46	48	20	11	31	27
1946–47	22	8	5	13	28
Totals	148	58	43	101	126

- promoted from Indianapolis during '41–'42
- first Red Wings game January 1, 1942
- played '42–'43 with Indianapolis, though called up for playoffs
- missed 1944–45 — Canadian Armed Forces
- traded December 1946 with Ray Powell to Chicago for Leo Reise and Pete Horeck

ANDY BROWN ("Moe") #31 GOALIE 6′ 185 *b.* Hamilton, Ontario, February 15, 1944

1971–72R	10	4–5–1	560	37	0	3.96
1972–73	7	2–1–2	337	20	0	3.56
Totals	17	6–6–3	897	57	0	3.81

- claimed June 7, 1971 from Baltimore (AHL) in Intra-League Draft
- first Red Wings games February 20, March 12/16/19/21/22/25/28/29, April 2, 1972
- played December 21/24/26/31, January 12/14/21, 1972–73
- traded February 25, 1973 to Penguins for a 3rd-round draft choice in 1973 (Nelson Pyatt) and cash

ARNIE BROWN #4 DEFENCE 5′11″ 185 *b.* Apsley, Ontario, January 28, 1942

1970–71	27	2	6	8	30
1971–72	77	2	23	25	84
Totals	104	4	29	33	114

- acquired February 2, 1971 from Rangers with Mike Robitaille and Tom Miller for Bruce MacGregor and Larry Brown
- traded October 4, 1972 with Gerry Gray to the Islanders for Dennis DeJordy and Don McLaughlin

DOUG BROWN #17 RIGHT WING 5′10″ 185 *b.* Southborough, Massachusetts, June 12, 1964

1994–95	45	9	12	21	16
1995–96	62	12	15	27	4
Totals	107	21	27	48	20

- claimed January 18, 1995 from Penguins in Waiver Draft
- currently with Red Wings

GERALD "GERRY" BROWN #10 – 14 – 18 LEFT WING 5′10″ 176 *b.* Edmonton, Alberta, July 7, 1917

1941–42R	13	4	4	8	0
1945–46L	10	0	1	1	2
Totals	23	4	5	9	2

- started '41–'42 with Indianapolis
- first Red Wings game February 12, 1942
- missed 1942–45 — Canadian Armed Forces
- traded 1946 to Toronto for Doug Baldwin and Ray Powell
- last Red Wings games November 10/11/15/17/18/24/25, December 2/9/12, 1945

LARRY BROWN #4 DEFENCE 6′2″ 210 *b.* Brandon, Manitoba, April 14, 1947

1970–71	33	1	4	5	8

- acquired October 31, 1970 from Rangers for Pete Stemkowski
- traded February 2, 1971 to Rangers with Bruce MacGregor for Mike Robitaille, Arnie Brown, and Tom Miller

PATRICK "CONNIE" BROWN #9 – 15 – 16 – 18 CENTRE 5′7″ 168 *b.* Van Kleek Hill, Ontario, January 11, 1917

1938–39R	20	1	0	1	0
1939–40	36	8	3	11	2
1940–41	3	1	2	3	0
1941–42	9	0	3	3	4
1942–43L	23	5	16	21	6
Totals	91	15	24	39	12

- signed October 21, 1938
- first Red Wings game January 26, 1939
- played most of '38–'39 with Pittsburgh; started '39–'40 with Indianapolis
- joined Canadian Army 1943–45 — never played in the NHL again
- last Red Wings game January 3, 1943

STAN BROWN #7 FORWARD 5′9″ 150 *b.* North Bay, Ontario, May 9, 1898 *d.* Unknown

1927–28L	24	2	0	2	4

- last Cougars game February 9, 1928

JEFF BRUBAKER ("Bru") #38 LEFT WING 6′2″ 210 *b.* Hagerstown, Maryland, February 24, 1958

1988–89L	1	0	0	0	0

- played November 20, 1988
- played most of '88–'89 with Adirondack; out of hockey after

ED BRÛNETEAU #9 – 10 – 15 – 18 – 22 RIGHT WING 5′9″ 172 *b.* St. Boniface, Manitoba, August 1, 1919

1940–41R	12	1	1	2	2
1943–44	2	0	1	1	0

MODERE "MUD" BRÛNETEAU

1944–45	42	12	13	25	6
1945–46	46	17	12	29	11
1946–47	60	9	14	23	14
1947–48	18	1	1	2	2
1948–49L	1	0	0	0	0
Totals	181	40	42	82	35

- first Red Wings games January 12/18/19/24/26/30, February 6/9/11/14/16, 1941
- last Red Wings game December 5, 1948

MODERE "MUD" BRÛNETEAU #9 – 14 – 17 RIGHT WING 5′11″ 185 *b.* St. Boniface, Manitoba, November 28, 1914 *d.* Houston, Texas, 1981

1935–36R	24	2	0	2	2
1936–37	42	9	7	16	18
1937–38	24	3	6	9	16
1938–39	20	3	7	10	0
1939–40	48	10	14	24	10
1940–41	45	11	17	28	12
1941–42	48	14	19	33	8
1942–43	50	23	22	45	2
1943–44	39	35	18	53	4
1944–45	43	23	24	47	6
1945–46L	28	6	4	10	2
Totals	411	139	138	277	80

- first Red Wings game November 10, 1935
- demoted March 4, 1938 to Pittsburgh
- retired after '45–'46 season
- last Red Wings game February 3, 1946

BILL BRYDGE #5 DEFENCE 5′9″ 195 *b.* Renfrew, Ontario, 1901 *d.* Kirkland Lake, Ontario, November 1949

1928–29	31	2	2	4	59

- acquired in 1927 from Toronto for Art Duncan
- sold November 22, 1929 to Americans for $5,000 after contract dispute with Detroit

JOHN BUCYK ("Chief") #20 LEFT WING 6′ 215 *b.* Edmonton, Alberta, May 12, 1935

1955–56R	38	1	8	9	20
1956–57	66	10	11	21	41
Totals	104	11	19	30	61

- first Red Wings game October 6, 1955
- played '53–'55 and part of '55–'56 with Edmonton (WHL)
- traded July 24, 1957 to Boston for Terry Sawchuk

TONY BUKOVICH #17 – 20 CENTRE 5′11″ 160 *b.* Painesdale, Michigan, August 30, 1918

1943–44R	30	0	1	1	0
1944–45L	14	7	2	9	6
Totals	44	7	3	10	6

- first Red Wings game October 31, 1943
- last Red Wings game March 18, 1945

HYMAN "HY" BULLER ("The Blueline Blaster") #17 – 18 – 22 DEFENCE 5′11″ 185 *b.* Montreal, Quebec, March 15, 1926 *d.* Cleveland, Ohio, September 1969

1943–44R	7	0	3	3	4
1944–45	2	0	0	0	2
Totals	9	0	3	3	6

- first Red Wings games December 7, March 7/11/12/16/18/19, 1943–44
- played October 29 & November 25, 1944

CHARLIE BURNS #21 CENTRE 5′11″ 170 *b.* Detroit, February 14, 1936

1958–59R	70	9	11	20	32

- first Red Wings game October 11, 1958
- lost June 1959 to Boston at Intra-League Draft

SHAWN BURR #11 LEFT WING/CENTRE 6′1″ 195 *b.* Sarnia, Ontario, July 1, 1966

1984–85R	9	0	0	0	2
1985–86	5	1	0	1	4
1986–87	80	22	25	47	107
1987–88	78	17	23	40	97
1988–89	79	19	27	46	78

1989–90	76	24	32	56	82
1990–91	80	20	30	50	112
1991–92	79	19	32	51	118
1992–93	80	10	25	35	74
1993–94	51	10	12	22	31
1994–95	42	6	8	14	60
Totals	659	148	214	362	765

- drafted 7th overall at 1984 Entry Draft
- first Red Wings games October 11/13/26/30, November 1/2/6/8/10, 1984
- played October 14/16, January 15/22/23, 1985–86
- played part of '84–'86 with Kitchener and Adirondack, and '89–'90 with Adirondack
- traded August 17, 1995 with a 3rd-round draft choice in 1996 (later traded to Boston — Jason Doyle) to Tampa Bay for Marc Bergevin and Ben Hankinson

CUMMING "CUMMY" BURTON #6 – 21 RIGHT WING 5′10″ 175
b. Sudbury, Ontario, May 12, 1936

1955–56R	3	0	0	0	0
1957–58	26	0	1	1	12
1958–59L	14	0	1	1	9
Totals	43	0	2	2	21

- first Red Wings games March 8/11/18, 1956
- last Red Wings game March 22, 1959
- career minor-leaguer with Edmonton ('56–'58), Seattle ('58–'59), Sudbury ('59–'62), Edmonton ('62–'63), and Pittsburgh ('62–'63)

EDDIE BUSH #5 – 15 DEFENCE 6′1″ 195
b. Collingwood, Ontario, July 11, 1918
d. London, Ontario, May 31, 1984

1938–39R	9	0	0	0	0
1941–42L	18	4	6	10	50
Totals	27	4	6	10	50

- signed October 21, 1938
- first Red Wings games February 26, March 2/5/7/9/11/12/14, 1939
- last Red Wings game March 19, 1943
- joined Royal Canadian Air Force 1942–45
- sold August 17, 1946 to St. Louis (AHL) for cash

WALT BUSWELL #12 DEFENCE 5′11″ 170
b. Montreal, Quebec, November 6, 1907
d. Unknown

1932–33R	46	2	4	6	16
1933–34	47	1	2	3	8
1934–35	47	1	3	4	32
Totals	140	4	9	13	56

- first Red Wings game November 10, 1932
- traded before '35–'36 season to Canadiens

AL CAMERON #26 DEFENCE 6′ 205
b. Edmonton, Alberta, October 21, 1955

1975–76R	38	2	8	10	49
1976–77	80	3	13	16	112
1977–78	63	2	7	9	94
1978–79	9	0	3	3	8
Totals	190	7	31	38	263

- selected 37th overall at 1975 Entry Draft
- first Red Wings game October 8, 1975
- lost June 13, 1979 to Winnipeg in Expansion Draft

CRAIG CAMERON #14 RIGHT WING 6′ 200
b. Edmonton, Alberta, July 19, 1945

1966–67R	1	0	0	0	0

- first and only Red Wings game February 18, 1967
- played part of '66–'67 with Memphis and Pittsburgh
- traded October 19, 1967 with Larry Hornung and Don Giesebrecht to St. Louis for John Brenneman

COLIN CAMPBELL ("Soupy") #4 DEFENCE 5′9″ 190 *b.* London, Ontario, January 28, 1953

1982–83	53	1	7	8	74
1983–84	68	3	4	7	108
1984–85L	57	1	5	6	124
Totals	178	5	16	21	306

- signed June 26, 1982 as a free agent from Vancouver Canucks
- last Red Wings game March 20, 1985
- retired July 30, 1985 to become assistant coach with Red Wings

TERRY CARKNER #2 DEFENCE 6′3″ 210
b. Smiths Falls, Ontario, March 7, 1966

1993–94	68	1	6	7	130
1994–95	20	1	2	3	21
Totals	88	2	8	10	151

- acquired October 5, 1993 from Flyers for Yves Racine and a 4th-round draft choice in 1994 (Sebastien Vallee)
- lost August 17, 1995 as a free agent to Florida

GENE CARRIGAN #15 – 17 CENTRE 6′1″ 200
b. Edmonton, Alberta, July 5, 1907
d. Unknown

- appeared only in the 1934 playoffs for Detroit

BILLY CARROLL #12 CENTRE 5′10″ 190
b. Toronto, Ontario, January 19, 1959

1985–86	21	2	4	6	11
1986–87L	31	1	2	3	6
Totals	52	3	6	9	17

- acquired December 28, 1985 from Edmonton for Bruce Eakin
- last Red Wings game March 15, 1987
- out of hockey after '86–'87

GREG CARROLL #25 CENTRE 6′ 185
b. Gimli, Manitoba, November 10, 1956

1978–79	36	2	9	11	8

- claimed on waivers January 6, 1979 from Washington
- lost October 30, 1979 as a free agent to Hartford

GORDON "DWIGHT" CARRUTHERS #2 DEFENCE 5′9″ 185 *b.* Lashburn, Saskatchewan, November 7, 1944

1965–66R	1	0	0	0	0

- first and only Red Wings game March 6, 1966

FRANK CARSON ("Gray Eagle"/"Frosty") #9 RIGHT WING 5′7″ 165
b. Parry Sound, Ontario, January 12, 1902
d. Parry Sound, Ontario, May 29, 1967

1931–32	31	10	14	24	31
1932–33	45	12	13	25	35
1933–34L	47	10	9	19	36
Totals	123	32	36	68	102

- acquired December 29, 1931 from Americans with Hap Emms for Tommy Filmore and Bert McInenly
- last Red Wings game March 18, 1934

JIMMY CARSON #10 – 12 CENTRE 6′ 200
b. Southfield, Michigan, July 20, 1968

1990–91	64	21	25	46	28
1991–92	80	34	35	69	30
Totals	144	55	60	115	58

- acquired November 2, 1989 with Kevin McClelland from Edmonton for Adam Graves, Petr Klima, Joe Murphy, and Jeff Sharples
- traded January 29, 1993 with Marc Potvin and Gary Shuchuk to Los Angeles for Paul Coffey, Sylvain Couturier, and Jim Hiller

JOE CARVETH ("Dad") #12 – 14 – 17 RIGHT WING 5′10″ 180 *b.* Regina, Saskatchewan, March 21, 1918 *d.* Unknown

1940–41R	19	2	1	3	2
1941–42	29	6	11	17	2
1942–43	43	18	18	36	6
1943–44	46	21	36	57	6
1944–45	50	26	28	54	10
1945–46	48	17	18	35	18
1950–51L	30	1	4	5	0
Totals	265	91	116	207	44

- first Red Wings game November 3, 1940
- played '39–'40 with Indianapolis
- missed much of '40–'41 with a broken leg
- traded summer 1946 to Boston for Roy Conacher
- acquired November 11, 1949 from Canadiens for Calum MacKay
- last Red Wings game December 25, 1950
- demoted January 1951 to Indianapolis

FRANTISEK "FRANK" CERNIK #21 LEFT WING/RIGHT WING 5′10″ 189 *b.* Novy Jicin, Czechoslovakia, June 3, 1953

1984–85L	49	5	4	9	13

- rights purchased July 6, 1984 from Quebec
- last Red Wings game April 7, 1985
- played '85–'86 in West Germany

JOHN CHABOT #16 CENTRE 6′2″ 200 *b.* Summerside, Prince Edward Island, May 18, 1962

1987–88	78	13	44	57	10
1988–89	52	2	10	12	6
1989–90	69	9	40	49	24
1990–91L	27	5	5	10	4
Totals	226	29	99	128	44

- signed as a free agent June 25, 1987
- played part of '90–'91 with Adirondack
- last Red Wings game February 23, 1991
- played '91–'92 with Merano (Italian League)

MILAN CHALUPA #7 DEFENCE 5′10″ 183 *b.* Oudolen, Czechoslovakia, July 4, 1953

1984–85R/L	14	0	5	5	6

- selected 49th overall at 1984 Entry Draft
- first and only Red Wings games October 11/13/14/17/18/ 20/24/26/30, November 1/2/6, December 7/9, 1984
- played one game with Adirondack in '84–'85; out of hockey after

BOB CHAMPOUX #22 GOALIE 5′10″ 175 *b.* St. Hilaire, Quebec, December 2, 1942

- signed as a free agent summer 1963
- appeared only in the 1964 playoffs for Detroit
- played '63–'64 with Cincinnati

GUY CHARRON #8 – 23 CENTRE 5′10″ 180 *b.* Verdun, Quebec, January 24, 1949

1970–71	24	8	4	12	4
1971–72	64	9	16	25	12
1972–73	75	18	18	36	23
1973–74	76	25	30	55	10
1974–75	77	14	39	53	27
Totals	316	74	107	181	76

- acquired January 13, 1971 with Mickey Redmond and Bill Collins from Canadiens for Frank Mahovlich
- traded December 14, 1974 with Claude Houde to Kansas City for Bart Crashley, Ted Snell, and Larry Giroux

LUDIC "LUDE" CHECK #15 FORWARD 154 *b.* Brandon, Manitoba, May 22, 1919

1943–44R	1	0	0	0	0

- first and only Red Wings game March 11, 1944
- played '44–'45 with Chicago

TIM CHEVELDAE #32 – 31 GOALIE 5′11″ 175 *b.* Melville, Saskatchewan, February 15, 1968

1988–89	2	0–2–0	122	9	0	4.43
1989–90	28	10–9–8	1600	101	0	3.79
1990–91	65	30–26–5	3615	214	2	3.55
1991–92	72	38–23–9	4236	226	2	3.20
1992–93	67	34–24–7	3880	210	4	3.25
1993–94	30	16–9–1	1572	91	1	3.47
Totals	264	128–93–30	15,025	851	9	3.40

- selected 64th overall at 1986 Entry Draft
- played February 2 & 9, 1989
- traded March 8, 1994 with Dallas Drake to Winnipeg for Sergei Bautin and Bob Essensa

REAL CHEVREFILS #14 LEFT WING 5′10″ 175 *b.* Timmins, Ontario, May 2, 1932 *d.* Windsor, Ontario, January 8, 1981

1955–56	38	3	4	7	24

- acquired June 3, 1955 from Boston with Gilles Boisvert, Ed Sandford, Norm Corcoran, and Warren Godfrey for Marcel Bonin, Terry Sawchuk, Vic Stasiuk, and Lorne Davis
- traded January 17, 1956 with Jerry Toppazzini to Boston for Lorne Ferguson and Murray Costello

ALAIN CHEVRIER #31 GOALIE 5′8″ 180
b. Cornwall, Ontario, April 23, 1961

1990–91L	3	0–2–0	108	11	0	6.11

- signed as a free agent July 5, 1990
- only Red Wings games October 20, November 8, and January 30, 1990–91
- played most of '90–'91 with San Diego

STEVE CHIASSON #3 DEFENCE 6′ 205
b. Barrie, Ontario, April 14, 1967

1986–87R	45	1	4	5	73
1987–88	29	2	9	11	57
1988–89	65	12	35	47	149
1989–90	67	14	28	42	114
1990–91	42	3	17	20	80
1991–92	62	10	24	34	136
1992–93	79	12	50	62	155
1993–94	82	13	33	46	122
Totals	471	67	200	267	886

- selected 50th overall at 1985 Entry Draft
- first Red Wings game October 9, 1986
- traded June 29, 1994 to Calgary for Mike Vernon

DINO CICCARELLI #22 RIGHT WING 5′10″ 185 *b.* Sarnia, Ontario, February 8, 1960

1992–93	82	41	56	97	81
1993–94	66	28	29	57	73
1994–95	42	16	27	43	39
1995–96	64	22	21	43	99
Totals	254	107	133	240	292

- acquired June 20, 1992 from Washington for Kevin Miller
- traded August 28, 1996 to Tampa Bay for a conditional draft choice in 1998

CHRIS CICHOCKI #15 RIGHT WING 5′11″ 185
b. Detroit, September 17, 1963

1985–86R	59	10	11	21	21
1986–87	2	0	0	0	2
Totals	61	10	11	21	23

- signed as a free agent June 28, 1985
- first Red Wings game October 10, 1985
- played December 11 & 17, 1986
- traded March 9, 1987 with a 3rd-round draft choice in 1987 (later traded to Buffalo — Andrew MacVicar) to New Jersey for Mel Bridgman

REJEAN CLOUTIER #4 – 16 DEFENCE 6′ 180
b. Windsor, Ontario, February 15, 1960

1979–80R/L	3	0	1	1	0

- signed as a free agent October 30, 1979
- first and only Red Wings games January 26/27/30, 1980
- played '81–'84 with Adirondack
- traded October 17, 1984 to Edmonton for Todd Bidner

ROLAND CLOUTIER #19 – 21 – 23
CENTRE 5′8″ 157 *b.* Rouyn-Noranda, Quebec, October 6, 1957

1977–78R	1	0	0	0	0
1978–79	19	6	6	12	2
Totals	20	6	6	12	2

- selected 178th overall at 1977 Entry Draft
- first Red Wings game February 28, 1978
- lost June 13, 1979 to Quebec in Expansion Draft

STEVE COATES #17 RIGHT WING 5′9″ 172
b. Toronto, Ontario, July 2, 1950

1976–77R/L	5	1	0	1	24

- acquired February 17, 1977 with Terry Murray, Bob Ritchie, and Dave Kelly from Flyers for Rick Lapointe and Mike Korney
- first and only Red Wings games February 19, March 3 & 31, April 2 & 3, 1977
- played '77–'78 with Kansas City and Maine

PAUL COFFEY #77 DEFENCE 6′ 190
b. Weston, Ontario, June 1, 1961

1992–93	30	4	26	30	27
1993–94	80	14	63	77	106
1994–95	45	14	44	58	72
1995–96	76	14	60	74	90
Totals	231	46	193	239	295

- acquired January 29, 1993 with Sylvain Couturier and Jim Hiller from Los Angeles for Jimmy Carson, Marc Potvin, and Gary Shuchuk
- traded October 9, 1996 with Keith Primeau and a 1st-round draft choice in 1997 to Hartford for Brendan Shanahan and Brian Glynn

BILL COLLINS #22 RIGHT WING 6′ 178
b. Ottawa, Ontario, July 13, 1943

1970–71	36	5	16	21	10
1971–72	71	15	25	40	38
1972–73	78	21	21	42	44
1973–74	54	13	15	28	37
Totals	239	54	77	131	129

- acquired January 13, 1971 with Guy Charron and Mickey Redmond from Canadiens for Frank Mahovlich
- traded February 14, 1974 with Garnet "Ace" Bailey and Ted Harris to St. Louis for Bryan Watson, Chris Evans, and Jean Hamel

BRIAN CONACHER #24 LEFT WING 6′3″ 197
b. Toronto, Ontario, August 31, 1941

1971–72	22	3	1	4	4

- claimed June 11, 1968 from Toronto at Intra-League Draft
- traded February 15, 1969 with Danny Lawson to Minnesota for Wayne Connelly
- played part of '71–'72 with Fort Worth
- played for Ottawa (WHA) '72–'73

CHARLIE CONACHER ("The Bomber") #17 RIGHT WING 6′1″ 195
b. Toronto, Ontario, December 20, 1910
d. Toronto, January 1, 1968

1938–39	40	8	15	23	29

- bought from Toronto summer 1938

CHARLIE CONACHER GOALIE

1938–39	1	0–0–0	4	0	0	0.00

JIM CONACHER ("Pencil") #18 CENTRE 5′10″ 155 *b.* Motherwell, Scotland, May 5, 1921

1945–46R	20	1	5	6	6
1946–47	33	16	13	29	2
1947–48	60	17	23	40	2
1948–49	4	1	0	1	2
Totals	117	35	41	76	12

- in Royal Canadian Air Force 1943–45
- played part of '45–'46 with Indianapolis
- first Red Wings game October 28, 1945
- played October 13/17/23/24, 1948
- traded October 24, 1948 with Bep Guidolin and Doug McCaig to Chicago for George Gee and Bud Poile

ROY CONACHER #9 LEFT WING 6′1″ 175
b. Toronto, Ontario, October 5, 1916
d. Unknown

1946–47	60	30	24	54	6

- acquired summer 1946 from Boston for Joe Carveth
- traded October 1947 to Rangers for Ed Slowinski

ALEX CONNELL ("The Ottawa Fireman") #1 GOALIE 5′9″ 150
b. Ottawa, Ontario, February 8, 1902

1931–32	48	18–20–10	3050	108	6	2.12

- on loan from Ottawa which did not field a team
- returned to Ottawa for '32–'33

WAYNE CONNELLY #17 RIGHT WING 5′10″ 170 *b.* Rouyn, Quebec, December 16, 1939

1968–69	19	4	9	13	0
1969–70	76	23	36	59	10
1970–71	51	8	13	21	12
Totals	146	35	58	93	22

- acquired February 15, 1969 from Minnesota for Dan Lawson and Brian Conacher
- traded February 6, 1971 with Garry Unger to St. Louis for Tim Ecclestone and Red Berenson

BOB CONNORS #5 – 10 DEFENCE
b. Unknown *d.* Unknown

1928–29	41	13	3	16	68
1929–30L	31	3	7	10	42
Totals	72	16	10	26	110

- last Cougars game February 2, 1930

BOB COOK ("Cookie") #12 RIGHT WING 6′ 190 *b.* Sudbury, Ontario, January 6, 1946
d. Unknown

1972–73	13	3	1	4	4

- bought November 21, 1971 from Vancouver Canucks
- played November 18/22/25/26/29, December 2/3/5/7/9/10/13/24, 1972
- traded January 17, 1973 with Ralph Stewart to the Islanders for Ken Murray and Brian Lavender

CARSON COOPER ("Shovel Shot") #8 – 10 FORWARD *b.* Cornwall, Ontario *d.* Hamilton, Ontario, April 7, 1955

1927–28	43	15	2	17	32
1928–29	44	18	9	27	14
1929–30	44	18	18	36	14
1930–31	43	14	14	28	10
1931–32L	48	3	5	8	11
Totals	222	68	48	116	81

- last Falcons game March 22, 1932
- retired after '31–'32 season

NORM CORCORAN #21 CENTRE 6′ 165 *b.* Toronto, Ontario, August 15, 1931

1955–56	2	0	0	0	0

- acquired June 3, 1955 from Boston with Gilles Boisvert, Ed Sandford, Real Chevrefils, and Warren Godfrey for Marcel Bonin, Terry Sawchuk, Vic Stasiuk, and Lorne Davis
- played October 8 & 15, 1955
- lost January 17, 1956 on waivers to Chicago

MURRAY COSTELLO ("Muzz") #19 CENTRE 6′3″ 190 *b.* South Porcupine, Ontario, February 24, 1934

1955–56	24	0	0	0	4
1956–57L	3	0	0	0	0
Totals	27	0	0	0	4

- acquired January 17, 1956 with Lorne Ferguson from Boston for Real Chevrefils and Jerry Toppazzini
- last Red Wings game October 11/13/14, 1956
- played most of '56–'57 with Edmonton (WHL); out of hockey after

GERRY COUTURE ("Doc") #2 – 10 – 16 – 18 – 20 CENTRE 6′2″ 185 *b.* Saskatoon, Saskatchewan, August 6, 1925 *d.* Unknown

1945–46R	43	3	7	10	18
1946–47	30	5	10	15	0
1947–48	19	3	6	9	2
1948–49	51	19	10	29	6
1949–50	70	24	7	31	21
1950–51	53	7	6	13	2
Totals	266	61	46	107	49

- first Red Wings game November 8, 1945
- played part of '46–'48 with Indianapolis
- traded June 19, 1951 to Canadiens for Bert Hirschfield

ABBIE COX #1 GOALIE *b.* Unknown *d.* Unknown

1933–34	2	0–0–1	109	5	0	2.75

- played December 17, 1933
- also played with Americans in '33–'34

DANNY COX #8 LEFT WING 5′10″ 180 *b.* Little Current, Ontario, October 12, 1903

1931–32	47	4	6	10	23

- on loan from Ottawa for '31–'32 as Senators did not field a team
- returned to Ottawa for '32–'33

WILLIAM "BART" CRASHLEY #4 – 8 – 15 – 24 DEFENCE 6′ 180 *b.* Toronto, Ontario, June 15, 1946

1965–66R	1	0	0	0	0
1966–67	2	0	0	0	2
1967–68	57	2	14	16	18
1968–69	1	0	0	0	0
1974–75	48	2	15	17	14
Totals	109	4	29	33	34

- Hamilton Red Wings graduate
- first Red Wings game February 6, 1966
- played October 19 & 22, 1966
- played October 17, 1968
- played part of '63–'64 and '66–'67 with Pittsburgh, '66–'67 with Memphis, '67–'68 with Fort Worth
- traded June 6, 1969 with Pete Mahovlich to Canadiens for Garry Monahan and Doug Piper
- acquired December 14, 1974 with Ted Snell and Larry Giroux from Kansas City for Guy Charron and Claude Houde
- traded June 23, 1975 with the rights to Marcel Dionne to Los Angeles for Dan Maloney, Terry Harper, and a 2nd-round draft choice in 1976 (later traded to Minnesota — Jim Roberts)

MURRAY CRAVEN #11 – 22 – 24
LEFT WING 6′3″ 190
b. Medicine Hat, Alberta, July 20, 1964

1982–83R	31	4	7	11	6
1983–84	15	0	4	4	6
Totals	46	4	11	15	12

- selected 17th overall at 1982 Entry Draft
- first Red Wings game December 29, 1982
- played much of '82–'84 with Medicine Hat
- traded October 19, 1984 with Joe Paterson to Flyers for Darryl Sittler

ROBERT "BOBBY" CRAWFORD #17
RIGHT WING 5′8″ 180 *b.* Long Island, New York, May 27, 1960

1982–83L	1	0	0	0	0

- first and only Red Wings game December 1, 1982

JIM CREIGHTON #15 FORWARD
b. Unknown *d.* Unknown

1930–31R/L	11	1	0	1	2

- played with Falcons November 13/16/20/23/27/29/30, December 7/9, 1930

DOUG CROSSMAN #29 – 39 DEFENCE 6′2″
190 *b.* Peterborough, Ontario, June 30, 1960

1990–91	17	3	4	7	17
1991–92	26	0	8	8	14
Totals	43	3	12	15	31

- acquired February 20, 1991 from Hartford for Doug Houda
- sold June 15, 1992 with Dennis Vial to Quebec for cash

GARY CROTEAU #11 LEFT WING 6′ 202
b. Sudbury, Ontario, June 20, 1946

1969–70	10	0	2	2	2

- acquired February 20, 1970 with Dale Rolfe and Larry Johnston from Los Angeles for Brian Gibbons and Garry Monahan
- played February 21/22/26, March 5/11/18/20/21/26, April 5, 1970
- lost June 9, 1970 to Oakland in Intra-League Draft

TROY CROWDER #25 RIGHT WING 6′4″ 215
b. Sudbury, Ontario, May 3, 1968

1991–92	7	0	0	0	35

- signed August 27, 1991 as a free agent; in return, New Jersey received Dave Barr and Randy McKay as equal compensation
- played October 3/5/10, March 29 & 31, April 12 & 14, 1991–92
- lost August 31, 1994 as a free agent to Los Angeles

ROGER CROZIER #1 – 22 – 30 GOALIE 5′8″
140 *b.* Bracebridge, Ontario, March 16, 1942

1963–64R	15	5–6–4	900	51	2	3.40
1964–65	70	40–23–7	4167	168	6	2.42
1965–66	64	28–24–12	3734	173	7	2.78
1966–67	58	22–30–4	3256	182	4	3.35
1967–68	34	9–18–2	1729	95	1	3.30
1968–69	38	11–16–3	1820	101	0	3.33
1969–70	34	16–6–9	1877	83	0	2.65
Totals	313	131–123–41	17483	853	20	2.93

- acquired June 5, 1963 with Ron Ingram from Chicago for Howie Young
- first Red Wings game November 30, 1963
- traded June 10, 1970 to Sabres for Tom Webster

WILF CUDE #1 GOALIE 5′9″ 146
b. Barrie, Wales, July 4, 1910
d. Montreal, Quebec, May 5, 1966

1933–34	29	15–6–8	1860	47	0	1.52

- contract bought in 1933 by Canadiens, but loaned to Detroit for most of the season

CHARLES "BARRY" CULLEN #8
RIGHT WING 6′ 175 *b.* Ottawa, Ontario, June 16, 1935

1959–60L	55	4	9	13	23

- acquired June 9, 1959 from Toronto for Johnny Wilson and Frank Roggeveen
- last Red Wings game March 20, 1960
- played '60–'64 with Buffalo, then retired

RAY CULLEN #15 CENTRE 5′11″ 180
b. Ottawa, Ontario, September 20, 1941

1966–67	27	8	8	16	8

- claimed June 15, 1966 from Rangers at Intra-League Draft
- lost June 6, 1967 to Minnesota in Expansion Draft

JIM CUMMINS #27 – 47 RIGHT WING 6′2″ 203 *b.* Dearborn, Michigan, May 17, 1970

1991–92R	1	0	0	0	7
1992–93	7	1	1	2	58
Totals	8	1	1	2	65

- acquired March 5, 1991 with Kevin Miller and Dennis Vial from Rangers for Joey Kocur and Per Djoos
- first Red Wings game March 8, 1992
- played October 30/31, December 31, January 8/11/13/23, 1992–93
- traded June 20, 1993 with Flyers' 4th-round draft choice in 1993 (previously acquired by Detroit — later traded to Boston — Charles Paquette) to Flyers for Greg Johnston and a 5th-round draft choice in 1994 (Frederic Deschenes)

IAN CUSHENAN #18 DEFENCE 6′1″ 195
b. Hamilton, Ontario, November 29, 1933

1963–64L	5	0	0	0	4

- signed as a free agent August 5, 1963
- only Red Wings games November 20/27/28/30 & December 1, 1963
- traded June 9, 1964 with John Miszuk and Art Stratten to Chicago for Ron Murphy and Aut Erickson

FRANK DALEY ("Dapper Dan") #14 DEFENCE
b. Port Arthur, Ontario, August 22, 1909

1928–29R/L	4	0	0	0	0

- first and only Cougars games March 5/9/10/14, 1929

JOE DALEY #1 GOALIE 5′10″ 160
b. Winnipeg, Manitoba, February 20, 1943

1971–72	29	11–10–5	1620	85	0	3.15

- lost June 6, 1967 to Penguins in Expansion Draft
- acquired May 25, 1971 from Sabres for Don Luce and Mike Robitaille
- signed with Winnipeg (WHA) for '72–'73

MATHIEU DANDENAULT #11 RIGHT WING 6′ 174 *b.* Sherbrooke, Quebec, February 3, 1976

1995–96R	34	5	7	12	6

- selected 49th overall at 1994 Entry Draft
- currently with Red Wings

BOB DAVIS ("Friday") #18 FORWARD
b. Lachine, Quebec, 1903 *d.* Unknown

1932–33R/L	3	0	0	0	0

- played February 26 & March 5, 1933
- played for Duluth, then the Olympics

LORNE DAVIS #15 RIGHT WING 5′11″ 190
b. Regina, Saskatchewan, July 20, 1930

1954–55	30	0	5	5	6

- acquired November 9, 1954 from Chicago for Metro Prystai
- traded June 3, 1955 to Boston with Marcel Bonin, Terry Sawchuk, and Vic Stasiuk for Gilles Boisvert, Ed Sandford, Real Chevrefils, Norm Corcoran, and Warren Godfrey

MAL DAVIS #14 – 18 – 19 LEFT WING 5′11″ 180 *b.* Lockeport, Nova Scotia, October 10, 1956

1980–81R	5	2	0	2	0

- signed as a free agent October 12, 1978
- first and only Red Wings games November 20/22/26/29, December 2, 1980
- played most of '78–'79 with Kansas City, '79–'81 with Adirondack
- lost as a free agent September 2, 1981 to Sabres

BILLY DEA #7 – 15 – 21 LEFT WING 5′11″ 175 *b.* Edmonton, Alberta, April 3, 1933

1956–57	69	15	15	30	14
1957–58	29	4	4	8	6
1969–70	70	10	3	13	6
1970–71L	42	6	3	9	2
Totals	210	35	25	60	28

- acquired August 18, 1955 with Dolph Kukulowicz from Rangers for Dave Creighton and Bronco Horvath
- traded December 17, 1957 with Earl Reibel, Lorne Ferguson, and Bill Dineen to Chicago for Bob Bailey, Nick Mickoski, Jack McIntyre, and Hec Lalande
- acquired October 28, 1969 from Penguins for Mike McMahon
- last Red Wings game January 21, 1971
- played part of '70–'71 with Fort Worth and all of '71–'72 with Tidewater
- retired to coach Detroit Junior Red Wings for '72–'73

DON DEACON #3 – 7 – 8 – 15 – 17 – 22 LEFT WING 5′9″ 190 *b.* Regina, Saskatchewan, June 2, 1913

1936–37R	4	0	0	0	2
1938–39	8	1	3	4	2
1939–40L	18	5	1	6	2
Totals	30	6	4	10	6

- first Red Wings games November 26, December 3/6/8, 1936
- last Red Wings game January 1, 1940

NELSON DEBENEDET #23 LEFT WING 6′1″ 195 *b.* Cardenona, Italy, December 31, 1947

1973–74R	15	4	1	5	2

- University of Toronto graduate
- first and only Red Wings games December 13/15/16/18/20/27/31, January 2/23/25/27/30, February 9/13/15, 1973–74
- played part of '73–'74 with Virginia
- traded May 27, 1974 to Penguins for Hank Nowak and a 3rd-round draft choice in 1974 (Dan Mandryk)

DENIS DeJORDY #27 – 30 GOALIE 5′9″ 185 *b.* St. Hyacinthe, Quebec, November 12, 1938

1972–73	24	8–11–3	1331	83	1	3.74
1973–74L	1	0–1–0	20	4	0	12.00
Totals	25	8–12–3	1351	87	1	3.86

- acquired October 4, 1972 with Don McLaughlin from the Islanders for Arnie Brown and Gerry Gray
- played most of '73–'74 with Baltimore
- last Red Wings game December 5, 1973
- hired September 5, 1974 as Red Wings goalie coach, first ever in the NHL

GILBERT DELORME #29 – 35 DEFENCE 6′1″ 205 *b.* Boucherville, Quebec, November 25, 1962

1986–87	24	2	3	5	33
1987–88	55	2	8	10	81
1988–89	42	1	3	4	51
Totals	121	5	14	19	165

- acquired January 17, 1987 from Quebec with Brent Ashton and Mark Kumpel for John Ogrodnick, Basil McRae, and Doug Shedden
- lost June 28, 1989 as a free agent to Penguins

ALEX DELVECCHIO #10 – 15 – 17 CENTRE 6′ 195 *b.* Fort William, Ontario, December 4, 1931

1950–51R	1	0	0	0	0
1951–52	65	15	22	37	22
1952–53	70	16	43	59	28
1953–54	69	11	18	29	34

ALEX DELVECCHIO

1954–55	69	17	31	48	37
1955–56	70	25	26	51	24
1956–57	48	16	25	41	8
1957–58	70	21	38	59	22
1958–59	70	19	35	54	6
1959–60	70	19	28	47	8
1960–61	70	27	35	62	26
1961–62	70	26	43	69	18
1962–63	70	20	44	64	8
1963–64	70	23	30	53	11
1964–65	68	25	42	67	16
1965–66	70	31	38	69	16
1966–67	70	17	38	55	10
1967–68	74	22	48	70	14
1968–69	72	25	58	83	8
1969–70	73	21	47	68	24
1970–71	77	21	34	55	6
1971–72	75	20	45	65	22
1972–73	77	18	53	71	13
1973–74L	11	1	4	5	2
Totals	1549	456	825	1281	383

- played with Oshawa Generals (OHA)
- first Red Wings game March 25, 1951
- played part of '51–'52 with Indianapolis
- last Red Wings games October 10/13/14/16/18/21/24/26/27/30, November 4, 1973
- retired November 7, 1973 to become Red Wings coach

AL DEWSBURY ("Dews") #4 – 5 – 21 – 22 – 24 DEFENCE 6′2″ 202 *b.* Goderich, Ontario, April 12, 1926

1946–47R	23	2	1	3	12
1949–50	11	2	2	4	2
Totals	34	4	3	7	14

- first Red Wings game November 2, 1946
- played much of '46–'50 with Indianapolis, '45–'46 and '47–'48 with Omaha
- traded July 13, 1950 with Harry Lumley, Jack Stewart, Don Morrison, and Pete Babando to Chicago for Jim Henry, Bob Goldham, Gaye Stewart, and Metro Prystai

ED DIACHUK #16 LEFT WING 6′1″ 195 *b.* Vergreville, Alberta, August 16, 1936

1960–61R/L	12	0	0	0	19

- first and only Red Wings games December 10/11/15/18/24/25/28/29/31, and January 1/4/5, 1960–61

BOB DILLABOUGH #11 – 12 – 19 – 22 – 24 CENTRE 5′10″ 180 *b.* Belleville, Ontario, April 14, 1941

1961–62R	5	0	0	0	2
1964–65	4	0	0	0	2
Totals	9	0	0	0	4

- Hamilton Red Wings graduate
- first Red Wings games November 2/5/9/11/12, 1961
- played October 15/17/18/24, 1964
- also played '62–'65 with Pittsburgh, '61–'62 with Hershey and Sudbury, '62–'63 with Edmonton
- traded May 31, 1965 with Al Langlois, Ron Harris, and Parker MacDonald to Boston for Ab McDonald, Bob McCord, and Ken Stephenson
- acquired June 8, 1971 with Irv Spencer from Vancouver Canucks for John Cunniff and Gary Bredin

CECIL "CEECE" DILLON #17 FORWARD 5′10″ 173 *b.* Toledo, Ohio, April 26, 1908 *d.* Unknown

1939–40L	44	7	10	17	12

- acquired summer 1939 from Rangers
- last Red Wings game March 17, 1940

BILL DINEEN #12 – 17 – 21 RIGHT WING 5′11″ 180 *b.* Arvida, Quebec, September 18, 1932

1953–54R	70	17	8	25	34
1954–55	69	10	9	19	36
1955–56	70	12	7	19	30
1956–57	51	6	7	13	12
1957–58	22	2	4	6	2
Totals	282	47	35	82	114

- St. Mike's graduate 1953
- first Red Wings game October 8, 1953
- rights acquired (while at St. Mike's) in 1953 with Lou Jankowski from Cleveland for Bob Bailey and John Bailey
- traded December 17, 1957 with Earl Reibel, Billy Dea, and Lorne Ferguson to Chicago for Bob Bailey, Nick Mickoski, Jack McIntyre, and Hec Lalande

PETER DINEEN #5 DEFENCE 5′11″ 190
b. Kingston, Ontario, November 19, 1960

1989–90L	2	0	0	0	5

- signed as a free agent September 16, 1987
- only Red Wings games December 3 & 5, 1989
- played most of ’87–’90 with Adirondack, ’90–’91 with San Diego, then retired

CONNIE DION #1 GOALIE 5′4″ 140 *b.* St. Remi de Tingwick, Quebec, August 11, 1918

1943–44R	26	17–7–2	1560	80	1	3.08
1944–45L	12	6–4–2	720	39	0	3.25
Totals	38	23–11–4	2280	119	1	3.13

- first Red Wings game January 13, 1944
- last Red Wings game November 26, 1944; Lumley took over as number one goalie

MARCEL DIONNE (“Beaver”/“Lou”) #5 – 12 CENTRE 5′8″ 185
b. Drummondville, Quebec, August 3, 1951

1971–72R	78	28	49	77	14
1972–73	77	40	50	90	21
1973–74	74	24	54	78	10
1974–75	80	47	74	121	14
Totals	309	139	227	366	59

- selected 2nd overall at 1971 Entry Draft
- first Red Wings game October 9, 1971
- rights traded June 23, 1975 with Bart Crashley to Los Angeles for Dan Maloney, Terry Harper, and a 2nd-round draft choice in 1976 (later traded to Minnesota — Jim Roberts)

PER DJOOS #36 DEFENCE 5′11″ 170
b. Mora, Sweden, May 11, 1968

1990–91R	26	0	12	12	16

- selected 127th overall at 1986 Entry Draft
- first Red Wings game October 4, 1990
- played part of ’90–’91 with Adirondack and Binghampton
- traded March 5, 1991 with Joey Kocur to Rangers for Jim Cummins, Kevin Miller, and Dennis Vial

GARY DOAK #19 – 24 DEFENCE 5′11″ 191
b. Goderich, Ontario, February 26, 1946

1965–66R	4	0	0	0	12
1972–73	44	0	5	5	51
Totals	48	0	5	5	63

- Hamilton Red Wings graduate
- first Red Wings games November 14, February 12/13/16, 1965–66
- played most of ’63–’66 with Pittsburgh
- traded February 18, 1966 with Bill Lesuk, Ron Murphy, and Steve Atkinson from Boston for Leo Boivin and Dean Prentice
- acquired May 25, 1972 with Rick Newell from Rangers for Joe Zanussi and a 1st-round draft choice in 1972 (Albert Blanchard)
- traded March 1, 1973 to Boston for Garnet “Ace” Bailey and future considerations (Murray Wing — June 4, 1973)

BOBBY DOLLAS #38 – 8 DEFENCE 6′2″ 212
b. Montreal, Quebec, January 31, 1965

1990–91	56	3	5	8	20
1991–92	27	3	1	4	20
1992–93	6	0	0	0	2
Totals	89	6	6	12	42

- signed October 18, 1990 as a free agent
- played much of ’91–’93 with Adirondack
- played December 27/29/31, January 21/23/27, 1992–93
- lost June 24, 1993 to Anaheim in Expansion Draft

CLARENCE “DOLLY” DOLSON #1 GOALIE *b.* Hespeler, Ontario, 1897
d. Good Friday, 1976

1928–29R	44	19–19–6	2750	63	10	1.37
1929–30	5	0–4–1	320	24	0	4.50
1930–31L	44	16–21–7	2750	105	6	2.29
Totals	93	35–44–13	5820	192	16	1.98

- signed from Stratford Nationals in 1928
- first Cougars game November 15, 1928
- played for London Tecumsehs in ’31–’32
- played November 14/17/19/24/26, 1929
- last Falcons game March 22, 1931

JOHN "RED" DORAN #5 – 17 DEFENCE
6′ 195 *b.* Belleville, Ontario, May 24, 1911
d. Unknown

1937–38	7	0	0	0	10

- acquired May 9, 1937 from Americans with $7,500 for Earl Robertson

LLOYD DORAN ("Red") #16 CENTRE
6′ 175 *b.* South Porcupine, Ontario, January 10, 1921

1946–47R/L	24	3	2	5	10

- first signed October 21, 1941
- served in Canadian Armed Forces 1942–46
- played most of '46–'48 with Indianapolis
- first Red Wings game November 30, 1946
- last Red Wings game February 1, 1947
- traded September 9, 1948 with Ralph Almas, Tony Licari, Barry Sullivan, and Thain Simon to St. Louis (AHL) for Joe Lund and Hec Highton

KEN DORATY ("Cagey") #11 – 17 FORWARD
5′7″ 133 *b.* Stittsville, Ontario, June 23, 1906
d. Moose Jaw, Saskatchewan, May 4, 1981

1937–38L	3	0	1	1	2

- recalled from Pittsburgh on January 10, 1938
- only Red Wings games January 11/13/15, 1938

KENT DOUGLAS #5 DEFENCE 5′10″ 189
b. Cobalt, Ontario, February 6, 1936

1967–68	36	7	10	17	46
1968–69	69	2	29	31	97
Totals	105	9	39	48	143

- acquired January 9, 1968 from Oakland for John Brenneman, Ted Hampson, and Bert Marshall
- sold June 20, 1969 to Vancouver Canucks

LES DOUGLAS #16 – 18 – 19 – 22 CENTRE
5′9″ 165 *b.* Perth, Ontario, December 5, 1918

1940–41R	18	1	2	3	2
1942–43	21	5	8	13	4
1945–46	1	0	0	0	0
1946–47L	12	0	2	2	2
Totals	52	6	12	18	8

- played junior with Detroit Pontiac Chiefs
- first Red Wings game November 3, 1940
- played much of '39–'43 and '45–'46 with Indianapolis
- missed 1943–45 — Royal Canadian Air Force
- played February 7, 1946
- last Red Wings games November 2/3/6/10/13/14/17/20/21/23/24/27, 1946
- sold outright to Buffalo in 1947; traded to Cleveland in 1949 for Gord Davidson

DALLAS DRAKE #28 CENTRE 6′ 180
b. Trail, British Columbia, February 4, 1969

1992–93R	72	18	26	44	93

- selected 116th overall at 1989 Entry Draft
- first Red Wings game October 6, 1992
- traded March 8, 1994 with Tim Cheveldae to Winnipeg for Sergei Bautin and Bob Essensa

KRIS DRAPER #33 CENTRE 5′11″ 185
b. Toronto, Ontario, May 24, 1971

1993–94	39	5	8	13	31
1994–95	36	2	6	8	22
1995–96	52	7	9	16	32
Totals	127	14	23	37	85

- acquired June 30, 1993 from Winnipeg for future considerations
- currently with Red Wings

RÉNÉ DRÔLET #24 RIGHT WING 5′7″ 155
b. Quebec City, Quebec, November 13, 1944

1974–75L	1	0	0	0	0

- claimed June 13, 1974 from Flyers in Reverse Draft
- first and only Red Wings game December 21, 1974
- played most of '74–'75 with Virginia, '75–'78 with Rochester

CLARENCE "CLARE" DROUILLARD
#10 – 15 CENTRE 5′7″ 150
b. Windsor, Ontario, March 2, 1914

1937–38R/L	10	0	1	1	0

- acquired February 26, 1936 from Windsor Bulldogs for Joe Bretto and cash
- traded December 22, 1937 to Boston with cash for Alex Motter
- first and only Red Wings games November 23/25/28, December 5/7/9/12/14/16/19, 1937

GILLES DUBE #25 LEFT WING 5′11″ 165
b. Sherbrooke, Quebec, June 2, 1927

- appeared for Detroit only in the 1954 playoffs

RON DUGUAY ("Doogie") #10 CENTRE
6′2″ 210 *b.* Sudbury, Ontario, July 6, 1957

1983–84	80	33	47	80	34
1984–85	80	38	51	89	51
1985–86	67	19	29	48	26
Totals	227	90	127	217	111

- acquired June 13, 1983 with Ed Mio and Eddie Johnstone from Rangers for Mike Blaisdell, Willie Huber, and Mark Osborne
- traded March 11, 1986 to Pittsburgh Penguins for Doug Shedden

LORNE DUGUID #14 LEFT WING 5′11″ 185
b. Bolton, Ontario, April 4, 1910
d. Toronto, Ontario, March 21, 1981

1934–35	34	3	3	6	9
1935–36	5	0	0	0	0
Totals	39	3	3	6	9

- played November 12/14/19/21/28, 1935
- traded to Boston during '35–'36 season

ART DUNCAN #8 DEFENCE
b. Sault Ste. Marie, Ontario, 1893
d. Aurora, Ontario, April 13, 1975

1926–27R	34	3	2	5	26

- manager/player when team moved from Victoria to play as Detroit Cougars
- first Cougars game November 18, 1926
- sold in 1927 to Toronto for Bill Brydge

BLAKE DUNLOP #11 CENTRE 5′10″ 170
b. Hamilton, Ontario, April 4, 1953

1983–84L	57	6	14	20	20

- signed as a free agent December 2, 1983
- last Red Wings game April 1, 1984
- retired after '83–'84 season

BRUCE EAKIN #32 CENTRE 5′11″ 190
b. Winnipeg, Manitoba, September 18, 1962

1985–86L	4	0	1	1	0

- signed as a free agent July 18, 1985
- only Red Wings games October 19/23/26/27, 1985
- traded December 28, 1985 to Edmonton for Bill Carroll

MURRAY EAVES #38 – 43 CENTRE 5′10″ 185
b. Calgary, Alberta, May 10, 1960

1987–88	7	0	1	1	2
1988–89L	1	0	0	0	0
Totals	8	0	1	1	2

- played December 9/11/14/16/18/26, and March 29, 1987–88

TIM ECCLESTONE #17 RIGHT WING 5′10″
195 *b.* Toronto, Ontario, September 24, 1947

1970–71	27	4	10	14	13
1971–72	72	18	35	53	33
1972–73	78	18	30	48	28
1973–74	14	0	5	5	6
Totals	191	40	80	120	80

- acquired February 6, 1971 with Red Berenson from St. Louis for Garry Unger and Wayne Connelly
- traded November 29, 1973 to Toronto for Pierre Jarry

ROY EDWARDS #1 – 30 GOALIE 5′8″ 165
b. Seneca Township, Ontario, March 12, 1937

1967–68R	41	15–15–8	2177	127	0	3.50
1968–69	40	18–11–6	2099	89	4	2.54
1969–70	47	24–15–6	2683	116	2	2.59
1970–71	38	11–19–7	2104	119	0	3.39
1972–73	52	22–17–7	3012	132	6	2.63
1973–74L	4	0–3–0	187	18	0	5.78
Totals	222	90–80–34	12262	601	12	2.94

- acquired September 7, 1967 from Penguins for Hank Bassen
- first Red Wings game November 9, 1967
- lost on waivers June 7, 1971 to Penguins
- bought October 6, 1972 from Penguins for cash
- last Red Wings games October 13/14/16/18, 1973
- lost on waivers May 20, 1975 to Sabres

MARTIN "PAT" EGAN ("Box Car") #5
DEFENCE 5′10″ 190
b. Blackie, Alberta, April 25, 1918

1943–44	23	4	15	19	40

- bought October 9, 1942 with Harry Watson when Brooklyn Americans folded
- missed 1942–43 — Canadian Armed Forces
- traded January 5, 1944 to Boston for Flash Hollett

GERRY EHMAN #19 RIGHT WING
6′ 190 *b.* Cudworth, Saskatchewan, November 3, 1932

1958–59	6	0	1	1	4

- claimed June 4, 1958 from Boston at Intra-League Draft
- played October 11/12/16/18/19/23, 1958
- sent to Hershey in November 1958
- lost December 1959 on waivers to Toronto

BORIS "BO" ELIK #17 LEFT WING 5′10″ 190
b. Geraldton, Ontario, October 17, 1929

1962–63R/L	3	0	0	0	0

- first and only Red Wings games December 29 & 31, January 1, 1962–63

DARREN ELIOT #31 GOALIE 6′1″ 175
b. Hamilton, Ontario, November 26, 1961

1987–88	3	0–0–1	97	9	0	5.57

- signed as a free agent June 30, 1987
- played October 17, January 18 & 23, 1987–88
- played most of '87–'88 with Adirondack
- lost 1988 as a free agent to Sabres

LEIGHTON "HAP" EMMS #11 LEFT WING
6′ 190 *b.* Barrie, Ontario, January 12, 1905
d. Niagara Falls, Ontario, October 22, 1988

1931–32	20	6	9	15	27
1932–33	41	9	13	22	63
1933–34	47	7	7	14	51
Totals	108	22	29	51	141

- acquired December 29, 1931 from Americans with Frank Carson for Tommy Filmore and Bert McInenly
- sold October 28, 1934 to Boston
- traded February 13, 1938 to Americans for John Sorrell

ANDERS ERIKSSON #34 CENTRE 5′10″ 183
b. Vastervik, Sweden, February 17, 1969

1995–96R	1	0	0	0	2

- selected 22nd overall at 1993 Entry Draft
- currently with Red Wings

BOB ERREY #21 – 12 LEFT WING 5′10″ 185
b. Montreal, Quebec, September 21, 1964

1994–95	30	6	11	17	31
1995–96	71	11	21	32	66
Totals	101	17	32	49	97

- acquired February 27, 1995 from San Jose for a 5th-round draft choice in 1995 (Michel Bros)
- currently with Red Wings

BOB ESSENSA #35 GOALIE 6′ 185
b. Toronto, Ontario, January 14, 1965

1993–94	13	4–7–2	778	34	1	2.62

- acquired March 8, 1994 with Sergei Bautin from Winnipeg for Tim Cheveldae and Dallas Drake
- loaned to San Diego January 27, 1995
- traded June 14, 1996 to Edmonton for future considerations

CHRIS EVANS #11 DEFENCE 5′9″ 180
b. Toronto, Ontario, September 14, 1946

1973–74	23	0	2	2	2

- acquired February 14, 1974 with Bryan Watson and Jean Hamel from St. Louis for Garnet "Ace" Bailey, Ted Harris, and Bill Collins
- lost June 12, 1974 to Kansas City in Expansion Draft

STEWART "STU" EVANS #3 – 8 – 14 DEFENCE
5′10″ 170 *b.* Ottawa, Ontario, June 19, 1908

1930–31R	43	1	4	5	14
1932–33	48	2	6	8	74
1933–34	17	0	0	0	20
Totals	108	3	10	13	108

- first Falcons game November 13, 1930
- traded in December 1933 to Maroons for Ted Graham

BOB FALKENBERG ("Steady") #3 – 5 – 22
DEFENCE 6′ 205
b. Stettler, Alberta, January 1, 1946

1966–67R	16	1	1	2	10
1967–68	20	0	3	3	10
1968–69	5	0	0	0	0
1970–71	9	0	1	1	6
1971–72	4	0	0	0	0
Totals	54	1	5	6	26

- first Red Wings game December 29, 1966
- played '65–'66 with Memphis, part of '66–'67 with Pittsburgh, '67–'69 and '70–'71 with Fort Worth, '68–'69 with Baltimore, '69–'70 with Cleveland, '71–'72 with Tidewater
- played October 11/17/20/27, November 2, 1968
- played October 11/13/15/17/25/29, November 8,and December 6, 1970
- played October 22/24/26/27, 1971
- joined Alberta (WHA) in '72–'73

ALEX FAULKNER #12 CENTRE 5′8″ 165
b. Bishops Falls, Newfoundland, May 21, 1936

1962–63	70	10	10	20	6
1963–64L	30	5	7	12	9
Totals	100	15	17	32	15

- claimed June 1962 from Toronto in Intra-League Draft
- last Red Wings game February 9, 1964
- retired August 1964

BERNIE FEDERKO #42 CENTRE 6′ 190
b. Foam Lake, Saskatchewan, May 12, 1956

1989–90L	73	17	40	57	24

- acquired June 15, 1989 from St. Louis with Tony McKegney for Adam Oates and Paul MacLean
- last Red Wings game April 1, 1990
- retired after '89–'90

SERGEI FEDOROV #91 CENTRE 6′1″ 190
b. Moscow, USSR, December 13, 1969

1990–91R	77	31	48	79	66
1991–92	80	32	54	86	72
1992–93	73	34	53	87	72
1993–94	82	56	64	120	34
1994–95	42	20	30	50	24
1995–96	78	39	68	107	48
Totals	432	212	317	529	316

- selected 74th overall at 1989 Entry Draft
- first Red Wings game October 4, 1990
- currently with Red Wings

BRENT FEDYK #7 – 14 – 15 – 28 – 39
RIGHT WING 6′ 195 *b.* Yorkton, Saskatchewan, March 8, 1967

1987–88R	2	0	1	1	2
1988–89	5	2	0	2	0
1989–90	27	1	4	5	24
1990–91	67	16	19	35	38
1991–92	61	5	8	13	42
Totals	162	24	32	56	106

- selected 8th overall at 1985 Entry Draft
- first Red Wings games December 27 & January 6, 1987–88
- played February 2/3, March 29/31, April 2, 1989
- traded October 1, 1992 to Flyers for a 4th-round draft choice in 1993 (later traded to Boston — Charles Paquette)

LORNE FERGUSON ("Fergie") #14 LEFT WING 6′ 185 *b.* Palmerston, Ontario, May 26, 1930

1955–56	31	8	7	15	12
1956–57	70	13	10	23	26
1957–58	15	1	3	4	0
Totals	116	22	20	42	38

- acquired January 17, 1956 with Murray Costello from Boston for Real Chevrefils and Jerry Toppazzini
- traded December 17, 1957 with Earl Reibel, Billy Dea, and Bill Dineen to Chicago for Bob Bailey, Nick Mickoski, Jack McIntyre, and Hec Lalande

MARK FERNER #27 – 21 DEFENCE 6′ 193
b. Regina, Saskatchewan, September 5, 1965

1994–95	3	0	0	0	0

- acquired April 4, 1995 with Stu Grimson and a 6th-round draft choice in 1996 (Magnus Nilsson) from Anaheim for Mike Sillinger and Jason York
- played April 13/21, May 3, 1995

VIACHESLAV FETISOV #44 – 2 DEFENCE
6′1″ 220 *b.* Moscow, USSR, April 20, 1958

1994–95	14	0	1	1	0
1995–96	69	7	35	42	96
Totals	83	7	36	43	96

- acquired April 3, 1995 from New Jersey for a 3rd-round draft choice in 1995 (David Gosselin)
- currently with Red Wings

GUYLE "GUY" FIELDER #21 CENTRE 5′9″ 165 *b.* Potlatch, Idaho, November 21, 1930

1957–58L	6	0	0	0	2

- acquired September 23, 1952 from Chicago with Steve Hrymnak and Red Almas for cash
- sold September 24, 1953 to Boston for cash
- bought June 5, 1957 from Boston for cash
- first and only Red Wings games October 10/12/13/17/20/24, 1957
- sent to Seattle in December '57; spent next 18 years in minors

TOM FILMORE #11 RIGHT WING 5′11″ 189 *b.* Thamesford, Ontario, 1906 *d.* Unknown

1930–31R	40	6	2	8	10
1931–32	9	0	0	0	2
Totals	49	6	2	8	12

- first Falcons game November 13, 1930
- played November 12/15/17/19/22/24/29, December 5/29, 1931
- traded December 29, 1931 to Americans with Bert McInenly for Frank Carson and Hap Emms

DUNCAN "DUNC" FISHER #12 RIGHT WING 5′8″ 165 *b.* Regina, Saskatchewan, August 30, 1927

1958–59L	7	0	0	0	0

- acquired April 1958 from Hershey for Hec Lalande and Don Poile
- first and only Red Wings games October 11/12/16/18/19/23/25, 1958
- played most of '58–'60 with Hershey, then retired

JOE FISHER #14 – 16 – 17 RIGHT WING 6′ 175 *b.* Medicine Hat, Alberta, July 4, 1916

1939–40R	34	2	4	6	2
1940–41	28	5	8	13	11
1941–42	3	0	0	0	0
1942–43L	1	1	0	1	0
Totals	66	8	12	20	13

- signed October 21, 1938
- first Red Wings game December 13, 1940
- played November 1/2/9, 1941
- played much of '39–'43 with Indianapolis
- last Red Wings game March 2, 1943
- joined Canadian Armed Forces in 1943–45 — never returned to the NHL

LIDIO "LEE" FOGOLIN #21 – 25 DEFENCE 5′11″ 200 *b.* Fort William, Ontario, February 27, 1926

1948–49R	43	1	2	3	59
1949–50	64	4	8	12	63
1950–51	19	0	1	1	16
Totals	126	5	11	16	138

- first Red Wings regular season game December 1, 1948
- Galt Red Wings graduate
- played much of '47–'49 with Indianapolis
- traded December 10, 1950 with Steve Black to Chicago for Bert Olmstead and Vic Stasiuk

RICK FOLEY #19 DEFENCE 6′4″ 225 *b.* Niagara Falls, Ontario, September 22, 1945

1973–74	7	0	0	0	4

- acquired May 15, 1973 from Flyers for Serge Lajeunesse
- only Red Wings games October 10/13/14/16/18/24/26, 1973
- played most of '73–'74 with Baltimore, '74–'75 with Syracuse
- began '75–'76 with Toronto Toros (WHA), then played 4 games with Baltimore before retiring December 12, 1975

MIKE FOLIGNO #17 RIGHT WING 6′2″ 195 *b.* Sudbury, Ontario, January 29, 1959

1979–80R	80	36	35	71	109
1980–81	80	28	35	63	210
1981–82	26	13	13	26	28
Totals	186	77	83	160	347

- selected 3rd overall at 1979 Entry Draft
- first Red Wings game October 10, 1979
- traded December 2, 1981 with Dale McCourt and Brent Peterson to Buffalo for Danny Gare, Jim Schoenfeld, and Derek Smith

BILL FOLK #18 – 19 DEFENCE 6′ 190
b. Regina, Saskatchewan, July 11, 1927

1951–52R	4	0	0	0	2
1952–53L	8	0	0	0	2
Totals	12	0	0	0	4

- first Red Wings games December 2/5/8/9, 1951
- last Red Wings games November 2/6/8/13/19/22/23/29, 1952
- career minor-leaguer '48–'61; suffered heart attack during opening of '61–'62 with Spokane — forced to retire

LEN FONTAINE #11 – 18 RIGHT WING 5′7″ 165 *b.* Quebec City, Quebec, February 25, 1948

1972–73R	39	8	10	18	6
1973–74	7	0	1	1	4
Totals	46	8	11	19	10

- signed May 1972 with Detroit
- first Red Wings game October 7, 1972
- played part of '72–'73 with Tidewater
- only Red Wings games October 10/13/14/16/18/24/26, 1973
- missed much of '73–'74 after foot surgery; played with Virginia to recuperate

VALERE "VAL" FONTEYNE #8 – 11 – 12 – 19 – 21 LEFT WING 5′9″ 155 *b.* Wetaskewin, Alberta, December 2, 1933

1959–60R	69	4	7	11	2
1960–61	66	6	11	17	4
1961–62	70	5	5	10	4
1962–63	67	6	14	20	2
1964–65	16	2	6	8	6
1965–66	59	5	10	15	0
1966–67	28	1	1	2	0
Totals	375	29	54	83	18

- played '55–'59 with Seattle, part of '65–'67 with Pittsburgh
- first Red Wings game October 10, 1959
- lost June 1963 to Rangers at Intra-League Draft
- claimed February 8, 1965 on waiver from Rangers
- missed much of '66–'67 with broken thumb
- lost June 6, 1967 to Penguins at Expansion Draft

DWIGHT FOSTER ("Dewey") #20 CENTRE 5′11″ 195 *b.* Toronto, Ontario, April 2, 1957

1982–83	58	17	22	39	58
1983–84	52	9	12	21	50
1984–85	50	16	16	32	56
1985–86L	55	6	12	18	48
Totals	215	48	62	110	212

- rights bought October 29, 1982 from New Jersey
- last Red Wings game March 9, 1986
- traded March 11, 1986 to Boston for Dave Donnelly

HARRY FOSTER ("Yip") #8 – 16 DEFENCE 6′ 198 *b.* Guelph, Ontario, November 25, 1907

1933–34	6	0	0	0	2
1934–35L	12	2	0	2	8
Totals	18	2	0	2	10

- played November 9/12/14/16/19/21, 1933
- last Red Wings games January 6/8/13/15/17/20/26/27/31, February 3/5/7, 1935

FRANK FOYSTON #10 CENTRE
b. Minesing, Ontario, February 2, 1891
d. Port Orchard, Washington, January 19, 1966

1926–27R	41	10	5	15	16
1927–28L	23	7	2	9	16
Totals	64	17	7	24	32

- came from Victoria when team moved to Detroit
- first Cougars game November 18, 1926
- last Cougars game March 24, 1928

BOBBY FRANCIS #16 CENTRE
5′9″ 175 *b.* North Battleford, Saskatchewan, December 5, 1958

1982–83R/L	14	2	0	2	0

- acquired December 2, 1982 from Calgary for the rights to Yves Courteau
- played part of '82–'83 with Adirondack, '83–'84 with Colorado, '84–'87 with Salt Lake
- first and only Red Wings games December 4/8/11/12/15/16/18/21/23/26/27, January 3/16/19, 1982–83

JIMMY FRANKS #1 GOALIE 5′11″ 156
b. Melville, Saskatchewan, November 8, 1914

1937–38R	1	1–0–0	60	3	0	3.00
1943–44	18	6–8–3	1080	73	1	4.06
Totals	19	7–8–3	1140	76	1	4.00

- first Red Wings game March 20, 1938
- traded to Boston during '43–'44

GORD FRASER #5 DEFENCE
b. Pembroke, Ontario

1927–28	30	3	1	4	50
1928–29	13	0	0	0	12
Totals	43	3	1	4	62

- acquired December 16, 1927 with $5,000 from Chicago for Duke Keats

FRANK FREDERICKSON #5 – 17
CENTRE 5′11″ 175
b. Winnipeg, Manitoba, June 11, 1895
d. Toronto, Ontario, May 28, 1979

1926–27R	16	4	6	10	12
1930–31	25	1	2	3	6
Totals	41	5	8	13	18

- came from Victoria when team moved to Detroit
- first Cougars game November 18, 1926
- traded during '26–'27 back to Victoria Cougars for Duke Keats
- signed November 24, 1930

TIM FRIDAY #4 DEFENCE 6′ 190
b. Burbank, California, March 5, 1961

1985–86R/L	23	0	3	3	6

- signed as a free agent June 5, 1985
- first Red Wings game October 10, 1985
- last Red Wings game January 5, 1986

MIROSLAV "MIRKO" FRYCER #14
RIGHT WING 6′ 200 *b.* Ostrava, Czechoslovakia, September 27, 1959

1988–89	23	7	8	15	47

- acquired June 11, 1988 from Toronto for Darren Veitch
- traded January 3, 1989 to Edmonton for a 10th round draft choice in 1989 (Rick Judson)

ROBBIE FTOREK ("Britz") #15 – 23
CENTRE 5′10″ 155 *b.* Needham, Massachusetts, January 2, 1952

1972–73R	3	0	0	0	0
1973–74	12	2	5	7	4
Totals	15	2	5	7	4

- first Red Wings games December 26/30/31, 1972
- played part of '72–'73 with Tidewater, '73–'74 with Virginia
- played '74–'75 with Phoenix (WHA)

BILL GADSBY ("Gads") #4 DEFENCE 6′ 185
b. Calgary, Alberta, August 8, 1927

1961–62	70	7	30	37	88
1962–63	70	4	24	28	116
1963–64	64	2	16	18	80
1964–65	61	0	12	12	122
1965–66L	58	5	12	17	72
Totals	323	18	94	112	478

- acquired June 1961 from Rangers for Leslie Hunt
- last Red Wings game April 3, 1966
- retired after '65–'66 season

JOSEPH "JODY" GAGE #16 – 17 – 21
RIGHT WING 6′ 190 *b.* Toronto, Ontario, November 29, 1959

1980–81R	16	2	2	4	22
1981–82	31	9	10	19	2
1983–84	3	0	0	0	0
Totals	50	11	12	23	24

- selected 45th overall at 1979 Entry Draft
- first Red Wings game October 10, 1980
- played November 9/23/25, 1983
- played most of '80–'84 and all of '84–'85 with Adirondack
- lost as a free agent July 31, 1985 to Sabres

ART GAGNE #7 – 11 RIGHT WING
b. Unknown *d.* Unknown

1931–32L	13	1	1	2	0

- loaned from Ottawa for '31–'32 when Senators did not field a team
- only Falcons games November 22/24/29, December 3/5/10/12/16/17/20/22/27/29, 1931
- retired after '31–'32

DAVE GAGNON #35 GOALIE 6′ 185
b. Windsor, Ontario, October 31, 1967

1990–91	2	0–0–0	35	6	0	10.59

- signed as a free agent June 11, 1990
- played most of '90–'91 with Adirondack and Hampton (ECHL)
- played January 25 & 28, 1991

JOHNNY GALLAGHER #2 – 3 – 16 – 17
DEFENCE 5′11″ 188 *b.* Kenora, Ontario, January 19, 1909 *d.* Unknown

1932–33	35	3	6	9	48
1933–34	1	0	0	0	0
1936–37	11	1	0	1	4
Totals	47	4	6	10	52

- acquired December 9, 1932 from Maroons for Reg Noble
- sold October 7, 1937 to Americans for $6,000

GERARD GALLANT #17 LEFT WING 5′10″
185 *b.* Summerside, Prince Edward Island, September 2, 1963

1984–85R	32	6	12	18	66
1985–86	52	20	19	39	106
1986–87	80	38	34	72	216
1987–88	73	34	39	73	242
1988–89	76	39	54	93	230
1989–90	69	36	44	80	254
1990–91	45	10	16	26	111
1991–92	69	14	22	36	187
1992–93	67	10	20	30	188
Totals	563	207	260	467	1600

- selected 107th overall at 1981 Entry Draft
- first Red Wings game January 22, 1985
- signed July 31, 1993 as a free agent by Tampa Bay

GEORGE GARDNER ("Bud") #25 – 30
GOALIE 5′10″ 160 *b.* Lachine, Quebec, October 8, 1942

1965–66R	1	1–0–0	60	1	0	1.00
1966–67	11	3–6–0	560	36	0	3.86
1967–68	12	3–2–2	534	32	0	3.60
Totals	24	7–8–2	1154	69	0	3.59

- first Red Wings game March 20, 1966
- claimed June 10, 1964 from Boston in Intra-League Draft
- claimed June 13, 1968 by Rochester in Reverse Draft

DANNY GARE #18 RIGHT WING 5′9″ 175
b. Nelson, British Columbia, May 14, 1954

1981–82	36	13	9	22	74
1982–83	79	26	35	61	107
1983–84	63	13	13	26	147
1984–85	71	27	29	56	163
1985–86	57	7	9	16	102
Totals	306	86	95	181	593

- acquired December 2, 1981 with Jim Schoenfeld and Derek Smith from Sabres for Mike Foligno, Dale McCourt, and Brent Peterson
- released outright June 2, 1986

JOHAN GARPENLOV #15 LEFT WING 5′11″
183 *b.* Stockholm, Sweden, March 21, 1968

1990–91R	71	18	22	40	18
1991–92	16	1	1	2	4
Totals	87	19	23	42	22

- selected 85th overall at 1986 Entry Draft
- first Red Wings game October 4, 1990
- traded March 9, 1992 to San Jose for Bob McGill and an 8th-round draft choice in 1992 (acquired from Vancouver Canucks — C.J. Denomme)

DAVE GATHERUM #1 GOALIE 5′8″ 170
b. Fort William, Ontario, March 28, 1932

1953–54R/L	3	2–0–1	180	3	1	1.00

- replaced injured Sawchuk October 11/16/17, 1953

FERN GAUTHIER #10 – 15 – 25 RIGHT WING 5′11″ 175 *b.* Chicoutimi, Quebec, August 31, 1919 *d.* Unknown

1945–46	30	9	8	17	6
1946–47	40	1	12	13	2
1947–48	35	1	5	6	2
1948–49L	41	3	2	5	2
Totals	146	14	27	41	12

- on September 12, 1945, Billy Reay was traded to the Canadiens for Ray Getliffe, Rollie Rossignol, and cash. Rather than report to Detroit, however, Getliffe retired. On October 19, 1945, to complete the deal, the Habs sent Gauthier to the Wings instead
- played part of ’45–’46 with Indianapolis
- last Red Wings game February 9, 1949
- traded September 1949 with Cliff Simpson, Ed Nicholson, and future considerations to St. Louis Flyers for Steve Black and Bill Brennan

GEORGE GEE #8 CENTRE 5′11″ 180 *b.* Stratford, Ontario, June 28, 1922 *d.* Wyandotte, January 1972

1948–49	47	7	11	18	27
1949–50	69	17	21	38	42
1950–51	70	17	20	37	19
Totals	186	41	52	93	88

- acquired October 1948 with Bud Poile from Chicago for Jim Conacher, Bep Guidolin, and Doug McCaig
- traded August 20, 1951 with Jim McFadden, Max McNab, Jim Peters, Clare Martin, and Rags Raglan to Chicago for Hugh Coflin and $75,000

ED GIACOMIN (“Fast Eddie”) #31 GOALIE 5′11″ 180 *b.* Sudbury, Ontario, June 6, 1939

1975–76	29	12–14–3	1740	100	2	3.45
1976–77	33	8–18–3	1980	119	2	3.61
1977–78L	9	3–5–1	516	27	0	3.14
Totals	71	23–37–7	4236	246	4	3.48

- claimed on waivers November 1, 1975 from Rangers
- last Red Wings games October 20/27, November 6/13/19/27, December 3/8/21, 1977
- retired after ’77–’78

ROY “GUS” GIESEBRECHT #4 – 14 – 19 CENTRE 6′ 177 *b.* Petawawa, Ontario, September 16, 1918

1938–39R	28	10	10	20	2
1939–40	30	4	7	11	2
1940–41	43	7	18	25	7
1941–42L	34	6	16	22	2
Totals	135	27	51	78	13

- signed October 21, 1938
- first Red Wings game December 29, 1938
- played part of ’38–’39 with Pittsburgh, part of ’39–’40 with Indianapolis
- joined Canadian Armed Forces in 1942–46, then retired from hockey after being discharged
- last Red Wings game February 8, 1942

GILLES GILBERT #1 – 30 GOALIE 6′1″ 175 *b.* St. Esprit, Quebec, March 31, 1949

1980–81	48	11–24–9	2618	175	0	4.01
1981–82	27	6–10–6	1478	105	0	4.26
1982–83L	20	4–14–1	1137	85	0	4.49
Totals	95	21–48–16	5233	365	0	4.18

- acquired July 15, 1980 from Boston for Rogie Vachon
- missed many games in ’82–’83 with serious “mystery” skin rash; played part of the season in Adirondack
- last Red Wings game March 30, 1983
- retired after ’82–’83

ART GIROUX #17 RIGHT WING 5′11″ 165 *b.* Strathmore, Alberta, June 6, 1907

1935–36L	4	0	2	2	0

- only Red Wings games February 20/23/27, March 1, 1936

LARRY GIROUX #3 – 4 – 22 DEFENCE 6′ 190 *b.* Weyburn, Saskatchewan, August 28, 1951

1974–75	39	2	20	22	60
1975–76	10	1	1	2	25
1976–77	2	0	0	0	2
1977–78	5	0	3	3	4
Totals	56	3	24	27	91

- acquired December 14, 1974 with Bart Crashley and Ted Snell from Kansas City for Guy Charron and Claude Houde
- played March 17 & 20, 1977
- played December 21/23/27/29/31, 1977
- lost October 9, 1978 to St. Louis in Waiver Draft

LORRY GLOECKNER #11 DEFENCE 6′2″ 210
b. Kindersley, Saskatchewan, January 25, 1956

1978–79R/L	13	0	2	2	6

- signed October 12, 1978 as a free agent
- first and only Red Wings games January 10/11/13/17/19/20/25/27/28/30, February 1/3/4, 1979
- played most of '78–'79 with Kansas City

FRED GLOVER #16 – 17 – 22 – 24
RIGHT WING 5′9″ 175 *b.* Toronto, Ontario, January 5, 1928

1949–50R	7	0	0	0	0
1951–52	54	9	9	18	25
Totals	61	9	9	18	25

- Galt Red Wings graduate
- first Red Wings games October 12/16/23/27/29 and November 2/6, 1949
- played much of '48–'52 with Indianapolis
- sold August 14, 1952 with Enio Sclisizzi to Chicago for cash

HOWIE GLOVER #15 RIGHT WING 5′11″ 195
b. Toronto, Ontario, February 14, 1935

1960–61	66	21	8	29	46
1961–62	39	7	8	15	44
Totals	105	28	16	44	90

- acquired June 7, 1960 from Chicago for Jim Morrison
- lost June 5, 1963 to Rangers at Intra-League Draft

WARREN GODFREY ("Rocky") #2 – 3 – 5 – 11 – 18 – 21 – 23 – 25 DEFENCE 6′1″ 190
b. Toronto, Ontario, March 23, 1931

1955–56	67	2	6	8	86
1956–57	69	1	8	9	103
1957–58	67	2	16	18	56
1958–59	69	6	4	10	44
1959–60	69	5	9	14	60
1960–61	63	3	16	19	62
1961–62	69	4	13	17	84
1963–64	4	0	0	0	2
1964–65	11	0	0	0	8
1965–66	26	0	4	4	22
1966–67	2	0	0	0	0
1967–68L	12	0	1	1	0
Totals	528	23	77	100	527

- acquired June 3, 1955 from Boston with Gilles Boisvert, Ed Sandford, Real Chevrefils, and Norm Corcoran for Marcel Bonin, Terry Sawchuk, Vic Stasiuk, and Lorne Davis
- lost June 1962 to Boston in Intra-League Draft
- acquired October 10, 1963 from Boston for Gerry Odrowski
- played part of '67–'68 with Fort Worth, '68–'69 with Rochester
- played December 5/7/8/11, 1963
- played March 4 & 5, 1967
- last Red Wings game January 24, 1968
- out of hockey after 1969

PETE GOEGAN #2 – 18 – 19 – 22 – 23
DEFENCE 6′1″ 200 *b.* Fort William, Ontario, March 6, 1934

1957–58R	14	0	2	2	28
1958–59	67	1	11	12	109
1959–60	21	3	0	3	6
1960–61	67	5	29	34	48
1961–62	39	5	5	10	24
1962–63	62	1	8	9	48
1963–64	12	0	0	0	8
1964–65	4	1	0	1	2
1965–66	13	0	2	2	14
1966–67	31	2	6	8	12
Totals	330	18	63	81	299

- acquired February 20, 1958 from Cleveland (AHL) for Gord Hollingworth
- first Red Wings game February 22, 1958
- traded February 16, 1962 to Rangers for Noel Price
- acquired October 8, 1962 from Rangers for Noel Price
- lost June 6, 1967 to Minnesota in Expansion Draft

EBENEZER "EBBIE" GOODFELLOW

BOB GOLDHAM ("Goldie") #2 DEFENCE
6′1″ 195 *b.* Georgetown, Ontario, May 12, 1922 *d.* Toronto, Ontario, September 6, 1991

1950–51	61	5	18	23	31
1951–52	69	0	14	14	24
1952–53	70	1	13	14	32
1953–54	69	1	15	16	50
1954–55	69	1	15	16	50
1955–56L	68	3	16	19	32
Totals	406	11	91	102	219

- acquired July 13, 1950 with Jim Henry, Gaye Stewart, and Metro Prystai from Chicago for Al Dewsbury, Harry Lumley, Jack Stewart, Don Morrison, and Pete Babando
- last regular season Red Wings game March 18, 1956
- retired April 10, 1956, immediately after last playoff game

LEROY GOLDSWORTHY ("Goldie") #7 – 16 – 17 RIGHT WING 6′ 190 *b.* Two Harbors, Minnesota, October 18, 1908

1930–31	13	1	0	1	2
1932–33	26	3	6	9	6
Totals	39	4	6	10	8

- acquired from London (Can Pro League) for Herb Stuart
- sent to Chicago for '33–'34

EBENEZER "EBBIE" GOODFELLOW ("Poker Face") #5 – 10 CENTRE 6′ 180 *b.* Ottawa, Ontario, April 9, 1907 *d.* Sarasota, Florida, September 10, 1965

1929–30R	44	17	17	34	54
1930–31	44	25	23	48	32
1931–32	48	14	16	30	56
1932–33	40	12	8	20	47
1933–34	48	13	13	26	45
1934–35	48	12	24	36	44
1935–36	48	5	18	23	69
1936–37	48	9	16	25	43
1937–38	29	0	7	7	18
1938–39	48	8	8	16	36
1939–40	43	11	17	28	31
1940–41	47	5	17	22	35
1941–42	8	2	2	4	2
1942–43L	11	1	4	5	4
Totals	554	134	190	324	516

- acquired October 14, 1928 from Americans for Johnny Sheppard and $12,500
- first Cougars game November 14, 1929
- played January 1/3/4/6/8/10/11/13, 1942
- last Red Wings games November 15/19/24/26/29, December 1/6/12/13/20/25, 1942
- retired after '42–'43

FRED GORDON #12 FORWARD
b. Unknown *d.* Unknown

1926–27R	36	5	5	10	28

- played with Saskatoon in '25–'26
- first Cougars game November 18, 1926
- sent to Boston in summer 1927

EDWARD "TED" GRAHAM #3 DEFENCE
5′10″ 173
b. Owen Sound, Ontario, June 30, 1906
d. Owen Sound, Ontario, December 7, 1978

1933–34	28	1	0	1	29
1934–35	24	0	2	2	26
Totals	52	1	2	3	55

- acquired January 1934 from Maroons for Stu Evans
- traded February 11, 1935 to St. Louis with $50,000 for Scotty Bowman and Syd Howe

DANNY GRANT #21 LEFT WING 5′10″ 188
b. Fredericton, New Brunswick, February 21, 1946

1974–75	80	50	37	87	28
1975–76	39	10	13	23	20
1976–77	42	2	10	12	4
1977–78	13	2	2	4	0
Totals	174	64	62	126	52

- acquired August 27, 1974 from Minnesota for Henry Boucha
- traded January 9, 1978 to Los Angeles for a 3rd-round draft choice in 1978 (Doug Derkson) and the rights to Barry Long

DOUG GRANT #30 – 31 GOALIE 6′1″ 200
b. Corner Brook, Newfoundland, July 27, 1948

1973–74R	37	15–16–2	2018	140	1	4.16
1974–75	7	1–5–0	380	34	0	5.37
1975–76	2	1–1–0	120	8	0	4.00
Totals	46	17–22–2	2518	182	1	4.34

- first Red Wings game October 10, 1973
- played part of '73–'75 with Virginia, '75–'76 with New Haven
- played November 13/20/23/24/27, December 5/18, 1974
- played February 6 & 7, 1976
- traded March 9, 1976 to St. Louis for future considerations (Rick Wilson — June 16, 1976)

LEO GRAVELLE ("The Gazelle") #20
RIGHT WING 5′8″ 158 *b.* Aylmer, Quebec, June 10, 1925

1950–51IL	17	1	2	3	6

- played part of '50–'51 with Indianapolis; joined QSHL from '51–'56
- acquired December 19, 1950 from Canadiens for Bert Olmstead (Olmstead was acquired December 10, 1950 with Vic Stasiuk from Chicago for Lee Fogolin and Steve Black, though never played a game with the Red Wings)
- last Red Wings game February 4, 1951

ADAM GRAVES #12 CENTRE 5′11″ 185
b. Toronto, Ontario, April 12, 1968

1987–88R	9	0	1	1	8
1988–89	56	7	5	12	60
1989–90	13	0	1	1	13
Totals	78	7	7	14	81

- selected 22nd overall at 1986 Entry Draft
- first Red Wings games October 9/17/23/28/30/31, November 3/6, January 8, 1987–88
- traded November 2, 1989 with Petr Klima, Joe Murphy, and Jeff Sharples to Edmonton for Jimmy Carson and Kevin McClelland

GERALD "GERRY" GRAY #30 GOALIE 6′ 168
b. Brantford, Ontario, January 28, 1948

1970–71R	7	1–4–1	380	30	0	4.74

- Hamilton Red Wings graduate
- first Red Wings games March 4/9/13/18/21/25/27, 1971
- played part of '68–'69 and '70–'71 with Fort Worth, '69–'70 with Cleveland
- traded October 4, 1972 with Arnie Brown to the Islanders for Dennis DeJordy and Don McLaughlin

HARRISON GRAY #22 GOALIE 5′11″ 165
b. Calgary, Alberta, September 5, 1941

1963–64R/L	1	0–0–0	40	5	0	7.50

- first and only Red Wings game November 28, 1963, replacing Sawchuk to start 2nd period
- played part of '63–'64 with Cincinnati

RED GREEN #12 FORWARD
b. Unknown *d.* Unknown

1928–29R/L	2	0	0	0	0

- first and only Cougars games February 23 & March 3, 1929

RICHARD "RICK" GREEN #5 DEFENCE 6′3″
220 *b.* Belleville, Ontario, February 20, 1956

1990–91	65	2	14	15	25

- acquired June 15, 1990 from Canadiens for a 5th-round draft choice in 1991 (Brad Layzell)
- traded May 26, 1991 to Islanders for Alan Kerr and future considerations

STU GRIMSON #32 LEFT WING 6′5″ 227
b. Kamloops, British Columbia, May 20, 1965

1994–95	11	0	0	0	37
1995–96	56	0	1	1	126
Totals	67	0	1	1	163

- selected 186th overall at 1983 Entry Draft
- not signed; re-entered draft and claimed by Calgary in 1985
- acquired April 4, 1995 with Mark Ferner and a 6th-round draft choice in 1996 (Magnus Nilsson) from Anaheim for Mike Sillinger and Jason York
- lost on waivers October 10, 1996

LLOYD GROSS #14 – 15 LEFT WING 5′8″ 175
b. Kitchener, Ontario, October 15, 1907

1933–34	13	1	0	1	6
1934–35L	6	1	0	1	2
Totals	19	2	0	2	8

- played February 13/15/18/20/22/25/27, March 1/3/8/11/15/18, 1934
- last Red Wings games December 13/16/20/22/23/25, 1934

DON GROSSO ("Count") #10 – 18 – 25
LEFT WING 5′11″ 170 *b.* Sault Ste. Marie, Ontario, April 12, 1915 *d.* Unknown

1939–40R	28	2	3	5	11
1940–41	45	8	7	15	14
1941–42	48	23	30	53	13
1942–43	50	15	17	32	10
1943–44	42	16	31	47	13
1944–45	20	6	10	16	16
Totals	233	70	98	168	77

- played '38–'39 with Kirkland Lake Blue Devils, but joined Detroit for '39 playoffs
- first regular season Red Wings game December 31, 1939
- missed much of '39–'40 with badly broken hand
- traded January 1945 with Cully Simon and Byron McDonald to Chicago for Earl Seibert

DANNY GRUEN #12 – 23 LEFT WING 5′11″
190 *b.* Thunder Bay, Ontario, June 26, 1952

1972–73R	2	0	0	0	0
1973–74	18	1	3	4	7
Totals	20	1	3	4	7

- selected 58th overall at 1972 Entry Draft
- first Red Wings games January 4 & 7, 1973
- left for WHA in April 1974
- rights sold February 1, 1977 to Colorado for cash
- signed August 17, 1977 as a free agent
- played '77–'79 with Kansas City

ARMAND "BEP" GUIDOLIN #14
LEFT WING 5′8″ 175 *b.* Thorold, Ontario, December 9, 1925

1947–48	58	12	10	22	78
1948–49	4	0	0	0	0
Totals	62	12	10	22	78

- acquired October 1947 from Boston for Billy Taylor
- played October 13/17/23/24, 1948
- traded October 1948 with Jim Conacher and Doug McCaig to Chicago for George Gee and Bud Poile

MARC HABSCHEID #25 RIGHT WING/CENTRE 6′ 185 *b.* Swift Current, Saskatchewan, March 1, 1963

1989–90	66	15	11	26	33
1990–91	46	9	8	17	22
Totals	112	24	19	43	55

- signed as a free agent June 9, 1989
- traded June 11, 1991 to Calgary for Brian MacLellan

LLOYD HADDON #18 DEFENCE 6′ 195
b. Sarnia, Ontario, August 10, 1938

1959–60R/L	8	0	0	0	2

- first and only Red Wings games February 11/13/14/20/21/28, March 12/20, 1960
- career minor-leaguer '58–'65

GORD HAIDY ("Adam") #20 RIGHT WING
5′10″ 185 *b.* Winnipeg, Manitoba, April 11, 1928

- appeared for Detroit only in the 1950 playoffs

HAROLD "SLIM" HALDERSON #3 DEFENCE
6′3″ 200 *b.* Winnipeg, Manitoba, January 6, 1900 *d.* Unknown

1926–27R	18	2	0	2	29

- came from Victoria when team moved to Detroit
- first Cougars game November 18, 1926
- traded January 10, 1927 to Toronto for Pete Bellefeuille

LEONARD "LEN" HALEY ("Comet") #22
RIGHT WING 5′7″ 168
b. Edmonton, Alberta, September 15, 1931

1959–60R	27	1	2	3	12
1960–61L	3	0	1	1	12
Totals	30	1	3	4	24

- first Red Wings game January 13, 1960
- last Red Wings games October 5/6/9, 1960
- career minor-leaguer '50–'69

BOB HALKIDIS #21 DEFENCE 5′11″ 205
b. Toronto, Ontario, March 5, 1966

1993–94	28	1	4	5	93
1994–95	4	0	1	1	6
Totals	32	1	5	6	99

- signed September 2, 1993 as a free agent
- played part of '93–'94 with Adirondack
- lost February 10, 1995 on waivers to Tampa Bay

GLENN HALL ("Mr. Goalie") #1 – 22
GOALIE 6′ 160 *b.* Humboldt, Saskatchewan, October 3, 1931

1952–53R	6	4–1–1	360	10	1	1.67
1954–55	2	2–0–0	120	2	0	1.00
1955–56	70	30–24–16	4200	148	12	2.11
1956–57	70	38–20–12	4200	157	4	2.24
Totals	148	74–45–29	8880	317	17	2.14

- played '51–'52 with Indianapolis and most of '52–'55 with Edmonton
- first Red Wings games December 27/28/31 and January 4/8/11, 1952–53
- played February 12 & 13, 1955
- traded July 1957 with Ted Lindsay to Chicago for Forbes Kennedy, Johnny Wilson, William Preston, and Hank Bassen

MURRAY HALL #14 – 20 – 25 CENTRE 6′ 175
b. Kirkland Lake, Ontario, November 24, 1940

1965–66	1	0	0	0	0
1966–67	12	4	3	7	4
Totals	13	4	3	7	4

- claimed June 10, 1964 from Chicago at Intra-League Draft
- played February 13, 1966
- sold May 8, 1967 with Albert Le Brun to Chicago to complete trade of December 20, 1966 in which Detroit acquired Howie Young from the Blackhawks

DOUG HALWARD #7 DEFENCE 6′1″ 200
b. Toronto, Ontario, November 1, 1955

1986–87	11	0	3	3	19
1987–88	70	5	21	26	130
1988–89	18	0	1	1	36
Totals	99	5	25	30	185

- acquired November 21, 1986 from Vancouver Canucks for a 6th-round draft choice in 1988 (Phil von Stefenelli)
- traded January 23, 1989 to Edmonton for a 12th-round draft choice in 1989 (Jason Glickman)

JEAN HAMEL #5 – 19 DEFENCE 5′11″ 195
b. Asbestos, Quebec, June 6, 1952

1973–74	22	0	3	3	40
1974–75	80	5	19	24	136
1975–76	77	3	9	12	129
1976–77	71	1	10	11	63
1977–78	32	2	6	8	34
1978–79	52	2	4	6	72
1979–80	49	1	4	5	43
1980–81	68	5	7	12	57
Totals	451	19	62	81	574

- acquired February 14, 1974 with Bryan Watson and Chris Evans from St. Louis for Garnet "Ace" Bailey, Ted Harris, and Bill Collins
- played part of '77–'78 with Kansas City
- claimed June 13, 1979 as fill in Expansion Draft
- signed October 6, 1981 as a free agent by Quebec

EDWARD "TED" HAMPSON #16 – 17 – 21
CENTRE 5′8″ 173 *b.* Togo, Saskatchewan, December 11, 1936

1963–64	7	0	1	1	0
1964–65	1	0	0	0	0
1966–67	65	13	35	48	4
1967–68	37	9	18	27	10
Totals	110	22	54	76	14

- claimed June 4, 1963 from Rangers at Intra-League Draft
- played October 10/13/16/19/20/24/27, 1963
- played November 18, 1964
- played much of '63–'67 with Pittsburgh
- traded January 9, 1968 with John Brenneman and Bert Marshall to Oakland for Kurt Douglas

GLEN HANLON #1 GOALIE 6′ 185
b. Brandon, Manitoba, February 20, 1957

1986–87	36	11–16–5	1963	104	1	3.18
1987–88	47	22–17–5	2623	141	4	3.23
1988–89	39	13–14–8	2092	124	1	3.56
1989–90	45	15–18–5	2290	154	1	4.03
1990–91L	19	4–6–3	862	46	0	3.20
Totals	186	65–71–26	9830	569	7	3.47

- acquired July 29, 1986 with a 3rd-round draft choice in 1987 (Dennis Holland), and a 3rd-round draft choice in 1988 (Guy Dupuis) from the Rangers for Kelly Kisio, Jim Leavins, and Lane Lambert
- last Red Wings game March 31, 1991
- played part of '90–'91 with San Diego, then retired

DAVE HANSON #17 DEFENCE 6′ 190
b. Cumberland, Wisconsin, April 12, 1954

1978–79	11	0	0	0	26

- selected 176th overall at 1975 Entry Draft
- played '76–'77 with Minnesota (WHA)
- signed as a free agent October 4, 1977
- loaned November 15, 1977 to Birmingham (WHA) with Steve Durbano and future considerations for Vaclav Nedomansky and Tim Sheehy
- returned to the NHL for the end of '78–'79 after starting in Birmingham (WHA)
- played much of '79–'80 with Birmingham (CHL) and Oklahoma City
- traded January 3, 1980 to Minnesota for future considerations

EMIL HANSON #3 – 16 DEFENCE 5′10″ 180
b. Centerville, South Dakota, November 18, 1907 *d.* Unknown

1932–33R/L	7	0	0	0	6

- first Red Wings game November 17, 1932

TERRANCE "TERRY" HARPER #2
DEFENCE 6′1″ 197
b. Regina, Saskatchewan, January 27, 1940

1975–76	69	8	25	33	59
1976–77	52	4	8	12	28
1977–78	80	2	17	19	85
1978–79	51	0	6	6	58
Totals	252	14	56	70	230

- acquired June 23, 1975 with Dan Maloney and a 2nd-round draft choice in 1976 (later traded to Minnesota — Jim Roberts) to Los Angeles for the rights to Marcel Dionne and Bart Crashley
- lost as a free agent March 10, 1980 to St. Louis

BILLY HARRIS ("Hinky") #14 CENTRE 6′ 165
b. Toronto, Ontario, July 29, 1935

1965–66	24	1	4	5	6

- acquired May 20, 1965 with Andy Bathgate and Gary Jarrett from Toronto for Marcel Pronovost, Ed Joyal, Larry Jeffrey, Lowell MacDonald, and Aut Erickson
- lost June 6, 1967 to Oakland in Expansion Draft

EDWARD HARRIS ("Ted") #19 DEFENCE 6′2″ 183 *b.* Winnipeg, Manitoba, July 18, 1936

1973–74	41	0	11	11	66

- acquired November 7, 1973 from Minnesota for Gary Bergman
- traded February 14, 1974 with Garnet "Ace" Bailey and Bill Collins to St. Louis for Bryan Watson, Chris Evans, and Jean Hamel

RON HARRIS #4 – 16 – 18 DEFENCE 5′9″ 190
b. Verdun, Quebec, June 30, 1942

1962–63R	1	0	1	1	0
1963–64	3	0	0	0	7
1968–69	73	3	13	16	91
1969–70	72	2	19	21	99
1970–71	42	2	8	10	65
1971–72	61	1	10	11	80
Totals	252	8	51	59	342

- Hamilton Red Wings graduate
- first Red Wings game December 13, 1962
- played December 11/14/15, 1963
- played part of '62–'63 with Pittsburgh, '63–'64 with Cincinnati, all of '64–'65 with Memphis and Pittsburgh
- traded May 31, 1965 with Bob Dillabough, Al Langlois, and Parker MacDonald to Boston for Ab McDonald, Bob McCord, and Ken Stephenson
- acquired May 27, 1968 with Bob Baun from Oakland for Gary Jarrett, Doug Roberts, Howie Young, and Chris Worthy
- lost June 6, 1972 to Atlanta in Expansion Draft

GERRY HART #3 – 18 – 21 DEFENCE 5′9″ 190
b. Flin Flon, Manitoba, January 1, 1948

1968–69R	1	0	0	0	2
1969–70	3	0	0	0	2
1970–71	64	2	7	9	148
1971–72	3	0	0	0	0
Totals	71	2	7	9	152

- first Red Wings game February 23, 1969
- played part of '68–'69 with Fort Worth and Baltimore, '69–'70 with Fort Worth, '71–'72 with Fort Worth and Tidewater
- played March 17 & 18, 1970
- played January 19/22/23, 1972
- lost June 6, 1972 to Islanders in Expansion Draft

HAROLD "GIZZY" HART #13
LEFT WING 5′9″ 171
b. Weyburn, Saskatchewan, June 1, 1903
d. Weyburn, Saskatchewan, June 22, 1964

1926–27R	6	0	0	0	0

- first Cougars game November 18, 1926
- traded December 1926 to Canadiens

DOUG HARVEY #5 DEFENCE 5′11″ 180
b. Montreal, Quebec, December 19, 1924
d. Montreal, Quebec, December 26, 1989

1966–67	2	0	0	0	0

- signed January 1967 as a free agent
- played January 11 & 12, 1967
- signed April 1968 as a free agent by St. Louis

FREDERIC "BUSTER" HARVEY #27
RIGHT WING 6′ 185 *b.* Fredericton, New Brunswick, April 2, 1950

1975–76	75	13	21	34	31
1976–77L	54	11	11	22	18
Totals	129	24	32	56	49

- acquired January 14, 1976 from Kansas City for Phil Roberts
- played part of '76–'77 with Kansas City (WHL), all of '77–'78 with Philadelphia (AHL)
- played March 17 & 18, 1970
- played January 19/22/23, 1972

ED HATOUM #18 – 20 RIGHT WING 5′10″ 185
b. Beirut, Lebanon, December 7, 1947

1968–69R	16	2	1	3	2
1969–70	5	0	2	2	2
Totals	21	2	3	5	4

- Hamilton Red Wings graduate
- first Red Wings game December 1, 1968
- played most of '68–'69 with Fort Worth and Baltimore, '69–'70 with Fort Worth
- played November 29/30, December 3/4, March 29, 1969–70
- lost June 10, 1970 to Vancouver Canucks in Expansion Draft

GEORGE HAY ("The Western Wizard") #4 – 7
LEFT WING *b.* Listowell, Ontario, January 10, 1898 *d.* Stratford, Ontario, July 13, 1975

1927–28	42	22	13	35	20
1928–29	42	11	8	19	14
1929–30	42	18	15	33	8
1930–31	44	8	10	18	24
1932–33	34	1	6	7	6
1933–34L	1	0	0	0	0
Totals	205	60	52	112	72

- bought summer 1927 with Percy Traub from Chicago for $15,000

JIM HAY ("Red Eye") #18 – 20
DEFENCE 5′11″ 185
b. Saskatoon, Saskatchewan, May 15, 1931

1952–53R	42	1	4	5	2
1953–54	12	0	0	0	0
1954–55L	21	0	1	1	20
Totals	75	1	5	6	22

- first Red Wings game December 13, 1952
- played part of '52–'53 with Edmonton, '53–'54 with Sherbrooke, '54–'55 with Quebec
- last Red Wings game March 16, 1955
- played '55–'71 in WHL

GALEN HEAD #15 RIGHT WING 5′10″ 170
b. Grand Prairie, Alberta, April 6, 1947

1967–68R/L	1	0	0	0	0

- lost June 12, 1969 to Salt Lake City in Reverse Draft
- first and only Red Wings game March 21, 1968

RICK HEALEY #5 DEFENCE 5′10″ 170
b. Vancouver, British Columbia, March 12, 1938

1960–61R/L	1	0	0	0	2

- first and only Red Wings game January 4, 1961
- played '59–'60 with Sudbury, most of '60–'61 with Sudbury, Hershey, and Edmonton, '61–'62 with Sault Ste. Marie

PAUL HENDERSON #19 – 22 LEFT WING 5′1″ 180 *b.* Kincardine, Ontario, January 28, 1943

1962–63R	2	0	0	0	9
1963–64	32	3	3	6	6
1964–65	70	8	13	21	30
1965–66	69	22	24	46	34
1966–67	46	21	19	40	10
1967–68	50	13	20	33	35
Totals	269	67	79	146	124

- Hamilton Red Wings graduate
- first Red Wings games March 23 & 24, 1963
- played half of '63–'64 with Pittsburgh
- missed six weeks in '66–'67 with throat infection
- traded March 3, 1968 with Norm Ullman and Floyd Smith to Toronto for Garry Unger, Pete Stemkowski, and the rights to Carl Brewer

JOHN "JACK" HENDRICKSON #2 – 16 – 21 DEFENCE 5′11″ 175 *b.* Kingston, Ontario, December 5, 1936

1957–58R	1	0	0	0	0
1958–59	3	0	0	0	2
1961–62L	1	0	0	0	2
Totals	5	0	0	0	4

- career minor-leaguer '56–'67
- first Red Wings game October 24, 1957
- played October 23/25/26, 1958
- last Red Wings game January 13, 1962

JIM "SAILOR" HERBERTS #7 – 11 – 12 FORWARD *b.* Collingwood, Ontario, 1897 *d.* Buffalo, New York, December 5, 1968

1928–29	40	9	5	14	34
1929–30L	23	1	3	4	4
Totals	63	10	8	18	38

- acquired April 8, 1928 from Toronto for Jack Arbour and $12,500
- last Cougars game March 18, 1930

ART HERCHENRATTER #19 LEFT WING 6′ 185
b. Kitchener, Ontario, November 24, 1917

1940–41R/L	10	1	2	3	2

- first and only Red Wings games December 25/29, January 1/4/5/7/9/12/14/19, 1940–41
- joined Royal Canadian Air Force 1943–45

BRYAN HEXTALL #12 CENTRE 5′11″ 185
b. Winnipeg, Manitoba, May 23, 1941

1975–76	21	0	4	4	29

- acquired June 5, 1975 from Atlanta for Dave Kryskow
- traded November 21, 1975 to Minnesota for Rick Chinnick

DENNIS HEXTALL #22 CENTRE 5′11″ 175
b. Winnipeg, Manitoba, April 17, 1943

1975–76	76	16	44	60	164
1976–77	78	14	32	46	158
1977–78	78	16	33	49	195
1978–79	20	4	8	12	33
Totals	252	50	117	167	550

- acquired February 27, 1976 from Minnesota for Bill Hogaboam and Jim Roberts
- signed February 7, 1979 as a free agent by Washington

GLENN HICKS #22 – 23 LEFT WING 5′10″ 177 *b.* Red Deer, Alberta, August 28, 1958

1979–80	50	1	2	3	43
1980–81L	58	5	10	15	84
Totals	108	6	12	18	127

- selected 28th overall at 1978 Entry Draft
- played '78–'79 with Winnipeg (WHA)
- reclaimed June 9, 1979 from Winnipeg prior to Expansion Draft
- played part of '80–'81 with Adirondack, '81–'82 with Tulsa, '82–'83 with Birmingham
- last Red Wings game April 5, 1981
- lost September 2, 1983 as a free agent to Minnesota

HAROLD "HAL" HICKS #9 – 16 DEFENCE
b. Ottawa, Ontario, December 10, 1900
d. Ottawa, Ontario, August 1965

1929–30	44	3	2	5	35
1930–31L	22	2	0	2	10
Totals	66	5	2	7	45

- last Falcons game January 11, 1931

TIM HIGGINS #20 RIGHT WING 6′1″ 185
b. Ottawa, Ontario, February 7, 1958

1986–87	77	12	14	26	124
1987–88	62	12	13	25	94
1988–89L	42	5	9	14	62
Totals	181	29	36	65	280

- acquired June 30, 1986 from New Jersey for Claude Loiselle
- played part of '88–'89 with Adirondack
- last Red Wings game March 19, 1989
- retired after '88–'89 season

JIM HILLER #14 RIGHT WING 6′2″ 200
b. Port Alberni, British Columbia, May 15, 1969

1992–93	21	2	6	8	19

- acquired January 29, 1993 with Paul Coffey and Sylvain Couturier from Los Angeles for Jimmy Carson, Mark Potvin, and Gary Shuchuk
- lost on waivers October 12, 1993 to Rangers

WILBERT "DUTCH" HILLER #18 LEFT WING 5′8″ 170 *b.* Kitchener, Ontario, May 11, 1915

1941–42	7	0	0	0	0

- bought April 8, 1941 from Rangers for $5,000
- played November 1/2/9/15/16/20/22, 1941
- traded November 1941 to Boston

LARRY HILLMAN #2 – 15 DEFENCE 6′ 181
b. Kirkland Lake, Ontario, February 5, 1937

1954–55R	7	0	0	0	2
1955–56	47	0	3	3	53
1956–57	16	1	2	3	4
Totals	70	1	5	6	59

- Hamilton Red Wings graduate
- first Red Wings games March 3/5/6/12/13/16/20, 1955
- played part of '55–'56 with Buffalo, '56–'57 with Edmonton
- lost June 1957 to Chicago in Intra-League Draft

JOHN HILWORTH ("Too Tall"/"Jasper") #4 – 19 – 29 DEFENCE 6′4″ 205 *b.* Jasper, Alberta, May 23, 1957

1977–78R	5	0	0	0	12
1978–79	37	1	1	2	66
1979–80L	15	0	0	0	11
Totals	57	1	1	2	89

- selected 55th overall at 1977 Entry Draft
- first Red Wings games October 13/15, February 9/19, March 9, 1977–78
- played much of '77–'79 with Kansas City
- last Red Wings games January 4/6/9/12/13/16/18/19/23/26/27/30, February 2/6/9, 1980

KEVIN HODSON #31 GOALIE 6′ 182
b. Winnipeg, Manitoba, March 27, 1972

1995–96	4	2–0–0	163	3	1	1.10

- signed as a free agent June 16, 1993
- currently with Red Wings

BILL HOGABOAM #15 – 22 – 23 CENTRE 5′11″ 170 *b.* Swift Current, Saskatchewan, September 5, 1949

1972–73	4	1	0	1	2
1973–74	47	18	23	41	12
1974–75	60	14	27	41	16
1975–76	50	21	16	37	30
1978–79	18	4	6	10	4
1979–80L	42	3	12	15	10
Totals	221	61	84	145	74

- acquired November 28, 1972 from Atlanta for Leon Rochefort
- played January 23/25, February 11/14, 1973
- traded February 27, 1976 with Jim Roberts to Minnesota for Dennis Hextall
- signed February 12, 1979 as a free agent
- played part of '79–'80 and all of '80–'81 and '82–'83 with Adirondack; played '81–'82 with Dallas
- last Red Wings game April 6, 1980

KEN HOLLAND #35 GOALIE 5′8″ 160 *b.* Vernon, British Columbia, November 10, 1955

1983–84	3	0–1–1	146	10	0	4.12

- signed as a free agent July 6, 1983
- first and only Red Wings games January 20, February 1/4, 1984

FRANK "FLASH" HOLLETT #5 DEFENCE 6′ 180 *b.* North Sydney, Nova Scotia, April 13, 1912

1943–44	27	6	12	18	34
1944–45	50	20	21	41	39
1945–46L	38	4	9	13	16
Totals	115	30	42	72	89

- acquired January 5, 1944 from Boston for Pat Egan
- last Red Wings game March 17, 1946
- retired after '45–'46 season

GORD HOLLINGWORTH ("Bucky") #18 – 19 – 21 DEFENCE 5′11″ 185 *b.* Verdun, Quebec, July 24, 1933 *d.* Unknown

1955–56	41	0	2	2	28
1956–57	25	0	1	1	16
1957–58L	27	1	2	3	22
Totals	93	1	5	6	66

- acquired June 3, 1955 with Jerry Toppazzini, John McCormack, and Dave Creighton from Chicago for Tony Leswick, Glen Skov, Johnny Wilson, and Ben Woit
- last Red Wings game December 29, 1957
- traded February 20, 1958 to Cleveland (AHL) for Pete Goegan

CHARLES "CHUCK" HOLMES #12 – 15 RIGHT WING 6′ 185 *b.* Edmonton, Alberta, September 21, 1934

1958–59R	15	0	3	3	6
1961–62L	8	1	0	1	4
Totals	23	1	3	4	10

- recalled from Hershey in November 1958 when Gerry Ehman demoted
- first Red Wings game October 30, 1958
- last Red Wings games January 31, February 1/3/4/7/10/11/15, 1962
- career minor-leaguer '54–'71

HAROLD "HAP" HOLMES #1 GOALIE *b.* Aurora, Ontario, April 15, 1889

1926–27	43	12–27–4	2685	100	6	2.23
1927–28L	44	18–19–6	2740	79	11	1.73
Totals	87	30–46–10	5425	179	17	1.98

- played in Victoria '26–'27
- last Cougars game March 24, 1928
- released October 10, 1928

TOMAS HOLMSTROM #15 LEFT WING 6′ 200 *b.* Pitea, Sweden, January 23, 1973

- selected 257th overall at 1994 Entry Draft
- currently with Red Wings

JOHN HOLOTA #18 CENTRE 5′6″ 160 *b.* Hamilton, Ontario, February 25, 1921 *d.* Denver, Colorado, March 10, 1951

1942–43R	12	2	0	2	0
1945–46L	3	0	0	0	0
Totals	15	2	0	2	0

- first Red Wings games November 5/7/14/15/19, January 7/9/10/14/16, 1942–43
- joined Canadian Army 1943–45
- last Red Wings games December 15/16/22, 1945

PETE HORECK #11 RIGHT WING 5′9″ 160
b. Massey, Ontario, June 15, 1923

1946–47	38	12	13	25	49
1947–48	50	12	17	29	44
1948–49	60	14	16	30	46
Totals	148	38	46	84	139

- acquired December 1946 with Leo Reise from Chicago for Adam Brown and Ray Powell
- traded August 16, 1949 with Bill Quackenbush to Boston for Pete Babando, Clare Martin, Lloyd Durham, and Jim Peters

DOUG HOUDA #22 – 27 – 33 DEFENCE 6′2″ 190 *b.* Blairmore, Alberta, June 3, 1966

1985–86R	6	0	0	0	4
1987–88	11	1	1	2	10
1988–89	57	2	11	13	67
1989–90	73	2	9	11	127
1990–91	22	0	4	4	43
Totals	169	5	25	30	251

- selected 28th overall at 1984 Entry Draft
- first Red Wings games October 10/12/16/17/23, November 2, 1985
- traded February 20, 1991 to Hartford for Doug Crossman

GORDIE HOWE ("Mr. Hockey") #9 – 17
RIGHT WING 6′ 205
b. Floral, Saskatchewan, March 31, 1928

1946–47R	58	7	15	22	52
1947–48	60	16	28	44	63
1948–49	40	12	25	37	57
1949–50	70	35	33	68	69
1950–51	70	43	43	86	74
1951–52	70	47	39	86	78
1952–53	70	49	46	95	57
1953–54	70	33	48	81	109
1954–55	64	29	33	62	68
1955–56	70	38	41	79	100
1956–57	70	44	45	89	72
1957–58	64	33	44	77	40
1958–59	70	32	46	78	57
1959–60	70	28	45	73	46
1960–61	64	23	49	72	30
1961–62	70	33	44	77	54
1962–63	70	38	48	86	100
1963–64	69	26	47	73	70
1964–65	70	29	47	76	104
1965–66	70	29	46	75	83
1966–67	69	25	40	65	53
1967–68	74	39	43	82	53
1968–69	76	44	59	103	58
1969–70	76	31	40	71	58
1970–71	63	23	29	52	38
Totals	1687	786	1023	1809	1643

- Galt Red Wings graduate
- first Red Wings game October 16, 1946
- retired '71–'73; joined Houston (WHA) for '73–'74

MARK HOWE #4 DEFENCE 5′11″ 185
b. Detroit, May 28, 1955

1992–93	60	3	31	34	22
1993–94	44	4	20	24	8
1994–95	18	1	5	6	10
Totals	122	8	56	64	40

- signed July 7, 1992 as a free agent
- retired after '94–'95

SYD HOWE #8 CENTRE 5′9″ 165
b. Ottawa, Ontario, September 18, 1911
d. Ottawa, Ontario, May 21, 1976

1934–35	14	8	12	20	11
1935–36	48	16	14	30	26
1936–37	42	17	10	27	10
1937–38	47	8	19	27	14
1938–39	48	16	20	36	11
1939–40	48	14	23	37	17
1940–41	48	20	24	44	8
1941–42	48	16	19	35	6
1942–43	50	20	35	55	10
1943–44	40	32	28	60	6
1944–45	46	17	36	53	6
1945–46L	26	4	7	11	9
Totals	505	188	247	435	134

- acquired February 11, 1935 with Scotty Bowman from St. Louis for Ted Graham and $50,000
- last Red Wings game February 7, 1946
- traded August 17, 1946 to St. Louis (AHL) for Dan Summers and cash

STEVE HRYMNAK #19 DEFENCE 5′11″ 178
b. Port Arthur, Ontario, March 3, 1926

- acquired September 23, 1952 from Chicago with Guy Fielder and Red Almas for cash
- appeared only in the 1953 playoffs for Detroit
- played '52–'58 in minors

WILHELM "WILLIE" HUBER ("Hubie") #7 DEFENCE 6′5″ 230 *b.* Strasskirchen, West Germany, January 15, 1958

1978–79R	68	7	24	31	114
1979–80	75	17	23	40	164
1980–81	80	15	34	49	130
1981–82	74	15	30	45	98
1982–83	74	14	29	43	106
Totals	371	68	140	208	612

- selected 9th overall at 1978 Entry Draft
- first Red Wings game October 11, 1978
- traded June 13, 1983 with Mike Blaisdell and Mark Osborne to Rangers for Ron Duguay, Ed Mio, and Ed Johnstone

RON HUDSON #15 – 17 – 19 RIGHT WING 5′10″ 175 *b.* Timmins, Ontario, April 18, 1914

1937–38R	33	5	2	7	2
1939–40L	1	0	0	0	0
Totals	34	5	2	7	2

- first Red Wings game December 25, 1937
- last Red Wings game February 9, 1940

BRENT HUGHES #24 DEFENCE 6′ 205
b. Bowmanville, Ontario, June 17, 1943

1973–74	69	1	21	22	92

- bought October 27, 1973 from St. Louis for cash
- lost June 12, 1974 to Kansas City in Expansion Draft

RUSTY HUGHES #14 DEFENCE *b.* Unknown

1929–30R/L	40	0	1	1	48

- first Cougars game November 14, 1929
- last Cougars game March 9, 1930

DENNIS HULL #19 LEFT WING 5′11″ 195
b. Pointe Anne, Ontario, November 19, 1944

1977–78L	55	5	9	14	6

- acquired December 2, 1977 from Chicago for a 4th-round draft choice in 1980 (Carey Wilson)
- last Red Wings game April 9, 1978
- retired September 7, 1978

MIROSLAV "MIRO" IHNACAK #35 LEFT WING 5′11″ 175 *b.* Poprad, Czechoslovakia, November 19, 1962

1988–89L	1	0	0	0	0

- signed November 18, 1988 as a free agent
- only Red Wings game February 3, 1989
- played most of '88–'89 with Adirondack, '89–'91 with Halifax

PETER ING #31 GOALIE 6′2″ 170
b. Toronto, Ontario April 28, 1969

1993–94	3	1–2–0	170	15	0	5.29

- acquired August 30, 1993 from Edmonton for a 7th-round draft choice in 1994 (Chris Wickenheiser)
- only Red Wings games October 8/9/13, 1993
- played most of '93–'95 with Adirondack, Las Vegas, and Fort Wayne

EARL INGARFIELD, JR. #21 CENTRE 5′10″ 175 *b.* Manhasset, New York, January 30, 1959

1980–81L	22	2	1	3	16

- acquired February 3, 1981 from Calgary for Dan Labraaten
- last Red Wings game March 31, 1981

RON INGRAM #2 DEFENCE 5′11″ 185
b. Toronto, Ontario, July 5, 1933

1963–64	50	3	6	9	50

- acquired June 5, 1963 with Roger Crozier from Chicago for Howie Young
- traded February 14, 1964 to Rangers for Al Langlois

HAROLD "HAL" JACKSON #4 – 5 – 19
DEFENCE 5′11″ 175
b. Cedar Springs, Ontario, August 1, 1917

1940–41	1	0	0	0	0
1942–43	4	0	4	4	6
1943–44	50	7	12	19	76
1944–45	50	5	6	11	45
1945–46	3	3	4	7	36
1946–47L	37	1	5	6	39
Totals	145	16	31	47	202

- St. Mike's graduate
- played '40–'44 witih Indianapolis
- played March 18, 1941
- played February 7, March 6/7/18, 1943
- last Red Wings game March 6, 1947
- retired after '46–'47

LOU JANKOWSKI #19 LEFT WING 6′ 184
b. Regina, Saskatchewan, June 27, 1931

1950–51R	1	0	1	1	0
1952–53	22	1	2	3	0
Totals	23	1	3	4	0

- first Red Wings game March 25, 1951
- played most of '51–'52 with Indianapolis, '52–'53 with Edmonton (WHL) and St. Louis (AHL)
- sold August 12, 1953 with Larry Zeidel and Larry Wilson to Chicago for cash

GARY JARRETT #8 – 15 LEFT WING 5′8″ 170
b. Toronto, Ontario, September 3, 1942

1966–67	4	0	0	0	0
1967–68	68	18	21	39	20
Totals	72	18	21	33	20

- acquired May 20, 1965 with Andy Bathgate and Billy Harris from Toronto for Marcel Pronovost, Ed Joyal, Larry Jeffrey, Lowell MacDonald, and Aut Erickson
- played November 24/26, February 25/26, 1966–67
- traded May 27, 1968 with Doug Roberts, Howie Young, and Chris Worthy to Oakland for Bob Baun and Ron Harris

PIERRE JARRY ("Pete") #17 LEFT WING 5′11″ 182 *b.* Montreal, Quebec, March 30, 1949

1973–74	52	15	23	38	17
1974–75	39	8	13	21	4
Totals	91	23	36	59	21

- acquired November 29, 1973 from Toronto for Tim Ecclestone
- traded November 25, 1975 to Minnesota for Don Martineau

LARRY JEFFREY #14 – 21 LEFT WING 5′11″ 189 *b.* Zurich, Ontario, October 12, 1940

1961–62R	18	5	3	8	20
1962–63	53	5	11	16	62
1963–64	58	10	18	28	87
1964–65	41	4	2	6	48
Totals	170	24	34	58	217

- Hamilton Red Wings graduate
- first Red Wings game February 11, 1962
- played part of '59–'60 with Hershey, '61–'62 with Edmonton, '62–'63 with Pittsburgh
- traded May 20, 1965 with Marcel Pronovost, Ed Joyal, Lowell MacDonald, and Aut Erickson to Toronto for Andy Bathgate, Billy Harris, and Gary Jarrett
- acquired June 17, 1969 from Rangers for Terry Sawchuk and Sandy Snow
- shattered his kneecap September 1969 during an exhibition game, ending his career

JOSEPH "BILL" JENNINGS #10 – 14 – 16
RIGHT WING 5′9″ 165 *b.* Toronto, Ontario, June 28, 1917

1940–41R	12	1	5	6	2
1941–42	16	2	1	3	6
1942–43	8	3	3	6	2
1943–44	33	6	11	17	10
Totals	69	12	20	32	20

- first Red Wings games February 14/22/23/27/28, March 2/4/6/8/13/16/18, 1941
- sold summer 1944 to Boston

AL JENSEN #31 GOALIE 5′10″ 180
b. Hamilton, Ontario, November 27, 1958

1980–81R	1	0–1–0	60	7	0	7.00

- selected 31st overall at 1978 Entry Draft
- first and only Red Wings game November 20, 1980
- traded July 23, 1981 to Washington for Mark Lofthouse

AL JOHNSON #15 – 17 RIGHT WING 5′11″ 185
b. Winnipeg, Manitoba, March 30, 1935

1960–61	70	16	21	37	14
1961–62	31	5	6	11	14
1962–63L	2	0	0	0	0
Totals	103	21	27	48	28

- bought January 1961 from Canadiens for $20,000
- played part of ’61–’62 with Hershey, ’62–’63 with Pittsburgh
- out of hockey after ’62–’63

BRIAN JOHNSON #24 RIGHT WING 6′1″ 185
b. Montreal, Quebec, April 1, 1960

1983–84R/L	3	0	0	0	5

- signed October 30, 1979 as a free agent
- played most of ’80–’81 and ’82–’84 with Adirondack, ’81–’82 with Dallas
- first and only Red Wings games October 9/15/19, 1983

DANNY JOHNSON #8 CENTRE 5′11″ 170
b. Winnipegosis, Manitoba, October 1, 1944
d. Unknown

1971–72	43	2	5	7	8

- acquired November 22, 1971 from Vancouver Canucks on waivers
- played with Winnipeg (WHA) ’72–’75 before retiring August 21, 1975

EARL JOHNSON #21 CENTRE 6′ 185
b. Fort Francis, Ontario, June 28, 1931

1953–54R/L	1	0	0	0	0

- career minor-leaguer ’51–’62
- first and only Red Wings game March 20, 1954

GREG JOHNSON #23 CENTRE 5′10″ 185
b. Thunder Bay, Ontario, March 16, 1971

1993–94R	52	6	11	17	22
1994–95	22	3	5	8	14
1995–96	60	18	22	40	30
Totals	134	27	38	65	66

- acquired June 20, 1993 with a 5th-round draft choice in 1994 (Frederic Deschenes) from Flyers for Jim Cummins and Flyers’ 4th-round draft choice in 1993 (previously acquired by Detroit — later traded to Boston — Charles Paquette)
- first Red Wings game October 5, 1993
- currently with Red Wings

LARRY JOHNSTON #3 DEFENCE 5′11″ 195
b. Kitchener, Ontario, July 20, 1943

1971–72	65	4	20	24	111
1972–73	73	1	12	13	169
1973–74	65	2	12	14	139
Totals	203	7	44	51	419

- acquired February 20, 1970 with Gary Croteau and Dale Rolfe from Los Angeles for Brian Gibbons and Garry Monahan
- released September 3, 1974

ED JOHNSTONE ("E.J."/"Ciggy") #7 – 17 – 34 RIGHT WING 5′9″ 175 *b.* Brandon, Manitoba, March 2, 1954

1983–84	45	12	11	23	54
1985–86	3	1	0	1	2
1986–87L	6	0	0	0	0
Totals	54	13	11	24	56

- acquired June 13, 1983 with Ron Duguay and Ed Mio from Rangers for Mike Blaisdell, Willie Huber, and Mark Osborne
- missed many games in '83–'84 with fractured cheekbone
- played all of '84–'85 and most of '85–'87 with Adirondack before retiring
- last Red Wings games November 8/9/12/13/15/19, 1986

GREG JOLY #22 – 24 DEFENCE 6′1″ 190 *b.* Calgary, Alberta, May 30, 1954

1976–77	53	1	11	12	14
1977–78	79	7	20	27	73
1978–79	20	0	4	4	6
1979–80	59	3	10	13	45
1980–81	17	0	2	2	10
1981–82	37	1	5	6	30
1982–83L	2	0	0	0	0
Totals	267	12	52	64	178

- acquired November 30, 1976 from Washington for Bryan Watson
- last Red Wings games October 16 & 17, 1982
- played most of '82–'83 and all of '83–'86 with Adirondack, then retired

ALVIN JONES ("Buck") #2 – 3 – 5 – 15 – 16 DEFENCE 6′ 180 *b.* Owen Sound, Ontario, August 17, 1918

1938–39R	11	0	1	1	6
1939–40	2	0	0	0	0
1941–42	21	2	1	3	8
Totals	34	2	2	4	14

- signed October 21, 1938
- first Red Wings games January 26, February 16/26, March 2/5/7/9/11/12/14/19, 1939
- sent to Toronto summer 1942

ED JOYAL #21 CENTRE 6′ 180 *b.* Edmonton, Alberta, May 8, 1940

1962–63R	14	2	8	10	0
1963–64	47	10	7	17	17
1964–65	46	8	14	22	4
Totals	107	20	29	49	21

- first Red Wings game January 24, 1963
- played most of '62–'63 with Pittsburgh
- traded May 20, 1965 with Marcel Pronovost, Larry Jeffrey, Lowell MacDonald, and Aut Erickson to Toronto for Andy Bathgate, Billy Harris, and Gary Jarrett

FRANCIS "RED" KANE #17 DEFENCE 5′11″ 190 *b.* Stratford, Ontario, January 19, 1923

1943–44R/L	2	0	0	0	0

- only Red Wings games December 16 & 19, 1943

AL KARLANDER #15 CENTRE 5′8″ 170 *b.* Lac la Hache, British Columbia, November 5, 1946

1969–70R	41	5	10	15	6
1970–71	23	1	4	5	10
1971–72	71	15	20	35	29
1972–73	77	15	22	37	25
Totals	212	36	56	92	70

- selected 17th overall at 1967 Amateur Draft
- first Red Wings game December 6, 1969
- played part of '69–'71 with Fort Worth
- left to play with New England (WHL) in '73–'74

JACK KEATING ("Red") #15 – 20 LEFT WING 6′ 180 *b.* Kitchener, Ontario, October 9, 1916

1938–39R	1	0	1	1	2
1939–40L	10	2	0	2	2
Totals	11	2	1	3	4

- signed October 21, 1938
- first Red Wings game January 5, 1939
- played most of '38–'39 with Pittsburgh, '39–'40 with Indianapolis
- last Red Wings games November 2/5/12/14/18/19/25/26/28, December 3, 1939

GORDON "DUKE" KEATS #5 CENTRE
b. Montreal, Quebec, March 1, 1895
d. Victoria, British Columbia, January 16, 1972

1926–27R	40	16	8	24	52
1927–28	5	0	2	2	6
Totals	45	16	10	26	58

- acquired from Victoria Cougars for Frank Frederickson
- first Cougars game January 9, 1927
- traded December 16, 1927 to Chicago for Gordon Fraser and $5,000

DAVE KELLY #25 RIGHT WING 6′2″ 205
b. Chatham, Ontario, September 20, 1952

1976–77R/L	16	2	0	2	4

- acquired February 17, 1977 with Steve Coates, Terry Murray, and Bob Ritchie from Flyers for Rick Lapointe and Mike Korney
- first and only Red Wings games February 19/20/23/24/26, March 15/17/20/23/24/26/27/29/31, April 2 & 3, 1977
- played part of '76–'77 with Kansas City, '77–'78 with Philadelphia
- out of hockey after '77–'78

LEONARD "RED" KELLY #4 – 20 CENTRE
6′ 195 *b.* Simcoe, Ontario, July 9, 1927

1947–48R	60	6	14	20	13
1948–49	59	5	11	16	10
1949–50	70	15	25	40	9
1950–51	70	17	37	54	24
1951–52	67	16	31	47	16
1952–53	70	19	27	46	8
1953–54	62	16	33	49	18
1954–55	70	15	30	45	28
1955–56	70	16	34	50	39
1956–57	70	10	25	35	18
1957–58	61	13	18	31	26
1958–59	67	8	13	21	34
1959–60	50	6	12	18	10
Totals	846	162	310	472	253

- St. Mike's graduate
- signed September 25, 1947
- first Red Wings game October 15, 1947
- traded February 5, 1960 with Billy McNeill to the Rangers for Bill Gadsby and Eddie Shack. However, both Kelly and McNeill refused to go. Five days later, Kelly was traded to Toronto for Marc Reaume

PETE KELLY #9 – 15 – 18 – 21 RIGHT WING
5′10″ 170 *b.* St. Vital, Manitoba, May 22, 1913

1935–36	48	6	8	14	30
1936–37	48	5	4	9	12
1937–38	9	0	1	1	2
1938–39	32	4	9	13	4
Totals	137	15	22	37	48

- acquired October 15, 1935 from Americans for Carl Voss
- started '37–'38 with Wings; demoted to Pittsburgh on December 2, 1937
- sold outright to Pittsburgh on October 6, 1939

FORBES KENNEDY ("Spud") #8 – 17 CENTRE
5′8″ 185 *b.* Dorchester, New Brunswick, August 18, 1935

1957–58	70	11	16	27	135
1958–59	67	1	4	5	49
1959–60	17	1	2	3	8
1961–62	14	1	0	1	8
Totals	168	14	22	36	200

- acquired July 1957 with Johnny Wilson, William Preston, and Hank Bassen from Chicago for Ted Lindsay and Glenn Hall
- traded December 1962 to Boston for André Pronovost

SHELDON KENNEDY #15 – 12 – 28 RIGHT WING 5′11″ 170 *b.* Brandon, Manitoba, June 15, 1969

1989–90R	20	2	7	9	10
1990–91	7	1	0	1	12
1991–92	27	3	8	11	24
1992–93	68	19	11	30	46
1993–94	61	6	7	13	30
Totals	183	31	33	64	122

- selected 80th overall at 1988 Entry Draft
- first Red Wings game November 24, 1989
- played January 22/25/26/28/30, February 2/4, 1991
- traded May 25, 1994 to Winnipeg for a 3rd-round draft choice in 1995 (Darryl Laplante)

ALAN KERR #18 RIGHT WING 5′11″ 195
b. Hazleton, British Columbia, March 28, 1964

1991–92	58	3	8	11	133

- acquired May 26, 1991 with future considerations from the Islanders for Rick Green
- traded June 18, 1993 to Winnipeg to complete deal of June 11, 1993 in which Paul Ysebaert went to the Jets for Aaron Ward and a 4th-round draft choice in 1993 (John Jakopin)

BRIAN KILREA ("Killer") #7 CENTRE 5′11″ 182 *b.* Ottawa, Ontario, October 21, 1934

1957–58R	1	0	0	0	0

- played part of '57–'58 with Edmonton, all of '59–'67 with Springfield before going to Los Angeles after expansion
- first and only Red Wings game March 4, 1958

HECTOR "HEC" KILREA ("Hurricane Hec") #7 – 12 – 15 LEFT WING 5′11″ 175
b. Blackburn, Ontario, June 11, 1907
d. Detroit, September 6, 1969

1931–32	47	13	3	16	28
1935–36	48	6	17	23	37
1936–37	48	6	9	15	20
1937–38	48	9	9	18	10
1938–39	48	8	9	17	8
1939–40L	12	0	0	0	0
Totals	251	42	47	89	103

- on loan for '31–'32 from Ottawa which did not field a team
- returned to Ottawa for '32–'33
- bought for $7,000 from Toronto after '34–'35 season
- last Red Wings games November 2/5/12/14/18/19/23/25/26/28, December 3, 1939
- retired after '39–'40

KEN KILREA #7 – 14 – 21 – 3 – 15 – 17 – 18 LEFT WING 6′ 170 *b.* Ottawa, Ontario, January 16, 1919 *d.* Destin, Florida, January 14, 1990

1938–39R	1	0	0	0	0
1939–40	40	10	8	18	4
1940–41	12	2	0	2	0
1941–42	21	3	12	15	4
1943–44L	14	1	3	4	0
Totals	88	16	23	39	8

- signed March 18, 1938
- first Red Wings game March 19, 1939
- recalled from Indianapolis on January 2, 1940
- played most of '38–'39 with Pittsburgh, part of '39–'40 with Indianapolis
- last Red Wings game March 19, 1944

WALTER "WALLY" KILREA #9 – 11 – 17 FORWARD 5′7″ 150 *b.* Ottawa, Ontario, February 18, 1909

1934–35	2	0	0	0	0
1935–36	44	4	10	14	10
1936–37	48	8	13	21	6
1937–38L	5	0	0	0	4
Totals	99	12	23	35	20

- acquired September 23, 1934 from Maroons for Gus Marker
- played December 25 & 30, 1934
- last Red Wings games November 7/13/14/18/21, 1937
- sold to Hershey in October 1938

KRIS KING #18 – 37 LEFT WING 5′11″ 210
b. Bracebridge, Ontario, February 18, 1966

1987–88R	3	1	0	1	2
1988–89	55	2	3	5	168
Totals	58	3	3	6	170

- signed March 23, 1987 as a free agent
- first Red Wings games December 27/30, January 8, 1987–88
- traded September 7, 1989 to Rangers for Chris McRae and a 5th-round draft choice in 1990 (Tony Burns)

SCOTT KING #31 – 38 GOALIE 6′1″ 170
b. Thunder Bay, Ontario, June 25, 1967

1990–91R	1	0–0–0	45	2	0	2.67
1991–92L	1	0–0–0	16	1	0	3.75
Totals	2	0–0–0	61	3	0	2.95

- selected 190th overall at 1986 Entry Draft
- first Red Wings game January 28, 1991
- also played with Adirondack ('90–'93), Hampton ('90–'91), and Toledo ('91–'93)
- last Red Wings game November 30, 1991
- out of hockey after '92–'93

MARK KIRTON ("Kirt") #16 – 23 CENTRE 5′10″ 170 *b.* Regina, Saskatchewan, February 3, 1958

1980–81	50	18	13	31	24
1981–82	74	14	28	42	62
1982–83	10	1	1	2	6
Totals	134	33	42	75	92

- acquired December 4, 1980 from Toronto for Jim Rutherford
- traded January 17, 1983 to Vancouver Canucks for Ivan Boldirev

KELLY KISIO #16 CENTRE 5′9″ 170 *b.* Peace River, Alberta, September 18, 1959

1982–83R	15	4	3	7	0
1983–84	70	23	37	60	34
1984–85	75	20	41	61	56
1985–86	76	21	48	69	85
Totals	236	68	129	197	175

- signed as a free agent March 2, 1983
- first Red Wings games March 3/5/6/10/12/13/16/19/20/23/26/27/30, April 1/3, 1983
- traded July 29, 1986 with Jim Leavins and Lane Lambert to Rangers for Glen Hanlon, a 3rd-round draft choice in 1987 (Dennis Holland), and a 3rd-round draft choice in 1988 (Guy Dupuis)

CHAPMAN "HOBIE" KITCHEN #11 DEFENCE *b.* Toronto, Ontario *d.* Unknown

1926–27L	17	0	2	2	42

- played '25–'26 with Maroons
- last Cougars game January 25, 1927
- out of NHL after '26–'27

PETR KLIMA #85 LEFT WING 6′ 190 *b.* Chomutov, Czechoslovakia, December 23, 1964

1985–86R	74	32	24	56	16
1986–87	77	30	23	53	42
1987–88	78	37	25	62	46
1988–89	51	25	16	41	44
1989–90	13	5	5	10	6
Totals	293	129	93	222	154

- selected 86th overall at 1983 Entry Draft
- first Red Wings game October 10, 1985
- traded November 2, 1989 with Adam Graves, Joe Murphy, and Jeff Sharples to Edmonton for Jimmy Carson and Kevin McClelland

JOEY KOCUR #26 RIGHT WING 6′ 195 *b.* Calgary, Alberta, December 21, 1964

1984–85R	17	1	0	1	64
1985–86	59	9	6	15	377
1986–87	77	9	9	18	276
1987–88	63	7	7	14	263
1988–89	60	9	9	18	213
1989–90	71	16	20	36	268
1990–91	52	5	4	9	253
Totals	399	56	55	111	1714

- selected 88th overall at 1983 Entry Draft
- first Red Wings game February 20, 1985
- traded March 5, 1991 with Per Djoos to Rangers for Jim Cummins, Kevin Miller, and Dennis Vial

STEVE KONROYD #8 DEFENCE 6′1″ 195 *b.* Scarborough, Ontario, February 10, 1961

1992–93	6	0	1	1	4

- acquired March 22, 1993 from Hartford for a 6th-round draft choice in 1993 (later re-acquired by Detroit — Tim Spitzig)
- played March 27/29, April 1/3/8/10, 1993
- traded March 21, 1994 to Ottawa for Daniel Berthiaume

VLADIMIR KONSTANTINOV #16 DEFENCE
5′11″ 176 *b.* Murmansk, Soviet Union, March 19, 1967

1991–92R	79	8	25	33	172
1992–93	82	5	17	22	137
1993–94	80	12	21	33	138
1994–95	47	3	11	14	101
1995–96	81	14	20	34	139
Totals	349	42	94	136	687

- selected 221st overall in 1989 Entry Draft
- first Red Wings game October 3, 1991
- currently with Red Wings

JIM KORN #26 DEFENCE 6′4″ 220
b. Hopkins, Minnesota, July 28, 1957

1979–80R	63	5	13	18	108
1980–81	63	5	15	20	246
1981–82	59	1	7	8	104
Totals	185	11	35	46	458

- selected 73rd overall at 1977 Entry Draft
- first Red Wings game October 28, 1979
- played part of '79–'81 with Adirondack
- traded March 8, 1982 to Toronto for a 4th-round draft choice in 1982 (Craig Coxe) and a 5th-round draft choice in 1983 (Joey Kocur)

MIKE KORNEY #2 – 19 RIGHT WING 6′3″ 195
b. Dauphin, Manitoba, September 15, 1953

1973–74R	2	0	0	0	0
1974–75	30	8	2	10	18
1975–76	27	1	7	8	23
Totals	59	9	9	18	41

- selected 59th overall at 1973 Entry Draft
- first Red Wings games January 30 & February 2, 1974
- traded February 17, 1977 with Rick Lapointe to Flyers for Steve Coates, Terry Murray, Bob Ritchie, and Dave Kelly

CHRIS KOTSOPOULOS #29 DEFENCE
6′3″ 215 *b.* Scarborough, Ontario, November 27, 1958

1989–90L	2	0	0	0	10

- signed June 23, 1989 as a free agent
- only Red Wings games October 7 & 8, 1989
- played part of '89–'90 with Adirondack, retiring at end of season

VYACHESLAV KOZLOV #13 CENTRE
5′10″ 172 *b.* Voskresensk, Soviet Union, May 3, 1972

1991–92R	7	0	2	2	2
1992–93	17	4	1	5	14
1993–94	77	34	39	73	50
1994–95	46	13	20	33	45
1995–96	82	36	37	73	70
Totals	229	87	99	186	181

- selected 45th overall at 1990 Entry Draft
- first Red Wings games March 12/14/15/17/20/22, April 12, 1992
- currently with Red Wings

DALE KRENTZ #28 – 39 LEFT WING 5′11″ 190 *b.* Steinbach, Manitoba, December 19, 1961

1986–87R	8	0	0	0	0
1987–88	6	2	0	2	5
1988–89L	16	3	3	6	4
Totals	30	5	3	8	9

- signed as a free agent June 5, 1985
- first Red Wings games January 17, February 14/17/18/20/22/24/26, 1987
- played December 30, March 12/13/27/29, April 2, 1987–88
- played part of '86–'90 with Adirondack
- last Red Wings game April 2, 1989
- played '90–'91 in German League

JIM KRULICKI #19 LEFT WING 5′11″ 180 *b.* Kitchener, Ontario, March 9, 1948

1970–71L	14	0	1	1	0

- acquired March 2, 1971 from Rangers for Dale Rolfe
- only Red Wings games March 4/6/7/9/13/14/16/18/20/21/24/27/28/31, 1971
- out of NHL after '70–'71

GORD KRUPPKE #8 – 40 – 44 DEFENCE 6′1″ 200 *b.* Slave Lake, Alberta, April 2, 1969

1990–91R	4	0	0	0	0
1992–93	10	0	0	0	20
1993–94	9	0	0	0	12
Totals	23	0	0	0	32

- selected 32nd overall in 1987 Entry Draft
- first Red Wings games January 30, February 1/2/4, 1991
- traded April 7, 1995 to Toronto for future considerations

MIKE KRUSHELNYSKI ("Krusher") #18 CENTRE 6′2″ 200 *b.* Montreal, Quebec, April 27, 1960

1994–95	20	2	3	5	6

- signed August 1, 1994 as a free agent
- retired after '94–'95

DAVE KRYSKOW #7 LEFT WING 5′10″ 175 *b.* Edmonton, Alberta, December 25, 1951

1974–75	69	10	19	29	87

- acquired February 8, 1975 from Washington for Jack Lynch
- traded June 5, 1975 to Atlanta for Bryan Hextall

MARK KUMPEL #18 RIGHT WING 6′ 190 *b.* Wakefield, Massachusetts, March 7, 1961

1986–87	5	0	1	1	0
1987–88	13	0	2	2	4
Totals	18	0	3	3	4

- acquired January 17, 1987 from Quebec with Brent Ashton and Gilbert Delorme for John Ogrodnick, Basil McRae, and Doug Shedden
- played March 21/22/28, April 1/4, 1987
- traded January 11, 1988 to Winnipeg for Jim Nill

LEO LABINE ("The Lion") #8 RIGHT WING 5′10″ 178 *b.* Haileybury, Ontario, July 22, 1931

1960–61	40	7	12	19	34
1961–62L	48	3	4	7	30
Totals	88	10	16	26	64

- acquired January 1961 with Vic Stasiuk from Boston for Gary Aldcorn, Murray Oliver, and Tom McCarthy
- last Red Wings game February 15, 1962
- played part of '61–'62 with Sudbury, '62–'67 with Los Angeles (WHL) before retiring

DAN LABRAATEN ("Rusty") #21 LEFT WING 6′ 190 *b.* Leksland, Sweden, June 9, 1951

1978–79	78	19	19	38	8
1979–80	76	30	27	57	8
1980–81	44	3	8	11	12
Totals	198	52	54	106	28

- signed October 12, 1978 as a free agent
- traded February 3, 1981 to Calgary for Earl Ingarfield

RANDY LADOUCEUR #19 – 29 DEFENCE 6′2″ 220 *b.* Brockville, Ontario, June 30, 1960

1982–83R	27	0	4	4	16
1983–84	71	3	17	20	58
1984–85	80	3	27	30	108
1985–86	78	5	13	18	195
1986–87	34	3	6	9	70
Totals	290	14	67	81	447

- signed November 1, 1979 as a free agent
- first Red Wings game November 16, 1982
- traded January 12, 1987 to Hartford for Dave Barr

MARK LAFOREST ("Trees") #31 GOALIE 5′11″ 190 *b.* Welland, Ontario, July 10, 1962

1985–86R	28	4–21–0	1383	114	1	4.95
1986–87	5	2–1–0	219	12	0	3.29
Totals	33	6–22–0	1602	126	1	4.72

- signed April 29, 1983 as a free agent
- first Red Wings game December 3, 1985
- last Red Wings games January 24/31, February 14/17, March 10, 1987
- traded June 13, 1987 to Flyers for a 2nd-round draft choice in 1987 (Bob Wilkie)

CLAUDE LAFORGE #8 – 14 – 16 – 17 – 21 LEFT WING 5′9″ 172 *b.* Sorel, Quebec, July 1, 1936

1958–59	57	2	5	7	18
1960–61	10	1	0	1	2
1961–62	38	10	9	19	20
1963–64	17	2	3	5	4
1964–65	1	0	0	0	2
Totals	123	15	17	32	46

- bought June 1958 from Canadiens
- played November 17, 1964
- played part of '58–'62 with Hershey, '62–'66 with Pittsburgh, '66–'68 with Quebec (AHL), before signing with Flyers after expansion

ROGER LAFRENIÈRE #17 LEFT WING 6′ 190 *b.* Montreal, Quebec, July 24, 1942

1962–63R	3	0	0	0	4

- Hamilton Red Wings graduate
- first & only Red Wings games February 23/24/26, 1963
- career minor-leaguer '62–'74

SERGE LAJEUNESSE #5 – 21 – 25 RIGHT WING 5′10″ 185 *b.* Montreal, Quebec, June 11, 1950

1970–71R	62	1	3	4	55
1971–72	7	0	0	0	20
1972–73	28	0	1	1	26
Totals	97	1	4	5	101

- selected 12th overall at 1970 Entry Draft
- first Red Wings game November 12, 1970
- traded May 15, 1973 to Flyers for Rick Foley

HEC LALANDE #7 CENTRE 5′9″ 157 *b.* North Bay, Ontario, November 24, 1934

1957–58L	12	0	2	2	2

- acquired December 17, 1957 with Bob Bailey, Nick Mickoski, and Jack McIntyre from Chicago for Earl Reibel, Billy Dea, Lorne Ferguson, and Bill Dineen
- only Red Wings games December 19/21/22/25/28/31, January 9/11/16/19, and February 8/9, 1957–58
- traded April 1958 with Don Poile to Hershey for Dunc Fisher

JOE LAMB #9 RIGHT WING 5′9″ 170 *b.* Sussex, New Brunswick, June 18, 1906 *d.* Unknown

1937–38L	12	3	1	4	6

- only Red Wings games February 13/20/24/27, March 1/3/6/10/13/15/17/20, 1938
- acquired January 24, 1938 from Americans for Red Beattie
- retired after '37–'38 season

MARK LAMB #8 DEFENCE 5′8″ 177 *b.* Ponteix, Saskatchewan, August 3, 1964

1986–87	22	2	1	3	8

- signed July 28, 1986 as a free agent
- lost October 5, 1987 to Edmonton in Waiver Draft

LANE LAMBERT #14 RIGHT WING 6′ 185 *b.* Melfort, Saskatchewan, November 18, 1964

1983–84R	73	20	15	35	115
1984–85	69	14	11	25	104
1985–86	34	2	3	5	130
Totals	176	36	29	65	349

- selected 25th overall at 1983 Entry Draft
- first Red Wings game October 5, 1983
- traded July 29, 1986 with Kelly Kisio and Jim Leavins to the Rangers for Glen Hanlon, a 3rd-round draft choice in 1987 (Dennis Holland), and a 3rd-round draft choice in 1988 (Guy Dupuis)

AL LANGLOIS ("Junior") #2 DEFENCE 6′ 205 *b.* Magog, Quebec, November 6, 1934

1963–64	17	1	6	7	13
1964–65	65	1	12	13	107
Totals	82	2	18	20	120

- acquired February 14, 1964 from Rangers for Ron Ingram
- traded May 31, 1965 with Bob Dillabough, Ron Harris, and Parker MacDonald to Boston for Ab McDonald, Bob McCord, and Ken Stephenson

MARTIN LAPOINTE #20 – 22 RIGHT WING 5′11″ 197 *b.* Lachine, Quebec, September 12, 1973

1991–92R	4	0	1	1	5
1992–93	3	0	0	0	0
1993–94	50	8	8	16	55
1994–95	39	4	6	10	73
1995–96	58	6	3	9	93
Totals	154	18	18	36	226

- selected 10th overall in 1991 Entry Draft
- first Red Wings games October 5, December 3/7/10, 1991
- currently with Red Wings

RICK LAPOINTE ("Jumbo") #4 DEFENCE 6′2″ 200 *b.* Victoria, British Columbia, August 2, 1955

1975–76R	80	10	23	33	95
1976–77	49	2	11	13	80
Totals	129	12	34	46	175

- selected 5th overall at 1975 Entry Draft
- first Red Wings game October 8, 1975
- traded February 17, 1977 with Mike Korney to Flyers for Steve Coates, Terry Murray, Bob Ritchie, and Dave Kelly

IGOR LARIONOV #8 CENTRE 5′9″ 170 *b.* Voskresensk, USSR, December 3, 1960

1995–96	69	21	50	71	34

- acquired October 24, 1995 with a conditional draft choice in 1998 from San Jose for Ray Sheppard
- currently with Red Wings

REED LARSON #28 DEFENCE 6′ 195 *b.* Minneapolis, Minnesota, July 30, 1956

1976–77R	14	0	1	1	23
1977–78	75	19	41	60	95
1978–79	79	18	49	67	169
1979–80	80	22	44	66	101
1980–81	78	27	31	58	153
1981–82	80	21	39	60	112
1982–83	80	22	52	74	104
1983–84	78	23	39	62	122

1984–85	77	17	45	62	139
1985–86	67	19	41	60	109
Totals	708	188	382	570	1127

- selected 22nd overall at 1976 Entry Draft
- first Red Wings games February 12/13/15/17/19/20/23/24/26, March 5/9/10/12/13, 1977
- traded March 10, 1986 to Boston for Mike O'Connell

BRIAN LAVENDER #11 – 18 LEFT WING 6′ 180 *b.* Edmonton, Alberta, April 20, 1947

1972–73	26	2	2	4	14
1973–74	4	0	0	0	11
Totals	30	2	2	4	25

- acquired January 17, 1973 with Ken Murray from the Islanders for Bob Cook and Ralph Stewart
- played November 10/11/14/17, 1973
- traded February 28, 1974 to Rangers for Claude Houde

DAN LAWSON #18 – 22 RIGHT WING 5′11″ 180 *b.* Toronto, Ontario, October 30, 1947

1967–68R	1	0	0	0	0
1968–69	44	5	7	12	21
Totals	45	5	7	12	21

- Hamilton Red Wings graduate
- first Red Wings game January 10, 1968
- played part of '68–'69 with Fort Worth
- traded February 15, 1969 with Brian Conacher to Minnesota for Wayne Connelly

REG LEACH ("Rifle") #27 RIGHT WING 6′ 180 *b.* Riverton, Manitoba, April 23, 1950

1982–83L	78	15	17	32	13

- signed as a free agent August 25, 1982
- last Red Wings game March 30, 1983
- played '83–'84 with Montana (CHL), then retired

JIM LEAVINS #4 DEFENCE 5′11″ 185 *b.* Dinsmore, Saskatchewan, July 28, 1960

1985–86R	37	2	11	13	26

- signed November 9, 1985 as a free agent
- first Red Wings game January 15, 1986
- traded July 29, 1986 with Kelly Kisio and Lane Lambert to Rangers for Glen Hanlon, a 3rd-round draft choice in 1987 (Dennis Holland), and a 3rd-round draft choice in 1988 (Guy Dupuis)

FERNAND "FERN" LEBLANC #12 – 18 CENTRE 5′9″ 170 *b.* Gaspesie, Quebec, January 12, 1956

1976–77R	3	0	0	0	0
1977–78	2	0	0	0	0
1978–79L	29	5	6	11	0
Totals	34	5	6	11	0

- selected 111th overall at 1976 Entry Draft
- first Red Wings games December 27, January 6, and March 1, 1976–77
- played December 8 & 10, 1977
- played most of '76–'79 with Kalamazoo and Kansas City
- last Red Wings game December 23, 1978

JEAN-PAUL "J.P." LEBLANC #12 – 18 – 21 CENTRE 5′10″ 175 *b.* South Durham, Quebec, October 20, 1946

1975–76	46	4	9	13	39
1976–77	74	7	11	18	40
1977–78	3	0	2	2	4
1978–79L	24	2	6	8	4
Totals	147	13	28	41	87

- acquired November 20, 1975 from Chicago for a 2nd-round draft choice in 1977 (Jean Savard)
- played most of '77–'79 with Kansas City
- last Red Wings game April 4, 1979

RENALD "RENE" LECLERC #8 – 15 RIGHT WING 5′11″ 165 *b.* Ville-de-Vanier, Quebec, November 12, 1947

1968–69R	43	2	3	5	62
1970–71	44	8	8	16	30
Totals	87	10	11	21	92

- selected 19th overall at 1964 Draft
- first Red Wings game December 11, 1968
- played much of '67–'72 with Fort Worth, part of '69–'70 with Cleveland, '71–'72 with San Diego and Tidewater
- joined WHA in 1972

HERB LEWIS

CLAUDE LEGRIS #31 GOALIE 5′9″ 160
b. Verdun, Quebec, November 6, 1956

1980–81R	3	0–1–0	63	4	0	3.81
1981–82L	1	0–0–1	28	0	0	0.00
Totals	4	0–1–1	91	4	0	2.64

- selected 120th overall at 1976 Entry Draft
- first Red Wings games March 24, April 4 & 5, 1981
- last Red Wings game November 11, 1981

REAL LEMIEUX #14 LEFT WING 5′11″ 180
b. Victoriaville, Quebec, January 3, 1945
d. Montreal, Quebec, October 25, 1975

1966–67R	1	0	0	0	0

- Hamilton Red Wings graduate
- first and only Red Wings game January 19, 1967
- played much of '64–'67 with Memphis
- lost June 6, 1967 to Los Angeles in Expansion Draft

TONY LESWICK ("Tough Tony") #8 – 12 LEFT WING 5′6″ 160 *b.* Humboldt, Saskatchewan, March 17, 1923

1951–52	70	9	10	19	93
1952–53	70	15	12	27	87
1953–54	70	6	18	24	90
1954–55	70	10	17	27	137
1957–58L	22	1	2	3	2
Totals	302	41	59	100	409

- acquired June 19, 1951 from Rangers for Gaye Stewart
- traded June 3, 1955 with Glen Skov, Johnny Wilson, and Ben Woit to Chicago for Gord Hollingworth, Jerry Toppazzini, John McCormack, & Dave Creighton
- last Red Wings game March 23, 1958
- contract bought August 1956 from Chicago

DAVE LEWIS #25 – 52 DEFENCE 6′2″ 205
b. Kindersley, Saskatchewan, July 3, 1953

1986–87	58	2	5	7	66
1987–88L	6	0	0	0	18
Totals	64	2	5	7	84

- signed July 27, 1986 as a free agent
- last Red Wings games October 8/12/16/21/31, November 4, 1987
- retired November 6, 1987 to become Red Wings assistant coach

HERB LEWIS ("Duke of Duluth") #4 – 7 – 9 LEFT WING 5′9″ 160
b. Calgary, Alberta, April 17, 1907
d. Indianapolis, Indiana, January 20, 1991

1928–29R	37	9	5	14	33
1929–30	44	20	11	31	36
1930–31	44	15	6	21	38
1931–32	48	5	14	19	21
1932–33	48	20	14	34	20
1933–34	43	16	15	31	15
1934–35	48	16	27	43	25
1935–36	45	14	23	37	25
1936–37	45	14	18	32	14
1937–38	42	13	18	31	12
1938–39L	39	6	10	16	8
Totals	483	148	161	309	247

- played '24–'28 with Duluth Hornets (AHL)
- first Cougars game November 15, 1928
- last Red Wings game March 19, 1939
- retired after '38–'39

NICK LIBETT #14 – 22 LEFT WING 6′1″ 195
b. Stratford, Ontario, December 9, 1945

1967–68R	22	2	1	3	12
1968–69	75	10	14	24	34
1969–70	76	20	20	40	39
1970–71	78	16	13	29	25
1971–72	77	31	22	53	50
1972–73	78	19	34	53	56
1973–74	67	24	24	48	37
1974–75	80	23	28	51	39
1975–76	80	20	26	46	71
1976–77	80	14	27	41	25
1977–78	80	23	22	45	46
1978–79	68	15	19	34	20
Totals	861	217	250	467	454

- Hamilton Red Wings graduate
- first Red Wings game February 10, 1968
- played part of '67–'68 with San Diego and Fort Worth
- traded August 3, 1979 to Penguins for Pete Mahovlich

TONY LICARI #19 RIGHT WING 5′7″ 147
b. Ottawa, Ontario, April 9, 1921

1946–47R/L	9	0	1	1	0

- first and only Red Wings games November 30, December 1/4/8/11/15/18/19/22, 1946
- traded September 9, 1948 with Ralph Almas, Lloyd Doran, Barry Sullivan, and Thain Simon to St. Louis (AHL) for Joe Lund and Hec Highton

NICKLAS LIDSTROM #5 DEFENCE 6′1″ 176
b. Vasteras, Sweden, April 28, 1970

1991–92R	80	11	49	60	22
1992–93	84	7	34	41	28
1993–94	84	10	46	56	26
1994–95	43	10	16	26	6
1995–96	81	17	50	67	20
Totals	372	55	195	250	102

- selected 53rd overall at 1989 Entry Draft
- first Red Wings game October 3, 1991
- currently with Red Wings

TED LINDSAY ("Terrible Ted") #7 – 14 – 15
LEFT WING 5′8″ 160 *b.* Renfrew, Ontario, July 29, 1925

1944–45R	45	17	6	23	43
1945–46	47	7	10	17	14
1946–47	59	27	15	42	57
1947–48	60	33	19	52	95
1948–49	50	26	28	54	97
1949–50	69	23	55	78	141
1950–51	67	24	35	59	110
1951–52	70	30	39	69	123
1952–53	70	32	39	71	111
1953–54	70	26	36	62	110
1954–55	49	19	19	38	85
1955–56	67	27	23	50	161
1956–57	70	30	55	85	103
1964–65L	69	14	14	28	173
Totals	862	335	393	728	1423

- St. Mike's graduate
- first Red Wings game October 29, 1944
- traded July 1957 with Glenn Hall to Chicago for Forbes Kennedy, Johnny Wilson, William Preston, and Hank Bassen
- rights purchased October 14, 1964 from Chicago
- last Red Wings game March 28, 1965
- retired April 15, 1965

CARL LISCOMBE ("Lefty") #7 – 10 – 15 – 17 LEFT WING 5′8″ 170
b. Perth, Ontario, May 17, 1915

1937–38R	42	14	10	24	30
1938–39	47	8	18	26	13
1939–40	30	2	7	9	4
1940–41	31	10	10	20	0
1941–42	47	13	17	30	30
1942–43	50	19	23	42	19
1943–44	50	36	37	73	17
1944–45	42	23	9	32	18
1945–46L	44	12	9	21	2
Totals	383	137	140	277	133

- Hamilton Tigers graduate
- first Red Wings game November 23, 1937
- last Red Wings game March 17, 1946
- sold August 17, 1946 to St. Louis (AHL) for cash

ED LITZENBERGER ("Litz") #14 RIGHT WING 6′3″ 194 *b.* Neudorf, Saskatchewan, July 15, 1932

1961–62	32	8	12	20	4

- acquired June 1961 from Chicago for Gerry Melnyk and Brian Smith
- sold December 1961 to Toronto for $20,000

CARL LISCOMBE

BILL LOCHEAD ("Whip") #23 LEFT WING 6′1″ 190 *b.* Forest, Ontario, October 13, 1954

1974–75R	65	16	12	28	34
1975–76	53	9	11	20	22
1976–77	61	16	14	30	39
1977–78	77	20	16	36	47
1978–79	40	4	7	11	20
Totals	296	65	60	125	162

- selected 9th overall at 1974 Entry Draft
- first Red Wings game October 9, 1974
- claimed on waivers February 9, 1979 by Rockies
- reclaimed June 9, 1979 from Winnipeg prior to Expansion Draft
- sold October 31, 1980 to Winnipeg

MARK LOFTHOUSE #10 – 17 RIGHT WING/CENTRE 6′2″ 195 *b.* New Westminster, British Columbia, April 21, 1957

1981–82	12	3	4	7	13
1982–83L	28	8	4	12	18
Totals	40	11	8	19	31

- acquired July 23, 1981 from Washington for Al Jensen
- last Red Wings game March 26, 1983
- lost August 10, 1983 as a free agent to Los Angeles

CLAUDE LOISELLE #8 – 10 – 15 – 21 CENTRE 5′11″ 195 *b.* Ottawa, Ontario, May 29, 1963

1981–82R	4	1	0	1	2
1982–83	18	2	0	2	15
1983–84	28	4	6	10	32
1984–85	30	8	1	9	45
1985–86	48	7	15	22	142
Totals	128	22	22	44	236

- selected 23rd overall at 1981 Entry Draft
- first Red Wings games February 7/13/20/21, 1982
- traded June 30, 1986 to New Jersey for Tim Higgins

BARRY LONG ("Marathon Man") #2 DEFENCE 6′2″ 210 *b.* Brantford, Ontario, January 3, 1949

1979–80	80	0	17	17	38

- acquired January 9, 1978 with a 3rd-round draft choice in 1978 (Doug Derkson) from Los Angeles for Danny Grant

CLEMENT "CLEM" LOUGHLIN #2 DEFENCE 6′ 180 *b.* Carroll, Manitoba, November 15, 1894

1926–27R	34	7	3	10	40
1927–28	43	1	2	3	21
Totals	77	8	5	13	61

- came from Victoria when team moved to Detroit
- first Cougars game November 18, 1926
- sold October 17, 1928 to Chicago

RON LOW #30 GOALIE 6′1″ 205 *b.* Birtle, Manitoba, June 21, 1950

1977–78	32	9–12–9	1816	102	1	3.37

- signed August 17, 1977 as a restricted free agent from Washington. As compensation, the Capitals received Walt McKechnie, a 3rd-round draft choice in 1978 (Joey Johnson), and a 2nd-round draft choice in 1979 (Errol Rausse). Detroit also received a 3rd-round draft choice in 1978 (Boris Fistric)
- lost June 13, 1979 to Quebec in Expansion Draft

PETE LOZINSKI #31 GOALIE 5′11″ 175 *b.* Hudson Bay, Saskatchewan, March 11, 1958

1980–81R/L	30	6–11–7	1459	105	0	4.32

- selected 219th overall at 1978 Entry Draft
- first Red Wings game December 27, 1980
- last Red Wings game April 5, 1981
- played part of '80–'83 with Adirondack

DAVE LUCAS #18 DEFENCE *b.* Downeyville, Ontario, March 22, 1932

1962–63R/L	1	0	0	0	0

- first and only Red Wings game February 24, 1963
- played '63–'64 with Johnstown Jets (EHL), then became player/coach

DON LUCE #11 CENTRE 6′2″ 185
b. London, Ontario, October 2, 1948

1970–71	58	3	11	14	18

- acquired November 2, 1970 from Rangers for Steve Andrascik
- traded May 25, 1971 with Mike Robitaille to Buffalo for Joe Daley

HARRY LUMLEY ("Apple Cheeks") #1 GOALIE 6′ 195 *b.* Owen Sound, Ontario, November 11, 1926

1943–44R	2	0–2–0	120	13	0	6.50
1944–45	37	24–10–3	2228	119	1	3.20
1945–46	50	20–20–10	3000	159	2	3.18
1946–47	52	22–20–10	3129	159	3	3.05
1947–48	60	30–18–12	3592	147	7	2.46
1948–49	60	34–19–7	3600	145	6	2.42
1949–50	63	33–16–14	3780	148	7	2.35
Totals	324	163–105–56	19449	890	26	2.75

- signed with Detroit from the Barrie Colts at age 16
- first Red Wings games December 19 & 22, 1943
- traded July 13, 1950 with Al Dewsbury, Jack Stewart, Don Morrison, and Pete Babando to Chicago for Jim Henry, Bob Goldham, Gaye Stewart, and Metro Prystai

LEN LUNDE #14 – 20 CENTRE 6′1″ 194
b. Campbell River, British Columbia, November 13, 1936

1958–59R	68	14	12	26	15
1959–60	66	6	17	23	10
1960–61	53	6	12	18	10
1961–62	23	2	9	11	4
Totals	210	28	50	78	39

- played much of '55–'58 and '61–'62 with Edmonton (WHL)
- first Red Wings game October 11, 1958
- traded June 5, 1962 with John McKenzie to Chicago for Doug Barkley

TORD LUNDSTROM #23 LEFT WING 5′11″ 176 *b.* Kiruna, Sweden, March 4, 1945

1973–74R/L	11	1	1	2	0

- first and only Red Wings games October 10/26/27/30, November 4/7/14/18/20/22, December 5, 1973
- played '72–'73 with Swedish National Team
- played most of '73–'74 in London, England

PAT LUNDY #8 – 17 CENTRE 5′10″ 168
b. Saskatoon, Saskatchewan, May 31, 1924

1945–46R	4	3	2	5	2
1946–47	59	17	17	34	10
1947–48	11	4	1	5	6
1948–49	15	4	3	7	4
Totals	89	28	23	51	22

- first Red Wings games March 13/14/16/17, 1946
- played much of '47–'50 with Indianapolis
- sold October 1, 1950 to Chicago for cash

CHRIS LUONGO #37 DEFENCE 6′ 180
b. Detroit, March 17, 1967

1990–91R	4	0	1	1	4

- selected 92nd overall at 1985 Entry Draft
- first Red Wings games January 22/25/26/28, 1991
- lost September 9, 1992 as a free agent to Ottawa

GEORGE LYLE ("Sparky") #18 LEFT WING 6′2″ 205 *b.* North Vancouver, British Columbia, November 24, 1953

1979–80	27	7	4	11	2
1980–81	31	10	14	24	28
1981–82	11	1	2	3	0
Totals	69	18	20	38	30

- selected 123rd overall at 1973 Entry Draft
- reclaimed June 9, 1979 from Hartford prior to Expansion Draft
- lost November 3, 1981 to Hartford on waivers

JACK LYNCH #3 – 21 DEFENCE 6′2″ 180
b. Toronto, Ontario, May 25, 1952

1973–74	35	3	9	12	27
1974–75	50	2	15	17	46
Totals	85	5	24	29	73

- acquired January 18, 1974 with Jim Rutherford from Penguins for Ron Stackhouse
- traded February 8, 1975 to Washington for Dave Kyrskow

VIC LYNN #3 DEFENCE 5′9″ 185 *b.* Saskatoon, Saskatchewan, January 26, 1925

1943–44R	3	0	0	0	4

- first and only Red Wings games December 16/19/22, 1943
- played most of '43–'44 with Indianapolis
- played '44–'45 with St. Louis (AHL), before signing with Canadiens for '45–'46

LOWELL MACDONALD #8 – 11 RIGHT WING 5′11″ 185 *b.* New Glasgow, Nova Scotia, August 30, 1941

1961–62R	1	0	0	0	2
1962–63	26	2	1	3	8
1963–64	10	1	4	5	0
1964–65	9	2	1	3	0
Totals	46	5	6	11	10

- Hamilton Red Wings graduate
- first Red Wings game December 30, 1961
- played part of '62–'65 with Pittsburgh
- traded May 20, 1965 with Marcel Pronovost, Ed Joyal, Larry Jeffrey, and Aut Erickson to Toronto for Andy Bathgate, Billy Harris, and Gary Jarrett

PARKER MACDONALD #14 – 19 – 20 LEFT WING 5′11″ 184 *b.* Sydney, Nova Scotia, June 14, 1933

1960–61	70	14	12	26	6
1961–62	32	5	7	12	8
1962–63	69	33	28	61	32
1963–64	68	21	25	46	25
1964–65	69	13	33	46	38
1965–66	37	5	12	17	24
1966–67	16	3	5	8	2
Totals	361	94	122	216	135

- claimed June 1960 from Rangers at Intra-League Draft
- traded May 31, 1965 with Bob Dillabough, Al Langlois, and Ron Harris to Boston for Ab McDonald, Bob McCord, and Ken Stephenson
- acquired December 30, 1965 from Boston for Pit Martin
- lost June 6, 1967 to Minnesota in Expansion Draft

BRUCE MACGREGOR ("The Redheaded Rocket") #12 – 16 RIGHT WING 5′10″ 180 *b.* Edmonton, Alberta, April 26, 1941

1960–61R	12	0	1	1	0
1961–62	65	6	12	18	16
1962–63	67	11	11	22	12
1963–64	63	11	21	32	15
1964–65	66	21	20	41	19
1965–66	70	20	14	34	28
1966–67	70	28	19	47	14
1967–68	71	15	24	39	13
1968–69	69	18	23	41	14
1969–70	73	15	23	38	24
1970–71	47	6	16	22	18
Totals	673	151	184	335	173

- first Red Wings games February 25/26/28, March 2/4/5/7/9/12/14/15/19, 1961
- played most of '60–'61 with Edmonton (WHL)
- traded February 2, 1971 to Rangers with Larry Brown for Mike Robitaille, Arnie Brown, and Tom Miller

CALUM MACKAY ("Baldy") #16 – 24 LEFT WING 5′9″ 185 *b.* Toronto, Ontario, January 1, 1927

1946–47R	5	0	0	0	0
1948–49	1	0	0	0	0
Totals	6	0	0	0	0

- first Red Wings games March 9/12/13/15/16, 1947
- played December 22, 1948
- played with Omaha '47–'48 and Indianapolis '47–'50
- traded November 11, 1949 to Canadiens for Joe Carveth

HOWARD "HAL" MACKIE #14 – 17 DEFENCE 5′8″ 175 *b.* Kitchener, Ontario, August 30, 1913

1936–37R	13	1	0	1	4
1937–38L	7	0	0	0	0
Totals	20	1	0	1	4

- first Red Wings game November 26, 1936
- last Red Wings games December 5/7/9/12/14/16/19, 1937

PAUL MACLEAN #15 RIGHT WING 6′2″ 218
b. Grostenquin, France, March 9, 1958

1988–89L	76	36	35	71	118

- acquired June 13, 1988 from Winnipeg for Brent Ashton
- last Red Wings game April 2, 1989
- traded June 15, 1989 with Adam Oates to St. Louis for Bernie Federko and Tony McKegney

RICK MACLEISH #23 CENTRE 5′11″ 185
b. Lindsay, Ontario, January 3, 1950

1983–84L	25	2	8	10	4

- acquired January 8, 1984 from Flyers for future considerations
- last Red Wings game March 31, 1984
- retired after '83–'84 season

BRIAN MACLELLAN #27 LEFT WING 6′3″ 215 *b.* Guelph, Ontario, October 27, 1958

1991–92L	23	1	5	6	28

- acquired June 11, 1991 from Calgary for Marc Habscheid
- last Red Wings game March 14, 1992
- retired after '91–'92 season

JOHN MACMILLAN #11 – 12 – 19
RIGHT WING 5′9″ 185
b. Lethbridge, Alberta, October 25, 1935

1963–64	20	0	3	3	6
1964–65L	3	0	1	1	0
Totals	23	0	4	4	6

- bought December 3, 1963 from Toronto
- last Red Wings games November 8/10/11, 1964
- played part of '63–'64 with Pittsburgh, '64–'66 with Memphis, '66–'71 with San Diego

FRANK MAHOVLICH ("Big M") #27
LEFT WING 6′ 205 *b.* Timmins, Ontario, January 10, 1938

1967–68	13	7	9	16	2
1968–69	76	49	29	78	38
1969–70	74	38	32	70	59
1970–71	35	14	18	32	30
Totals	198	108	88	196	129

- acquired March 3, 1968 with Garry Unger, Pete Stemkowski, and the rights to Carl Brewer for Paul Henderson, Norm Ullman, and Floyd Smith
- traded January 13, 1971 to Canadiens for Mickey Redmond, Guy Charron, and Bill Collins

PETE MAHOVLICH ("Little M") #11 – 21 – 24
CENTRE 6′5″ 210 *b.* Timmins, Ontario, October 10, 1946

1965–66R	3	0	1	1	0
1966–67	34	1	3	4	16
1967–68	15	6	4	10	13
1968–69	30	2	2	4	21
1979–80	80	16	50	66	69
1980–81	24	1	4	5	26
Totals	186	26	64	90	145

- selected 2nd overall at 1963 Draft
- first Red Wings games December 28, March 23 & 27, 1965–66
- played part of '66–'67 with Pittsburgh, '67–'69 with Fort Worth
- traded June 6, 1969 with Bart Crashley to Canadiens for Garry Monahan and Doug Piper
- acquired August 3, 1979 from Penguins for Nick Libett
- played part of '80–'82 with Adirondack
- contract bought out August 25, 1982

DAN MALONEY #7 LEFT WING 6′2″ 195
b. Barrie, Ontario, September 24, 1950

1975–76	77	27	39	66	203
1976–77	34	13	13	26	64
1977–78	66	16	29	45	151
Totals	177	56	81	137	418

- acquired June 23, 1975 with Terry Harper and a 2nd-round draft choice in 1976 (later traded to Minnesota — Jim Roberts) to Los Angeles for Bart Crashley and the rights to Marcel Dionne
- traded March 13, 1978 with a 2nd-round draft choice in 1980 (Craig Muni) to Toronto for Errol Thompson, a 1st-round draft choice in 1978 (Brent Peterson), a 2nd-round draft choice in 1978 (Al Jensen) and a 1st-round draft choice in 1980 (Mike Blaisdell)

STEVE MALTAIS #34 LEFT WING 6′2″ 210
b. Arvida, Quebec, January 25, 1969

1993–94	4	0	1	1	0

- acquired June 8, 1993 from Tampa Bay for Dennis Vial
- played February 5/8/11/15, 1994
- played most of '93–'94 with Adirondack, '94–'95 with Chicago (IHL)

KIRK MALTBY #18 RIGHT WING 6′ 180
b. Guelph, Ontario, December 22, 1972

1995–96	6	1	0	1	6

- acquired March 20, 1996 from Edmonton for Dan McGillis
- currently with Red Wings

RANDY MANERY #12 – 24 DEFENCE 6′ 185
b. Leamington, Ontario, January 10, 1949

1970–71R	2	0	0	0	0
1971–72	1	0	0	0	0
Totals	3	0	0	0	0

- Hamilton Red Wings graduate
- first Red Wings games April 3 & 4, 1971
- played January 30, 1972
- played most of '69–'72 with Forth Worth
- lost June 6, 1972 to Atlanta in Expansion Draft

KEN MANN #17 RIGHT WING 5′11″ 200
b. Hamilton, Ontario, September 5, 1953

1975–76R/L	1	0	0	0	0

- also played with Kalamazoo ('75–'77) and Kansas City ('76–'77)
- first and only Red Wings game February 25, 1976

BOB MANNO #23 – 33 DEFENCE/LEFT WING 6′ 185 *b.* Niagara Falls, Ontario, October 31, 1956

1983–84	62	9	13	22	60
1984–85L	74	10	22	32	32
Totals	136	19	35	54	92

- signed as a free agent August 2, 1983
- last Red Wings game April 7, 1985
- joined Merano (Italian League) for '85–'86

LOU MARCON #19 – 21 DEFENCE 5′9″ 178
b. Fort William, Ontario, May 28, 1935

1958–59R	21	0	1	1	12
1959–60	38	0	3	3	30
1962–63L	1	0	0	0	0
Totals	60	0	4	4	42

- first Red Wings game February 5, 1959
- last Red Wings game February 26, 1963
- career minor-leaguer '56–'68

AUGUST "GUS" MARKER #14 – 15 – 16 FORWARD *b.* Wetaskewin, Alberta, August 1, 1907

1932–33R	15	1	1	2	8
1933–34	7	1	0	1	2
Totals	22	2	1	3	10

- called up from Detroit Olympics in '32–'33 and '33–'34
- first Red Wings game November 10, 1932
- traded September 23, 1934 to Maroons for Wally Kilrea

BRAD MARSH #20 DEFENCE 6′3″ 220
b. London, Ontario, March 31, 1958

1990–91	20	1	3	4	16
1991–92	55	3	5	8	53
Totals	75	4	8	12	69

- acquired February 4, 1991 from Toronto for an 8th-round draft choice in 1991 (Robb McIntyre)
- sold June 10, 1992 to Toronto for cash

GARY MARSH #14 LEFT WING 5′9″ 172
b. Toronto, Ontario, March 9, 1946

1967–68R	6	1	3	4	4

- Hamilton Red Wings graduate
- first and only Red Wings games December 14/16/17/20/23 and January 17, 1967–68
- played '65–'67 with Memphis, '67–'68 with Fort Worth
- lost June 6, 1968 when put on Toronto reserve list

BERT MARSHALL #3 – 5 DEFENCE 6′3″ 205
b. Kamloops, British Columbia, November 22, 1943

1965–66R	61	0	19	19	45
1966–67	57	0	10	10	68
1967–68	37	1	5	6	56
Totals	155	1	34	35	169

- first Red Wings game November 14, 1965
- played '63–'64 with Cincinnati, '64–'65 with Memphis, and most of '65–'66 with Pittsburgh
- traded January 9, 1968 with John Brenneman and Ted Hampson to Oakland for Kent Douglas

CLARE MARTIN #3 DEFENCE 5′11″ 180
b. Waterloo, Ontario, February 25, 1922

1949–50	64	2	5	7	14
1950–51	50	1	6	7	12
Totals	114	3	11	14	26

- acquired August 16, 1949 with Pete Babando, Lloyd Durham, and Jim Peters from Boston for Pete Horeck and Bill Quackenbush
- traded August 20, 1951 with George Gee, Jim McFadden, Max McNab, Jim Peters, and Rags Raglan to Chicago for Hugh Coflin and $75,000

HUBERT "PIT" MARTIN #8 – 12 – 15
CENTRE 5′9″ 170 *b.* Noranda, Quebec, December 9, 1943

1961–62R	1	0	1	1	0
1963–64	50	9	12	21	21
1964–65	58	8	9	17	32
1965–66	10	1	1	2	0
Totals	119	18	23	41	53

- Hamilton Red Wings graduate
- first Red Wings game January 24, 1962
- played part of '62–'64 and '65–'66 with Pittsburgh
- traded December 30, 1965 to Boston for Parker MacDonald

DON MARTINEAU #20 – 29 RIGHT WING
6′ 190 *b.* Kimberley, British Columbia, April 25, 1952

1975–76	9	0	1	1	0
1976–77L	1	0	0	0	0
Totals	10	0	1	1	0

- acquired November 25, 1975 from Minnesota for Pierre Jarry
- played January 3/4/6/8/10/13/14/18/22, 1976
- played '76–'78 with Kansas City (CHL)
- last Red Wings game March 17, 1977

STEVE MARTINSON #36 LEFT WING 6′1″ 205
b. Minnetonka, Minnesota, June 21, 1959

1987–88R	10	1	1	2	84

- signed October 3, 1987 as a free agent
- first and only Red Wings games October 9/12, November 4/7/11, December 9/11/27, January 6/8, 1987–88
- played part of '87–'88 with Adirondack
- lost August 2, 1988 as a free agent to Canadiens

CHARLIE MASON ("Dutch") #18
FORWARD 5′10″ 160 *b.* Seaforth, Ontario, February 1, 1912 *d.* Unknown

1938–39	4	0	1	1	0

- played '37–'38 with Americans
- played November 10/13/15/17, 1938
- traded during '38–'39 to Chicago

ROLAND MATTE #9 – 15 DEFENCE 5′10″ 178
b. Bourget, Ontario, March 15, 1909

1929–30R/L	12	0	1	1	0

- first and only Cougars games February 4/6/9/13/16/18/23, March 2/6/8/15/18, 1930

GARY McADAM #19 LEFT WING
5′11″ 175 *b.* Smiths Falls, Ontario, December 31, 1955

1980–81	40	5	14	19	27

- acquired January 8, 1981 from Penguins for Errol Thompson
- traded November 10, 1981 with a 4th-round draft choice in 1983 (John Bekkers) to Calgary for Eric Vail

JEROME "JUD" McATEE #11 – 17 – 18 LEFT WING 5′9″ 170 *b.* Stratford, Ontario, February 5, 1920

1942–43R	1	0	0	0	0
1943–44	1	0	2	2	0
1944–45L	44	15	11	26	6
Totals	46	15	13	28	6

- signed October 17, 1940
- first Red Wings game November 1, 1942
- played December 4, 1943
- last Red Wings game March 18, 1944

STAN McCABE #12 – 14 DEFENCE
b. Ottawa, Ontario

1929–30R	25	7	3	10	23
1930–31	44	2	1	3	22
Totals	69	9	4	13	45

- first Cougars game January 5, 1930

DOUG McCAIG #4 – 5 – 17 – 18 – 21 – 22 DEFENCE 6′ 180 *b.* Guelph, Ontario, February 24, 1919

1941–42R	9	0	1	1	6
1945–46	6	0	1	1	12
1946–47	47	2	4	6	64
1947–48	29	3	3	6	37
1948–49	1	0	0	0	0
Totals	92	5	9	14	119

- played much of '40–'42 with Indianapolis
- first Red Wings games November 1/2/9/15/16/20/22/23/25, 1941
- played October 13, 1948
- missed 1942–45 — Royal Canadian Air Force
- played most of '45–'46 with Indianapolis
- traded October 1948 with Jim Conacher and Bep Guidolin to Chicago for George Gee and Bud Poile
- acquired September 18, 1951 from Chicago for Max Quackenbush

RICK McCANN #8 – 18 – 22 – 24 CENTRE
5′9″ 178 *b.* Hamilton, Ontario, May 27, 1944

1967–68R	3	0	0	0	0
1968–69	3	0	0	0	0
1969–70	18	0	1	1	4
1970–71	5	0	0	0	0
1971–72	1	0	0	0	0
1974–75L	13	1	3	4	2
Totals	43	1	4	5	6

- played on Canadian national team
- first Red Wings games December 6/7/9, 1967
- played March 27/29/30, 1969
- played October 11/13, March 4/6/7, 1970–71
- played November 27, 1971
- last Red Wings games November 20/23/24/27/28/30, December 4/5/7/8/27/28/29, 1974
- played '66–'67 with Memphis, most of '67–'70 with Fort Worth, '70–'71 with Baltimore, '71–'73 with Tidewater, '73–'74 in London, England, '74–'75 with Virginia, and '75–'76 with New Haven

TOM McCARTHY #19 – 21 LEFT WING 6′1″ 190 *b.* Toronto, Ontario, September 15, 1934

1956–57R	3	0	0	0	0
1957–58	18	2	1	3	4
1958–59	15	2	3	5	4
Totals	36	4	4	8	8

- recalled from Hershey in November 1958 when Dunc Fisher demoted
- first Red Wings games October 18/21/25, 1956
- traded January 1961 with Gary Aldcorn and Murray Oliver to Boston for Vic Stasiuk and Leo Labine

DARREN McCARTY #25 RIGHT WING
6′1″ 210 *b.* Burnaby, British Columbia, April 1, 1972

1993–94R	67	9	17	26	181

1994–95	31	5	8	13	88
1995–96	63	15	14	29	158
Totals	161	29	39	68	427

- selected 46th overall at 1992 Entry Draft
- first Red Wings game October 5, 1993
- currently with Red Wings

KEVIN McCLELLAND #18 RIGHT WING 6′2″ 205 *b.* Oshawa, Ontario, July 4, 1962

1989–90	61	4	5	9	183
1990–91	3	0	0	0	7
Totals	64	4	5	9	190

- acquired November 2, 1989 with Jimmy Carson from Edmonton for Adam Graves, Petr Klima, Joe Murphy, and Jeff Sharples
- played part of '90–'91 with Adirondack
- lost September 2, 1991 as a free agent to Toronto

BOB McCORD #2 – 3 – 24 – 25 DEFENCE 6′1″ 202 *b.* Matheson, Ontario, March 30, 1934

1965–66	9	0	2	2	16
1966–67	14	1	2	3	27
1967–68	3	0	0	0	2
Totals	26	1	4	5	45

- acquired May 31, 1965 with Ab McDonald and Ken Stephenson from Boston for Bob Dillabough, Al Langlois, Ron Harris, and Parker MacDonald
- traded October 19, 1967 to Minnesota for Jean-Guy Talbot

DALE McCOURT ("Chief") #10 CENTRE 5′10″ 180 *b.* Falconbridge, Ontario, January 26, 1957

1977–78R	76	33	39	72	10
1978–79	79	28	43	71	14
1979–80	80	30	51	81	12
1980–81	80	30	56	86	50
1981–82	26	13	14	27	12
Totals	341	134	203	337	98

- selected 1st overall at 1977 Entry Draft
- first Red Wings game October 13, 1977
- lost August 8, 1978 to Los Angeles as compensation for Red Wings signing of Rogie Vachon
- refused to go; sued the NHL
- as a result, traded by Los Angeles back to Detroit for Andre St. Laurent, a 1st-round draft choice in 1980 (Larry Smith) and a 1st-round draft choice in 1981 (Doug Smith)
- traded December 2, 1981 with Mike Foligno and Brent Peterson to Buffalo for Jim Schoenfeld, Danny Gare, and Derek Smith

BILL McCREARY #20 LEFT WING 5′10″ 172 *b.* Sundridge, Ontario, December 2, 1934

1957–58	3	1	0	1	2

- claimed June 5, 1956 from Rangers at Intra-League Draft
- played October 12/13/17, 1957
- played '56–'57 with Edmonton, '57–'58 with Hershey and Edmonton

PAT McCREAVY #18 RIGHT WING 5′11″ 165 *b.* Owen Sound, Ontario, January 16, 1918

1941–42L	34	5	8	13	0

- last Red Wings game March 19, 1942
- joined Royal Canadian Air Force 1942–45 — never played in the NHL again

BYRON "BRAD" McCRIMMON #2 DEFENCE 5′11″ 197 *b.* Dodsland, Saskatchewan, March 29, 1959

1990–91	64	0	13	13	81
1991–92	79	7	22	29	118
1992–93	60	1	14	15	71
Totals	203	8	49	57	270

- acquired June 15, 1990 from Calgary for a 2nd-round draft choice in 1990 (later traded to New Jersey — David Harlock)
- traded June 1, 1993 to Hartford for a 6th-round draft choice in 1993 (Tim Spitzig)

BRIAN "BOOM BOOM" McCUTCHEON #8 – 27 – 29 LEFT WING 5′10″ 180
b. Toronto, Ontario, August 3, 1949

1974–75R	17	3	1	4	2
1975–76	8	0	0	0	5
1976–77L	12	0	0	0	0
Totals	37	3	1	4	7

- first Red Wings game November 20, 1974
- played most of '75–'76 with New Haven, '76–'78 with Kansas City
- last Red Wings games November 4/7/9/10/13/17/19/21/24/25/27/28, 1976

ALVIN "AB" McDONALD ("Ab") #12 – 22 LEFT WING 6′2″ 194
b. Winnipeg, Manitoba, February 18, 1936

1965–66	43	6	16	22	6
1966–67	12	2	0	2	2
1971–72	19	2	3	5	0
Totals	74	10	19	29	8

- acquired May 31, 1965 with Bob McCord and Ken Stephenson from Boston for Bob Dillabough, Al Langlois, Ron Harris, and Parker MacDonald
- lost June 6, 1967 to Penguins in Expansion Draft
- acquired May 12, 1971 witih Bob Wall and Mike Lowe from St. Louis for Carl Brewer (sent to the Blues February 22, 1971)
- signed with Winnipeg Jets (WHA) on August 15, 1972

BYRON "BUTCH" McDONALD #11 – 12 LEFT WING 6′ 185 *b.* Moose Jaw, Saskatchewan, November 21, 1916
d. Burks Falls, Ontario, July 19, 1991

1939–40R	37	1	6	7	2
1944–45	3	1	1	2	0
Totals	40	2	7	9	2

- played '38–'39 with Pittsburgh, and '39–'40 with Indianapolis
- first Red Wings game December 8, 1939
- traded January 1945 with Don Grosso and Cully Simon to Chicago for Earl Seibert

WILFRED "BUCKO" McDONALD #3 DEFENCE 5′9″ 205 *b.* Fergus, Ontario, October 31, 1911

1934–35R	16	1	2	3	8
1935–36	48	4	6	10	32
1936–37	47	3	5	8	20
1937–38	47	3	7	10	14
1938–39	14	0	0	0	2
Totals	172	11	20	31	76

- acquired during '34–'35 from Toronto
- first Red Wings game February 10, 1935
- traded December 19, 1938 to Toronto for Bill Thomson and $10,000

AL McDONOUGH #17 RIGHT WING 6′1″ 175
b. Hamilton, Ontario, June 6, 1950

1977–78L	13	2	2	4	4

- signed as a free agent August 17, 1977 from Atlanta for future considerations
- only Red Wings games October 26/27, November 2/6/9/12/13/16/18/19/23/26/27, 1977
- retired September 8, 1978

BILL McDOUGALL #43 CENTRE 6′ 185
b. Mississauga, Ontario, August 10, 1966

1990–91R	2	0	1	1	0

- signed January 9, 1990 as a free agent
- first and only Red Wings games February 27 & March 1, 1991
- played part of '90–'91 with Adirondack, '91–'92 with Cape Breton and Adirondack
- traded February 22, 1992 to Edmonton for Max Middendorf

PETE McDUFFE #30 GOALIE 5′9″ 180
b. Milton, Ontario, February 16, 1948

1975–76	4	0–3–1	240	22	0	5.50

- acquired August 22, 1975 with Glen Burdon from Kansas City for Gary Bergman and Bill McKenzie
- played October 15/19/25, January 22, 1975–76
- played part of '75–'76 with New Haven, '76–'77 with Rhode Island and New Haven, before joining Indianapolis (WHA) for '77–'78

MIKE McEWEN #7 DEFENCE 6′1″ 185
b. Hornepayne, Ontario, August 10, 1956

1985–86	29	0	10	10	16

- signed as a free agent August 12, 1985
- traded December 26, 1985 to Rangers for Steve Richmond

JIM McFADDEN #4 – 16 CENTRE 5′7″ 178
b. Belfast, Ireland, April 15, 1920

1947–48R	60	24	24	48	12
1948–49	55	12	20	32	10
1949–50	68	14	16	30	8
1950–51	70	14	18	32	10
Totals	253	64	78	142	40

- joined Detroit from Buffalo for 1947 playoffs
- first regular season Red Wings game October 15, 1947
- traded August 20, 1951 with George Gee, Max McNab, Jim Peters, Clare Martin and Rags Raglan to Chicago for Hugh Coflin and $75,000

BOB McGILL ("Big Daddy") #4 DEFENCE 6′1″
193 *b.* Edmonton, Alberta, April 27, 1962

1991–92	12	0	0	0	21

- acquired March 9, 1992 with an 8th-round draft choice in 1992 (previously acquired from Vancouver Canucks — C.J. Denomme) from San Jose for Johan Garpenlov
- played March 12/14/15/17/20/22/24/28/29/31, April 12/14, 1992
- lost June 18, 1992 to Tampa Bay in Expansion Draft

TOM McGRATTON #25 GOALIE 6′2″ 170
b. Brantford, Ontario, October 19, 1927

1947–48R/L	1	0–0–0	8	1	0	7.80

- first and only Red Wings game November 9, 1947

BERT McINENLY #9 DEFENCE 5′9″ 160
b. Quebec City, Quebec, May 6, 1906
d. Unknown

1930–31R	44	3	5	8	48
1931–32	17	0	1	1	16
Totals	61	3	6	9	64

- first Falcons game November 13, 1930
- traded December 29, 1931 to Americans with Tommy Filmore for Frank Carson and Hap Emms

JACK McINTYRE ("Jake") #14 – 15 – 16
LEFT WING 5′11″ 190 *b.* Brussels, Ontario, September 8, 1930

1957–58	41	15	7	22	4
1958–59	55	15	14	29	14
1959–60L	49	8	7	15	6
Totals	145	38	28	66	24

- acquired December 17, 1957 with Bob Bailey, Nick Mickoski, and Hec Lalande from Chicago for Earl Reibel, Billy Dea, Lorne Ferguson, and Bill Dineen
- last Red Wings game March 20, 1960
- played part of '58–'61 with Hershey; sold November 1961 to Pittsburgh

ALVIN "DOUG" McKAY #27 LEFT WING 5′9″
165 *b.* Hamilton, Ontario, May 28, 1929

- appeared only in the 1950 playoffs for Detroit

RANDY McKAY #14 – 25 – 29 RIGHT WING
6′1″ 185 *b.* Montreal, Quebec, January 25, 1967

1988–89R	3	0	0	0	0
1989–90	33	3	6	9	51
1990–91	47	1	7	8	183
Totals	83	4	13	17	234

- selected 113th overall at 1985 Entry Draft
- first Red Wings games February 2/3/5, 1989
- lost September 9, 1991 with Dave Barr to New Jersey as equal compensation for Detroit signing Troy Crowder

WALT McKECHNIE ("McKech") #11 CENTRE
6′2″ 200 *b.* London, Ontario, June 19, 1947

1974–75	23	6	11	17	6
1975–76	80	26	56	82	85
1976–77	80	25	34	59	50
1981–82	74	18	37	55	35
1982–83	64	14	29	43	42
Totals	321	89	167	256	218

- acquired February 18, 1975 with a 3rd-round draft choice in 1975 (Clark Hamilton) from Boston for Earl Anderson and Hank Nowak
- traded August 17, 1977 with a 3rd-round draft choice in 1978 (Jay Johnston) and a 2nd-round draft choice in 1979 (Errol Rausse) to Washington for the rights to Ron Low, and a 3rd-round draft choice in 1979 (Borris Fistric) as compensation for Detroit signing restricted free agent Low
- signed as a free agent August 13, 1981
- lost August 5, 1983 as a free agent to Minnesota

TONY McKEGNEY #7 LEFT WING 6′1″ 200
b. Montreal, Quebec, February 15, 1958

1989–90	14	2	1	3	8

- acquired June 15, 1989 with Bernie Federko from St. Louis for Adam Oates and Paul MacLean
- traded December 4, 1989 to Quebec for Greg C. Adams and Robert Picard

DON McKENNEY #20 CENTRE 6′ 175
b. Smiths Falls, Ontario, April 30, 1934

1965–66	24	1	6	7	0

- claimed June 8, 1965 on waivers from Toronto
- lost June 6, 1967 to St. Louis in Expansion Draft

BILL McKENZIE #1 – 30 GOALIE 5′11″ 180
b. St. Thomas, Ontario, March 12, 1949

1973–74R	13	4–4–4	720	43	1	3.58
1974–75	13	1–9–2	740	58	0	4.70
Totals	26	5–13–6	1460	101	1	4.15

- Port Huron Wings graduate
- first Red Wings games December 18/20/22/26/27/30/31, January 9/12/16/23/30, February 2, 1973–74
- played part of ’73–’75 with Virginia, 2 games with London Lions (England)
- traded August 22, 1975 with Gary Bergman to Kansas City for Pete McDuffe and Glen Burdon

JOHN McKENZIE (“Pie Face”) #21
RIGHT WING 5′9″ 175 *b.* High River, Alberta, December 12, 1937

1959–60	59	8	12	20	50
1960–61	16	3	1	4	13
Totals	75	11	13	24	63

- claimed June 10, 1959 from Chicago at Intra-League Draft
- traded June 5, 1962 with Len Lunde to Chicago for Doug Barkley

ANDREW McKIM #14 CENTRE 5′8″ 175
b. St. John, New Brunswick, July 6, 1970

1994–95	2	0	0	0	2

- signed August 31, 1994 as a free agent
- played February 10 & 12, 1995
- played most of ’94–’95 with Adirondack
- played ’95–’96 with Canadian National Team
- currently with Red Wings

ROLAND “ROLLIE” McLENAHAN
(“The Mighty Mite”) #21 DEFENCE 5′7″ 170 *b.* Fredericton, New Brunswick, October 26, 1921 *d.* Unknown

1945–46R/L	9	2	1	3	10

- first Red Wings game February 2, 1946
- last Red Wings game March 17, 1946
- career minor-leaguer ’45–’51; out of hockey after 1951

AL “MOOSE” McLEOD #2 DEFENCE 5′11″
200 *b.* Medicine Hat, Alberta, June 17, 1949

1973–74R	26	2	2	4	24

- first Red Wings game February 9, 1974
- played most of ’73–’74 with Virginia
- jumped to Phoenix (WHA) for ’74–’75

DON McLEOD #1 – 30 GOALIE 6′ 190
b. Trail, British Columbia, August 24, 1946

1970–71R	14	3–7–0	698	60	0	5.16

- first Red Wings games November 28/29, December 5/6/10/12/13/16/19/20/27/31, January 2, April 4, 1970–71
- played part of ’69–’71 with Forth Worth
- lost to Flyers at 1971 Intra-League Draft

MIKE McMAHON #21 DEFENCE 5′11″ 175
b. Quebec City, Quebec, August 30, 1941

1969–70	2	0	0	0	0

- claimed on waivers October 14, 1969 from Chicago
- played April 11 & 12, 1970
- traded October 28, 1969 to Penguins for Billy Dea

MAX McNAB #10 – 11 – 19 – 20 – 27
CENTRE 6′2″ 170 *b.* Watson, Saskatchewan, June 21, 1924

1947–48R	12	2	2	4	2
1948–49	51	10	13	23	14
1949–50L	65	4	4	8	8
Totals	128	16	19	35	24

- played junior with Saskatoon Elks in '46–'47
- first Red Wings games October 15/19/29, November 1/2/6/8/9/15/16/19/23, 1947
- last Red Wings game March 26, 1950
- played parts of '46–'47 and all of '50–'51 with Indianapolis, but joined Red Wings for '51 playoffs
- played part of '46–'48 with Omaha
- traded August 20, 1951 with George Gee, Jim McFadden, Jim Peters, Clare Martin, and Rags Raglan to Chicago for Hugh Coflin and $75,000

BILLY McNEILL #14 – 15 – 19 – 21
RIGHT WING 5′10″ 185 *b.* Edmonton, Alberta, January 26, 1936

1956–57R	64	5	10	15	34
1957–58	35	5	10	15	29
1958–59	54	2	5	7	32
1959–60	47	5	13	18	33
1962–63	42	3	7	10	12
1963–64L	15	1	1	2	2
Totals	257	21	46	67	142

- Edmonton Oil Kings graduate (played '52–'59)
- first Red Wings game October 18, 1956
- traded February 5, 1960 with Red Kelly to the Rangers for Eddie Shack and Bill Gadsby; refused to join Rangers, so retired
- claimed June 8, 1960 by Rangers at Intra-League Draft
- re-acquired before the start of '62–'63
- last Red Wings game December 1, 1963

STUART "STU" McNEILL #12 – 22 FORWARD
b. Port Arthur, Ontario, September 25, 1938

1957–58R	2	0	0	0	0
1958–59	3	1	1	2	2
1959–60L	5	0	0	0	0
Totals	10	1	1	2	2

- first Red Wings games February 15/16, 1958
- played March 14/21/22, 1959
- played October 10/11/15/18/22, 1959

BASIL McRAE #18 – 23 LEFT WING 6′2″ 205
b. Beaverton, Ontario, January 5, 1961

1985–86	4	0	0	0	5
1986–87	36	2	2	4	193
Totals	40	2	2	4	198

- signed as a free agent June 18, 1985
- played October 19/23/26, January 15, 1985–86
- traded January 17, 1987 to Quebec with John Ogrodnick and Doug Shedden for Brent Ashton, Gilbert Delorme, and Mark Kumpel

CHRIS McRAE #5 LEFT WING 6′ 200
b. Beaverton, Ontario, August 26, 1965

1989–90L	7	1	0	1	45

- acquired September 7, 1989 with a 5th-round draft choice in 1990 (Tony Burns) from Rangers for Kris King
- played part of '89–'91 with Adirondack, '91–'92 with Fort Wayne, then out of hockey
- last Red Wings game February 28, March 2/3/5/8/31, April 1, 1990

HARRY MEEKING #4 LEFT WING
b. Kitchener, Ontario, November 4, 1894
d. Unknown

1926–27	6	0	0	0	4

- came from Victoria when team moved to Detroit
- traded January 1927 to Boston

TOM MELLOR #24 – 25 DEFENCE 6′1″ 185
b. Cranston, Rhode Island, January 27, 1950

1973–74R	25	2	4	6	25
1974–75L	1	0	0	0	0
Totals	26	2	4	6	25

- selected 68th overall at 1970 Entry Draft
- first Red Wings game October 10, 1973
- last Red Wings game December 3, 1974
- played part of '73–'75 with Virginia, 6 games with London Lions (England) in '73–'74, '75–'77 with Toledo

MICHAEL "GERRY" MELNYK #14 – 21
CENTRE 5′10″ 180 *b.* Edmonton, Alberta, September 16, 1934

1959–60R	63	10	10	20	12
1960–61	70	9	16	25	2
Totals	133	19	26	45	14

- played most of '52–'59 with Edmonton (WHL)
- recalled for 1956 playoffs
- first regular season Red Wings game October 10, 1959
- traded June 1961 with Brian Smith to Chicago for Ed Litzenberger

BARRY MELROSE #2 – 26 DEFENCE 6′ 205
b. Kelvington, Saskatchewan, July 15, 1956

1983–84	21	0	1	1	74
1985–86L	14	0	0	0	70
Totals	35	0	1	1	144

- signed as a free agent July 5, 1983
- last Red Wings games January 5/7/10/11/13/15/18/19/22/23/25/28/31, February 1, 1986
- also played with Adirondack '83–'87 before retiring

HOWIE MENARD #12 CENTRE 5′8″ 160
b. Timmins, Ontario, April 28, 1942

1963–64R	3	0	0	0	0

- Hamilton Red Wings graduate
- first and only Red Wings games February 15/16/19, 1964
- played '62–'63 with Pittsburgh, most of '63–'64 with Cincinnati, '64–'65 with Memphis
- contract bought by Springfield summer '65 for $10,000

GLENN MERKOSKY #22 – 44 CENTRE 5′10″
175 *b.* Edmonton, Alberta, April 8, 1959

1985–86	17	0	2	2	0
1989–90L	3	0	0	0	0
Totals	20	0	2	2	0

- signed as a free agent July 1, 1985
- played most of '85–'91 with Adirondack
- last Red Wings games March 17/20/27, 1990
- out of hockey after '90–'91

CORRADO MICALEF #1 – 30 – 31 GOALIE
5′8″ 172 *b.* Montreal, Quebec, April 20, 1961

1981–82R	18	4–10–1	809	63	0	4.67
1982–83	34	11–13–5	1755	106	2	3.62
1983–84	14	5–8–1	808	52	0	3.86
1984–85	36	5–19–7	1856	136	0	4.40
1985–86L	11	1–9–1	565	52	0	5.52
Totals	113	26–59–15	5793	409	2	4.24

- selected 44th overall at 1981 Entry Draft
- first Red Wings game October 17, 1981
- played most of '82–'87 with Adirondack, then out of hockey
- last Red Wings games October 10/12/16/17/19/23/26, February 16, March 26, April 2/6, 1985–86

NICK MICKOSKI #11 LEFT WING 6′1″ 193
b. Winnipeg, Manitoba, December 7, 1927

1957–58	37	8	12	20	30
1958–59	66	11	15	26	20
Totals	103	19	27	46	50

- acquired December 17, 1957 with Bob Bailey, Jack McIntyre, and Hec Lalande from Chicago for Earl Reibel, Billy Dea, Lorne Ferguson, and Bill Dineen
- traded August 25, 1959 to Boston for Jim Morrison

HUGH MILLAR #5 – 19 DEFENCE 5′8″ 200
b. Edmonton, Alberta, April 3, 1921

1946–47R/L	4	0	0	0	0

- first and only Red Wings games October 20/26/27 and March 23, 1946–47

GREG MILLEN #34 GOALIE 5′9″ 175
b. Toronto, Ontario, June 25, 1957

1991–92L	10	3–2–3	487	22	0	2.71

- acquired December 26, 1991 from Rangers for an 8th-round draft choice in 1992 (Colin Schmidt)
- last Red Wings games January 3/29/31, February 3/7/15, March 3/14/15/17, 1992
- played part of '91–'92 with Maine and San Diego before retiring

KEVIN MILLER #23 CENTRE 5'10" 191
b. Lansing, September 9, 1965

1990–91	11	5	2	7	4
1991–92	80	20	26	46	53
Totals	91	25	28	53	57

- acquired March 5, 1991 with Jim Cummins and Dennis Vial from Rangers for Joey Kocur and Per Djoos
- traded June 20, 1992 to Washington for Dino Ciccarelli

PERRY MILLER #3 DEFENCE 6'1" 194
b. Winnipeg, Manitoba, June 24, 1952

1977–78	62	4	17	21	120
1978–79	75	5	23	28	156
1979–80	16	0	3	3	41
1980–81	64	1	8	9	70
Totals	217	10	51	61	387

- signed July 8, 1977 as a free agent
- played part of '79–'81 with Adirondack, then out of hockey

TOM MILLER #12 CENTRE 6' 187
b. Kitchener, Ontario, March 31, 1947

1970–71R	29	1	7	8	9

- acquired February 2, 1971 from Rangers with Mike Robitaille and Arnie Brown for Bruce MacGregor and Larry Brown
- first Red Wings game February 3, 1971
- lost June 8, 1971 to Buffalo in Intra-League Draft

EDDIE MIO #41 GOALIE 5'10" 180
b. Windsor, Ontario, January 31, 1954

1983–84	24	7–11–3	1295	95	1	4.40
1984–85	7	1–3–2	376	27	0	4.31
1985–86L	18	2–7–0	788	83	0	6.32
Totals	49	10–21–5	2459	205	1	5.00

- acquired June 13, 1983 with Ron Duguay and Ed Johnstone from Rangers for Mike Blaisdell, Willie Huber, and Mark Osborne
- played parts of '83–'86 with Adirondack
- last Red Wings game April 5, 1986
- given unconditional release June 2, 1986

JOHN MISZUK #5 – 18 DEFENCE 6' 200
b. Naliboki, Poland, September 29, 1940

1963–64R	42	0	2	2	30

- Hamilton Red Wings graduate
- first Red Wings game December 11, 1963
- played parts of '61–'63 with Edmonton, '62–'64 with Pittsburgh
- traded June 9, 1964 with Art Stratton and Ian Cushenan to Chicago for Ron Murphy and Aut Erickson

BILL MITCHELL #3 DEFENCE 5'10" 185
b. Toronto, Ontario, September 6, 1912

1963–64R/L	1	0	0	0	0

- first and only Red Wings game February 23, 1964

ROBERT "RON" MOFFATT ("Atlas") #15 – 16 – 17 – 18 FORWARD *b.* West Hope, North Dakota, 1893 *d.* Unknown

1932–33R	24	1	1	2	6
1933–34	5	0	0	0	2
1934–35L	7	0	0	0	0
Totals	36	1	1	2	8

- promoted from the Olympics when Emms broke his hand during '32–'33
- first Red Wings game January 12, 1933
- sold outright February 23, 1936 to Windsor Bulldogs
- last Red Wings games January 13/15/17/20/26/27/31, 1935

JOHN MOKOSAK #5 – 37 DEFENCE 5'11" 200
b. Edmonton, Alberta, September 7, 1963

1988–89R	8	0	1	1	14
1989–90L	33	0	1	1	82
Totals	41	0	2	2	96

- signed as a free agent August 29, 1988
- first Red Wings games February 2/5/9/11/21/25/26, April 2, 1989
- last Red Wings game February 6, 1990
- played much of '88–'90 with Adirondack
- lost July 16, 1990 as a free agent to Boston

GARRY MONAHAN #11 LEFT WING 6′ 185
b. Barrie, Ontario, October 20, 1946

1969–70	51	3	4	7	24

- acquired June 6, 1969 with Doug Piper from Canadiens for Pete Mahovlich and Bart Crashley
- traded February 20, 1970 with Brian Gibbons to Los Angeles for Gary Croteau, Dale Rolfe, and Larry Johnston

HENRY MONTEITH ("Hank") #11 – 15 – 19 LEFT WING 5′10″ 180 *b.* Stratford, Ontario, October 2, 1945

1968–69R	34	1	9	10	6
1969–70	9	0	0	0	4
1970–71L	34	4	3	7	0
Totals	77	5	12	17	10

- first Red Wings game December 4, 1968
- last Red Wings game February 27, 1971
- played most of '68–'71 with Fort Worth

ALFRED "ALFIE" MOORE #1 GOALIE
b. Toronto, Ontario

1939–40L	1	0–1–0	60	3	0	3.00

- first and only Red Wings game January 9, 1940

DON MORRISON #17 CENTRE 5′10″ 165
b. Saskatoon, Saskatchewan, July 14, 1923

1947–48R	40	10	15	25	6
1948–49	13	0	1	1	0
Totals	53	10	16	26	6

- first Red Wings game December 13, 1947
- played '45–'47 with Omaha, parts of '47–'50 with Indianapolis
- traded July 13, 1950 with Al Dewsbury, Harry Lumley, Jack Stewart, and Pete Babando to Chicago for Jim Henry, Bob Goldham, Gaye Stewart, and Metro Prystai

JIM MORRISON #2 – 18 DEFENCE 5′10″ 183
b. Montreal, Quebec, October 11, 1931

1959–60	70	3	23	26	62

- acquired August 25, 1959 from Boston for Nick Mickoski
- traded June 7, 1960 to Chicago for Howie Glover

ROD MORRISON #21 RIGHT WING 5′9″ 160
b. Saskatoon, Saskatchewan, October 7, 1925

1947–48R/L	34	8	7	15	4

- first Red Wings game December 10, 1947
- played '43–'44 with Indianapolis
- missed 1944–45 — Canadian Armed Forces
- played '45–'46 with Omaha, most of '46–'51 with Indianapolis

DEAN MORTON #5 DEFENCE 6′1″ 196
b. Peterborough, Ontario, February 27, 1968

1989–90R/L	1	1	0	1	2

- selected 148th overall at 1986 Entry Draft
- first and only Red Wings game October 5, 1989
- played most of '89–'91 with Adirondack and San Diego

GUS MORTSON #18 DEFENCE 5′11″ 190
b. New Liskeard, Ontario, January 24, 1925

1958–59L	36	0	1	1	22

- acquired August 1958 from Chicago for future considerations (three players)
- last Red Wings game January 15, 1959
- claimed by Buffalo on waivers January 1959

ALEX MOTTER #3 – 7 – 14 CENTRE 6′ 175
b. Melville, Saskatchewan, June 20, 1913

1937–38	33	5	17	22	6
1938–39	42	5	11	16	17
1939–40	37	7	12	19	28
1940–41	47	13	12	25	18
1941–42	30	2	4	6	20
1942–43L	50	6	4	10	42
Totals	239	38	60	98	131

- acquired December 22, 1937 from Boston for Clarence Drouillard and cash
- last Red Wings game March 18, 1943
- retired after '42–'43 season

JOHN MOWERS #1 – 20 GOALIE 5′11″ 185
b. Niagara Falls, Ontario, October 29, 1916

1940–41R	48	21–16–11	3040	102	4	2.13
1941–42	47	19–25–3	2880	144	5	3.06
1942–43	50	25–14–11	3010	124	6	2.47
1946–47L	7	0–6–1	420	29	0	4.14
Totals	152	65–61–26	9350	399	15	2.56

- signed January 1940, and finished season with Omaha
- first Red Wings game November 3, 1940
- missed 1943–46 — Royal Canadian Air Force
- last Red Wings games October 23/26 and December 11/15/18/19/22, 1946
- back problems forced him to retire early in '46–'47

WAYNE MULOIN #19 DEFENCE 5′8″ 176
b. Toronto, Ontario, December 24, 1941

1963–64R	3	0	1	1	2

- Edmonton Oil Kings graduate (played '60–'63)
- first and only Red Wings games January 29 & February 1 & 2, 1964
- played most of '63–'64 with Cincinnati, '64–'65 with St. Paul
- drafted by Rangers in summer 1965

DON MURDOCH ("Murder") #14
RIGHT WING 5′11″ 180 *b.* Cranbrook, British Columbia, October 25, 1956

1981–82L	49	9	13	22	23

- acquired August 21, 1981 from Minnesota with Greg Smith and a 1st-round draft choice in 1982 (Murray Craven) for a 1st-round draft choice in 1982 (Brian Bellows)
- played part of '81–'82 with Adirondack; in minors until '86
- last Red Wings game January 30, 1982

BRIAN MURPHY #17 CENTRE 6′3″ 195
b. Toronto, Ontario, August 20, 1947

1974–75R/L	2	0	0	0	0

- first and only Red Wings games November 28 & December 18, 1974
- played most of '74–'75 with Virginia, '75–'76 with Rochester

JOE MURPHY #10 RIGHT WING 6′1″ 190
b. London, Ontario, October 16, 1967

1986–87R	5	0	1	1	2
1987–88	50	10	9	19	37
1988–89	26	1	7	8	28
1989–90	9	3	1	4	4
Totals	90	14	18	32	71

- selected 1st overall at 1986 Entry Draft
- first Red Wings games October 11/15/17/18/24, 1986
- traded November 2, 1989 with Adam Graves, Petr Klima, and Jeff Sharples to Edmonton for Jimmy Carson and Kevin McClelland

RON MURPHY #12 LEFT WING 5′11″ 185
b. Hamilton, Ontario, April 10, 1933

1964–65	58	20	19	39	32
1965–66	32	10	7	17	10
Totals	90	30	26	56	42

- acquired June 9, 1964 with Aut Erickson from Chicago for John Miszuk, Art Stratton, and Ian Cushenan
- traded February 18, 1966 with Gary Doak, Bill Lesuk, and Steve Atkinson for Leo Boivin and Dean Prentice

KEN MURRAY #24 DEFENCE 6′ 180
b. Toronto, Ontario, January 22, 1948

1972–73	31	1	1	2	36

- acquired January 17, 1973 with Brian Lavender from the Islanders for Bob Cook and Ralph Stewart
- lost June 12, 1974 to Kansas City in Expansion Draft

TERRENCE "TERRY" MURRAY #4 DEFENCE
6′2″ 190 *b.* Shawville, Quebec, July 20, 1950

1976–77	59	0	20	20	24

- acquired February 17, 1977 with Steve Coates, Bob Ritchie, and Dave Kelly from Flyers for Rick Lapointe and Mike Korney
- sold to Flyers November 1, 1977

JIM NAHRGANG #3 – 24 DEFENCE 6′ 185
b. Millbank, Ontario, April 17, 1951

1974–75R	1	0	0	0	0
1975–76	3	0	1	1	0

1976–77L	53	5	11	16	34
Totals	57	5	12	17	34

- selected 86th overall at 1971 Entry Draft
- first Red Wings game March 29, 1975
- played January 22/24/25, 1976
- played most of '74–'75 with Virginia, '75–'76 with New Haven, '76–'78 with Kansas City, '77–'78 with Philadelphia
- last Red Wings game April 3, 1977

VACLAV NEDOMANSKY ("Big Ned") #20 RIGHT WING 6'2" 205 *b.* Hodonin, Czechoslovakia, March 14, 1944

1977–78	63	11	17	28	2
1978–79	60	38	35	73	19
1979–80	79	35	39	74	13
1980–81	74	12	20	32	30
1981–82	68	12	28	40	22
Totals	344	108	139	247	86

- acquired November 15, 1977 from Birmingham (WHA) with Tim Sheehy for Steve Durbano, Dave Hanson, and future considerations
- contract bought out August 25, 1982

RICK NEWELL #23 – 25 DEFENCE 5'11" 180 *b.* Winnipeg, Manitoba, February 18, 1948

1972–73R	3	0	0	0	0
1973–74	4	0	0	0	0
Totals	7	0	0	0	0

- acquired May 24, 1972 with Gary Doak from Rangers for Joe Zanussi and a 1st-round draft choice in 1972 (Albert Blanchard)
- first Red Wings games October 26/28, January 14, 1972–73
- played most of '72–'73 with Tidewater, '73–'74 with Virginia and London Lions (England)
- jumped to Phoenix (WHA) for '74–'75

JOHN NEWMAN #15 DEFENCE *b.* Unknown

1930–31R/L	8	1	1	2	0

- first and only Falcons games February 14/17/26, March 8/12/15/19/22, 1931

EDDIE NICHOLSON #23 DEFENCE 5'7" 171 *b.* Portsmouth, Ontario, September 9, 1923

1947–48R/L	1	0	0	0	0

- first and only Red Wings game March 21, 1948
- traded September 1949 with Fern Gauthier, Cliff Simpson, and future considerations to St. Louis Flyers for Steve Black and Bill Brennan

JIM NIEKAMP #3 – 20 DEFENCE 6' 170 *b.* Detroit, March 11, 1946

1970–71R	24	0	2	2	27
1971–72	5	0	0	0	0
Totals	29	0	2	2	27

- first Red Wings game November 26, 1970
- played '67–'69 with Fort Worth, '69–'70 with Cleveland, '70–'71 with Baltimore, '71–'72 with Tidewater
- played October 9/10/16/17/20, 1971
- traded March 6, 1972 to Vancouver Canucks for Ralph Stewart

JIM NILL #8 RIGHT WING 6' 185 *b.* Hanna, Alberta, April 11, 1958

1987–88	36	3	11	14	55
1988–89	71	8	7	15	83
1989–90L	15	0	2	2	18
Totals	122	11	20	31	156

- acquired January 11, 1988 from Winnipeg for Mark Kumpel
- last Red Wings games October 7/8/12/14/15/19, December 16/20/23/29, January 2/4/6/9/12, 1989–90
- played '89–'91 with Adirondack, then out of hockey

REGINALD "REG" NOBLE #3 LEFT WING 5'8" 180 *b.* Collingwood, Ontario, June 23, 1895 *d.* Alliston, Ontario, January 19, 1962

1927–28	44	6	8	14	63
1928–29	44	6	4	10	52
1929–30	43	6	4	10	72
1930–31	44	2	5	7	42
1931–32	48	3	3	6	72
1932–33	5	0	0	0	6
Totals	228	23	24	47	307

- played '26–'27 with Maroons
- traded December 1932 to Maroons for Johnny Gallagher

THEODORE "TED" NOLAN #8 – 29
CENTRE 6′ 185 *b.* Sault Ste. Marie, Ontario, April 7, 1958

1981–82R	41	4	13	17	45
1983–84	19	1	2	3	26
Totals	60	5	15	20	71

- selected 78th overall at 1978 Entry Draft
- first Red Wings game January 3, 1982
- played most of '79–'84 with Adirondack, '84–'85 with Rochester
- lost as a free agent March 7, 1985 to Sabres

LEE NORWOOD #23 DEFENCE 6′1″ 198
b. Oakland, California, February 2, 1960

1986–87	57	6	21	27	163
1987–88	51	9	22	31	131
1988–89	66	10	32	42	100
1989–90	64	8	14	22	95
1990–91	21	3	7	10	50
Totals	259	36	96	132	539

- acquired August 7, 1986 from St. Louis for Larry Trader
- traded November 27, 1990 with a 4th-round draft choice in 1992 (Scott McCabe) to New Jersey for Paul Ysebaert

HENRY "HANK" NOWAK #11 LEFT WING 6′1″ 195 *b.* Oshawa, Ontario, November 24, 1950

1974–75	56	8	14	22	69

- acquired May 27, 1974 with a 3rd-round draft choice in 1974 (Dan Mandryk) from Penguins for Nelson Debenedet
- traded February 18, 1975 with Earl Anderson to Boston for Walt McKechnie and a 3rd-round draft choice in 1975 (Clark Hamilton)

ADAM OATES #21 – 34 CENTRE 5′11″ 189
b. Weston, Ontario, August 27, 1962

1985–86R	38	9	11	20	10
1986–87	76	15	32	47	21
1987–88	63	14	40	54	20
1988–89	69	16	62	78	14
Totals	246	54	145	199	65

- signed June 28, 1985 as a free agent
- first Red Wings game October 10, 1985
- traded June 15, 1989 with Paul MacLean to St. Louis for Bernie Federko and Tony McKegney

RUSS OATMAN #7 FORWARD 5′10″ 195
b. Tilsonburg, Ontario, February 19, 1905
d. Keswick, Ontario, October 25, 1964

1926–27R	14	3	0	3	12

- came from Victoria when team moved to Detroit
- first Cougars game November 27, 1926
- traded January 1927 to Maroons

MIKE O'CONNELL #2 DEFENCE 5′9″ 180
b. Chicago, Illinois, November 25, 1955

1985–86	13	1	7	8	16
1986–87	77	5	26	31	70
1987–88	48	6	13	19	38
1988–89	66	1	15	16	41
1989–90L	66	4	14	18	22
Totals	270	17	75	92	187

- acquired March 10, 1986 from Boston for Reed Larson
- retired after '89–'90 season
- last Red Wings game March 27, 1990

GERRY ODROWSKI ("Snowy"/"The Hook") #18 – 22 DEFENCE 5′11″ 190 *b.* Trout Creek, Ontario, October 4, 1938

1960–61R	68	1	4	5	45
1961–62	69	1	6	7	24
1962–63	1	0	0	0	0
Totals	138	2	10	12	69

- played '59–'60 with Sudbury
- first Red Wings game October 5, 1960
- played February 28, 1963
- traded October 10, 1963 to Boston for Warren Godfrey

JOHN OGRODNICK #25 – 18 LEFT WING
6′ 204 *b.* Ottawa, Ontario, June 20, 1959

1979–80R	41	8	24	32	8
1980–81	80	35	35	70	14
1981–82	80	28	26	54	28
1982–83	80	41	44	85	30

1983–84	64	42	36	78	14
1984–85	79	55	50	105	30
1985–86	76	38	32	70	18
1986–87	39	12	28	40	6
1992–93	19	6	6	12	2
Totals	558	265	281	546	150

- selected 66th overall at 1979 Entry Draft
- first Red Wings game January 12, 1980
- traded January 17, 1987 to Quebec with Basil McRae and Doug Shedden for Brent Ashton, Gilbert Delorme, and Mark Kumpel
- signed as a free agent September 29, 1992
- played part of '92–'93 with Adirondack, then retired

MURRAY OLIVER #7 – 8 – 17 CENTRE
5′9″ 170 *b.* Hamilton, Ontario, November 14, 1937

1957–58R	1	0	1	1	0
1959–60	54	20	19	39	6
1960–61	49	11	12	23	8
Totals	104	31	32	63	14

- first Red Wings game February 1, 1958
- played part of '58–'60 with Edmonton
- traded January 1961 with Gary Aldcorn and Tom McCarthy to Boston for Vic Stasiuk and Leo Labine

DENNIS OLSON #15 CENTRE 6′ 182
b. Kenora, Ontario, November 9, 1934

1957–58R/L	3	0	0	0	0

- first and only Red Wings games November 7/9/10, 1957
- played most of '57–'58 with Seattle, Edmonton, and Victoria

JIMMY ORLANDO #4 – 5 – 16 – 17 DEFENCE
5′11″ 185 *b.* Montreal, Quebec, February 27, 1916 *d.* Montreal, Quebec, October 24, 1992

1936–37R	10	0	1	1	8
1937–38	6	0	0	0	4
1939–40	48	1	3	4	54
1940–41	48	1	10	11	99
1941–42	48	1	7	8	111
1942–43L	40	4	3	7	99
Totals	200	7	24	31	375

- recalled from Pittsburgh on January 25, 1937 after Roulston broke his ankle
- first Red Wings games January 31, February 2/4/7/9/11/14/18/21/25, 1937
- played most of '36–'37 with Pittsburgh, '37–'38 with Springfield
- last Red Wings game March 18, 1943
- retired after '42–'43

MARK OSBORNE ("Ozzie") #23 LEFT WING
6′2″ 205 *b.* Toronto, Ontario, August 13, 1961

1981–82R	80	26	41	67	61
1982–83	80	19	24	43	83
Totals	160	45	65	110	144

- selected 46th overall in 1980 Entry Draft
- first Red Wings game October 6, 1981
- traded June 13, 1983 with Mike Blaisdell and Willie Huber to Rangers for Ron Duguay, Ed Mio, and Ed Johnstone

CHRIS OSGOOD #30 GOALIE 5′10″ 175
b. Peace River, Alberta, November 26, 1972

1993–94R	41	23–8–5	2206	105	2	2.86
1994–95	19	14–5–0	1087	41	1	2.26
1995–96	50	39–6–5	2933	106	5	2.17
Totals	110	76–19–10	6226	252	8	2.43

- selected 54th overall in 1991 Entry Draft
- first Red Wings game October 15, 1993
- currently with Red Wings

MARTY PAVELICH

CHRIS OSGOOD

1995–96	50	1	2	3	4

- scored a goal March 6, 1996 vs. Hartford

PETER PALANGIO #7 LEFT WING 5′11″ 175 *b.* North Bay, Ontario, October 10, 1908

1927–28	14	3	0	3	8

- released by Canadiens after '26–'27
- played '28–'29 with Canadiens

BRAD PARK #22 DEFENCE 6′ 200 *b.* Toronto, Ontario, July 6, 1948

1983–84	80	5	53	58	85
1984–85L	67	13	30	43	53
Totals	147	18	83	101	138

- signed August 9, 1983 as a free agent
- last Red Wings game April 7, 1985
- retired after '84–'85 season

JOE PATERSON #7 – 8 – 29 LEFT WING 6′2″ 207 *b.* Toronto, Ontario, June 25, 1960

1980–81R	38	2	5	7	53
1981–82	3	0	0	0	0
1982–83	33	2	1	3	14
1983–84	41	2	5	7	148
Totals	115	6	11	17	215

- selected 87th overall at 1979 Entry Draft
- first Red Wing game January 8, 1981
- played much of '80–'84 with Adirondack
- traded October 19, 1984 with Murray Craven to Flyers for Darryl Sittler

GEORGE PATTERSON ("Paddy") #15 RIGHT WING 6′1″ 176 *b.* Kingston, Ontario, May 22, 1906 *d.* Kingston, Ontario, January 22, 1977

1934–35	7	0	1	1	0

- played '33–'34 with Boston
- traded during '34–'35 to St. Louis Eagles

ARTHUR "BUTCH" PAUL #14 – 22 CENTRE 5′11″ 160 *b.* Rocky Mountain House, Alberta, September 11, 1943 *d.* Memphis, March 1966

1964–65R/L	3	0	0	0	0

- Edmonton Oil Kings graduate
- first and only Red Wings games December 3/5/6, 1964
- played part of '63–'64 with Cincinnati, '64–'65 with Pittsburgh
- killed April 1966 when struck by a car

MARTY PAVELICH ("Sabu"/"Blackie") #11 – 15 – 19 LEFT WING 5′10″ 170 *b.* Sault Ste. Marie, Ontario, November 6, 1927

1947–48R	41	4	8	12	10
1948–49	60	10	16	26	40
1949–50	65	8	15	23	58
1950–51	67	9	20	29	41
1951–52	68	17	19	36	54
1952–53	64	13	20	33	49
1953–54	65	9	20	29	57
1954–55	70	15	15	30	59
1955–56	70	5	13	18	38
1956–57L	64	3	13	16	48
Totals	634	93	159	252	454

- Galt Red Wings graduate
- first Red Wings game December 10, 1947
- played '47–'48 and '49–'50 with Indianapolis
- last Red Wings game March 24, 1957
- retired after '56–'57

JIM PAVESE #25 DEFENCE 6′2″ 205 *b.* New York, New York, May 8, 1962

1987–88	7	0	3	3	21
1988–89	39	3	6	9	130
Totals	46	3	9	12	151

- acquired March 8, 1988 from Rangers for future considerations
- traded March 7, 1989 to Hartford for Torrie Robertson

MARK PEDERSON #18 LEFT WING 6′2″ 196
b. Prelate, Saskatchewan, January 14, 1968

1993–94	2	0	0	0	2

- signed August 23, 1993 as a free agent
- played February 5 & 8, 1994
- lost August 13, 1994 to Dallas as a free agent

BERT PEER #17 RIGHT WING
b. Port Credit, Ontario, November 12, 1910

1939–40R/L	1	0	0	0	0

- first and only Red Wings game March 15, 1940

BOB "MICHIE" PERREAULT ("The Glove") #1 GOALIE 5′8″ 170 *b.* Trois-Rivières, Quebec, January 28, 1931

1958–59	3	2–1–0	180	9	0	3.00

- called up from Hershey for three games (January 21/24/25, 1959) when Sawchuk injured
- lost June 6, 1962 to Boston in Intra-League Draft

JIM PETERS SR. #10 – 20 – 19 RIGHT WING 5′11″ 165 *b.* Verdun, Quebec, October 2, 1922

1949–50	70	14	16	30	20
1950–51	68	17	21	38	14
1953–54L	26	0	4	4	10
Totals	164	31	41	72	44

- acquired August 16, 1949 with Pete Babando, Clare Martin, and Lloyd Durham from Boston for Pete Horeck and Bill Quackenbush
- traded August 20, 1951 with George Gee, Jim McFadden, Max McNab, Clare Martin, and Rags Raglan to Chicago for Hugh Coflin and $75,000
- last Red Wings game March 21, 1954

JIM PETERS, JR. #11 – 16 – 21 – 25 CENTRE 6′2″ 185 *b.* Montreal, Quebec, June 20, 1944

1964–65R	1	0	0	0	0
1965–66	6	1	1	2	2
1966–67	2	0	0	0	0
1967–68	45	5	6	11	8
Totals	54	6	7	13	10

- Hamilton Red Wings graduate
- first Red Wings game November 11, 1964
- played February 25 & 26, 1967
- played December 18/19/23/26/28, March 31, 1965–66
- played part of '63–'64 with Cincinnati, '64–'67 with Memphis, '66–'67 with Pittsburgh, and '67–'68 with Fort Worth
- traded October 10, 1968 to Los Angeles for Terry Sawchuk

BRENT PETERSON #12 – 27 CENTRE 6′ 190
b. Calgary, Alberta, February 15, 1958

1979–80R	18	1	2	3	2
1980–81	53	6	18	24	24
1981–82	15	1	0	1	6
Totals	86	8	20	28	32

- selected 12th overall at 1978 Entry Draft
- first Red Wings game January 4, 1980
- traded December 2, 1981 with Mike Foligno and Dale McCourt to Sabres for Danny Gare, Jim Schoenfeld, and Derek Smith

GORD PETTINGER ("Gosh"/"Pet") #11 – 15 CENTRE 6′ 175 *b.* Regina, Saskatchewan, November 17, 1911

1933–34	48	3	14	17	14
1934–35	13	2	3	5	2
1935–36	33	8	7	15	6
1936–37	48	7	15	22	13
1937–38	11	1	3	4	4
Totals	153	21	42	63	39

- acquired October 11, 1933 from Rangers for cash
- played part of '33–'34 with Olympics
- traded December 19, 1937 to Boston for Red Beattie

ROBERT PICARD #7 DEFENCE 6′2″ 207
b. Montreal, Quebec, May 25, 1957

1989–90L	20	0	3	3	20

- acquired December 4, 1989 with Greg C. Adams from Quebec for Tony McKegney
- last Red Wings game April 1, 1990
- retired after '89–'90 season

ALEX PIRUS #14 RIGHT WING 6′1″ 205
b. Toronto, Ontario, January 12, 1955

1979–80L	4	0	2	2	0

- bought January 3, 1980 from Minnesota
- only Red Wings games February 6/9/16/23, 1980
- sold June 6, 1980 to Minnesota

ROB PLUMB #17 – 18 LEFT WING 5′8″ 166
b. Kingston, Ontario, August 29, 1957

1977–78R/L	7	2	1	3	0

- selected 163rd overall at 1977 Entry Draft
- first and only Red Wings games October 13/20/22/29, November 5/6/9, 1977
- played most of '77–'80 with Kansas City, Adirondack, and Kalamazoo

NELSON "NELLIE" PODOLSKY #15
LEFT WING 5′10″ 170 *b.* Winnipeg, Manitoba, December 19, 1925

1948–49R/L	1	0	0	0	0

- first and only Red Wings game December 5, 1948

DON POILE #15 – 19 – 20 CENTRE
b. Fort William, Ontario, June 1, 1932

1954–55R	4	0	0	0	0
1957–58L	62	7	9	16	12
Totals	66	7	9	16	12

- played most of '52–'58 with Edmonton
- first Red Wings games October 9/17/21/23, 1954
- last Red Wings game March 22, 1958
- traded April 1958 with Hec Lalande to Hershey for Dunc Fisher

NORMAN "BUD" POILE #14 CENTRE 6′ 185
b. Fort William, Ontario, February 10, 1924

1948–49	60	21	21	42	8

- acquired October 1948 with George Gee from Chicago for Jim Conacher, Bep Guidolin, and Doug McCaig
- sold August 16, 1949 to Rangers

DENNIS POLONICH ("Polo") #8 – 22
CENTRE/RIGHT WING 5′6″ 165 *b.* Foam Lake, Saskatchewan, December 4, 1953

1974–75R	4	0	0	0	0
1975–76	57	11	12	23	302
1976–77	79	18	28	46	274
1977–78	79	16	19	35	254
1978–79	62	10	12	22	208
1979–80	66	2	8	10	127
1980–81	32	2	2	4	77
1982–83L	11	0	1	1	0
Totals	390	59	82	141	1242

- selected 118th overall at 1973 Entry Draft
- first Red Wings games December 31, January 16/18/19, 1974–75
- played '73–'74 with London Lions (England), part of '74–'75 with Virginia, part of '75–'76 with Kalamazoo, '80–'85 with Adirondack, '85–'87 with Muskegan
- last Red Wings games October 6/8/9/14/16/17/20/23, November 2/6/7, 1982

POUL "PAUL" POPIEL #3 DEFENCE 5′8″ 170
b. Sollested, Denmark, February 28, 1943

1968–69	62	2	13	15	82
1969–70	32	0	4	4	31
Totals	94	2	17	19	113

- acquired November 12, 1968 from Los Angeles for Ron Anderson
- lost June 10, 1970 to Vancouver Canucks in Expansion Draft

MARC POTVIN #20 – 46 RIGHT WING 6′1″ 185 *b.* Ottawa, Ontario, January 29, 1967

1990–91R	9	0	0	0	55
1991–92	5	0	1	0	52
Totals	14	0	1	1	107

- selected 169th overall at 1986 Entry Draft
- first Red Wings games January 16, March 13/14/16/22/23/27/30/31, 1991
- played October 25/26/28/30, November 2, 1991
- played most of '90–'92 with Adirondack
- traded January 29, 1993 with Jimmy Carson and Gary Shuchuk to Los Angeles for Paul Coffey, Sylvain Couturier, and Jim Hiller

DEAN PRENTICE ("Deano") #20
LEFT WING 5′11″ 180 *b.* Schumacher, Ontario, October 5, 1932

1965–66	19	6	9	15	8
1966–67	68	23	22	45	18
1967–68	69	17	38	55	42
1968–69	74	14	20	34	18
Totals	230	60	89	149	86

- acquired February 18, 1966 with Leo Boivin from Boston for Ron Murphy, Gary Doak, Bill Lesuk, and Steve Atkinson
- lost June 11, 1969 to Penguins in Intra-League Draft

GARRY "NOEL" PRICE #2 DEFENCE 6′ 185
b. Brockville, Ontario, December 9, 1935

1961–62	20	0	1	1	6

- acquired February 16, 1962 from Rangers for Pete Goegan
- traded October 8, 1962 to Rangers for Pete Goegan

KEITH PRIMEAU #55 CENTRE 6′4″ 220
b. Toronto, Ontario, November 24, 1971

1990–91R	58	3	12	15	106
1991–92	35	6	10	16	83
1992–93	73	15	17	32	152
1993–94	78	31	42	73	173
1994–95	45	15	27	42	99
1995–96	74	27	25	52	168
Totals	363	97	133	230	781

- selected 3rd overall in 1990 Entry Draft
- first Red Wings game October 6, 1990
- traded October 9, 1996 with Paul Coffey and a 1st-round draft choice in 1997 to Hartford for Brendan Shanahan and Brian Glynn

BOB PROBERT #24 LEFT WING 6′3″ 215
b. Windsor, Ontario, June 5, 1965

1985–86R	44	8	13	21	186
1986–87	63	13	11	24	221
1987–88	74	29	33	62	398
1988–89	25	4	2	6	106
1989–90	4	3	0	3	21
1990–91	55	16	23	39	315
1991–92	63	20	24	44	276
1992–93	80	14	29	43	292
1993–94	66	7	10	17	275
Totals	474	114	145	259	2090

- selected 46th overall in 1983 Entry Draft
- first Red Wings game November 6, 1985
- lost July 23, 1994 as a free agent to Chicago

ANDRE PRONOVOST #15 – 21
LEFT WING 5′9″ 165 *b.* Shawinigan Falls, Quebec, July 9, 1936

1962–63	47	13	5	18	20
1963–64	70	7	16	23	23
1964–65	3	0	1	1	0
Totals	120	20	22	42	43

- acquired December 1962 from Boston for Forbes Kennedy
- played November 18/21/22, 1964
- lost June 6, 1967 to Minnesota in Expansion Draft

MARCEL PRONOVOST #3 – 18 – 21 – 22 – 23
DEFENCE 6′ 190 *b.* Lac la Tortue, Quebec, June 15, 1930

1950–51R	37	1	6	7	20
1951–52	69	7	11	18	50
1952–53	68	8	19	27	72
1953–54	57	6	12	18	50
1954–55	70	9	25	34	90
1955–56	68	4	13	17	46
1956–57	70	7	9	16	38
1957–58	62	2	18	20	52
1958–59	69	11	21	32	44
1959–60	69	7	17	24	38
1960–61	70	6	11	17	44
1961–62	70	4	14	18	30
1962–63	69	4	9	13	48
1963–64	67	3	17	20	20
1964–65	68	1	15	16	45
Totals	983	80	217	297	687

- played '49–'50 with Omaha, but joined Detroit for '50 playoffs
- first regular season game October 11, 1950
- played part of '50–'51 with Indianapolis
- traded May 20, 1965 with Ed Joyal, Larry Jeffrey, Lowell MacDonald and Aut Erickson to Toronto for Andy Bathgate, Billy Harris, and Gary Jarrett

METRO PRYSTAI #10 – 12 – 14 – 15 – 17
CENTRE 5′9″ 170 *b.* Yorkton, Saskatchewan, November 7, 1927

1950–51	62	20	17	37	27
1951–52	69	21	22	43	16
1952–53	70	16	34	50	12
1953–54	70	12	15	27	26

1954–55	12	2	3	5	9
1955–56	63	12	16	28	10
1956–57	70	7	15	22	16
1957–58L	15	1	1	2	4
Totals	431	91	123	214	120

- acquired July 13, 1950 with Jim Henry, Bob Goldham, and Gaye Stewart from Chicago for Al Dewsbury, Harry Lumley, Jack Hewatt, Don Morrison, and Pete Babando
- traded November 9, 1954 to Chicago for Lorne Davis
- acquired October 24, 1955 from Chicago for Ed Sandford
- last Red Wings game January 30, 1958
- played part of '58–'59 with Edmonton, but a leg injury forced him to retire

CLIFF "FIDO" PURPUR #8 – 10 RIGHT WING *b.* Grand Fork, North Dakota, October 26, 1916

- appeared only in the 1945 playoffs for Detroit

CHRIS PUSEY #31 GOALIE 6′ 180 *b.* Brantford, Ontario, June 30, 1966

1985–86R/L	1	0-0-0	40	3	0	4.50

- selected 106th overall at 1983 Entry Draft
- first and only Red Wings game October 19, 1985
- played '85–'87 with Adirondack and Indianapolis

JAMIE PUSHOR #4 DEFENCE 6′3″ 192 *b.* Lethbridge, Alberta, February 11, 1973

1995–96R	5	0	1	1	17

- selected 32nd overall at 1991 Entry Draft
- currently with Red Wings

FREDERICK "NELSON" PYATT #22 – 23 – 26 CENTRE 6′ 175 *b.* Port Arthur, Ontario, September 9, 1953

1973–74R	5	0	0	0	0
1974–75	9	0	0	0	0
Totals	14	0	0	0	0

- selected 39th overall at 1973 Entry Draft
- first Red Wings games October 13/14, March 27/31, April 3, 1973–74
- played most of '73–'74 with London Lions (England), part of '74–'75 with Virginia
- played October 9/12/13/19/22/23/29, November 1 & 2, 1974
- traded February 28, 1975 to Washington for a 3rd-round draft choice in 1975 (Alan Cameron)

HUBERT "BILL" QUACKENBUSH ("Quack") #3 – 15 – 16 DEFENCE 5′11″ 180 *b.* Toronto, Ontario, March 2, 1922

1942–43R	10	1	1	2	4
1943–44	43	4	14	18	6
1944–45	50	7	14	21	10
1945–46	48	11	10	21	6
1946–47	44	5	17	22	6
1947–48	58	6	16	22	17
1948–49	60	6	17	23	0
Totals	313	40	89	129	49

- first Red Wings games November 1/5/7/14/29, December 1/6/12/13/15, 1942
- played part of '42–'44 with Indianapolis
- traded August 16, 1949 with Pete Horeck to Boston for Pete Babando, Clare Martin, Lloyd Durham, and Jim Peters

YVES RACINE #33 DEFENCE 6′ 185 *b.* Matane, Quebec, February 7, 1969

1989–90R	28	4	9	13	23
1990–91	62	7	40	47	33
1991–92	61	2	22	24	94
1992–93	80	9	31	40	80
Totals	231	22	102	124	230

- selected 14th overall in 1987 Entry Draft

- first Red Wings game February 2, 1990
- traded October 5, 1993 with a 4th-round draft choice in 1994 (Sebastien Vallee) to Flyers for Terry Carkner

CLARE RAGLAN ("Rags") #22 DEFENCE 6′1″ 177 *b.* Pembroke, Ontario, September 4, 1927

1950–51R	33	3	1	4	14

- first Red Wings game December 6, 1950
- played all of '49–'50 and much of '50–'51 with Indianapolis
- traded August 20, 1951 with George Gee, Jim McFadden, Max McNab, Jim Peters, and Clare Martin to Chicago for Hugh Coflin and $75,000

MIKE RAMSEY #15 DEFENCE 6′3″ 195 *b.* Minneapolis, Minnesota, December 3, 1960

1994–95	33	1	2	3	23
1995–96	47	2	4	6	35
Totals	80	3	6	9	58

- signed August 3, 1994 as a free agent

MATT RAVLICH #18 DEFENCE 5′10″ 185 *b.* Sault Ste. Marie, Ontario, July 12, 1938

1969–70	46	0	6	6	33

- claimed June 11, 1969 from Chicago in Intra-League Draft
- lost February 20, 1970 on waivers to Los Angeles

MARC REAUME #4 DEFENCE 6′1″ 185 *b.* Lasalle, Quebec, February 7, 1934

1959–60	9	0	1	1	2
1960–61	38	0	1	1	8
Totals	47	0	2	2	10

- acquired February 10, 1960 from Toronto for Red Kelly
- lost June 9, 1964 to Toronto at Intra-League Draft

BILLY REAY #8 – 10 – 15 CENTRE 5′7″ 155 *b.* Winnipeg, Manitoba, August 21, 1918

1943–44R	2	2	0	2	2
1944–45	2	0	0	0	0
Totals	4	2	0	2	2

- first Red Wings game January 13, 1944
- played most of '43–'45 as player/coach with Quebec Aces
- traded September 12, 1945 to Canadiens for Ray Getliffe, Rollie Rossignol, and cash. Rather than report to Detroit, however, Getliffe retired. On October 19, 1945, to complete the deal, the Habs send Fern Gauthier to the Wings instead

MICHAEL "MICKEY" REDMOND ("Mick") #20 RIGHT WING 5′11″ 185 *b.* Kirkland Lake, Ontario, December 27, 1947

1970–71	21	6	8	14	7
1971–72	78	42	28	70	34
1972–73	76	52	41	93	24
1973–74	76	51	26	77	14
1974–75	29	15	12	27	18
1975–76L	37	11	17	28	10
Totals	317	177	132	309	107

- acquired January 13, 1971 with Guy Charron and Bill Collins from Canadiens for Frank Mahovlich
- missed much of '74–'75 with back surgery for ruptured disc
- placed on waivers February 8, 1976, but because of injury President Campbell disallowed the move
- last Red Wings game January 18, 1976
- retired after '75–'76 because of recurring injury

EARL "DUTCH" REIBEL #8 – 14 CENTRE 5′8″ 160 *b.* Kitchener, Ontario, July 21, 1930

1953–54R	69	15	33	48	18
1954–55	70	25	41	66	15
1955–56	68	17	39	56	10
1956–57	70	13	23	36	6
1957–58	29	4	5	9	4
Totals	306	74	141	215	53

- first Red Wings game October 8, 1953
- played '50–'51 with Omaha, '51–'52 with Indianapolis, '52–'53 with Edmonton
- traded December 17, 1957 with Billy Dea, Lorne Ferguson, and Bill Dineen to Chicago for Bob Bailey, Nick Mickoski, Jack McIntyre, and Hec Lalande

GERRY REID #24 CENTRE 6′ 160 *b.* Owen Sound, Ontario, October 13, 1928

- appeared only in the 1949 playoffs for Detroit

LEO REISE JR. #5 DEFENCE *b.* Stoney Creek, Ontario, June 7, 1922

1946–47	31	4	6	10	14
1947–48	58	5	4	9	30
1948–49	59	3	7	10	60
1949–50	70	4	17	21	46
1950–51	68	5	16	21	46
1951–52	54	0	11	11	34
Totals	340	21	61	82	230

- acquired December, 1946 with Pete Horeck from Chicago for Adam Brown and Ray Powell
- traded August 18, 1952 to Rangers for Reg Sinclair, rights to John Morrison, and cash

DAVE RICHARDSON #21 LEFT WING 5′8″ 175 *b.* St. Boniface, Manitoba, December 11, 1940

1967–68L	1	0	0	0	0

- first and only Red Wings game December 25, 1967

TERRY RICHARDSON #1 – 30 GOALIE 6′1″ 190 *b.* Powell River, British Columbia, May 7, 1953

1973–74R	9	1–4–0	315	28	0	5.33
1974–75	4	1–2–0	202	23	0	6.83
1975–76	1	0–1–0	60	7	0	7.00
1976–77	5	1–3–0	269	18	0	4.01
Totals	19	3–10–0	846	76	0	5.39

- selected 11th overall at 1973 Entry Draft
- first Red Wings games October 24/26/30, November 7/22/29, December 1/2/16, 1973
- played part of '73–'74 with Virginia and London Lions (England), part of '74–'75 with Virginia, part of '75–'76 with Springfield and New Haven, part of '76–'77 with Kalamazoo, all of '77–'78 with Kansas City
- played October 12/23, March 29/30, 1974–75
- played February 8, 1976
- played February 15/20/24, March 9/23, 1977
- lost July 26, 1978 as a free agent to St. Louis

STEVE RICHMOND #7 DEFENCE 6′1″ 205 *b.* Chicago, Illinois, December 11, 1959

1985–86	29	1	2	3	82

- acquired December 26, 1985 from Rangers for Mike McEwen
- traded August 18, 1986 to New Jersey for Sam St. Laurent

VINCENT RIENDEAU #37 GOALIE 5′10″ 185 *b.* St. Hyacinthe, Quebec, April 20, 1966

1991–92	2	2–0–0	87	2	0	1.38
1992–93	22	13–4–2	1193	64	0	3.22
1993–94	8	2–4–0	345	23	0	4.00
Totals	32	17–8–2	1625	89	0	3.29

- acquired October 18, 1991 from St. Louis for Rick Zombo
- traded January 17, 1994 to Boston for a 5th-round draft choice in 1995 (Chad Wilchynski)

DENNIS RIGGIN #1 GOALIE 5′11″ 156 *b.* Kincardine, Ontario, April 11, 1936

1959–60R	9	2–6–1	540	32	1	3.56
1962–63L	9	3–4–1	445	22	0	2.97
Totals	18	5–10–2	985	54	1	3.29

- played most of '55–'63 with Edmonton, part of '62–'63 with Pittsburgh
- played February 4/6/7/11/13/14/18/20/21, 1960
- played December 5/6/8/9, January 10/12/13/17/19, 1962–63
- forced to retire after serious eye injury

JACK RILEY ("Shovel Shot") CENTRE 5′10″ 160 *b.* Berckenia, Ireland, December 29, 1910

1932–33R	1	0	0	0	0

- played most of '32–'33 with Olympics
- sold to Canadiens in summer 1933

JIM RILEY #11 LEFT WING *b.* Bayfield, New Brunswick, May 25, 1897

1926–27R/L	17	0	2	2	14

- first Cougars game February 12, 1927

BOB RITCHIE #27 LEFT WING 5′10″ 170 *b.* Laverlochere, Quebec, February 20, 1955

1976–77	17	6	2	8	10
1977–78L	11	2	2	4	0
Totals	28	8	4	12	10

- acquired February 17, 1977 with Steve Coates, Terry Murray, and Dave Kelly from Flyers for Rick Lapointe and Mike Korney
- played most of '76–'77 with Springfield, '77–'78 with Kansas City
- last Red Wings games October 13/15/18/20/22/29, November 2/5/12/13/16, 1977

JOHN "WAYNE" RIVERS #15 RIGHT WING 5'10" 180 *b.* Hamilton, Ontario, February 1, 1942

1961–62R	2	0	0	0	0

- Hamilton Red Wings graduate
- first and only Red Wings games January 27 & 28, 1962
- played part of '61–'62 and most of '62–'63 with Hershey
- lost June 1963 to Boston in Intra-League Draft

JOHN ROSS ROACH ("Little Napoleon"/ "The Port Perry Woodpecker") #1 GOALIE 5'5" 130 *b.* Port Perry, Ontario, June 23, 1900 *d.* Windsor, Ontario, July 9, 1973

1932–33	48	25–15–8	2970	93	10	1.88
1933–34	18	9–8–1	1030	45	1	2.62
1934–35L	23	7–11–5	1460	62	4	2.55
Totals	89	41–34–14	5460	200	15	2.20

- bought summer 1932 from Rangers
- last Red Wings game March 17, 1935
- retired after '34–'35 season

PHIL ROBERTO #27 RIGHT WING 6'1" 190 *b.* Niagara Falls, Ontario, January 1, 1949

1974–75	53	13	29	42	32
1975–76	74	8	22	30	110
Totals	127	21	51	72	142

- acquired December 30, 1974 with a 3rd-round draft choice in 1975 (Blair Davidson) from St. Louis for Red Berenson
- traded January 14, 1976 to Kansas City for Buster Harvey

DOUG ROBERTS #14 – 25 – 26 DEFENCE 6'2" 190 *b.* Detroit, October 28, 1942

1965–66R	1	0	0	0	0
1966–67	13	3	1	4	25
1967–68	37	8	9	17	12
1973–74	57	12	25	37	33
1974–75	26	4	4	8	8
Totals	134	27	39	66	78

- first Red Wings game March 31, 1966
- played part of '65–'67 with Memphis, '67–'68 with Fort Worth
- traded May 27, 1968 with Gary Jarrett, Howie Young, and Chris Worthy to Oakland for Bob Baun and Ron Harris
- bought November 23, 1973 from Boston for cash
- jumped to New England (WHA) for '75–'76

EARL ROBERTSON #1 GOALIE 5'10" 165 *b.* Bingorgh, Saskatchewan, November 24, 1910

- appeared only in the 1937 playoffs for Detroit
- purchased October 21, 1936 for $1,500
- traded May 9, 1937 to Americans for Red Doran and $7,500

FRED ROBERTSON #14 DEFENCE 5'10" 198 *b.* Carlisle, England, October 22, 1911

1933–34L	24	1	0	1	12

- bought from Toronto on November 13, 1933 for $6,500
- last Red Wings game January 18, 1934

TORRIE ROBERTSON #14 LEFT WING 5'11" 200 *b.* Victoria, British Columbia, August 2, 1961

1988–89	12	2	2	4	63
1989–90L	42	1	5	6	112
Totals	54	3	7	10	175

- acquired March 7, 1989 from Hartford for Jim Pavese
- played part of '89–'90 with Adirondack
- last Red Wings game February 6, 1990
- played '90–'91 with Rochester and Albany, then out of hockey

MIKE ROBITAILLE #21 DEFENCE 5′11″ 195
b. Midland, Ontario, February 12, 1948

1970–71	23	4	8	12	22

- acquired February 2, 1971 from Rangers with Arnie Brown and Tom Miller for Bruce MacGregor and Larry Brown
- traded May 25, 1971 with Don Luce to Buffalo for Joe Daley

EARL ROCHE #11 LEFT WING 5′11″ 175
b. Prescott, Ontario, February 22, 1910
d. Montreal, Quebec, August 15, 1965

1934–35L	13	3	3	6	0

- bought December 31, 1934 from Buffalo for cash
- only Red Wings games January 1/3/6/8/13/15/17/20/26/27/31, February 3/5/7/10, 1935

MICHAEL "DESSE" ROCHE #14
RIGHT WING 5′6″ 188 *b.* Kemptville, Ontario, February 1, 1909

1934–35L	13	3	3	6	0

- bought December 31, 1934 from Buffalo for cash
- only Red Wings games January 1/3/6/8/13/15/17/20/26/27/31, February 3/5/7/10, 1935

DAVE ROCHEFORT #23 CENTRE 6′ 180
b. Red Deer, Alberta, July 22, 1946

1966–67R/L	1	0	0	0	0

- first and only Red Wings game March 28, 1967
- Edmonton Oil Kings graduate
- played '66–'67 with Memphis and Pittsburgh, '67–'68 with Fort Worth, '68–'69 with Baltimore, '69–'70 with Oklahoma City and Salt Lake

LEON ROCHEFORT #11 RIGHT WING 6′ 185
b. Cap-de-la-Madeleine, Quebec, May 4, 1939

1971–72	64	17	12	29	10
1972–73	20	2	4	6	2
Totals	84	19	16	35	12

- acquired May 25, 1971 from Canadiens for Kerry Ketter and cash
- traded November 28, 1972 to Atlanta for Bill Hogaboam

HARVEY "ROCKY" ROCKBURN #2 DEFENCE
b. Unknown *d.* Unknown

1929–30R	36	4	0	4	97
1930–31	42	0	1	1	118
Totals	78	4	1	5	215

- first Cougars game November 14, 1929
- played '32–'33 with Ottawa

DALE ROLFE #3 – 18 DEFENCE 6′4″ 210
b. Timmins, Ontario, April 30, 1940

1969–70	20	2	9	11	12
1970–71	44	3	9	12	48
Totals	64	5	18	23	60

- acquired February 20, 1970 with Gary Croteau and Larry Johnston from Los Angeles for Brian Gibbons and Garry Monahan
- traded March 2, 1971 to Rangers for Jim Krulicki

ROLLIE "ROSIE" ROSSIGNOL #16 – 18
RIGHT WING 168 lbs. *b.* Edmundston, New Brunswick, October 18, 1921

1943–44R	1	0	1	1	0
1945–46L	8	1	2	3	4
Totals	9	1	3	4	4

- first Red Wings game March 11, 1944
- traded September 12, 1945 to Canadiens with Billy Reay, Ray Getliffe, and cash. Rather than report to Detroit, however, Getliffe decided to retire. On October 19, 1945, to complete the deal, the Habs send Fern Gauthier to the Wings instead
- re-acquired by Wings during '45–'46
- last Red Wings games January 3/6/10/12/13/20/26/27, 1946
- sold August 17, 1946 to St. Louis (AHL) for cash

WILLIAM "ROLLY" ROULSTON #2 – 16 – 18
DEFENCE 6′ 180 *b.* Toronto, Ontario, April 12, 1911 *d.* Unknown

1935–36R	1	0	0	0	0
1936–37	21	0	5	5	10
1937–38L	2	0	1	1	0
Totals	24	0	6	6	10

- first Red Wings game March 22, 1936
- broke leg January 25, 1937 and missed rest of season
- last Red Wings games January 11/13, 1938

BOB ROUSE #3 DEFENCE 6′1″ 210
b. Surrey, British Columbia, June 18, 1964

1994–95	48	1	7	8	36
1995–96	58	0	6	6	48
Totals	106	1	13	14	84

- signed August 5, 1994 as a free agent
- currently with Red Wings

TOM ROWE #8 – 12 RIGHT WING 6′ 190
b. Lynn, Massachusetts, May 23, 1956

1982–83L	51	6	10	16	44

- signed August 9, 1982 as a free agent
- last Red Wings game April 3, 1983
- lost August 23, 1983 as a free agent to Edmonton

BERNIE RUELLE #14 – 18 LEFT WING
5′9″ 165 *b.* Houghton, Michigan, November 23, 1920

1943–44R/L	2	1	0	1	0

- first and only Red Wings games October 31 & November 7, 1943

PAT RUPP #22 GOALIE
b. Detroit, August 12, 1942

1963–64R/L	1	0–1–0	60	4	0	4.00

- first and only Red Wings game March 22, 1964 when Sawchuk rested for playoffs

JIM RUTHERFORD ("Roach"/"Rut")
#1 – 27 – 29 – 30 GOALIE 5′8″ 168
b. Beeton, Ontario, February 17, 1949

1970–71R	29	6–15–3	1498	94	1	3.77
1973–74	25	9–11–4	1420	86	0	3.63
1974–75	59	20–29–10	3478	217	2	3.74
1975–76	44	13–25–6	2640	158	4	3.59
1976–77	48	7–34–6	2740	180	0	3.94
1977–78	43	20–17–4	2468	134	1	3.26
1978–79	32	13–14–5	1892	103	1	3.27
1979–80	23	6–13–3	1326	92	1	4.16
1980–81	10	2–6–2	600	43	0	4.30
1982–83	1	0–1–0	60	7	0	7.00
Totals	314	96–165–43	18122	1114	10	3.69

- selected 10th overall at 1969 Draft
- first Red Wings game October 23, 1970
- lost June 8, 1971 to Penguins in Intra-League Draft
- acquired January 18, 1974 with Jack Lynch from Penguins for Ron Stackhouse
- traded December 4, 1980 to Toronto for Mark Kirton
- signed September 27, 1982 as a free agent
- played November 7, 1982
- retired February 11, 1983

ANDRÉ ST. LAURENT ("Ace") #16 – 34
CENTRE 5′10″ 180 *b.* Rouyn-Noranda, Quebec, February 16, 1953

1977–78	77	31	39	70	108
1978–79	76	18	31	49	124
1983–84	19	1	3	4	17
Totals	172	50	73	123	249

- acquired October 20, 1977 from the Islanders for Michel Bergeron
- traded August 22, 1979 with a 1st-round draft choice in 1980 (Larry Murphy) and a 1st-round draft choice in 1981 (Doug Smith) to Los Angeles for Dale McCourt
- acquired October 24, 1983 from Penguins for future considerations
- played most of '83–'85 with Adirondack

SAM ST. LAURENT #32 – 34 – 35 GOALIE 5′10″ 190 *b.* Arvida, Quebec, February 16, 1959

1986–87	6	1–2–2	342	16	0	2.81
1987–88	6	2–2–0	294	16	0	3.27
1988–89	4	0–1–1	141	9	0	3.83
1989–90	14	2–6–1	607	38	0	3.76
Totals	30	5–11–4	1384	79	0	3.42

- acquired August 18, 1986 from New Jersey for Steve Richmond
- sold June 26, 1990 to Rangers for cash

BORJE SALMING ("King"/"B.J.") #21 DEFENCE 6′1″ 193 *b.* Kiruna, Sweden, April 17, 1951

1989–90L	49	2	17	19	52

- signed as a free agent June 12, 1989
- last Red Wings game April 1, 1990
- retired after '89–'90 to play in Sweden

BARRY SALOVAARA #19 – 28 DEFENCE 5′8″ 175 *b.* Cookesville, Ontario, January 7, 1948

1974–75R	27	0	2	2	18
1975–76L	63	2	11	13	52
Totals	90	2	13	15	70

- first Red Wings game November 13, 1974
- played much of '74–'75 with Virginia, '75–'76 with New Haven
- last Red Wings game April 4, 1976
- out of hockey after '75–'76

ED SANDFORD ("Sandy") #12 LEFT WING 6′1″ 190 *b.* New Toronto, Ontario, August 20, 1928

1955–56	4	0	0	0	0

- acquired June 3, 1955 from Boston with Gilles Boisvert, Real Chevrefils, Norm Corcoran, and Warren Godfrey for Marcel Bonin, Terry Sawchuk, Vic Stasiuk, and Lorne Davis
- played October 6/8/9/22, 1955
- traded October 24, 1955 to Chicago for Metro Prystai

BOB SAUVE #31 GOALIE 5′8″ 165 *b.* Ste. Genevieve, Quebec, June 17, 1955

1981–82	41	11–25–4	2365	165	0	4.19

- acquired December 2, 1981 from Sabres for future considerations
- lost June 1, 1982 as a free agent to Sabres

TERRY SAWCHUK ("Ukie") #1 – 29 GOALIE 6′ 195 *b.* Winnipeg, Manitoba, December 28, 1929 *d.* Long Beach, New York, May 31, 1970

1949–50R	7	4–3–0	420	16	1	2.29
1950–51	70	44–13–13	4200	139	11	1.99
1951–52	70	44–14–12	4200	133	12	1.90
1952–53	63	32–15–16	3780	120	9	1.90
1953–54	67	35–19–13	4000	129	12	1.94
1954–55	68	40–17–11	4040	132	12	1.96
1957–58	70	29–29–12	4200	207	3	2.96
1958–59	67	23–36–8	4020	209	5	3.12
1959–60	58	24–20–14	3480	156	5	2.69
1960–61	37	12–16–8	2080	113	2	3.26
1961–62	43	14–21–8	2580	143	5	3.33
1962–63	48	23–16–7	2775	119	3	2.57
1963–64	53	24–20–7	3140	138	5	2.64
1968–69	13	3–4–3	641	28	0	2.62
Totals	734	351–243–132	43556	1782	85	2.45

- Windsor Spitfires graduate
- first Red Wings games January 8/11/14/15/18/21/22, 1950
- played most of '49–'50 with Indianapolis
- traded June 3, 1955 to Boston with Marcel Bonin, Vic Stasiuk, and Lorne Davis for Gilles Boisvert, Ed Sandford, Real Chevrefils, Norm Corcoran, and Warren Godfrey
- acquired July 24, 1957 from Boston for John Bucyk
- claimed June 10, 1964 by Toronto at Intra-League Draft
- acquired October 10, 1968 from Los Angeles for Jim Peters, Jr.
- traded June 17, 1969 with Sandy Snow to Rangers for Larry Jeffrey

KEVIN SCHAMEHORN #18 – 25 RIGHT WING 5′9″ 185 *b.* Calgary, Alberta, July 28, 1956

1976–77R	3	0	0	0	9
1979–80	2	0	0	0	4
Totals	5	0	0	0	13

- selected 58th overall at 1976 Entry Draft
- first Red Wings games December 31, January 4 & 6, 1976–77
- played October 28 & 31, 1979
- lost October 18, 1980 as a free agent to Los Angeles

JIM SCHOENFELD #2 DEFENCE 6′2″ 210
b. Galt, Ontario, September 4, 1952

1981–82	39	5	9	14	69
1982–83	57	1	10	11	18
Totals	96	6	19	25	87

- acquired December 2, 1981 with Danny Gare and Derek Smith from Sabres for Mike Foligno, Dale McCourt, and Brent Peterson
- lost as a free agent August 19, 1983 to Boston

DWIGHT SCHOFIELD #20 DEFENCE 6′3″ 195
b. Watham, Massachusetts, March 25, 1956

1976–77R	3	1	0	1	2

- selected 76th overall at 1976 Entry Draft
- played most of '76–'82 in minors
- lost September 20, 1982 as a free agent to Canadiens

ENIO SCLISIZZI ("Sils") (sometimes called James Enio) #15 – 16 – 20 – 21 – 23 LEFT WING 5′10″ 168 *b.* Milton, Ontario, August 1, 1925

1947–48R	4	1	0	1	0
1948–49	50	9	8	17	24
1949–50	4	0	0	0	2
1951–52	9	2	1	3	0
Totals	67	12	9	21	26

- first Red Wings games October 15 & March 17/20/21, 1947–48
- played October 12/16/19/23, 1949
- played January 10/12/15/17/19/20/24/26/27, 1952
- played most of '46–'52 with Indianapolis
- sold August 14, 1952 with Fred Glover to Chicago for cash

EARL SEIBERT #17 DEFENCE 6′2″ 198
b. Kitchener, Ontario, December 7, 1910
d. Kitchener, Ontario, December 27, 1965

1944–45	25	5	9	14	10
1945–46L	18	0	3	3	18
Totals	43	5	12	17	28

- acquired January 1945 from Chicago for Don Grosso, Cully Simon, and Byron McDonald
- last Red Wings game December 22, 1945
- retired after '45–'46 to coach at Springfield

RICHARD "RIC" SEILING #16 RIGHT WING/CENTRE 6′1″ 180 *b.* Elmira, Ontario, December 15, 1957

1986–87L	74	3	8	11	49

- acquired October 7, 1986 from Sabres for future considerations
- played '87–'88 with Adirondack, then retired
- last Red Wings game March 25, 1987

BRENDAN SHANAHAN #14 LEFT WING 6′3″ 218 *b.* Mimico, Ontario, January 23, 1969

- acquired October 9, 1996 with Brian Glynn from Hartford for Paul Coffey, Keith Primeau, and a 1st-round draft choice in 1997
- currently with Red Wings

DANIEL SHANK #34 RIGHT WING 5′10″ 190
b. Montreal, Quebec, May 12, 1967

1989–90R	57	11	13	24	143
1990–91	7	0	1	1	14
Totals	64	11	14	25	157

- signed May 26, 1989 as a free agent
- first Red Wings game November 3, 1989
- played December 4/7/11/13/15/20/23, 1990

- traded December 18, 1991 to Hartford for Chris Tancill

JEFF SHARPLES #4 – 32 – 34 DEFENCE
6′1″ 195 *b.* Terrace, British Columbia, July 28, 1967

1986–87R	3	0	1	1	2
1987–88	56	10	25	35	42
1988–89	46	4	9	13	26
Totals	105	14	35	49	70

- selected 29th overall at 1985 Entry Draft
- first Red Wings games October 11/18/24, 1986
- traded November 2, 1989 with Adam Graves, Petr Klima, and Joe Murphy to Edmonton for Jimmy Carson and Kevin McClelland

DOUG SHEDDEN #14 CENTRE 6′ 185
b. Wallaceburg, Ontario, April 29, 1961

1985–86	11	2	3	5	2
1986–87	33	6	12	18	6
Totals	44	8	15	23	8

- acquired March 11, 1986 from Penguins for Ron Duguay
- traded January 17, 1987 to Quebec with John Ogrodnick and Basil McRae for Brent Ashton, Gilbert Delorme, and Mark Kumpel

BOBBY SHEEHAN #17 CENTRE 5′7″ 155
b. Weymouth, Massachusetts, January 11, 1949

1976–77	34	5	4	9	2

- signed October 8, 1976 as a free agent
- lost October 1, 1978 to Rangers as a free agent

TIM SHEEHY #29 RIGHT WING 6′1″ 185
b. Fort Francis, Ontario, September 3, 1948

1977–78	15	0	0	0	0

- acquired November 15, 1977 with Vaclav Nedomansky from Birmingham (WHA) for Steve Durbano, Dave Hanson, and future considerations
- played most of '77–'78 with Kansas City and New England (WHA), '78–'79 with Springfield
- traded February 1979 to Hartford for future considerations

FRANK SHEPPARD #10 – 15 C
b. Montreal, Quebec, Octobe

1927–28R/L	8	1	1

- only Cougars games Novem December 11/13/15/17, 1927

JAKE "JOHNNY" SHEPPARD
5′7″ 165 *b.* Montreal, Queb 1907

1926–27R	43	13
1927–28	44	10
Totals	87	23

- first Cougars game Novembe
- sold October 14, 1928 to Goodfellow and $12,500

RAY SHEPPARD #26 RIG
b. Pembroke, Ontario, M

onov and a conditional

JOHN SHERF #9 – 1
5′11″ 178 *b.* Calume

1935–36R	1
1936–37	1
1937–38	6
1938–39	3
1943–44L	8
Totals	19

- first Red Wings gam
- played March 14, 19
- played November 4
- traded January 17, 1
- played February 12
- sold October 18, 19
- recalled briefly in '
- last Red Wings gam 13/14/21, Decemb

" SHERRITT ("Moose") #3
' 195 *b.* Oakville, Manitoba,

	0	0	0	12

h Portage La Prairie Terriers
ith Harringay Greyhounds (BIHA)
Wings games October 31, Novem-
8/21, 1943
–'45 with Indianapolis, then sold
e '45–'46 season

LEFT WING 6′ 180
berta, November 15, 1945

	2	1	3	22

e October 17, 1970
University of Denver, Omaha,
with Fort Worth
o St. Louis for Richard Sentes

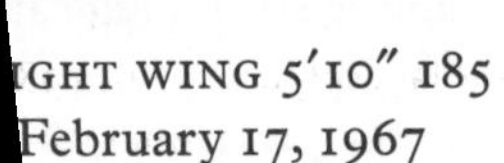

IGHT WING 5′10″ 185
February 17, 1967

	2	3	6

38 Supplemental Draft
arch 16/22/23/27/30/31,

ith Jimmy Carson and
for Paul Coffey, Sylvain

G 5′11″ 190
, January 1, 1958

	5	14	32

waivers from Boston
26, 1985
e agent to Winnipeg

MIKE SILLINGER #23 – 12 CENTRE 5′10″ 191
b. Regina, Saskatchewan, June 29, 1971

1990–91R	3	0	1	1	0
1992–93	51	4	17	21	16
1993–94	62	8	21	29	10
Totals	116	12	39	51	26

- selected 11th overall at 1989 Entry Draft
- played most of '90–'91 with Regina, most of '91–'92 and part of '92–'93 with Adirondack
- played with Detroit only in playoffs during '91–'92
- first Red Wings games October 4/7/13, 1990
- traded April 4, 1995 with Jason York to Anaheim for Mark Ferner, Stu Grimson, and a 6th-round draft choice in 1996 (Magnus Nilsson)

JOHN "CULLY" SIMON #2 – 15 – 18
DEFENCE 5′10″ 190
b. Brockville, Ontario, May 8, 1918

1942–43R	34	1	1	2	34
1943–44	46	3	7	10	52
1944–45	21	0	2	2	26
Totals	101	4	10	14	112

- first Red Wings game December 17, 1942
- traded January 1945 with Don Grosso and Byron McDonald to Chicago for Earl Seibert

THAIN SIMON #21 DEFENCE 6′ 200
b. Brockville, Ontario, April 24, 1922

1946–47R/L	3	0	0	0	0

- first and only Red Wings games October 16/19 and November 3, 1946
- traded September 9, 1948 with Red Almas, Lloyd Doran, Tony Licari, and Barry Sullivan to St. Louis (AHL) for Joe Lund and Hec Highton

CLIFF SIMPSON #19 – 25 CENTRE
5′11″ 175 *b.* Toronto, Ontario, April 4, 1923
d. Unknown

1946–47R/L	6	0	1	1	0

- played most of '42–'49 with Indianapolis, but missed 1943–45 — Canadian Armed Forces
- first and only Red Wings regular season games October 16/19/20/23/26/27, 1946
- joined Detroit for '48 playoffs

- traded September 1949 with Fern Gauthier, Ed Nicholson, and future considerations to St. Louis Flyers for Steve Black and Bill Brennan

REGINALD "REG" SINCLAIR #14 RIGHT WING 6′ 165 *b.* Lachine, Quebec, March 6, 1925

1952–53L	69	11	12	23	36

- acquired August 18, 1952 with John Morrison from Rangers for Leo Reise, Jr.
- last Red Wings game March 22, 1953
- out of hockey after '52–'53 season

DARRYL SITTLER ("Sitt") #27 CENTRE 6′ 190 *b.* Kitchener, Ontario, September 18, 1950

1984–85L	61	11	16	27	37

- acquired October 19, 1984 from Flyers for Joe Paterson and Murray Craven
- last Red Wings game April 7, 1985
- retired August 8, 1985

BJORNE SKAARE #25 CENTRE 6′ 180 *b.* Oslo, Norway, October 29, 1948 *d.* Unknown

1978–79R/L	1	0	0	0	0

- selected 62nd overall at 1978 Entry Draft
- first and only Red Wings game November 29, 1978
- played most of '78–'79 with Kansas City

GLEN SKOV #12 – 14 – 20 CENTRE 6′1″ 185 *b.* Wheatley, Ontario, January 26, 1931

1949–50R	2	0	0	0	0
1950–51	19	7	6	13	13
1951–52	70	12	14	26	48
1952–53	70	12	15	27	54
1953–54	70	17	10	27	95
1954–55	70	14	16	30	53
Totals	301	62	61	123	263

- played most of '50–'51 with Omaha
- first Red Wings games February 4 & 5, 1950
- traded June 3, 1955 with Tony Leswick, Johnny Wilson, and Ben Woit to Chicago for Gord Hollingworth, Jerry Toppazzini, John McCormack, and Dave Creighton

AL SMITH #30 GOALIE 6′1″ 200 *b.* Toronto, Ontario, November 10, 1945

1971–72	43	18–20–4	2500	135	4	3.24

- claimed June 8, 1971 from Penguins at Intra-League Draft
- signed with New England (WHA) on August 7, 1972

ALEX SMITH ("Boots") #2 DEFENCE 5′11″ 176 *b.* Bootle, England, April 2, 1904 *d.* Ottawa, Ontario, November 29, 1963

1931–32	48	6	8	14	47

- on loan from Ottawa for '31–'32 which did not field a team
- returned to Ottawa for '32–'33

BRAD SMITH ("Motor City Smitty") #11 – 17 – 21 – 27 – 72 RIGHT WING 6′1″ 195 *b.* Windsor, Ontario, April 13, 1958

1980–81	20	5	2	7	93
1981–82	33	2	0	2	80
1982–83	1	0	0	0	0
1983–84	8	2	1	3	36
1984–85	1	1	0	1	5
Totals	63	10	3	13	214

- acquired February 24, 1981 from Calgary for future considerations (Rick Vasko — deal completed May 28, 1981)
- played October 9, 1982
- played November 26/30, December 3/4/7/10/11/13, 1983
- played April 7, 1985
- lost July 2, 1985 as a free agent to Toronto

BRIAN SMITH #16 – 19 LEFT WING 6′ 180 *b.* Creighton Mine, Ontario, December 6, 1937

1957–58R	4	0	1	1	0
1959–60	31	2	5	7	2
1960–61L	26	0	2	2	10
Totals	61	2	8	10	12

- career minor-leaguer '57–'68
- first Red Wings games February 1/2/8/9, 1958
- last Red Wings game December 4, 1960
- traded June 1961 with Gerry Melnyk to Chicago for Ed Litzenberger

CARL SMITH #21 FORWARD
b. Cache Bay, Ontario, September 18, 1917

1943–44R/L	7	1	1	2	2

- first and only Red Wings games November 18/21/25/28, December 2/7/12, 1943

DALTON SMITH ("Nakina") #15 CENTRE 5′10″ 150 *b.* Cache Bay, Ontario, June 26, 1915

1943–44L	10	1	2	3	0

- only Red Wings games December 16/19/22/23/26/28/30, January 2/15/16, 1943–44

DEREK SMITH #24 CENTRE/LEFT WING 5′11″ 180 *b.* Quebec City, Quebec, July 31, 1954

1981–82	49	6	14	20	10
1982–83L	42	7	4	11	12
Totals	91	13	18	31	22

- acquired December 2, 1981 with Jim Schoenfeld and Danny Gare from Sabres for Mike Foligno, Dale McCourt, and Brent Peterson
- played part of '82–'83 and all of '83–'84 with Adirondack, then retired
- last Red Wings game February 9, 1983

FLOYD SMITH ("Smitty") #8 – 17 RIGHT WING 5′10″ 180 *b.* Perth, Ontario, May 16, 1935

1962–63	51	9	17	26	10
1963–64	52	18	13	31	22
1964–65	67	16	29	45	44
1965–66	66	21	28	49	20
1966–67	54	11	14	25	8
1967–68	57	18	21	39	14
Totals	347	93	122	215	118

- claimed June 1962 from Rangers at Intra-League Draft
- traded March 3, 1968 with Paul Henderson and Norm Ullman to Toronto for Carl Brewer, Garry Unger, and Pete Stemkowski

GREG SMITH #5 DEFENCE 6′ 195
b. Ponoka, Alberta, July 8, 1955

1981–82	69	10	22	32	79
1982–83	73	4	26	30	79
1983–84	75	3	20	23	108
1984–85	73	2	18	20	117
1985–86	62	5	19	24	84
Totals	352	24	105	129	467

- acquired August 21, 1981 with the rights to Don Murdoch and a 1st-round draft choice in 1982 (Murray Craven) from Minnesota for a 1st-round draft choice in 1982 (Brian Bellows)
- traded March 10, 1986 with John Barrett to Washington for Darren Veitch

NORM SMITH #1 GOALIE 5′7″ 165
b. Toronto, Ontario, March 18, 1908

1934–35	25	12–11–2	1550	52	2	2.01
1935–36	48	24–16–8	3030	103	6	2.04
1936–37	48	25–14–9	2980	102	6	2.05
1937–38	47	11–25–11	2930	130	3	2.66
1938–39	4	0–4–0	240	12	0	3.00
1943–44	5	3–1–1	240	11	0	2.75
1944–45L	1	1–0–0	60	3	0	3.00
Totals	178	76–71–31	11030	413	17	2.25

- acquired from St. Louis Eagles prior to '34–'35
- quit the team November 23, 1938
- played December 16/23/26, January 2/9, 1943–44
- played November 28, 1944
- played a few games '43–'45 at team's request when WWII affected lineup

RICHARD "RICK" SMITH #2 DEFENCE 5′11″ 200 *b.* Kingston, Ontario, June 29, 1948

1980–81	11	0	2	2	6

- claimed October 10, 1980 from Boston in Waiver Draft
- played October 10/11/15/16/18/23/25/26/28/29, November 1, 1980
- lost November 7, 1980 to Washington on waivers

TED SNELL #8 RIGHT WING 5′9″ 190
b. Ottawa, Ontario, May 28, 1946

1974–75L	20	0	4	4	6

- acquired December 14, 1974 with Bart Crashley and Larry Giroux from Kansas City for Guy Charron and Claude Houde
- last Red Wings game February 5, 1975
- played part of '74–'75 with Virginia; retired at season's end

HAROLD SNEPSTS #27 DEFENCE 6′3″ 210
b. Edmonton, Alberta, October 24, 1954

1985–86	35	0	6	6	75
1986–87	54	1	13	14	129
1987–88	31	1	4	5	67
Totals	120	2	23	25	271

- signed as a free agent August 19, 1985
- lost as a free agent October 6, 1988 to Vancouver Canucks

WILLIAM "SANDY" SNOW #15 RIGHT WING 5′11″ 175 *b.* Glace Bay, Nova Scotia, November 11, 1946

1968–69R/L	3	0	0	0	2

- Hamilton Red Wings graduate
- first and only Red Wings games November 16/20/23, 1968
- played part of '65–'66 with Memphis, '67–'69 with Fort Worth
- traded June 17, 1969 with Terry Sawchuk to Rangers for Larry Jeffrey

DENNIS SOBCHUK #14 CENTRE 6′2″ 180
b. Lang, Saskatchewan, January 12, 1954

1979–80	33	4	6	10	0

- acquired September 4, 1979 from Flyers for a 3rd-round draft choice in 1981 (David Michayluk)
- released after '79–'80

KEN SOLHEIM #26 LEFT WING 6′3″ 210
b. Hythe, Alberta, March 27, 1961

1982–83	10	0	0	0	2

- acquired March 8, 1983 from Minnesota for future considerations
- played March 10/12/13/16/19/20/23/30, April 1/3, 1983
- played most of '83–'84 with Adirondack
- signed by Minnesota for '84–'85

BOB SOLINGER #20 LEFT WING 5′10″ 190
b. Star City, Saskatchewan, December 23, 1925

1959–60L	1	0	0	0	0

- only Red Wings game January 23, 1960
- career minor-leaguer '45–'64
- played part of '59–'60 with Edmonton (WHL), '61–'62 with San Francisco, '62–'64 with Los Angeles (WHL), then retired

JOHN SORRELL ("Long John") #4 – 9 – 10 – 12 – 17 LEFT WING 6′ 152 *b.* Chesterville, Ontario, January 16, 1906 *d.* Unknown

1930–31IR	39	9	7	16	10
1931–32	48	8	5	13	22
1932–33	47	14	10	24	11
1933–34	47	21	10	31	8
1934–35	47	20	16	36	12
1935–36	48	13	15	28	8
1936–37	48	8	16	24	4
1937–38	23	3	7	10	0
Totals	347	96	86	182	75

- signed from London (IL) in 1930
- first Falcons game November 13, 1930
- sent to Pittsburgh in December 1937; recalled December 31
- traded February 13, 1938 to Americans for Hap Emms

FRED SPECK #8 – 15 CENTRE 5′9″ 160
b. Thorold, Ontario, July 22, 1947

1968–69R	5	0	0	0	2
1969–70	5	0	0	0	0
Totals	10	0	0	0	2

- Hamilton Red Wings graduate
- first Red Wings games November 28, December 5/7/8/11, 1968
- played much of '67–'70 with Forth Worth, part of '69–'70 with San Diego
- played January 22/24, February 12/14/15, 1970
- lost June 8, 1971 to Vancouver Canucks in Intra-League Draft

TED SPEERS #11 RIGHT WING 5′11″ 200
b. Ann Arbor, Michigan, January 28, 1961

1985–86R/L	4	1	1	2	0

- signed as a free agent September 14, 1983
- first and only Red Wings games March 3/5/6/9, 1986
- played most of '83–'87 with Adirondack

IRV SPENCER #11 – 15 – 21 DEFENCE 5′10″ 180 *b.* Sudbury, Ontario, December 4, 1937

1963–64	25	3	0	3	8
1967–68	5	0	1	1	4
Totals	30	3	1	4	12

- claimed June 1963 from Boston at Intra-League Draft
- played part of '63–'69 with Pittsburgh, Memphis, and Fort Worth, '69–'70 with San Diego
- played January 20/27/28, February 1/8, 1968
- acquired June 8, 1971 with Bob Dillabough from Vancouver Canucks for John Cunniff and Gary Bredin

RON STACKHOUSE ("Stack") #21 DEFENCE 6′3″ 210 *b.* Haliburton, Ontario, August 26, 1949

1971–72	73	5	25	30	81
1972–73	78	5	29	34	82
1973–74	33	2	14	16	33
Totals	184	12	68	80	196

- acquired October 22, 1971 from California for Tom Webster
- traded January 18, 1974 to Penguins for Jack Lynch and Jim Rutherford

ED STANKIEWICZ #21 – 25 RIGHT WING 5′9″ 175 *b.* Kitchener, Ontario, December 1, 1929

1953–54R	1	0	0	0	2
1955–56L	5	0	0	0	0
Totals	6	0	0	0	2

- career minor-leaguer '51–'63
- first Red Wings game March 20, 1954
- last Red Wings games October 22/26/29/30 and November 2, 1955

WILFRED "WILF" STARR ("Twinkie") #14 – 15 – 16 FORWARD 5′11″ 190 *b.* St. Boniface, Manitoba, July 22, 1909

1933–34	28	2	2	4	17
1934–35	29	1	1	2	0
1935–36L	9	1	0	1	0
Totals	66	4	3	7	17

- acquired summer 1933 from Americans
- last Red Wings games February 18/20/23/27, March 1/5/7/8/12, 1936
- out of hockey after '35–'36

VIC STASIUK #11 – 19 – 22 LEFT WING 6′1″ 185 *b.* Lethbridge, Alberta, May 23, 1929

1951–52	58	5	9	14	19
1952–53	3	0	0	0	0
1953–54	42	5	2	7	4
1954–55	59	8	11	19	67
1960–61	21	10	13	23	16
1961–62	59	15	28	43	45
1962–63L	36	6	11	17	37
Totals	278	49	74	123	188

- acquired December 10, 1950 with Bert Olmstead from Chicago for Steve Black and Lee Fogolin
- played October 9/12/19, 1952
- traded June 3, 1955 to Boston with Marcel Bonin, Terry Sawchuk, and Lorne Davis for Gilles Boisvert, Ed Sandford, Real Chevrefils, Norm Corcoran, and Warren Godfrey
- acquired January 1961 with Leo Labine from Boston for Gary Aldcorn, Murray Oliver, and Tom McCarthy
- last Red Wings game March 24, 1963
- demoted December-January 1962–63 to Pittsburgh; played with Hornets until '65, '65–'66 with Memphis, then retired

RAY STASZAK #8 RIGHT WING 6′ 200 *b.* Philadelphia, Pennsylvania, December 1, 1962

1985–86R/L	4	0	1	1	7

- signed as a free agent July 31, 1985
- played part of '85–'86 with Adirondack
- first and only Red Wings games October 10/12/14/17, 1985
- contract bought out June 9, 1986

FRANK STEELE #11 DEFENCE *b.* Unknown

1930–31R/L	1	0	0	0	0

- first and only Falcons game December 25, 1930

GREG STEFAN #29 – 30 GOALIE 5′11″ 180
b. Brantford, Ontario, February 11, 1961

1981–82R	2	0–2–0	120	10	2	5.00
1982–83	35	6–16–9	1847	139	0	4.52
1983–84	50	19–22–2	2600	152	2	3.51
1984–85	46	21–19–3	2635	190	0	4.33
1985–86	37	10–20–5	2068	155	1	4.50
1986–87	43	20–17–3	2351	135	1	3.45
1987–88	33	17–9–5	1854	95	1	3.07
1988–89	46	21–17–3	2499	167	0	4.01
1989–90L	7	1–5–0	359	24	0	4.01
Totals	299	115–127–30	16333	1067	7	3.92

- selected 128th overall at 1981 Entry Draft
- first Red Wings games March 24 & 25, 1982
- played part of '89–'91 with Adirondack
- last Red Wings games November 6/9/14/16/18/21/27, 1989

PETE STEMKOWSKI ("Stemmer") #19 – 23 CENTRE 6′1″ 210 *b.* Winnipeg, Manitoba, August 25, 1943

1967–68	13	3	6	9	4
1968–69	71	21	31	52	81
1969–70	76	25	24	49	114
1970–71	10	2	2	4	8
Totals	170	51	63	114	207

- acquired March 3, 1968 with Carl Brewer and Garry Unger from Toronto for Paul Henderson, Norm Ullman, and Floyd Smith
- traded October 31, 1970 to Rangers for Larry Brown

BLAIR STEWART #18 – 22 – 25 LEFT WING 5′11″ 185 *b.* Winnipeg, Manitoba, March 15, 1953

1973–74R	17	0	4	4	16
1974–75	19	0	5	5	38
Totals	36	0	9	9	54

- selected 75th overall at 1973 Entry Draft
- first Red Wings game October 30, 1973
- traded March 9, 1975 to Washington for Mike Bloom

JAMES "GAYE" STEWART #11 LEFT WING 5′11″ 175 *b.* Fort William, Ontario, June 28, 1923

1950–51	67	18	13	31	18

- acquired July 13, 1950 with Jim Henry, Bob Goldham, and Metro Prystai from Chicago for Al Dewsbury, Harry Lumley, Jack Stewart, Don Morrison, and Pete Babando
- traded June 19, 1951 to Rangers for Tony Leswick

JACK STEWART ("Black Jack"/"Jack the Bouncer") #2 – 3 – 16 – 18 – 19 DEFENCE 5′11″ 185 *b.* Pilot Mound, Manitoba, May 6, 1917 *d.* Detroit, May 25, 1983

1938–39R	33	0	1	1	18
1939–40	47	1	0	1	40
1940–41	47	2	6	8	56
1941–42	44	4	7	11	93
1942–43	44	2	9	11	68
1945–46	47	4	11	15	73
1946–47	55	5	9	14	83
1947–48	60	5	14	19	83
1948–49	60	4	11	15	96
1949–50	66	3	11	14	86
Totals	503	30	79	109	696

- played '36–'37 with Portage La Prairie
- first Red Wings game November 6, 1938
- played part of '38–'39 with Pittsburgh
- missed 1943–45 — Royal Canadian Air Force
- traded July 13, 1950 with Al Dewsbury, Harry Lumley, Don Morrison, and Pete Babando to Chicago for Jim Henry, Bob Goldham, Gaye Stewart, and Metro Prystai

GORD STRATE #18 – 19 – 21 DEFENCE 6′1″ 190 *b.* Edmonton, Alberta, May 28, 1935

1956–57R	5	0	0	0	4
1957–58	45	0	0	0	24
1958–59L	11	0	0	0	6
Totals	61	0	0	0	34

- Edmonton Oil Kings graduate
- first Red Wings games January 24/26/27/31 & February 2, 1957
- last Red Wings games January 15/17/18/21/25/29/31, February 1/5/7/8, 1959
- career minor-leaguer '54–'62

ART STRATTON #8 CENTRE 6′1″ 175
b. Winnipeg, Manitoba, October 8, 1935

1963–64	5	0	3	3	2

- drafted summer 1963 from Buffalo (AHL)
- played October 10/13/16/19/20, 1963
- traded June 9, 1964 with John Miszuk and Ian Cushenan to Chicago for Ron Murphy and Aut Erickson

HERB STUART #14 GOALIE
b. Unknown *d.* Unknown

1926–27R/L	3	0–1–0	180	5	0	1.67

- first and only Cougars games November 18, February 15/17, 1926–27
- traded to London (Can Pro League) for Leroy Goldsworthy

BARRY SULLIVAN ("Big Ben") #11
RIGHT WING 6′ 205 *b.* Preston, Ontario, September 21, 1926

1947–48R/L	1	0	0	0	0

- first and only Red Wings game February 3, 1948
- played '45–'46 and '47–'48 with Omaha, '46–'47 with Indianapolis
- traded September 9, 1948 with Red Almas, Lloyd Doran, Tony Licari, Barry Sullivan, and Thain Simon to St. Louis (AHL) for Joe Lund and Hec Highton

BILL SUTHERLAND #8 – 18 LEFT WING
5′10″ 176 *b.* Regina, Saskatchewan, November 10, 1934

1971–72L	5	0	1	1	2

- bought November 9, 1971 from St. Louis for cash
- only Red Wings games November 20 & 21, February 16/19/20, 1971–72
- played part of '71–'72 with Tidewater
- jumped to Winnipeg (WHA) for '72–'73 season

JOHN TAFT #11 DEFENCE 6′2″ 185
b. Minneapolis, Minnesota, March 8, 1954

1978–79R/L	15	0	2	2	4

- selected 81st overall at 1974 Entry Draft
- signed as a free agent May 12, 1977
- first and only Red Wings games November 29, December 1/2/6/7/9/10/13/14/16/17/20/22/23, January 7, 1978–79
- played much of '77–'79 with Kansas City, '79–'80 with Adirondack, '80–'83 with Salt Lake
- lost July 14, 1980 as a free agent to St. Louis

JEAN-GUY TALBOT #3 DEFENCE
5′11″ 170 *b.* Cap-de-la-Madeleine, Quebec, July 11, 1932

1967–68	32	0	3	3	10

- acquired October 19, 1967 from Minnesota for Bob McCord
- lost January 13, 1968 on waivers to St. Louis

CHRIS TANCILL #18 – 48 CENTRE 5′10″ 185
b. Livonia, Michigan, February 7, 1968

1991–92	1	0	0	0	0
1992–93	4	1	0	1	2
Totals	5	1	0	1	2

- acquired December 18, 1991 from Hartford for Daniel Shank
- played March 5, 1992
- played December 31, January 2/4/19, 1992–93
- lost August 28, 1993 as a free agent

BILLY TAYLOR ("Billy the Kid") #7 CENTRE
5′9″ 150 *b.* Winnipeg, Manitoba, May 3, 1919 *d.* Oshawa, Ontario, June 12, 1990

1946–47	60	17	46	63	35

- acquired summer 1946 from Toronto for Harry Watson
- traded October 1947 to Boston for Bep Guidolin

EDWARD "TED" TAYLOR #18
LEFT WING 6′ 175 *b.* Brandon, Manitoba, February 25, 1942

1966–67	2	0	0	0	0

- claimed June 15, 1966 from Canadiens at Intra-League Draft
- played February 18 & 19, 1967
- lost June 6, 1967 to Minnesota at Expansion Draft

TIM TAYLOR #38 – 37 CENTRE 6′1″ 188 *b.* Stratford, Ontario, February 6, 1969

1993–94R	1	1	0	1	0
1994–95	22	0	4	4	16
1995–96	72	11	14	25	39
Totals	95	12	18	30	55

- signed July 28, 1993 as a free agent
- first Red Wings game December 18, 1993
- currently with Red Wings

HARVEY TENO #1 GOALIE *b.* Windsor, Ontario, February 15, 1915

1938–39R/L	5	2–3–0	300	15	0	3.00

- signed October 21, 1938
- first and only Red Wings games November 17/20/24/26/27, 1938
- played most of '38–'39 with Pittsburgh
- sold outright to Pittsburgh on October 6, 1939

LARRY THIBEAULT #15 LEFT WING 5′7″ 180 *b.* Charletone, Ontario, October 2, 1918

1944–45R	4	0	2	2	0

- first Red Wings games October 29, November 5/11/12, 1944
- played one game with Canadiens in '45–'46

CECIL THOMPSON ("Tiny") #1 GOALIE 5′10″ 160 *b.* Sandon, British Columbia, May 31, 1905 *d.* Calgary, Alberta, February 9, 1981

1938–39	39	16–17–6	2396	101	4	2.53
1939–40L	46	16–24–6	2830	120	3	2.54
Totals	85	32–41–12	5226	221	7	2.54

- bought November 28, 1938 from Boston
- last Red Wings game March 17, 1940
- retired after '39–'40 season

LORAN "ERROL" THOMPSON ("Spud") #12 LEFT WING 5′8″ 180 *b.* Summerside, Prince Edward Island, May 28, 1950

1977–78	14	5	1	6	2
1978–79	70	23	31	54	26
1979–80	77	34	14	48	22
1980–81	39	14	12	26	52
Totals	200	76	58	134	102

- acquired March 13, 1978 with a 1st-round draft choice in 1978 (Brent Peterson), a 2nd-round draft choice in 1978 (Al Jensen), and a 1st-round draft choice in 1980 (Mike Blaisdell) from Toronto for Dan Maloney and a 2nd-round draft choice in 1980 (Craig Muni)
- traded January 8, 1981 to Penguins for Gary McAdam

BILLY THOMSON #9 – 11 – 17 CENTRE 5′9″ 162 *b.* Ayshire, Scotland, March 23, 1914

1938–39R	4	0	0	0	0
1943–44	5	2	2	4	0
Totals	9	2	2	4	0

- acquired December 19, 1938 with $10,000 from Toronto for Bucko McDonald
- first Red Wings game February 9, 1939
- began '43–'44 with Chicago; out of hockey after season's end

JERRY TOPPAZZINI ("Topper") #19 RIGHT WING 5′11″ 180 *b.* Copper Cliff, Ontario, July 29, 1931

1955–56	40	1	7	8	31

- acquired June 3, 1955 with Gord Hollingworth, John McCormack, and Dave Creighton from Chicago for Tony Leswick, Glen Skov, Johnny Wilson, and Ben Woit

- traded January 17, 1956 with Real Chevrefils to Boston for Lorne Ferguson and Murray Costello

LARRY TRADER #2 – 24 – 26 DEFENCE 6′1″ 180 *b.* Barry's Bay, Ontario, July 7, 1963

1982–83R	15	0	2	2	6
1984–85	40	3	7	10	39
Totals	55	3	9	12	45

- selected 86th overall at 1981 Entry Draft
- first Red Wings games October 6/8/9/14/16/17/20/24/28/30, November 7/10/13/18/21, 1982
- played most of '82–'86 with Adirondack
- traded August 7, 1986 to St. Louis for Lee Norwood

PERCY TRAUB ("Puss") #2 – 14 DEFENCE *b.* Unknown *d.* Unknown

1927–28	44	3	1	4	75
1928–29L	44	0	0	0	46
Totals	88	3	1	4	121

- bought summer 1927 with George Hay from Chicago for $15,000
- last Cougars game March 14, 1929
- retired after '28–'29 season

DAVE TROTTIER #15 LEFT WING 5′10″ 170 *b.* Pembroke, Ontario, June 25, 1906 *d.* Halifax, Nova Scotia, November 1956

1938–39L	11	1	1	2	16

- retired after '38–'39
- only Red Wings games December 18/22/24/25/29, January 1/2/5/8/10/15/19, 1938–39

JOE TURNER #1 GOALIE *b.* Windsor, Ontario, 1909 *d.* Holland, 1945

1941–42R/L	1	0-0-1	60	3	0	3.00

- only Red Wings game February 5, 1942
- joined United States Marine Corps — killed in action January 1945 in Holland

NORM ULLMAN #7 – 16 CENTRE 5′10″ 185 *b.* Provost, Alberta, December 26, 1935

1955–56R	66	9	9	18	26
1956–57	64	16	36	52	47
1957–58	69	23	28	51	38
1958–59	69	22	36	58	42
1959–60	70	24	34	58	42
1960–61	70	28	42	70	34
1961–62	70	26	38	64	54
1962–63	70	26	30	56	53
1963–64	61	21	30	51	55
1964–65	70	42	41	83	70
1965–66	70	31	41	72	35
1966–67	68	26	44	70	26
1967–68	58	30	25	55	26
Totals	875	324	434	758	548

- played '53–'55 with Edmonton Oil Kings
- first Red Wings game October 6, 1955
- traded March 3, 1968 with Paul Henderson and Floyd Smith to Toronto for Carl Brewer, Garry Unger, and Pete Stemkowski

GARRY UNGER ("Iron Man") #7 – 16 CENTRE 6′ 185 *b.* Edmonton, Alberta, December 7, 1947

1967–68	13	5	10	15	2
1968–69	76	24	20	44	33
1969–70	76	42	24	66	67
1970–71	51	13	14	27	63
Totals	216	84	68	152	165

- acquired March 3, 1968 with the rights to Carl Brewer and Pete Stemkowski from Toronto for Paul Henderson, Norm Ullman, and Floyd Smith
- traded February 6, 1971 with Wayne Connelly to St. Louis for Tim Ecclestone and Red Berenson

ROGATIEN "ROGIE" VACHON ("Bono") #30 – 40 5′7″ 165 *b.* Palmarolle, Quebec, September 8, 1945

1978–79	50	10–27–11	2908	189	0	3.90
1979–80	59	20–30–8	3474	209	4	3.61
Totals	109	30–57–19	6382	398	4	3.74

- signed August 8, 1978 as a restricted free agent; Los Angeles received Dale McCourt as compensation
- traded July 15, 1980 to Boston for Gilles Gilbert

ERIC VAIL ("Big Train") #19 LEFT WING 6′2″ 210 *b.* Timmins, Ontario, September 16, 1953

1981–82L	52	10	14	24	35

- acquired November 10, 1981 from Calgary for Gary McAdam and a 4th-round draft choice in 1983 (John Bekkers)

- played part of '81–'82 with Oklahoma City and Adirondack, all of '82–'83 with Adirondack, then retired
- last Red Wings game April 4, 1982

RICK VASKO ("Moose") #3 – 4 DEFENCE
6′ 185 *b.* St. Catharines, Ontario, January 12, 1957

1977–78R	3	0	0	0	7
1979–80	8	0	0	0	2
1980–81L	20	3	7	10	20
Totals	31	3	7	10	29

- selected 37th overall at 1977 Entry Draft
- first Red Wings games December 15/17/18, 1977
- played most of '77–'81 with Kansas City and Adirondack
- last Red Wings game November 22, 1980
- sent May 28, 1981 to Calgary to complete trade for Brad Smith (February 24, 1981)

DARREN VEITCH #5 DEFENCE 5′11″ 195
b. Saskatoon, Saskatchewan, April 24, 1960

1985–86	13	0	5	5	2
1986–87	77	13	45	58	52
1987–88	63	7	33	40	45
Totals	153	20	83	103	99

- acquired March 10, 1986 from Washington for John Barrett and Greg Smith
- traded June 11, 1988 to Toronto for Miroslav Frycer

MIKE VERNON #29 GOALIE 5′9″ 165
b. Calgary, Alberta, February 24, 1963

1994–95	30	19–6–4	1807	76	1	2.52
1995–96	32	21–7–2	1855	70	3	2.26
Totals	62	40–13–6	3662	146	4	2.39

- acquired June 29, 1994 from Calgary for Steve Chiasson
- currently with Red Wings

DENNIS VIAL #29 – 36 DEFENCE 6′1″ 215
b. Sault Ste. Marie, Ontario, April 10, 1969

1990–91	9	0	0	0	16
1991–92	27	1	0	1	72
1992–93	9	0	1	1	20
Totals	45	1	1	2	108

- acquired March 5, 1991 with Jim Cummins and Kevin Miller from Rangers for Joey Kocur and Per Djoos
- sold June 15, 1992 with Doug Crossman to Quebec for cash
- bought September 9, 1992 from Quebec for cash
- traded June 8, 1993 to Tampa Bay for Steve Maltais

DOUG VOLMAR #19 – 23 – 27 CENTRE
6′1″ 215 *b.* Cleveland Heights, Ohio, January 9, 1945

1970–71R	2	0	1	1	2
1971–72	39	9	5	14	8
Totals	41	9	6	15	10

- first Red Wings games November 26 & 28, 1970
- played most of '69–'70 with Fort Worth, part with San Diego, '70–'71 with Springfield, '71–'72 with Tidewater
- lost June 5, 1972 to Los Angeles at Intra-League Draft

CARL VOSS #3 – 7 – 16 CENTRE 5′8″ 168
b. Chelsea, Massachusetts, January 6, 1907
d. Lake Park, Florida, September 13, 1994

1932–33	38	6	14	20	6
1933–34	8	0	2	2	2
Totals	46	6	16	22	8

- bought December 1932 from Rangers
- traded November 26, 1933 to Ottawa for Cooney Weiland

JOHN "JACK" WALKER #6 LEFT WING
b. Silver Mountain, Ontario, November 28, 1888 *d.* Seattle, Washington, February 16, 1950

1926–27R	37	3	4	7	6
1927–28L	43	2	4	6	12
Totals	80	5	8	13	18

- came from Victoria when team moved to Detroit
- first Cougars game November 18, 1926
- last Cougars game March 24, 1928

BOB WALL #4 – 5 – 16 – 19 – 23 DEFENCE 5′10″ 202 *b.* Richmond Hill, Ontario, December 1, 1942

1964–65R	1	0	0	0	0
1965–66	8	1	1	2	8
1966–67	31	2	2	4	26
1971–72	45	2	4	6	9
Totals	85	5	7	12	43

- first Red Wings game October 15, 1964
- lost June 6, 1967 to Los Angeles at Expansion Draft
- acquired May 12, 1971 with Ab McDonald and Mike Lowe to complete February 22, 1971 deal which sent Carl Brewer to St. Louis

WES WALZ #26 CENTRE 5′10″ 185 *b.* Calgary, Alberta, May 15, 1970

1995–96	2	0	0	0	0

- currently with Red Wings

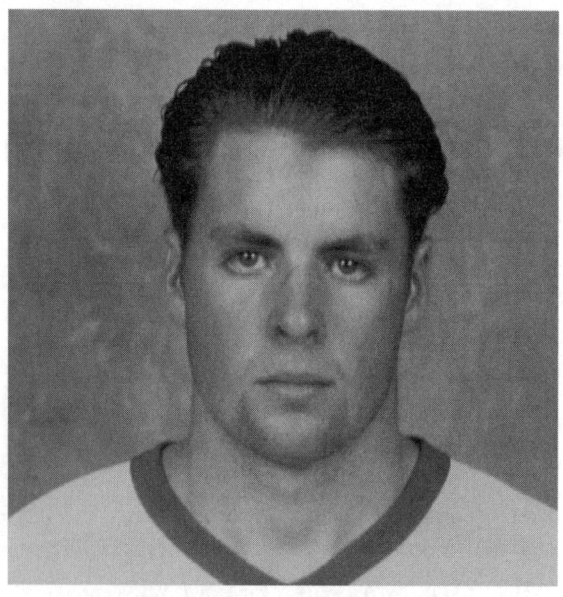

AARON WARD #29 – 8 DEFENCE 6′2″ 200 *b.* Windsor, Ontario, January 17, 1973

1993–94R	5	1	0	1	4
1994–95	1	0	1	1	2
Totals	6	1	1	2	6

- acquired June 11, 1993 with a 4th-round draft choice in 1993 (John Jakopin) from Winnipeg for Paul Ysebaert and future considerations (Alan Kerr — June 18, 1993)
- first Red Wings games October 5/8/13/21/23, 1993
- played March 17, 1995
- played most of '93–'96 with Adirondack
- currently with Red Wings

EDDIE WARES #11 DEFENCE 5′10″ 182 *b.* Calgary, Alberta, March 19, 1915

1937–38	21	9	7	16	2
1938–39	28	8	8	16	10
1939–40	33	2	6	8	19
1940–41	42	10	16	26	34
1941–42	43	9	29	38	31
1942–43	47	12	18	30	10
Totals	214	50	84	134	106

- acquired January 17, 1938 from Rangers for Johnny Sherf
- broke shoulder March 10, 1941; missed rest of year
- missed 1943–46 — Canadian Armed Forces
- sold October 11, 1945 to Chicago for cash

BRYAN WATSON ("Bugsy") #18 DEFENCE 5′10″ 175 *b.* Bancroft, Ontario, November 14, 1942

1965–66	70	2	7	9	133
1966–67	48	0	1	1	66
1973–74	21	0	4	4	99
1974–75	70	1	13	14	238
1975–76	79	0	18	18	322
1976–77	14	0	1	1	39
Totals	302	3	44	47	897

- claimed June 9, 1965 from Chicago in Intra-League Draft
- lost June 6, 1967 to Minnesota in Expansion Draft
- acquired February 14, 1974 with Chris Evans and Jean Hamel from St. Louis for Garnet "Ace" Bailey, Ted Harris, and Bill Collins
- traded November 30, 1976 to Washington for Greg Joly

HARRY WATSON ("Whipper") #17 – 19 LEFT WING 6′1″ 203 *b.* Saskatoon, Saskatchewan, May 6, 1923

1942–43	50	13	18	31	10
1945–46	44	14	10	24	4
Totals	94	27	28	55	14

- bought October 9, 1942 with Pat Egan when Brooklyn Americans folded
- missed 1943–45 — Royal Canadian Air Force
- traded summer 1946 to Toronto for Billy Taylor

JIM WATSON ("Watty") #2 – 3 – 11 – 18 – 21 – 24 DEFENCE 6′2″ 195 *b.* Malartic, Quebec, June 28, 1943

1963–64R	1	0	0	0	0
1964–65	1	0	0	0	2
1965–66	2	0	0	0	4
1967–68	61	0	3	3	87
1968–69	8	0	1	1	4
1969–70	4	0	0	0	0
Totals	77	0	4	4	97

- Hamilton Red Wings graduate
- first Red Wings game January 29, 1964
- played January 3, 1965
- played most of '63–'64 with Cincinnati, '64–'65 with Pittsburgh, '65–'66 with Memphis, '66–'67 with San Diego
- played December 12 & 15, 1965
- played November 6/7/9/13, January 4/5/9, March 27, 1968–69
- played January 17/18/22/24, 1970
- lost June 10, 1970 to Sabres at Intra-League Draft

BRIAN WATTS #15 LEFT WING 6′ 180 *b.* Hagersville, Ontario, September 10, 1947

1975–76R/L	4	0	0	0	0

- selected 7th overall at 1964 Draft
- first and only Red Wings games March 21/24/30/31, 1976

TOM WEBSTER #8 – 16 RIGHT WING 5′10″ 170 *b.* Kirkland Lake, Ontario, October 4, 1948

1970–71	78	30	37	67	40
1971–72	12	3	2	5	10
1979–80L	1	0	0	0	0
Totals	91	33	39	72	50

- acquired June 10, 1970 from Sabres for Roger Crozier
- traded October 22, 1971 to California for Ron Stackhouse
- signed as a free agent September 15, 1979
- played most of '79–'80 with Adirondack
- last Red Wings game October 13, 1979

RALPH "COONEY" WEILAND #7 CENTRE 5′7″ 150 *b.* Egmondville, Ontario, November 5, 1904 *d.* Florida, July 1985

1933–34	39	11	19	30	6

- acquired November 26, 1933 from Ottawa for Carl Voss
- traded 1936 to Boston for Marty Barry

STAN WEIR ("Stash") #14 CENTRE 6′1″ 180 *b.* Ponoka, Alberta, March 17, 1952

1982–83L	57	15	24	29	2

- bought September 14, 1982 from Edmonton Oilers for cash
- last Red Wings game April 3, 1983
- played '83–'84 with Montana, '84–'85 with Milwaukee, then retired

CARL WETZEL #22 GOALIE 6′1″ 170 *b.* Detroit, December 12, 1938

1964–65R	2	0–1–0	33	4	0	7.27

- out of hockey '62–'64; signed as a free agent in 1964
- first and only Red Wings games December 26 & January 2, 1964–65
- played part of '64–'65 with Pittsburgh, '65–'66 with Quebec (AHL) and Houston (CPHL)

BOB WHITELAW #17 – 20 DEFENCE 5′11″ 185 *b.* Motherwell, Scotland, October 5, 1916

1940–41R	23	0	2	2	2
1941–42L	9	0	0	0	0
Totals	32	0	2	2	2

- first Red Wings game December 25, 1940
- last Red Wings games November 27, December 4/7/14/18/21/25/27/28, 1941–42

ARCHIE WILDER #15 LEFT WING 5′9″ 155 *b.* Melville, Saskatchewan, April 30, 1917

1940–41R/L	18	0	2	2	2

- played '39–'40 with Indianapolis
- first Red Wings game November 3, 1940
- last Red Wings game December 22, 1940

BOB WILKIE #28 CENTRE 6′2″ 200 *b.* Calgary, Alberta, February 11, 1969

1990–91R	8	1	2	3	2

- selected 41st overall at 1987 Entry Draft
- first and only Red Wings games October 6/13/18/20, January 11/12/14, 1990–91
- played most of '89–'93 with Adirondack
- traded February 2, 1993 to Flyers for future considerations

CARL "BURR" WILLIAMS #2 – 17 DEFENCE 5′10″ 183 *b.* Okemah, Oklahoma, August 30, 1909

1933–34R	4	0	1	1	12
1936–37L	2	0	0	0	4
Totals	6	0	1	1	16

- first Red Wings games March 8/11/15/18, 1934
- bought December 31, 1934 from Buffalo for cash
- last Red Wings games December 8/10, 1936

DAVE "TIGER" WILLIAMS #55 LEFT WING 5′11″ 190 *b.* Weyburn, Saskatchewan, February 3, 1954

1984–85	55	3	8	11	158

- acquired August 8, 1984 from Vancouver Canucks for Rob McClanahan
- traded March 12, 1985 to Los Angeles for future considerations

FRED WILLIAMS ("Fats") #15 CENTRE 5′11″ 178 *b.* Saskatoon, Saskatchewan, July 1, 1956

1976–77R/L	44	2	5	7	10

- selected 4th overall at 1976 Entry Draft
- first Red Wings game October 7, 1976
- last Red Wings game April 3, 1977
- played with Rhode Island, Kansas City, and Philadelphia in '76–'78

JOHNNY WILSON ("Iron Man") #8 – 11 – 16 – 17 – 23 LEFT WING 5′10″ 175 *b.* Kincardine, Ontario, June 14, 1929

1949–50R	1	0	0	0	0
1951–52	28	4	5	9	18
1952–53	70	23	19	42	22
1953–54	70	17	17	34	22
1954–55	70	12	15	27	14
1957–58	70	12	27	39	14
1958–59	70	11	17	28	18
Totals	379	79	100	179	108

- Windsor Spitfires graduate
- first Red Wings game February 15, 1950
- played most of '49–'50 with Omaha, '50–'52 with Indianapolis
- traded June 3, 1955 with Tony Leswick, Glen Skov, and Ben Woit to Chicago for Gord Hollingworth, Jerry Toppazzini, John McCormack, and Dave Creighton
- acquired July 1957 with Forbes Kennedy, William Preston, and Hank Bassen from Chicago for Ted Lindsay and Glenn Hall
- traded June 9, 1959 with Frank Roggeveen to Toronto for Barry Cullen

LARRY WILSON #15 – 17 – 20 CENTRE 5′11″ 170 *b.* Kincardine, Ontario, October 23, 1930 *d.* Queensbury, New York, August 16, 1979

1949–50R	1	0	0	0	2
1951–52	5	0	0	0	4
1952–53	15	0	4	4	6
Totals	21	0	4	4	12

- first Red Wings game February 15, 1950
- played most of '49–'50 with Omaha and '50–'52 with Indianapolis
- sold August 12, 1953 with Lou Jankowski and Larry Zeidel to Chicago for cash

RICK WILSON #19 DEFENCE 6′1″ 195 *b.* Prince Albert, Saskatchewan, August 10, 1950

1976–77L	77	3	13	16	56

- acquired June 16, 1976 from St. Louis to complete Blues' acquiring Doug Grant (March 9, 1976)

- played '77–'78 with Philadelphia (AHL), then out of hockey
- last Red Wings game April 3, 1977

ROSS "LEFTY" WILSON #1 GOALIE 5′11″ 178
b. Toronto, Ontario, October 15, 1919

1953–54	1	0–0–0	20	0	0	0.00

- first and only Red Wings game October 10, 1953, playing 3rd period in place of injured Sawchuk

MURRAY WING #3 DEFENCE 5′11″ 180
b. Thunder Bay, Ontario, October 14, 1950

1973–74R/L	1	0	1	1	0

- acquired March 1, 1973 with Garnet "Ace" Bailey from Boston for Gary Doak
- first and only Red Wings game April 7, 1974
- played most of '73–'74 with London Lions (England)

EDDIE WISEMAN #8 – 9 – 17 RIGHT WING 5′7″ 160 *b.* Newcastle, New Brunswick, December 28, 1912 *d.* Unknown

1932–33R	47	8	8	16	16
1933–34	47	5	9	14	13
1934–35	40	11	13	24	14
1935–36	1	0	0	0	0
Totals	135	24	30	54	43

- played with the Olympics
- first Red Wings game November 10, 1932
- played November 12, 1935
- sold to Americans early in '35–'36 season

BENEDICT "BENNY" WOIT #3 – 5 – 22 DEFENCE 5′11″ 190 *b.* Fort William, Ontario, January 7, 1928

1950–51R	2	0	0	0	0
1951–52	58	3	8	11	20
1952–53	70	1	5	6	40
1953–54	70	0	2	2	38
1954–55	62	2	3	5	22
Totals	262	6	18	24	120

- St. Mike's graduate
- first Red Wings games February 10 & 11, 1951
- played most of '48–'51 with Indianapolis
- played two games in '50–'51 when Red Kelly injured
- traded June 3, 1955 with Tony Leswick, Glen Skov, and Johnny Wilson to Chicago for Gord Hollingworth, Jerry Toppazzini, John McCormack, and Dave Creighton

STEVE WOJCIECHOWSKI ("Wochy") #10 – 16 – 17 RIGHT WING 5′8″ 160 *b.* Fort William, Ontario, December 25, 1922

1944–45R	49	19	20	39	17
1946–47L	5	0	0	0	0
Totals	54	19	20	39	17

- played with Winnipeg Army
- first Red Wings game October 29, 1944
- played '45–'46 with Omaha and Indianapolis, most of '46–'47 with Indianapolis
- last Red Wings games October 16/19/23/26/27, 1946
- sold June 15, 1947 to Cleveland

MIKE WONG #19 – 22 CENTRE 6′3″ 205
b. Minneapolis, Minnesota, January 14, 1955

1975–76R/L	22	1	1	2	12

- selected 77th overall at 1975 Entry Draft
- first Red Wings game October 11, 1975
- played part of '75–'76 with Kalamazoo, '76–'77 with Rhode Island and Kalamazoo, then out of hockey

PAUL WOODS ("Woodsy") #15 LEFT WING 5′10″ 170 *b.* Hespeler, Ontario, April 12, 1955

1977–78R	80	19	23	42	52
1978–79	80	14	23	37	59
1979–80	79	6	20	26	24
1980–81	67	8	16	24	45
1981–82	75	10	17	27	48
1982–83	63	13	20	33	30
1983–84L	57	2	5	7	18
Totals	501	72	124	196	276

- claimed October 1977 from Canadiens in Waiver Draft
- first Red Wings game October 13, 1977
- played '84–'85 with Adirondack, then retired
- last Red Wings game March 28, 1984

LARRY WRIGHT #25 CENTRE 6′1″ 180 *b.* Regina, Saskatchewan, October 8, 1951

1977–78L	66	3	6	9	13

- signed October 22, 1977 as a free agent after playing '76–'77 in Germany
- played '78–'79 with Kansas City
- last Red Wings game April 6, 1978

JASON YORK #38 – 27 – 40 DEFENCE 6′1″ 192 *b.* Ottawa, Ontario, May 20, 1970

1992–93R	2	0	0	0	0
1993–94	7	1	2	3	2
Totals	9	1	2	3	2

- selected 129th overall in 1990 Entry Draft
- first Red Wings games December 3 & 5, 1992
- played February 16, March 23/29, April 3/5/9/10, 1994
- traded April 4, 1995 with Mike Sillinger to Anaheim for Mark Ferner, Stu Grimson, and a 6th-round draft choice in 1996 (Magnus Nilsson)

DOUG YOUNG ("The Gleichen Cowboy") #2 – 14 DEFENCE 5′9″ 190 *b.* Medicine Hat, Alberta, October 1, 1908 *d.* Unknown

1931–32R	47	10	2	12	45
1932–33	48	5	6	11	59
1933–34	48	4	0	4	36
1934–35	48	4	6	10	37
1935–36	48	5	12	17	54
1936–37	10	0	0	0	6
1937–38	48	3	5	8	24
1938–39	44	1	5	6	15
Totals	341	32	36	68	276

- signed prior to '31–'32 season
- first Falcons game November 12, 1931
- missed much of '36–'37 with a badly broken ankle suffered December 6
- sold October 18, 1939 to Pittsburgh

DOUG YOUNG GOALIE

1933–34	1	0–0–0	21	1	0	2.86

HOWIE YOUNG #2 – 4 – 20 – 22 DEFENCE 6′ 190 *b.* Toronto, Ontario, August 2, 1937

1960–61R	29	0	8	8	108
1961–62	30	0	2	2	67
1962–63	64	4	5	9	273
1966–67	44	3	14	17	100
1967–68	62	2	17	19	112
Totals	229	9	46	55	660

- played part of '60–'61 with Hershey, '61–'62 with Edmonton (WHL)
- first Red Wings game January 14, 1961
- traded June 5, 1963 to Chicago for Roger Crozier and Ron Ingram
- acquired December 20, 1966 from Chicago for future considerations (deal completed May 8, 1967 when Detroit sold Murray Hall and Albert LeBrun to the Blackhawks)
- traded May 27, 1968 with Gary Jarrett, Doug Roberts, and Chris Young to Oakland for Bob Baun and Ron Harris

WARREN YOUNG #35 CENTRE 6′3″ 195 *b.* Toronto, Ontario, January 11, 1956

1985–86L	79	22	24	46	161

- signed as a free agent July 10, 1985
- last Red Wings game April 6, 1986
- sold October 8, 1986 to Penguins for cash

PAUL YSEBAERT #21 CENTRE 6′1″ 190 *b.* Sarnia, Ontario, May 15, 1966

1990–91	51	15	18	33	16
1991–92	79	35	40	75	55
1992–93	80	34	28	62	42
Totals	210	84	86	170	113

- acquired November 27, 1990 from New Jersey for Lee Norwood and a 4th-round draft choice in 1992 (Scott McCabe)
- traded June 11, 1993 with future considerations (Alan Kerr — June 18, 1993) to Winnipeg for Aaron Ward and a 4th-round draft choice in 1993 (John Jakopin)

STEVE YZERMAN

STEVE YZERMAN ("Stevie Y"/"Stevie Wonderful") #19 CENTRE 5′11″ 183 *b.* Cranbrook, British Columbia, May 9, 1965

1983–84R	80	39	48	87	33
1984–85	80	30	59	89	58
1985–86	51	14	28	42	16
1986–87	80	31	59	90	43
1987–88	64	50	52	102	44
1988–89	80	65	90	155	61
1989–90	79	62	65	127	79
1990–91	80	51	57	108	34
1991–92	79	45	58	103	64
1992–93	84	58	79	137	44
1993–94	58	24	58	82	36
1994–95	47	12	26	38	40
1995–96	80	36	59	95	64
Totals	942	517	738	1255	616

- selected 4th overall at 1983 Entry Draft
- first Red Wings game October 5, 1983
- currently with Red Wings

LAZARUS "LARRY" ZEIDEL ("The Rock") #18 – 19 DEFENCE 5′11″ 185 *b.* Montreal, Quebec, June 1, 1928

1951–52R	19	1	0	1	14
1952–53	9	0	0	0	8
Totals	28	1	0	1	22

- first Red Wings game October 14, 1951
- played most of '51–'52 with Indianapolis, '52–'53 with Edmonton
- sold August 12, 1953 with Lou Jankowski and Larry Wilson to Chicago for cash

ED ZENIUK #18 DEFENCE 5′11″ 180 *b.* Landis, Saskatchewan, March 8, 1933

1954–55R/L	2	0	0	0	0

- career minor leaguer '53–'56
- first and only Red Wings games December 30 and January 9, 1954–55

RICK ZOMBO #4 – 11 – 23 DEFENCE 6′1″ 195 *b.* Des Plaines, Illinois, May 8, 1963

1984–85R	1	0	0	0	0
1985–86	14	0	1	1	16
1986–87	44	1	4	5	59
1987–88	62	3	14	17	96
1988–89	75	1	20	21	106
1989–90	77	5	20	25	95
1990–91	77	4	19	23	55
1991–92	3	0	0	0	15
Totals	353	14	78	92	442

- selected 149th overall at 1981 Entry Draft
- first Red Wings game March 10, 1985
- played October 3/5/10, 1991
- played much of '84–'87 with Adirondack
- traded October 18, 1991 to St. Louis for Vincent Riendeau

RALPH "RUDY" ZUNICH #20 DEFENCE *b.* Calumet, Michigan, November 24, 1910

1943–44R/L	2	0	0	0	2

- first and only Red Wings games October 31 & November 4, 1943

RED WINGS REGISTER BY BIRTHPLACE

Total number of players since 1926 778

FROM DETROIT 11

G. Abel, Blum, Burns, Cichoki, M. Howe, Luongo, Niekamp, Ramsey, Roberts, Rupp, Wetzel

BY COUNTRY

Canada 652

USA.................................. 61

E. Anderson, Babando, Bessone, Bissett, Bolduc, Boucha, Boyd, D. Brown, Brubaker, Bukovich, J. Carson, Crawford, Cummins, Dillon, Fielder, Friday, Ftorek, Goldsworthy, D. Hanson, E. Hanson, Ingarfield, Korn, Kumpel, Larson, Martinson, Mellor, K. Miller, Moffatt, Norwood, O'Connell, Pavese, Purpur, Richmond, Rowe, Ruelle, Schofield, Sheehan, Sherf, Short, Silk, Speers, Staszak, Taft, Tancill, Volmar, Voss, B. Williams, Wong, Zombo, Zunich

Sweden 9

T. Bergman, Djoos, Eriksson, Garpenlov, Holmstrom, Labraaten, Lidstrom, Lundstrom, Salming

Czechoslovakia 6

Cernik, Chalupa, Frycer, Ihnacak, Klima, Nedomansky

USSR 6

Bautin, Fedorov, Fetisov, Konstantinov, Kozlov, Larionov

Scotland 5

T. Anderson, Adam Brown, J. Conacher, B. Thomson, Whitelaw

England................................ 3

Beattie, F. Robertson, Alex Smith

Ireland 2

McFadden, Jack Riley

Denmark 1

Popiel

France 1

MacLean

Italy 1

Debenedet

Lebanon 1

Hatoum

Norway.................................. 1

Skaare

Poland 1

Miszuk

West Germany 1

Huber

Yugoslavia 1

Boldirev

Unknown 15

Bellefeuille, Briden, Connors, A. Cox, Creighton, Gagne, Gordon, Red Green, R. Hughes, Kitchen, Newman, Rockburn, Steele, Stuart, Traub

BY PROVINCE IN CANADA

Ontario 335

Saskatchewan 70

S. Abel, Aldcorn, K. Allen, Almas, D. Anderson, M. Armstrong, Ashton, G. Bailey, Baun, Berenson, Besler, Blaisdell, Carruthers, Carveth, Cheveldae, Couture, L. Davis, Deacon, Ehman, Federko, Fedyk, Ferner, D. Fisher, Folk, Francis, Franks, L. Giroux, Gloeckner, Habscheid, G. Hall, Hampson, Harper, H. Hart, J. Hay, Hogaboam, G. Howe, Jankowski, Kirton, Lambert, Leavins, Leswick, D. Lewis, Litzenberger, Lozinski, Lundy, Lynn, McCrimmon, Butch McDonald, McNab, Melrose, D. Morrison, R. Morrison, Motter, Pederson, Pettinger, Polonich, Prystai, E. Robertson, Sillinger, Sobchuk, Solinger,

Sutherland, Veitch, H. Watson, Wilder, D. Williams, F. Williams, R. Wilson, Wright, Zeniuk

Alberta 72
Achtymichuk, R. Anderson, Asmundson, Barkley, Bassen, Berry, Bladon, G. Brown, Bucyk, A. Cameron, C. Cameron, Carrigan, Craven, Dea, Diachuk, Eaves, Egan, Falkenberg, J. Fisher, Fonteyne, Gadsby, A. Giroux, H. Gray, Haley, Head, G. Hicks, Hilworth, C. Holmes, Houda, Joly, Joyal, Kisio, Kocur, Kotanen, Kruppke, Kryskow, M. Lamb, Lavender, H. Lewis, MacGregor, MacMillan, Marker, McGill, J. McKenzie, A. McLeod, B. McNeill, Melnyk, Merkosky, Millar, Mokosak, Nill, Osgood, Paul, Peterson, Pushor, D. Rochefort, Schamehorn, Shires, Shuchuk, G. Smith, Snepts, Solheim, Stasiuk, Strate, Ullman, Unger, Vernon, Walz, Wares, Weir, Wilkie, D. Young

Manitoba 46
Baldwin, Bathgate, Bowman, L. Brown, E. Brûneteau, M. Brûneteau, G. Carroll, Check, J. Daley, Eakin, Frederickson, Haidy, Halderson, Hanlon, E. Harris, G. Hart, B. Hextall, D. Hextall, Hodson, A. Johnson, D. Johnson, Johnstone, P. Kelly, S. Kennedy, Korney, Krentz, Leach, Loughlin, Low, A. McDonald, Mickoski, P. Miller, Newell, Podolsky, Reay, D. Richardson, Sawchuk, Sherritt, Starr, Stemkowski, B. Stewart, J. Stewart, Stratton, B. Taylor, Ted Taylor

Quebec 81
Aubry, Bergeron, Bergevin, Boileau, Boisvert, Bonin, Buller, Buswell, Champoux, Charron, Roland Cloutier, Connelly, Cude, Dandenault, B. Davis, DeJordy, Delorme, B. Dineen, Dion, Dionne, Dollas, Drôlet, Dube, Errey, Fontaine, Gardner, Gauthier, Gilbert, Gravelle, Hamel, R. Harris, D. Harvey, Hollingworth, Jarry, B. Johnson, Keats, Krushelnyski, Laforge, Lafrenière, Lajeunesse, Langlois, M. Lapointe, F. Leblanc, J.P. Leblanc, Leclerc, Legris, Lemieux, Maltais, Martin, McInenly, R. McKay, McKegney, McMahon, Micalef, J. Morrison, T. Murray, Orlando, Perreault, Peters, Sr., Peters, Jr., Picard, A. Pronovost, M. Pronovost, Racine, Reaume, Riendeau, Ritchie, L. Rochefort, A. St. Laurent, S. St. Laurent, Sauve, Shank, F. Sheppard, J. Sheppard, Sinclair, Derek Smith, Talbot, Vachon, J. Watson, Zeidel

British Columbia 25
G. Adams, Aivazoff, Drake, Gare, Grimson, Healey, J. Hiller, Holland, Karlander, Kerr, R. Lapointe, Lofthouse, Lunde, Lyle, Marshall, Martineau, McCarty, D. McLeod, Murdoch, T. Richardson, T. Robertson, Rouse, Sharples, C. Thompson, Yzerman

New Brunswick 10
Bowness, Danny Grant, B. Harvey, F. Kennedy, J. Lamb, McKim, McLenahan, Jim Riley, Rossignol, Wiseman

Nova Scotia 8
Amadio, Barry, Bourque, M. Davis, Hollett, L. MacDonald, P. MacDonald, Snow

Newfoundland 2
Faulkner, Doug Grant

Prince Edward Island 3
Chabot, Gallant, E. Thompson

BY CITY IN ONTARIO
(listed alphabetically)

Apsley 1
Arnie Brown

Aurora 1
H. Holmes

Bancroft 1
B. Watson

Barrie 4
Chiasson, Emms, Maloney, Monahan

Barry's Bay 1
Trader

Beaverton 2
B. McRae, C. McRae

Beeton 1
Rutherford

Belleville 3
Dillabough, J. Doran, Rick Green

Blackburn 1
H. Kilrea

Bolton 1
Duguid

Bourget 1
Matte

Bowmanville 1
B. Hughes

Bracebridge 2
Crozier, K. King

Brantford 5
G. Gray, Long, McGratton, Pusey, Stefan

Brockville 4
Ladouceur, Price, J. Simon, T. Simon

Brussels 1
McIntyre

Cache Bay 2
C. Smith, Dalton Smith

Cedar Springs 1
Jackson

Charletone 1
Thibeault
Chatham 1
D. Kelly
Chesterville 1
Sorrell
Cobalt 1
K. Douglas
Collingwood 4
Brophy, Bush, Herberts, Noble
Cookesville 1
Salovaara
Copper Cliff 1
Toppazzini
Cornwall 2
Chevrier, Cooper
Creighton Mine 1
Brian Smith
Downeyville 1
Lucas
Egmondville 1
Weiland
Elmira 1
Seiling
Falconbridge 1
McCourt
Fergus 1
Bucko McDonald
Forest 1
Lochead
Fort Erie 1
Brenneman
Fort Francis 2
E. Johnson, Sheehy
Fort William 11
Black, Delvecchio, Fogolin, Gatherum, Goegan, Marcon, B. Poile, D. Poile, G. Stewart, Woit, Wojciechowski,
Galt 1
Schoenfeld
Georgetown 1
Goldham
Geraldton 1
Elik
Goderich 1
Dewsbury, Doak
Guelph 4
H. Foster, MacLellan, Maltby, McCaig
Hagersville 1
Watts
Haileybury 1
Labine
Haliburton 1
Stackhouse
Hamilton 14
Bester, Andy Brown, Cushenan, Dunlop, Eliot, Holota, Jensen, Mann, McCann, McDonough, D. McKay, R. Murphy, Oliver, Rivers
Hespeler 2
Dolson, Woods
Hornepayne 1
McEwen
Kenora 2
B. Bailey, Olson
Kitchener 13
Behling, Gross, Herchenratter, D. Hiller, L. Johnson, Keating, Krulicki, Mackie, T. Miller, Reibel, Seibert, Sittler, Stankiewicz
Kemptville 1
D. Roche
Kenora 2
G. Bergman, Gallagher
Kincardine 4
Henderson, Riggin, J. Wilson, L. Wilson
Kingston 5
P. Dineen, Hendrickson, Patterson, Plumb, R. Smith
Kirkland Lake 4
M. Hall, Hillman, Redmond, Webster
Leamington 1
Manery
Lindsay 1
MacLeish
Little Current 1
D. Cox
Listowel 1
G. Hay
London 5
Campbell, Luce, B. Marsh, McKechnie, J. Murphy
Massey 1
Horeck
Matheson 1
McCord
Midland 1
Robitaille
Millbank 1
Nahrgang
Milton 1
McDuffe, Sclisizzi
Mimico 1
Shanahan
Minesing 1
Foyston
Mississauga 1
McDougall
New Liskeard 1
Mortson
New Toronto 1
Sandford

Niagara Falls 4
Foley, Manno, Mowers, Roberto
North Bay 3
S. Brown, Lalande, Palangio
Oshawa 3
Bathe, McClelland, Nowak
Ottawa 19
Barrett, Beveridge, Bloom, Collins, Connell, Barry Cullen, R. Cullen, S. Evans, Goodfellow, H. Hicks, Higgins, S. Howe, B. Kilrea, K. Kilrea, W. Kilrea, Licari, Loiselle, McCabe, Ogrodnick, Potvin, Snell, York
Owen Sound 5
Graham, Jones, Lumley, McCreavy, Reid
Palmerston 1
Ferguson
Parry Sound 1
F. Carson
Pembroke 4
Fraser, Raglan, R. Sheppard, Trottier
Perth 3
L. Douglas, Liscombe, F. Smith
Petawawa 1
Giesebrecht
Peterborough 2
Crossman, Morton
Pointe Anne 1
Hull
Port Arthur 4
F. Daley, Hrymnak, S. McNeill, Pyatt
Port Credit 1
Peer
Port Perry 1
Roach
Portsmouth 1
Nicholson
Prescott 2
Boivin, E. Roche
Preston 1
Sullivan
Renfrew 2
Brydge, Lindsay
Richmond Hill 1
Wall
St. Catharines 1
Vasko
St. Thomas 1
B. McKenzie
Sarnia 4
Burr, Ciccarelli, Haddon, Ysebaert
Sault Ste. Marie 6
Duncan, Grosso, Nolan, Pavelich, Ravelich, Vial
Scarborough 2
Konroyd, Kotsopoulos
Schumacher 1
Prentice
Seaforth 1
Mason
Seneca Township 1
Edwards
Silver Mountain 1
Walker
Simcoe 1
R. Kelly
Smiths Falls 3
Carkner, McAdam, McKenney
South Porcupine 2
Costello, L. Doran
Stittsville 1
Doraty
Stoney Creek 1
Reise
Stratford 6
Gee, Kane, Libett, McAtee, Monteith, Tim Taylor
Sudbury 10
A. Arbour, Aurie, Burton, Cook, Croteau, Crowder, Duguay, Foligno, Giacomin, Spencer
Sundridge 1
McCreary
Thamesford 1
Filmore
Thorold 2
Guidolin, Speck
Thunder Bay 4
Gruen, G. Johnson, S. King, Wing
Tilsonburg 1
Oatman
Timmins 7
Chevrefils, Hudson, F. Mahovlich, P. Mahovlich, Menard, Rolfe, Vail
Toronto 52
Barr, Bennett, Brewer, B. Carroll, Coates, B. Conacher, C. Conacher, R. Conacher, Corcoran, Crashley, Draper, Ecclestone, Essensa, C. Evans, D. Foster, Gage, F. Glover, H. Glover, Godfrey, Graves, Halkidis, Halward, B. Harris, Ing, Ingram, Jarrett, Jennings, Lawson, Lynch, MacKay, G. Marsh, McCarthy, McCutcheon, Millen, Mitchell, Moore, Muloin, B. Murphy, K. Murray, Osborne, Park, Paterson, Pirus, Primeau, B. Quackenbush, Roulston, Simpson, Al Smith, N. Smith, R. Wilson, H. Young, W. Young
Trenton 1
Bridgman
Trout Creek 1
Odrowski
Van Kleek Hill 1
C. Brown

Wabushene 1
J. Arbour
Wallaceburg. 1
Shedden
Waterloo 1
Martin
Welland 1
Laforest
Weston. 2
Coffey, Oates
Wheatley 1
Skov
Windsor 9
Rejean Cloutier, Drouillard, Gagner, Mio, Probert, Brad Smith, Teno, Turner, Ward
Zurich 1
Jeffrey

RED WINGS BY NUMBERS

1

Red Almas, Hank Bassen, Bill Beveridge, Gilles Boisvert, Claude Bourque, Alex Connell, Abbie Cox, Roger Crozier, Wilf Cude, Joe Daley, Connie Dion, Dolly Dolson, Roy Edwards, Jim Franks, Dave Gatherum, Gilles Gilbert, Glenn Hall, Glen Hanlon, Harry Holmes, Harry Lumley, Bill McKenzie, Don McLeod, Corrado Micalef, Alfie Moore, John Mowers, Bob Perreault, Terry Richardson, Dennis Riggin, John Ross Roach, Earl Robertson, Jim Rutherford, Terry Sawchuk, Norm Smith, Harvey Teno, Cecil Thompson, Joe Turner, Lefty Wilson

2

Al Arbour, John Barrett, Dick Behling, Gary Bergman, Terry Carkner, Dwight Carruthers, Gerry Couture, Viacheslav Fetisov, John Gallagher, Warren Godfrey, Pete Goegan, Bob Goldham, Terry Harper, Jack Hendrickson, Larry Hillman, Ron Ingram, Buck Jones, Mike Korney, Al Langlois, Barry Long, Clem Loughlin, Bob McCord, Brad McCrimmon, Al McLeod, Barry Melrose, Jim Morrison, Mike O'Connell, Noel Price, Harvey Rockburn, Rolly Roulston, Jim Schoenfeld, Cully Simon, Alex Smith, Rick Smith, Jack Stewart, Larry Trader, Percy Traub, Jim Watson, Burr Williams, Doug Young, Howie Young

3

Murray Armstrong, John Barrett, Pete Bellefeuille, Gary Bergman, Scotty Bowman, Steve Chiasson, Don Deacon, Stu Evans, Bob Falkenberg, John Gallagher, Larry Giroux, Warren Godfrey, Ted Graham, Slim Halderson, Emil Hanson, Gerry Hart, Larry Johnston, Buck Jones, Ken Kilrea, Jack Lynch, Vic Lynn, Bert Marshall, Clare Martin, Bob McCord, Bucko McDonald, Perry Miller, Bill Mitchell, Alex Motter, Jim Nahrgang, Jim Niekamp, Reg Noble, Paul Popiel, Marcel Pronovost, Bill Quackenbush, Dale Rolfe, Bob Rouse, Gord Sherritt, Jack Stewart, Jean-Guy Talbot, Rick Vasco, Carl Voss, Jim Watson, Murray Wing, Ben Woit

4

Sid Abel, Bob Baun, Thommie Bergman, Tom Bladon, Leo Boivin, Archie Briden, Arnie Brown, Larry Brown, Colin Campbell, Rejean Cloutier, Bart Crashley, Al Dewsbury, Tim Friday, Bill Gadsby, Gus Giesebrecht, Larry Giroux, Ron Harris, George Hay, John Hilworth, Mark Howe, Hal Jackson, Red Kelly, Rick Lapointe, Jim Leavins, Herb Lewis, Doug McCaig, Jim McFadden, Bob McGill, Harry Meeking, Terry Murray, Jimmy Orlando, Jamie Pushor, Marc Reaume, Jeff Sharples, John Sorrell, Rick Vasco, Bob Wall, Howie Young, Rick Zombo

5

Al Arbour, Doug Barkley, Dick Behling, Pete Bessone, Carl Brewer, Bill Brydge, Eddie Bush Doug McCaig, Bob Connors, Al Dewsbury, Peter Dineen, Marcel Dionne, John Doran, Kent Douglas, Pat Egan, Bob Falkenberg, Gord Fraser, Frank Frederickson, Warren Godfrey, Ebbie Goodfellow, Rick Green, Jean Hamel, Doug Harvey, Rich Healey, Flash Hollett, Hal Jackson, Buck Jones, Duke Keats, Serge Lajeunesse, Nicklas Lidstrom, Bert Marshall, Chris McRae, Hugh Millar, John Miszuk, John Mokosak, Dean Morton, Jimmy Orlando, Leo Reise, Greg Smith, Darren Veitch, Bob Wall, Ben Woit

6

Larry Aurie, Cummy Burton, Jack Walker

7

Sid Abel, Marty Barry, Red Berenson, Tom Bissett, Stan Brown, Milan Chalupa, Billy Dea, Don Deacon, Brent Fedyk, Art Gagne, Leroy Goldsworthy, Doug Halward, George Hay, Jim Herberts, Willie Huber, Ed Johnstone, Brian Kilrea, Hec Kilrea, Ken Kilrea, Dave Kryskow, Hec Lalande, Herb Lewis, Ted Lindsay, Carl Liscombe, Dan Maloney, Mike McEwen, Tony McKegney, Alex Motter, Russ Oatman, Murray Oliver, Pete Palangio, Joe Paterson, Robert Picard, Steve Richmond, Billy Taylor, Norm Ullman, Garry Unger, Carl Voss, Cooney Weiland

8

Guy Charron, Rene Leclerc, Carson Cooper, Danny Cox, Bart Crashley, Barry Cullen, Don Deacon, Bobby Dollas, Art Duncan, Stu Evans, Val Fonteyne, Harry Foster, George Gee, Syd Howe, Gary Jarrett,

Danny Johnson, Forbes Kennedy, Steve Konroyd, Gord Kruppke, Leo Labine, Claude Laforge, Mark Lamb, Igor Larionov, Tony Leswick, Claude Loiselle, Pat Lundy, Lowell MacDonald, Pit Martin, Rick McCann, Brian McCutcheon, Jim Nill, Ted Nolan, Murray Oliver, Joe Paterson, Dennis Polonich, Cliff Purpur, Billy Reay, Dutch Reibel, Tom Rowe, Dave Silk, Floyd Smith, Ted Snell, Fred Speck, Ray Staszak, Art Stratton, Bill Sutherland, Aaron Ward, Tom Webster, Johnny Wilson, Eddie Wiseman

9

Sid Abel, Tom Anderson, Ossie Asmundson, Connie Brown, Ed Brûneteau, Mud Brûneteau, Frank Carson, Roy Conacher, Harold Hicks, Gordie Howe, Pete Kelly, Wally Kilrea, Joe Lamb, Herb Lewis, Roland Matte, Bert McInenly, Johnny Sheppard, John Sherf, John Sorrell, Billy Thomson, Eddie Wiseman

10

Gerry Brown, Ed Brûneteau, Jimmy Carson, Bob Connors, Carson Cooper, Gerry Couture, Alex Delvecchio, Clarence Drouillard, Ron Duguay, Frank Foyston, Fern Gauthier, Ebbie Goodfellow, Don Grosso, Bill Jennings, Carl Liscombe, Mark Lofthouse, Claude Loiselle, Dale McCourt, Max McNab, Joe Murphy, Jim Peters, Metro Prystai, Cliff Purpur, Billy Reay, Frank Sheppard, John Sorrell, Steve Wojciechowski

11

Gerry Abel, Sid Abel, Gary Aldcorn, Red Beattie, Scotty Bowman, Rick Bowness, Bernie Brophy, Adam Brown, Shawn Burr, Murray Craven, Gary Croteau, Mathieu Dandenault, Bob Dillabough, Ken Doraty, Blake Dunlop, Hap Emms, Chris Evans, Tom Filmore, Len Fontaine, Val Fonteyne, Art Gagne, Lorry Gloeckner, Warren Godfrey, Jim Herberts, Pete Horeck, Wally Kilrea, Hobie Kitchen, Brian Lavender, Don Luce, Lowell MacDonald, John MacMillan, Pete Mahovlich, Jud McAtee, Byron McDonald, Walt McKechnie, Max McNab, Nick Mickoski, Gary Monahan, Hank Monteith, Hank Nowak, Marty Pavelich, Jim Peters, Jr., Gord Pettinger, Jim Riley, Earl Roche, Leon Rochefort, Brad Smith, Ted Speers, Irv Spencer, Vic Stasiuk, Frank Steele, Gaye Stewart, Barry Sullivan, John Taft, Billy Thomson, Eddie Wares, Jim Watson, Johnny Wilson, Rick Zombo

12

Sid Abel, Gene Achtymichuk, Larry Aurie, Garnet Bailey, Pete Bellefeuille, Ivan Boldirev, Henry Boucha, Walt Buswell, Billy Carroll, Jimmy Carson, Joe Carveth, Bob Cook, Bob Dillabough, Bill Dineen, Marcel Dionne, Bob Errey, Alex Faulkner, Dunc Fisher, Val Fonteyne, Fred Gordon, Adam Graves, Red Green, Dan Gruen, Jim Herberts, Bryan Hextall, Chuck Holmes, Sheldon Kennedy, Hec Kilrea, Fern Leblanc, J.P. Leblanc, Tony Leswick, Bruce MacGregor, John MacMillan, Randy Manery, Pit Martin, Stan McCabe, Ab McDonald, Byron McDonald, Stu McNeill, Howie Menard, Tom Miller, Ron Murphy, Brent Peterson, Metro Prystai, Tom Rowe, Ed Sandford, Mike Sillinger, Glen Skov, John Sorrell, Errol Thompson

13

Harold Hart, Vyacheslav Kozlov

14

Sid Abel, Brent Ashton, Pete Babando, Mike Blaisdell, Gerry Brown, Mud Brûneteau, Craig Cameron, Joe Carveth, Real Chevrefils, Frank Daley, Mal Davis, Lorne Duguid, Stu Evans, Brent Fedyk, Lorne Ferguson, Joe Fisher, Miroslav Frycer, Gus Giesebrecht, Lloyd Gross, Bep Guidolin, Murray Hall, Billy Harris, Jim Hiller, Rusty Hughes, Larry Jeffrey, Bill Jennings, Ken Kilrea, Claude Laforge, Lane Lambert, Real Lemieux, Nick Libett, Ted Lindsay, Ed Litzenberger, Len Lunde, Parker MacDonald, Hal Mackie, Gus Marker, Gary Marsh, Stan McCabe, Jack McIntyre, Randy McKay, Andrew McKim, Billy McNeill, Gerry Melnyk, Alex Motter, Don Murdoch, Butch Paul, Alex Pirus, Bud Poile, Metro Prystai, Dutch Reibel, Doug Roberts, Fred Robertson, Torrie Robertson, Desse Roche, Bernie Ruelle, Brendan Shanahan, Doug Shedden, Reg Sinclair, Glen Skov, Dennis Sobchuk, Wilf Starr, Herb Stuart, Percy Traub, Stan Weir, Doug Young

15

Ron Anderson, Jack Arbour, Pete Bellefeuille, Frank Bennett, Phil Besler, Mel Bridgman, Connie Brown, Ed Brûneteau, Eddie Bush, Gene Carrigan, Lude Check, Chris Cichocki, Bart Crashley, Jim Creighton, Ray Cullen, Lorne Davis, Billy Dea, Don Deacon, Alex Delvecchio, Clarence Drouillard, Brent Fedyk, Robbie Ftorek, Johan Garpenlov, Fern Gauthier, Howie Glover, Lloyd Gross, Galen Head, Larry Hillman, Bill Hogaboam, Chuck Holmes, Tomas Holmstrom, Ron Hudson, Gary Jarrett, Al Johnson, Buck Jones, Al Karlander, Jack Keating, Pete Kelly, Sheldon Kennedy, Hec Kilrea, Ken Kilrea, Rene Leclerc, Ted Lindsay, Carl Liscombe, Claude Loiselle, Paul MacLean, Gus Marker, Pit Martin, Roland Matte, Jack McIntyre, Billy McNeill, Ron Moffatt, Hank Monteith, John Newman, Dennis Olson, Paddy Patterson,

Marty Pavelich, Gord Pettinger, Nelson Podolsky, Don Poile, Andre Pronovost, Metro Prystai, Bill Quackenbush, Mike Ramsey, Billy Reay, Wayne Rivers, Enio Sclisizzi, Frank Sheppard, John Sherf, Cully Simon, Dalton Smith, Sandy Snow, Fred Speck, Irv Spencer, Wilf Starr, Larry Thibeault, Dave Trottier, Brian Watts, Archie Wilder, Fred Williams, Larry Wilson, Paul Woods

16

Earl Anderson, Dick Behling, Michel Bergeron, Henry Boucha, Scott Bowman, Yank Boyd, Adam Brown, Connie Brown, John Chabot, Rejean Cloutier, Gerry Couture, Ed Diachuk, Lloyd Doran, Les Douglas, Joe Fisher, Harry Foster, Bobby Francis, Jody Gage, John Gallagher, Fred Glover, Leroy Goldsworthy, Ted Hampson, Emil Hanson, Ron Harris, Jack Hendrickson, Harold Hicks, Bill Jennings, Buck Jones, Mark Kirton, Kelly Kisio, Vladimir Konstantinov, Claude Laforge, Bruce MacGregor, Calum MacKay, Gus Marker, Jim McFadden, Jake McIntyre, Ron Moffatt, Jimmy Orlando, Bill Quackenbush, Rollie Rossignol, Rollie Roulston, Enio Sclisizzi, Ric Seiling, Brian Smith, Andre St. Laurent, Wilf Starr, Jack Stewart, Norm Ullman, Garry Unger, Carl Voss, Bob Wall, Tom Webster, Johnny Wilson, Steve Wojciechowski

17

Red Almas, Pete Bessone, Marcel Bonin, Doug Brown, Mud Brûneteau, Tony Bukovich, Hy Buller, Gene Carrigan, Joe Carveth, Steve Coates, Charlie Conacher, Wayne Connelly, Bob Crawford, Don Deacon, Alex Delvecchio, Cecil Dillon, Bill Dineen, John Doran, Ken Doraty, Tim Ecclestone, Bo Elik, Joe Fisher, Mike Foligno, Frank Frederickson, Jody Gage, John Gallagher, Gerard Gallant, Art Giroux, Fred Glover, Leroy Goldsworthy, Ted Hampson, Dave Hanson, Gordie Howe, Ron Hudson, Pierre Jarry, Al Johnson, Ed Johnstone, Frank Kane, Forbes Kennedy, Ken Kilrea, Wally Kilrea, Claude Laforge, Roger Lafrenière, Carl Liscombe, Mark Lofthouse, Pat Lundy, Hal Mackie, Ken Mann, Jud McAtee, Doug McCaig, Al McDonough, Ron Moffatt, Don Morrison, Brian Murphy, Murray Oliver, Jimmy Orlando, Bert Peer, Rob Plumb, Metro Prystai, Earl Seibert, Bobby Sheehan, John Sherf, Brad Smith, Floyd Smith, John Sorrell, Billy Thompson, Harry Watson, Bob Whitelaw, Burr Williams, Johnny Wilson, Larry Wilson, Eddie Wiseman, Steve Wojciechowski

18

Keith Allen, Dale Anderson, Al Arbour, Doug Baldwin, Gary Bergman, Connie Brown, Gerry Brown, Ed Brûneteau, Hy Buller, Jim Conacher, Gerry Couture, Ian Cushenan, Bob Davis, Mal Davis, Bill Folk, Len Fontaine, Danny Gare, Warren Godfrey, Pete Goegan, Don Grosso, Lloyd Haddon, Ron Harris, Gerry Hart, Ed Hatoum, Jim Hay, Dutch Hiller, Bucky Hollingworth, John Holota, Les Douglas, Pete Kelly, Alan Kerr, Kris King, Mike Krushelnyski, Mark Kumpel, Brian Lavender, Dan Lawson, Fern Leblanc, J.P. Leblanc, Dave Lucas, George Lyle, Kirk Maltby, Charlie Mason, Jud McAtee, Doug McCaig, Rick McCann, Kevin McClelland, Pat McCreavy, Basil McRae, John Miszuk, Ron Moffatt, Jim Morrison, Gus Mortson, Gerry Odrowski, John Ogrodnick, Mark Pederson, Rob Plumb, Marcel Pronovost, Matt Ravlich, Dale Rolfe, Rollie Rossignol, Rollie Roulston, Bernie Ruelle, Kevin Schamehorn, John Sherf, Blair Stewart, Jack Stewart, Gord Strate, Bill Sutherland, Chris Tancill, Ted Taylor, Bryan Watson, Bryan Watson, Jim Watson, Cully Wilson, Larry Zeidel, Ed Zeniuk

19

Sid Abel, Keith Allen, Dave Amadio, Steve Black, John Blum, Marc Boileau, Ivan Boldirev, Dan Bolduc, Roland Cloutier, Murray Costello, Mal Davis, Bob Dillabough, Gary Doak, Les Douglas, Gerry Ehman, Rick Foley, Bill Folk, Val Fonteyne, Gus Giesebrecht, Pete Goegan, Jean Hamel, Ted Harris, Paul Henderson, Art Herchenratter, John Hilworth, Bucky Hollingworth, Steve Hrymnak, Ron Hudson, Dennis Hull, Hal Jackson, Lou Jankowski, Mike Korney, Jim Krulicki, Randy Ladouceur, Tony Licari, Parker MacDonald, John MacMillan, Lou Marcon, Gary McAdam, Tom McCarthy, Max McNab, Billy McNeill, Hugh Millar, Hank Monteith, Wayne Muloin, Marty Pavelich, Don Poile, Barry Salovaara, Cliff Simpson, Brian Smith, Vic Stasiuk, Pete Stemkowski, Jack Stewart, Gord Strate, Jerry Toppazzini, Eric Vail, Doug Volmar, Bob Wall, Harry Watson, Rick Wilson, Mike Wong, Steve Yzerman, Larry Zeidel

20

Sid Abel, Bob Bailey, Marcel Bonin, Johnny Bucyk, Tony Bukovich, Greg C. Adams, Gerry Couture, Dwight Foster, Leo Gravelle, Gord Haidy, Murray Hall, Ed Hatoum, Jim Hay, Tim Higgins, Jack Keating, Red Kelly, Martin Lapointe, Len Lunde, Parker MacDonald, Brad Marsh, Don Martineau, Bill McCreary, Don McKenney, Max McNab, John Mowers, Vaclav Nedomansky, Jim Niekamp, Jim Peters, Don Poile, Marc Potvin, Dean Prentice, Mickey Redmond, Dwight Schofield, Enio Sclisizzi, Glen Skov, Bob Solinger, Bob Whitelaw, Larry Wilson, Howie Young, Rudy Zunich

21

Bob Bailey, Andy Bathgate, Mike Blaisdell, John Brenneman, Charlie Burns, Cummy Burton, Frank Cernik, Roland Cloutier, Norm Corcoran, Billy Dea, Al Dewsbury, Bill Dineen, Gilles Dube, Bob Errey, Mark Ferner, Guyle Fielder, Lee Fogolin, Val Fonteyne, Jody Gage, Warren Godfrey, Danny Grant, Bob Halkidis, Ted Hampson, Gerry Hart, Jack Hendrickson, Bucky Hollingworth, Earl Ingarfield, Larry Jeffrey, Earl Johnson, Ed Joyal, Pete Kelly, Ken Kilrea, Dan Labraaten, Claude Laforge, Serge Lajeunesse, J.P. Leblanc, Claude Loiselle, Jack Lynch, Pete Mahovlich, Lou Marcon, Doug McCaig, Tom McCarthy, John McKenzie, Rollie McLenahan, Mike McMahon, Billy McNeill, Gerry Melnyk, Rod Morrison, Adam Oates, Jim Peters Jr., Andre Pronovost, Marcel Pronovost, Dave Richardson, Mike Robitaille, Borje Salming, Enio Sclisizzi, Thain Simon, Brad Smith, Carl Smith, Irv Spencer, Ron Stackhouse, Ed Stankiewicz, Gord Strate, Jim Watson, Paul Ysebaert

22

Ron Anderson, Dave Barr, Ed Brûneteau, Hy Buller, Bob Champoux, Dino Ciccarelli, Bill Collins, Murray Craven, Roger Crozier, Don Deacon, Al Dewsbury, Bob Dillabough, Les Douglas, Bob Falkenberg, Larry Giroux, Fred Glover, Pete Goegan, Harrison Gray, Len Haley, Glenn Hall, Paul Henderson, Dennis Hextall, Glenn Hicks, Bill Hogaboam, Doug Houda, Greg Joly, Martin Lapointe, Dan Lawson, Nick Libett, Doug McCaig, Rick McCann, Ab McDonald, Stu McNeill, Glenn Merkosky, Gerry Odrowski, Brad Park, Butch Paul, Dennis Polonich, Marcel Pronovost, Nelson Pyatt, Clare Raglan, Pat Rupp, Vic Stasiuk, Blair Stewart, Carl Wetzel, Ben Woit, Mike Wong, Howie Young

23

Gary Bergman, Guy Charron, Roland Cloutier, Nelson Debenedet, Robbie Ftorek, Warren Godfrey, Pete Goegan, Dan Gruen, Glenn Hicks, Bill Hogaboam, Greg Johnson, Mark Kirton, Bill Lochead, Tord Lundstrom, Rick MacLeish, Bob Manno, Basil McRae, Kevin Miller, Rick Newell, Ed Nicholson, Lee Norwood, Mark Osborne, Marcel Pronovost, Nelson Pyatt, Dave Rochefort, Enio Sclisizzi, Jim Shires, Mike Sillinger, Pete Stemkowski, Doug Volmar, Bob Wall, Johnny Wilson, Rick Zombo

24

Pierre Aubry, Frank Bathe, Leo Boivin, Brian Conacher, Bart Crashley, Murray Craven, Al Dewsbury, Bob Dillabough, Gary Doak, Rene Drôlet, Fred Glover, Brent Hughes, Brian Johnson, Greg Joly, Calum MacKay, Pete Mahovlich, Randy Manery, Rick McCann, Bob McCord, Tom Mellor, Ken Murray, Jim Nahrgang, Bob Probert, Gerry Reid, Derek Smith, Larry Trader, Jim Watson

25

Hank Bassen, Mike Bloom, Greg Carroll, Troy Crowder, Gilles Dube, Lee Fogolin, George Gardner, Fern Gauthier, Warren Godfrey, Tom Gratton, Don Grosso, Marc Habscheid, Murray Hall, Dave Kelly, Serge Lajeunesse, Dave Lewis, Darren McCarty, Bob McCord, Randy McKay, Tom Mellor, Rick Newell, John Ogrodnick, Jim Pavese, Jim Peters, Sr., Jim Peters, Jr., Doug Roberts, Kevin Schamehorn, Cliff Simpson, Bjorn Skaare, Ed Stankiewicz, Blair Stewart, Larry Wright

26

Al Cameron, Joey Kocur, Jim Korn, Barry Melrose, Nelson Pyatt, Doug Roberts, Ray Sheppard, Steve Short, Ken Solheim, Larry Trader, Wes Walz

27

Micah Aivazoff, Pierre Aubry, Marc Bergevin, Jim Cummins, Dennis DeJordy, Mark Ferner, Buster Harvey, Doug Houda, Reg Leach, Brian MacLellan, Frank Mahovlich, Brian McCutcheon, Doug McKay, Max McNab, Brent Peterson, Bob Ritchie, Phil Roberto, Jim Rutherford, Darryl Sittler, Brad Smith, Harold Snepsts, Doug Volmar, Jason York

28

Dallas Drake, Brent Fedyk, Sheldon Kennedy, Dale Krentz, Reed Larson, Barry Salovaara, Bob Wilkie

29

Sergei Bautin, Fred Berry, Doug Crossman, Gilbert Delorme, John Hilworth, Chris Kotsopoulos, Randy Ladouceur, Don Martineau, Brian McCutcheon, Randy McKay, Ted Nolan, Joe Paterson, Jim Rutherford, Terry Sawchuk, Tim Sheehy, Greg Stefan, Mike Vernon, Dennis Vial, Aaron Ward

30

Hank Bassen, Roger Crozier, Denis DeJordy, Roy Edwards, George Gardner, Gilles Gilbert, Doug Grant, Gerry Gray, Ron Low, Pete McDuffe, Bill McKenzie, Don McLeod, Corrado Micalef, Chris Osgood, Terry Richardson, Jim Rutherford, Al Smith, Greg Stefan, Rogie Vachon

31

Andy Brown, Tim Cheveldae, Alain Chevrier, Darren Eliot, Ed Giacomin, Doug Grant, Kevin Hodson, Peter Ing, Al Jensen, Scott King, Mark Laforest, Claude Legris, Pete Lozinski, Corrado Micalef, Chris Pusey, Bob Sauve

32
Tim Cheveldae, Bruce Eakin, Stu Grimson, Jeff Sharples, Sam St. Laurent

33
Brent Ashton, John Blum, Chris Draper, Doug Houda, Bob Manno, Yves Racine

34
Ed Johnstone, Steve Maltais, Greg Millen, Adam Oates, Daniel Shank, Jeff Sharples, Andre St. Laurent, Sam St. Laurent

35
Allan Bester, Gilbert Delorme, Bob Essensa, Dave Gagnon, Ken Holland, Miroslav Ihnacak, Sam St. Laurent, Warren Young

36
Per Djoos, Steve Martinson, Dennis Vial

37
Kris King, Chris Luongo, John Mokosak, Vincent Riendeau, Tim Taylor

38
Jeff Brubaker, Bobby Dollas, Murray Eaves, Scott King, Tim Taylor, Jason York

39
Doug Crossman, Brent Fedyk, Dale Krentz

40
Gord Kruppke, Rogie Vachon, Jason York

41
Ed Mio

42
Bernie Federko

43
Murray Eaves, Bill McDougall

44
Viacheslav Fetisov, Gord Kruppke, Glenn Merkosky

46
Marc Potvin

47
Jim Cummins

48
Gary Shuchuk, Chris Tancill

52
Dave Lewis

55
Keith Primeau, Tiger Williams

72
Brad Smith

77
Paul Coffey

85
Petr Klima

91
Sergei Fedorov

UNKNOWN
Jack Riley

HOW THEY HOLD THE STICK

PLAYERS WHO SHOOT LEFT

G. Abel, S. Abel, Achtymichuk, G. Adams, Aivazoff, Aldcorn, Allen, D. Anderson, T. Anderson, A. Arbour, Armstrong, Ashton, Aubry, Aurie, Babando, G. Bailey, Baldwin, Barrett, Barry, Bathe, Bautin, Beattie, Berenson, Bergevin, G. Bergman, T. Bergman, Berry, Bessone, Bissett, Black, Bloom, Boileau, Boivin, Boldirev, Bolduc, Bonin, Bowman, Brewer, Bridgman, Adam Brown, Andy Brown, Arnie Brown, G. Brown, L. Brown, P. Brown, S. Brown, Brubaker, Bucyk, Bukovich, Buller, Burns, Burr, Buswell, Cameron, Campbell, Carkner, Carrigan, B. Carroll, C. Carroll, Chabot, Charron, Check, Chevrefils, Chiasson, Rejean Cloutier, Roland Cloutier, Coffey, B. Conacher, J. Conacher, R. Conacher, D. Cox, Craven, Crossman, Croteau, Cushenan, M. Davis, Dea, Deacon, Debenedet, Delvecchio, Dewsbury, Diachuk, Dillabough, Dillon, Djoos, Dollas, J. Doran, L. Doran, K. Douglas, L. Douglas, Drake, Draper, Drouillard, Dube, Eakin, Elik, Emms, Eriksson, Errey, C. Evans, S. Evans, Falkenberg, Faulkner, Federko, Fedorov, Ferguson, Ferner, Fetisov, Fielder, Fogolin, Foley, Folk, Fonteyne, Foster, Foyston, Frederckson, Ftorek, Gadsby, Gallagher, Gallant, Garpenlov, Gee, Giesebrecht, Gloeckner, Godfrey, Goegan, Goldsworthy, Goodfellow, Graham, Danny Grant, Graves, Rick Green, Grimson, Gross, Grosso, Gruen, Guidolin, Haddon, Halkidis, Halward, Hamel, Hampson, D. Hanson, E. Hanson, B. Harris, E. Harris, Gerry Hart, D. Harvey, Hay, Healey, Herchenratter, B. Hextall, D. Hextall, G. Hicks, D. Hiller, Hillman, Hollett, Hollingworth, Holmstrom, Holota, Horeck, M. Howe, S. Howe, Hrymnak, B. Hughes, D. Hull, M. Ihnacak, Ingarfield, Jarrett, Jarry, Jeffrey, D. Johnson, E. Johnson, G. Johnson, Joly, Joyal, Kane, Karlander, Keating, R. Kelly, Kennedy, H. Kilrea, K. Kilrea, K. King, Kirton, Kisio, Klima, Konroyd, Korn, Kozlov, Krentz, Krulicki, Krushelnyski, Kryskow, Ladouceur, Laforge, Lafrenière, Lalande, M. Lamb, Langlois, R. Lapointe, Larionov, Lavender, Leavins, F. Leblanc, J.P. Leblanc, Lemieux, D. Lewis, H. Lewis, Libett, Lidstrom, Lindsay, Liscombe, Loiselle, Long, Lucas, Luce, Lundstrom, Lyle, Lynn, P. MacDonald, MacKay, MacLeish, MacLellan, MacMillan, F. Mahovlich, P. Mahovlich, Maloney, Maltais, Manno, B. Marsh, G. Marsh, Marshall, Martinson, MacAdam, McAtee, McCann, McCarthy, McCreary, McCrimmon, McCutcheon, A. McDonald, B. McDonald, W. McDonald, McEwen, McFadden, McInenly, McIntyre, A. McKay, McKechnie, McKegney, McKenney, McLenahan, A. McLeod, McMahon, McNab, B. McRae, C. McRae, Merkosky, Mickoski, Millar, P. Miller, T. Miller, Miszuk, Mokosak, Monahan, Monteith, J. Morrison, Mortson, Motter, Muloin, B. Murphy, J. Murphy, R. Murphy, Nedomansky, Newell, Nicholson, Noble, Nolan, Norwood, Nowak, Oatman, Odrowski, Ogrodnick, Oliver, Orlando, Osborne, Palangio, Park, Paterson, Pavelich, Pavese, Peterson, Peters, Jr., Pettinger, Picard, Plumb, Podolsky, Poile, Popiel, Prentice, Price, Primeau, Probert, A. Pronovost, M. Pronovost, Prystai, Pyatt, B. Quackenbsh, Racine, Raglan, Ramsey, Ravlich, Reaume, Reay, Reise, D. Richardson, Richmond, Jack Riley, Jim Riley, Ritchie, Roberts, F. Robertson, T. Robertson, E. Roche, Rochefort, Rolfe, Roulston, Ruelle, Salming, Schoenfeld, Schofield, Sclisizzi, Sharples, Sheehan, F. Sheppard, J. Sheppard, Sherf, Sherritt, Shires, Short, C. Simon, T. Simon, Sittler, Skaare, Skov, Alex Smith, Brian Smith, Dalton Smith, Derek Smith, G. Smith, R. Smith, Snepsts, Sobchuk, Solheim, Solinger, Sorrell, Speck, Spencer, Starr, Stasiuk, Stemkowski, B. Stewart, G. Stewart, J. Stewart, Strate, Stratton, Sutherland, Taft, Talbot, Tancill, Ted Taylor, Tim Taylor, Thibeault, Thompson, Trader, Ullman, Unger, Vail, Vasko, Vial, Voss, J. Walker, Wall, H. Watson, J. Watson, Watts, Weiland, Weir, Whitelaw, Wilder, F. Williams, T. Williams, J. Wilson, L. Wilson, Rick Wilson, Wong, Woods, Wright, Young, Ysebaert, Zeidel, Zeniuk

Hec Kilrea

PLAYERS WHO SHOOT RIGHT

Amadio, E. Anderson, R. Anderson, Asmundson, Aurie, B. Bailey, Barkley, Barr, Bathgate, Baun, Behling, Bergeron, Besler, Bladon, Blaisdell, Blum, Boucha, Bowness, Boyd, D. Brown, E. Brûneteau, M. Brûneteau, Burton, Bush, C. Cameron, Carruthers, F. Carson, J. Carson, Carveth, Cernik, Chalupa, Ciccarelli, Cichocki, Coates, Collins, C. Conacher, Connelly, Cook, Cooper, Corcoran, Costello, Couture, Crashley, Crawford, Crowder, B. Cullen, R. Cullen, Cummins, Dandenault, L. Davis, Delorme, B. Dineen, P. Dineen, Dionne, Doak, Doraty, Drôlet, Duguay, Duncan, Dunlop, Eaves, Ecclestone, Egan, Ehman, Fedyk, Filmore, D. Fisher, J. Fisher, Foligno, Fontaine, D. Foster, Francis, Friday, Frycer, Gage, Gagne, Gare, Gauthier, A. Giroux, L. Giroux, F. Glover, H. Glover, Goldham, Gravelle, Habscheid, Haidy, Halderson, Haley, M. Hall, Harper, R. Harris, B. Harvey, Hatoum, J. Hay, Head, Henderson, Hendrickson, Herberts, Higgins, J. Hiller, Hilworth, Hogaboam, C. Holmes, Houda, G. Howe, Huber, Hudson, Ingram, H. Jackson, Jankowski, Jennings, A. Johnson, B. Johnson, L. Johnson, E. Johnstone, Jones, Keats, D. Kelly, P. Kelly, Kennedy, Kerr, B. Kilrea, W. Kilrea, Kocur, Konstantinov, Korney, Kotsopoulos, Kruppke, Kumpel, Labine, Labraaten, Lajeunesse, J. Lamb, Lambert, M. Lapointe, Larson, Lawson, Leach, R. Leclerc, Leswick, Litzenberger, Lochead, Lofthouse, Lunde, Lundy, Luongo, Lynch, L. MacDonald, MacGregor, MacLean, Maltby, Manery, Mann, Marcon, Marker, C. Martin, P. Martin, Martineau, Matte, McCaig, McCarty, McClelland, McCourt, McCreavy, McDonough, McDougall, McGill, McKay, J. McKenzie, McKim, B. McNeill, S. McNeill, Mellor, Melnyk, Melrose, Menard, Miller, Mitchell, D. Morrison, R. Morrison, Morton, Murdoch, K. Murray, T. Murray, Nahrgang, Niekamp, Nill, Oates, O'Connell, Olson, Paul, Peters, Peterson, Pirus, Poile, Polonich, Potvin, Pushor, Redmond, Reibel, Reid, Rivers, Roberto, Robitaille, Roche, L. Rochefort, Rossignol, Rouse, Rowe, A. St. Laurent, Salovaara, Sandford, Schamehorn, Seibert, Shanahan, Shank, Shedden, Sheehy, R. Sheppard, Shuchuk, Silk, Sillinger, Simpson, Sinclair, Brad Smith, F. Smith, Snell, Snow, Speers, Stackhouse, Stankiewicz, Staszak, Sullivan, B. Taylor, B. Thomson, Toppazzini, Veitch, Volmar, Walz, Wares, B. Watson, Webster, Wilkie, B. Williams, Wing, Wiseman, Woit, Wojciechowski, York, D. Young, H. Young, Yzerman, Zombo

UNKNOWN

J. Arbour, Bennett, Brophy, Connors, B. Davis, Duguid, Fraser, Gordon, Green, Hart, Hicks, Hughes, Kitchen, Licari, Loughlin, Mackie, McCabe, Moffatt, Newman, Patterson, Peer, Purpur, Rockburn, Rupp, C. Smith, Steele, Stuart, Traub, Trottier, Turner, Zunich

GOALIES WHO CATCH WITH THEIR LEFT HAND

Bassen, Bester, Beverdige, Boisvert, Champoux, Cheveldae, Chevrier, Cox, Cude, Daley, DeJordy, Essensa, Franks, Gagnon, Gardner, Gatherum, Gilbert, Doug Grant, G. Gray, H. Gray, G. Hall, Hodson, Holland, H. Holmes, Ing, Jensen, S. King, Laforest, Legris, Low, Lumley, McDuffe, McGratton, D. McLeod, Millen, Mowers, Osgood, Perreault, Pusey, Riendeau, Riggin, Roach, Rutherford, S. St. Laurent, Sauve, Sawchuk, Al Smith, N. Smith, Stefan, Teno, Vachon, Vernon, Wetzel, L. Wilson

GOALIES WHO CATCH WITH THEIR RIGHT HAND

Almas, Connell, Crozier, Dion, Edwards, Eliot, Giacomin, Hanlon, Lozinski, Micalef, Millen, Moore, Richardson, C. Thompson

UNKNOWN

Bourque, Dolson, Rupp

COACHING REGISTER
PLAYOFFS

(games/won/lost/tied/series record)

SID ABEL

1958	4	0	4	0	0–1
1960	6	2	4	0	0–1
1961	11	6	5	0	1–1
1963	11	5	6	0	1–1
1964	14	7	7	0	1–1
1965	7	3	4	0	0–1
1966	12	6	6	0	1–1
1970	4	0	4	0	0–1
Totals	69	29	40	0	4–8

JACK ADAMS

1929	2	0	2	0	0–1
1932	2	0	1	1	0–1
1933	4	2	2	0	1–1
1934	9	4	5	0	1–1
1936	7	6	1	0	2–0
1937	10	6	4	0	2–0
1939	6	3	3	0	1–1
1940	5	2	3	0	1–1
1941	9	4	5	0	2–1
1942	12	7	5	0	2–1
1943	10	8	2	0	2–0
1944	5	1	4	0	0–1
1945	14	7	7	0	1–1
1946	5	1	4	0	0–1
1947	5	1	4	0	0–1
Totals	105	52	52	1	15–12

SCOTTY BOWMAN

1994	7	3	4	0	0–1
1995	18	12	6	0	3–1
1996	19	10	9	0	2–1
Totals	44	25	19	0	5–3

JACQUES DEMERS

1987	16	9	7	0	2–1
1988	16	9	7	0	2–1
1989	6	2	4	0	0–1
Totals	38	20	18	0	4–3

TOMMY IVAN

1948	10	4	6	0	1–1
1949	11	4	7	0	1–1
1950	14	8	6	0	2–0
1951	6	2	4	0	0–1
1952	8	8	0	0	2–0
1953	6	2	4	0	0–1
1954	12	8	4	0	2–0
Totals	67	36	31	0	8–4

BOBBY KROMM

1978	7	3	4	0	1–1

BRYAN MURRAY

1991	7	3	4	0	0–1
1992	11	4	7	0	1–1
1993	7	3	4	0	0–1
Totals	25	10	15	0	1–3

NICK POLANO

1984	4	1	3	0	0–1
1985	3	0	3	0	0–1
Totals	7	1	6	0	0–2

JIMMY SKINNER

1955	11	8	3	0	2–0
1956	10	5	5	0	1–1
1957	5	1	4	0	0–1
Totals	26	14	12	0	3–2

Jack Adams

ALL-TIME COACHING RECORDS PLAYOFFS

STANLEY CUPS

Jack Adams	3
Tommy Ivan	3
Jimmy Skinner	1

MOST SEASONS

Jack Adams	15
Sid Abel	8
Tommy Ivan	7

MOST GAMES

Jack Adams	105
Sid Abel	69
Tommy Ivan	67
Scotty Bowman	44

MOST WINS

Jack Adams	52
Tommy Ivan	36
Sid Abel	29
Scotty Bowman	25

MOST LOSSES

Jack Adams	52
Sid Abel	40
Tommy Ivan	31
Scotty Bowman	19

WINNING PERCENTAGE — ALL COACHES — PLAYOFFS

.568	Scotty Bowman
.538	Jimmy Skinner
.537	Tommy Ivan
.526	Jacques Demers
.495	Jack Adams
.429	Bobby Kromm
.420	Sid Abel
.400	Bryan Murray
.143	Nick Polano

ALL-TIME RED WINGS PLAYOFF REGISTER

indicates the number of Stanley Cups that player has won as a member of the Red Wings
"R" indicates a player's rookie season

SID ABEL

1939R	6	1	1	2	2
1940	5	0	3	3	21
1941	9	2	2	4	2
1942	12	4	2	6	6
1943	10	5	8	13	4
1946	3	0	0	0	0
1947	3	1	1	2	2
1948	10	0	3	3	16
1949	11	3	3	6	6
1950	14	6	2	8	6
1951	6	4	3	7	0
1952	7	2	2	4	12
Totals	96	28	30	58	77

GARY ALDCORN

1960	6	1	2	3	4

KEITH ALLEN

1954R	5	0	0	0	0

RALPH ALMAS

1947R	5	1–3	258	13	0	3.02

DALE ANDERSON

1957R	2	0	0	0	0

AL ARBOUR

1956	4	0	1	1	0
1957	5	0	0	0	6
1958	4	0	1	1	4
Totals	13	0	2	2	10

■ name appears on 1954 Cup although he did not participate in playoffs

MURRAY ARMSTRONG

1944	5	0	2	2	0
1945	14	4	2	6	2
1946	5	0	2	2	0
Totals	24	4	6	10	2

BRENT ASHTON

1987	16	4	9	13	6
1988	16	7	5	12	10
Totals	32	11	14	25	16

PIERRE AUBRY

1984	3	0	0	0	2

LARRY AURIE

1929	2	1	0	1	2
1932	2	0	0	0	0
1933	4	1	0	1	4
1934	9	3	7	10	2
1936	7	1	2	3	2
Totals	24	6	9	15	10

PETE BABANDO

1950	8	2	2	4	2

BOB BAILEY

1957	5	0	2	2	2
1958	4	0	0	0	16
Totals	9	0	2	2	18

DOUG BARKLEY

1963	11	0	3	3	16
1964	14	0	5	5	33
1965	5	0	1	1	14
Totals	30	0	9	9	63

DAVE BARR

1987	13	1	0	1	14
1988	16	5	7	12	22
1989	6	3	1	4	6
Totals	35	9	8	17	42

JOHN BARRETT

1984	4	0	0	0	4
1985	3	0	1	1	11
Totals	7	0	1	1	15

MARTY BARRY

1936	7	2	4	6	6
1937	10	4	7	11	2
Totals	17	6	11	17	8

HANK BASSEN

1961	4	1–2	220	9	0	2.45
1966	1	0–1	55	2	0	2.18
Totals	5	1–3	275	11	0	2.40

ANDY BATHGATE

1966	12	6	3	9	6

BOB BAUN

1970	4	0	0	0	6

GARY BERGMAN

1965R	5	0	1	1	4
1966	12	0	3	3	14
1970	4	0	1	1	2
Totals	21	0	5	5	20

THOMMIE BERGMAN

1978	7	0	2	2	2

MARC BERGEVIN

1996	17	1	0	1	14

ALLAN BESTER

1991	1	0–0	20	1	0	3.00

STEVE BLACK

1950R	13	0	0	0	13

LEO BOIVIN

1966	12	0	1	1	16

IVAN BOLDIREV

1984	4	0	5	5	4
1985	2	0	1	1	0
Totals	6	0	6	6	4

MARCEL BONIN

1953R	5	0	1	1	0
1955	11	0	2	2	4
Totals	16	0	3	3	4

SCOTTY BOWMAN

1936	7	2	1	3	2
1937	10	0	1	1	4
1939	4	0	0	0	0
Totals	21	2	2	4	6

RICK BOWNESS

1978	4	0	0	0	2

CARL BREWER

1970	4	0	0	0	2

MEL BRIDGMAN

1987	16	5	2	7	28
1988	16	4	1	5	12
Totals	32	9	3	12	40

BERNIE BROPHY

1929	2	0	0	0	2

ADAM BROWN

1942R	12	0	2	2	4
1943	6	1	1	2	2
1944	5	0	0	0	8
1946	5	1	1	2	0
Totals	28	2	4	6	14

DOUG BROWN

1995	18	4	8	12	2
1996	13	3	3	6	11
Totals	31	7	11	18	6

GERRY BROWN

1942R	12	2	1	3	4

CONNIE BROWN

1940	5	2	1	3	0
1941	4	0	2	2	0
Totals	9	2	3	5	0

■ name appears on 1943 Cup although he did not participate in playoffs

ED BRÛNETEAU

1941R	3	0	0	0	2
1945	14	5	2	7	0
1946	4	1	0	1	0
1947	4	1	4	5	0
1948	6	0	0	0	0
Totals	31	7	6	13	2

MUD BRÛNETEAU

1936R	7	2	2	4	0
1937	10	2	0	2	4
1939	1	0	0	0	0
1940	5	3	2	5	0
1941	9	2	1	3	2
1942	12	5	1	6	6
1943	9	5	4	9	0
1944	5	1	2	3	2
1945	14	3	2	5	2
Totals	72	23	14	37	16

BILL BRYDGE

1929	2	0	0	0	4

JOHNNY BUCYK

1956R	10	1	1	2	8
1957	5	0	1	1	0
Totals	15	1	2	3	8

TONY BUKOVICH

1945	6	0	1	1	0

SHAWN BURR

1987	16	7	2	9	20
1988	9	3	1	4	14
1989	6	1	2	3	6
1991	7	0	4	4	15
1992	11	1	5	6	10
1993	7	2	1	3	2
1994	7	2	0	2	6
1995	16	0	2	2	6
Totals	79	16	17	33	79

CUMMY BURTON

1956R	3	0	0	0	0

EDDIE BUSH

1942	11	1	6	7	23

WALT BUSWELL

1933R	4	0	0	0	4
1934	9	0	1	1	2
Totals	13	0	1	1	6

AL CAMERON

1978	7	0	1	1	2

COLIN CAMPBELL

1984	4	0	0	0	21

TERRY CARKNER

1994	7	0	0	0	4

GENE CARRIGAN

1934	4	0	0	0	0

FRANK CARSON

1932	2	0	0	0	2
1933	4	0	1	1	0
1934	6	0	1	1	5
Totals	12	0	2	2	7

JIMMY CARSON

1991	7	2	1	3	4
1992	11	2	3	5	0
Totals	18	4	4	8	4

JOE CARVETH

1942	9	4	0	4	0
1943	10	6	2	8	4
1944	5	2	1	3	8
1945	14	5	6	11	2
1946	5	0	1	1	0
1950	14	2	4	6	6
Totals	57	19	14	33	20

■ name appears on 1950 Cup although he did not participate in playoffs

JOHN CHABOT

1988	16	4	15	19	2
1989	6	1	1	2	0
Totals	22	5	16	21	2

BOB CHAMPOUX

1964	1	1–0	55	4	0	4.36

TIM CHEVELDAE

1991	7	3–4	398	22	0	3.32
1992	11	3–7	597	25	2	2.51
1993	7	3–4	423	24	0	3.40
Totals	25	9–15	1418	71	2	3.00

STEVE CHIASSON

1987R	2	0	0	0	19
1988	9	2	2	4	31
1989	5	2	1	3	6
1991	5	3	1	4	19
1992	11	1	5	6	12
1993	7	2	2	4	19
1994	7	2	3	5	2
Totals	46	12	14	26	108

DINO CICCARELLI

1993	7	4	2	6	16
1994	7	5	2	7	14
1995	16	9	2	11	22
1996	17	6	2	8	26
Totals	47	24	8	32	78

PAUL COFFEY

1993	7	2	9	11	2
1994	7	1	6	7	8
1995	18	6	12	18	10
1996	17	5	9	14	30
Totals	49	14	36	50	50

CHARLIE CONACHER

1939	5	2	5	7	2

JIM CONACHER

1946R	5	1	1	2	0
1947	5	2	1	3	2
1948	9	2	0	2	2
Totals	19	5	2	7	4

ROY CONACHER

1947	5	4	4	8	2

ALEX CONNELL

1932	2	0–1–1	120	3	0	1.50

WAYNE CONNELLY

1970	4	1	3	4	2

BOB CONNORS

1929	2	0	0	0	10

CARSON COOPER

1929	2	0	0	0	0
1932	2	0	0	0	0
Totals	4	0	0	0	0

MURRAY COSTELLO

1956	4	0	0	0	0

GERRY COUTURE

1945R	2	0	0	0	0
1946	5	0	2	2	0
1947	1	0	0	0	0
1949	10	2	0	2	2
1950	14	5	4	9	2
1951	6	1	1	2	0
Totals	38	8	7	15	4

DANNY COX

1932	2	0	0	0	2

DOUG CROSSMAN

1991	6	0	5	5	6

TROY CROWDER

1992	1	0	0	0	0

ROGER CROZIER

1964R	2	0–1	108	5	0	2.50
1965	7	3–4	420	23	0	3.29
1966	12	6–5	666	26	1	2.36
1970	1	0–1	34	3	0	5.00
Totals	22	9–11	1228	57	1	2.79

WILF CUDE

1934	9	4–5	593	21	1	2.12

BARRY CULLEN

1960	4	0	0	0	2

FRANK DALEY

1929R	2	0	0	0	0

BILLY DEA

1957	5	2	0	2	2
1970	4	0	1	1	2
Totals	9	2	1	3	4

DON DEACON

1939	2	2	1	3	0

GILBERT DELORME

1987	16	0	2	2	14
1988	15	0	3	3	22
1989	6	0	1	1	2
Totals	37	0	6	6	38

ALEX DELVECCHIO

1952R	8	0	3	3	4
1953	6	2	4	6	2
1954	12	2	7	9	7
1955	11	7	8	15	2
1956	10	7	3	10	2
1957	5	3	2	5	2
1958	4	0	1	1	0
1960	6	2	6	8	0
1961	11	4	5	9	0
1963	11	3	6	9	2
1964	14	3	8	11	0
1965	7	2	3	5	4
1966	12	0	11	11	4
1970	4	0	2	2	0
Totals	121	35	69	104	29

AL DEWSBURY

1947R	2	0	0	0	4
1948	1	0	0	0	0
1950	4	0	3	3	8
Totals	7	0	3	3	12

BOB DILLABOUGH

1963	1	0	0	0	0
1964	1	0	0	0	0
1965	4	0	0	0	0
Totals	6	0	0	0	0

CECIL DILLON

1940	5	1	0	1	0

BILL DINEEN

1954R	12	0	0	0	2
1955	11	0	1	1	8
1956	10	1	0	1	8
1957	4	0	0	0	0
Totals	37	1	1	2	18

CONRAD DION

1944R	5	1–4	300	17	0	3.40

BOBBY DOLLAS

1991	7	1	0	1	13
1992	2	0	1	1	0
Totals	9	1	1	2	13

CLARENCE "DOLLY" DOLSON

1929R	2	0–2	120	7	0	3.50

LES DOUGLAS

1943	10	3	2	5	2

DALLAS DRAKE

1993R	7	3	3	6	6

KRIS DRAPER

1994	7	2	2	4	4
1995	18	4	1	5	12
1996	18	4	2	6	18
Totals	43	10	5	15	34

GILLES DUBE

1954	1	0	0	0	0

RON DUGUAY

1984	4	2	3	5	2
1985	3	1	0	1	7
Totals	7	3	3	6	9

BLAKE DUNLOP

1984	4	0	1	1	4

ROY EDWARDS

1970	4	0–3	206	11	0	3.20

HAP EMMS

1932	2	0	0	0	2
1933	4	0	0	0	8
1934	8	0	0	0	2
Totals	14	0	0	0	12

ANDERS ERIKSSON

1996	3	0	0	0	0

BOB ERREY

1995	18	1	5	6	30
1996	14	0	4	4	8
Totals	32	1	9	10	38

BOB ESSENSA

1994	2	0–2	109	9	0	4.95

STU EVANS

1933	4	0	0	0	6

ALEX FAULKNER

1963	8	5	0	5	2
1964	4	0	0	0	0
Totals	12	5	0	5	2

SERGEI FEDOROV

1991R	7	1	5	6	4
1992	11	5	5	10	8
1993	7	3	6	9	23
1994	7	1	7	8	6
1995	17	7	17	24	6
1996	19	2	18	20	10
Totals	68	19	58	77	57

BRENT FEDYK

1991	6	1	0	1	2
1992	1	0	0	0	2
Totals	7	1	0	1	4

LORNE FERGUSON

1956	10	1	2	3	12
1957	5	1	0	1	6
Totals	15	2	2	4	18

VIACHESLAV FETISOV

1995	18	0	8	8	14
1996	19	1	4	5	34
Totals	37	1	12	13	48

GUYLE FIELDER

1953	4	0	0	0	0

JOE FISHER

1940R	5	1	1	2	0
1941	5	1	0	1	6
1943	1	0	0	0	0
Totals	11	2	1	3	6

LEE FOGOLIN

1948R	2	0	1	1	6
1949	9	0	0	0	4
1950	10	0	0	0	16
Totals	21	0	1	1	26

VAL FONTEYNE

1960R	6	0	4	4	0
1961	11	2	3	5	0
1963	11	0	0	0	0
1965	5	0	1	1	0
1966	12	1	0	1	4
Totals	45	3	8	11	4

DWIGHT FOSTER

1984	3	0	1	1	0
1985	3	0	0	0	0
Totals	6	0	1	1	0

JIMMY FRANKS

1937R	1	0–1	30	2	0	4.00

BILL GADSBY

1963	11	1	4	5	36
1964	14	0	4	4	22
1965	7	0	3	3	8
1966	12	1	3	4	12
Totals	44	2	14	16	78

JOHNNY GALLAGHER

1933	4	1	1	2	4
1937	10	1	0	1	15
Totals	14	2	1	3	19

GERARD GALLANT

1985R	3	0	0	0	11
1987	16	8	6	14	43
1988	16	6	9	15	55
1989	6	1	2	3	40
1992	11	2	2	4	25
1993	6	1	2	3	4
Totals	58	18	21	39	178

DANNY GARE

1984	4	2	0	2	38
1985	2	0	0	0	10
Totals	6	2	0	2	48

JOHAN GARPENLOV

1991R	6	0	1	1	4

FERN GAUTHIER

1946	5	3	0	3	2
1947	3	1	0	1	0
1948	10	1	1	2	5
Totals	18	5	1	6	7

GEORGE GEE

1949	10	1	3	4	22
1950	14	3	6	9	0
1951	6	0	1	1	0
Totals	30	4	10	14	22

GUS GIESEBRECHT

1939R	6	0	2	2	0
1941	9	2	1	3	0
1942	2	0	0	0	0
Totals	17	2	3	5	0

LARRY GIROUX

1978	2	0	0	0	2

FRED GLOVER

1949R	2	0	0	0	0
1951	2	0	0	0	0
Totals	4	0	0	0	0

HOWIE GLOVER

1961	11	1	2	3	2

WARREN GODFREY

1957	5	0	0	0	6
1958	4	0	0	0	0
1960	6	1	0	1	10
1961	11	0	2	2	18
1965	4	0	1	1	2
1966	4	0	0	0	0
Totals	34	1	3	4	36

PETE GOEGAN

1958R	4	0	0	0	18
1960	6	1	0	1	13
1961	11	0	1	1	18
1963	11	0	2	2	12
1966	1	0	0	0	0
Totals	33	1	3	4	61

BOB GOLDHAM

1951	6	0	1	1	2
1952	8	0	1	1	8
1953	6	1	1	2	2
1954	12	0	2	2	2
1955	11	0	4	4	4
1956	10	0	3	3	4
Totals	53	1	12	13	22

LEROY GOLDSWORTHY

1933	2	0	0	0	0

EBBIE GOODFELLOW

1932	2	0	0	0	0
1933	4	1	0	1	11
1934	9	4	3	7	12
1936	7	1	0	1	4
1937	9	2	2	4	12
1939	6	0	0	0	8
1940	5	0	2	2	9
1941	3	0	1	1	9
Totals	45	8	8	16	65

■ name appears on 1943 Cup as player/coach during regular season

TED GRAHAM

1934	9	3	1	4	8

ADAM GRAVES

1989	5	0	0	0	4

RICK GREEN

1991	3	0	0	0	0

STU GRIMSON

1995	11	1	0	1	26
1996	2	0	0	0	0
Totals	13	1	0	1	26

LLOYD GROSS

1934	1	0	0	0	0

DON GROSSO

1939R	4	1	2	3	7
1940	5	0	0	0	2
1941	9	1	4	5	0
1942	12	8	6	14	19
1943	10	4	2	6	10
1944	5	1	0	1	0
Totals	45	15	14	29	38

BEP GUIDOLIN

1948	2	0	0	0	4

MARC HABSCHEID

1991	5	0	0	0	0

LLOYD HADDON

1960R	1	0	0	0	0

GORD HAIDY

1950	1	0	0	0	0

LEN HALEY

1960R	6	1	3	4	6

BOB HALKIDIS

1994	1	0	0	0	2

GLENN HALL

1956	10	5–5	604	28	0	2.80
1957	5	1–4	300	15	0	3.00
Totals	15	6–9	904	43	0	2.85

MURRAY HALL

1965	1	0	0	0	0
1966	1	0	0	0	0
Totals	2	0	0	0	0

DOUG HALWARD

1988	8	1	4	5	18

JEAN HAMEL

1978	7	0	0	0	10

GLEN HANLON

1987	8	5–2	467	13	2	1.67
1988	8	4–3	431	22	1	3.06
1989	2	0–1	78	7	0	5.38
Totals	18	9–6	976	42	3	2.58

TERRY HARPER

1978	7	0	1	1	4

RON HARRIS

1970	4	0	0	0	8

GEORGE HAY

1929	2	1	0	1	0
1933	4	0	1	1	0
Totals	6	1	1	2	0

JIM HAY 🏆

1953R	4	0	0	0	2
1955	5	1	0	1	0
Totals	9	1	0	1	2

PAUL HENDERSON

1964	14	2	3	5	6
1965	7	0	2	2	0
1966	12	3	3	6	10
Totals	33	5	8	13	16

JIM HERBERTS

1929	1	0	0	0	2

DENNIS HEXTAL

1978	7	1	1	2	10

TIM HIGGINS

1987	12	0	1	1	16
1988	13	1	0	1	26
1989	1	0	0	0	0
Totals	26	1	1	2	42

JIM HILLER

1993	2	0	0	0	4

LARRY HILLMAN 🏆

1955R	3	0	0	0	0
1956	10	0	1	1	6
Totals	13	0	1	1	6

FLASH HOLLETT

1944	5	0	0	0	6
1945	14	3	4	7	6
1946	5	0	2	2	0
Totals	24	3	6	9	12

GORDON HOLLINGWORTH

1956	3	0	0	0	2

PETE HORECK

1947	5	2	0	2	6
1948	10	3	7	10	12
1949	11	1	1	2	10
Totals	26	6	8	14	28

DOUG HOUDA

1989	6	0	1	1	0

GORDIE HOWE 🏆🏆🏆🏆

1947R	5	0	0	0	18
1948	10	1	1	2	11
1949	11	8	3	11	19
1950	1	0	0	0	7
1951	6	4	3	7	4
1952	8	2	5	7	2
1953	6	2	5	7	2
1954	12	4	5	9	31
1955	11	9	11	20	24
1956	10	3	9	12	8
1957	5	2	5	7	6
1958	4	1	1	2	0
1960	6	1	5	6	4
1961	11	4	11	15	10
1963	11	7	9	16	22
1964	14	9	10	19	16
1965	7	4	2	6	20
1966	12	4	6	10	12
1970	4	2	0	2	2
Totals	154	67	91	158	218

MARK HOWE

1993	7	1	3	4	2
1994	6	0	1	1	0
1995	3	0	0	0	0
Totals	16	1	4	5	2

SYD HOWE 🏆🏆🏆

1936	7	3	3	6	2
1937	10	2	5	7	0
1939	6	3	1	4	4
1940	5	2	2	4	2
1941	9	1	7	8	0
1942	12	3	5	8	0
1943	7	1	2	3	0
1944	5	2	2	4	0
1945	7	0	0	0	2
Totals	67	17	27	44	10

STEVE HRYMNAK

1953	2	0	0	0	0

DENNIS HULL

1978	7	0	0	0	2

HAL JACKSON 🏆

1941	5	0	0	0	7
1943	6	0	1	1	4
1944	5	0	0	0	11
1945	14	1	1	2	10
1946	5	0	0	0	6
Totals	35	1	2	3	38

LOU JANKOWSKI

1953	1	0	0	0	0

LARRY JEFFREY

1963	9	3	3	6	8
1964	14	1	6	7	28
1965	2	0	0	0	0
Totals	25	4	9	13	36

BILL JENNINGS

1941R	9	2	2	4	0
1944	4	0	0	0	0
Totals	13	2	2	4	0

AL JOHNSON

1961	11	2	2	4	6

GREG JOHNSON

1994R	7	2	2	4	2
1995	1	0	0	0	0
1996	13	3	1	4	8
Totals	21	5	3	8	10

ED JOHNSTONE

1984	2	0	0	0	0

GREG JOLY

1978	5	0	0	0	8

BUCK JONES

1939R	6	0	1	1	10

ED JOYAL

1963R	11	1	0	1	2
1964	14	2	3	5	10
1965	7	1	1	2	4
Totals	32	4	4	8	16

AL KARLANDER

1970R	4	0	1	1	0

RED KELLY

1948R	10	3	2	5	2
1949	11	1	1	2	6
1950	14	1	3	4	2
1951	6	0	1	1	0
1952	5	1	0	1	0
1953	6	0	4	4	0
1954	12	5	1	6	0
1955	11	2	4	6	17
1956	10	2	4	6	2
1957	5	1	0	1	0
1958	4	0	1	1	2
Totals	94	16	21	37	31

PETE KELLY

1936	7	1	1	2	2
1937	8	2	0	2	0
1939	4	0	0	0	0
Totals	19	3	1	4	2

FORBES KENNEDY

1958	4	1	0	1	12

SHELDON KENNEDY

1993	7	1	1	2	2
1994	7	1	2	3	0
Totals	14	2	3	5	2

ALAN KERR

1992	9	2	0	2	17

HEC KILREA

1932	2	0	0	0	0
1936	7	0	3	3	2
1937	10	3	1	4	2
1939	6	1	2	3	0
Totals	25	4	6	10	4

KEN KILREA

1939R	3	1	1	2	4
1940	5	1	1	2	0
1941	5	0	0	0	0
1944	2	0	0	0	0
Totals	15	2	2	4	4

WALLY KILREA

1936	7	2	2	4	2
1937	10	0	2	2	4
Totals	17	2	4	6	6

KRIS KING

1989	2	0	0	0	2

KELLY KISIO

1984	4	1	0	1	4
1985	3	0	2	2	2
Totals	7	1	2	3	6

PETR KLIMA

1987	13	1	2	3	4
1988	12	10	8	18	10
1989	6	2	4	6	19
Totals	31	13	14	27	33

JOEY KOCUR

1985R	3	1	0	1	5
1987	16	2	3	5	71
1988	10	0	1	1	13
1989	3	0	1	1	6
Totals	32	3	5	8	95

STEVE KONROYD

1993	1	0	0	0	0

VLADIMIR KONSTANTINOV

1992R	11	0	1	1	16
1993	7	0	1	1	8
1994	7	0	2	2	4
1995	18	1	1	2	22
1996	19	4	5	9	28
Totals	62	5	10	15	78

VYACHESLAV KOZLOV

1993	4	0	2	2	2
1994	7	2	5	7	12
1995	18	9	7	16	10
1996	19	5	7	12	10
Totals	48	16	21	37	34

DALE KRENTZ

1988	2	0	0	0	0

MIKE KRUSHELNYSKI

1995	8	0	0	0	0

MARK KUMPEL

1987	8	0	0	0	4

LEO LABINE

1961	11	3	2	5	4

RANDY LADOUCEUR

1984	4	1	0	1	6
1985	3	1	0	1	0
Totals	7	2	0	2	6

MARK LAMB

1987	11	0	0	0	11

LANE LAMBERT

1984R	4	0	0	0	10

AL LANGLOIS

1964	14	0	0	0	12
1965	6	1	0	1	4
Totals	20	1	0	1	16

MARTIN LAPOINTE

1992R	3	0	1	1	4
1994	4	0	0	0	6
1995	2	0	1	1	8
1996	11	1	2	3	12
Totals	20	1	4	5	30

IGOR LARIONOV

1996	19	6	7	13	6

REED LARSON

1978	7	0	2	2	4
1984	4	2	0	2	21
1985	3	1	2	3	20
Totals	14	3	4	7	45

JEAN-PAUL LEBLANC

1978	2	0	0	0	0

TONY LESWICK

1952	8	3	1	4	22
1953	6	1	0	1	11
1954	12	3	1	4	18
1955	11	1	2	3	20
1958	4	0	0	0	0
Totals	41	8	4	12	71

DAVE LEWIS

1987	14	0	4	4	10

HERB LEWIS

1932	2	0	0	0	0
1933	4	1	0	1	0
1934	9	5	2	7	2
1936	7	2	3	5	0
1937	10	4	3	7	4
1939	6	1	2	3	0
Totals	38	13	10	23	6

NICK LIBETT

1970	4	2	0	2	2
1978	7	3	1	4	0
Totals	11	5	1	6	2

NICKLAS LIDSTROM

1992R	11	1	2	3	0
1993	7	1	0	1	0
1994	7	3	2	5	0
1995	18	4	12	16	8
1996	19	5	9	14	10
Totals	62	14	25	39	18

TED LINDSAY

1945R	14	2	0	2	6
1946	5	0	1	1	0
1947	5	2	2	4	10
1948	10	3	1	4	6
1949	11	2	6	8	31
1950	13	4	4	8	16
1951	6	0	1	1	8
1952	8	5	2	7	8
1953	6	4	4	8	6
1954	12	4	4	8	14
1955	11	7	12	19	12
1956	10	6	3	9	22
1957	5	2	4	6	8
1965	7	3	0	3	34
Totals	123	44	44	88	181

CARL LISCOMBE

1939	3	0	0	0	2
1941	9	4	3	7	12
1942	12	6	6	12	2
1943	10	6	8	14	2
1944	5	1	0	1	2
1945	14	4	2	6	0
1946	4	1	0	1	0
Totals	57	22	19	41	20

BILL LOCHEAD

1978	7	3	0	3	6

CLAUDE LOISELLE

1985	3	0	2	2	0

RON LOW

1978	4	1–3	240	17	0	4.25

HARRY LUMLEY

1945	14	7–7	871	31	2	2.21
1946	5	1–4	310	16	1	3.20
1948	10	4–6	600	30	0	3.00
1949	11	4–7	726	26	0	2.36
1950	14	8–6	910	28	3	2.00
Totals	54	24–30	3417	131	6	2.30

LEN LUNDE

1960	6	1	2	3	0
1961	10	2	0	2	0
Totals	16	3	2	5	0

PAT LUNDY

1946R	2	1	0	1	0
1947	5	1	0	1	2
1948	5	1	1	2	0
1949	4	0	0	0	0
Totals	16	3	1	4	2

LOWELL MACDONALD

1963	1	0	0	0	2

PARKER MACDONALD

1961	9	1	0	1	0
1963	11	3	2	5	2
1964	14	3	3	6	2
1965	7	1	1	2	6
1966	9	0	0	0	2
Totals	50	8	6	14	12

BRUCE MACGREGOR

1961R	8	1	2	3	6
1963	10	1	4	5	6
1964	14	5	2	7	12
1965	7	0	2	2	2
1966	12	1	4	5	2
1970	4	1	0	1	2
Totals	55	9	14	23	50

HOWARD MACKIE

1937R	8	0	0	0	0

PAUL MACLEAN

1989	5	1	1	2	8

RICK MACLEISH

1984	1	0	0	0	0

JOHN MACMILLAN

1964	4	0	1	1	2

FRANK MAHOVLICH

1970	4	0	0	0	2

KIRK MALTBY

1996	8	0	1	1	4

BOB MANNO

1984	4	0	3	3	0
1985	3	1	0	1	0
Totals	7	1	3	4	0

GUS MARKER

1934	3	0	0	0	2

BRAD MARSH

1991	1	0	0	0	0
1992	3	0	0	0	0
Totals	4	0	0	0	0

BERT MARSHALL

1966R	12	1	3	4	16

CLARE MARTIN

1950	10	0	1	1	0
1951	2	0	0	0	0
Totals	12	0	1	1	0

PIT MARTIN

1964	14	1	4	5	14
1965	3	0	1	1	2
Totals	17	1	5	6	16

JEROME McATEE

1945	14	2	1	3	0

DOUG McCAIG

1942R	2	0	0	0	6
1947	5	0	1	1	4
Totals	7	0	1	1	10

DARREN McCARTY

1994R	7	2	2	4	8
1995	18	3	2	5	14
1996	19	3	2	5	20
Totals	44	8	6	14	42

DALE McCOURT

1978R	7	4	2	6	2

PAT McCREAVY

1942	11	1	1	2	4

BRAD McCRIMMON

1991	7	1	1	2	21
1992	11	0	1	1	8
Totals	18	1	2	3	29

AB McDONALD

1966	10	1	4	5	2

BYRON McDONALD

1940R	5	0	2	2	0

BUCKO McDONALD

1936	7	3	0	3	10
1937	10	0	0	0	2
Totals	17	3	0	3	12

BILL McDOUGALL

1991R	1	0	0	0	0

JIM McFADDEN

1947R	4	0	2	2	0
1948	10	5	3	8	10
1949	8	0	1	1	6
1950	14	2	3	5	8
1951	6	0	0	0	0
Totals	42	7	9	16	24

BOB McGILL

1992	8	0	0	0	14

JACK McINTYRE

1958	4	1	1	2	0
1960	6	1	1	2	0
Totals	10	2	2	4	0

DOUG McKAY

1950	1	0	0	0	0

RANDY McKAY

1989R	2	0	0	0	2
1991	5	0	1	1	41
Totals	7	0	1	1	43

JOHN McKENZIE

1960	2	0	0	0	0

ROLLIE McLENAHAN

1946R	2	0	0	0	0

MAX McNAB

1948R	3	0	0	0	2
1949	10	1	0	1	2
1950	10	0	0	0	0
1951	2	0	0	0	0
Totals	25	1	0	1	4

BILLY McNEILL

1958	4	1	1	2	4

JERRY MELNYK

1956	6	0	0	0	0
1960	6	3	0	3	0
1961	11	1	0	1	2
Totals	23	4	0	4	2

CORRADO MICALEF

1984	1	0–0	7	2	0	17.14
1985	2	0–0	42	6	0	8.57
Totals	3	0–0	49	8	0	9.80

NICK MICKOSKI

1958	4	0	0	0	4

HUGH MILLAR

1947R	1	0	0	0	0

KEVIN MILLER

1991	7	3	2	5	20
1992	9	0	2	2	4
Totals	16	3	4	7	24

ED MIO

1984	1	0–1	63	3	0	2.86

JOHN MISZUK

1964R	3	0	0	0	2

RON MOFFATT

1933R	4	0	0	0	0
1934	3	0	0	0	0
Totals	7	0	0	0	0

HANK MONTEITH

1970	4	0	0	0	0

DON MORRISON

1948R	3	0	1	1	0

JIM MORRISON

1960	6	0	2	2	0

ROD MORRISON

1948R	3	0	0	0	0

ALEX MOTTER

1939	4	0	1	1	0
1940	5	1	1	2	15
1941	9	1	3	4	4
1942	12	1	3	4	12
1943	5	0	1	1	2
Totals	35	3	9	12	33

JOHN MOWERS

1941R	9	4–5	561	20	0	2.22
1942	12	7–5	720	38	0	3.17
1943	10	8–2	679	22	2	2.20
1947	1	0–1	46	5	0	6.52
Totals	32	19–13	2006	85	2	2.54

JOE MURPHY

1988	8	0	1	1	6

RON MURPHY

1965	5	0	1	1	4

VACLAV NEDOMANSKY

1978	7	3	5	8	0

JIM NILL

1988	16	6	1	7	62
1989	6	0	0	0	25
Totals	22	6	1	7	87

REG NOBLE

1929	2	0	0	0	2
1932	2	0	0	0	0
Totals	4	0	0	0	2

LEE NORWOOD

1987	16	1	6	7	31
1988	16	2	6	8	40
1989	6	1	2	3	16
Totals	38	4	14	18	87

ADAM OATES

1987	16	4	7	11	6
1988	16	8	12	20	6
1989	6	0	8	8	2
Totals	38	12	27	39	14

MIKE O'CONNELL

1987	16	1	4	5	14
1988	10	0	4	4	8
1989	6	0	0	0	4
Totals	32	1	8	9	26

GERRY ODROWSKI

1961R	10	0	0	0	4
1963	2	0	0	0	2
Totals	12	0	0	0	6

JOHN OGRODNICK

1984	4	0	0	0	0
1985	3	1	1	2	0
1993	1	0	0	0	0
Totals	8	1	1	2	0

MURRAY OLIVER

1960	6	1	0	1	4

JIMMY ORLANDO

1940	5	0	0	0	15
1941	9	0	2	2	31
1942	12	0	4	4	45
1943	10	0	3	3	14
Totals	36	0	9	9	105

CHRIS OSGOOD

1994R	6	3–2	307	12	1	2.35
1995	2	0–0	68	2	0	1.76
1996	15	8–7	936	33	2	2.12
Totals	23	11–9	1311	47	3	2.15

BRAD PARK

1984	3	0	3	3	0
1985	3	0	0	0	11
Totals	6	0	3	3	11

JOE PATERSON

1984	3	0	0	0	7

MARTY PAVELICH

1948R	10	2	2	4	6
1949	9	0	1	1	8
1950	14	4	2	6	13
1951	6	0	1	1	2
1952	8	2	2	4	2
1953	6	2	1	3	7
1954	12	2	2	4	4
1955	11	1	3	4	12
1956	10	0	1	1	14
1957	5	0	0	0	0
Totals	91	13	15	28	68

JIM PAVESE

1988	4	0	1	1	15

JIM PETERS SR.

1950	8	0	2	2	0
1951	6	0	0	0	0
1954	10	0	0	0	0
Totals	24	0	2	2	0

GORD PETTINGER

1934	7	1	0	1	2
1936	7	2	2	4	0
1937	10	0	2	2	2
Totals	24	3	4	7	4

NELSON PODOLSKY

1949R	7	0	0	0	4

BUD POILE

1949	10	0	1	1	2

DON POILE

1958	4	0	0	0	0

DENNIS POLONICH

1978	7	1	0	1	19

PAUL POPIEL

1970	1	0	0	0	0

MARC POTVIN

1991R	6	0	0	0	32
1992	1	0	0	0	0
Totals	7	0	0	0	32

DEAN PRENTICE

1966	12	5	5	10	4

KEITH PRIMEAU

1991R	5	1	1	2	25
1992	11	0	0	0	14
1993	7	0	2	2	26
1994	7	0	2	2	6
1995	17	4	5	9	45
1996	17	1	4	5	28
Totals	64	6	14	20	144

BOB PROBERT

1987	16	3	4	7	63
1988	16	8	13	21	51
1991	6	1	2	3	50
1992	11	1	6	7	28
1993	7	0	3	3	10
1994	7	1	1	2	8
Totals	63	14	29	43	210

ANDRE PRONOVOST

1963	11	1	4	5	6
1964	14	4	3	7	26
Totals	25	5	7	12	32

MARCEL PRONOVOST

1950R	9	0	1	1	10
1951	6	0	0	0	0
1952	8	0	1	1	10
1953	6	0	0	0	6
1954	12	2	3	5	12
1955	11	1	2	3	6
1956	10	0	2	2	8
1957	5	0	0	0	6
1958	4	0	1	1	4
1960	6	1	1	2	2
1961	9	2	3	5	0
1963	11	1	4	5	8
1964	14	0	2	2	14
1965	7	0	3	3	4
Totals	118	7	23	30	90

METRO PRYSTAI

1951	3	1	0	1	0
1952	8	2	5	7	0
1953	6	4	4	8	2
1954	12	2	3	5	0
1956	9	1	2	3	6
1957	5	2	0	2	0
Totals	43	12	14	26	8

CLIFFORD PURPUR

1945	7	0	1	1	4

BILL QUACKENBUSH

1944	2	1	0	1	0
1945	14	0	2	2	2
1946	5	0	1	1	0
1947	5	0	0	0	2
1948	10	0	2	2	0
1949	11	1	1	2	0
Totals	47	2	6	8	4

YVES RACINE

1991	7	2	0	2	0
1992	11	2	1	3	10
1993	7	1	3	4	27
Totals	25	5	4	9	37

MIKE RAMSEY

1995	15	0	1	1	4
1996	15	0	4	4	10
Totals	30	0	5	5	14

MARC REAUME

1960	2	0	0	0	0

EARL REIBEL

1954R	9	1	3	4	0
1955	11	5	7	12	2
1956	10	0	2	2	2
1957	5	0	2	2	0
Totals	35	6	14	20	4

GERRY REID

1949	2	0	0	0	2

LEO REISE

1947	5	0	1	1	4
1948	10	2	1	3	12
1949	11	1	0	1	4
1950	14	2	0	2	19
1951	6	2	3	5	2
1952	6	1	0	1	27
Totals	52	8	5	13	68

VINCENT RIENDEAU

1992	2	1–0	73	4	0	3.29

JOHN ROSS ROACH

1933	4	2–2	240	8	1	2.00

EARL ROBERTSON

1937	6	3–2	340	8	2	1.41

TORRIE ROBERTSON

1989	6	1	0	1	17

DALE ROLFE

1970	4	0	2	2	8

BOB ROUSE

1995	18	0	3	3	8
1996	7	0	1	1	4
Totals	25	0	4	4	12

JIM RUTHERFORD

1978	3	2–1	180	12	0	4.00

ANDRE ST. LAURENT

1978	7	1	1	2	4

SAM ST. LAURENT

1988	1	0–0	10	1	0	6.00

TERRY SAWCHUK

1951	6	2–4	463	13	1	2.17
1952	8	8–0	480	5	4	0.63
1953	6	2–4	372	21	1	3.50
1954	12	8–4	751	20	2	1.67
1955	11	8–3	660	26	1	2.36
1958	4	0–4	252	19	0	4.75
1960	6	2–4	405	20	0	3.33
1961	7	5–2	465	18	1	2.45
1963	11	5–6	660	36	0	3.27
1964	13	6–6	695	31	1	2.78
Totals	85	46–37	5203	209	11	2.41

JAMES SCLISIZZI

1947R	1	0	0	0	0
1948	6	0	0	0	4
1949	6	0	0	0	2
Totals	13	0	0	0	6

EARL SEIBERT

1945	14	2	1	3	4

RIC SEILING

1987	7	0	0	0	5

JEFF SHARPLES

1987R	2	0	0	0	2
1988	4	0	3	3	4
1989	1	0	0	0	0
Totals	7	0	3	3	6

RAY SHEPPARD

1992	11	6	2	8	4
1993	7	2	3	5	0
1994	7	2	1	3	4
1995	17	4	3	7	5
Totals	42	14	9	23	13

JOHN SHERF

1937	5	0	1	1	2
1939	3	0	0	0	0
Totals	8	0	1	1	2

GARY SHUCHUK

1991R	3	0	0	0	0

MIKE SILLINGER

1991R	3	0	1	1	0
1992	8	2	2	4	2
Totals	11	2	3	5	2

CULLY SIMON

1943R	9	1	0	1	4
1944	5	0	0	0	2
Totals	14	1	0	1	6

CLIFF SIMPSON

1947R	1	0	0	0	0
1948	1	0	0	0	2
Totals	2	0	0	0	2

DARRYL SITTLER

1985	2	0	2	2	0

GLEN SKOV

1951	6	0	0	0	0
1952	8	1	4	5	16
1953	6	1	0	1	2
1954	12	1	2	3	16
1955	11	2	0	2	8
Totals	43	5	6	11	42

ALEX SMITH

1932	2	0	0	0	4

BRAD SMITH

1985	3	0	1	1	5

BRIAN SMITH

1960	5	0	0	0	0

FLOYD SMITH

1963	11	2	3	5	4
1964	14	4	3	7	4
1965	7	1	3	4	4
1966	12	5	2	7	4
Totals	44	12	11	23	16

GREG SMITH

1984	4	1	0	1	8
1985	3	0	0	0	7
Totals	7	1	0	1	15

NORM SMITH

1936	7	6–1	598	12	2	1.71
1937	5	3–1	282	6	1	1.57
Totals	12	9–2	880	18	3	1.23

HAROLD SNEPSTS

1987	11	0	2	2	18
1988	10	0	0	0	40
Totals	21	0	2	2	58

JOHN SORRELL

1932	2	1	0	1	0
1933	4	2	2	4	4
1934	8	0	2	2	0
1936	7	3	4	7	0
1937	10	2	4	6	2
Totals	31	8	12	20	6

IRV SPENCER

1964	11	0	0	0	0
1965	1	0	0	0	4
1966	3	0	0	0	2
Totals	15	0	0	0	6

WILF STARR

1934	7	0	2	2	2

VIC STASIUK

1952	7	0	2	2	0
1955	11	5	3	8	6
1961	11	2	5	7	4
1963	11	3	0	3	4
Totals	40	10	10	20	14

■ named appears on 1954 Cup although he did not participate in playoffs

GREG STEFAN

1984	3	1–2	210	8	0	2.29
1985	3	0–3	138	17	0	7.39
1987	9	4–5	508	24	0	2.83
1988	10	5–4	531	32	1	3.62
1989	5	2–3	294	18	0	3.67
Totals	30	12–17	1681	99	1	3.53

PETE STEMKOWSKI

1970	4	1	1	2	6

GAYE STEWART

1951	6	0	2	2	4

JACK STEWART

1940	5	0	0	0	0
1941	9	1	2	3	8
1942	12	0	1	1	12
1943	10	1	2	3	35
1946	5	0	0	0	14
1947	5	0	1	1	12
1948	9	1	3	4	6
1949	11	1	1	2	32
1950	14	1	4	5	20
Totals	80	5	14	19	139

BILLY TAYLOR

1947	5	1	5	6	4

TIM TAYLOR

1995	6	0	1	1	12
1996	18	0	4	4	4
Totals	24	0	5	5	16

CECIL THOMPSON

1939	6	3–3	374	15	1	2.50
1940	5	2–3	300	12	0	2.40
Totals	11	5–6	674	27	1	2.40

ERROL THOMPSON

1978	7	2	1	3	2

BILLY THOMSON

1944	2	0	0	0	0

LARRY TRADER

1985	3	0	0	0	0

PERCY TRAUB

1929	2	0	0	0	0

NORM ULLMAN

1956R	10	1	3	4	13
1957	5	1	1	2	6
1958	4	0	2	2	4
1960	6	2	2	4	0
1961	11	0	4	4	4
1963	11	4	12	16	14
1964	14	7	10	17	6
1965	7	6	4	10	2
1966	12	6	9	15	12
Totals	80	27	47	74	61

GARRY UNGER

1970	4	0	1	1	6

DARREN VEITCH

1987	12	3	4	7	8
1988	11	1	5	6	6
Totals	23	4	9	13	14

MIKE VERNON

1995	18	12–6	1063	41	1	2.31
1996	4	2–2	243	11	0	2.72
Totals	22	14–8	1306	52	1	2.39

DOUG VOLMAR

1970	2	1	0	1	0

CARL VOSS

1933	4	1	1	2	0

BOB WALL

1965R	1	0	0	0	0
1966	6	0	0	0	2
Totals	7	0	0	0	2

EDDIE WARES

1939	6	1	0	1	8
1940	5	0	0	0	0
1941	2	0	0	0	0
1942	12	1	3	4	22
1943	10	3	3	6	4
Totals	35	5	6	11	34

BRYAN WATSON

1966	12	2	0	2	30

HARRY WATSON

1943	7	0	0	0	0
1946	5	2	0	2	0
Totals	12	2	0	2	0

COONEY WEILAND

1934	9	2	2	4	4

BOB WHITELAW

1941R	9	0	0	0	0

BURR WILLIAMS

1934R	7	0	0	0	8

JOHNNY WILSON

1950R	8	0	1	1	0
1951	1	0	0	0	0
1952	8	4	1	5	5
1953	6	2	5	7	0
1954	12	3	0	3	0
1955	11	0	1	1	0
1958	4	2	1	3	0
Totals	50	11	9	20	5

LARRY WILSON

1950R	4	0	0	0	0

EDDIE WISEMAN

1933R	2	0	0	0	0
1934	9	0	1	1	4
Totals	11	0	1	1	4

STEVE WOJCIECHOWSKI

1945R	6	0	1	1	0

BENNY WOIT

1951R	4	0	0	0	2
1952	8	1	1	2	2
1953	6	1	3	4	0
1954	12	0	1	1	8
1955	11	0	1	1	6
Totals	41	2	6	8	18

PAUL WOODS

1978R	7	0	5	5	4

DOUG YOUNG

1932R	2	0	0	0	2
1933	4	1	1	2	0
1934	9	0	0	0	10
1936	7	0	2	2	0
1939	6	0	2	2	4
Totals	28	1	5	6	16

HOWIE YOUNG

1961R	11	2	2	4	30
1963	8	0	2	2	16
Totals	19	2	4	6	46

PAUL YSEBAERT

1991	2	0	2	2	0
1992	10	1	0	1	10
1993	7	3	1	4	2
Totals	19	4	3	7	12

STEVE YZERMAN

1984R	4	3	3	6	0
1985	3	2	1	3	2
1987	16	5	13	18	8
1988	3	1	3	4	6
1989	6	5	5	10	2
1991	7	3	3	6	4
1992	11	3	5	8	12
1993	7	4	3	7	4
1994	3	1	3	4	0
1995	15	4	8	12	0
1996	18	8	12	20	4
Totals	93	39	59	98	42

LARRY ZEIDEL

1952R	5	0	0	0	0

RICK ZOMBO

1987	7	0	1	1	9
1988	16	0	6	6	55
1989	6	0	1	1	16
1991	7	1	0	1	10
Totals	36	1	8	9	90

MOST GOALS — PLAYOFFS

(home team in bold)

FOR

Date / Game / Series	Detroit	Opponent
April 7, 1936 Game 2 finals Detroit led 2–0, won Cup 3–1	**Detroit** 9	Toronto 4
March 29, 1947 Game 2 semi-finals Detroit tied series 1–1, lost 4–1	Detroit 9	**Toronto** 1
April 10, 1988 Game 4 1st round Detroit led series 3–1, won 4–2	Detroit 8	**Toronto** 0
May 5, 1996 Game 2 quarter-finals Detroit led series 2–0, won 4–3	**Detroit** 8	St. Louis 3
March 23, 1939 Game 2 quarter-finals Detroit tied series 1–1, won 2–1	**Detroit** 7	Canadiens 3
March 24, 1953 Game 1 semi-finals Detroit led series 1–0, lost 4–2	**Detroit** 7	Boston 0
March 22, 1955 Game 1 semi-finals Detroit led series 1–0, won 4–0	**Detroit** 7	Toronto 4
April 5, 1955 Game 2 finals Detroit led series 2–0, won Cup 4–3	**Detroit** 7	Canadiens 1
April 7, 1963 Game 6 semi-finals Detroit won series 4–2	**Detroit** 7	Chicago 4
April 7, 1964 Game 6 semi-finals Detroit tied series 3–3, won 4–3	**Detroit** 7	Chicago 2
April 10, 1966 Game 2 semi-finals Detroit tied series 1–1, won 4–2	Detroit 7	**Chicago** 0
April 29, 1993 Game 6 1st round Detroit tied series 3–3, Toronto won 4–3	Detroit 7	**Toronto** 3
April 28, 1994 Game 6 preliminary round Detroit tied series 3–3, San Jose won 4–3	**Detroit** 7	San Jose 1

AGAINST

Date / Game		
April 14, 1942 Game 5 finals Toronto trailed 3–2, won Cup 4–3	**Toronto** 9	Detroit 3
April 10, 1985 Game 1, 1st round Chicago led 1–0, won 3–0	**Chicago** 9	Detroit 5
March 25, 1958 Game 1 semi-finals Canadiens led series 1–0, won 4–0	**Canadiens** 8	Detroit 1
April 23, 1978 Game 4 quarter-finals Canadiens led 3–1, won 4–1	Canadiens 8	**Detroit** 0
May 11, 1988 Game 5 semi-finals Edmonton won series 4–1	**Edmonton** 8	Detroit 4
April 13, 1985 Game 3 1st round Chicago won 3–0	Chicago 8	**Detroit** 2
March 28, 1944 Game 4 semi-finals Chicago led 3–1, won series 4–1	**Chicago** 7	Detroit 1
April 14, 1948 Game 4 finals Toronto won Cup 4–0	Toronto 7	**Detroit** 2
April 23, 1987 Game 2 quarter-finals Toronto led series 2–0, Detroit won 4–3	Toronto 7	**Detroit** 2
April 13, 1989 Game 6 preliminary round Chicago won series 4–2	**Chicago** 7	Detroit 1

MOST GOALS — BOTH TEAMS — PLAYOFFS

Goals	Date	Score
14	April 10, 1985	**Chicago** 9 Detroit 5
13	April 7, 1936	**Detroit** 9 Toronto 4
12	April 14, 1942	**Toronto** 9 Detroit 3
	May 11, 1988	**Edmonton** 8 Detroit 4
11	March 22, 1955	**Detroit** 7 Toronto 4
	April 7, 1963	**Detroit** 7 Chicago 4
	April 12, 1988	Toronto 6 **Detroit** 5
	May 5, 1996	**Detroit** 8 St. Louis 3

PENALTY-FREE GAMES
PLAYOFFS

April 16, 1942 — Game 6, best-of-seven finals
Toronto 3 at Detroit 0

The 1932 Falcons at Windsor Station.

TEAM RECORDS
SERIES SCORING

MOST GOALS
7–Game Series

30	1993 vs. Toronto
27	1955 vs. Canadiens
	1994 vs. San Jose
24	1964 vs. Chicago

MOST GOALS ALLOWED
7–Game Series

25	1942 vs. Toronto
24	1991 vs. St. Louis
	1993 vs. Toronto
23	1965 vs. Chicago

MOST GOALS — BOTH TEAMS
7–Game Series

54	1993 vs. Toronto
48	1994 vs. San Jose
47	1955 vs. Canadiens
44	1942 vs. Toronto
	1945 vs. Boston
	1991 vs. St. Louis

MOST GOALS
6–Game Series

32	1988 vs. Toronto
25	1963 vs. Chicago
22	1966 vs. Chicago
21	1953 vs. Boston

MOST GOALS ALLOWED
6–Game Series

25	1989 vs. Chicago
21	1953 vs. Boston
20	1960 vs. Toronto
	1988 vs. Toronto
	1996 vs. Colorado

FEWEST GOALS
7–Game Series

9	1945 vs. Toronto
10	1950 vs. Toronto
14	1954 vs. Canadiens
17	1949 vs. Canadiens
	1964 vs. Toronto

FEWEST GOALS ALLOWED
7–Game Series

9	1945 vs. Toronto
11	1950 vs. Toronto
12	1954 vs. Canadiens
14	1949 vs. Canadiens

FEWEST GOALS — BOTH TEAMS
7–Game Series

18	1945 vs. Toronto
21	1950 vs. Toronto
26	1954 vs. Canadiens
31	1949 vs. Canadiens

FEWEST GOALS
6–Game Series

12	1951 vs. Canadiens
	1961 vs. Chicago
14	1966 vs. Canadiens
16	1960 vs. Toronto
	1996 vs. Colorado

FEWEST GOALS ALLOWED
6–Game Series

10	1966 vs. Chicago
	1996 vs. Winnipeg
12	1948 vs. Rangers
13	1951 vs. Canadiens

MOST GOALS — BOTH TEAMS
6–Game Series

52 1988 vs. Toronto
44 1963 vs. Chicago
43 1989 vs. Chicago
42 1953 vs. Boston

FEWEST GOALS — BOTH TEAMS
6–Game Series

25 1951 vs. Canadiens
29 1948 vs. Rangers
30 1996 vs. Winnipeg
31 1961 vs. Chicago

MOST GOALS
5–Game Series

21 1988 vs. St. Louis
17 1995 vs. Dallas
16 1988 vs. Edmonton
15 1954 vs. Toronto
1961 vs. Toronto

FEWEST GOALS
5–Game Series

8 1944 vs. Chicago
9 1937 vs. Rangers
1956 vs. Canadiens
10 1946 vs. Boston
1957 vs. Boston
1963 vs. Toronto
1978 vs. Canadiens
1987 vs. Edmonton

MOST GOALS ALLOWED
5–Game Series

24 1987 vs. Canadiens
23 1988 vs. Edmonton
18 1947 vs. Toronto
1956 vs. Canadiens

FEWEST GOALS ALLOWED
5–Game Series

8 1937 vs. Canadiens
1937 vs. Rangers
1954 vs. Toronto
1961 vs. Toronto
10 1956 vs. Toronto
1995 vs. Dallas

MOST GOALS — BOTH TEAMS
5–Game Series

39 1988 vs. Edmonton
35 1988 vs. St. Louis
34 1978 vs. Canadiens
32 1947 vs. Toronto

FEWEST GOALS — BOTH TEAMS
5–Game Series

17 1937 vs. Rangers
1995 vs. Dallas
1937 vs. Canadiens
21 1937 vs. Canadiens
23 1934 vs. Toronto
1954 vs. Toronto
1961 vs. Toronto

MOST GOALS
4–Game Series

24 1995 vs. San Jose
18 1936 vs. Toronto
16 1943 vs. Boston
1970 vs. Chicago

FEWEST GOALS
4–Game Series

5 1949 vs. Toronto
6 1941 vs. Boston
1958 vs. Canadiens
1992 vs. Chicago

MOST GOALS ALLOWED
4-Game Series

19 1958 vs. Canadiens
18 1948 vs. Toronto
16 1995 vs. New Jersey
13 1984 vs. St. Louis

FEWEST GOALS ALLOWED
4-Game Series

2 1952 vs. Canadiens
3 1952 vs. Toronto
5 1943 vs. Boston

MOST GOALS — BOTH TEAMS
4-Game Series

30 1995 vs. San Jose
29 1936 vs. Toronto
25 1948 vs. Toronto
1958 vs. Canadiens
1984 vs. St. Louis

FEWEST GOALS — BOTH TEAMS
4-Game Series

13 1952 vs. Canadiens
16 1934 vs. Chicago
1952 vs. Toronto
17 1949 vs. Toronto
1992 vs. Chicago

MOST GOALS
3-Game Series

9 1940 vs. Americans
8 1939 vs. Toronto
1942 vs. Canadiens
1985 vs. Chicago

FEWEST GOALS
3-Game Series

6 1936 vs. Maroons
1941 vs. Rangers

MOST GOALS ALLOWED
3-Game Series

23 1985 vs. Chicago
10 1939 vs. Toronto

FEWEST GOALS ALLOWED
3-Game Series

1 1936 vs. Maroons
6 1941 vs. Rangers

MOST GOALS — BOTH TEAMS
3-Game Series

31 1985 vs. Chicago
18 1939 vs. Toronto

FEWEST GOALS — BOTH TEAMS
3-Game Series

7 1936 vs. Maroons
12 1941 vs. Rangers

MOST GOALS
2-Game Series

9 1942 vs. Boston
8 1978 vs. Atlanta

FEWEST GOALS
2-Game Series

1 1932 vs. Maroons
2 1929 vs. Toronto
1940 vs. Toronto

MOST GOALS ALLOWED
2-Game Series

7 1929 vs. Toronto
6 1933 vs. Rangers

FEWEST GOALS ALLOWED
2-Game Series

2 1933 vs. Maroons
1941 vs. Chicago
3 1932 vs. Maroons

MOST GOALS — BOTH TEAMS
2–Game Series

14	1942 vs. Boston
13	1978 vs. Atlanta

FEWEST GOALS — BOTH TEAMS
2–Game Series

4	1932 vs. Maroons
7	1932 vs. Maroons
	1940 vs. Toronto
	1941 vs. Chicago

YEARS THE RED WINGS LED THE LEAGUE PLAYOFFS

POINTS — INDIVIDUAL

1933–34 Larry Aurie.......... 10
1936–37 Marty Barry.......... 11
1941–42 Don Grosso.......... 14
1942–43 Carl Liscombe.......... 14
1944–45 Joe Carveth.......... 11
1948–49 Gordie Howe.......... 11
1951–52 Ted Lindsay
Gordie Howe
Metro Prystai.......... 7
(tied with one other)
1954–55 Gordie Howe.......... 20
1960–61 Gordie Howe.......... 15
(tied with one other)
1962–63 Gordie Howe
Norm Ullman.......... 16
1963–64 Gordie Howe.......... 19
1965–66 Norm Ullman.......... 15
1994–95 Sergei Fedorov.......... 24

GOALS — INDIVIDUAL

1936–37 Marty Barry.......... 4
(tied with one other)
1941–42 Don Grosso.......... 8
1942–43 Carl Liscombe.......... 6
(tied with two others)
1948–49 Gordie Howe.......... 8
1951–52 Ted Lindsay.......... 5
1954–55 Gordie Howe.......... 9
1963–64 Gordie Howe.......... 9
1965–66 Norm Ullman.......... 6
(tied with one other)

ASSISTS — INDIVIDUAL

1933–34 Larry Aurie.......... 7
(tied with one other)
1936–37 Marty Barry.......... 7
1940–41 Syd Howe.......... 7
1944–45 Joe Carveth.......... 6
1947–48 Pete Horeck.......... 7
(tied with one other)
1948–49 Ted Lindsay.......... 6
(tied with one other)
1949–50 George Gee.......... 6
(tied with one other)
1951–52 Metro Prystai
Gordie Howe.......... 5
1954–55 Ted Lindsay.......... 12
1962–63 Norm Ullman.......... 12
1965–66 Alex Delvecchio.......... 11

PENALTY MINUTES — INDIVIDUAL

1936–37 Johnny Gallagher.......... 15
(tied with one other)
1940–41 Jimmy Orlando.......... 31
1941–42 Jimmy Orlando.......... 55
1942–43 Jack Stewart.......... 35
1948–49 Jack Stewart.......... 32
1951–52 Leo Reise.......... 27
1953–54 Gordie Howe.......... 31
1960–61 Howie Young.......... 30
1962–63 Bill Gadsby.......... 36

PENALTY MINUTES — TEAM

1941–42	205
1947–48	116
1948–49	164
1949–50	148
1951–52	118
1962–63	170

GOALS AGAINST AVERAGE

1935–36	Norm Smith	1.71
1942–43	John Mowers	2.20
1944–45	Harry Lumley	2.21
1951–52	Terry Sawchuk	0.62

SHUTOUTS

1935–36	2 (tied with one other)
1942–43	2
1945–46	1
1949–50	3 (tied with one other)
1951–52	4
1954–55	1 (tied with one other)
1965–66	1 (tied with one other)
1986–87	2 (tied with one other)
1987–88	2
1991–92	2 (tied with two others)

Norm Smith

CAREER PLAYOFF RECORDS

MOST SEASONS

Gordie Howe	19
Alex Delvecchio	14
Ted Lindsay	14
Marcel Pronovost	14
Sid Abel	12
Steve Yzerman	11
Red Kelly	11
Marty Pavelich	10
Terry Sawchuk	10
Mud Brûneteau	9
Syd Howe	9
Jack Stewart	9
Norm Ullman	9

MOST GAMES — PLAYOFFS — CAREER

Gordie Howe	154
Ted Lindsay	123
Alex Delvecchio	121
Marcel Pronovost	118
Sid Abel	96
Steve Yzerman	93
Marty Pavelich	91
Terry Sawchuk	84
Jack Stewart	80
Norm Ullman	80
Shawn Burr	79
Red Kelly	74
Mud Brûneteau	72
Syd Howe	68
Sergei Fedorov	68
Bob Probert	63
Vladimir Konstantinov	62
Joe Carveth	60

By Position:

CENTRE

Alex Delvecchio	121
Steve Yzerman	93
Sid Abel	93
Norm Ullman	80

LEFT WING

Ted Lindsay	123
Marty Pavelich	91
Shawn Burr	79

RIGHT WING

Gordie Howe	154
Mud Brûneteau	72
Bob Probert	63
Joe Carveth	60

DEFENCE

Marcel Pronovost	118
Jack Stewart	80
Vladimir Konstantinov	62
Bob Goldham	53

MOST POINTS — PLAYOFFS — CAREER

Gordie Howe	158
Alex Delvecchio	104
Steve Yzerman	98
Ted Lindsay	90
Sergei Fedorov	77
Norm Ullman	74
Sid Abel	56
Paul Coffey	50
Syd Howe	44
Bob Probert	43
Carl Liscombe	40
Gerard Gallant	39
Adam Oates	39
Vyacheslav Kozlov	37
Mud Brûneteau	37
Red Kelly	37
Joe Carveth	34
Shawn Burr	33

Ted Lindsay

By Position:

CENTRE

Alex Delvecchio	104
Steve Yzerman	98
Sergei Fedorov	77
Norm Ullman	74

LEFT WING

Ted Lindsay	90
Carl Liscombe	40
Gerard Gallant	39
Shawn Burr	33

RIGHT WING

Gordie Howe	158
Bob Probert	43
Mud Brûneteau	37
Joe Carveth	34

DEFENCE

Paul Coffey	50
Marcel Pronovost	30
Steve Chiasson	26

MOST GOALS — PLAYOFFS — CAREER

Gordie Howe . . . 67
Ted Lindsay . . . 46
Steve Yzerman . . . 39
Alex Delvecchio . . . 35
Sid Abel . . . 28
Norm Ullman . . . 27
Dino Ciccarelli . . . 24
Mud Brûneteau . . . 23
Carl Liscombe . . . 22
Sergei Fedorov . . . 19
Joe Carveth . . . 19
Gerard Gallant . . . 18

By Position:

CENTRE
Steve Yzerman . . . 39
Alex Delvecchio . . . 35
Sid Abel . . . 28
Norm Ullman . . . 27

LEFT WING
Ted Lindsay . . . 46
Carl Liscombe . . . 22
Gerard Gallant . . . 18

RIGHT WING
Gordie Howe . . . 67
Dino Ciccarelli . . . 24
Mud Brûneteau . . . 23
Joe Carveth . . . 19

DEFENCE
Paul Coffey . . . 14
Steve Chiasson . . . 12

MOST ASSISTS — PLAYOFFS — CAREER

Gordie Howe . . . 91
Alex Delvecchio . . . 69
Steve Yzerman . . . 59
Sergei Fedorov . . . 58
Norm Ullman . . . 47
Ted Lindsay . . . 44
Paul Coffey . . . 36
Bob Probert . . . 29
Sid Abel . . . 30
Syd Howe . . . 27
Adam Oates . . . 27
Nicklas Lidstrom . . . 25
Marcel Pronovost . . . 23
Gerard Gallant . . . 21
Red Kelly . . . 21
Vyacheslav Kozlov . . . 21

By Position:

CENTRE
Alex Delvecchio . . . 69
Steve Yzerman . . . 59
Sergei Fedorov . . . 58
Norm Ullman . . . 47

LEFT WING
Ted Lindsay . . . 44
Gerard Gallant . . . 21
Carl Liscombe . . . 19

RIGHT WING
Gordie Howe . . . 91
Bob Probert . . . 29
Larry Aurie . . . 16

DEFENCE
Paul Coffey . . . 36
Marcel Pronovost . . . 23
Steve Chiasson . . . 14
Bill Gadsby . . . 14
Jack Stewart . . . 14
Lee Norwood . . . 14

MOST PENALTY MINUTES — PLAYOFFS — CAREER

Gordie Howe 218
Bob Probert 210
Ted Lindsay 181
Gerard Gallant 178
Keith Primeau 144
Jack Stewart 139
Steve Chiasson 108
Jimmy Orlando 105
Joey Kocur 95
Marcel Pronovost 90
Rick Zombo 90
Jim Nill 87
Lee Norwood 87
Shawn Burr 79
Dino Ciccarelli 78
Vladimir Konstantinov 78
Bill Gadsby 78
Sid Abel 77

By Position:

CENTRE
Keith Primeau 144
Sid Abel 77
Ebbie Goodfellow 67

LEFT WING
Ted Lindsay 181
Gerard Gallant 178
Shawn Burr 79
Tony Leswick 71

RIGHT WING
Gordie Howe 218
Bob Probert 210
Joey Kocur 95
Jim Nill 87

DEFENCE
Jack Stewart 139
Steve Chiasson 108
Jimmy Orlando 105
Marcel Pronovost 90

MOST POINTS — PLAYOFF SEASON

Sergei Fedorov ('95) 24
Bob Probert ('88) 21
Gordie Howe ('55) 20
Adam Oates ('88) 20
Sergei Fedorov ('96) 20
Steve Yzerman ('96) 20
Ted Lindsay ('55) 19
Gordie Howe ('64) 19
John Chabot ('88) 19
Steve Yzerman ('87) 18
Petr Klima ('88) 18
Paul Coffey ('95) 18
Norm Ullman ('64) 17
Gordie Howe ('63) 16
Norm Ullman ('63) 16
Vyacheslav Kozlov ('95) 16
Nicklas Lidstrom ('96) 16
Alex Delvecchio ('55) 15
Gordie Howe ('61) 15
Norm Ullman ('66) 15
Gerard Gallant ('88) 15

By Position:

CENTRE
Sergei Fedorov ('95) 24
Adam Oates ('88) 20
Sergei Fedorov ('96) 20
Steve Yzerman ('96) 20

LEFT WING
Ted Lindsay ('55) 19
Petr Klima ('88) 18
Gerard Gallant ('88) 15

RIGHT WING
Bob Probert ('88) 21
Gordie Howe ('55) 20
Gordie Howe ('64) 19
Gordie Howe ('63) 16

DEFENCE

Paul Coffey ('95) 18
Nicklas Lidstrom ('96) 16
Paul Coffey ('96) 14

MOST GOALS — PLAYOFF SEASON

Petr Klima ('88) 10
Gordie Howe ('55) 9
Gordie Howe ('64) 9
Dino Ciccarelli ('95) 9
Don Grosso ('42) 8
Gordie Howe ('49) 8
Gerard Gallant ('87) 8
Adam Oates ('88) 8
Bob Probert ('88) 8
Alex Delvecchio ('55) 7
Ted Lindsay ('55) 7
Alex Delvecchio ('56) 7
Gordie Howe ('63) 7
Norm Ullman ('64) 7
Shawn Burr ('87) 7
Brent Ashton ('88) 7
Sergei Fedorov ('95) 7

By Position:

CENTRE

Don Grosso ('42) 8
Adam Oates ('88) 8
Steve Yzerman ('96) 8
Alex Delvecchio ('55) 7

LEFT WING

Petr Klima ('88) 10
Gerard Gallant ('87) 8
Ted Lindsay ('55) 7
Brent Ashton ('88) 7

RIGHT WING

Gordie Howe ('55) 9
Gordie Howe ('64) 9
Dino Ciccarelli ('95) 9
Gordie Howe ('49) 8

DEFENCE

Paul Coffey ('95) 6
Paul Coffey ('96) 5
Vladimir Konstantinov ('96) 4

MOST ASSISTS — PLAYOFF SEASON

Sergei Fedorov ('96) 18
Sergei Fedorov ('95) 17
John Chabot ('88) 15
Steve Yzerman ('87) 13
Bob Probert ('88) 13
Ted Lindsay ('55) 12
Norm Ullman ('63) 12
Adam Oates ('88) 12
Paul Coffey ('95) 12
Steve Yzerman ('96) 12
Gordie Howe ('55) 11
Gordie Howe ('61) 11
Alex Delvecchio ('66) 11
Gordie Howe ('64) 10
Norm Ullman ('64) 10

By Position:

CENTRE

Sergei Fedorov ('96) 18
Sergei Fedorov ('95) 17
John Chabot ('88) 15
Steve Yzerman ('87) 13

LEFT WING
Ted Lindsay ('55) 12
Gerard Gallant ('88) 9
Brent Ashton ('87) 9

RIGHT WING
Bob Probert ('88) 13
Gordie Howe ('55) 11
Gordie Howe ('61) 11
Gordie Howe ('64) 10

DEFENCE
Paul Coffey ('95) 12
Paul Coffey ('93) 9
Nicklas Lidstrom ('96) 9
Paul Coffey ('96) 9

MOST PENALTY MINUTES — PLAYOFF SEASON

Joey Kocur ('87) 71
Bob Probert ('87) 63
Jim Nill ('88) 62
Gerard Gallant ('88) 55
Rick Zombo ('88) 55
Bob Probert ('88) 51
Bob Probert ('91) 50
Jimmy Orlando ('42) 45
Keith Primeau ('95) 45
Gerard Gallant ('87) 43
Randy McKay ('91) 41
Harold Snepsts ('88) 40
Lee Norwood ('88) 40
Gerard Gallant ('89) 40

By Position:

CENTRE
Keith Primeau ('95) 45
Keith Primeau ('93) 26
Keith Primeau ('91) 25
Sergei Fedorov ('93) 23

LEFT WING
Gerard Gallant ('88) 55
Gerard Gallant ('87) 43
Marc Potvin ('91) 32
Ted Lindsay ('49) 31

RIGHT WING
Joey Kocur ('87) 71
Bob Probert ('87) 63
Jim Nill ('88) 62
Bob Probert ('88) 51

DEFENCE
Rick Zombo ('88) 55
Jimmy Orlando ('42) 45
Harold Snepsts ('88) 40
Lee Norwood ('88) 40

ALL GOALIE RECORDS — PLAYOFFS

MOST GAMES

Terry Sawchuk	85
Harry Lumley	54
John Mowers	32
Greg Stefan	30
Tim Cheveldae	25
Chris Osgood	23
Mike Vernon	22
Roger Crozier	22

MOST WINS

Terry Sawchuk	47
Harry Lumley	24
John Mowers	19
Mike Vernon	14
Greg Stefan	12
Chris Osgood	11
Tim Cheveldae	9
Roger Crozier	9
Glen Hanlon	9
Norm Smith	9

MOST LOSSES

Terry Sawchuk	37
Harry Lumley	30
Greg Stefan	17
Tim Cheveldae	15
John Mowers	13
Roger Crozier	12
Chris Osgood	9
Glenn Hall	9
Mike Vernon	8
Glen Hanlon	6
Cecil Thompson	6

MOST SHUTOUTS

Here is a complete list of the goalies who have registered the 36 playoff shutouts for the Red Wings:

Terry Sawchuk	11
Harry Lumley	6
Chris Osgood	3
Glen Hanlon	3
Norm Smith	3
John Mowers	2
Earl Robertson	2
Greg Stefan	1
Mike Vernon	1
Roger Crozier	1
Wilf Cude	1
Cecil Thompson	1
John Ross Roach	1

GOALS AGAINST AVERAGE
(minimum 10 games played)

Norm Smith	1.28
Chris Osgood	2.15
Harry Lumley	2.26
Cecil Thompson	2.32
Mike Vernon	2.39
John Mowers	2.45
Terry Sawchuk	2.51
Roger Crozier	2.59
Glen Hanlon	2.58
Glenn Hall	2.86

Cecil Thompson

MOST ASSISTS — CAREER
(all goalies)

Tim Cheveldae	4
Greg Stefan	3
Bob Essensa	2
Jim Rutherford	1

MOST ASSISTS — SEASON

Greg Stefan ('86–'87)	2
Tim Cheveldae ('92–'93)	2
Bob Essensa ('93–'94)	2

MOST PENALTY MINUTES — CAREER
(all goalies)

Tim Cheveldae	8
Chris Osgood	6
Greg Stefan	4
Glen Hanlon	2
Mike Vernon	2

MOST PENALTY MINUTES — SEASON

Tim Cheveldae ('91–'92)	6
Greg Stefan ('88–'89)	4
Chris Osgood ('95–'96)	4
Glen Hanlon ('86–'87)	2
Tim Cheveldae ('92–'93)	2
Chris Osgood ('93–'94)	2

GOAL-SCORING RECORDS— INDIVIDUAL — PLAYOFFS

FOUR GOAL GAMES

1945	April 3	Carl Liscombe vs. Boston Bruins in 5–3 win at the Olympia
1955	April 5	Ted Lindsay vs. Montreal Canadiens in 7–1 Detroit win at the Olympia

HAT TRICKS

1939	March 23	Syd Howe vs. Montreal Canadiens in 7–3 Detroit win at the Olympia
1943	April 1	Mud Brûneteau vs. Boston Bruins in 6–2 Detroit win at the Olympia
1943	April 7	Don Grosso vs. Boston Bruins in 4–0 Detroit win at the Garden
1955	April 10	Gordie Howe vs. Montreal Canadiens in 5–1 Detroit win at the Olympia
1964	March 29	Norm Ullman vs. Chicago Blackhawks in 5–4 Detroit win at the Stadium
1964	April 7	Norm Ullman vs. Chicago Blackhawks in 7–2 Detroit win at the Olympia
1965	April 11	Norm Ullman vs. Chicago Blackhawks in 4–2 Detroit win at the Olympia
1988	April 7	Petr Klima vs. Toronto Maple Leafs in 6–2 Detroit win at the Joe Louis Arena
1988	April 21	Petr Klima vs. St. Louis Blues in 6–0 Detroit win at the Joe Louis Arena
1989	April 6	Steve Yzerman vs. Chicago Blackhawks in 5–4 Chicago win at the Joe Louis Arena
1991	April 4	Steve Yzerman vs. St. Louis Blues in 6–3 Detroit win at the St. Louis Arena
1992	April 24	Ray Sheppard vs. Minnesota North Stars in 5–4 Minnesota win at the Met Centre
1993	April 29	Dino Ciccarelli vs. Toronto Maple Leafs in 7–3 Detroit win at Maple Leaf Gardens
1995	May 11	Dino Ciccarelli vs. Dallas Stars in 5–1 Detroit win at Reunion Arena
1996	May 8	Steve Yzerman vs. St. Louis Blues in 5–4 St. Louis win at the Kiel Centre

MOST POINTS — GAME — PLAYOFFS

5	Eddie Bush (1 goal, 4 assists)	April 9, 1942
	Roy Conacher (2 goals, 3 assists)	March 29, 1947
	Norm Ullman (2 goals, 3 assists)	April 7, 1963
	Norm Ullman (3 goals, 2 assists)	April 7, 1964
	Steve Yzerman (2 goals, 3 assists)	May 5, 1996
4	John Sorrell (2 goals, 2 assists)	April 7, 1936
	Marty Barry (4 assists)	March 23, 1937
	Carl Liscombe (2 goals, 2 assists)	March 26, 1942
	Sid Abel (4 assists)	April 1, 1943
	Carl Liscombe (4 goals)	April 3, 1945
	Ted Lindsay (2 goals, 2 assists)	March 24, 1953
	Ted Lindsay (4 goals)	April 5, 1955
	Gordie Howe (1 goal, 3 assists)	April 5, 1955
	Earl Reibel (4 assists)	April 5, 1955
	Gordie Howe (1 goal, 3 assists)	April 10, 1966
	Petr Klima (3 goals, 1 assist)	April 21, 1988
	Steve Yzerman (1 goal, 3 assists)	April 11, 1989
	Paul Coffey (1 goal, 3 assists)	April 29, 1993
	Sergei Fedorov (1 goal, 3 assists)	May 21, 1995
	Sergei Fedorov (4 assists)	April 23, 1996

MOST ASSISTS — GAME — PLAYOFFS

4	Marty Barry	March 23, 1937
	Eddie Bush	April 9, 1942
	Sid Abel	April 1, 1943
	Earl Reibel	April 5, 1955
	Sergei Fedorov	April 23, 1996
	Sergei Fedorov	May 23, 1996
3	Larry Aurie	March 24, 1934
	Syd Howe	April 7, 1936
	Charlie Conacher	March 23, 1939
	Roy Conacher	March 29, 1947
	Billy Taylor	March 29, 1947
	Pete Horeck	March 26, 1948
	Alex Delvecchio	March 22, 1955
	Gordie Howe	April 5, 1955
	Gordie Howe	April 7, 1963
	Norm Ullman	April 7, 1963
	Norm Ullman	April 10, 1966
	Alex Delvecchio	April 14, 1966
	Paul Woods	April 13, 1978
	Adam Oates	April 7, 1988
	Adam Oates	May 7, 1988
	Paul Coffey	April 21, 1993
	Paul Coffey	April 29, 1993
	Sergei Fedorov	May 21, 1995
	Bob Errey	May 5, 1996

MOST POINTS — PERIOD — PLAYOFFS

4	Carl Liscombe (2 goals, 2 assists)	3rd period, March 26, 1942
3	Syd Howe (1 goal, 2 assists)	3rd period, April 14, 1942
	Roy Conacher (2 goals, 1 assist)	3rd period, March 29, 1947
	Billy Taylor (3 assists)	3rd period, March 29, 1947
	Red Kelly (1 goal, 2 assists)	1st period, April 4, 1948
	Ted Lindsay (1 goal, 2 assists)	1st period, March 24, 1953
	Marty Pavelich (2 goals, 1 assist)	1st period, March 24, 1953
	Gordie Howe (2 goals, 1 assist)	3rd period, March 22, 1955
	Ted Lindsay (3 goals)	2nd period, April 5, 1955
	Norm Ullman (1 goal, 2 assists)	2nd period, April 7, 1964
	Alex Delvecchio (3 assists)	3rd period, April 14, 1966
	Vaclav Nedomansky (1 goal, 2 assists)	1st period, April 11, 1978
	Ray Sheppard (2 goals, 1 assist)	1st period, April 24, 1992
	Sergei Fedorov (1 goal, 2 assists)	3rd period, May 21, 1995
	Vyacheslav Kozlov (2 goals, 1 assist)	1st period, May 27, 1995
	Steve Yzerman (1 goal, 2 assists)	1st period, May 5, 1996

MOST GOALS — PERIOD — PLAYOFFS

3	Ted Lindsay	2nd period, April 5, 1955

MOST ASSISTS — PERIOD — PLAYOFFS

3	Billy Taylor	3rd period, March 29, 1947
	Alex Delvecchio	3rd period, April 14, 1966

POWER-PLAY AND SHORT-HANDED GOALS — PLAYOFFS

MOST POWER-PLAY GOALS — CAREER — PLAYOFFS

Gordie Howe	16
Dino Ciccarelli	16
Steve Yzerman	12
Alex Delvecchio	12
Ted Lindsay	9
Norm Ullman	9
Nicklas Lidstrom	7
Steve Chiasson	7

MOST POWER-PLAY GOALS — SEASON — PLAYOFFS

Alex Delvecchio ('55)	6
Gordie Howe ('55)	6
Dino Ciccarelli ('95)	6
Dino Ciccarelli ('96)	6
Andy Bathgate ('66)	5
Bob Probert ('88)	5

MOST POWER-PLAY GOALS — GAME — PLAYOFFS

3	Syd Howe	March 23, 1939
	Gordie Howe	April 10, 1955

MOST SHORT-HANDED GOALS — CAREER — PLAYOFFS

Gordie Howe	4
Paul Coffey	3
Chris Draper	3
Sergei Fedorov	3

MOST SHORT-HANDED GOALS — SEASON — PLAYOFFS

Sergei Fedorov ('92)	2
Paul Coffey ('96)	2

SPEED RECORDS
PLAYOFFS

FASTEST GOAL FROM START OF GAME

9 seconds — Gordie Howe, April 1, 1954 vs. Toronto

FASTEST TWO GOALS FROM START OF GAME

55 seconds — Ted Lindsay (:23)
Bob Goldham (:55)
April 2, 1953

FASTEST TWO GOALS — INDIVIDUAL

5 seconds* — April 11, 1965, 2nd period vs. Chicago
Norm Ullman scored at 17:35 & 17:40

* NHL record

FASTEST THREE GOALS

1:30 March 29, 1947, 3rd period vs. Toronto
Jim Conacher (17:30)
Roy Conacher (18:30)
Ed Brûneteau (19:00)
Detroit 9 Toronto 1

1:36 April 28, 1994, 1st period, vs. San Jose
Steve Chiasson (15:20)
Ray Sheppard (16:33)
Vyacheslav Kozlov (16:56)

FASTEST THREE GOALS — BOTH TEAMS

1:08 2nd period, April 7, 1963 vs. Chicago
Bobby Hull 3:53 (Chicago)
Larry Jeffrey 4:12 (Detroit)
Alex Delvecchio 5:01 (Detroit)

FASTEST FOUR GOALS

4:46 March 23, 1939, 3rd period vs. Canadiens
Syd Howe (13:44)
Syd Howe (14:39)
Sid Abel (17:02)
Eddie Wares (18:30)
Detroit 7 Canadiens 3

FASTEST FOUR GOALS — BOTH TEAMS

1:49 3rd period, March 24, 1934 vs. Toronto
Hec Kilrea 11:12 (Toronto)
Charlie Conacher 12:16 (Toronto)
Ted Graham 12:49 (Detroit)
Larry Aurie 13:01 (Detroit)

MOST GOALS — PERIOD — TEAM

6 3rd period March 29, 1947

MOST POWER-PLAY GOALS — TEAM — GAME

4 March 23, 1939 vs. Canadiens
April 4, 1965 vs. Chicago
April 10, 1966 vs. Chicago
April 29, 1993 vs. Toronto

MOST POWER-PLAY GOALS — TEAM — PERIOD

3 April 11, 1978 vs. Atlanta

MOST SHORT-HANDED GOALS — TEAM — GAME

2 April 5, 1936 vs. Toronto
Syd Howe
Bucko McDonald

April 29, 1993 vs. Toronto
Steve Yzerman
Paul Ysebaert

MOST SHORT-HANDED GOALS — TEAM — PERIOD

2 April 29, 1993 vs. Toronto
Steve Yzerman
Paul Ysebaert

MOST PENALTY MINUTES — TEAM — GAME

152* April 12, 1991 vs. St. Louis
* NHL record

MOST PENALTY MINUTES — TEAM — PERIOD

114 April 12, 1991 vs. St. Louis

MOST PENALTIES — TEAM — GAME

33* April 12, 1991 vs. St. Louis

* ties NHL record

MOST PENALTIES — TEAM — PERIOD

20 April 12, 1991 vs. St. Louis

Sid Abel

EMPTY-NET GOALS
PLAYOFFS

1.	March 31, 1942	Don Grosso (unassisted)	19:54
2.	March 28, 1943	Sid Abel (Liscombe, Orlando)	19:59
3.	April 10, 1952	Ted Lindsay (Abel)	18:44*
4.	March 27, 1954	Marcel Pronovost (unassisted)	18:38
5.	April 10, 1954	Red Kelly (unassisted)	19:53
6.	March 22, 1955	Tony Leswick (Pavelich, Goldham)	19:33
7.	April 3, 1955	Ted Lindsay (G. Howe)	19:42
8.	March 29, 1956	Ted Lindsay (G. Howe, M. Pronovost)	19:35
9.	March 28, 1961	Val Fonteyne (Goegan, Ullman)	19:55
10.	April 8, 1961	Alex Delvecchio (Stasiuk, G. Howe)	19:22
11.	April 11, 1978	Andre St. Laurent (Harper)	19:59
12.	May 1, 1987	Shawn Burr (Kocur, Delorme)	19:49
13.	May 7, 1988	Mel Bridgman (Zombo, Chabot)	18:33
14.	April 8, 1991	Kelly Miller (unassisted)	19:42
15.	April 26, 1992	Jimmy Carson (Burr)	18:51
16.	April 28, 1996	Keith Primeau (unassisted)	19:45

* the last part of the game was played without the electronic clock. However, referee Chadwick later ruled that 21:00 had been played in the 3rd. Thus, Abel's goal, originally recorded as 19:44, was moved back to 18:44.

PENALTY SHOTS — PLAYOFFS

FOR

1988 April 9 Petr Klima scored on Allan Bester (Toronto) in 6–3 Detroit win at Maple Leaf Gardens

AGAINST

1937 April 15 Alex Shibicky (Rangers) stopped by Earl Robertson in 3–0 Detroit win at the Olympia

RED WINGS WHOSE FIRST NHL GAME WAS A PLAYOFF GAME

Jimmy Franks*	March 27, 1937 vs. Canadiens
Don Grosso	March 21, 1939 vs. Canadiens
Gerry Couture	April 12, 1945 vs. Toronto
Jim McFadden**	March 29, 1947 vs. Toronto
Enio Sclisizzi	April 5, 1947 vs. Toronto
Lee Fogolin	April 11, 1948 vs. Toronto
Fred Glover	April 8, 1949 vs. Toronto
Marcel Pronovost	April 6, 1950 vs. Toronto
Guyle Fielder	March 24, 1953 vs. Boston
Gerry Melnyk	March 27, 1956 vs. Toronto

* Franks is the only Red Wings goalie ever to make his NHL debut in the playoffs. He replaced Norm Smith at 10:28 of the 2nd, March 27, 1937 and allowed two goals.
** Jim McFadden is the only Red Wing ever to register a point in his first ever NHL game, a playoff game. On March 29, 1947 he registered two assists in a 9–1 Detroit win over the Leafs at Maple Leaf Gardens.

Jim McFadden

SHOTS ON GOAL RECORDS
PLAYOFFS

MOST SHOTS — GAME

66	March 27, 1960 vs. Toronto
52	April 26, 1996 vs. Winnipeg
51	April 10, 1985 vs. Chicago
	June 6, 1995 vs. Chicago

MOST SHOTS AGAINST — GAME

52	March 27, 1960 by Toronto
50	April 27, 1987 by Toronto

MOST SHOTS — PERIOD

20	3rd period	March 20, 1956 vs. Toronto
	3rd period	April 11, 1970 vs. Chicago

MOST SHOTS AGAINST — PERIOD

21	2nd period	April 27, 1987 by Toronto
19	1st period	April 8, 1970 by Chicago

FEWEST SHOTS — GAME

16	May 3, 1988 vs. Edmonton
	April 8, 1989 vs. Chicago
	June 24, 1995 vs. New Jersey
17	June 17, 1995 vs. New Jersey
18	May 7, 1987 vs. Edmonton
	April 12, 1991 vs. St. Louis
	June 20, 1995 vs. New Jersey
19	April 16, 1961 vs. Chicago
	May 11, 1987 vs. Edmonton
	April 13, 1989 vs. Chicago

FEWEST SHOTS AGAINST — GAME

12	May 29, 1995 by San Jose
14	June 1, 1995 by Chicago
	April 17, 1996 by Winnipeg
15	April 9, 1987 by Chicago
	May 21, 1995 by San Jose
16	April 27, 1988 by St. Louis
17	April 30, 1994 by San Jose
	May 23, 1995 by San Jose
	May 25, 1996 by Colorado
18	April 2, 1963 by Chicago

FEWEST SHOTS — PERIOD

1	3rd period	June 24, 1995 vs. New Jersey
2	2nd period	April 21, 1988 vs. St. Louis
	2nd period	April 25, 1988 vs. St. Louis
	1st period	April 8, 1991 vs. St. Louis
	3rd period	April 28, 1992 vs. Minnesota
3	1st period	April 13, 1985 vs. Chicago
	3rd period	April 21, 1993 vs. Toronto
	1st period	May 3, 1988 vs. Edmonton
	1st period	May 11, 1988 vs. Edmonton
	2nd period	May 14, 1996 vs. St. Louis
	3rd period	June 1, 1995 vs. Chicago
	1st period	May 27, 1996 vs. Colorado

FEWEST SHOTS AGAINST — PERIOD

1	3rd period	June 1, 1995 by Chicago
2	1st period	April 8, 1961 by Chicago
	2nd period	May 29, 1995 by San Jose
	2nd period	June 11, 1995 by Chicago
3	1st period	April 4, 1957 by Boston
	3rd period	April 8, 1984 by St. Louis
	2nd period	April 25, 1987 by Toronto
	2nd period	April 19, 1988 by St. Louis
	2nd period	April 20, 1992 by Minnesota
	1st period	May 7, 1995 by Dallas
	1st period	May 29, 1995 by San Jose
	3rd period	June 4, 1995 by Chicago
	1st period	June 20, 1995 by New Jersey
	3rd period	April 17, 1996 by Winnipeg
	1st period	April 26, 1996 by Winnipeg

MOST SHOTS — BOTH TEAMS — GAME

118	March 27, 1960 vs. Toronto (Detroit 66, Toronto 52)

FEWEST SHOTS — BOTH TEAMS — GAME

37	April 21, 1988 (Detroit 18, St. Louis 19)
38	June 1, 1995 (Detroit 24, Chicago 14)
41	April 4, 1957 vs. Boston (Detroit 26, Boston 15)
	April 19, 1988 (St. Louis 19, Detroit 22)
	May 23, 1996 (Detroit 22, Colorado 19)
42	June 24, 1995 (New Jersey 26, Detroit 16)
44	March 25, 1961 vs. Toronto (Toronto 20, Detroit 24)
	May 11, 1987 (Edmonton 20, Detroit 24)

MOST SHOTS — BOTH TEAMS — PERIOD

35	3rd period	April 14, 1961 (Chicago 24, Detroit 11)
33	1st period	April 4, 1963 (Chicago 18, Detroit 15)
31	1st period	April 10, 1985 (Detroit 18, Chicago 13)

FEWEST SHOTS — BOTH TEAMS — PERIOD

4	3rd period	June 1, 1995 (Detroit 3, Chicago 1)
7	2nd period	April 19, 1988 (Detroit 4, St. Louis 3)
	3rd period	April 28, 1992 (Minnesota 5, Detroit 2)
8	2nd period	April 21, 1988 (St. Louis 6, Detroit 2)
	1st period	May 27, 1996 (Colorado 5, Detroit 3)
	2nd period	May 14, 1996 (St. Louis 5, Detroit 3)
9	2nd period	April 2, 1957 (Boston 5, Detroit 4)
	2nd period	April 24, 1994 (San Jose 5, Detroit 4)
	3rd period	May 23, 1995 (San Jose 4, Detroit 5)

10-3-6-2
OTTAWA
OTTAWA. 1904
OTTAWA. 1904
S. CLEGHORN A. JOLIAT O. CLEGHORN
GEO VEZINA H. MORENZ
B. COUTU B. BOUCHER S. MANTHA

Stanley Cup

STANLEY CUP FINALS APPEARANCES

Detroit has appeared in the Stanley Cup Finals 19 times (7–12).

(h) indicates the Cup was presented in Detroit;
(a) means the Cup was won in the opponents' rink.

WON

1936 vs. Toronto . . . . . 3–1 (a)
1937 vs. Rangers . . . . . 3–2 (h)
1943 vs. Boston . . . . . 4–0 (a)
1950 vs. Rangers . . . . . 4–3 (h)
1952 vs. Canadiens . . . . . 4–0 (h)
1954 vs. Canadiens . . . . . 4–3 (h)
1955 vs. Canadiens . . . . . 4–3 (h)

LOST

1934 vs. Chicago . . . . . 3–1 (a)
1941 vs. Boston . . . . . 4–0 (h)
1942 vs. Toronto . . . . . 4–3 (a)
1945 vs. Toronto . . . . . 4–3 (h)
1948 vs. Toronto . . . . . 4–0 (h)
1949 vs. Toronto . . . . . 4–0 (a)
1956 vs. Canadiens . . . . . 4–1 (a)
1961 vs. Chicago . . . . . 4–2 (h)
1963 vs. Toronto . . . . . 4–1 (a)
1964 vs. Toronto . . . . . 4–3 (a)
1966 vs. Canadiens . . . . . 4–2 (h)
1995 vs. New Jersey . . . . . 4–0 (a)

STANLEY CUP WINNING GOALS

1936 Marty Barry
1937 Marty Barry
1943 Joe Carveth
1950 Pete Babando (OT)
1952 Metro Prystai
1954 Tony Leswick (OT)
1955 Gordie Howe

1936 STANLEY CUP FINALS

Game 1, best-of-five
April 5, 1936
Toronto 1 at Detroit 3

FIRST PERIOD

Detroit McDONALD (unassisted) .... 4:53 (sh)

Detroit S. HOWE (YOUNG) 5:37

Detroit W. KILREA (BRÛNETEAU) 12:05

Toronto BOLL (THOMS, C. CONACHER) .. 12:15

penalty: Detroit, Aurie (tripping)

SECOND PERIOD

penalty: Toronto, Shill

THIRD PERIOD

penalty: Toronto, Horner (tripping)

IN GOAL
Smith (Detroit)
Hainsworth (Toronto)

REFEREES: Smith and Stewart

ATTENDANCE: 12,763

Game 2, best-of-five
(Detroit leads 1–0)
April 7, 1936
Toronto 4 at Detroit 9

FIRST PERIOD

Detroit KILREA (SORRELL)............... 1:30

Detroit BARRY (BOWMAN) 4:25

Detroit LEWIS (SORRELL, BARRY) 10:05

Toronto BOLL (THOMS)................. 12:35

Detroit McDONALD (H. KILREA)......... 16:55

penalty: Toronto, Clancy (hooking)
penalty: Detroit, Barry (high-sticking)
penalty: Toronto, Horner (high-sticking)
penalty: Detroit, McDonald (tripping)

SECOND PERIOD

Detroit SORRELL (BARRY, S. HOWE)... 7:15 (pp)

Detroit PETTINGER (S. HOWE, YOUNG) ... 9:10

Toronto PRIMEAU (SHILL)............... 14:00

penalty: Toronto, Horner (tripping)
penalty: Toronto, Shill (roughing)
penalty: Toronto, Davidson (tripping)

THIRD PERIOD

Detroit SORRELL (W. KILREA, BRÛNETEAU)...................... 7:30

Toronto THOMS (BOLL, DAVIDSON) 9:40

Detroit PETTINGER (H. KILREA, S. HOWE)......................... 12:05

Toronto DAVIDSON (FINNIGAN, H. JACKSON) 16:10

Detroit McDONALD (unassisted)........... 17:15

IN GOAL
Smith (Detroit)
Hainsworth (Toronto)

REFEREES: Smith and Stewart

ATTENDANCE: 12,456

Game 3, best-of-five
(Detroit leads 2–0)
April 9, 1936
Detroit 3 at Toronto 4

FIRST PERIOD

Detroit BOWMAN (PETTINGER)........... 9:25

SECOND PERIOD

Detroit BRÛNETEAU (unassisted)........... 1:06

penalty: Detroit, Bowman (roughing)
penalty: Toronto, Shill (roughing)

THIRD PERIOD

Detroit S. HOWE (PETTINGER, P. KELLY) . 11:15

Toronto PRIMEAU (DAVIDSON, HORNER) . 13:10

Toronto R. KELLY (FINNIGAN) 15:21

Toronto R. KELLY (PRIMEAU) 19:18

penalty: Toronto, Day (holding)
penalty: Detroit, McDonald (tripping)

OVERTIME

Toronto BOLL (HORNER, A. JACKSON) 0:31

IN GOAL
Smith (Detroit)
Hainsworth (Toronto)

REFEREES: Smith and Stewart

ATTENDANCE: 13,802

Game 4, best-of-five
(Detroit leads 2–1)
April 11, 1936
Detroit 3 at Toronto 2

FIRST PERIOD

Toronto PRIMEAU (unassisted) 18:11

penalty: Toronto, Horner (tripping)
penalty: Toronto, Day
penalty: Toronto, H. Jackson

SECOND PERIOD

Detroit GOODFELLOW (SORRELL) 9:55

Detroit BARRY (LEWIS) 10:38

penalty: Toronto, Conacher
penalty: Detroit, Goodfellow
penalty: Detroit, S. Howe
penalty: Toronto, Blair

THIRD PERIOD

Detroit P. KELLY (LEWIS) 9:45

Toronto THOMS (unassisted) 10:57

IN GOAL
Smith (Detroit)
Hainsworth (Toronto)

REFEREES: Smith and Stewart

ATTENDANCE: 14,728

Detroit wins Stanley Cup 3–1

1937 STANLEY CUP FINALS

Game 1, best-of-five
April 6, 1937
Detroit 1 at Rangers 5

FIRST PERIOD

Rangers KEELING (COOPER, MURDOCH) . 5:23

Rangers PATRICK (BOUCHER, COULTER) . 9:40

Rangers COOPER (DILLON, KEELING) . . . 18:43

penalty: Detroit, Cooper (tripping)

SECOND PERIOD

Rangers BOUCHER (JOHNSON). 18:55

THIRD PERIOD

Detroit S. HOWE (GOODFELLOW, PETTINGER) 17:12

Rangers PATRICK (BOUCHER, DILLON) . . 18:22

penalty: Detroit, Gallagher (tripping)
penalty: Detroit, Goodfellow (fighting)
penalty: Rangers, Heller (fighting)
penalty: Detroit, W. Kilrea (roughing)
penalty: Rangers, Watson (roughing)

IN GOAL
Smith (Detroit)
Kerr (Rangers)

REFEREES: Ion and Mitchell

ATTENDANCE: 16,000

Game 2, best-of-five
(Rangers lead 1–0)
April 8, 1937
Rangers 2 at Detroit 4

FIRST PERIOD

Detroit SORRELL (unassisted). . . . . 9:22 (pp)

Detroit BRÛNETEAU (S. HOWE) 12:07

Detroit GALLAGHER (W. KILREA, SHERF) 13:31

penalty: Rangers, Patrick (high-sticking)

SECOND PERIOD

Detroit LEWIS (S. HOWE, GOODFELLOW) 11:02

Rangers PRATT (N. COLVILLE, M. COLVILLE) 15:06

Rangers KEELING (COULTER). 18:18

THIRD PERIOD

penalty: Detroit, Goodfellow (tripping)
penalty: Rangers, Watson (tripping)

IN GOAL
Robertson (Detroit)
Kerr (Rangers)

REFEREES: Campbell and Dye

ATTENDANCE: 13,491

Game 3, best-of-five
(series tied 1–1)
April 11, 1937
Rangers 1 at Detroit 0

FIRST PERIOD

penalty: Rangers, Cooper (holding)
penalty: Detroit, Gallagher (tripping)

SECOND PERIOD

Rangers N. COLVILLE (PRATT) . . . . 0:23 (pp)

penalty: Detroit, Brûneteau (roughing)
penalty: Rangers, Cooper (roughing)
penalty: Detroit, Brûneteau (roughing)
penalty: Rangers, Pratt (roughing)

THIRD PERIOD

penalty: Detroit, Gallagher (tripping)
penalty: Detroit, Goodfellow (fighting)
penalty: Rangers, Pratt (fighting)
penalty: Detroit, Lewis (high-sticking)
penalty: Rangers, Pratt (high-sticking)

IN GOAL
Robertson (Detroit)
Kerr (Rangers)

REFEREES: Smith and Stewart

ATTENDANCE: 13,735

Game 4, best-of-five
(Rangers lead 2–1)
April 13, 1937
Rangers 0 at Detroit 1

FIRST PERIOD

no scoring
no penalties

SECOND PERIOD

penalty: Rangers, Johnson (tripping) 19:27

THIRD PERIOD

Detroit BARRY (S. HOWE, SORRELL) 12:43

IN GOAL
Robertson (Detroit)
Kerr (Rangers)

REFEREES: Ion and Mitchell

ATTENDANCE: 13,515

Game 5, best-of-five
(series tied 2–2)
April 15, 1937
Rangers 0 at Detroit 3

FIRST PERIOD

Detroit BARRY (S. HOWE) . . . . 19:22 (pp)

penalty: Rangers, Cooper
penalty: Detroit, Sorrell
penalty: Detroit, Sherf (tripping)
penalty: Rangers, Coulter (high-sticking)
penalty: Detroit, Pettinger (high-sticking)
penalty: Rangers, Cooper (holding)

SECOND PERIOD

Detroit SORRELL (BARRY, H. KILREA) 9:36

penalty: Detroit, Lewis (holding)
penalty: Rangers, Cooper (high-sticking)
penalty: Detroit, W. Kilrea (high-sticking)
*penalty:*Rangers, Coulter (tripping)
*penalty:*Detroit, Bowman (charging)

THIRD PERIOD

Detroit BARRY (SORRELL) 2:22

penalty: Rangers, Coulter (boarding)
penalty: Detroit, Gallagher (charging)

IN GOAL
Robertson (Detroit)
Kerr (Rangers)

REFEREES: Ion and Stewart

ATTENDANCE: 14,102

Detroit wins Stanley Cup 3–2

1943 STANLEY CUP FINALS

Game 1, best-of-seven
April 1, 1943
Boston 2 at Detroit 6

FIRST PERIOD

Detroit STEWART (ABEL, LISCOMBE) 1:15

Boston A. JACKSON (CAIN).............. 18:13

SECOND PERIOD

Detroit BRÛNETEAU (ABEL, H. JACKSON) . 1:12

Detroit ABEL (unassisted)................. 15:43

Detroit CARVETH (DOUGLAS)........... 19:06

penalty: Boston, A. Jackson (major)
penalty: Detroit, Orlando

THIRD PERIOD

Detroit BRÛNETEAU (ABEL, LISCOMBE) .. 1:21

Detroit BRÛNETEAU (ABEL, STEWART) .. 16:24

Boston DeMARCO (GALLINGER, GUIDOLIN) 17:53

penalty: Detroit, Stewart

IN GOAL
Mowers (Detroit)
Brimsek (Boston)

REFEREE: Chadwick

LINESMEN: Babcock and Hedges

ATTENDANCE: 12,652

Game 2, best-of-seven
(Detroit leads 1–0)
April 4, 1943
Boston 3 at Detroit 4

FIRST PERIOD

penalty: Boston, Cowley
penalty: Detroit, H. Jackson
penalty: Boston, Gallinger
penalty: Boston, Shewchuk

SECOND PERIOD

Boston CRAWFORD (CHAMBERLAIN) 10:16

Boston A. JACKSON (COWLEY, CAIN)..... 11:04

Detroit DOUGLAS (ORLANDO) 17:06

penalty: Detroit, Wares
penalty: Boston, A. Jackson
penalty: Detroit, Stewart
penalty: Detroit, Orlando
penalty: Boston, Hollett

THIRD PERIOD

Detroit CARVETH (ORLANDO) 5:55

Detroit LISCOMBE (ABEL)................ 6:21

Detroit HOWE (WARES).................. 13:16

Boston H. JACKSON (COWLEY, HOLLETT) 16:38

IN GOAL
Mowers (Detroit)
Brimsek (Boston)

REFEREE: Clancy

LINESMEN: Babcock and Hedges

ATTENDANCE: 13,827

Game 3, best-of-seven
(Detroit leads 2–0)
April 7, 1943
Detroit 4 at Boston 0

FIRST PERIOD

Detroit GROSSO (WARES)................ 3:26

Detroit GROSSO (LISCOMBE) 10:16

penalty: Boston, Chamberlain
penalty: Detroit, Abel (interference)
penalty: Boston, Crawford
penalty: Boston, Boyd
penalty: Detroit, Stewart

SECOND PERIOD

penalty: Boston, Chamberlain
penalty: Detroit, Douglas
penalty: Detroit, Grosso
penalty: Boston, Guidolin

THIRD PERIOD

Detroit DOUGLAS (MOTTER) 8:03

Detroit GROSSO (WARES)................ 18:41

penalty: Detroit, Liscombe

IN GOAL
Mowers (Detroit)
Brimsek (Boston)

REFEREE: Lamport

LINESMEN: Babcock and Hedges

ATTENDANCE: 14,480

Game 4, best-of-seven
(Detroit leads 3–0)
April 8, 1943
Detroit 2 at Boston 0

FIRST PERIOD

Detroit CARVETH (unassisted) 12:09

penalty: Boston, Guidolin
penalty: Boston, Guidolin
penalty: Detroit, Carveth (roughing)
penalty: Detroit, Orlando (high-sticking)
Boston, Gallinger (high-sticking)
Detroit, Grosso (boarding)
Boston, Chamberlain (boarding)

SECOND PERIOD

Detroit LISCOMBE (unassisted) 2:45

penalty: Detroit, John Stewart (2)
penalty: Detroit, Jackson (roughing)
Boston, H. Jackson (roughing)

THIRD PERIOD

penalty: Boston, Guidolin (high-sticking)
penalty: Detroit, A. Brown (roughing)
Boston, Shewchuk (roughing)
penalty: Detroit, Stewart (tripping)
penalty: Detroit, Orlando (tripping)

IN GOAL
Mowers (Detroit)
Brimsek (Boston)

REFEREE: Chadwick

LINESMEN: Babcock and Hedges

ATTENDANCE: 12,954

Detroit wins Stanley Cup 4–0

1950 STANLEY CUP FINALS

Game 1, best-of-seven
April 11, 1950
Rangers 1 at Detroit 4

FIRST PERIOD

Rangers O'CONNOR (GORDON, MICKOSKI) 5:58

penalty: Detroit, Pronovost
penalty: Rangers, Fisher
penalty: Detroit, Reise
penalty: Rangers, Kyle
penalty: Detroit, Pavelich

SECOND PERIOD

penalty: Rangers, Egan (charging)
Rangers, Stanley (charging) 4:30

Detroit CARVETH (BABANDO, GEE) . . . 4:43 (pp)

penalty: Rangers, Walter Kyle (2)

penalty: Detroit, Kelly (hooking) 6:30

Detroit GEE (J. WILSON) 9:32

Detroit McFADDEN (COUTURE) 10:06

Detroit COUTURE (McFADDEN, PRONOVOST) 13:56

THIRD PERIOD

penalty: Detroit, Babando
penalty: Detroit, Stewart
penalty: Rangers, Fisher (minor and misconduct)

IN GOAL
Lumley (Detroit)
Rayner (Rangers)

REFEREE: Chadwick

LINESMEN: Babcock and McLean

ATTENDANCE: 13,415

Game 2, best-of-seven
(Detroit leads 1–0)
April 13, 1950
Rangers 3 Detroit 1 (at Toronto)

FIRST PERIOD

penalty: Detroit, Carveth

SECOND PERIOD

Detroit COUTURE (PAVELICH) 2:05

Rangers EGAN (unassisted) 10:39

penalty: Detroit, Abel

THIRD PERIOD

Rangers LAPRADE (STANLEY) 3:04

Rangers LAPRADE (unassisted) 11:20

IN GOAL
Lumley (Detroit)
Rayner (Rangers)

REFEREE: Gravel

LINESMEN: Hayes and Keeling

ATTENDANCE: 12,866

Game 3, best-of-seven
(series tied 1–1)
April 15, 1950
Detroit 4 Rangers 0 (at Toronto)

FIRST PERIOD

Detroit COUTURE (KELLY) . . . . 14:13 (pp)

Detroit GEE (DEWSBURY) . . . . 19:08 (pp)

penalty: Detroit, Stewart
penalty: Rangers, Gordon
penalty: Rangers, Kyle (2)
penalty: Detroit, Dewsbury
penalty: Rangers, Stanley

SECOND PERIOD

Detroit ABEL (unassisted) 19:16

penalty: Detroit, Reise
penalty: Detroit, McFadden

THIRD PERIOD

Detroit PAVELICH (KELLY) 16:55

penalty: Rangers, Slowinski
penalty: Detroit, Stewart (2)
penalty: Rangers, Kyle (kicking)
penalty: Detroit, Dewsbury

IN GOAL
Lumley (Detroit)
Rayner (Rangers)

REFEREE: Chadwick

LINESMEN: Babcock and McLean

ATTENDANCE: 13,781

Game 4, best-of-seven
(Detroit leads 2–1)
April 18, 1950
Rangers 4 at Detroit 3

FIRST PERIOD

Detroit LINDSAY (STEWART) 6:31

Detroit ABEL (LINDSAY) 16:48

penalty: Detroit, Dewsbury
penalty: Rangers, Leswick

SECOND PERIOD

Rangers O'CONNOR (KALETA, MICKOSKI) 19:59

penalty: Detroit, Fogolin
penalty: Detroit, Reise

THIRD PERIOD

Detroit PAVELICH (PETERS, STEWART) . . . 3:22

Rangers LAPRADE (FISHER, LESWICK) 8:09

Rangers KYLE (KALETA) 16:26

OVERTIME

Rangers RALEIGH (KALETA) 8:34

IN GOAL
Lumley (Detroit)
Rayner (Rangers)

REFEREE: Gravel

LINESMEN: Hayes and Keeling

ATTENDANCE: 13,557

Game 5, best-of-seven
(series tied 2–2)
April 20, 1950
Rangers 2 at Detroit 1

FIRST PERIOD

penalty: Detroit, Stewart

SECOND PERIOD

Rangers FISHER (LESWICK) 7:44

penalty: Rangers, Eddolls

THIRD PERIOD

Detroit LINDSAY (ABEL, CARVETH) 18:10

OVERTIME

Rangers RALEIGH (SLOWINSKI, LUND) . . . 1:38

IN GOAL
Lumley (Detroit)
Rayner (Rangers)

REFEREE: Chadwick

LINESMEN: Babcock and McLean

ATTENDANCE: 12,610

Game 6, best-of-seven
(Rangers lead 3–2)
April 22, 1950
Rangers 4 at Detroit 5

FIRST PERIOD

Rangers STANLEY (KALETA, MICKOSKI). . . 3:45

Rangers FISHER (LAPRADE, LESWICK) 7:35

Detroit LINDSAY (STEWART) 19:18

penalty: Detroit, Reise
penalty: Detroit, Pronovost
penalty: Rangers, Egan
penalty: Detroit, Lindsay

SECOND PERIOD

penalty: Detroit, Carveth (hooking). 2:30

Rangers LUND (EGAN, SLOWINSKI) . . 3:18 (pp)

Detroit ABEL (CARVETH, LINDSAY). 5:38

Detroit COUTURE (BABANDO, GEE). 16:07

THIRD PERIOD

Rangers LESWICK (FISHER, LAPRADE) 1:54

Detroit LINDSAY (ABEL). 4:13

Detroit ABEL (CARVETH, DEWSBURY) 10:34

IN GOAL
Lumley (Detroit)
Rayner (Rangers)

REFEREE: Gravel

LINESMEN: Hayes and Keeling

ATTENDANCE: 12,054

Game 7, best-of-seven
(series tied 3–3)
April 23, 1950
Rangers 3 at Detroit 4

FIRST PERIOD

Rangers STANLEY (LESWICK) . . . . 11:14 (pp)

Rangers LESWICK (LAPRADE,
O'CONNOR) . . . . 12:18 (pp)

penalty: Detroit, Pavelich (2)
penalty: Detroit, Lindsay (2)
penalty: Rangers, Laprade
penalty: Rangers, O'Connor
penalty: Rangers, Slowinski

SECOND PERIOD

penalty: Rangers, Stanley (cross-checking) 5:00

Detroit BABANDO (KELLY, COUTURE) 5:09 (pp)

Detroit ABEL (DEWSBURY) . . . . 5:30 (pp)

Rangers O'CONNOR (MICKOSKI) 11:42
Detroit McFADDEN (PETERS) 15:57

THIRD PERIOD

penalty: Rangers, Kyle
penalty: Detroit, Dewsbury

1ST OVERTIME

no scoring

no penalties

2ND OVERTIME

Detroit BABANDO (GEE) 8:31

IN GOAL

Lumley (Detroit)
Rayner (Rangers)

REFEREE: Chadwick

LINESMEN: Hayes and McLean

ATTENDANCE: 13,095

Detroit wins Stanley Cup 4–3

1952 STANLEY CUP FINALS

Game 1, best-of-seven
April 10, 1952
Detroit 3 at Canadiens 1

FIRST PERIOD

penalty: Detroit, Woit 16:49

SECOND PERIOD

Detroit LESWICK (PAVELICH) 3:27

penalty: Detroit, Goldham 6:15
penalty: Canadiens, Mazur 10:48
penalty: Detroit, Lindsay 12:39
penalty: Canadiens, Harvey 19:21

THIRD PERIOD

penalty: Canadiens, Richard (roughing)
Detroit, Skov (roughing) 1:38

Detroit LESWICK (SKOV) 7:59

Canadiens JOHNSON (CURRY, OLMSTEAD) 11:01

Detroit LINDSAY (ABEL) . . . . 18:44 (en)

IN GOAL
Sawchuk (Detroit)
McNeil (Canadiens)

REFEREE: Chadwick

LINESMEN: Hayes and Morrison

ATTENDANCE: 14,533

Game 2, best-of-seven
(Detroit leads 1–0)
April 12, 1952
Detroit 2 at Canadiens 1

FIRST PERIOD

penalty: Canadiens, Masnick 2:06
penalty: Detroit, Leswick
Canadiens, Moore 5:43
penalty: Detroit, Goldham 8:54
penalty: Detroit, Leswick 9:13
penalty: Canadiens, Lach (roughing)
Detroit, Lindsay (roughing) 11:15

Detroit PAVELICH (LESWICK, SKOV) 16:09

penalty: Detroit, Leswick (misconduct)
Detroit, Skov (misconduct) 17:02

Canadiens LACH (GEOFFRION) 18:37

penalty: Canadiens, Harvey (slashing) 19:33

SECOND PERIOD

Detroit LINDSAY (unassisted) 0:43

penalty: Canadiens, Moore 3:59
penalty: Canadiens, Moore 10:27
penalty: Canadiens, Bouchard
Detroit, Leswick 19:17

THIRD PERIOD

penalty: Detroit, Abel 4:51
penalty: Canadiens, Masnick 7:28

IN GOAL
Sawchuk (Detroit)
McNeil (Canadiens)

REFEREE: Gravel

LINESMEN: Babcock and Hayes

ATTENDANCE: 14,549

Game 3, best-of-seven
(Detroit leads 2–0)
April 13, 1952
Canadiens 0 at Detroit 3

FIRST PERIOD

penalty: Canadiens, Harvey (holding) 3:09

Detroit G. HOWE (STASIUK) . . . . 4:31 (pp)

penalty: Detroit, Pronovost 15:12
penalty: Detroit, Leswick
Canadiens, Moore 16:35
penalty: Canadiens, Olmstead 18:20

SECOND PERIOD

penalty: Canadiens, Lach 1:59
penalty: Canadiens, Moore
Detroit, Pavelich 6:16

Detroit LINDSAY (G. HOWE) 9:13

penalty: Canadiens, Bouchard 10:42
penalty: Detroit, G. Howe
Canadiens, Mazur 17:20

THIRD PERIOD

Detroit G. HOWE (PAVELICH) 6:54

IN GOAL
Sawchuk (Detroit)
McNeil (Canadiens)

REFEREE: Storey

LINESMEN: Babcock and Morrison

ATTENDANCE: 14,018

Game 4, best-of-seven
(Detroit leads 3–0)
April 15, 1952
Canadiens 0 at Detroit 3

FIRST PERIOD

penalty: Canadiens, Bouchard 0:24
penalty: Detroit, Leswick 4:09
penalty: Canadiens, Richard (holding) 4:59
Detroit PRYSTAI (DELVECCHIO, J. WILSON) 6:50
penalty: Canadiens, Masnick 14:28
penalty: Detroit, Leswick 18:10

SECOND PERIOD

penalty: Detroit, Delvecchio 9:35
penalty: Canadiens, Moore 11:45
Detroit SKOV (PRYSTAI) 19:39

THIRD PERIOD

Detroit PRYSTAI (unassisted) 7:35

IN GOAL
Sawchuk (Detroit)
McNeil (Canadiens)

REFEREE: Chadwick

LINESMEN: Hayes and Morrison

ATTENDANCE: 14,090

Detroit wins Stanley Cup 4–0

1954 STANLEY CUP FINALS

Game 1, best-of-seven
April 4, 1954
Canadiens 1 at Detroit 3

FIRST PERIOD

penalty: Canadiens, St. Laurent 0:52
penalty: Canadiens, Olmstead................ 5:53
penalty: Detroit, Skov 11:25
penalty: Canadiens, Moore (hooking)......... 12:54

Detroit LINDSAY (REIBEL, DELVECCHIO)................. 13:44 (pp)

penalty: Detroit, Pronovost 14:52
penalty: Detroit, Lindsay (minor and misconduct)........................ 17:39
penalty: Canadiens, Richard 19:04

SECOND PERIOD

penalty: Canadiens, Richard (minor and misconduct)........................... 1:49
penalty: Detroit, Pavelich 5:38
penalty: Canadiens, T. Johnson 7:28
penalty: Detroit, Skov (tripping)............ 12:04

Canadiens GEOFFRION (HARVEY, MASNICK) 12:16

THIRD PERIOD

penalty: Canadiens, St. Laurent (boarding) 0:59

Detroit REIBEL (LINDSAY, G. HOWE) .. 1:52 (pp)

penalty: Detroit, Pronovost (tripping).......... 5:47

Detroit KELLY (PAVELICH, LESWICK)..... 7:13

IN GOAL
Sawchuk (Detroit)
Plante (Canadiens)

REFEREE: Chadwick

LINESMEN: Babcock and Davies

ATTENDANCE: 13,959

Game 2, best-of-seven
(Detroit leads 1–0)
April 6, 1954
Canadiens 3 at Detroit 1

FIRST PERIOD

penalty: Canadiens, Bouchard (high-sticking)
penalty: Detroit, Leswick (high-sticking) 1:11
penalty: Canadiens, Geoffrion (tripping)....... 6:19
penalty: Detroit, G. Howe (tripping) 11:12
penalty: Canadiens, Harvey (holding) 11:24
penalty: Detroit, G. Howe (high-sticking) 13:42
penalty: Detroit, Leswick (slashing).......... 14:01

Canadiens MOORE (GEOFFRION, BÉLIVEAU) .... 15:03 (pp)

Canadiens RICHARD (MOORE) .... 15:28 (pp)

Canadiens RICHARD (MOORE) .... 15:59 (pp)

penalty: Canadiens, Mosdell 16:36

SECOND PERIOD

penalty: Canadiens, MacPherson (interference) . 6:12

Detroit DELVECCHIO (unassisted) ...... 6:37 (pp)

penalty: Canadiens, Bouchard (hooking)...... 13:31

THIRD PERIOD

no scoring

no penalties

IN GOAL
Sawchuk (Detroit)
Plante (Canadiens)

REFEREE: Storey

LINESMEN: Babcock and Davies

ATTENDANCE: 14,026

Game 3, best-of-seven
(series tied 1–1)
April 8, 1954
Detroit 5 at Canadiens 2

FIRST PERIOD

Detroit DELVECCHIO (G. HOWE)......... 0:42

penalty: Canadiens, Meger................. 3:30
penalty: Detroit, Woit 6:30
penalty: Canadiens, Richard................ 7:41
penalty: Detroit, Lindsay 9:40
penalty: Canadiens, MacPherson............ 11:57

Detroit LINDSAY (KELLY) 17:06

SECOND PERIOD

Detroit J. WILSON (PRYSTAI, GOLDHAM) .. 4:57

THIRD PERIOD

penalty: Canadiens, Olmstead 0:22
penalty: Canadiens, T. Johnson
Detroit, Sawchuk 2:45
penalty: Canadiens, Geoffrion (slashing) 6:49

Canadiens T. JOHNSON (unassisted). . . . . 7:19 (sh)

Detroit PRYSTAI (DELVECCHIO) 7:59

Detroit G. HOWE (DELVECCHIO, WOIT) . . 11:32

Canadiens ST. LAURENT (MacKAY) 15:02

penalty: Canadiens, Moore 17:32
penalty: Detroit, G. Howe
(minor and misconduct) 17:32

IN GOAL

Sawchuk (Detroit)
Plante (Canadiens)

REFEREE: Chadwick

LINESMEN: Hayes and Morrison

ATTENDANCE: 14,481

Game 4, best-of-seven
(Detroit leads 2–1)
April 10, 1954
Detroit 2 at Canadiens 0

FIRST PERIOD

penalty: Canadiens, Davis 1:03
penalty: Canadiens, Olmstead 7:55
penalty: Detroit, Pronovost 11:48
penalty: Canadiens, Curry. 15:57

SECOND PERIOD

penalty: Detroit, Woit. 1:37
penalty: Canadiens, Richard 2:05

Detroit J. WILSON (PRYSTAI). . . . . 2:09 (pp)

penalty: Detroit, G. Howe (slashing major) 4:12
penalty: Detroit, Leswick. 15:24
penalty: Canadiens, Richard 17:38

THIRD PERIOD

penalty: Canadiens, Geoffrion (slashing
and misconduct) 10:47

Detroit KELLY (unassisted) . . . . 19:53 (en)

IN GOAL

Sawchuk (Detroit)
Plante (Canadiens)

REFEREE: Storey

LINESMEN: Hayes and Morrison

ATTENDANCE: 14,583

Game 5, best-of-seven
(Detroit leads 3–1)
April 11, 1954
Canadiens 1 at Detroit 0

FIRST PERIOD

penalty: Canadiens, Olmstead 11:52
penalty: Canadiens, Béliveau (roughing)
Canadiens, T. Johnson (roughing)
Detroit, Leswick (roughing)
Detroit, Pavelich (roughing) 16:27

SECOND PERIOD

no scoring

no penalties

THIRD PERIOD

penalty: Canadiens, T. Johnson 8:21
penalty: Detroit, G. Howe 10:33
penalty: Canadiens (too many men) 15:10

OVERTIME

Canadiens MOSDELL (unassisted). 5:45

IN GOAL

Sawchuk (Detroit)
McNeil (Canadiens)

REFEREE: Chadwick

LINESMEN: Hayes and Morrison

ATTENDANCE: 14,623

Game 6, best-of-seven
(Detroit leads 3–2)
April 13, 1954
Detroit 1 at Canadiens 4

FIRST PERIOD

penalty: Canadiens, Masnick 2:46
penalty: Canadiens, Davis 10:41

SECOND PERIOD

penalty: Canadiens, St. Laurent. 4:22
penalty: Canadiens, Moore
Detroit, Pronovost 8:45

Canadiens GEOFFRION (BÉLIVEAU) 12:07

Canadiens CURRY (OLMSTEAD,
MASNICK) 13:07

Canadiens CURRY (LACH, MAZUR) 14:25

penalty: Detroit, Skov. 15:32
penalty: Detroit, Skov. 19:50

THIRD PERIOD

Detroit PRYSTAI (unassisted) 5:11

Canadiens RICHARD (LACH) 10:06

penalty: Canadiens, Moore 16:49

IN GOAL

Sawchuk (Detroit)
McNeil (Canadiens)

REFEREE: Storey

LINESMEN: Babcock and Davies

ATTENDANCE: 14,622

Game 7, best-of-seven
(series tied 3–3)
April 16, 1954
Canadiens 1 at Detroit 2

FIRST PERIOD

Canadiens CURRY (MASNICK) 9:17

penalty: Canadiens, Harvey (holding) 14:20
penalty: Detroit, Skov (hooking) 17:11

SECOND PERIOD

penalty: Canadiens, Masnick (hooking) 0:20

Detroit KELLY (DELVECCHIO, LINDSAY) . . . . 1:17 (pp)

THIRD PERIOD

no scoring

no penalties

OVERTIME

Detroit LESWICK (SKOV) 4:29

IN GOAL

Sawchuk (Detroit)
McNeil (Canadiens)

REFEREE: Chadwick

LINESMEN: Hayes and Morrison

ATTENDANCE: 15,792

Detroit wins Stanley Cup 4–3

1955 STANLEY CUP FINALS

Game 1, best-of-seven
April 3, 1955
Canadiens 2 at Detroit 4

FIRST PERIOD

penalty: Detroit, Leswick 1:54
penalty: Canadiens, Johnson 4:11
penalty: Canadiens, Béliveau
penalty: Detroit, Leswick 10:10
penalty: Detroit, Lindsay 15:09

SECOND PERIOD

penalty: Detroit, Pavelich 2:52

Canadiens CURRY (MacKAY, MOSDELL) ... 5:09

penalty: Canadiens, Harvey 6:27
penalty: Canadiens, Bouchard (interference) .. 12:16

Detroit DELVECCHIO (G. HOWE, LINDSAY) .... 14:00 (pp)

THIRD PERIOD

Canadiens CURRY (MacKAY, MOSDELL) ... 8:57

penalty: Canadiens, St. Laurent (hooking) 11:04

Detroit STASIUK (G. HOWE, LINDSAY) ... 13:05

penalty: Detroit, G. Howe (slashing) 16:12

Detroit PAVELICH (unassisted) .... 17:07 (sh)

Detroit LINDSAY (G. HOWE) 19:42

IN GOAL
Sawchuk (Detroit)
Plante (Canadiens)

REFEREE: Chadwick

LINESMEN: Babcock and Davies

ATTENDANCE: 13,862

Game 2, best-of-seven
(Detroit leads 1–0)
April 5, 1955
Canadiens 1 at Detroit 7

FIRST PERIOD

penalty: Detroit, Lindsay (high-sticking) 1:58

Detroit PRONOVOST (GOLDHAM) .... 2:15 (sh)

Detroit LINDSAY (G. HOWE, REIBEL) 9:57

penalty: Canadiens, St. Laurent (tripping) 11:55
penalty: Canadiens, Bouchard (high-sticking)
penalty: Detroit, Reibel (high-sticking) 13:52

Detroit DELVECCHIO (STASIUK, GOLDHAM) 16:00

Detroit G. HOWE (REIBEL) 17:11

SECOND PERIOD

Detroit LINDSAY (G. HOWE, REIBEL) 8:10

penalty: Canadiens, Johnson (tripping and misconduct) 14:19
penalty: Canadiens, St. Laurent (tripping) 14:53

Detroit LINDSAY (DELVECCHIO) ..... 15:48 (pp)

Detroit LINDSAY (REIBEL, G. HOWE) 19:34

THIRD PERIOD

penalty: Detroit, G. Howe (spearing)
penalty: Canadiens, Moore (slashing, misconduct, game misconduct) 4:21

Canadiens MOSDELL (ST. LAURENT, CURRY) 12:32

penalty: Canadiens, Bouchard (high-sticking)
penalty: Detroit, Leswick (high-sticking) 16:19

IN GOAL
Sawchuk (Detroit)
Plante (Canadiens)

REFEREE: Storey

LINESMEN: Davies and Hayes

ATTENDANCE: 13,942

Game 3, best-of-seven
(Detroit leads 2–0)
April 7, 1955
Detroit 2 at Canadiens 4

FIRST PERIOD

penalty: Detroit, Pavelich (roughing)
penalty: Canadiens, St. Laurent (roughing) 2:56
penalty: Detroit, G. Howe (holding) 6:55

Canadiens GEOFFRION (BÉLIVEAU, OLMSTEAD) .... 8:30 (pp)

Canadiens GEOFFRION (unassisted) .... 8:42 (pp)

penalty: Detroit, Sawchuk (slashing) 11:14
penalty: Canadiens, Olmstead (hooking and misconduct) 12:22
penalty: Canadiens, Moore (slashing) 14:55
penalty: Detroit, G. Howe (high-sticking and misconduct) 15:08
penalty: Canadiens, Geoffrion (high-sticking) . 17:37

Detroit KELLY (STASIUK) . . . . 18:13 (pp)

penalty: Canadiens, Curry (tripping) 19:06

SECOND PERIOD

penalty: Canadiens, Béliveau (high-sticking) . . . 4:32
penalty: Detroit, Bonin (high-sticking) 7:02
penalty: Canadiens, Moore (interference) 7:26

Canadiens GEOFFRION (BÉLIVEAU) 14:23

Detroit STASIUK (PAVELICH, DELVECCHIO) 16:16

THIRD PERIOD

penalty: Canadiens, Mosdell (tripping) 1:23

Canadiens LECLAIR (MOORE) 7:50

penalty: Canadiens, Béliveau (high-sticking) . . 16:45

IN GOAL
Sawchuk (Detroit)
Plante (Canadiens)

REFEREE: Chadwick

LINESMEN: Hayes and Morrison

ATTENDANCE: Unknown

Game 4, best-of-seven
(Detroit leads 2–1)
April 9, 1955
Detroit 3 at Canadiens 5

FIRST PERIOD

Canadiens MacKAY (HARVEY, MOSDELL) . . 0:40

penalty: Canadiens, Béliveau (high-sticking) . . . 1:12

Detroit REIBEL (KELLY) 12:38

penalty: Detroit, Pavelich (holding) 15:31

SECOND PERIOD

Canadiens GEOFFRION (unassisted) 0:40

Canadiens BÉLIVEAU (unassisted) 8:25

Canadiens JOHNSON (unassisted) 9:07

penalty: Canadiens, Béliveau (high-sticking)
Detroit, Pavelich (slashing) 13:27
penalty: Canadiens, Leclair (hooking) 17:26
penalty: Detroit, Skov (interference) 20:00

THIRD PERIOD

Canadiens CURRY (MacKAY) 2:33

Detroit REIBEL (LINDSAY, G. HOWE) 3:40

Detroit HAY (REIBEL) 12:00

IN GOAL
Sawchuk (Detroit)
Plante (Canadiens)

REFEREE: Storey

LINESMEN: Hayes and Morrison

ATTENDANCE: 13,569

Game 5, best-of-seven
(series tied 2–2)
April 10, 1955
Canadiens 1 at Detroit 5

FIRST PERIOD

penalty: Canadiens, Bouchard 4:33
penalty: Detroit, Pronovost (slashing) 6:57

Canadiens, BÉLIVEAU (HARVEY, MOORE) . . . . 8:01 (pp)

penalty: Detroit, G. Howe 8:54

Detroit SKOV (unassisted) 12:59

penalty: Canadiens, St. Laurent 16:55

Detroit G. HOWE (unassisted) . . . . 18:49 (pp)

SECOND PERIOD

penalty: Detroit, Woit 3:04
penalty: Canadiens, MacKay (interference) 11:41

Detroit G. HOWE (LINDSAY, DELVECCHIO) . . . . 12:39 (pp)

penalty: Detroit, Bonin (hooking) 14:42

Detroit G. HOWE (LINDSAY, KELLY) . . 16:20 (sh)

THIRD PERIOD

Detroit STASIUK (DELVECCHIO, BONIN) . 2:09

penalty: Detroit, Woit 7:21
penalty: Canadiens, Ronty 10:29
penalty: Detroit, Kelly (slashing, fighting major, misconduct)
penalty: Canadiens, Bouchard (slashing, fighting major, misconduct)
. . . . 12:17
Detroit, Pavelich 19:36

IN GOAL
Sawchuk (Detroit)
Plante (Canadiens)

REFEREE: Chadwick

LINESMEN: Davies and Morrison

ATTENDANCE: 14,284

Game 6, best-of-seven
(Detroit leads 3–2)
April 12, 1955
Detroit 3 at Canadiens 6

FIRST PERIOD

Canadiens BÉLIVEAU (HARVEY) 7:30
penalty: Canadiens, Gamble 9:48
Detroit DELVECCHIO (STASIUK) 13:36

SECOND PERIOD

penalty: Detroit, Skov (interference).......... 3:10
Canadiens LECLAIR (GEOFFRION, HARVEY) .... 3:45 (pp)
penalty: Detroit, Leswick (high-sticking) 4:29
Canadiens GEOFFRION (BÉLIVEAU, HARVEY) .... 5:21 (pp)
penalty: Detroit, G. Howe (high-sticking)..... 10:07
penalty: Canadiens, Béliveau (elbowing)...... 15:00
penalty: Canadiens, Olmstead (high-sticking) . 15:28
Detroit DELVECCHIO (LINDSAY, PRONOVOST) .... 15:54 (pp)
Canadiens GEOFFRION (BÉLIVEAU, BOUCHARD)...................... 18:18
penalty: Detroit, Sawchuk (misconduct)...... 18:18

THIRD PERIOD

Canadiens CURRY (MacKAY, MOSDELL) ... 9:19
penalty: Canadiens, Bouchard (hooking) 11:43
Detroit KELLY (LESWICK, PAVELICH).... 16:25
Canadiens MacKAY (MOSDELL) 18:55

IN GOAL
Sawchuk (Detroit)
Plante (Canadiens)

REFEREE: Storey

LINESMEN: Hayes and Morrison

ATTENDANCE: 13,599

Game 7, best-of-seven
(series tied 3–3)
April 14, 1955
Canadiens 1 at Detroit 3

FIRST PERIOD

penalty: Detroit, Lindsay (holding) 1:12
penalty: Canadiens, Bouchard (interference).... 5:16
penalty: Canadiens, Harvey (hooking)......... 7:19
penalty: Detroit, Pavelich (holding) 11:51
penalty: Canadiens, Bouchard (slashing)
penalty: Detroit, G. Howe (slashing) 19:34

SECOND PERIOD

Detroit DELVECCHIO (KELLY) 7:12
penalty: Detroit, Leswick (slashing)........... 7:44
penalty: Canadiens (too many men) 9:50
penalty: Canadiens, Mosdell (hooking) 15:25
Detroit G. HOWE (PRONOVOST).......... 19:49

THIRD PERIOD

Detroit DELVECCHIO (unassisted) 2:59
penalty: Detroit, Stasiuk (interference) 3:36
penalty: Canadiens, Mosdell (cross-checking).. 10:23
penalty: Canadiens, Johnson (slashing) 11:36
penalty: Detroit, Dineen (tripping) 12:28
penalty: Detroit, Goldham (tripping).......... 14:09
Canadiens CURRY (GEOFFRION, BÉLIVEAU).................... 14:35 (pp)

IN GOAL
Sawchuk (Detroit)
Plante (Canadiens)

REFEREE: Chadwick

LINESMEN: Hayes and Morrison

ATTENDANCE: 15,141

Detroit wins Stanley Cup 4–3

STANLEY CUP CHAMPIONS

1935–1936

Johnny Sorrell, Syd Howe, Marty Barry, Herbie Lewis, Mud Brûneteau, Wally Kilrea, Hec Kilrea, Gord Pettinger, Bucko McDonald, Scotty Bowman, Pete Kelly, Doug Young, Ebbie Goodfellow, Norm Smith, Jack Adams (general manager/coach), Honey Walker (trainer)

1936–1937

Norm Smith, Pete Kelly, Larry Aurie, Herbie Lewis, Hec Kilrea, Mud Brûneteau, Syd Howe, Wally Kilrea, Jimmy Franks, Bucko McDonald, Gord Pettinger, Ebbie Goodfellow, Johnny Gallagher, Scotty Bowman, Johnny Sorrell, Marty Barry, Earl Robertson, Johnny Sherf, Howard Mackie, Jack Adams (general manager/coach), Honey Walker (trainer)

1942–1943

Jack Stewart, Jimmy Orlando, Sid Abel, Alex Motter, Harry Watson, Joe Carveth, Mud Brûneteau, Eddie Wares, John Mowers, Cully Simon, Don Grosso, Carl Liscombe, Connie Brown, Syd Howe, Les Douglas, Hal Jackson, Joe Fisher, Jack Adams (general manager), Ebbie Goodfellow (player/coach), Honey Walker (trainer)

1949–1950

Harry Lumley, Jack Stewart, Leo Reise, Clare Martin, Al Dewsbury, Lee Fogolin, Marcel Pronovost, Red Kelly, Ted Lindsay, Sid Abel, Gordie Howe, George Gee, Jimmy Peters, Marty Pavelich, Jim McFadden, Pete Babando, Max McNab, Gerry Couture, Joe Carveth, Steve Black, Johnny Wilson, Larry Wilson, Jack Adams (general manager), Tommy Ivan (coach), Carl Mattson (trainer)

1951–1952

Terry Sawchuk, Bob Goldham, Ben Woit, Red Kelly, Leo Reise, Marcel Pronovost, Ted Lindsay, Tony Leswick, Gordie Howe, Metro Prystai, Marty Pavelich, Sid Abel, Glen Skov, Alex Delvecchio, Johnny Wilson, Vic Stasiuk, Larry Zeidel, Jack Adams (general manager), Tommy Ivan (coach), Carl Mattson (trainer)

1953–1954

Terry Sawchuk, Red Kelly, Bob Goldham, Ben Woit, Marcel Pronovost, Al Arbour, Keith Allen, Ted Lindsay, Tony Leswick, Gordie Howe, Alex Delvecchio, Marty Pavelich, Metro Prystai, Glen Skov, Johnny Wilson, Bill Dineen, Jim Peters, Earl Reibel, Vic Stasiuk, Jack Adams (general manager), Tommy Ivan (coach), Carl Mattson (trainer)

1954–1955

Terry Sawchuk, Red Kelly, Bob Goldham, Marcel Pronovost, Ben Woit, Jim Hay, Larry Hillman, Ted Lindsay, Tony Leswick, Gordie Howe, Alex Delvecchio, Marty Pavelich, Glen Skov, Earl Reibel, Johnny Wilson, Bill Dineen, Vic Stasiuk, Marcel Bonin, Jack Adams (general manager), Jimmy Skinner (coach), Carl Mattson (trainer)

Tommy Ivan

COACHING REGISTER
STANLEY CUP FINALS

(games played/won/lost/series)

SID ABEL

1961	6	2	4	0–1
1963	5	1	4	0–1
1964	7	3	4	0–1
1966	6	2	4	0–1
Totals	24	8	16	0–4

JACK ADAMS

1934	4	1	3	0–1
1936	4	3	1	1–0
1937	5	3	2	1–0
1941	4	0	4	0–1
1942	7	3	4	0–1
1943	4	4	0	1–0
1945	7	3	4	0–1
Totals	35	17	18	3–4

SCOTTY BOWMAN

1995	4	0	4	0–1

TOMMY IVAN

1948	4	0	4	0–1
1949	4	0	4	0–1
1950	7	4	3	1–0
1952	4	4	0	1–0
1954	7	4	3	1–0
Totals	26	12	14	3–2

JIMMY SKINNER

1955	7	4	3	1–0
1956	5	1	4	0–1
Totals	12	5	7	1–1

PLAYER REGISTER — STANLEY CUP FINALS

PLAYER	YRS	GA	G	A	P	PIM
Sid Abel	7	34	9	11	20	25
Keith Allen	1	3	0	0	0	0
Larry Aurie	2	8	2	3	5	2
Pete Babando	1	5	2	2	4	2
Doug Barkley	1	12	0	3	3	14
Marty Barry	3	11	5	3	8	8
Gary Bergman	1	6	0	1	1	4
Steve Black	1	6	0	0	0	0
Leo Boivin	1	6	0	0	0	6
Marcel Bonin	1	7	0	1	1	4
Adam Brown	2	9	0	1	1	6
Doug Brown	1	4	0	3	3	2
Gerry Brown	1	7	2	0	2	4
Ed Brûneteau	3	12	2	1	3	0
Mud Brûneteau	6	30	8	4	12	8
Tony Bukovich	1	1	0	0	0	0
Shawn Burr	1	2	0	0	0	0
Cummy Burton	1	1	0	0	0	0
Eddie Bush	1	6	1	5	6	16
Walt Buswell	1	4	0	1	1	2
Gene Carrigan	1	3	0	0	0	0
Joe Carveth	4	25	7	4	11	6
Dino Ciccarelli	1	4	1	1	2	6
Jim Conacher	1	4	1	0	1	0
Murray Costello	1	2	0	0	0	0
Doc Couture	2	10	4	2	6	0
Alex Delvecchio	8	47	16	22	38	2
Bill Dineen	3	19	1	0	1	6
Les Douglas	1	4	2	1	3	2
Kris Draper	1	4	0	0	0	4
Gilles Dube	1	2	0	0	0	0
Hap Emms	1	3	0	0	0	2
Alex Faulkner	2	6	2	0	2	2
Sergei Fedorov	1	4	3	2	5	0
Viacheslav Fetisov	1	4	0	3	3	0
Joe Fisher	1	1	0	0	0	0
Lee Fogolin	3	9	0	1	1	8
Val Fonteyne	3	17	0	2	2	0
Bill Gadsby	3	18	1	3	4	28
John Gallagher	1	5	1	0	1	8
Fern Gauthier	1	4	1	0	1	5
George Gee	2	11	3	5	8	14
Gus Giesebrecht	2	6	0	1	1	0
Fred Glover	1	2	0	0	0	0
Howie Glover	1	6	1	0	1	0
Warren Godfrey	2	7	0	1	1	10
Pete Goegan	2	11	0	0	0	16
Bob Goldham	4	23	0	3	3	8
Ebbie Goodfellow	3	12	1	2	3	20
Ted Graham	1	4	0	1	1	4
Stu Grimson	1	2	0	0	0	2
Don Grosso	3	15	7	5	12	14
Bep Guidolin	1	1	0	0	0	2
Murray Hall	1	1	0	0	0	0
Jim Hay	3	19	2	7	9	12
Larry Hillman	1	5	0	0	0	2
Gord Hollingworth	1	2	0	0	0	2
Pete Horeck	2	8	3	3	6	12
Gordie Howe	10	55	18	32	50	94
Mark Howe	1	2	0	0	0	0
Syd Howe	6	28	8	12	20	4
Harold Jackson	3	15	0	1	1	8
Bill Jennings	1	4	1	1	2	0
Al Johnson	1	6	1	2	3	0
Ed Joyal	2	12	3	1	4	6
Red Kelly	6	30	4	6	10	19
Pete Kelly	2	7	1	1	2	0
Ken Kilrea	1	2	0	0	0	0
Wally Kilrea	2	9	2	2	4	4
Vladimir Konstantinov	1	4	0	0	0	8
Vyacheslav Kozlov	1	4	1	0	1	0
Leo Labine	1	6	1	0	1	0
Al Langlois	1	7	0	0	0	8
Martin Lapointe	1	2	0	1	1	8
Tony Leswick	3	18	3	3	6	32
Herbie Lewis	3	13	4	3	7	6
Nicklas Lidstrom	1	4	0	2	2	0
Ted Lindsay	8	44	19	15	34	48
Carl Liscombe	4	22	6	8	14	9
Len Lunde	1	5	1	0	1	0
Pat Lundy	1	1	0	1	1	0
Parker MacDonald	4	24	3	1	4	14
Bruce MacGregor	4	24	5	4	9	12
Howard Mackie	1	3	0	0	0	0
John MacMillan	1	4	0	1	1	2
Bert Marshall	1	6	0	2	2	8
Clare Martin	1	3	0	0	0	0
Pit Martin	1	7	1	2	3	10
Jud McAtee	1	7	0	0	0	0
Darren McCarty	1	4	0	0	0	4
Ab McDonald	1	4	1	2	3	2
Pat McCreavy	1	6	1	1	2	2
Bucko McDonald	2	9	3	0	3	4
Jim McFadden	3	15	3	3	6	6
Doug McKay	1	1	0	0	0	0

Max McNab	3	10	0	0	0	4
Gerry Melnyk	1	6	0	0	0	0
Ron Moffat	1	2	0	0	0	0
Rod Morrison	1	1	0	0	0	0
Alex Motter	3	12	1	2	3	8
Gerry Odrowski	2	8	0	0	0	6
Jimmy Orlando	3	15	0	5	5	53
Marty Pavelich	7	36	4	8	12	38
Jim Peters	2	11	0	2	2	0
Gord Pettinger	3	12	3	3	6	2
Nelson Podolsky	1	3	0	0	0	
Bud Poile	1	3	0	0	0	0
Keith Primeau	1	3	0	0	0	8
Andre Pronovost	2	12	0	3	3	8
Marcel Pronovost	8	45	1	8	9	26
Metro Prystai	3	15	4	3	7	4
Cliff Purpur	1	4	0	0	0	4
Bill Quackenbush	3	15	1	2	3	2
Mike Ramsey	1	2	0	0	0	0
Earl Reibel	3	16	3	7	10	4
Gerry Reid	1	2	0	0	0	2
Leo Reise	4	17	1	0	1	14
Bob Rouse	1	4	0	0	0	0
Enio Sclisizzi	2	4	0	0	0	2
Earl Seibert	1	7	0	0	0	2
Ray Sheppard	1	3	0	1	1	0
John Sherf	1	5	0	1	1	2
Cully Simon	1	3	0	0	0	0
Glen Skov	3	18	2	3	5	26
Floyd Smith	3	18	6	3	9	4
John Sorrell	3	13	4	5	9	2
Irv Spencer	2	8	0	0	0	0
Wilf Starr	1	3	0	1	1	2
Vic Stasiuk	4	20	5	6	11	6
Jack Stewart	6	29	2	7	9	34
Tim Taylor	1	2	0	0	0	2
Norm Ullman	5	28	6	12	18	23
Bob Wall	1	4	0	0	0	2
Eddie Wares	3	14	0	6	6	22
Bryan Watson	1	6	0	0	0	12
Harry Watson	1	1	0	0	0	0
Cooney Weiland	1	4	1	1	2	2
Bob Whitelaw	1	4	0	0	0	0
Burr Williams	1	2	0	0	0	0
Johnny Wilson	5	27	3	2	5	2
Larry Wilson	1	2	0	0	0	0
Eddie Wiseman	1	3	0	0	0	0
Benny Woit	3	18	0	1	1	10
Steve Wojciechowski	1	2	0	0	0	0
Howie Young	2	8	1	1	2	18
Steve Yzerman	1	4	1	0	1	0
Larry Zeidel	1	3	0	0	0	0

GOALIES

	YRS	G	W-L	MINS	GA	SO	AVG
Hank Bassen	2	5	1–3	274	11	0	2.41
Roger Crozier	1	6	2–3	308	16	0	3.12
Wilf Cude	1	4	1–3	291	9	0	1.86
Glenn Hall	1	5	1–4	300	18	0	3.60
Harry Lumley	3	15	3–12	932	39	2	2.51
John Mowers	3	15	7–8	900	42	2	2.80
Chris Osgood	1	1	1–0	32	1	0	1.88
Earl Robertson	1	5	2–2	280	8	2	1.71
Terry Sawchuk	6	33	17–16	1960	83	3	2.54
Norm Smith	2	5	4–1	261	11	0	2.53
Mike Vernon	1	4	0–4	240	14	0	4.08

FINALS RECORDS

MOST STANLEY CUP FINALS APPEARANCES

Gordie Howe	10	Alex Delvecchio	8
Ted Lindsay	8	Sid Abel	7
Marcel Pronovost	8	Marty Pavelich	7

MOST GAMES

Gordie Howe	55	Marty Pavelich	36
Alex Delvecchio	47	Sid Abel	34
Marcel Pronovost	45	Mud Brûneteau	30
Ted Lindsay	44	Red Kelly	30

MOST POINTS

Gordie Howe	50	Sid Abel	20
Alex Delvecchio	38	Syd Howe	20
Ted Lindsay	34		

MOST GOALS

Ted Lindsay	19	Sid Abel	9
Gordie Howe	18	Mud Brûneteau	8
Alex Delvecchio	16		

MOST ASSISTS

Gordie Howe	32	Syd Howe	12
Alex Delvecchio	22	Norm Ullman	12
Ted Lindsay	15	Sid Abel	11

MOST PENALTY MINUTES

Gordie Howe	94	Tony Leswick	32
Jimmy Orlando	53	Bill Gadsby	28
Ted Lindsay	48	Marcel Pronovost	26
Marty Pavelich	38	Glen Skov	26
Jack Stewart	34		

ALL PLAYOFF OVERTIME GAMES

(length of overtime played listed in brackets from longest to shortest)

SIX OVERTIME PERIODS

March 24, 1936	Detroit	1	Mud Brûneteau (116:30)
	Maroons	0	

- Game 1 best-of-five semi-finals at Montreal
- Detroit took 1–0 series lead, won 3–0

FOUR OVERTIME PERIODS

March 23, 1943	Toronto	3	Jack McLean (70:18)
	Detroit	2	

- Game 2 best-of-seven semi-finals at Detroit
- Toronto tied series 1–1; Detroit won 4–2

March 27, 1951	Canadiens	3	Maurice Richard (61:09)
	Detroit	2	

- Game 1 best-of-seven semi-finals at Detroit
- Canadiens took 1–0 series lead, won 4–2

THREE OVERTIME PERIODS

April 1, 1937	Detroit	2	Hec Kilrea (51:49)
	Canadiens	1	

- Game 5 best-of-five semi-finals at Montreal
- Detroit eliminated Canadiens 3–2

March 22, 1949	Detroit	2	Max McNab (44:52)(pp)
	Canadiens	1	

- Game 1 best-of-seven semi-finals at Detroit
- Detroit took 1–0 series lead, won 4–3

March 27, 1960	Toronto	5	Frank Mahovlich (43:00)
	Detroit	4	

- Game 3 best-of-seven semi-finals at Detroit
- Toronto took 2–1 series lead, won 4–2

March 29, 1951	Canadiens	1	Maurice Richard (42:20)
	Detroit	0	

- Game 2 best-of-seven semi-finals at Detroit
- Canadiens took 2–0 series lead, won 4–2

TWO OVERTIME PERIODS

April 7, 1984 .... St. Louis 4 Mark Reeds (37:07)
Detroit 3

- Game 3 best-of-five first round at Detroit
- St. Louis took 2–1 series lead, won 3–1

April 10, 1934 .... Chicago 1 Mush March (30:05)
Detroit 0

- Game 4 best-of-five finals at Chicago
- Chicago won Stanley Cup 3–1

June 6, 1995 .... Detroit 4 Vladimir Konstantinov (29:25)
Chicago 3

- Game 3 best-of-seven semi-finals at Chicago
- Detroit took 3–0 series lead, won 4–1

April 23, 1950 .... Detroit 4 Pete Babando (28:31)
Rangers 3

- Game 7 best-of-seven finals at Detroit
- Detroit won Stanley Cup 4–3

March 22, 1961 .... Toronto 3 George Armstrong (24:51)
Detroit 2

- Game 1 best-of-seven semi-finals at Toronto
- Toronto took 1–0 series lead; Detroit won 4–1

June 11, 1995................. Detroit 2 Vyacheslav Kozlov (22:25)
Chicago 1

- Game 5 best-of-seven semi-finals at Detroit
- Detroit eliminated Chicago 4–1

May 16, 1996................. Detroit 1 Steve Yzerman (21:15)
St. Louis 0

- Game 7 best-of-seven quarter-finals at Detroit
- Detroit eliminated St. Louis 4–3

April 3, 1934 .... Chicago 2 Paul Thompson (21:10)
Detroit 1

- Game 1 best-of-five finals at Detroit
- Chicago took 1–0 lead, won Stanley Cup 3–1

April 1, 1954 .... Detroit 4 Ted Lindsay (21:01)
Toronto 3

- Game 5 best-of-seven semi-finals at Detroit
- Detroit eliminated Toronto 4–1

April 4, 1950 .... Detroit 2 Leo Reise (20:38)
Toronto 1

- Game 4 best-of-seven semi-finals at Toronto
- Detroit tied series 2–2, won 4–3

ONE OVERTIME PERIOD

Date	Team	Score	Goal
April 8, 1949	Toronto	3	Joe Klukay (17:31)
	Detroit	2	

- Game 1 best-of-seven finals at Detroit
- Toronto took 1–0 lead, won Stanley Cup 4–0

Date	Team	Score	Goal
May 19, 1996	Colorado	3	Mike Keane (17:31)
	Detroit	2	

- Game 1 best-of-seven semi-finals at Detroit
- Colorado took 1–0 lead, won series 4–2

Date	Team	Score	Goal
March 29, 1945	Detroit	3	Mud Brûneteau (17:12)
	Boston	2	

- Game 5 best-of-seven semi-finals at Detroit
- Detroit took 3–2 series lead, won 4–3

Date	Team	Score	Goal
April 28, 1992	Detroit	1	Sergei Fedorov (16:13)
	Minnesota	0	

- Game 6 best-of-seven preliminary round at Minnesota
- Detroit tied series 3–3, won 4–3

Date	Team	Score	Goal
April 6, 1989	Chicago	5	Duane Sutter (14:36)
	Detroit	4	

- Game 2 best-of-seven preliminary round at Detroit
- Chicago tied series 1–1, won 4–2

Date	Team	Score	Goal
April 21, 1945	Detroit	1	Ed Brûneteau (14:16)
	Toronto	0	

- Game 6 best-of-seven finals at Toronto
- Detroit tied series 3–3; Toronto won Stanley Cup 4–3

Date	Team	Score	Goal
March 29, 1953	Boston	2	Jack McIntyre (12:29)
	Detroit	1	

- Game 3 best-of-seven semi-finals at Boston
- Boston took 2–1 series lead, won 4–2

Date	Team	Score	Goal
March 20, 1941	Detroit	2	Gus Giesebrecht (12:01)
	Rangers	1	

- Game 1 best-of-three quarter-finals at Detroit
- Detroit took 1–0 series lead, won 2–1

Date	Team	Score	Goal
March 30, 1958	Canadiens	2	Andre Pronovost (11:52)
	Detroit	1	

- Game 3 best-of-seven semi-finals at Detroit
- Canadiens took 3–0 series lead, won 4–0

Date	Team	Score	Goal
May 9, 1988	Edmonton	4	Jari Kurri (11:02)
	Detroit	3	

- Game 4 best-of-seven semi-finals at Detroit
- Edmonton took 3–1 series lead, won 4–1

Date	Team	Score	Goal
March 28, 1946	Boston	4	Don Gallinger (9:51)
	Detroit	3	

- Game 5 best-of-five semi-finals at Boston
- Boston eliminated Detroit 3–2

Date	Team	Score	Goal
April 27, 1987	Toronto	3	Mike Allison (9:31)
	Detroit	2	

- Game 4 best-of-seven quarter-finals at Toronto
- Toronto took 3–1 series lead; Detroit won 4–3

Date	Team	Score	Goal
March 30, 1943	Detroit	3	Adam Brown (9:21)
	Toronto	2	

- Game 6 best-of-seven semi-finals at Toronto
- Detroit eliminated Toronto 4–2

Date	Team	Score	Goal
March 30, 1941	Detroit	2	Gus Giesebrecht (9:15)
	Chicago	1	

- Game 2 best-of-three semi-finals at Chicago
- Detroit eliminated Chicago 2–0

Date	Team	Score	Goal
April 9, 1950	Detroit	1	Leo Reise (8:39)
	Toronto	0	

- Game 7 best-of-seven semi-finals at Detroit
- Detroit eliminated Toronto 4–3

Date	Team	Score	Goal
April 18, 1950	Rangers	4	Don Raleigh (8:34)
	Detroit	3	

- Game 4 best-of-seven finals at Detroit
- Rangers tied series 2–2; Detroit won Stanley Cup 4–3

Date	Team	Score	Goal
April 2, 1964	Chicago	3	Murray Balfour (8:21)
	Detroit	2	

- Game 4 best-of-seven semi-finals at Detroit
- Chicago tied series 2–2; Detroit won 4–3

Date	Team	Score	Goal
April 14, 1964	Detroit	4	Larry Jeffrey (7:52)
	Toronto	3	

- Game 2 best-of-seven finals at Toronto
- Detroit tied series 1–1; Toronto won Stanley Cup 4–3

Date	Team	Score	Goal
March 26, 1939	Detroit	1	Marty Barry (7:47)(pp)
	Canadiens	0	

- Game 3 best-of-three quarter-finals at Detroit
- Detroit eliminated Canadiens 2–1

Date	Team	Score	Goal
April 11, 1954	Canadiens	1	Ken Mosdell (5:45)
	Detroit	0	

- Game 5 best-of-seven finals at Detroit
- Canadiens trailed 3–2; Detroit won Stanley Cup 4–3

April 1, 1939	Toronto	5	Gord Drillon (5:42)
	Detroit	4	

- Game 3 best-of-three semi-finals at Toronto
- Toronto eliminated Detroit 2–1

April 11, 1987	Detroit	4	Shawn Burr (4:51)
	Chicago	3	

- Game 3 best-of-seven first round at Chicago
- Detroit took 3–0 series lead, won 4–0

April 16, 1954	Detroit	2	Tony Leswick (4:29)
	Canadiens	1	

- Game 7 best-of-seven finals at Detroit
- Detroit won Stanley Cup 4–3

March 24, 1956	Detroit	5	Ted Lindsay (4:22)
	Toronto	4	

- Game 3 best-of-seven semi–finals at Toronto
- Detroit took 3–0 series lead, won 4–1

May 8, 1996	St. Louis	5	Igor Kravchuk (3:23)
	Detroit	4	

- Game 3 best-of-seven quarter-finals at St. Louis
- St. Louis trailed 2–1; Detroit won 4–3

March 26, 1947	Toronto	3	Howie Meeker (3:05)
	Detroit	2	

- Game 1 best-of-seven semi-finals at Toronto
- Toronto took 1–0 series lead, won 4–1

March 24, 1949	Canadiens	4	Gerry Plamondon (2:59)
	Detroit	3	

- Game 2 best-of-seven semi-finals at Detroit
- Canadiens tied series 1–1; Detroit won 4–3

April 8, 1984	St. Louis	3	Jorgen Petersson (2:42)
	Detroit	2	

- Game 4 best-of-five first round at Detroit
- St. Louis eliminated Detroit 3–1

May 1, 1993	Toronto	4	Nikolai Borschevsky (2:35)
	Detroit	3	

- Game 7 best-of-seven first round at Detroit
- Toronto eliminated Detroit 4–3

May 5, 1966	Canadiens	3	Henri Richard (2:20)
	Detroit	2	

- Game 6 best-of-seven finals at Detroit
- Canadiens won Stanley Cup 4–2

April 27, 1993	Toronto	5	Mike Foligno (2:05)
	Detroit	4	

- Game 5 best-of-seven first round at Detroit
- Toronto took 3–2 series lead, won 4–3

March 29, 1960	Detroit	2	Gerry Melnyk (1:54)(pp)
	Toronto	1	

- Game 4 best-of-seven semi-finals at Detroit
- Detroit tied series 2–2; Toronto won 4–2

April 23, 1964	Toronto	4	Bobby Baun (1:43)
	Detroit	3	

- Game 6 best-of-seven finals at Detroit
- Toronto tied series 3–3, won Stanley Cup 4–3

April 20, 1950	Rangers	2	Don Raleigh (1:38)
	Detroit	1	

- Game 5 best-of-seven finals at Detroit
- Rangers took 3–2 series lead; Detroit won Stanley Cup 4–3

March 22, 1934	Detroit	2	Herbie Lewis (1:33)(pp)
	Toronto	1	

- Game 1 best-of-five semi-finals at Toronto
- Detroit took 1–0 series lead, won 3–2

April 22, 1992	Detroit	5	Yves Racine (1:15)
	Minnesota	4	

- Game 3 best-of-seven preliminary round at Minnesota
- Detroit trailed series 2–1, won 4–3

June 1, 1995	Detroit	2	Nicklas Lidstrom (1:01)
	Chicago	1	

- Game 1 best-of-seven semi-finals at Detroit
- Detroit took 1–0 series lead, won 4–1

April 12, 1988	Toronto	6	Ed Olczyk (:34)
	Detroit	5	

- Game 5 best-of-seven first round at Detroit
- Toronto trailed series 3–2; Detroit won 4–2

April 9, 1936	Toronto	4	Buzz Boll (:31)
	Detroit	3	

- Game 3 best-of-five finals at Toronto
- Detroit led 2–1, won Stanley Cup 3–1

March 19, 1940	Detroit	2	Syd Howe (:25)
	Americans	1	

- Game 1 best-of-three quarter-finals at Detroit
- Detroit took 1–0 series lead, won 2–1

OVERTIME RECORD BY TEAM

vs.

Team	Record	Team	Record
Toronto	9–12	Maroons	1–0
Chicago	5–4	Boston	1–2
Canadiens	4–6	Edmonton	0–1
Minnesota	2–0	St. Louis	1–3
Rangers	2–2	Colorado	0–1
Americans	1–0	Totals	26–31

YEAR-BY-YEAR OVERTIME RECORD
(won/loss record in brackets)

YEAR	GAMES TOTAL	GAMES OVERTIME	YEAR	GAMES TOTAL	GAMES OVERTIME
1927	—	—	1963	11	0
1928	—	—	1964	14	3 (1–2)
1929	2	0	1965	7	0
1930	—	—	1966	12	1 (0–1)
1931	—	—	1967	—	—
1932	2	0	1968	—	—
1933	4	0	1969	—	—
1934	9	3 (1–2)	1970	4	0
1935	—	—	1971	—	—
1936	7	2 (1–1)	1972	—	—
1937	10	1 (1–0)	1973	—	—
1938	—	—	1974	—	—
1939	6	2 (1–1)	1975	—	—
1940	5	1 (1–0)	1976	—	—
1941	9	2 (2–0)	1977	—	—
1942	12	0	1978	8	0
1943	10	2 (1–1)	1979	—	—
1944	5	0	1980	—	—
1945	14	2 (2–0)	1981	—	—
1946	5	1 (0–1)	1982	—	—
1947	5	1 (0–1)	1983	—	—
1948	10	0	1984	4	2 (0–2)
1949	11	3 (1–2)	1985	3	0
1950	14	5 (3–2)	1986	—	—
1951	6	2 (0–2)	1987	16	2 (1–1)
1952	8	0	1988	16	2 (0–2)
1953	6	1 (0–1)	1989	6	1 (0–1)
1954	12	3 (2–1)	1990	—	—
1955	11	0	1991	7	0
1956	12	1 (1–0)	1992	11	2 (2–0)
1957	5	0	1993	7	2 (0–2)
1958	4	1 (0–1)	1994	7	0
1959	—	—	1995	18	3 (3–0)
1960	6	2 (1–1)	1996	19	3 (1–2)
1961	11	1 (0–1)	Total playoff games	391	
1962	—	—	Total overtime games	57 (26–31)	

COACHING REGISTER
PLAYOFF OVERTIME GAMES

SID ABEL

1958	1	0	1
1960	2	1	1
1961	1	0	1
1964	3	1	2
1966	1	0	1
Totals	8	2	6

JACK ADAMS

1934	3	1	2
1936	2	1	1
1937	1	1	0
1939	2	1	1
1940	1	1	0
1941	2	2	0
1943	2	1	1
1945	2	2	0
1946	1	0	1
1947	1	0	1
Totals	17	10	7

SCOTTY BOWMAN

1995	3	3	0
1996	3	1	2
Totals	6	4	2

JACQUES DEMERS

1987	2	1	1
1988	2	0	2
1989	1	0	1
Totals	5	1	4

TOMMY IVAN

1949	3	1	2
1950	5	3	2
1951	2	0	2
1953	1	0	1
1954	3	2	1
Totals	14	6	8

BRYAN MURRAY

1992	2	2	0
1993	2	0	2
Totals	4	2	2

NICK POLANO

1984	2	0	2

JIMMY SKINNER

1956	1	1	0

PLAYER OVERTIME REGISTER

	GP	G	A	P	PIM
Sid Abel	18	0	0	0	2
Gary Aldcorn	2	0	0	0	0
Keith Allen	3	0	0	0	0
Ralph Almas	1	0	0	0	0
Al Arbour	1	0	0	0	0
Murray Armstrong	3	0	0	0	0
Brent Ashton	4	0	1	1	0
Pierre Aubry	1	0	0	0	0
Larry Aurie	5	0	0	0	0
Pete Babando	1	1	0	1	0
Doug Barkley	3	0	0	0	0
Dave Barr	5	0	0	0	0
John Barrett	2	0	0	0	0
Marty Barry	5	1	1	2	0
Andy Bathgate	1	0	0	0	0
Marc Bergevin	3	0	0	0	0
Gary Bergman	1	0	0	0	0
Steve Black	5	0	0	0	0
Leo Boivin	1	0	0	0	0
Ivan Boldirev	2	0	0	0	0
Marcel Bonin	1	0	0	0	0
Ralph Bowman	4	0	0	0	0
Mel Bridgman	4	0	0	0	2
Adam Brown	2	1	0	1	0
Doug Brown	5	0	1	1	0
Connie Brown	1	0	0	0	0
Ed Brûneteau	2	1	0	1	0
Mud Brûneteau	10	2	1	3	0
Ed Brûneteau	3	0	0	0	0
Johnny Bucyk	1	0	0	0	0
Tony Bukovich	1	0	0	0	0
Shawn Burr	11	1	0	1	0
Cummy Burton	1	0	0	0	0
Walter Buswell	3	0	0	0	0
Colin Campbell	2	0	0	0	0
Gene Carrigan	2	0	0	0	0
Jimmy Carson	2	0	0	0	0
Frank Carson	1	0	0	0	0
Joe Carveth	10	0	1	1	0
John Chabot	3	0	0	0	0
Tim Cheveldae	4	0	0	0	0
Tim Cheveldae	3	0	0	0	0
Steve Chiasson	4	0	0	0	0
Steve Chiasson	1	0	0	0	0
Dino Ciccarelli	8	0	0	0	0
Paul Coffey	8	0	0	0	0
Roy Conacher	1	0	0	0	0
Charlie Conacher	2	0	1	1	0
Jim Conacher	2	0	0	0	0
Murray Costello	1	0	0	0	0
Gerry Couture	11	0	0	0	0
Roger Crozier	2	0	0	0	0
Roger Crozier	1	0	0	0	0
Wilf Cude	3	0	0	0	0
Barry Cullen	2	0	0	0	0
Don Deacon	1	0	0	0	0
Gilbert Delorme	4	0	0	0	0
Gilbert Delorme	1	0	0	0	0
Alex Delvecchio	13	0	0	0	0
Al Dewsbury	4	0	0	0	0
Bob Dillabough	1	0	0	0	0
Cecil Dillon	1	0	0	0	0
Bill Dineen	4	0	0	0	0
Bobby Dollas	1	0	0	0	0
Les Douglas	2	0	0	0	0
Dallas Drake	2	0	0	0	0
Chris Draper	5	0	0	0	0
Gilles Dube	1	0	0	0	0
Ron Duguay	2	0	0	0	0
Blake Dunlop	2	0	0	0	0
Hap Emms	3	0	0	0	0
Bob Errey	6	0	0	0	2
Sergei Fedorov	8	1	1	2	0
Lorne Ferguson	1	0	0	0	0
Viacheslav Fetisov	6	0	1	1	0
Guyle Fielder	1	0	0	0	0
Joe Fisher	3	0	0	0	0
Lee Fogolin	8	0	0	0	0
Val Fonteyne	4	0	1	1	0
Dwight Foster	2	0	0	0	0
Bill Gadsby	4	0	0	0	2
Johnny Gallagher	1	0	0	0	0
Gerard Gallant	9	0	0	0	0
Danny Gare	2	0	0	0	0
Fern Gauthier	1	0	0	0	0

George Gee	10	0	3	3	2
Gus Giesebrecht	4	2	0	2	0
Howie Glover	1	0	0	0	0
Fred Glover	3	0	0	0	0
Warren Godfrey	5	0	0	0	0
Pete Goegan	1	0	0	0	5
Pete Goegan	3	0	0	0	0
Bob Goldham	8	0	1	1	0
Ebbie Goodfellow	10	0	1	1	7
Ted Graham	3	0	0	0	0
Stu Grimson	1	0	0	0	0
Lloyd Gross	1	0	0	0	0
Don Grosso	6	0	1	1	0
Lloyd Haddon	2	0	0	0	0
Gord Haidy	1	0	0	0	0
Len Haley	2	0	0	0	0
Glenn Hall	1	0	0	0	0
Doug Halward	1	0	0	0	0
Glen Hanlon	3	0	0	0	0
George Hay	1	0	0	0	0
Paul Henderson	4	0	0	0	0
Tim Higgins	3	0	0	0	0
Jim Hiller	1	0	0	0	0
Larry Hillman	1	0	0	0	0
Flash Hollett	3	0	1	1	0
Gord Hollingworth	1	0	0	0	0
Pete Horeck	4	0	0	0	0
Doug Houda	1	0	0	0	0
Gordie Howe	19	0	4	4	6
Syd Howe	11	1	2	3	0
Mark Howe	2	0	0	0	0
Steve Hrymnak	1	0	0	0	0
Hal Jackson	5	0	0	0	0
Larry Jeffrey	3	1	0	1	0
Bill Jennings	2	0	0	0	0
Greg Johnson	1	0	0	0	0
Earl Johnson	1	0	0	0	0
Al Johnson	1	0	0	0	0
Ed Johnstone	1	0	0	0	0
Buck Jones	2	0	0	0	0
Ed Joyal	3	0	0	0	0
Red Kelly	16	0	0	0	0
Pete Kelly	5	0	0	0	0
Forbes Kennedy	1	0	0	0	0
Sheldon Kennedy	2	0	0	0	0
Alan Kerr	2	0	0	0	0
Hec Kilrea	5	1	1	2	0
Wally Kilrea	3	0	0	0	0
Ken Kilrea	3	0	0	0	0
Kris King	1	0	0	0	0
Kelly Kisio	2	0	0	0	0
Petr Klima	4	0	0	0	0
Joey Kocur	3	0	0	0	0
Steve Konroyd	1	0	0	0	0
Vladimir Konstantinov	10	1	0	1	0
Vyacheslav Kozlov	6	1	0	1	0
Leo Labine	1	0	0	0	0
Randy Ladouceur	2	0	0	0	0
Mark Lamb	2	0	0	0	0
Lane Lambert	2	0	0	0	0
Al Langlois	3	0	0	0	0
Martin Lapointe	4	0	0	0	0
Igor Larionov	3	0	0	0	0
Reed Larson	2	0	0	0	0
Tony Leswick	5	1	0	1	2
Dave Lewis	2	0	1	1	0
Herb Lewis	7	1	2	3	0
Nicklas Lidstrom	10	1	0	1	0
Ted Lindsay	19	2	1	3	0
Carl Liscombe	7	0	0	0	0
Harry Lumley	11	0	0	0	0
Len Lunde	3	0	0	0	0
Pat Lundy	1	0	0	0	0
Parker MacDonald	5	0	0	0	0
Bruce MacGregor	5	0	0	0	0
Howard Mackie	1	0	0	0	0
Paul MacLean	1	0	0	0	0
Rick MacLeish	1	0	0	0	0
John MacMillan	1	0	0	0	0
Kirk Maltby	1	0	0	0	0
Bob Manno	2	0	0	0	0
Gus Marker	2	0	0	0	0
Brad Marsh	1	0	0	0	0
Bert Marshall	1	0	0	0	0
Clare Martin	3	0	0	0	0
Hubie Martin	3	0	0	0	0
Jud McAtee	2	0	0	0	0
Doug McCaig	1	0	0	0	0
Darren McCarty	6	0	0	0	0
Brad McCrimmon	2	0	0	0	0
Bucko McDonald	3	0	0	0	0
Ab McDonald	1	0	0	0	0
Byron McDonald	1	0	0	0	0
Jim McFadden	10	0	0	0	0
Bob McGill	1	0	0	0	0
Jack McIntyre	3	0	0	0	0
Rollie McLenahan	1	0	0	0	0
Max McNab	9	1	0	1	0
Billy McNeill	1	0	0	0	0
Gerry Melnyk	3	0	1	1	0

Nick Mickoski	1	0	0	0	0
Kevin Miller	1	0	0	0	0
Ed Mio	1	0	0	0	0
Ed Mio	1	0	0	0	0
John Miszuk	1	0	0	0	0
Ron Moffatt	1	0	0	0	0
Jim Morrison	2	0	0	0	0
Alex Motter	5	0	0	0	0
John Mowers	4	0	0	0	0
Joe Murphy	1	0	0	0	0
Jim Nill	3	0	0	0	0
Lee Norwood	5	0	0	0	2
Mike O'Connell	5	0	0	0	0
Adam Oates	5	0	0	0	0
Gerry Odrowski	1	0	0	0	0
John Ogrodnick	2	0	0	0	0
Murray Oliver	2	0	0	0	0
Jimmy Orlando	5	0	0	0	0
Chris Osgood	2	0	0	0	0
Brad Park	1	0	0	0	0
Joe Paterson	1	0	0	0	0
Marty Pavelich	15	0	0	0	0
Jim Peters	8	0	0	0	0
Eric Pettinger	5	0	0	0	0
Nellie Podolsky	1	0	0	0	0
Don Poile	1	0	0	0	0
Bud Poile	3	0	0	0	0
Dean Prentice	1	0	0	0	0
Keith Primeau	10	0	1	1	4
Bob Probert	8	0	0	0	0
Marcel Pronovost	18	0	1	1	0
Andre Pronovost	3	0	0	0	0
Metro Prystai	5	0	0	0	0
Cliff Purpur	2	0	0	0	0
Bill Quackenbush	7	0	0	0	0
Yves Racine	4	1	0	1	0
Mike Ramsey	3	0	0	0	0
Earl Reibel	2	0	0	0	0
Leo Reise	11	2	0	2	0
Vincent Riendeau	1	0	0	0	0
Torrie Robertson	1	0	0	0	0
Bob Rouse	4	0	0	0	0
Terry Sawchuk	13	0	0	0	0
Enio Sclisizzi	2	0	0	0	0
Earl Seibert	2	0	0	0	0
Ric Seiling	1	0	0	0	0
Jeff Sharples	1	0	0	0	0
Ray Sheppard	7	0	0	0	0
John Sherf	1	0	0	0	0
Mike Sillinger	1	0	0	0	0
Cully Simon	2	0	0	0	0
Glen Skov	6	0	1	1	0
Floyd Smith	4	0	0	0	0
Greg Smith	2	0	0	0	0
Brian Smith	2	0	0	0	0
Norm Smith	3	0	0	0	0
Neil Smith	3	0	0	0	0
Harold Snepsts	4	0	0	0	0
John Sorrell	5	0	0	0	0
Irv Spencer	3	0	0	0	0
Wilf Starr	2	0	0	0	0
Vic Stasiuk	1	0	0	0	0
Greg Stefan	3	0	0	0	0
Jack Stewart	15	0	0	0	0
Gaye Stewart	2	0	0	0	0
Tim Taylor	4	0	0	0	0
Billy Taylor	1	0	0	0	0
Cecil Thompson	3	0	0	0	0
Norm Ullman	8	0	1	1	0
Darren Veitch	4	0	0	0	0
Mike Vernon	4	0	0	0	0
Eddie Wares	5	0	0	0	0
Harry Watson	3	0	0	0	0
Bryan Watson	1	0	0	0	0
Cooney Weiland	3	0	0	0	0
Bob Whitelaw	2	0	0	0	0
Burr Williams	2	0	0	0	0
Johnny Wilson	9	0	0	0	0
Larry Wilson	1	0	0	0	0
Eddie Wiseman	3	0	0	0	0
Benny Woit	5	0	0	0	0
Howie Young	1	0	0	0	2
Doug Young	7	0	0	0	0
Paul Ysebaert	4	0	0	0	0
Steve Yzerman	13	1	0	1	4
Rick Zombo	3	0	0	0	0

MOST OVERTIME GAMES

Player	Games
Gordie Howe	19
Ted Lindsay	19
Sid Abel	18
Marcel Pronovost	18
Red Kelly	16
Marty Pavelich	15
Jack Stewart	15
Terry Sawchuk	13
Steve Yzerman	13

MOST OVERTIME GOALS

Player	Goals
Mud Brûneteau	2
Gus Giesebrecht	2
Ted Lindsay	2
Leo Reise	2

MOST OVERTIME ASSISTS

Gordie Howe	4
George Gee	3
Syd Howe	2
Herbie Lewis	2

MOST OVERTIME POINTS

Gordie Howe	4
Mud Brûneteau	3
Ted Lindsay	3
Syd Howe	3
Herbie Lewis	3
George Gee	3

MOST OVERTIME PENALTY MINUTES

Ebbie Goodfellow	7
Gordie Howe	6
Pete Goegan	5
Keith Primeau	4

RECORDS FOR ALL GOALIES IN OVERTIME

MINUTES PLAYED

Terry Sawchuk	246:46
Harry Lumley	174:41
Neil Smith	168:50
John Mowers	100:55
Mike Vernon	56:14
Wilf Cude	52:48
Greg Stefan	52:17
Chris Osgood	38:46
Glen Hanlon	25:24
Tim Cheveldae	20:53
Cecil Thompson	13:54
Glenn Hall	4:22
Ralph Almas	3:05
Ed Mio	2:42
Roger Crozier	2:20
Vincent Riendeau	1:15

WON/LOSS RECORD

Harry Lumley	6–5
Terry Sawchuk	5–8
John Mowers	3–1
Mike Vernon	3–1
Norm Smith	2–1
Cecil Thompson	2–1
Glenn Hall	1–0
Vincent Riendeau	1–0
Chris Osgood	1–1
Tim Cheveldae	1–2
Wilf Cude	1–2
Glen Hanlon	1–2
Ralph Almas	0–1
Roger Crozier	0–1
Ed Mio	0–1
Greg Stefan	0–3

TROPHY WINNERS

ART ROSS TROPHY

Given to the NHL by Arthur Ross, former manager and coach of the Boston Bruins, in 1947 to honour the player with the most points in the regular season (if there is a tie, the following rules decide the winner: (a) most goals; (b) fewest games played; (c) player who scores the first goal of the season).

1950	Ted Lindsay
1951	Gordie Howe
1952	Gordie Howe
1953	Gordie Howe
1954	Gordie Howe
1957	Gordie Howe
1963	Gordie Howe

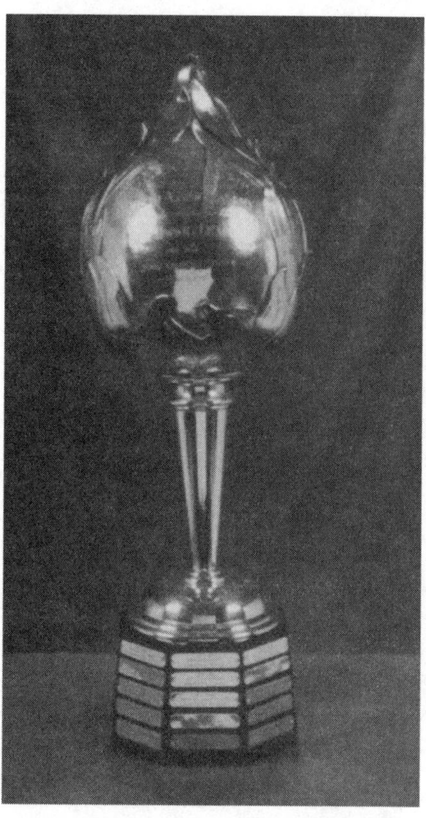

HART MEMORIAL TROPHY

Begun in 1923–24, the Hart Trophy was retired and replaced by the Hart Memorial Trophy beginning with the '59–'60 season. It was inaugurated by Dr. David Hart in memory of his father Cecil Hart, manager and coach of the Canadiens, and is presented to the player most valuable to his team.

1940	Ebbie Goodfellow
1949	Sid Abel
1952	Gordie Howe
1953	Gordie Howe
1957	Gordie Howe
1958	Gordie Howe
1960	Gordie Howe
1963	Gordie Howe
1994	Sergei Fedorov

VEZINA TROPHY

Inaugurated in 1926–27 by former owners of the Canadiens (Leo Dandurand, Louis Letourneau, and Joe Cattarinich) to honour Georges Vezina. Up until 1981–82 it was awarded to the goaltenders who allowed the fewest goals against during the regular season. Since then, it has been given to the goalie deemed to be the best in the league.

1937	Norm Smith
1943	John Mowers
1952	Terry Sawchuk
1953	Terry Sawchuk
1955	Terry Sawchuk

JAMES NORRIS MEMORIAL TROPHY

This trophy was first presented in 1953 by the four children of James Norris in memory of their father, owner of the Detroit Red Wings. It is given to the best defenceman in the league.

1954	Red Kelly
1995	Paul Coffey

CALDER MEMORIAL TROPHY

From 1937–1943 NHL President Frank Calder presented an annual trophy to the League's outstanding rookie. After his death, the Calder Memorial Trophy was presented in his honour. A player cannot have played more than 25 games in any previous season, or 6 or more games in any two previous seasons in any professional league. Since 1990–91, a player cannot have turned 26 by September 15 of his eligible year.

1933	Carl Voss
1948	Jim McFadden
1951	Terry Sawchuk
1956	Glenn Hall
1965	Roger Crozier

LADY BYNG MEMORIAL TROPHY

Given in 1925 by Lady Byng, wife of then Governor-General. After Frank Boucher (Rangers) won the award seven of eight times (1928–35, except 1932), he was given the trophy and a new Byng was donated in 1936. Upon Lady Byng's death in 1949, the trophy became the Lady Byng Memorial Trophy. It is awarded to the player who combines a high level of play with "sportsmanship and gentlemanly conduct."

1937	Marty Barry
1949	Bill Quackenbush
1951	Red Kelly
1953	Red Kelly
1954	Red Kelly
1956	Earl Reibel
1959	Alex Delvecchio
1966	Alex Delvecchio
1969	Alex Delvecchio
1975	Marcel Dionne

FRANK J. SELKE TROPHY

Presented in 1977 by the Board of Directors of the NHL to honour Frank J. Selke. It is given to the forward who "best excels in the defensive aspects of the game."

1994	Sergei Fedorov

CONN SMYTHE TROPHY

Begun in 1964, this award was given to the NHL by the Toronto Maple Leafs in honour of the team's founder, owner, coach, manager, and director. It is awarded to the player most valuable to his team in the playoffs.

1966	Roger Crozier

LESTER B. PEARSON AWARD

Begun in 1970–71, it is presented by the NHLPA in honour of the former Prime Minister of Canada and given to the league's most valuable player as selected by members of the NHL Players' Association.

1989	Steve Yzerman
1994	Sergei Fedorov

BILL MASTERTON TROPHY

First presented in 1968 by the NHL Writers' Association in memory of Bill Masterton, a member of the Minnesota North Stars who died as a result of an on-ice injury January 15, 1968. It is given to the player who "best exemplifies the qualities of perseverance, sportsmanship, and dedication to hockey."

1984	Brad Park

LESTER PATRICK TROPHY

First presented to the NHL by the New York Rangers in 1966 in memory of their long-serving coach and general manager and given for "outstanding service to hockey in the United States."

1966	Jack Adams
1967	Gordie Howe
1974	Alex Delvecchio
1975	Bruce A. Norris
1991	Mike Ilitch

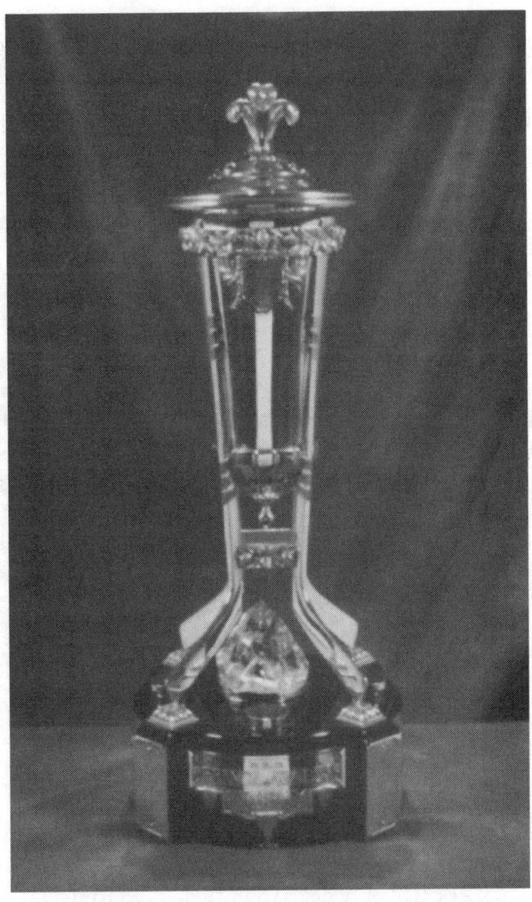

JACK ADAMS AWARD

First presented by the NHL Broadcasters' Association in 1974 in honour of Jack Adams and awarded to the coach who has "contributed the most to his team's success."

1978	Bobby Kromm
1987	Jacques Demers
1988	Jacques Demers

PRINCE OF WALES TROPHY

Awarded to the NHL champions from 1924–27. From 1927–38, it was given to the champions of the American Division and from 1938–67 was once again awarded to the league champion of the 6–team NHL.

1934	Detroit Red Wings
1936	Detroit Red Wings
1937	Detroit Red Wings
1943	Detroit Red Wings
1949	Detroit Red Wings
1950	Detroit Red Wings
1951	Detroit Red Wings
1952	Detroit Red Wings
1953	Detroit Red Wings
1954	Detroit Red Wings
1955	Detroit Red Wings
1957	Detroit Red Wings
1965	Detroit Red Wings

O'BRIEN TROPHY

First presented by M.J. O'Brien in 1910 to the champion of the National Hockey Association until the NHL took the trophy over in 1917 when the NHA folded. In 1924 it was decided the Prince of Wales Trophy would go to the league champion so the O'Brien was not awarded. But in 1928 the O'Brien was given to the winner of the Canadian Division of the NHL. This was done until 1939 after which it was given to the loser in the Stanley Cup finals. The trophy was permanently retired after the 1949–50 season.

1941	Detroit Red Wings
1942	Detroit Red Wings
1945	Detroit Red Wings
1948	Detroit Red Wings
1949	Detroit Red Wings

DETROIT RED WINGS TROPHIES

FRANK J. MURPHY MEMORIAL TROPHY

Awarded annually to the player scoring the most goals during the regular season. It was first presented in 1944–45 by Mrs. Constance Murphy in memory of her husband, former Lieutenant-Governor of the State of Michigan. It was later re-named the James D. Norris Trophy, but was retired after 1981 when the Norris family sold the club.

1944–45	Joe Carveth
1945–46	Adam Brown
1946–47	Roy Conacher
1947–48	Ted Lindsay
1948–49	Sid Abel
1949–50	Gordie Howe
1950–51	Gordie Howe
1951–52	Gordie Howe
1952–53	Gordie Howe
1953–54	Gordie Howe
1954–55	Gordie Howe
1955–56	Gordie Howe
1956–57	Gordie Howe
1957–58	Gordie Howe
1958–59	Gordie Howe
1959–60	Gordie Howe
1960–61	Norm Ullman
1961–62	Gordie Howe
1962–63	Gordie Howe
1963–64	Gordie Howe
1964–65	Norm Ullman
1965–66	Norm Ullman & Alex Delvecchio
1966–67	Bruce MacGregor
1967–68	Gordie Howe
1968–69	Frank Mahovlich
1969–70	Garry Unger
1970–71	Tom Webster
1971–72	Mickey Redmond
1972–73	Mickey Redmond
1973–74	Mickey Redmond
1974–75	Danny Grant
1975–76	Michel Bergeron
1976–77	Walt McKechnie

HARRY A. GORMLEY TROPHY

Presented annually to the player leading the team in point scoring for the season. First presented in 1941–42 by the heirs of the late Harry Gormley. It was later re-named the Bruce A. Norris Trophy but was retired after 1981 when the Norris family sold the club.

1941–42	Don Grosso
1942–43	Syd Howe
1943–44	Carl Liscombe
1944–45	Joe Carveth
1945–46	Joe Carveth
1946–47	Billy Taylor
1947–48	Ted Lindsay
1948–49	Ted Lindsay & Sid Abel
1949–50	Ted Lindsay
1950–51	Gordie Howe
1951–52	Gordie Howe
1952–53	Gordie Howe
1953–54	Gordie Howe
1954–55	Earl Reibel
1955–56	Gordie Howe
1956–57	Gordie Howe
1957–58	Gordie Howe
1958–59	Gordie Howe
1959–60	Gordie Howe
1960–61	Gordie Howe
1961–62	Gordie Howe
1962–63	Gordie Howe
1963–64	Gordie Howe
1964–65	Norm Ullman
1965–66	Gordie Howe
1966–67	Norm Ullman
1967–68	Gordie Howe
1968–69	Gordie Howe
1969–70	Gordie Howe
1970–71	Tom Webster
1971–72	Marcel Dionne
1972–73	Mickey Redmond
1973–74	Marcel Dionne
1974–75	Marcel Dionne
1975–76	Walt McKechnie
1976–77	Walt McKechnie
1977–78	Dale McCourt
1978–79	Vaclav Nedomansky
1979–80	Dale McCourt
1980–81	Dale McCourt

HOCKEY WRITERS TROPHY

Presented to the club's most valuable player as selected by the Writers' Association, originally donated by the late Harry Jacobson in 1941–42. When he passed away, the writers adopted it.

1941–42	John Mowers
1942–43	Jack Stewart
1943–44	Carl Liscombe
1944–45	Syd Howe
1945–46	Bill Quackenbush
1946–47	Ted Lindsay
1947–48	Sid Abel
1948–49	Sid Abel
1949–50	Sid Abel
1950–51	Red Kelly
1951–52	Gordie Howe
1952–53	Gordie Howe
1953–54	Red Kelly
1954–55	Bob Goldham
1955–56	Gordie Howe
1956–57	Gordie Howe
1957–58	Gordie Howe
1958–59	Gordie Howe
1959–60	Gordie Howe
1960–61	Gordie Howe
1961–62	Gordie Howe
1962–63	Gordie Howe
1963–64	Terry Sawchuk
1964–65	Norm Ullman
1965–66	Gordie Howe
1966–67	Gordie Howe
1967–68	Gordie Howe
1968–69	Gordie Howe
1969–70	Roy Edwards
1970–71	Gordie Howe
1971–72	Marcel Dionne
1972–73	Roy Edwards
1973–74	Jim Rutherford
1974–75	Marcel Dionne
1975–76	Dan Maloney
1976–77	*no winner*
1977–78	Andre St. Laurent
1978–79	Vaclav Nedomansky
1979–80	Reed Larson
1980–81	Reed Larson

STU EVANS TROPHY

Emblematic of the most sportsmanlike Red Wing

1942–43	Mud Brûneteau
1943–44	Bill Quackenbush
1944–45	Murray Armstrong
1945–46	Carl Liscombe
1946–47	Bill Quackenbush
1947–48	Jim McFadden
1948–49	Bill Quackenbush
1949–50	Red Kelly
1950–51	Red Kelly
1951–52	Bob Goldham
1952–53	Metro Prystai
1953–54	Johnny Wilson
1954–55	Earl Reibel
1955–56	Marty Pavelich
1956–57	Alex Delvecchio
1957–58	Johnny Wilson
1958–59	Alex Delvecchio
1959–60	Gary Aldcorn
1960–61	Norm Ullman
1961–62	Alex Delvecchio
1962–63	Parker MacDonald
1963–64	Bruce MacGregor
1964–65	Alex Delvecchio
1965–66	Alex Delvecchio
1966–67	Ted Hampson
1967–68	Alex Delvecchio
1968–69	Alex Delvecchio
1969–70	Wayne Connelly
1970–71	Alex Delvecchio
1971–72	Alex Delvecchio
1972–73	Alex Delvecchio
1973–74	Red Berenson
1974–75	Nick Libett
1975–76	Walt McKechnie
1976–77	J.P. Leblanc
1977–78	Reed Larson
1978–79	Paul Woods
1979–80	Errol Thompson
1980–81	John Ogrodnick

GEORGE VANDERVREKEN MEMORIAL (FOR 'EM CLUB) TROPHY

In recognition of the team's unsung hero

1950–51	Carl Mattson
1951–52	Fred Huber
1952–53	Lefty Wilson
1953–54	Bob Goldham
1954–55	Marty Pavelich
1955–56	Marcel Pronovost
1956–57	Al Arbour
1957–58	Forbes Kennedy
1958–59	Warren Godfrey
1959–60	Norm Ullman
1960–61	Pete Goegan
1961–62	Val Fonteyne
1962–63	Doug Barkley
1963–64	Andre Pronovost
1964–65	Floyd Smith
1965–66	Val Fonteyne
1966–67	Ted Hampson
1967–68	Alex Delvecchio
1968–69	Dean Prentice
1969–70	Wayne Connelly
1970–71	Lefty Wilson
1971–72	Larry Johnston
1972–73	Bill Collins
1973–74	Bill Hogaboam
1974–75	Jean Hamel
1975–76	Nick Libett
1976–77	Dennis Hextall
1977–78	Terry Harper
1978–79	Jean Hamel
1979–80	Barry Long
1980–81	Mark Kirton

DETROIT SPORTS BROADCASTERS ASSOCIATION PLAQUE

To the player adjudged to be the finest rookie on the team

1948–49	Max McNab
1949–50	Steve Black
1950–51	Terry Sawchuk
1951–52	Glen Skov
1952–53	Marcel Bonin
1953–54	Bill Dineen
1954–55	*not awarded*
1955–56	Glenn Hall
1956–57	Billy Dea
1957–58	Don Poile
1958–59	Len Lunde
1959–60	Murray Oliver
1960–61	Hank Bassen
1961–62	Bruce MacGregor
1962–63	Doug Barkley
1963–64	Pit Martin
1964–65	Roger Crozier
1965–66	Bert Marshall
1966–67	*not awarded*
1967–68	Roy Edwards & Gary Jarrett
1968–69	Paul Popiel
1969–70	Al Karlander
1970–71	Tom Webster
1971–72	Marcel Dionne
1972–73	Henry Boucha
1973–74	Bill Hogaboam
1974–75	Bill Lochead
1975–76	Michel Bergeron
1976–77	Jim Nahrgang
1977–78	Dale McCourt
1978–79	Willie Huber
1979–80	Mike Foligno
1980–81	John Barrett

GENERAL MANAGERS

1926–27	Art Duncan
1927–62	Jack Adams (resigned April 26, 1962)
1962–71	Sid Abel (appointed April 26, 1962; resigned January 6, 1971)
1971–74	Ned Harkness (appointed January 8, 1971; resigned February 6, 1974)
1974–77	Alex Delvecchio (hired May 21, 1974; fired March 16, 1977)
1977–80	Ted Lindsay (hired March 16, 1977; stepped down April 1980 to coach team)
1980–82	Jimmy Skinner (hired April 1980)
1982–90	Jim Devellano (hired July 12, 1982; moved to senior vice-president July 13, 1990)
1990–94	Bryan Murray (hired July 13, 1990; fired June 1994)
1994–present	Scotty Bowman

Ned Harkness

CAPTAINS

1926–27	Art Duncan
1927–30	Reg Noble
1930–31	George Hay
1931–32	Carson Cooper
1932–33	Larry Aurie
1933–34	Herbie Lewis
1934–35	Ebbie Goodfellow
1935–38	Doug Young
1938–41	Ebbie Goodfellow
1941–42	Ebbie Goodfellow & Syd Howe
1942–43	Sid Abel
1943–44	Mud Brûneteau & Flash Hollett
1944–45	Flash Hollett
1945–46	Flash Hollett & Sid Abel
1946–52	Sid Abel
1952–56	Ted Lindsay
1956–58	Red Kelly
1958–62	Gordie Howe
1962–73	Alex Delvecchio
1973–74	Alex Delvecchio/Nick Libett/Red Berenson/Gary Bergman/Ted Harris/ Mickey Redmond/Larry Johnston
1974–75	Marcel Dionne
1975–76	Danny Grant & Terry Harper
1976–77	Danny Grant & Dennis Polonich
1977–78	Dan Maloney & Dennis Hextall
1978–79	Dennis Hextall/Nick Libett/Paul Woods
1979–80	Dale McCourt
1980–81	Errol Thompson & Reed Larson
1981–82	Reed Larson
1982–86	Danny Gare
1986–present	Steve Yzerman

Steve Yzerman

HOCKEY HALL OF FAME HONOURED MEMBERS

(list is alphabetical; first year indicates year of induction, years in brackets indicate service as a Red Wing unless otherwise noted)

PLAYERS

1969 SID ABEL (1938–43; 1945–52)
1959 JACK ADAMS (inducted as a player)
1996 AL ARBOUR (inducted as a Builder, played with the Red Wings 1953–54; 1956–58)
1965 MARTY BARRY (1935–39)
1978 ANDY BATHGATE (1965–67)
1986 LEO BOIVIN (1965–67)
1981 JOHN BUCYK (1955–57)
1961 CHARLIE CONACHER (1938–39)
1958 ALEX CONNELL (1931–32)
1977 ALEX DELVECCHIO (1950–74)
1992 MARCEL DIONNE (1971–75)
1958 FRANK FOYSTON (Cougars, 1926–28)
1958 FRANK FREDERICKSON (Cougars, 1926–27; Falcons 1930–31)
1970 BILL GADSBY (1961–66)
1987 ED GIACOMIN (1975–78)
1963 EBBIE GOODFELLOW (1929–43)
1975 GLENN HALL (1952–53; 1954–57)
1973 DOUG HARVEY (1966–67)
1958 GEORGE HAY (1927–34)
1972 HAP HOLMES (Cougars, 1926–28)
1972 GORDIE HOWE (1946–71)
1965 SYD HOWE (1934–46)
1958 DUKE KEATS (Cougars, 1927–28)
1969 RED KELLY (1947–60)
1989 HERBIE LEWIS (1928–39)
1966 TED LINDSAY (1944–57; 1964–65)
1980 HARRY LUMLEY (1943–50)
1981 FRANK MAHOVLICH (1967–71)
1962 REG NOBLE (1927–33)
1988 BRAD PARK (1983–85)
1978 MARCEL PRONOVOST (1949–65)
1976 BILL QUACKENBUSH (1942–49)
1996 BORJE SALMING (1989–90)
1971 TERRY SAWCHUK (1949–55; 1957–64; 1968–69)
1964 EARL SEIBERT (1944–46)
1989 DARRYL SITTLER (1984–85)
1964 JACK STEWART (1938–43; 1945–50)
1959 CECIL THOMPSON (1939–40)
1982 NORM ULLMAN (1955–68)
1960 JACK WALKER (Cougars, 1926–28)
1971 COONEY WEILAND (1933–35)

BUILDERS

1991 SCOTTY BOWMAN
1974 TOMMY IVAN
1969 BRUCE A. NORRIS
1958 JAMES NORRIS
1962 JAMES D. NORRIS
1990 BUD POILE
1974 CARL VOSS
1987 JOHN A. ZEIGLER JR.

BROADCASTERS

1985 BUDD LYNCH (1949–75)
1991 BRUCE MARTYN (1964–95)

DETROIT RED WINGS HALL OF FAME

1944 SID ABEL
1945 JACK ADAMS
1944 LARRY AURIE

1944 MARTY BARRY
1944 MUD BRÛNETEAU
1978 JOE CARVETH
1949 CARSON COOPER
1978 ALEX DELVECCHIO
1978 BILL GADSBY
1944 EBBIE GOODFELLOW
1947 DON GROSSO
1944 GEORGE HAY
1985 GORDIE HOWE
1944 SYD HOWE
1977 TOMMY IVAN
1978 RED KELLY
1944 HERB LEWIS
1962 TED LINDSAY
1964 CARL LISCOMBE
1978 CARL MATTSON
1961 BUCKO MCDONALD
1946 JOHN MOWERS
1944 REG NOBLE
1968 BRUCE A. NORRIS
1959 JAMES NORRIS
1968 JAMES D. NORRIS
1962 JIMMY ORLANDO
1978 MARCEL PRONOVOST
1961 BILL QUACKENBUSH
1977 MARGUERITE NORRIS RIKER
1971 TERRY SAWCHUK
1977 JIMMY SKINNER
1963 NORM SMITH
1944 JACK STEWART
1954 FRANK WALKER
1951 DOUG YOUNG

RETIRED NUMBERS

1 TERRY SAWCHUK
(jersey retired March 6, 1994)

7 TED LINDSAY
(jersey retired November 10, 1991)

9 GORDIE HOWE
(jersey retired March 12, 1972)

10 ALEX DELVECCHIO
(jersey retired November 10, 1991)

12 SID ABEL
(jersey retired April 29, 1995)

Al Arbour (left) and Borje Salming will be inducted into the Hockey Hall of Fame on November 25, 1996 with Bobby Bauer and Bob Cole. The evening will be hosted by the Hall of Fame in Toronto.

ALL SCORES AND DATES FOR ALL REGULAR SEASON GAMES

- all shutouts are recorded, noted with the goalie's name enclosed in square brackets, i.e. "[Sawchuk]" means Terry Sawchuk registered a shutout that game
- all empty-net goals for and against are recorded
- all overtime goals for and against are recorded
- significant goalie changes and game events are also recorded wherever possible
- scorers in all 1–0 games are recorded

1926–1927

November 18 Boston 2 at Detroit 0 [C. Stewart] (both goals in 1st)
20 Detroit 1 at Pirates 4 (all goals in 3rd)
24 Detroit 1 at Chicago 0 [Holmes] (Frederickson 15:00 3rd)
27 Americans 2 at Detroit 4
30 Detroit 4 at Maroons 0 [Holmes]

December 4 Rangers 0 at Detroit 1 [Holmes] (Laughlin 2nd)
9 Ottawa 3 at Detroit 1
11 Americans 4 at Detroit 2
14 Detroit 2 at Boston 7
16 Detroit 5 at Ottawa 0 [Holmes]
19 Detroit 1 at Rangers 1 (20:00 OT)

	23	Canadiens 3 at Detroit 2 (Joliat 12:50 OT)
	25	Detroit 0 at Chicago 2 [Lehman]
	30	Maroons 2 at Detroit 0 [Benedict]
January	1	Pirates 3 at Detroit 2
	4	Toronto 2 at Detroit 1
	6	Detroit 3 at Pirates 1
	9	Detroit 1 at Rangers 4 (Bill Cook awarded a goal in the 1st when goalie Holmes threw his stick)
	11	Detroit 1 at Americans 0 [Holmes] (Keats 3:46 OT)
	13	Boston 2 at Detroit 3
	15	Detroit 1 at Toronto 1 (20:00 OT)
	18	Detroit 3 at Canadiens 5
	22	Detroit 0 at Pirates 1 [Worters] (Milks 2:21 OT)
	25	Detroit 1 at Maroons 2 (Oatman 18:00 OT)
	27	Detroit 1 at Ottawa 3
	29	Detroit 0 at Rangers 2 [Chabot]
February	1	Chicago 3 at Detroit 4 (Foyston 7:00 OT)
	8	Detroit 0 at Boston 2 [Winkler]
	12	Canadiens 4 at Detroit 1
	16	Toronto 1 at Detroit 5
	17	Ottawa 2 at Detroit 1
	19	Chicago 4 at Detroit 1
	22	Detroit 2 at Boston 3
	24	Maroons 2 at Detroit 0 [Benedict]
March	1	Detroit 0 at Canadiens 3 [Hainsworth]
	5	Detroit 2 at Toronto 4
	8	Chicago 4 at Detroit 1
	10	Pirates 1 at Detroit 7
	13	Rangers 2 at Detroit 2 (20:00 OT)
	15	Detroit 1 at Americans 0 [Holmes] (Walker 5:45 1st)
	17	Rangers 2 at Detroit 0 [Chabot]
	19	Boston 3 at Detroit 1
	22	Detroit 3 at Chicago 3 (20:00 OT)
	26	Pirates 6 at Detroit 4

1927–1928

November	15	Detroit 6 at Pirates 0 [Holmes]
	19	Detroit 2 at Boston 5
	22	Ottawa 2 at Detroit 1
	26	Detroit 0 at Chicago 0 (10:00 OT) [Holmes (D) / Gardiner (C)]
	27	Canadiens 0 at Detroit 2 [Holmes]
December	1	Chicago 1 at Detroit 3
	4	Rangers 3 at Detroit 1
	8	Americans 1 at Detroit 2
	10	Detroit 4 at Maroons 1
	11	Boston 2 at Detroit 1 (Gainor 1:45 OT)
	13	Detroit 1 at Canadiens 6
	15	Detroit 2 at Rangers 1
	17	Detroit 1 at Toronto 0 [Holmes] (Cooper 7:00 OT)
	18	Pittsburgh 3 at Detroit 3 (10:00 OT)
	27	Detroit 4 at Americans 4 (10:00 OT)
	29	Maroons 0 at Detroit 3 [Holmes]
	31	Detroit 2 at Ottawa 6
January	3	Detroit 4 at Rangers 2
	5	Canadiens 2 at Detroit 1
	7	Detroit 2 at Pirates 0 [Holmes] (both goals in 1st)
	12	Toronto 2 at Detroit 1
	15	Rangers 2 at Detroit 1
	18	Detroit 0 at Chicago 2 [Lehman]
	22	Boston 2 at Detroit 3 (Hay OT)
	26	Detroit 0 at Rangers 3 [Chabot]
	29	Chicago 2 at Detroit 4
February	4	Detroit 0 at Toronto 2 [Roach]
	7	Detroit 2 at Boston 4
	9	Detroit 2 at Americans 2 (10:00 OT)
	12	Pirates 1 at Detroit 0 [Worters] (Darragh)
	16	Detroit 1 at Maroons 0 [Holmes] (Foyston 11:50 1st)
	19	Chicago 2 at Detroit 1
	23	Ottawa 0 at Detroit 0 (10:00 OT) [Connell (O) / Holmes (D)]
	26	Rangers 0 at Detroit 0 (10:00 OT) [Chabot (R) / Holmes (D)]
March	1	Americans 1 at Detroit 4
	3	Detroit 3 at Pirates 2
	6	Toronto 1 at Detroit 3
	8	Maroons 3 at Detroit 2 (H. Smith 5:45 OT)
	10	Detroit 1 at Ottawa 3
	13	Detroit 0 at Boston 3 [Winkler]
	15	Detroit 1 at Canadiens 0 [Holmes] (Noble 6:16 2nd)
	17	Detroit 7 at Chicago 0 [Holmes]
	18	Pirates 1 at Detroit 0 [Worters]
	24	Boston 2 at Detroit 7

1928–1929

November
15 Rangers 2 at Detroit 0 [Roach] (Boucher credited with a goal when H. Lewis threw his stick)
18 Pirates 1 at Detroit 3
22 Boston 0 at Detroit 2 [Dolson]
24 Detroit 1 at Ottawa 1 (10:00 OT) (both goals in 1st)
29 Maroons 1 at Detroit 1 (10:00 OT) (both goals in 2nd)

December
2 Americans 1 at Detroit 2
8 Detroit 3 at Pirates 0 [Dolson]
9 Rangers 2 at Detroit 2 (10:00 OT)
11 Detroit 1 at Maroons 2
13 Ottawa 1 at Detroit 1 (10:00 OT)
16 Detroit 0 at Rangers 3 [Roach]
18 Detroit 1 at Boston 3
20 Canadiens 1 at Detroit 5
23 Detroit 2 at Americans 0 [Dolson] (both goals in 3rd)
27 Detroit 0 at Canadiens 3 [Hainsworth]
29 Detroit 3 at Toronto 4
30 Chicago 1 at Detroit 3

January
1 Detroit 2 at Chicago 1
6 Detroit 3 at Chicago 1
10 Pirates 1 at Detroit 4
12 Detroit 2 at Boston 3
13 Detroit 0 at Rangers 1 [Roach] (Abel 11:13 2nd)
17 Boston 1 at Detroit 1 (10:00 OT)
19 Detroit 0 at Pirates 3 [Miller]
20 Toronto 1 at Detroit 2
22 Detroit 1 at Maroons 0 [Dolson] (Hay 5:10 OT)
27 Americans 2 at Detroit 1

February
5 Chicago 1 at Detroit 0 [Gardiner] (Gottselig 1:18 1st)
7 Detroit 2 at Canadiens 2 (Patterson (C) 5:20 / Cooper (D) 9:30 OT)
9 Detroit 2 at Ottawa 0 [Dolson]
10 Pirates 0 at Detroit 3 [Dolson] (all goals in 3rd)
12 Detroit 0 at Boston 1 [Thompson] (Gainer 14:54 3rd)
14 Detroit 1 at Americans 1 (10:00 OT)
17 Toronto 0 at Detroit 2 [Dolson]
19 Ottawa 2 at Detroit 1
21 Detroit 1 at Rangers 0 [Dolson] (Cooper 14:22 2nd)
23 Detroit 0 at Chicago 0 (10:00 OT) [Dolson (D) / Gardiner (C)]
26 Chicago 0 at Detroit 3 [Dolson]

March
2 Detroit 4 at Pirates 3 (Herbert 2:55 OT)
3 Rangers 3 at Detroit 2
5 Maroons 1 at Detroit 3
9 Detroit 0 at Toronto 3 [Chabot]
10 Canadiens 1 at Detroit 1 (Morenz (C) 7:30 / Noble (D) 8:30 OT)
14 Boston 5 at Detroit 1

1929–1930

November
14 Boston 5 at Detroit 2
17 Detroit 5 at Rangers 5 (10:00 OT)
19 Ottawa 6 at Detroit 4
24 Detroit 0 at Chicago 4 [Gardiner]
26 Detroit 3 at Ottawa 4 (Finnigan 4:00 OT)
28 Detroit 7 at Maroons 6
30 Detroit 0 at Toronto 1 [Chabot] (Primeau 11:15 1st)

December
1 Rangers 3 at Detroit 4
5 Americans 2 at Detroit 3
7 Detroit 1 at Boston 2
10 Detroit 3 at Canadiens 5 (Morenz 1:10 / Morenz 4:06 OT)
15 Toronto 3 at Detroit 5
19 Chicago 3 at Detroit 4
22 Pirates 1 at Detroit 6
24 Detroit 3 at Americans 5
26 Detroit 1 at Pirates 3
29 Maroons 6 at Detroit 2

January
2 Canadiens 0 at Detroit 4 [Beveridge]
5 Detroit 4 at Chicago 0 [Beveridge]
9 Chicago 1 at Detroit 1 (10:00 OT) (Ingram (C) tied game at 19:35)
12 Pirates 2 at Detroit 3
14 Detroit 0 at Rangers 3 [Roach]
16 Detroit 1 at Canadiens 6
19 Boston 5 at Detroit 4
23 Detroit 2 at Maroons 2 (10:00 OT)
25 Detroit 2 at Toronto 1
26 Rangers 3 at Detroit 7
30 Detroit 2 at Americans 3

February 1 Detroit 2 at Pirates 3
2 Chicago 4 at Detroit 1
4 Detroit 1 at Boston 3
6 Detroit 1 at Rangers 1 (10:00 OT) (both goals in 2nd)
9 Pirates 1 at Detroit 8
13 Maroons 6 at Detroit 3 (Ward 5:45 / Stewart 8:55 / Stewart 9:40 OT)
16 Boston 4 at Detroit 2
18 Canadiens 2 at Detroit 0 [Hainsworth]
23 Detroit 2 at Chicago 1
27 Ottawa 3 at Detroit 3 (Kilrea (O) 4:45 / Goodfellow (D) 4:56 OT)
March 2 Rangers 2 at Detroit 2 (10:00 OT)
6 Americans 1 at Detroit 0 [Worters] (Himes 14:25 3rd)
8 Detroit 2 at Ottawa 3
9 Toronto 2 at Detroit 1
15 Detroit 2 at Boston 5
18 Detroit 4 at Pirates 2

1930–1931

November 13 Rangers 0 at Detroit 1 [Dolson] (Goodfellow 19:45 2nd)
16 Quakers 1 at Detroit 5
20 Detroit 0 at Ottawa 1 [Connell] (Lamb 1:45 1st)
23 Boston 2 at Detroit 2 (10:00 OT)
27 Canadiens 2 at Detroit 3
29 Detroit 2 at Toronto 4
30 Americans 2 at Detroit 2 (Hughes :40 (A) / Lewis (D) 9:32 OT)
December 7 Detroit 2 at Chicago 3
9 Chicago 0 at Detroit 1 [Dolson] (Goodfellow 17:25 3rd)
11 Detroit 2 at Maroons 3
13 Detroit 3 at Quakers 2
14 Detroit 0 at Rangers 3 [Roach]
16 Detroit 2 at Boston 3
18 Ottawa 0 at Detroit 3 [Dolson]
21 Detroit 4 at Americans 6
25 Toronto 1 at Detroit 10
28 Maroons 2 at Detroit 2 (10:00 OT)
January 4 Detroit 2 at Chicago 1
6 Detroit 6 at Canadiens 2
8 Rangers 1 at Detroit 0 [Roach] (B. Cook 5:17 1st)
11 Boston 4 at Detroit 1
13 Detroit 1 at Maroons 6
17 Detroit 5 at Quakers 2
18 Detroit 2 at Americans 2 (10:00 OT)
20 Quakers 2 at Detroit 5
25 Detroit 1 at Rangers 0 [Dolson] (Cooper 11:51 3rd)
27 Maroons 2 at Detroit 1
February 1 Toronto 0 at Detroit 2 [Dolson] (both goals in 3rd)
3 Detroit 2 at Boston 7
5 Detroit 4 at Ottawa 5
8 Ottawa 0 at Detroit 2 [Dolson]
12 Rangers 1 at Detroit 1 (10:00 OT)
14 Detroit 1 at Toronto 1 (10:00 OT) (both goals in 3rd)
17 Quakers 2 at Detroit 0 [Cude] (both goals in 3rd)
19 Detroit 5 at Chicago 4 (Sorrell 5:30 OT)
22 Chicago 1 at Detroit 1 (10:00 OT)
26 Detroit 0 at Canadiens 5 [Hainsworth]
March 1 Americans 2 at Detroit 1 (Himes 4:15 OT)
8 Canadiens 2 at Detroit 0 [Hainsworth] (both goals in 1st)
10 Detroit 2 at Rangers 3 (B. Cook 8:56 OT)
12 Detroit 5 at Quakers 7
15 Boston 2 at Detroit 5 (Goodfellow 1:01 / Lewis 3:22 / Aurie 8:12 OT)
17 Detroit 2 at Boston 4
22 Chicago 2 at Detroit 1

1931–1932

November 12 Americans 5 at Detroit 2
15 Detroit 2 at Rangers 1
17 Detroit 0 at Boston 1 [Thompson] (Clapper 5:55 3rd)
19 Maroons 1 at Detroit 3 (Sorrell :58 / Aurie 9:55 OT)
22 Detroit 1 at Americans 2
24 Detroit 1 at Maroons 6
29 Canadiens 2 at Detroit 3 (Goodfellow 2:27 OT)

December 3 Rangers 1 at Detroit 1 (10:00 OT) (both goals in 1st)
5 Detroit 0 at Canadiens 4 [Hainsworth]
10 Boston 1 at Detroit 1 (10:00 OT)
12 Detroit 1 at Toronto 3
16 Detroit 1 at Chicago 4 (Wentworth :45 / Romnes 3:45 / Lowery 7:00 OT)
17 Chicago 1 at Detroit 4
20 Detroit 2 at Americans 2 (10:00 OT)
22 Detroit 2 at Boston 6
27 Americans 0 at Detroit 1 [Connell] (Kilrea 11:45 3rd)
29 Detroit 2 at Maroons 4

January 1 Detroit 0 at Rangers 3 [Roach] (all goals in 3rd)
3 Toronto 2 at Detroit 3 (Sorrell 3:05 OT)
6 Detroit 2 at Chicago 4
7 Boston 0 at Detroit 0 (10:00 OT) [Thompson (B) / Connell (D)]
10 Canadiens 1 at Detroit 3
12 Detroit 4 at Toronto 7
14 Chicago 0 at Detroit 2 [Connell]
17 Rangers 2 at Detroit 4
21 Maroons 3 at Detroit 4
23 Detroit 2 at Boston 0 [Connell]
24 Detroit 3 at Rangers 4
27 Detroit 1 at Chicago 2 (Gottselig 1:55 OT)
28 Chicago 2 at Detroit 4
30 Detroit 3 at Canadiens 4

February 2 Detroit 3 at Maroons 4
7 Toronto 1 at Detroit 3
14 Chicago 1 at Detroit 3
16 Detroit 2 at Rangers 2 (10:00 OT)
18 Boston 0 at Detroit 0 (10:00 OT) [Thompson (B) / Connell (D)]
21 Canadiens 1 at Detroit 1 (10:00 OT)
23 Detroit 1 at Canadiens 2
25 Detroit 5 at Toronto 3
28 Maroons 1 at Detroit 2

March 3 Rangers 2 at Detroit 1
6 Detroit 2 at Americans 2 (10:00 OT)
8 Detroit 0 at Boston 2 [Thompson]
13 Americans 0 at Detroit 1 [Connell] (Aurie 16:34 2nd)
16 Detroit 1 at Chicago 1 (10:00 OT) (both goals in 1st)
17 Boston 1 at Detroit 1 (10:00 OT) (both goals in 3rd)
20 Toronto 3 at Detroit 2
22 Rangers 4 at Detroit 5

1932–1933

November 10 Chicago 1 at Detroit 3
12 Detroit 0 at Ottawa 2 [Connell]
15 Americans 2 at Detroit 6
17 Detroit 0 at Canadiens 1 [Hainsworth] (Larochelle 8:11 OT)
22 Canadiens 2 at Detroit 4
27 Toronto 2 at Detroit 1
29 Detroit 3 at Maroons 5

December 1 Rangers 4 at Detroit 2
4 Ottawa 0 at Detroit 2 [Roach] (both goals in 2nd)
8 Detroit 1 at Chicago 3
13 Maroons 7 at Detroit 4
17 Detroit 0 at Toronto 3 [Chabot]
18 Boston 1 at Detroit 2
20 Detroit 4 at Rangers 1
22 Detroit 0 at Boston 7 [Thompson]
25 Chicago 0 at Detroit 4 [Roach]
27 Detroit 3 at Americans 1
29 Detroit 3 at Canadiens 3 (10:00 OT)

January 1 Toronto 2 at Detroit 2 (10:00 OT) (Sorrell (D) tied game at 19:19)
3 Detroit 1 at Ottawa 0 [Roach] (Emms 16:55 3rd)
5 Canadiens 1 at Detroit 6 (all goals in 3rd)
7 Detroit 6 at Toronto 1
8 Boston 1 at Detroit 3
12 Maroons 0 at Detroit 4 [Roach]
15 Detroit 1 at Americans 1 (10:00 OT)
17 Rangers 0 at Detroit 2 [Roach] (both goals in 3rd)
22 Americans 0 at Detroit 2 [Roach]
26 Ottawa 1 at Detroit 1 (10:00 OT)
28 Detroit 1 at Maroons 4
31 Detroit 2 at Rangers 1

February 2 Detroit 1 at Boston 1 (10:00 OT) (both goals in 1st)
5 Chicago 0 at Detroit 1 [Roach] (Lewis 16:37 3rd)
9 Detroit 4 at Chicago 1
12 Detroit 2 at Americans 2 (10:00 OT)

	14	Detroit 2 at Canadiens 6
	16	Maroons 2 at Detroit 2 (10:00 OT)
	18	Detroit 1 at Toronto 4
	19	Boston 1 at Detroit 2
	23	Rangers 0 at Detroit 3 [Roach] (all goals in 3rd)
	26	Americans 1 at Detroit 1 (10:00 OT) (both goals in 2nd)
	28	Detroit 3 at Maroons 6
March	2	Detroit 3 at Ottawa 2
	5	Ottawa 0 at Detroit 2 [Roach]
	7	Detroit 1 at Boston 4
	9	Detroit 2 at Rangers 3
	12	Canadiens 1 at Detroit 3
	16	Toronto 0 at Detroit 1 [Roach] (Emms 9:56 1st)
	19	Detroit 4 at Chicago 2

1933–1934

November	9	Detroit 1 at Canadiens 2 (all goals in 3rd)
	12	Americans 2 at Detroit 5
	14	Detroit 4 at Boston 2
	16	Detroit 1 at Rangers 2
	19	Rangers 1 at Detroit 4
	21	Detroit 3 at Ottawa 2
	23	Boston 6 at Detroit 0 [Thompson]
	26	Canadiens 2 at Detroit 4
	30	Chicago 1 at Detroit 2
December	3	Toronto 3 at Detroit 0 [Hainsworth]
	5	Detroit 1 at Maroons 1 (10:00 OT)
	10	Maroons 1 at Detroit 3
	12	Chicago 1 at Detroit 4
	14	Detroit 0 at Chicago 4 [Gardiner] (game delayed 20 minutes after Roach (D) injured) (all goals on power-play)
	17	Americans 4 at Detroit 4 (10:00 OT)
	19	Detroit 1 at Americans 0 [Roach] (Weiland 13:24 1st)
	23	Detroit 0 at Canadiens 3 [Cude]
	25	Ottawa 6 at Detroit 3
	30	Detroit 1 at Toronto 8
January	4	Rangers 1 at Detroit 3
	7	Ottawa 0 at Detroit 2 [Cude]
	9	Detroit 1 at Rangers 2
	11	Detroit 1 at Maroons 1 (10:00 OT) (both goals in 1st)
	14	Boston 0 at Detroit 2 [Cude]
	18	Maroons 1 at Detroit 1 (10:00 OT)
	20	Detroit 4 at Ottawa 5
	21	Toronto 2 at Detroit 4 (Lewis 4:17 / Lewis 9:55 OT)
	23	Detroit 3 at Boston 1
	25	Detroit 1 at Americans 1 (Weiland (D) :26 / Klein (A) 4:21 OT)
	27	Detroit 2 at Toronto 2 (10:00 OT)
	28	Canadiens 3 at Detroit 3 (10:00 OT)
February	1	Boston 2 at Detroit 2 (10:00 OT)
	4	Toronto 1 at Detroit 2
	8	Detroit 1 at Chicago 1 (10:00 OT) (both goals in 3rd)
	11	Ottawa 0 at Detroit 3 [Cude]
	13	Detroit 6 at Maroons 1
	15	Detroit 1 at Americans 1 (10:00 OT) (both goals in 1st)
	18	Ottawa 1 at Detroit 2 (Wiseman 4:10 OT)
	20	Detroit 4 at Boston 1
	22	Detroit 1 at Rangers 3
	25	Americans 1 at Detroit 2 (Lewis 6:07 OT)
	27	Rangers 1 at Detroit 5
March	1	Maroons 4 at Detroit 1
	3	Detroit 4 at Toronto 6
	8	Detroit 3 at Chicago 0 [Cude]
	11	Chicago 2 at Detroit 3 (Pettinger 8:54 OT)
	15	Detroit 4 at Canadiens 1
	18	Canadiens 2 at Detroit 1

1934–1935

November	11	Boston 4 at Detroit 2
	15	Rangers 2 at Detroit 8
	17	Detroit 3 at Canadiens 0 [N. Smith]
	20	Detroit 0 at Boston 1 [Thompson] (Gagnon 4:25 2nd)
	22	Detroit 3 at Rangers 4 (Murdoch 7:15 OT)
	24	Detroit 2 at Toronto 3
	25	Eagles 1 at Detroit 4
	29	Detroit 1 at Maroons 2
December	2	Toronto 0 at Detroit 3 [N. Smith]
	9	Eagles 1 at Detroit 3 (Anderson 5:08 / Lewis 8:06 OT)
	11	Detroit 0 at Chicago 4 [Chabot]
	13	Detroit 11 at Eagles 2
	16	Americans 2 at Detroit 2 (10:00 OT)

20 Maroons 1 at Detroit 1 (10:00 OT)
22 Detroit 3 at Boston 4
23 Detroit 2 at Americans 1
25 Chicago 2 at Detroit 1
27 Detroit 2 at Eagles 5
30 Americans 0 at Detroit 0 (10:00 OT) [Worters (A) / Roach (D)]

January 1 Detroit 1 at Toronto 0 [Roach] (Weiland 18:15 1st)
3 Detroit 2 at Rangers 3
6 Canadiens 2 at Detroit 6
8 Detroit 2 at Chicago 1
13 Toronto 2 at Detroit 0 [Hainsworth]
15 Detroit 1 at Maroons 0 (Sorrell 1:45 OT) [Roach]
17 Detroit 3 at Americans 3 (10:00 OT)
20 Eagles 6 at Detroit 1
26 Detroit 0 at Toronto 0 (10:00 OT) [Roach (D) / Hainsworth (T)]
27 Boston 2 at Detroit 2 (10:00 OT)
31 Canadiens 4 at Detroit 4 (10:00 OT)

February 3 Detroit 3 at Rangers 5
5 Detroit 2 at Boston 4
7 Detroit 1 at Canadiens 4
10 Maroons 2 at Detroit 1 (Cain 4:57 OT)
14 Chicago 3 at Detroit 0 [Chabot] (all goals in 3rd)
16 Detroit 3 at Maroons 7
17 Rangers 5 at Detroit 3 (Keeling 3:45 / Dillon 9:57 OT)
21 Maroons 1 at Detroit 3
24 Toronto 2 at Detroit 4
26 Detroit 2 at Americans 3
28 Chicago 1 at Detroit 5

March 3 Americans 1 at Detroit 3
7 Rangers 1 at Detroit 6
9 Detroit 5 at Canadiens 3
10 Boston 2 at Detroit 1 (Shore 5:40 OT)
12 Detroit 2 at Eagles 3
14 Detroit 4 at Chicago 3
17 Canadiens 2 at Detroit 6

1935–1936

November 10 Rangers 1 at Detroit 1 (10:00 OT)
14 Chicago 0 at Detroit 0 (10:00 OT) [Karakas (C) / N. Smith (D)]
19 Detroit 2 at Rangers 2 (10:00 OT)
21 Detroit 1 at Americans 3 (Schriner 7:46 / Schriner 8:28 OT)
24 Toronto 1 at Detroit 2
28 Canadiens 0 at Detroit 0 (10:00 OT) [Cude (C) / N. Smith (D)]
30 Detroit 2 at Maroons 3

December 5 Boston 1 at Detroit 2
7 Detroit 3 at Canadiens 2
8 Americans 1 at Detroit 1 (10:00 OT)
12 Detroit 3 at Chicago 1
14 Detroit 4 at Toronto 2 (Lewis 4:01 / Brûneteau 7:27 OT)
15 Rangers 2 at Detroit 4
17 Detroit 1 at Boston 4
19 Detroit 3 at Americans 1
22 Maroons 2 at Detroit 2 (10:00 OT)
25 Chicago 2 at Detroit 0 [Karakas] (both goals in 2nd)
29 Boston 4 at Detroit 3 (Cowley 5:55 OT)

January 1 Detroit 4 at Chicago 2
5 Canadiens 2 at Detroit 5
7 Detroit 2 at Rangers 1
12 Maroons 0 at Detroit 6 [N. Smith]
16 Detroit 1 at Chicago 4
19 Toronto 0 at Detroit 4 [N. Smith]
23 Rangers 2 at Detroit 4
25 Detroit 1 at Toronto 6
28 Detroit 0 at Boston 2 [Thompson]
30 Chicago 4 at Detroit 3

February 1 Detroit 3 at Canadiens 1
4 Detroit 4 at Rangers 4 (Keeling (R) 1:12 / Sorrell (D) 6:40 OT)
6 Detroit 1 at Chicago 0 [N. Smith] (Sorrell 10:20 2nd)
11 Maroons 3 at Detroit 7
13 Boston 0 at Detroit 1 [N. Smith] (Barry 5:40 2nd)
15 Detroit 2 at Toronto 3 (Thoms 8:15 OT)
18 Detroit 2 at Boston 1
20 Detroit 3 at Maroons 6
23 Americans 3 at Detroit 4
27 Rangers 2 at Detroit 4

March 1 Canadiens 1 at Detroit 3
5 Detroit 4 at Americans 1
7 Detroit 3 at Maroons 5
8 Boston 5 at Detroit 2

	10	Detroit 0 at Boston 1 [Thompson] (Runge 4:58 OT)
	12	Detroit 3 at Rangers 4 (Heller 8:13 OT)
	14	Detroit 1 at Canadiens 1 (10:00 OT) (both goals in 1st)
	15	Toronto 2 at Detroit 1 (Conacher 7:30 OT)
	19	Chicago 3 at Detroit 5
	22	Americans 2 at Detroit 7

1936–1937

November	5	Detroit 3 at Toronto 1
	8	Rangers 2 at Detroit 5
	14	Detroit 2 at Maroons 2 (10:00 OT)
	15	Maroons 2 at Detroit 2 (10:00 OT)
	19	Detroit 0 at Rangers 1 [Kerr] (Dillon 14:10 1st)
	22	Toronto 2 at Detroit 4
	26	Chicago 2 at Detroit 0 [Karakas]
	29	Americans 2 at Detroit 0 [Worters]
December	3	Rangers 0 at Detroit 2 [N. Smith]
	6	Detroit 3 at Americans 3 (10:00 OT)
	8	Detroit 4 at Boston 3
	10	Canadiens 1 at Detroit 2
	13	Detroit 2 at Chicago 1 (Barry 7:00 OT)
	15	Detroit 3 at Canadiens 4
	20	Boston 3 at Detroit 4
	25	Chicago 1 at Detroit 1 (10:00 OT)
	27	Canadiens 5 at Detroit 2
	31	Americans 2 at Detroit 4
January	1	Detroit 2 at Chicago 4
	3	Toronto 2 at Detroit 4
	5	Detroit 3 at Boston 2
	7	Detroit 4 at Americans 2
	10	Boston 2 at Detroit 4
	12	Detroit 1 at Canadiens 4
	14	Detroit 2 at Rangers 0 [N. Smith]
	17	Detroit 2 at Chicago 0 [N. Smith]
	19	Chicago 2 at Detroit 7
	23	Detroit 1 at Maroons 1 (10:00 OT)
	24	Maroons 1 at Detroit 2
	31	Detroit 2 at Boston 1
February	2	Detroit 4 at Rangers 4 (10:00 OT)
	4	Rangers 2 at Detroit 2 (10:00 OT)
	7	Boston 0 at Detroit 8 [N. Smith]
	9	Detroit 2 at Americans 3
	11	Detroit 2 at Canadiens 3
	14	Toronto 3 at Detroit 3 (10:00 OT)
	18	Detroit 1 at Toronto 3
	21	Chicago 0 at Detroit 6 [N. Smith]
	25	Detroit 3 at Chicago 1
	28	Canadiens 0 at Detroit 0 (10:00 OT) [Cude (C) / N. Smith (D)]
March	2	Detroit 7 at Maroons 4
	4	Rangers 1 at Detroit 2
	7	Americans 3 at Detroit 1
	9	Detroit 1 at Boston 6
	11	Detroit 4 at Rangers 2
	14	Boston 1 at Detroit 2
	20	Detroit 2 at Toronto 3
	21	Maroons 5 at Detroit 1

1937–1938

November	4	Detroit 2 at Toronto 2 (10:00 OT)
	7	Rangers 3 at Detroit 0 [Kerr]
	13	Detroit 2 at Canadiens 5
	14	Canadiens 1 at Detroit 2
	18	Detroit 1 at Chicago 3
	21	Toronto 5 at Detroit 0 [Broda]
	23	Detroit 1 at Americans 3
	25	Chicago 1 at Detroit 4
	28	Maroons 3 at Detroit 1
December	5	Americans 2 at Detroit 1
	7	Detroit 3 at Boston 2
	9	Detroit 2 at Maroons 5
	12	Rangers 5 at Detroit 2
	14	Detroit 1 at Rangers 3
	16	Detroit 1 at Chicago 3
	19	Boston 4 at Detroit 2
	25	Detroit 1 at Toronto 1 (10:00 OT) (both goals in 2nd)
	26	Toronto 3 at Detroit 1
	30	Chicago 2 at Detroit 2 (10:00 OT)
January	2	Boston 4 at Detroit 1
	4	Detroit 3 at Canadiens 0 [N. Smith]
	6	Detroit 1 at Americans 1 (10:00 OT)
	9	Detroit 1 at Rangers 4
	11	Detroit 2 at Boston 6
	13	Detroit 3 at Rangers 3 (10:00 OT)
	15	Detroit 2 at Maroons 2 (10:00 OT)
	16	Maroons 1 at Detroit 1 (10:00 OT)
	20	Chicago 2 at Detroit 4
	23	Americans 2 at Detroit 3
	27	Detroit 3 at Chicago 4

29 Detroit 1 at Toronto 4
30 Boston 2 at Detroit 2 (10:00 OT)
February 1 Detroit 0 at Boston 2 [Thompson]
3 Detroit 6 at Americans 1
6 Canadiens 0 at Detroit 8 [N. Smith]
10 Rangers 4 at Detroit 0 [Kerr]
13 Americans 2 at Detroit 2 (10:00 OT)
20 Detroit 1 at Chicago 0 [N. Smith] (Motter 4:04 2nd)
24 Maroons 2 at Detroit 2 (10:00 OT)
27 Canadiens 1 at Detroit 1 (10:00 OT)
March 1 Detroit 1 at Boston 6
3 Detroit 3 at Rangers 4
6 Boston 3 at Detroit 4
10 Detroit 2 at Maroons 3
13 Chicago 1 at Detroit 5
15 Detroit 2 at Canadiens 3
17 Toronto 7 at Detroit 2
20 Rangers 3 at Detroit 4

1938–1939

November 6 Boston 4 at Detroit 1
10 Americans 2 at Detroit 1
13 Rangers 4 at Detroit 3
15 Detroit 0 at Rangers 2 [Kerr] (both goals in 2nd)
17 Detroit 7 at Canadiens 1
20 Detroit 1 at Boston 4 (all goals in 3rd)
24 Chicago 2 at Detroit 4
26 Detroit 0 at Toronto 5 [Broda]
27 Canadiens 3 at Detroit 2
December 1 Detroit 4 at Chicago 1
4 Toronto 0 at Detroit 1 [Thompson] (Brûneteau 14:33 3rd)
8 Americans 1 at Detroit 1 (Liscombe (D) 3:45 / Wiseman (A) 5:54 OT)
11 Detroit 2 at Canadiens 4 (Haynes (C) awarded goal when Young threw his stick)
13 Detroit 1 at Americans 5
18 Boston 2 at Detroit 0 [Brimsek] (both goals in 3rd)
20 Detroit 2 at Rangers 6
22 Detroit 3 at Chicago 3 (10:00 OT)
24 Detroit 0 at Toronto 2 [Broda]
25 Canadiens 1 at Detroit 4
29 Chicago 1 at Detroit 4
January 1 Detroit 1 at Boston 4
2 Detroit 0 at Rangers 3 [Kerr]
5 Detroit 6 at Americans 6 (10:00 OT)
8 Detroit 1 at Canadiens 1 (10:00 OT) (both goals in 2nd)
10 Canadiens 0 at Detroit 3 [Thompson]
15 Toronto 0 at Detroit 1 [Thompson] (Giesebrecht 17:22 2nd)
19 Rangers 3 at Detroit 4
22 Boston 5 at Detroit 0 [Brimsek] (all goals in 3rd)
26 Detroit 1 at Chicago 0 [Thompson] (Brown 18:48 2nd)
28 Detroit 0 at Toronto 6 [Broda]
29 Toronto 2 at Detroit 2 (10:00 OT)
February 5 Americans 3 at Detroit 7
9 Chicago 4 at Detroit 2
12 Detroit 0 at Americans 1 [Robertson] (Schriner 9:27 3rd)
14 Detroit 1 at Boston 2
16 Detroit 1 at Chicago 1 (10:00 OT) (both goals in 3rd)
19 Boston 1 at Detroit 4
21 Detroit 3 at Rangers 7
23 Rangers 4 at Detroit 2
26 Toronto 1 at Detroit 5
March 2 Americans 3 at Detroit 7
5 Detroit 4 at Americans 2
7 Detroit 0 at Boston 3 [Brimsek]
9 Detroit 2 at Canadiens 3
11 Detroit 1 at Toronto 5
12 Canadiens 1 at Detroit 2 (all goals in 1st)
14 Rangers 2 at Detroit 3
19 Chicago 2 at Detroit 3 (Marty Barry Night)

1939–1940

November 2 Detroit 2 at Chicago 3
5 Rangers 1 at Detroit 1 (10:00 OT)
12 Boston 1 at Detroit 2
14 Detroit 4 at Americans 2
18 Detroit 0 at Toronto 3 [Broda]
19 Toronto 7 at Detroit 1
23 Americans 2 at Detroit 3
25 Detroit 6 at Canadiens 4
26 Chicago 4 at Detroit 2
28 Detroit 1 at Rangers 4
December 3 Canadiens 3 at Detroit 1

8 Boston 3 at Detroit 0 [Brimsek] (all goals in 3rd)
10 Americans 3 at Detroit 2
12 Detroit 1 at Boston 3
14 Detroit 2 at Rangers 2 (10:00 OT)
17 Rangers 0 at Detroit 0 (10:00 OT) [Kerr (R) / Thompson (D)]
21 Detroit 0 at Americans 3 [Robertson]
23 Detroit 1 at Toronto 5
25 Canadiens 1 at Detroit 3
31 Toronto 3 at Detroit 2

January
1 Detroit 0 at Chicago 1 [Goodman] (Gottselig 19:22 2nd)
4 Detroit 3 at Canadiens 2
7 Detroit 0 at Rangers 3 [Kerr]
9 Detroit 1 at Boston 3
12 Americans 2 at Detroit 4
14 Detroit 0 at Americans 1 [Robertson] (N. Stewart 5:04 2nd)
18 Detroit 2 at Toronto 2 (10:00 OT)
21 Toronto 2 at Detroit 3
26 Chicago 1 at Detroit 1 (10:00 OT)
28 Boston 2 at Detroit 4

February
1 Rangers 0 at Detroit 2 [Thompson]
4 Detroit 1 at Chicago 1 (10:00 OT)
6 Detroit 3 at Americans 1
8 Detroit 2 at Canadiens 1
9 Chicago 3 at Detroit 0 [Goodman]
11 Canadiens 3 at Detroit 2 (Blake 5:31 OT)
13 Detroit 3 at Boston 10
15 Detroit 1 at Rangers 3
18 Rangers 0 at Detroit 2 [Thompson] (both goals in 3rd)
22 Toronto 2 at Detroit 1
25 Americans 1 at Detroit 4
29 Detroit 1 at Toronto 3

March
3 Boston 3 at Detroit 6
5 Detroit 2 at Boston 7
9 Detroit 0 at Canadiens 3 [Bourque]
10 Canadiens 2 at Detroit 5
15 Chicago 4 at Detroit 3
17 Detroit 1 at Chicago 3

1940–1941

November
3 Americans 2 at Detroit 4
9 Detroit 0 at Toronto 3 [Broda]
10 Rangers 2 at Detroit 2 (10:00 OT)
16 Detroit 3 at Rangers 3 (10:00 OT)
17 Detroit 2 at Americans 0 [Mowers]
19 Detroit 4 at Boston 4 (10:00 OT)
21 Canadiens 1 at Detroit 2
24 Boston 1 at Detroit 1 (10:00 OT)
29 Chicago 1 at Detroit 3

December
1 Toronto 3 at Detroit 1
5 Detroit 5 at Chicago 1
7 Detroit 2 at Canadiens 3
8 Detroit 3 at Rangers 1
13 Rangers 2 at Detroit 3 (D. Grosso 5:21 OT)
15 Canadiens 2 at Detroit 1 (Demers 8:41 OT)
17 Detroit 2 at Americans 3 (Anderson 5:11 OT)
19 Americans 1 at Detroit 1 (10:00 OT) (both goals in 1st)
22 Boston 5 at Detroit 3
25 Toronto 2 at Detroit 3
29 Chicago 1 at Detroit 2

January
1 Detroit 4 at Chicago 1
4 Detroit 3 at Toronto 1
5 Canadiens 0 at Detroit 3 [Mowers]
7 Detroit 1 at Boston 1 (10:00 OT)
9 Detroit 3 at Americans 3 (10:00 OT)
12 Detroit 1 at Chicago 2
14 Detroit 3 at Rangers 3 (10:00 OT)
18 Detroit 1 at Canadiens 2
19 Rangers 2 at Detroit 1
24 Americans 2 at Detroit 4 (Wares 7:45 / S. Howe 9:39 OT)
26 Toronto 2 at Detroit 0 [Broda]
30 Detroit 1 at Toronto 2

February
6 Detroit 4 at Canadiens 4 (10:00 OT)
9 Boston 2 at Detroit 2 (10:00 OT)
11 Detroit 0 at Boston 4 [Brimsek]
14 Chicago 1 at Detroit 2
16 Canadiens 1 at Detroit 2 (Canadiens played the first 24:09 of the game without registering a shot on Detroit goal)
22 Detroit 2 at Toronto 6
23 Toronto 0 at Detroit 3 [Mowers]
27 Detroit 0 at Chicago 1 [LoPresti] (Dahlstrom 12:38 3rd)
28 Americans 4 at Detroit 5 (Rayner (A) left at 12:47 of 3rd; Brannigan, defenceman, played the rest of the game without allowing a goal)

March 2 Rangers 2 at Detroit 4 (Fisher 2:24 / S. Howe 5:20 OT)
4 Detroit 0 at Rangers 6 [Kerr]
6 Detroit 6 at Americans 1
8 Detroit 4 at Canadiens 0 [Mowers]
13 Chicago 2 at Detroit 3
16 Boston 2 at Detroit 2 (10:00 OT)
18 Detroit 1 at Boston 4

1941–1942

November 1 Detroit 3 at Canadiens 2
2 Americans 3 at Detroit 3 (Knott (A) 4:11 / Stewart (D) 5:24 OT)
9 Rangers 3 at Detroit 1
15 Detroit 1 at Toronto 2
16 Detroit 2 at Chicago 3
20 Toronto 4 at Detroit 3 (Goldup (T) :47 / Carr (T) 3:18 / Abel (D) 9:19 OT)
22 Detroit 2 at Americans 1
23 Boston 4 at Detroit 2
25 Detroit 1 at Boston 7
27 Chicago 1 at Detroit 4
29 Detroit 1 at Rangers 4
December 4 Americans 3 at Detroit 4
7 Canadiens 2 at Detroit 3
14 Toronto 4 at Detroit 0 [Broda]
18 Detroit 3 at Americans 4 (Thurier :39 OT)
21 Boston 2 at Detroit 2 (10:00 OT)
25 Americans 2 at Detroit 3 (Abel 5:02 OT)
27 Detroit 3 at Toronto 5
28 Rangers 3 at Detroit 1
January 1 Detroit 3 at Chicago 0 [Mowers]
3 Detroit 1 at Canadiens 4
4 Canadiens 0 at Detroit 10 [Mowers]
6 Detroit 2 at Rangers 3
8 Detroit 4 at Americans 5
10 Detroit 6 at Toronto 4
11 Detroit 5 at Chicago 6
13 Detroit 1 at Boston 2
18 Americans 5 at Detroit 3
22 Boston 3 at Detroit 4
24 Rangers 3 at Detroit 2
25 Detroit 2 at Rangers 11
29 Chicago 0 at Detroit 2 [Mowers] (Syd Howe Night)
February 5 Toronto 3 at Detroit 3 (10:00 OT)
7 Detroit 1 at Canadiens 3
8 Detroit 0 at Boston 3 [Brimsek]
12 Detroit 2 at Chicago 4
14 Detroit 2 at Toronto 4
15 Canadiens 0 at Detroit 5 [Mowers]
19 Chicago 1 at Detroit 6
22 Toronto 0 at Detroit 3 [Mowers]
24 Detroit 3 at Americans 2
26 Detroit 4 at Rangers 7
March 1 Detroit 3 at Boston 3 (10:00 OT)
5 Rangers 2 at Detroit 5
8 Boston 1 at Detroit 3
14 Detroit 3 at Canadiens 4
15 Canadiens 1 at Detroit 4
19 Chicago 4 at Detroit 6

1942–1943

November 1 Boston 0 at Detroit 3 [Mowers]
5 Rangers 5 at Detroit 12
7 Detroit 2 at Toronto 5
8 Chicago 3 at Detroit 3 (10:00 OT)
14 Detroit 5 at Canadiens 2
15 Canadiens 1 at Detroit 3
19 Detroit 2 at Chicago 6
22 Detroit 4 at Rangers 4
24 Detroit 4 at Canadiens 4
26 Toronto 1 at Detroit 2
29 Canadiens 3 at Detroit 7
December 1 Detroit 2 at Boston 5
6 Toronto 2 at Detroit 2
12 Detroit 4 at Toronto 5
13 Boston 1 at Detroit 1
15 Detroit 2 at Boston 3
17 Detroit 3 at Chicago 1
20 Canadiens 3 at Detroit 4
25 Rangers 3 at Detroit 1
27 Chicago 1 at Detroit 6
31 Detroit 2 at Rangers 0 [Mowers] (both goals in 1st)
January 1 Detroit 2 at Boston 2 (all goals in 1st)
3 Boston 3 at Detroit 2
7 Rangers 2 at Detroit 2
9 Detroit 4 at Toronto 0 [Mowers] (all goals in 3rd)
10 Detroit 1 at Chicago 2
14 Detroit 4 at Rangers 1

	16	Chicago 1 at Detroit 1
	17	Detroit 2 at Chicago 2 (Abel (D) tied game at 19:59)
	21	Boston 2 at Detroit 3
	24	Rangers 0 at Detroit 7 [Mowers]
	26	Detroit 5 at Boston 3
	30	Detroit 3 at Canadiens 3
	31	Canadiens 4 at Detroit 3
February	4	Detroit 3 at Toronto 2
	7	Toronto 3 at Detroit 5
	13	Detroit 2 at Canadiens 5
	14	Canadiens 1 at Detroit 2
	18	Detroit 5 at Rangers 4
	21	Boston 0 at Detroit 4 [Mowers]
	25	Detroit 2 at Canadiens 4
	27	Rangers 1 at Detroit 7
	28	Detroit 5 at Rangers 1
March	2	Detroit 1 at Boston 3
	6	Chicago 0 at Detroit 5 [Mowers]
	7	Detroit 3 at Chicago 3
	11	Toronto 1 at Detroit 2
	13	Detroit 1 at Toronto 3
	14	Toronto 5 at Detroit 3
	18	Chicago 5 at Detroit 6

1943–1944

October	31	Rangers 3 at Detroit 8
November	4	Toronto 5 at Detroit 5
	7	Boston 4 at Detroit 6
	11	Detroit 2 at Toronto 2 (Carr (T) tied game at 19:43)
	13	Detroit 1 at Canadiens 4
	14	Canadiens 2 at Detroit 0 [Durnan]
	18	Detroit 3 at Rangers 1
	21	Chicago 2 at Detroit 5
	25	Detroit 3 at Chicago 4
	28	Toronto 4 at Detroit 6
December	2	Detroit 5 at Toronto 6
	4	Detroit 2 at Canadiens 8
	7	Detroit 6 at Boston 6
	12	Canadiens 5 at Detroit 1
	16	Detroit 4 at Toronto 1
	19	Detroit 2 at Rangers 6
	22	Detroit 1 at Chicago 7
	23	Rangers 3 at Detroit 5
	26	Boston 4 at Detroit 4
	28	Detroit 2 at Boston 5
	30	Detroit 3 at Canadiens 8
January	2	Canadiens 5 at Detroit 2
	6	Detroit 5 at Rangers 0 [Franks]
	9	Chicago 2 at Detroit 4
	13	Detroit 2 at Canadiens 2
	15	Detroit 6 at Toronto 4
	16	Toronto 1 at Detroit 4
	20	Chicago 3 at Detroit 4
	23	Rangers 0 at Detroit 15 [Dion]
	25	Detroit 6 at Boston 3
	29	Boston 1 at Detroit 6
	30	Detroit 2 at Chicago 3
February	3	Rangers 2 at Detroit 12
	5	Detroit 1 at Toronto 3
	6	Toronto 2 at Detroit 3
	10	Detroit 8 at Rangers 3
	13	Detroit 4 at Boston 1
	17	Canadiens 3 at Detroit 2
	20	Boston 5 at Detroit 6
	24	Detroit 3 at Rangers 3
	27	Canadiens 5 at Detroit 1
March	2	Rangers 5 at Detroit 6
	4	Chicago 2 at Detroit 6
	5	Detroit 1 at Chicago 6
	7	Detroit 8 at Boston 4
	11	Detroit 3 at Canadiens 4
	12	Toronto 1 at Detroit 4
	16	Boston 9 at Detroit 10
	18	Chicago 3 at Detroit 6
	19	Detroit 0 at Chicago 2 [Karakas]

1944–1945

October	29	Boston 1 at Detroit 7
November	2	Rangers 3 at Detroit 10
	4	Detroit 2 at Canadiens 3
	5	Canadiens 3 at Detroit 2
	11	Detroit 2 at Rangers 5
	12	Toronto 2 at Detroit 4
	15	Detroit 8 at Toronto 4
	18	Detroit 2 at Rangers 2
	19	Boston 3 at Detroit 4
	23	Canadiens 3 at Detroit 3
	25	Chicago 4 at Detroit 7
	26	Detroit 5 at Chicago 6
	28	Detroit 6 at Boston 3
December	7	Detroit 3 at Rangers 2
	10	Boston 6 at Detroit 7
	16	Detroit 1 at Toronto 1
	17	Detroit 1 at Chicago 2

	19	Detroit 6 at Boston 3
	21	Rangers 3 at Detroit 11
	23	Detroit 5 at Toronto 4
	25	Toronto 4 at Detroit 6
	28	Detroit 1 at Canadiens 9
	31	Chicago 2 at Detroit 6
January	1	Detroit 4 at Chicago 2
	4	Detroit 4 at Rangers 4
	6	Detroit 5 at Toronto 2
	7	Boston 4 at Detroit 8
	13	Detroit 3 at Canadiens 8
	14	Toronto 0 at Detroit 3 [Lumley]
	18	Rangers 3 at Detroit 7 (game delayed 2 hours, 43 minutes because of late arriving train from New York)
	21	Canadiens 6 at Detroit 3
	23	Detroit 5 at Boston 4
	27	Chicago 1 at Detroit 5
	28	Detroit 4 at Chicago 2
February	3	Detroit 2 at Canadiens 5
	4	Canadiens 3 at Detroit 1
	10	Detroit 2 at Canadiens 5
	11	Detroit 3 at Boston 2
	14	Rangers 2 at Detroit 4
	18	Toronto 1 at Detroit 6
	22	Detroit 3 at Rangers 5
	24	Chicago 2 at Detroit 4
	25	Detroit 3 at Chicago 1
March	4	Boston 4 at Detroit 10
	8	Rangers 3 at Detroit 7
	11	Toronto 3 at Detroit 2
	13	Detroit 2 at Boston 2
	15	Canadiens 1 at Detroit 2
	17	Detroit 4 at Toronto 3
	18	Chicago 5 at Detroit 3

1945–1946

October	28	Boston 0 at Detroit 7 [Lumley]
November	3	Detroit 1 at Canadiens 3
	4	Rangers 1 at Detroit 4
	8	Toronto 2 at Detroit 3
	10	Detroit 0 at Rangers 2 [Henry]
	11	Canadiens 1 at Detroit 4
	15	Chicago 2 at Detroit 5
	17	Detroit 6 at Toronto 5
	18	Detroit 5 at Chicago 3
	24	Detroit 1 at Canadiens 2
	25	Rangers 4 at Detroit 1
December	2	Detroit 2 at Boston 2
	9	Canadiens 1 at Detroit 2 (all goals in 3rd)
	12	Detroit 2 at Boston 2
	15	Detroit 1 at Toronto 3
	16	Detroit 4 at Chicago 6
	22	Chicago 6 at Detroit 4
	23	Detroit 4 at Chicago 4
	25	Toronto 3 at Detroit 6
	26	Detroit 3 at Rangers 2
	30	Boston 3 at Detroit 3
January	1	Detroit 0 at Boston 4 [Bibeault]
	3	Rangers 3 at Detroit 3
	6	Chicago 2 at Detroit 3
	10	Boston 1 at Detroit 2
	12	Detroit 3 at Toronto 9
	13	Canadiens 1 at Detroit 3
	20	Toronto 3 at Detroit 1
	26	Boston 4 at Detroit 2
	27	Detroit 2 at Rangers 5
February	2	Detroit 1 at Canadiens 5
	3	Canadiens 0 at Detroit 2 [Lumley]
	7	Rangers 2 at Detroit 4
	9	Detroit 1 at Toronto 4
	10	Toronto 2 at Detroit 2
	13	Detroit 0 at Boston 3 [Brimsek]
	16	Chicago 3 at Detroit 3
	17	Detroit 2 at Chicago 2
	20	Detroit 2 at Canadiens 1
	21	Detroit 2 at Rangers 2
	24	Boston 3 at Detroit 4
	28	Rangers 1 at Detroit 4
March	2	Detroit 3 at Canadiens 3
	3	Canadiens 2 at Detroit 4
	6	Detroit 2 at Boston 4
	10	Detroit 2 at Rangers 3
	13	Detroit 4 at Chicago 9
	14	Chicago 3 at Detroit 7
	16	Detroit 3 at Toronto 7
	17	Toronto 11 at Detroit 7

1946–1947

October	16	Toronto 3 at Detroit 3
	19	Detroit 3 at Toronto 6
	20	Rangers 3 at Detroit 1
	23	Chicago 6 at Detroit 5
	26	Detroit 2 at Canadiens 7

	27	Canadiens 1 at Detroit 2
November	2	Detroit 4 at Rangers 7
	3	Rangers 1 at Detroit 3
	6	Boston 3 at Detroit 3
	10	Canadiens 3 at Detroit 6
	13	Detroit 2 at Boston 5
	14	Detroit 3 at Canadiens 4
	17	Chicago 2 at Detroit 5
	20	Detroit 8 at Chicago 6
	21	Rangers 1 at Detroit 3
	23	Detroit 4 at Toronto 2
	24	Toronto 5 at Detroit 0 [Broda]
	27	Canadiens 6 at Detroit 1
	30	Detroit 1 at Canadiens 4
December	1	Detroit 3 at Boston 3
	4	Detroit 0 at Chicago 0 [Lumley (D) / Bibeault (C)]
	8	Toronto 5 at Detroit 4
	11	Detroit 1 at Rangers 1
	15	Detroit 2 at Boston 3
	18	Detroit 2 at Chicago 5
	19	Detroit 1 at Toronto 3
	22	Canadiens 4 at Detroit 2
	25	Toronto 2 at Detroit 1
	28	Rangers 2 at Detroit 2 (Laycoe (R) tied game at 19:53)
	31	Detroit 5 at Rangers 4
January	1	Detroit 1 at Toronto 2 (all goals in 2nd)
	5	Boston 1 at Detroit 3
	8	Detroit 4 at Canadiens 2
	9	Chicago 6 at Detroit 4
	12	Boston 1 at Detroit 5
	15	Detroit 3 at Rangers 4
	18	Detroit 4 at Toronto 7
	19	Canadiens 2 at Detroit 2
	23	Chicago 2 at Detroit 8
	26	Detroit 3 at Boston 4
	29	Detroit 1 at Boston 4
February	1	Boston 2 at Detroit 2
	8	Detroit 3 at Canadiens 4
	9	Rangers 2 at Detroit 5
	15	Chicago 1 at Detroit 5
	16	Detroit 2 at Chicago 3
	20	Boston 0 at Detroit 3 [Lumley]
	22	Canadiens 3 at Detroit 7
	23	Detroit 2 at Rangers 2
	27	Toronto 3 at Detroit 3
March	1	Detroit 5 at Toronto 4
	2	Detroit 3 at Chicago 1
	6	Detroit 1 at Canadiens 1
	9	Detroit 0 at Boston 6 [Brimsek]
	12	Detroit 4 at Rangers 2
	13	Boston 3 at Detroit 2
	15	Chicago 3 at Detroit 8
	16	Detroit 10 at Chicago 6
	19	Rangers 0 at Detroit 2 [Lumley]
	23	Toronto 5 at Detroit 3

1947–1948

October	15	Chicago 2 at Detroit 4
	18	Detroit 2 at Toronto 2
	19	Detroit 2 at Toronto 0 [Lumley]
	26	Canadiens 4 at Detroit 2
	29	Detroit 5 at Chicago 2
November	1	Detroit 3 at Rangers 4
	2	Boston 1 at Detroit 2
	6	Rangers 1 at Detroit 2 (all goals in 1st)
	8	Detroit 3 at Canadiens 1
	9	Toronto 6 at Detroit 0 [Broda] (McGratton (D) replaced Lumley at 12:00 of 3rd)
	15	Detroit 3 at Toronto 5
	16	Detroit 3 at Boston 2
	19	Rangers 6 at Detroit 5
	22	Chicago 5 at Detroit 8
	23	Detroit 9 at Chicago 3
	27	Boston 1 at Detroit 4
	30	Canadiens 1 at Detroit 1
December	6	Detroit 0 at Canadiens 4 [Durnan]
	7	Detroit 1 at Rangers 3
	10	Toronto 2 at Detroit 2
	13	Chicago 3 at Detroit 4
	14	Detroit 1 at Rangers 1
	17	Detroit 7 at Chicago 1
	20	Detroit 4 at Toronto 4 (Lynn (T) tied game at 19:53)
	21	Detroit 6 at Boston 5
	25	Rangers 2 at Detroit 0 [Henry]
	28	Boston 0 at Detroit 3 [Lumley]
	31	Chicago 0 at Detroit 4 [Lumley]
January	1	Detroit 4 at Chicago 1
	4	Canadiens 2 at Detroit 6
	7	Rangers 0 at Detroit 6 [Lumley]
	8	Detroit 1 at Canadiens 1 (both goals in 3rd)

10 Boston 4 at Detroit 1
11 Toronto 2 at Detroit 2
14 Detroit 3 at Boston 3
18 Chicago 5 at Detroit 4
21 Detroit 4 at Rangers 3
24 Detroit 5 at Canadiens 1
25 Canadiens 0 at Detroit 1 [Lumley] (D. Morrison 14:32 3rd)
28 Detroit 4 at Boston 2
31 Detroit 2 at Toronto 3

February 1 Toronto 0 at Detroit 3 [Lumley]
3 Detroit 4 at Chicago 1
4 Rangers 4 at Detroit 4 (Abel (D) tied game at 19:30)
7 Detroit 5 at Canadiens 3
8 Boston 3 at Detroit 1
15 Detroit 1 at Boston 3
18 Detroit 3 at Rangers 1 (all goals in 2nd)
21 Detroit 2 at Toronto 3
22 Canadiens 3 at Detroit 4
28 Detroit 5 at Canadiens 2

March 3 Rangers 2 at Detroit 4
6 Canadiens 2 at Detroit 2
7 Detroit 2 at Rangers 2
9 Detroit 1 at Chicago 4
10 Chicago 2 at Detroit 7
14 Boston 5 at Detroit 1
17 Detroit 0 at Boston 0 [Lumley (D) / Brimsek (B)]
20 Detroit 3 at Toronto 5
21 Toronto 5 at Detroit 2

1948–1949

October 13 Chicago 1 at Detroit 3
17 Rangers 0 at Detroit 7 [Lumley]
23 Detroit 0 at Canadiens 0 [Lumley (D) / Durnan (C)]
24 Toronto 1 at Detroit 2
27 Detroit 3 at Rangers 2
30 Detroit 1 at Toronto 2
31 Canadiens 1 at Detroit 4

November 6 Detroit 0 at Canadiens 2 [Durnan] (both goals in 2nd)
7 Boston 3 at Detroit 7
10 Detroit at Boston (game stopped after nine minutes because of poor ice conditions and replayed the next night)
11 Detroit 1 at Boston 4
14 Detroit 3 at Chicago 1
17 Rangers 4 at Detroit 4
21 Canadiens 3 at Detroit 0 [Durnan]
24 Boston 5 at Detroit 3
27 Chicago 5 at Detroit 3
28 Detroit 9 at Chicago 6

December 1 Toronto 3 at Detroit 5
4 Detroit 3 at Boston 2
5 Detroit 3 at Rangers 1
8 Detroit 4 at Toronto 3
11 Rangers 3 at Detroit 5
12 Detroit 0 at Rangers 2 [Rayner]
15 Detroit 1 at Chicago 5
18 Detroit 3 at Canadiens 5
19 Toronto 1 at Detroit 5
22 Detroit 2 at Boston 5
25 Detroit 1 at Toronto 2
26 Canadiens 1 at Detroit 3
29 Boston 2 at Detroit 10

January 1 Detroit 3 at Chicago 5
2 Chicago 3 at Detroit 5
6 Boston 3 at Detroit 2
8 Detroit 4 at Canadiens 1
9 Toronto 2 at Detroit 2
12 Detroit 4 at Rangers 1
16 Canadiens 2 at Detroit 3
19 Chicago 1 at Detroit 2
22 Detroit 2 at Toronto 2
23 Toronto 1 at Detroit 2
26 Rangers 5 at Detroit 1
29 Detroit 5 at Canadiens 2
30 Detroit 4 at Boston 0 [Lumley]

February 2 Chicago 4 at Detroit 6
3 Detroit 4 at Chicago 2
6 Canadiens 0 at Detroit 1 [Lumley] (Horeck 18:38 1st)
9 Rangers 0 at Detroit 8 [Lumley]
12 Detroit 1 at Toronto 3
13 Detroit 4 at Boston 4
16 Detroit 0 at Rangers 4 [Rayner]
21 Boston 2 at Detroit 2
26 Detroit 0 at Canadiens 1 [Durnan] (Leger 8:40 1st)
27 Detroit 2 at Rangers 3

March 2 Detroit 1 at Boston 1
5 Chicago 5 at Detroit 6
6 Detroit 6 at Chicago 2

9 Toronto 0 at Detroit 5 [Lumley]
13 Boston 6 at Detroit 2
16 Rangers 2 at Detroit 6
19 Detroit 5 at Toronto 2
20 Canadiens 1 at Detroit 2

1949–1950

October 12 Boston 1 at Detroit 2
16 Toronto 5 at Detroit 1
19 Rangers 1 at Detroit 6
23 Chicago 3 at Detroit 3
27 Detroit 3 at Chicago 1
29 Detroit 1 at Canadiens 0 [Lumley] (Black 16:30 1st)
30 Canadiens 4 at Detroit 1
November 2 Boston 3 at Detroit 5
5 Detroit 4 at Toronto 3
6 Rangers 0 at Detroit 7 [Lumley]
12 Detroit 7 at Boston 5
13 Detroit 1 at Rangers 1
16 Chicago 1 at Detroit 4
19 Detroit 5 at Toronto 2
20 Toronto 2 at Detroit 5
23 Rangers 3 at Detroit 4
24 Detroit 3 at Chicago 3
26 Chicago 7 at Detroit 2
27 Canadiens 6 at Detroit 2
30 Boston 0 at Detroit 3 [Lumley]
December 1 Detroit 2 at Toronto 0 [Lumley] (both goals in 1st)
3 Detroit 5 at Canadiens 3
4 Toronto 2 at Detroit 1
7 Detroit 2 at Boston 1
10 Rangers 1 at Detroit 0 [Rayner] (Laprade 4:18 3rd)
11 Detroit 1 at Rangers 2
14 Detroit 5 at Boston 2
17 Detroit 3 at Canadiens 4
18 Detroit 5 at Chicago 3
21 Toronto 1 at Detroit 7
25 Canadiens 2 at Detroit 4
28 Boston 2 at Detroit 2
31 Detroit 5 at Toronto 1
January 1 Toronto 0 at Detroit 5 [Lumley]
4 Detroit 1 at Rangers 2
8 Boston 4 at Detroit 3
11 Detroit 1 at Boston 2
14 Rangers 2 at Detroit 4
15 Detroit 1 at Rangers 0 [Sawchuk] (Abel 9:15 3rd)
18 Detroit 5 at Chicago 4
21 Chicago 3 at Detroit 5
22 Toronto 1 at Detroit 0 [Broda] (Smith 14:47 2nd)
25 Boston 4 at Detroit 4
26 Detroit 1 at Canadiens 1
28 Detroit 1 at Canadiens 1 (both goals in 2nd)
29 Detroit 1 at Boston 4
February 1 Canadiens 3 at Detroit 3
4 Detroit 3 at Toronto 3
5 Rangers 5 at Detroit 5
8 Chicago 2 at Detroit 9
11 Detroit 9 at Boston 4
12 Detroit 0 at Rangers 4 [Rayner]
15 Detroit 0 at Chicago 3 [Brimsek]
18 Detroit 2 at Toronto 3
20 Canadiens 0 at Detroit 2 [Lumley] (both goals in 3rd)
23 Detroit 1 at Canadiens 1
26 Detroit 4 at Chicago 1
March 1 Detroit 5 at Rangers 2
4 Detroit 2 at Toronto 3
6 Canadiens 2 at Detroit 2 (Sid Abel Night)
8 Detroit 5 at Boston 3
9 Detroit 1 at Rangers 3
11 Chicago 1 at Detroit 5
12 Detroit 4 at Chicago 2
15 Canadiens 1 at Detroit 4
16 Detroit 2 at Canadiens 2
18 Boston 1 at Detroit 1 (both goals in 1st)
19 Toronto 0 at Detroit 5 [Lumley]
22 Rangers 7 at Detroit 8
26 Chicago 5 at Detroit 4

1950–1951

October 11 Rangers 2 at Detroit 3
15 Toronto 4 at Detroit 4
21 Detroit 0 at Canadiens 2 [McNeil]
22 Canadiens 2 at Detroit 3
25 Detroit 0 at Toronto 1 [Broda] (Gardiner 11:22 3rd)
28 Chicago 1 at Detroit 3
29 Boston 0 at Detroit 2 [Sawchuk] (both goals in 1st)

November 2 Rangers 2 at Detroit 2
5 Boston 2 at Detroit 4
8 Detroit 3 at Boston 3
11 Detroit 3 at Toronto 1
12 Canadiens 0 at Detroit 4 [Sawchuk]
16 Detroit 5 at Chicago 1
18 Detroit 2 at Boston 1
19 Detroit 3 at Rangers 3
23 Toronto 2 at Detroit 1
25 Chicago 1 at Detroit 4
26 Detroit 0 at Chicago 5 [Lumley]
29 Detroit 3 at Boston 6

December 2 Detroit 7 at Canadiens 1
3 Canadiens 4 at Detroit 1
6 Detroit 9 at Rangers 0 [Sawchuk]
9 Rangers 0 at Detroit 5 [Sawchuk]
10 Toronto 2 at Detroit 3
13 Detroit 4 at Toronto 3
14 Boston 2 at Detroit 4
16 Detroit 4 at Boston 1
17 Detroit 3 at Rangers 3
19 Chicago 1 at Detroit 6
23 Detroit 4 at Canadiens 4
25 Rangers 1 at Detroit 4
28 Canadiens 1 at Detroit 8
30 Detroit 3 at Toronto 1
31 Toronto 4 at Detroit 2
(McCormack 19:58 en)

January 3 Detroit 3 at Rangers 5
4 Chicago 0 at Detroit 1 [Sawchuk]
(Gee 4:08 3rd)
6 Detroit 2 at Canadiens 5
7 Boston 0 at Detroit 3 [Sawchuk]
9 Toronto 3 at Detroit 3
13 Rangers 2 at Detroit 4
14 Canadiens 2 at Detroit 3
17 Detroit 4 at Chicago 2
18 Chicago 2 at Detroit 3
(Abel won game at 19:39)
21 Toronto 0 at Detroit 0
[Rollins (T) / Sawchuk (D)]
23 Detroit 8 at Chicago 2
25 Boston 3 at Detroit 3
27 Detroit 0 at Boston 3 [Gelineau]
28 Detroit 3 at Rangers 5

February 1 Rangers 2 at Detroit 3
4 Canadiens 3 at Detroit 3
7 Chicago 3 at Detroit 11
8 Detroit 4 at Chicago 3
10 Detroit 2 at Toronto 1
11 Detroit 2 at Boston 1
17 Detroit 2 at Canadiens 1
19 Boston 2 at Detroit 2
(Pronovost tied game at 19:18)
21 Detroit 2 at Toronto 2
25 Detroit 2 at Rangers 6
28 Detroit 1 at Boston 1

March 3 Detroit 3 at Canadiens 1
5 Toronto 1 at Detroit 3
7 Detroit 3 at Toronto 0 [Sawchuk]
10 Rangers 2 at Detroit 3
11 Detroit 7 at Chicago 0 [Sawchuk]
15 Boston 0 at Detroit 4 [Sawchuk]
17 Chicago 2 at Detroit 8
18 Detroit 4 at Chicago 3
21 Detroit 4 at Rangers 1
24 Detroit 2 at Canadiens 3
25 Canadiens 0 at Detroit 5 [Sawchuk]

1951–1952

October 11 Boston 0 at Detroit 1 [Sawchuk]
(Skov 6:49 1st)
14 Toronto 3 at Detroit 2
18 Detroit 6 at Chicago 1
20 Canadiens 0 at Detroit 3 [Sawchuk]
22 Detroit 3 at Canadiens 1
27 Detroit 2 at Toronto 1
29 Toronto 2 at Detroit 2

November 1 Boston 3 at Detroit 2
3 Detroit 3 at Canadiens 2
4 Rangers 2 at Detroit 4
6 Detroit 0 at Boston 0
[Sawchuk (D) / Henry (B)]
7 Detroit 4 at Rangers 4
10 Detroit 3 at Toronto 3
11 Canadiens 3 at Detroit 3
15 Chicago 1 at Detroit 3
18 Detroit 5 at Rangers 2
(Pronovost 19:40 en)
20 Detroit 2 at Boston 0 [Sawchuk]
(R. Kelly 19:27 en)
22 Rangers 1 at Detroit 2
24 Chicago 6 at Detroit 2
25 Detroit 5 at Chicago 2

29 Boston 1 at Detroit 1

December 2 Toronto 2 at Detroit 1

5 Detroit 2 at Toronto 2

8 Detroit 3 at Canadiens 0 [Sawchuk]

9 Canadiens 2 at Detroit 3

13 Toronto 1 at Detroit 3

15 Chicago 0 at Detroit 3 [Sawchuk]

16 Detroit 3 at Rangers 1

18 Detroit 5 at Boston 5

20 Detroit 6 at Chicago 4
(R. Kelly 19:31 en)

23 Canadiens 0 at Detroit 4 [Sawchuk]

25 Rangers 1 at Detroit 2

26 Detroit 0 at Rangers 1 [Rayner]
(Slowinski 3:04 1st)

29 Chicago 1 at Detroit 3

31 Canadiens 5 at Detroit 3

January 2 Detroit 0 at Rangers 1 [Rayner]
(Raleigh 12:00 1st)

6 Boston 2 at Detroit 4

10 Rangers 2 at Detroit 5

12 Detroit 3 at Toronto 5

13 Toronto 1 at Detroit 2

17 Boston 0 at Detroit 5 [Sawchuk]

19 Detroit 4 at Canadiens 0 [Sawchuk]

20 Rangers 3 at Detroit 2

24 Toronto 2 at Detroit 2

26 Chicago 3 at Detroit 2

27 Detroit 2 at Chicago 0 [Sawchuk]
(both goals in 3rd)
(Lindsay 19:40 en)

29 Detroit 1 at Boston 3

February 2 Detroit 2 at Canadiens 2

3 Rangers 3 at Detroit 4

7 Canadiens 3 at Detroit 5

10 Detroit 2 at Boston 0 [Sawchuk]

13 Detroit 3 at Toronto 1
(G. Howe 19:18 en)

14 Detroit 3 at Chicago 2

18 Boston 2 at Detroit 4

20 Detroit 1 at Rangers 1

23 Detroit 3 at Toronto 1
(Abel 19:55 en)

24 Detroit 2 at Chicago 1

26 Detroit 4 at Boston 3

28 Detroit 2 at Canadiens 3

March 2 Detroit 6 at Rangers 4

3 Chicago 2 at Detroit 3

6 Boston 1 at Detroit 2

8 Detroit 3 at Toronto 6

9 Toronto 1 at Detroit 6

11 Detroit 2 at Boston 3

15 Chicago 1 at Detroit 6

16 Detroit 4 at Chicago 0
(afternoon game)

20 Rangers 3 at Detroit 7

22 Detroit 3 at Canadiens 3

23 Canadiens 2 at Detroit 7

1952–1953

October 9 Rangers 3 at Detroit 5

11 Detroit 1 at Canadiens 2

12 Toronto 4 at Detroit 4

14 Detroit 1 at Chicago 1

16 Chicago 0 at Detroit 7 [Sawchuk]

19 Canadiens 1 at Detroit 6

22 Detroit 4 at Toronto 5

25 Detroit 0 at Canadiens 9 [McNeil]

26 Detroit 2 at Rangers 3

30 Boston 1 at Detroit 4

November 2 Toronto 4 at Detroit 2

4 Detroit at Chicago
(postponed to Dec. 6 because of U.S. election)

6 Detroit 0 at Boston 2 [Henry]

8 Detroit 3 at Toronto 3

9 Rangers 1 at Detroit 3

13 Boston 0 at Detroit 3 [Sawchuk]

16 Detroit 5 at Boston 2

19 Detroit 2 at Rangers 2

22 Chicago 1 at Detroit 10

23 Detroit 0 at Chicago 3 [Rollins]

27 Canadiens 2 at Detroit 2

29 Detroit 3 at Toronto 1

30 Toronto 1 at Detroit 4

December 4 Rangers 3 at Detroit 5

6 Detroit 2 at Chicago 0 [Sawchuk]
(rescheduled from Nov. 4)
(played at Indianapolis)

7 Boston 1 at Detroit 1

11 Detroit 10 at Boston 1

13 Detroit 3 at Toronto 1

14 Canadiens 0 at Detroit 0
[McNeil (C) / Sawchuk (D)]

18 Toronto 1 at Detroit 1

20 Rangers 1 at Detroit 1
(both goals in 3rd)

21 Detroit 5 at Rangers 2

25 Chicago 3 at Detroit 3

27 Detroit 2 at Canadiens 2
28 Boston 1 at Detroit 7
31 Canadiens 2 at Detroit 0 [McNeil]

January
4 Chicago 3 at Detroit 5
8 Boston 0 at Detroit 4 [Hall]
11 Toronto 2 at Detroit 5
14 Detroit 2 at Rangers 3
15 Detroit 4 at Boston 0 [Sawchuk]
17 Detroit 1 at Canadiens 1 (both goals in 3rd)
18 Canadiens 3 at Detroit 2
22 Rangers 8 at Detroit 2
24 Detroit 0 at Toronto 2 [Lumley]
25 Canadiens 3 at Detroit 3
29 Detroit 5 at Chicago 2
31 Chicago 0 at Detroit 4 [Sawchuk]

February
1 Toronto 1 at Detroit 5
5 Rangers 3 at Detroit 3
7 Detroit 3 at Canadiens 1 (G. Howe 19:52 en)
8 Detroit 5 at Boston 3
11 Detroit 2 at Rangers 2
12 Detroit 1 at Boston 3
15 Detroit 4 at Chicago 1
16 Chicago 1 at Detroit 3
18 Detroit 0 at Toronto 2 [Lumley] (both goals in 3rd) (Flaman 19:55 en)
19 Detroit 4 at Canadiens 1
22 Detroit 2 at Rangers 1
26 Detroit at Chicago (postponed to Mar. 21)
28 Detroit 4 at Canadiens 3

March
2 Boston 2 at Detroit 10
5 Rangers 1 at Detroit 7
7 Detroit 3 at Toronto 0 [Sawchuk]
8 Toronto 1 at Detroit 3
11 Detroit 2 at Rangers 0 [Sawchuk] (both goals in 2nd)
12 Detroit 2 at Boston 2 (all goals in 1st)
14 Chicago 3 at Detroit 1
15 Detroit 0 at Chicago 0 [Sawchuk (D) / Rollins (C)]
19 Boston 1 at Detroit 6
21 Detroit 3 at Chicago 4 (rescheduled from Feb. 26)
22 Canadiens 1 at Detroit 1

1953–1954

October
8 Rangers 1 at Detroit 4
10 Detroit 1 at Canadiens 4 (Wilson (D) replaced Sawchuk at 3:57 of 3rd)
11 Toronto 0 at Detroit 4 [Gatherum]
16 Detroit 2 at Chicago 2 (all goals in 3rd)
17 Chicago 1 at Detroit 2
18 Canadiens 0 at Detroit 4 [Sawchuk]
21 Detroit 1 at Toronto 1
24 Detroit 0 at Canadiens 1 [McNeil] (Mazur 18:11 1st)
25 Toronto 0 at Detroit 2 [Sawchuk] (both goals in 1st)
31 Boston 3 at Detroit 1

November
1 Canadiens 1 at Detroit 5
7 Detroit 2 at Toronto 2
8 Rangers 2 at Detroit 2
11 Detroit 2 at Boston 2 (G. Howe tied game at 19:35)
14 Detroit 3 at Rangers 2
15 Rangers 1 at Detroit 4
19 Boston 2 at Detroit 3
21 Detroit 0 at Canadiens 1 [McNeil] (Geoffrion 4:02 1st)
22 Detroit 3 at Rangers 2
26 Toronto 0 at Detroit 2 [Sawchuk]
28 Chicago 0 at Detroit 9 [Sawchuk]
29 Detroit 9 at Chicago 4

December
3 Rangers 0 at Detroit 4 [Sawchuk] (all goals in 2nd)
5 Detroit 0 at Toronto 3 [Lumley]
6 Chicago 5 at Detroit 0 [Rollins]
9 Detroit 3 at Rangers 3
10 Detroit 3 at Boston 6
12 Boston 1 at Detroit 7
13 Canadiens 3 at Detroit 4
17 Chicago 1 at Detroit 5
18 Detroit 3 at Chicago 1 (played in Indianapolis)
20 Detroit 4 at Boston 2
23 Detroit 1 at Rangers 2
26 Detroit 2 at Toronto 4
27 Boston 1 at Detroit 2
31 Canadiens 2 at Detroit 2

January
1 Detroit 2 at Chicago 4
3 Toronto 0 at Detroit 0 [Lumley (T) / Sawchuk (D)]

7 Boston 1 at Detroit 3
10 Canadiens 1 at Detroit 2
13 Detroit 3 at Rangers 1
(G. Howe 19:30 en)
14 Detroit 2 at Boston 1
17 Rangers 3 at Detroit 2
21 Detroit 1 at Canadiens 0 [Sawchuk]
(Prystai 5:25 3rd)
23 Detroit 1 at Toronto 4
24 Toronto 0 at Detroit 2 [Sawchuk]
28 Rangers 3 at Detroit 3
30 Chicago 2 at Detroit 4
(Skov 19:24 en)
31 Detroit 5 at Chicago 1

February 4 Boston 0 at Detroit 5 [Sawchuk]
6 Detroit 4 at Boston 2
7 Detroit 1 at Boston 1
(both goals in 2nd)
10 Detroit 2 at Rangers 3
14 Detroit 5 at Chicago 0 [Sawchuk]
(all goals in 3rd)
15 Chicago 2 at Detroit 3
17 Detroit 0 at Toronto 0
[Sawchuk (D) / Lumley (T)]
18 Detroit 2 at Canadiens 4
20 Detroit 0 at Canadiens 2 [Plante]
(both goals in 2nd)
22 Canadiens 0 at Detroit 3 [Sawchuk]
25 Detroit 3 at Chicago 2
28 Detroit at Boston
(postponed to Mar. 16)

March 4 Toronto 3 at Detroit 3
6 Detroit 3 at Toronto 1
(all goals in 1st)
7 Canadiens 2 at Detroit 2
11 Chicago 2 at Detroit 6
13 Rangers 5 at Detroit 2
14 Detroit 0 at Rangers 2 [Bower]
16 Detroit 2 at Boston 4
(rescheduled from Feb. 28)
18 Boston 3 at Detroit 3
20 Detroit 1 at Canadiens 6
21 Toronto 1 at Detroit 6

1954–1955

October 7 Toronto 1 at Detroit 2
9 Rangers 0 at Detroit 4 [Sawchuk]
13 Detroit 3 at Canadiens 2
16 Canadiens 3 at Detroit 1
17 Detroit 5 at Chicago 2
21 Boston 3 at Detroit 5
23 Chicago 4 at Detroit 2
27 Detroit 2 at Rangers 5
30 Boston 0 at Detroit 4 [Sawchuk]

November 3 Detroit 1 at Toronto 1
4 Detroit 3 at Boston 2
6 Detroit 1 at Canadiens 4
7 Rangers 0 at Detroit 1 [Sawchuk]
(Lindsay 2:33 1st)
11 Toronto 1 at Detroit 0 [Lumley]
(Smith 19:44 2nd)
13 Detroit 0 at Toronto 1 [Lumley]
(Smith :42 3rd)
14 Canadiens 1 at Detroit 4
20 Chicago 0 at Detroit 5 [Sawchuk]
21 Detroit 1 at Chicago 0 [Sawchuk]
(G. Howe 10:18 2nd)
25 Toronto 0 at Detroit 2 [Sawchuk]
27 Detroit 1 at Canadiens 4
28 Detroit 2 at Boston 6

December 1 Detroit 6 at Rangers 1
2 Canadiens 4 at Detroit 1
4 Detroit 0 at Toronto 1 [Lumley]
(Stewart 3:28 3rd)
5 Chicago 1 at Detroit 4
9 Rangers 2 at Detroit 3
11 Rangers 1 at Detroit 4
12 Detroit 4 at Chicago 3
15 Detroit 3 at Rangers 3
16 Detroit 4 at Boston 2
18 Boston 1 at Detroit 4
19 Canadiens 5 at Detroit 0 [Plante]
22 Detroit 2 at Rangers 2
25 Detroit 3 at Toronto 2
26 Toronto 1 at Detroit 1
30 Toronto 1 at Detroit 4

January 1 Detroit 1 at Canadiens 4
2 Canadiens 2 at Detroit 3
6 Boston 3 at Detroit 3
8 Chicago 0 at Detroit 1 [Sawchuk]
(Dineen 13:50 3rd)
9 Detroit 6 at Chicago 2
(played at St. Louis)
13 Boston 0 at Detroit 4 [Sawchuk]
15 Detroit 4 at Canadiens 3
16 Rangers 0 at Detroit 3 [Sawchuk]
19 Detroit 0 at Rangers 2 [Worsley]
20 Detroit 2 at Boston 3
22 Detroit 1 at Toronto 3

23 Toronto 0 at Detroit 4 [Sawchuk]
27 Rangers 3 at Detroit 3
29 Detroit 2 at Chicago 2 (played at St. Louis)
30 Canadiens 1 at Detroit 7

February 3 Boston 1 at Detroit 1
5 Detroit 4 at Boston 8
6 Detroit 2 at Boston 2
12 Detroit 2 at Toronto 1
13 Detroit 5 at Chicago 1
15 Chicago 2 at Detroit 3
17 Detroit 2 at Canadiens 4
20 Detroit 5 at Rangers 0 [Sawchuk]
21 Boston 2 at Detroit 2
26 Detroit 1 at Toronto 1 (both goals in 3rd)
27 Detroit 3 at Chicago 2

March 3 Chicago 1 at Detroit 6
5 Rangers 2 at Detroit 6
6 Detroit 2 at Rangers 1
12 Chicago 2 at Detroit 3
13 Toronto 1 at Detroit 6
16 Detroit 5 at Boston 4
17 Detroit 4 at Canadiens 1 (forfeited to Detroit at end of first period) (the worst moment in the history of hockey in Montreal — the "Richard Riot," so termed because of the mayhem created by fans, with League President Clarence Campbell in attendance, at the Forum after suspending Rocket Richard for the last two games of the regular season and all of the playoffs)
20 Canadiens 0 at Detroit 6 [Sawchuk]

1955–1956

October 6 Chicago 3 at Detroit 2
8 Detroit 2 at Toronto 4
9 Rangers 3 at Detroit 2
15 Detroit 4 at Chicago 1
16 Toronto 0 at Detroit 6 [Hall]
20 Chicago 2 at Detroit 2
22 Boston 0 at Detroit 0 [Sawchuk (B) / Hall (D)]
26 Detroit 2 at Rangers 6
29 Detroit 1 at Canadiens 2
30 Canadiens 2 at Detroit 2

November 2 Detroit 1 at Toronto 3
3 Rangers 1 at Detroit 1 (both goals in 2nd)
5 Detroit 3 at Chicago 3
6 Toronto 1 at Detroit 4
10 Chicago 2 at Detroit 2
12 Detroit 0 at Canadiens 3 [Plante]
13 Detroit 0 at Boston 0 [Hall (D) / Sawchuk (B)]
16 Detroit 3 at Rangers 3
19 Chicago 1 at Detroit 4
20 Detroit 1 at Chicago 1 (both goals in 1st)
24 Canadiens 2 at Detroit 3
27 Toronto 2 at Detroit 1 (all goals in 1st)
30 Detroit 3 at Toronto 3

December 3 Detroit 5 at Boston 0 [Hall]
4 Detroit 3 at Rangers 7
8 Boston 2 at Detroit 2
10 Detroit 2 at Canadiens 4
11 Rangers 0 at Detroit 2 [Hall]
15 Toronto 0 at Detroit 4 [Hall]
18 Canadiens 0 at Detroit 2 [Hall]
22 Detroit 3 at Boston 2
24 Detroit 2 at Canadiens 4
25 Toronto 1 at Detroit 1 (both goals in 1st)
29 Boston 3 at Detroit 4
31 Detroit 2 at Toronto 2

January 1 Chicago 1 at Detroit 5
4 Detroit 4 at Rangers 5
5 Detroit 5 at Canadiens 2
8 Boston 3 at Detroit 4 (first Sunday game ever at the Olympia)
12 Rangers 0 at Detroit 6 [Hall]
14 Detroit 3 at Chicago 1 (played at St. Louis)
15 Canadiens 0 at Detroit 2 [Hall] (both goals in 3rd)
19 Boston 2 at Detroit 4
21 Detroit 2 at Toronto 4
22 Toronto 1 at Detroit 4 (Lefty Wilson, the Wings' trainer, played the last 13:01 in *Toronto*'s goal after Leaf starter Lumley was injured)
26 Rangers 2 at Detroit 3

	27	Detroit 7 at Chicago 0 [Hall]
	29	Canadiens 1 at Detroit 1
February	2	Canadiens 2 at Detroit 0 [Plante] (both goals in 3rd)
	4	Detroit 1 at Canadiens 2
	5	Detroit 1 at Boston 3
	7	Chicago 2 at Detroit 3
	11	Detroit 2 at Boston 3
	12	Detroit 1 at Rangers 2
	14	Rangers 3 at Detroit 5
	18	Detroit 6 at Toronto 1
	19	Detroit 3 at Chicago 5
	21	Boston 1 at Detroit 4 (G. Howe 19:23 en / Delvecchio 19:39 en)
	25	Detroit 1 at Canadiens 5
	26	Detroit 2 at Rangers 3
	28	Rangers 1 at Detroit 4
March	1	Detroit 2 at Boston 0 [Hall] (both goals in 3rd)
	3	Detroit 2 at Toronto 2
	4	Canadiens 6 at Detroit 4
	8	Boston 2 at Detroit 4
	10	Chicago 0 at Detroit 2 [Hall] (both goals in 2nd)
	11	Detroit 3 at Chicago 2
	13	Detroit 0 at Boston 4 [Sawchuk]
	15	Detroit 2 at Rangers 2
	18	Toronto 2 at Detroit 0 [Lumley]

1956–1957

October	11	Chicago 1 at Detroit 3
	13	Detroit 4 at Toronto 1 (R. Kelly 19:35 en)
	14	Rangers 1 at Detroit 2
	18	Toronto 3 at Detroit 3
	21	Boston 3 at Detroit 3
	25	Chicago 1 at Detroit 3
	28	Canadiens 1 at Detroit 4
November	1	Detroit 3 at Canadiens 4
	3	Detroit 2 at Toronto 1
	8	Detroit 1 at Boston 3
	10	Detroit 6 at Rangers 4
	11	Detroit 3 at Chicago 1 (Lindsay 19:41 en)
	15	Toronto 2 at Detroit 4
	17	Detroit 2 at Canadiens 6
	18	Canadiens 3 at Detroit 8
	22	Toronto 2 at Detroit 2 (Barry Cullen (T) tied game at 18:45 with extra attacker)
	24	Chicago 2 at Detroit 3
	25	Detroit 3 at Chicago 3
	29	Rangers 1 at Detroit 4
December	1	Detroit 0 at Toronto 4 [Chadwick]
	2	Canadiens 0 at Detroit 1 [Hall] (Dineen 5:16 2nd)
	6	Boston 2 at Detroit 3
	8	Detroit 3 at Boston 5
	9	Detroit 2 at Rangers 4
	13	Rangers 1 at Detroit 2
	15	Chicago 1 at Detroit 5
	16	Detroit 1 at Chicago 3
	20	Detroit 1 at Boston 1
	22	Detroit 1 at Canadiens 1 (both goals in 2nd)
	23	Canadiens 3 at Detroit 3
	25	Rangers 1 at Detroit 8
	27	Detroit 5 at Boston 3
	30	Boston 4 at Detroit 2 (Mackell 19:52 en)
	31	Detroit 1 at Rangers 0 [Hall] (G. Howe 12:02 2nd)
January	2	Detroit 2 at Toronto 0 [Hall]
	5	Detroit 0 at Canadiens 1 (Beliveau 1:25 1st)
	6	Toronto 1 at Detroit 2
	10	Boston 2 at Detroit 1
	12	Rangers 5 at Detroit 4 (afternoon game)
	13	Detroit 3 at Rangers 2
	17	Detroit 2 at Boston 2
	19	Detroit 3 at Chicago 2 (afternoon game)
	20	Rangers 2 at Detroit 5
	24	Chicago 2 at Detroit 6
	26	Detroit 4 at Toronto 1
	27	Toronto 1 at Detroit 3
	31	Detroit 3 at Canadiens 5
February	2	Detroit 5 at Rangers 4 (Murphy (R) at 19:31 with extra attacker)
	3	Canadiens 3 at Detroit 3
	7	Boston 1 at Detroit 0 [Simmons] (McKenney 13:52 1st)
	9	Chicago 0 at Detroit 3 [Hall]
	10	Detroit 2 at Chicago 2
	14	Rangers 2 at Detroit 3

16 Detroit 3 at Toronto 1
17 Boston 2 at Detroit 6
21 Detroit 3 at Canadiens 3
23 Detroit 3 at Chicago 4 (afternoon game)
24 Toronto 2 at Detroit 1
28 Canadiens 3 at Detroit 0 [Plante]

March
2 Detroit 1 at Canadiens 5
3 Detroit 1 at Rangers 1 (both goals in 3rd)
7 Detroit 4 at Boston 2
9 Detroit 2 at Boston 4 (afternoon game)
10 Detroit 1 at Rangers 4
12 Detroit 4 at Chicago 3
14 Chicago 2 at Detroit 3
17 Canadiens 1 at Detroit 2
21 Boston 2 at Detroit 0 [Simmons]
23 Detroit 5 at Toronto 3 (Lindsay 19:50 en)
24 Toronto 1 at Detroit 4

1957–1958

October
10 Rangers 3 at Detroit 2
12 Detroit 5 at Toronto 3
13 Canadiens 6 at Detroit 0 [Hodge]
17 Boston 5 at Detroit 1
20 Toronto 1 at Detroit 3
24 Boston 3 at Detroit 4
27 Chicago 3 at Detroit 0 [Hall]
29 Detroit 0 at Chicago 1 [Hall] (Thomson 12:56 3rd)
30 Detroit 4 at Rangers 0 [Sawchuk]

November
2 Detroit 3 at Canadiens 6
3 Detroit 0 at Boston 4 [Simmons]
5 Rangers 1 at Detroit 1
7 Detroit 0 at Canadiens 6 [Plante]
9 Detroit 3 at Toronto 3
10 Detroit 2 at Boston 4
16 Detroit 1 at Chicago 0 [Sawchuk] (Ullman 3:03 3rd)
17 Chicago 3 at Detroit 2
20 Detroit 1 at Rangers 1 (both goals in 1st)
23 Detroit 2 at Toronto 1
24 Canadiens 3 at Detroit 3
28 Toronto 3 at Detroit 3 (Duff (T) tied game at 19:15 with extra attacker)
30 Detroit 3 at Rangers 1

December
1 Rangers 5 at Detroit 1
5 Detroit 2 at Boston 7
7 Detroit 2 at Canadiens 1
8 Canadiens 3 at Detroit 1
12 Boston 2 at Detroit 3
14 Rangers 4 at Detroit 4
15 Detroit 2 at Rangers 4
19 Toronto 2 at Detroit 3
21 Detroit 5 at Chicago 3
22 Chicago 0 at Detroit 2 [Sawchuk] (both goals in 2nd)
25 Detroit 1 at Boston 4
28 Detroit 0 at Canadiens 6 [Plante]
29 Boston 2 at Detroit 2
31 Chicago 2 at Detroit 3

January
1 Detroit 3 at Chicago 4
4 Detroit 1 at Canadiens 2 (Olmstead (C) won game at 19:34)
5 Toronto 2 at Detroit 3
9 Boston 1 at Detroit 6
11 Chicago 1 at Detroit 4
12 Detroit 3 at Rangers 2
16 Chicago 2 at Detroit 3
18 Detroit 1 at Toronto 2
19 Rangers 6 at Detroit 1
25 Detroit 3 at Boston 5 (McKenney 19:36 en)
26 Canadiens 2 at Detroit 4
30 Detroit 0 at Canadiens 7 [Plante]

February
1 Detroit 2 at Toronto 9
2 Toronto 1 at Detroit 3
6 Canadiens 1 at Detroit 1
8 Rangers 5 at Detroit 2
9 Detroit 2 at Chicago 1 (Mickoski won game at 19:48)
13 Detroit 0 at Boston 5 [Lumley]
15 Detroit 6 at Toronto 3
16 Toronto 1 at Detroit 4
22 Boston 1 at Detroit 6
23 Canadiens 3 at Detroit 3

March
1 Detroit 2 at Canadiens 2
2 Detroit 4 at Rangers 4
4 Boston 2 at Detroit 1
8 Detroit 3 at Chicago 4
9 Detroit 4 at Rangers 2
11 Rangers 2 at Detroit 2
15 Detroit 3 at Toronto 1
16 Detroit 6 at Boston 3

18 Toronto 2 at Detroit 4
20 Detroit 4 at Chicago 5
22 Chicago 6 at Detroit 4
23 Canadiens 2 at Detroit 4

1958–1959

October 11 Detroit 0 at Canadiens 2 [Plante] (both goals in 1st)
12 Rangers 0 at Detroit 3 [Sawchuk]
16 Chicago 7 at Detroit 2
18 Detroit 3 at Chicago 1
19 Toronto 1 at Detroit 3
23 Boston 1 at Detroit 3
25 Detroit 0 at Toronto 3 [Bower]
26 Canadiens 5 at Detroit 3
30 Rangers 1 at Detroit 4
November 1 Detroit 1 at Boston 3
2 Detroit 2 at Rangers 1
8 Chicago 4 at Detroit 3
9 Toronto 2 at Detroit 0 [Chadwick] (both goals in 1st)
12 Detroit 3 at Boston 1
14 Detroit 4 at Toronto 1
16 Detroit 2 at Chicago 3
18 Boston 0 at Detroit 6 [Sawchuk]
20 Detroit 4 at Canadiens 4
22 Detroit 1 at Boston 2
23 Detroit 3 at Rangers 1 (Delvecchio 19:28 en)
26 Detroit 5 at Toronto 2
27 Toronto 2 at Detroit 3 (all goals in 3rd)
29 Detroit 2 at Canadiens 6
30 Canadiens 7 at Detroit 0 [Plante]
December 4 Boston 0 at Detroit 4 [Sawchuk]
6 Detroit 4 at Chicago 3
7 Chicago 2 at Detroit 2 (Delvecchio (D) tied game at 19:50 with extra attacker)
10 Detroit 2 at Rangers 1
13 Detroit 2 at Canadiens 2 (G. Howe scores 400th goal)
14 Canadiens 6 at Detroit 1
18 Rangers 2 at Detroit 0 [Worsley]
21 Detroit 2 at Chicago 4 (Balfour 19:43 en)
25 Toronto 2 at Detroit 0 [Chadwick]
28 Boston 3 at Detroit 5
31 Chicago 4 at Detroit 2
January 3 Boston 8 at Detroit 2
4 Canadiens 2 at Detroit 2
7 Detroit 1 at Toronto 3 (Duff 19:45 en)
10 Detroit 3 at Rangers 3
11 Toronto 6 at Detroit 6
15 Detroit 0 at Boston 3 [Simmons]
17 Detroit 1 at Toronto 2
18 Rangers 4 at Detroit 2
21 Detroit 3 at Chicago 2
24 Chicago 0 at Detroit 2 [Perreault]
25 Canadiens 7 at Detroit 3
29 Detroit 4 at Canadiens 1
31 Detroit 4 at Boston 5
February 1 Detroit 4 at Rangers 5
5 Rangers 5 at Detroit 0 [Worsley]
7 Detroit 1 at Toronto 4
8 Canadiens 3 at Detroit 1
12 Rangers 0 at Detroit 1 [Sawchuk] (McIntyre 8:03 3rd)
15 Toronto 2 at Detroit 4
19 Detroit 0 at Canadiens 7 [Plante]
21 Chicago 2 at Detroit 5
22 Boston 4 at Detroit 1
25 Detroit 3 at Rangers 6
28 Detroit 4 at Toronto 2 (Kelly 19:21 en)
March 1 Detroit 1 at Chicago 3
3 Boston 2 at Detroit 2
5 Detroit 0 at Boston 3 [Lumley]
7 Detroit 2 at Canadiens 10
8 Detroit 2 at Rangers 4
10 Canadiens 5 at Detroit 5
14 Detroit 2 at Boston 4
15 Detroit 4 at Chicago 1
17 Chicago 0 at Detroit 2 [Sawchuk]
21 Rangers 5 at Detroit 2
22 Toronto 6 at Detroit 4

1959–1960

October 10 Detroit 1 at Canadiens 1
11 Rangers 2 at Detroit 4 (Ullman 19:45 en)
14 Detroit 2 at Chicago 0 [Sawchuk] (both goals in 1st)
15 Chicago 1 at Detroit 2 (all goals in 2nd)
18 Toronto 0 at Detroit 3 [Sawchuk]

22 Boston 1 at Detroit 4 (M. Pronovost 19:02 en / G. Howe 19:35 en)
25 Canadiens 2 at Detroit 1
28 Detroit 3 at Rangers 3
29 Detroit 1 at Boston 2
31 Detroit 2 at Canadiens 2

November 1 Chicago 1 at Detroit 2
5 Boston 8 at Detroit 3
7 Detroit 2 at Toronto 2
8 Rangers 3 at Detroit 3
12 Detroit 6 at Boston 5
14 Detroit 4 at Rangers 0 [Sawchuk]
15 Detroit 3 at Chicago 5
16 Chicago 2 at Detroit 3
18 Detroit 2 at Toronto 3
21 Detroit 3 at Boston 3
22 Detroit 5 at Rangers 3
26 Canadiens 4 at Detroit 2
28 Detroit 0 at Canadiens 1 [Plante] (Beliveau 19:32 2nd)
29 Toronto 4 at Detroit 1

December 5 Boston 3 at Detroit 4
6 Canadiens 4 at Detroit 4
9 Detroit 2 at Chicago 0 [Sawchuk]
12 Detroit 3 at Canadiens 2
13 Toronto 2 at Detroit 4
17 Chicago 2 at Detroit 3
19 Detroit 2 at Toronto 4
20 Detroit 4 at Boston 2
25 Rangers 5 at Detroit 2
27 Canadiens 3 at Detroit 1 (all goals in 3rd) (H. Richard 19:30 en)
31 Toronto 4 at Detroit 2

January 1 Detroit 4 at Chicago 4
3 Boston 3 at Detroit 4
6 Detroit 1 at Toronto 3
9 Detroit 3 at Rangers 3
10 Rangers 4 at Detroit 3
13 Detroit 2 at Chicago 5
16 Chicago 1 at Detroit 3
17 Toronto 3 at Detroit 4
21 Boston 2 at Detroit 5
23 Detroit 2 at Canadiens 4
24 Rangers 2 at Detroit 2
28 Canadiens 4 at Detroit 2
30 Detroit 2 at Boston 3
31 Detroit 3 at Rangers 3

February 4 Rangers 3 at Detroit 1 (Howell 19:53 en)
6 Detroit 4 at Toronto 6 (Stewart 19:27 en)
7 Chicago 0 at Detroit 5 [Riggin]
11 Detroit 2 at Boston 3
13 Detroit 1 at Toronto 7
14 Toronto 3 at Detroit 1
18 Detroit 3 at Canadiens 3 (Ullman (D) tied game at 19:59)
20 Boston 1 at Detroit 4
21 Canadiens 6 at Detroit 3
24 Detroit 2 at Rangers 2
27 Detroit 4 at Toronto 3
28 Detroit 2 at Chicago 5

March 1 Boston 2 at Detroit 3
5 Detroit 2 at Canadiens 2
6 Detroit 1 at Rangers 3
8 Canadiens 0 at Detroit 3 [Sawchuk]
12 Detroit 1 at Boston 5
13 Detroit 1 at Chicago 1
15 Chicago 3 at Detroit 2
19 Rangers 3 at Detroit 6
20 Toronto 3 at Detroit 2

1960–1961

October 5 Detroit 1 at Chicago 1
6 Chicago 4 at Detroit 2
9 Toronto 3 at Detroit 3
11 Detroit 3 at Boston 3
13 Detroit 3 at Canadiens 4
16 Canadiens 4 at Detroit 6
20 Boston 0 at Detroit 5 [Sawchuk]
22 Detroit 2 at Toronto 1
23 Toronto 3 at Detroit 1
26 Detroit 3 at Rangers 4
30 Chicago 1 at Detroit 2

November 3 Boston 5 at Detroit 8
6 Rangers 2 at Detroit 5
9 Detroit 4 at Rangers 3
10 Detroit 4 at Boston 1
12 Detroit 2 at Canadiens 4
13 Detroit 1 at Chicago 7
15 Chicago 2 at Detroit 3
16 Detroit 3 at Toronto 3
19 Detroit 4 at Boston 6
20 Detroit 4 at Rangers 3

24 Canadiens 1 at Detroit 3
26 Detroit 3 at Toronto 3
(Pronovost (D) tied game at 19:35 with extra attacker)
27 Toronto 0 at Detroit 2 [Sawchuk]
December 1 Boston 3 at Detroit 2
4 Rangers 4 at Detroit 1
7 Detroit 3 at Rangers 1
(Delvecchio 19:35 en)
10 Detroit 4 at Canadiens 6
11 Canadiens 5 at Detroit 1
15 Rangers 1 at Detroit 1
18 Detroit 3 at Chicago 2
24 Detroit 4 at Toronto 4
25 Chicago 3 at Detroit 0 [Hall]
28 Detroit 4 at Rangers 3
29 Detroit 1 at Canadiens 1
31 Chicago 3 at Detroit 0 [Hall]
January 1 Detroit 0 at Chicago 3 [Hall]
4 Detroit 4 at Toronto 6
5 Toronto 4 at Detroit 1
8 Boston 3 at Detroit 5
(Johnson 19:34 en)
11 Detroit 2 at Chicago 2
14 Rangers 2 at Detroit 2
15 Canadiens 4 at Detroit 4
(Turner (C) tied game at 19:48)
19 Detroit 2 at Boston 4
21 Detroit 3 at Canadiens 2
22 Rangers 5 at Detroit 3
26 Chicago 2 at Detroit 2
28 Detroit 3 at Canadiens 3
(G. Howe tied game at 19:35)
29 Detroit 3 at Boston 1
February 2 Toronto 5 at Detroit 0 [Bower]
4 Detroit 2 at Toronto 4
5 Canadiens 2 at Detroit 7
8 Detroit 2 at Chicago 5
9 Rangers 2 at Detroit 4
12 Toronto 4 at Detroit 2
(Keon 18:46 en)
18 Boston 1 at Detroit 5
19 Canadiens 4 at Detroit 2
(Marshall 19:32 en)
23 Boston 3 at Detroit 3
25 Detroit 1 at Toronto 3
(all goals in 2nd)
26 Toronto 2 at Detroit 2
28 Chicago 1 at Detroit 3
March 2 Detroit 2 at Boston 4
4 Detroit 4 at Canadiens 6
5 Detroit 3 at Rangers 8
7 Boston 1 at Detroit 3
9 Detroit 5 at Boston 2
12 Detroit 3 at Rangers 7
14 Rangers 2 at Detroit 5
15 Detroit 2 at Chicago 2
19 Canadiens 2 at Detroit 0 [Plante]
(Provost 19:59 en)

1961–1962

October 12 Toronto 4 at Detroit 2
14 Chicago 3 at Detroit 3
15 Detroit 2 at Chicago 2
19 Boston 3 at Detroit 7
21 Rangers 4 at Detroit 4
22 Detroit 5 at Rangers 4
26 Detroit 0 at Boston 4 [Head]
28 Detroit 5 at Canadiens 7
29 Canadiens 6 at Detroit 3
November 2 Rangers 0 at Detroit 1 [Sawchuk]
(G. Howe 4:48 2nd)
5 Toronto 3 at Detroit 2
9 Boston 1 at Detroit 2
(Ullman won game at 19:06)
11 Detroit 1 at Toronto 5
12 Canadiens 0 at Detroit 3 [Sawchuk]
15 Detroit 0 at Chicago 2 [Hall]
18 Detroit 1 at Toronto 6
19 Detroit 6 at Boston 2
22 Detroit 0 at Rangers 4 [Worsley]
23 Detroit 3 at Canadiens 5
(Provost 19:27 en)
26 Detroit 1 at Chicago 4
30 Boston 1 at Detroit 3
December 2 Detroit 2 at Canadiens 3
3 Toronto 1 at Detroit 3
(Ullman 19:48 en)
7 Rangers 3 at Detroit 3
9 Chicago 0 at Detroit 3 [Sawchuk]
10 Detroit 3 at Chicago 2
14 Boston 0 at Detroit 5 [Sawchuk]
17 Canadiens 1 at Detroit 3
20 Detroit 1 at Rangers 6
21 Detroit 2 at Boston 4
23 Detroit 1 at Canadiens 6
25 Rangers 6 at Detroit 4
28 Chicago 2 at Detroit 2

30 Detroit 4 at Toronto 6
31 Toronto 2 at Detroit 4
January 4 Chicago 1 at Detroit 1 (both goals in 2nd)
6 Boston 2 at Detroit 6
7 Canadiens 2 at Detroit 2
13 Detroit 3 at Toronto 4
14 Rangers 1 at Detroit 2 (all goals in 3rd)
18 Detroit 3 at Boston 5
20 Detroit 2 at Canadiens 2
21 Canadiens 5 at Detroit 3
24 Detroit 3 at Rangers 0 [Sawchuk]
27 Detroit 2 at Toronto 4
28 Toronto 2 at Detroit 2
31 Detroit 1 at Chicago 4
February 1 Chicago 7 at Detroit 4
3 Detroit 1 at Canadiens 8
4 Boston 0 at Detroit 6 [Bassen]
7 Detroit 2 at Rangers 2
10 Detroit 2 at Boston 2
11 Toronto 0 at Detroit 5 [Bassen]
15 Rangers 3 at Detroit 4
18 Canadiens 2 at Detroit 4
21 Detroit 4 at Chicago 6
24 Chicago 6 at Detroit 1
25 Toronto 8 at Detroit 2
March 3 Detroit 2 at Canadiens 2
4 Detroit 4 at Rangers 2
6 Rangers 5 at Detroit 4
8 Detroit 3 at Boston 0 [Bassen]
10 Detroit 0 at Toronto 2 [Simmons]
11 Detroit 2 at Boston 2 (all goals in 1st)
14 Detroit 2 at Rangers 3
15 Boston 4 at Detroit 0 [Gamble]
18 Chicago 1 at Detroit 4
20 Detroit 0 at Chicago 3 [Hall]
24 Detroit 2 at Toronto 2
25 Canadiens 5 at Detroit 2

1962–1963

October 11 Detroit 2 at Rangers 1
13 Detroit 0 at Chicago 0 [Sawchuk (D) / Hall (C)]
14 Canadiens 1 at Detroit 3
18 Boston 3 at Detroit 5
21 Chicago 1 at Detroit 3
25 Detroit 3 at Boston 3 (Spencer (B) tied game at 19:30 with extra attacker)
28 Toronto 0 at Detroit 2 [Sawchuk] (G. Howe 19:27 en)
November 1 Rangers 0 at Detroit 4 [Sawchuk]
3 Detroit 7 at Toronto 3
4 Chicago 1 at Detroit 3
8 Detroit 1 at Canadiens 4
10 Detroit 3 at Boston 3
11 Detroit 3 at Rangers 2
14 Detroit 2 at Chicago 4
17 Detroit 2 at Toronto 3
18 Detroit 3 at Boston 1
22 Canadiens 3 at Detroit 0 [Plante]
24 Detroit 1 at Chicago 1 (both goals in 2nd)
25 Chicago 2 at Detroit 3
29 Rangers 5 at Detroit 0 [Worsley]
December 2 Toronto 3 at Detroit 1 (Pulford 19:54 en)
5 Detroit 3 at Rangers 3
6 Boston 3 at Detroit 5
8 Detroit 1 at Canadiens 2
9 Toronto 3 at Detroit 4
13 Rangers 2 at Detroit 3 (all goals in 1st)
15 Chicago 1 at Detroit 3 (Ullman 18:56 en)
16 Detroit 2 at Rangers 5
20 Boston 5 at Detroit 3 (Burns 19:38 en)
23 Canadiens 2 at Detroit 2
25 Toronto 1 at Detroit 2
26 Detroit 4 at Toronto 5
29 Detroit 1 at Canadiens 5
31 Rangers 1 at Detroit 1
January 1 Detroit 2 at Chicago 4
6 Boston 5 at Detroit 5
10 Detroit 3 at Canadiens 2
12 Detroit 1 at Toronto 2
13 Rangers 2 at Detroit 4
17 Boston 3 at Detroit 5 (G. Howe 19:56 en)
19 Detroit 1 at Canadiens 5
20 Toronto 2 at Detroit 2
24 Canadiens 1 at Detroit 1
26 Chicago 3 at Detroit 0 [Hall] (all goals in 2nd) (afternoon game)

	27	Detroit 5 at Boston 3 (Ullman 19:59 en)
	30	Detroit 6 at Rangers 1
February	2	Detroit 4 at Boston 4
	3	Canadiens 6 at Detroit 2
	6	Detroit 3 at Chicago 3
	7	Boston 3 at Detroit 3
	10	Toronto 1 at Detroit 2
	13	Detroit 2 at Toronto 6
	16	Boston 1 at Detroit 3
	17	Canadiens 6 at Detroit 1
	21	Chicago 5 at Detroit 3 (Hull 19:19 en)
	23	Detroit 2 at Chicago 3
	24	Detroit 3 at Rangers 2
	26	Rangers 4 at Detroit 3
	28	Detroit 3 at Boston 5
March	2	Detroit 7 at Canadiens 1
	3	Detroit 3 at Rangers 2
	5	Canadiens 4 at Detroit 3
	9	Detroit 3 at Toronto 5
	10	Detroit 4 at Boston 3
	14	Rangers 4 at Detroit 9
	16	Detroit 3 at Canadiens 5
	17	Chicago 2 at Detroit 4 (Pronovost 19:45 en)
	19	Detroit 5 at Chicago 1
	23	Detroit 2 at Toronto 1
	24	Toronto 2 at Detroit 3

1963–1964

October	10	Chicago 3 at Detroit 5 (Delvecchio 19:54 en)
	13	Boston 0 at Detroit 3 [Sawchuk]
	16	Detroit 0 at Rangers 3 [Plante]
	19	Detroit 1 at Toronto 2
	20	Toronto 2 at Detroit 3
	24	Chicago 2 at Detroit 2
	27	Canadiens 6 at Detroit 4
	29	Detroit 1 at Chicago 5
	31	Rangers 1 at Detroit 4
November	2	Detroit 1 at Canadiens 5
	3	Detroit 1 at Boston 4
	7	Rangers 0 at Detroit 1 [Sawchuk] (P. MacDonald 12:38 3rd)
	10	Canadiens 0 at Detroit 3 [Sawchuk] (all goals in 2nd)
	16	Detroit 1 at Boston 1
	17	Detroit 2 at Rangers 5
	20	Detroit 2 at Chicago 5
	24	Detroit at Boston (postponed to Jan. 7)
	27	Detroit 2 at Rangers 3
	28	Canadiens 7 at Detroit 3 (Gray replaced Sawchuk at start of 2nd)
	30	Detroit 1 at Toronto 1
December	1	Toronto 4 at Detroit 1
	5	Boston 2 at Detroit 4
	7	Detroit 2 at Canadiens 5
	8	Toronto 5 at Detroit 3
	11	Detroit 3 at Toronto 1
	14	Chicago 4 at Detroit 5
	15	Detroit 4 at Chicago 4
	18	Detroit 1 at Rangers 1 (both goals in 2nd)
	19	Boston 0 at Detroit 3 [Crozier]
	21	Detroit 0 at Toronto 2 [Bower] (both goals in 1st)
	22	Canadiens 6 at Detroit 1
	25	Rangers 3 at Detroit 4
	28	Detroit 1 at Canadiens 1
	29	Boston 1 at Detroit 2 (G. Howe scored 600th goal)
	31	Toronto 5 at Detroit 4
January	4	Detroit 2 at Rangers 5
	5	Canadiens 3 at Detroit 3
	7	Detroit 5 at Boston 0 [Crozier]
	9	Chicago 3 at Detroit 5
	11	Detroit 3 at Chicago 6
	12	Rangers 3 at Detroit 5
	16	Detroit 1 at Boston 5
	18	Detroit 2 at Canadiens 0 [Sawchuk]
	19	Rangers 3 at Detroit 1
	25	Chicago 3 at Detroit 5 (afternoon game)
	26	Detroit 2 at Rangers 3
	29	Detroit 2 at Chicago 2
February	1	Detroit 3 at Canadiens 9
	2	Toronto 2 at Detroit 2
	5	Detroit 2 at Chicago 4 (Wharram 19:27 en)
	6	Chicago 0 at Detroit 4 [Sawchuk]
	8	Detroit 3 at Boston 2 (afternoon game)
	9	Rangers 2 at Detroit 4 (MacGregor 19:18 en)
	13	Boston 1 at Detroit 4

15 Detroit 4 at Canadiens 1
16 Canadiens 5 at Detroit 2 (Provost 19:23 en)
19 Detroit 1 at Toronto 1
22 Boston 2 at Detroit 3 (afternoon game)
23 Canadiens 2 at Detroit 3
27 Detroit 2 at Chicago 4
29 Detroit 1 at Boston 2

March 1 Detroit 2 at Rangers 2
3 Toronto 2 at Detroit 3
5 Detroit 7 at Canadiens 5
7 Detroit 2 at Toronto 4
8 Detroit 5 at Boston 3
12 Boston 1 at Detroit 2
15 Chicago 3 at Detroit 5
19 Rangers 3 at Detroit 9
21 Detroit 3 at Toronto 5
22 Toronto 4 at Detroit 1

1964–1965

October 15 Toronto 5 at Detroit 3
17 Detroit 2 at Chicago 4
18 Chicago 2 at Detroit 3
21 Detroit 1 at Rangers 0 [Crozier] (Ullman 8:30 3rd)
24 Detroit 1 at Canadiens 1 (both goals in 3rd)
25 Detroit 4 at Boston 0 [Crozier]
29 Boston 0 at Detroit 2 [Crozier]

November 1 Toronto 2 at Detroit 4
5 Rangers 1 at Detroit 3
8 Canadiens 1 at Detroit 2
10 Detroit 3 at Boston 3 (Leiter (B) tied game at 19:23)
11 Detroit 1 at Toronto 3 (Pulford 19:51 en)
14 Detroit 2 at Canadiens 4
15 Detroit 6 at Rangers 2
17 Rangers 2 at Detroit 1
18 Detroit 1 at Chicago 3 (Hull 19:54 en)
21 Detroit 3 at Boston 1
22 Detroit 3 at Rangers 3
26 Canadiens 1 at Detroit 3
29 Toronto 1 at Detroit 1

December 3 Boston 2 at Detroit 4
5 Detroit 2 at Toronto 10
6 Canadiens 1 at Detroit 4
12 Chicago 3 at Detroit 2
13 Detroit 0 at Chicago 5 [DeJordy]
16 Detroit 7 at Rangers 3
17 Boston 5 at Detroit 3
20 Toronto 1 at Detroit 3
25 Canadiens 2 at Detroit 2
26 Detroit 3 at Canadiens 6 (Crozier replaced Wetzel at 10:40 of 2nd)
27 Rangers 1 at Detroit 3
31 Chicago 1 at Detroit 1 (both goals in 1st)

January 2 Detroit 1 at Toronto 3
3 Boston 1 at Detroit 8
6 Detroit 5 at Canadiens 4
7 Detroit 2 at Boston 5
9 Chicago 7 at Detroit 4 (afternoon game)
10 Detroit 2 at Chicago 3
16 Detroit 4 at Toronto 2
17 Rangers 4 at Detroit 2
21 Boston 0 at Detroit 3 [Crozier]
24 Toronto 1 at Detroit 4
30 Chicago 1 at Detroit 3 (G. Howe 19:50 en)
31 Detroit 4 at Rangers 1

February 4 Detroit 1 at Boston 3
6 Detroit 3 at Canadiens 1
7 Canadiens 0 at Detroit 6 [Crozier]
10 Detroit 2 at Chicago 5
11 Chicago 3 at Detroit 5
13 Detroit 1 at Toronto 2
14 Rangers 2 at Detroit 6
17 Detroit 0 at Canadiens 2 [Hodge]
20 Rangers 2 at Detroit 3 (afternoon game)
21 Toronto 2 at Detroit 3
24 Detroit 2 at Chicago 3
27 Boston 1 at Detroit 4 (afternoon game)
28 Canadiens 1 at Detroit 5

March 3 Detroit 2 at Chicago 0 [Crozier] (Ullman 19:54 en)
6 Detroit 4 at Boston 3
7 Detroit 6 at Rangers 5
9 Canadiens 2 at Detroit 3 (Delvecchio won game at 19:55)
10 Detroit 4 at Toronto 2
13 Detroit 2 at Canadiens 4
14 Detroit 5 at Boston 2

18 Boston 3 at Detroit 10 (ten different Detroit scorers)
19 Detroit 6 at Rangers 6
21 Chicago 1 at Detroit 5
25 Rangers 4 at Detroit 7
27 Detroit 4 at Toronto 1
28 Toronto 4 at Detroit 0 [Bower] (Keon 19:57 en)

1965–1966

October
23 Detroit 1 at Canadiens 8
24 Toronto 0 at Detroit 3 [Crozier]
28 Chicago 5 at Detroit 1
30 Detroit 3 at Toronto 4
31 Canadiens 2 at Detroit 2

November
4 Boston 1 at Detroit 8
7 Detroit 2 at Rangers 3
10 Detroit 2 at Chicago 5
11 Rangers 3 at Detroit 3
14 Canadiens 2 at Detroit 2
20 Detroit 4 at Boston 2
21 Detroit 3 at Rangers 3
23 Chicago 3 at Detroit 2
25 Detroit 1 at Chicago 3 (Mikita 19:46 en)
27 Detroit 2 at Canadiens 3
28 Detroit 5 at Boston 3

December
2 Boston 2 at Detroit 10
4 Detroit 5 at Toronto 3 (Henderson 19:58 en)
5 Toronto 1 at Detroit 5
9 Rangers 3 at Detroit 7
11 Detroit 4 at Rangers 2 (afternoon game)
12 Detroit 5 at Boston 3
15 Detroit 3 at Toronto 5 (Shack 19:44 en)
16 Boston 0 at Detroit 2 [Crozier]
18 Chicago 1 at Detroit 3
19 Detroit 4 at Chicago 5 (Stapleton (C) won game at 19:50)
23 Rangers 2 at Detroit 4
25 Detroit 3 at Canadiens 4
26 Canadiens 0 at Detroit 1 [Crozier] (Delvecchio 19:04 3rd)
28 Detroit 1 at Boston 0 [Crozier] (Henderson 4:47 2nd)
31 Chicago 4 at Detroit 1

January
2 Toronto 0 at Detroit 4 [Crozier]
6 Boston 3 at Detroit 5
8 Detroit 3 at Toronto 1
9 Canadiens 2 at Detroit 4
15 Rangers 4 at Detroit 4 (afternoon game)
16 Toronto 0 at Detroit 4 [Crozier]
20 Canadiens 2 at Detroit 5
22 Detroit 3 at Canadiens 0 [Crozier]
23 Rangers 1 at Detroit 5
26 Detroit 3 at Rangers 4
29 Detroit 4 at Chicago 4 (Delvecchio (D) tied game at 19:58)
30 Chicago 5 at Detroit 1

February
3 Detroit 4 at Boston 2
5 Detroit 2 at Canadiens 2
6 Boston 3 at Detroit 3
9 Detroit 1 at Chicago 2
10 Rangers 2 at Detroit 6
12 Detroit 3 at Toronto 3 (Henderson (D) tied game at 19:59 with extra attacker)
13 Canadiens 4 at Detroit 3
16 Detroit 4 at Boston 5
19 Boston 5 at Detroit 1
20 Toronto 1 at Detroit 4
23 Detroit 0 at Rangers 5 [Maniago]
26 Chicago 4 at Detroit 1 (afternoon game)
27 Canadiens 5 at Detroit 3 (G. Tremblay 19:58 en)

March
2 Detroit 4 at Chicago 5
5 Detroit 2 at Canadiens 7
6 Detroit 1 at Rangers 1
9 Detroit 0 at Toronto 1 [Gamble] (Mahovlich 17:24 1st)
12 Detroit 1 at Canadiens 4
13 Detroit 8 at Boston 4
16 Detroit 1 at Chicago 4
17 Boston 2 at Detroit 4 (Delvecchio 19:43 en)
20 Toronto 1 at Detroit 6
23 Detroit 2 at Rangers 1
26 Detroit 1 at Toronto 3
27 Chicago 1 at Detroit 1 (both goals in 2nd)
31 Rangers 3 at Detroit 5

April
3 Toronto 3 at Detroit 3

1966–1967

October 19 Detroit 2 at Boston 6
22 Chicago 7 at Detroit 4
23 Detroit 1 at Chicago 4
26 Detroit 2 at Toronto 3
27 Rangers 3 at Detroit 5
30 Boston 1 at Detroit 8

November 3 Toronto 2 at Detroit 2
5 Detroit 1 at Canadiens 3
6 Canadiens 0 at Detroit 6 [Crozier]
10 Chicago 0 at Detroit 3 [Crozier]
12 Toronto 3 at Detroit 3
13 Detroit 2 at Rangers 5
19 Detroit 2 at Chicago 7
20 Detroit 2 at Boston 5
22 Canadiens 3 at Detroit 0 [Hodge]
24 Detroit 3 at Boston 8
26 Detroit 1 at Canadiens 3

December 1 Boston 1 at Detroit 4
3 Detroit 2 at Toronto 5
4 Detroit 1 at Chicago 4
8 Rangers 4 at Detroit 2
10 Detroit 1 at Canadiens 5
11 Toronto 1 at Detroit 4 (G. Howe 19:48 en)
14 Detroit 1 at Rangers 4
15 Boston 0 at Detroit 4 [Crozier]
18 Rangers 0 at Detroit 5 [Crozier]
21 Detroit 4 at Chicago 6
25 Canadiens 4 at Detroit 0 [Hodge]
27 Detroit 4 at Boston 4
29 Detroit 2 at Rangers 4
31 Boston 1 at Detroit 3

January 1 Canadiens 1 at Detroit 4
5 Chicago 4 at Detroit 6
7 Detroit 3 at Canadiens 4
8 Toronto 1 at Detroit 3 (all goals in 3rd)
11 Detroit 1 at Chicago 6
12 Chicago 1 at Detroit 4
14 Detroit 2 at Toronto 5
15 Rangers 2 at Detroit 0 [Giacomin] (Howell 19:54 en)
19 Toronto 2 at Detroit 6
21 Detroit 5 at Toronto 4
22 Rangers 2 at Detroit 7
26 Chicago 4 at Detroit 3
29 Detroit 4 at Rangers 2

February 2 Boston 3 at Detroit 4
5 Canadiens 1 at Detroit 6
8 Detroit 5 at Toronto 2
11 Rangers 3 at Detroit 6 (afternoon game)
12 Detroit 2 at Chicago 3 (afternoon game)
14 Detroit 3 at Boston 6
16 Chicago 5 at Detroit 1
18 Detroit 2 at Canadiens 3
19 Canadiens 1 at Detroit 3 (afternoon game) (Delvecchio 19:53 en)
22 Detroit 0 at Rangers 1 [Giacomin] (Nevin 1:10 1st)
23 Toronto 4 at Detroit 2
25 Detroit 0 at Toronto 4 [Sawchuk]
26 Boston 3 at Detroit 3 (Stewart (B) tied game at 19:51 with extra attacker) (afternoon game)

March 4 Detroit 2 at Canadiens 6
5 Detroit 5 at Boston 3 (Prentice 19:12 en)
8 Detroit 3 at Rangers 1
12 Detroit 3 at Boston 7
15 Detroit 4 at Toronto 2
18 Boston 5 at Detroit 3 (afternoon game)
19 Toronto 6 at Detroit 5 (afternoon game)
23 Rangers 1 at Detroit 4
25 Detroit 1 at Canadiens 4
26 Chicago 2 at Detroit 4
28 Detroit 2 at Chicago 7
29 Detroit 5 at Rangers 10

April 2 Canadiens 4 at Detroit 2

1967–1968

October 11 Detroit 4 at Boston 4
14 Detroit 2 at Canadiens 6
15 Rangers 2 at Detroit 3
18 Detroit 3 at Toronto 2
19 Boston 6 at Detroit 3
22 St. Louis 0 at Detroit 1 [Crozier] (Henderson 15:01 3rd)
26 Oakland 2 at Detroit 8
28 Detroit 3 at Philadelphia 1
29 Chicago 1 at Detroit 5

November 2 Toronto 9 at Detroit 3
4 Detroit 2 at St. Louis 3
5 Los Angeles 6 at Detroit 4
9 Pittsburgh 1 at Detroit 5
12 Canadiens 1 at Detroit 3
16 Detroit 1 at Oakland 1 (both goals in 1st)
17 Detroit 4 at Los Angeles 1
19 Detroit 2 at Chicago 2
22 Detroit 2 at Philadelphia 4
25 Detroit 2 at Toronto 3
26 Detroit 5 at Boston 7
29 Detroit 3 at Rangers 1
30 Toronto 3 at Detroit 3

December 3 Pittsburgh 1 at Detroit 6
6 Detroit 3 at Rangers 3
7 Detroit 2 at Canadiens 2
9 Rangers 2 at Detroit 3
14 Chicago 3 at Detroit 1
16 Detroit 3 at Canadiens 4
17 Canadiens 6 at Detroit 8
20 Detroit 0 at Rangers 2 [Giacomin] (both goals in 3rd) (Goyette 19:48 en)
23 Detroit 3 at Toronto 5
25 Toronto 3 at Detroit 1
28 Philadelphia 3 at Detroit 5
30 Detroit 5 at Pittsburgh 2
31 Boston 4 at Detroit 6 (Ullman 19:44 en)

January 4 Oakland 3 at Detroit 9
6 Detroit 2 at Chicago 6
7 Canadiens 4 at Detroit 3
10 Detroit 1 at Toronto 2
11 Detroit 4 at Boston 5
13 Chicago 4 at Detroit 4
17 Detroit 1 at Canadiens 6
20 Detroit 5 at Pittsburgh 8
21 Toronto 2 at Detroit 0 [Gamble] (both goals in 2nd)
24 Detroit 4 at Chicago 2
25 St. Louis 4 at Detroit 4
27 Philadelphia 2 at Detroit 3 (afternoon game)
28 Detroit 1 at Minnesota 2 (afternoon game)

February 1 Los Angeles 8 at Detroit 6 (Lemieux 19:48 en)
3 Minnesota 1 at Detroit 8
4 Detroit 4 at Boston 5
8 Rangers 3 at Detroit 2
10 Boston 1 at Detroit 1 (afternoon game) (both goals in 2nd)
11 Detroit 3 at Rangers 3
15 Canadiens 2 at Detroit 0 [Vachon] (Provost 19:43 en)
17 Chicago 7 at Detroit 4
18 Detroit 1 at Chicago 7 (afternoon game)
22 Boston 3 at Detroit 2
24 Minnesota 1 at Detroit 3 (afternoon game)
29 Rangers 4 at Detroit 2

March 3 Canadiens 2 at Detroit 5
6 Detroit 1 at Rangers 6
9 Detroit 5 at Toronto 7
10 Detroit 7 at Boston 5 (F. Mahovlich 19:34 en)
12 Detroit 2 at Los Angeles 2
13 Detroit 4 at Oakland 2
16 Detroit 6 at St. Louis 3
17 Detroit 1 at Minnesota 5 (afternoon game)
21 Toronto 5 at Detroit 2
23 Detroit 4 at Canadiens 7
24 Boston 3 at Detroit 5
28 Chicago 1 at Detroit 3
30 Rangers 3 at Detroit 1
31 Detroit 5 at Chicago 5

1968–1969

October 11 Detroit 2 at Boston 4 (D. Smith 19:49 en)
13 Toronto 2 at Detroit 1
17 Rangers 2 at Detroit 7
20 Canadiens 4 at Detroit 2
27 Chicago 3 at Detroit 4
31 Boston 5 at Detroit 7 (F. Mahovlich 19:22 en)

November 2 Detroit 1 at Canadiens 2
3 St. Louis 4 at Detroit 4
6 Detroit 6 at Chicago 5
7 Minnesota 2 at Detroit 5
9 Detroit 4 at Minnesota 6
10 Canadiens 4 at Detroit 4 (Prentice (D) tied game at 19:16)
13 Detroit 1 at Oakland 2
14 Detroit 5 at Los Angeles 2

16 Detroit 1 at St. Louis 1 (Delvecchio tied game at 19:38 with extra attacker)
20 Detroit 2 at Canadiens 3
23 Detroit 5 at Toronto 2
27 Detroit 5 at Philadelphia 2
28 St. Louis 3 at Detroit 1

December
1 Philadelphia 3 at Detroit 3
4 Detroit 7 at Pittsburgh 2 (G. Howe scored 700th goal)
5 Rangers 2 at Detroit 4
7 Detroit 1 at Boston 4
8 Detroit 5 at Rangers 2
11 Detroit 3 at Los Angeles 6
12 Detroit 0 at Oakland 6 [Smith]
14 Oakland 1 at Detroit 3 (afternoon game)
15 Minnesota 2 at Detroit 5
19 Chicago 2 at Detroit 0 [DeJordy] (both goals in 3rd)
21 Detroit 3 at Toronto 8
22 Toronto 2 at Detroit 3
25 Detroit 3 at Pittsburgh 6
27 Philadelphia 3 at Detroit 3
29 Boston 3 at Detroit 3
31 Minnesota 3 at Detroit 6

January
1 Detroit 1 at Chicago 4
4 Detroit 1 at St. Louis 3
5 Pittsburgh 1 at Detroit 2
9 Los Angeles 2 at Detroit 6
11 Rangers 2 at Detroit 3
12 Oakland 1 at Detroit 5
15 Detroit 4 at Canadiens 0 [Edwards]
16 Pittsburgh 2 at Detroit 3
18 Detroit 1 at Toronto 1 (both goals in 2nd)
19 Detroit 1 at Philadelphia 3
23 Boston 2 at Detroit 2
25 Oakland 3 at Detroit 5 (afternoon game) (MacGregor 19:45 en)
26 Toronto 2 at Detroit 3
29 Detroit 0 at Rangers 2 [Giacomin] (both goals in 1st)

February
1 St. Louis 2 at Detroit 0 [Plante] (Roberts 19:38 en)
2 Detroit 2 at Boston 4
4 Detroit 2 at Philadelphia 0 [Edwards] (Delvecchio 19:48 en)
6 Chicago 1 at Detroit 6
8 Detroit 3 at Chicago 1 (rescheduled from March 9)
9 Los Angeles 0 at Detroit 5 [Edwards] (afternoon game)
13 Canadiens 3 at Detroit 1
15 Detroit 2 at Minnesota 6
16 Los Angeles 3 at Detroit 6
19 Detroit 1 at Rangers 1
20 Pittsburgh 0 at Detroit 3 [Edwards]
22 Detroit 2 at Pittsburgh 3
23 Philadelphia 1 at Detroit 9
26 Detroit 2 at Canadiens 7

March
1 Detroit 4 at Minnesota 2
2 Canadiens 2 at Detroit 4
5 Detroit 2 at Boston 2
6 Rangers 4 at Detroit 1
8 Boston 4 at Detroit 7
9 Detroit at Chicago (moved up to February 8)
15 Detroit 2 at St. Louis 3
16 Detroit 4 at Rangers 6 (Nevin 19:09 en)
19 Detroit 4 at Oakland 4
20 Detroit 2 at Los Angeles 4
22 Detroit 1 at Toronto 3
27 Toronto 4 at Detroit 2
29 Chicago 1 at Detroit 1 (both goals in 2nd)
30 Detroit 5 at Chicago 9

1969–1970

October
11 Toronto 2 at Detroit 3
15 Detroit 4 at Chicago 1
16 Minnesota 3 at Detroit 2
19 St. Louis 2 at Detroit 4 (G. Howe 19:19 en)
23 Detroit 2 at Philadelphia 2
25 Rangers 4 at Detroit 1
29 Detroit 5 at Los Angeles 2
31 Detroit 3 at Oakland 1

November
2 Pittsburgh 3 at Detroit 4
5 Detroit 4 at Pittsburgh 2
6 St. Louis 5 at Detroit 2
8 Boston 2 at Detroit 3
12 Detroit 2 at Rangers 4
13 Detroit 1 at Boston 3
15 Detroit 2 at Minnesota 2
19 Detroit 5 at Canadiens 5

22 Detroit 0 at Toronto 4 [Gamble]
26 Detroit 1 at Philadelphia 1 (both goals in 1st)
27 Los Angeles 1 at Detroit 5
29 Chicago 4 at Detroit 5
30 Oakland 1 at Detroit 0 [Smith] (Jarrett 14:44 3rd)

December 3 Detroit 1 at Pittsburgh 2
4 Boston 4 at Detroit 4
6 Detroit 5 at St. Louis 1
7 Detroit 1 at Chicago 5
11 Minnesota 2 at Detroit 2
13 Detroit 3 at Toronto 1
14 Canadiens 2 at Detroit 5
16 Detroit 4 at St. Louis 6
20 Detroit 3 at Canadiens 2
21 Toronto 3 at Detroit 0 [Gamble]
26 Canadiens 3 at Detroit 3
28 Oakland 3 at Detroit 5
31 Boston 1 at Detroit 5

January 3 Detroit 6 at Philadelphia 1
4 Chicago 0 at Detroit 4 [Edwards]
7 Detroit 0 at Chicago 7 [Esposito]
10 Detroit 5 at Pittsburgh 3
17 Philadelphia 3 at Detroit 5 (afternoon game) (F. Mahovlich 19:54 en)
18 Los Angeles 1 at Detroit 3 (afternoon game)
22 Chicago 4 at Detroit 3
24 Detroit 5 at St. Louis 2
25 Canadiens 4 at Detroit 1
29 Philadelphia 3 at Detroit 4
31 Detroit 2 at Los Angeles 1

February 1 Detroit 3 at Oakland 2 (afternoon game)
4 Detroit 1 at Rangers 5
5 Toronto 1 at Detroit 4
7 Detroit 2 at Boston 2
8 Philadelphia 5 at Detroit 3 (afternoon game)
12 St. Louis 2 at Detroit 5
14 Detroit 5 at Canadiens 2
15 Pittsburgh 4 at Detroit 2
18 Detroit 1 at Minnesota 1
19 Rangers 3 at Detroit 3
21 Detroit 7 at Toronto 5
22 Canadiens 1 at Detroit 0 [Vachon] (Cournoyer 13:23 2nd)
26 Oakland 1 at Detroit 7
28 Rangers 3 at Detroit 3 (MacGregor (D) tied game at 19:36)

March 4 Detroit 2 at Rangers 0 [Edwards]
5 Pittsburgh 3 at Detroit 5
7 Detroit 4 at Canadiens 2 (G. Howe 19:57 en)
8 Minnesota 2 at Detroit 2
11 Detroit 3 at Toronto 1
15 Detroit 5 at Boston 5
17 Los Angeles 2 at Detroit 3
18 Detroit 6 at Minnesota 2
20 Detroit 2 at Oakland 3
21 Detroit 4 at Los Angeles 1
26 Chicago 1 at Detroit 0 [Esposito] (Martin 10:15 3rd)
28 Detroit 5 at Boston 5 (afternoon game)
29 Boston 2 at Detroit 2 (afternoon game)

April 1 Detroit 5 at Chicago 2
2 Toronto 2 at Detroit 4
4 Rangers 2 at Detroit 6 (Stemkowski 19:10 en)
5 Detroit 5 at Rangers 9 (G. Howe 17:29 en / Libett 19:05 en) (afternoon game)

1970–1971

October 10 California 3 at Detroit 5
11 Detroit 3 at Boston 7
13 Detroit 3 at Canadiens 4
15 Chicago 2 at Detroit 1
17 Detroit 3 at Minnesota 2
18 Minnesota 2 at Detroit 1
23 Detroit 3 at Buffalo 4
25 Canadiens 3 at Detroit 3
28 Detroit 1 at Rangers 4
29 Boston 3 at Detroit 5

November 1 Toronto 5 at Detroit 4
4 Detroit 2 at Chicago 4
5 Philadelphia 1 at Detroit 3
8 Pittsburgh 3 at Detroit 3
12 Detroit 1 at St. Louis 2
15 Detroit 4 at Los Angeles 4 (Bergman (D) tied game at 19:55)
17 Detroit 5 at Vancouver 2
21 Detroit 1 at Pittsburgh 6

22 Detroit 4 at Philadelphia 2
(F. Mahovlich 19:21 en)
26 Vancouver 2 at Detroit 4
28 Detroit 4 at Toronto 9
29 Canadiens 3 at Detroit 5

December
3 Los Angeles 4 at Detroit 4
5 Detroit 0 at St. Louis 3 [Wakely]
6 St. Louis 4 at Detroit 2
10 Philadelphia 1 at Detroit 3
(Webster 19:54 en)
12 Buffalo 3 at Detroit 5
13 Detroit 2 at Boston 6
16 Detroit 2 at California 4
(Roberts 19:47 en)
19 Detroit 1 at Pittsburgh 9
20 California 7 at Detroit 3
23 Boston 2 at Detroit 1
26 Rangers 4 at Detroit 7
(Connelly 19:36 en)
27 Detroit 2 at Buffalo 5
31 Chicago 8 at Detroit 3

January
2 Detroit 0 at Toronto 13
[Plante & Gamble share shutout]
3 California 2 at Detroit 3
7 Detroit 4 at Buffalo 7
9 Buffalo 2 at Detroit 3
10 Toronto 3 at Detroit 2
14 Pittsburgh 2 at Detroit 2
16 Philadelphia 4 at Detroit 2
17 Minnesota 2 at Detroit 0 [Edwards]
21 Detroit 0 at Chicago 2 [Esposito]
23 Detroit 2 at Canadiens 6
24 Vancouver 3 at Detroit 7
28 St. Louis 1 at Detroit 1
30 Los Angeles 3 at Detroit 3
31 Detroit 1 at Philadelphia 3
(all goals in 3rd)
(Dornhoefer 19:59 en)

February
3 Detroit 4 at Minnesota 4
(Libett (D) tied game at 19:31)
4 Rangers 1 at Detroit 0 [Villemure]
(Gilbert 3:47 2nd)
7 Detroit 5 at California 2
(afternoon game)
10 Detroit 2 at Los Angeles 5
(Flett 19:30 en)
12 Detroit 3 at Vancouver 5
(Paiement 19:48 en)
14 Los Angeles 0 at Detroit 4
[Rutherford]
18 Minnesota 3 at Detroit 5
20 Buffalo 5 at Detroit 6
21 Detroit 1 at Rangers 4
(afternoon game)
25 St. Louis 3 at Detroit 1
27 Detroit 2 at Minnesota 4
28 Pittsburgh 2 at Detroit 4

March
4 Detroit 2 at Philadelphia 2
6 Rangers 2 at Detroit 2
(Libett (D) tied game at 19:45)
7 Canadiens 4 at Detroit 1
(afternoon game)
11 Detroit 3 at Vancouver 7
13 Detroit 2 at Los Angeles 5
14 Detroit 8 at California 5
(afternoon game)
16 Boston 11 at Detroit 4
18 Detroit 3 at Boston 7
20 Detroit 1 at St. Louis 2
21 Detroit 0 at Chicago 2 [Esposito]
(afternoon game)
24 Detroit 2 at Pittsburgh 8
25 Vancouver 3 at Detroit 4
27 Detroit 2 at Canadiens 9
28 Toronto 1 at Detroit 2
(afternoon game)
31 Detroit 2 at Toronto 2

April
3 Chicago 4 at Detroit 1
4 Detroit 0 at Rangers 6
[Giacomin]

1971–1972

October
9 Minnesota 4 at Detroit 2
10 Detroit 1 at Chicago 2
16 Detroit 2 at St. Louis 9
17 St. Louis 3 at Detroit 5
20 Detroit 3 at Boston 4
22 Toronto 2 at Detroit 5
24 California 6 at Detroit 3
(Pinder 19:32 en)
26 Chicago 5 at Detroit 2
27 Detroit 4 at Rangers 7
30 Detroit 0 at Canadiens 3
[K. Dryden]
(all goals in 3rd)
31 Pittsburgh 1 at Detroit 3

November
1 Detroit 2 at Toronto 6
4 Buffalo 4 at Detroit 4

6 Boston 2 at Detroit 1
(afternoon game)
(all goals in 3rd)
7 Detroit 3 at Buffalo 3
10 Detroit 2 at Minnesota 1
13 Detroit 6 at Philadelphia 3
(afternoon game)
16 Detroit 2 at St. Louis 2
20 Detroit 1 at Los Angeles 3
(Lonsberry 19:54 en)
21 Detroit 2 at Vancouver 2
(afternoon game)
24 Detroit 1 at California 6
27 Rangers 1 at Detroit 3
28 Canadiens 2 at Detroit 4

December 1 Detroit 2 at Pittsburgh 4
2 Detroit 1 at Philadelphia 1
(both goals in 2nd)
4 Los Angeles 1 at Detroit 5
5 St. Louis 2 at Detroit 1
8 Detroit 2 at Canadiens 4
11 Philadelphia 3 at Detroit 6
14 Detroit 4 at Vancouver 3
17 Detroit 3 at California 3
18 Detroit 2 at Los Angeles 4
(Lemieux 19:34 en)
22 Vancouver 0 at Detroit 3 [A. Smith]
25 Detroit 3 at Toronto 5
26 Minnesota 1 at Detroit 5
29 Detroit 7 at Buffalo 3
31 California 3 at Detroit 6

January 2 Canadiens 4 at Detroit 6
5 Detroit 2 at Minnesota 4
7 Detroit 4 at California 4
9 Pittsburgh 2 at Detroit 4
(Libett 19:25 en)
11 Philadelphia 0 at Detroit 5
[A. Smith]
15 Los Angeles 4 at Detroit 7
16 Detroit 2 at Boston 9
19 Minnesota 4 at Detroit 1
22 Buffalo 2 at Detroit 3
(afternoon game)
23 St. Louis 1 at Detroit 3
27 Detroit 3 at Buffalo 1
(Libett 19:13 en)
29 Los Angeles 4 at Detroit 4
(Dionne (D) tied game at 18:50
with extra attacker)
30 Detroit 2 at Chicago 4

February 1 Toronto 0 at Detroit 4 [A. Smith]
(Berenson 19:32 en)
3 Detroit 4 at Philadelphia 5
5 Detroit 2 at Boston 3
(afternoon game)
6 California 2 at Detroit 8
10 Buffalo 2 at Detroit 4
12 Chicago 3 at Detroit 3
16 Detroit 2 at Minnesota 4
(Grant 19:59 en)
19 Detroit 6 at Pittsburgh 2
(afternoon game)
20 Detroit 3 at Rangers 4
22 Toronto 4 at Detroit 5
24 Vancouver 0 at Detroit 2
[A. Smith]
26 Detroit 1 at Canadiens 8
(afternoon game)
27 Philadelphia 3 at Detroit 1
(afternoon game)
29 Vancouver 2 at Detroit 8

March 2 Detroit 4 at Pittsburgh 7
(Schock 18:48 en / Schock
19:26 en)
4 Boston 5 at Detroit 4
5 Pittsburgh 3 at Detroit 6
8 Detroit 1 at Toronto 5
11 Rangers 4 at Detroit 2
(afternoon game)
12 Chicago 3 at Detroit 2
(afternoon game)
16 Rangers 2 at Detroit 1
19 Canadiens 6 at Detroit 7
21 Detroit 7 at Vancouver 5
22 Detroit 6 at Los Angeles 3
25 Detroit 3 at St. Louis 5
28 Boston 3 at Detroit 6
29 Detroit 2 at Rangers 2

April 2 Detroit 1 at Chicago 6

1972–1973

October 7 Rangers 3 at Detroit 5
11 Boston 3 at Detroit 4
14 Philadelphia 0 at Detroit 5
[R. Edwards]
15 Los Angeles 2 at Detroit 8
21 Detroit 3 at Toronto 1
22 Toronto 2 at Detroit 6
26 Detroit 1 at Philadelphia 2

28 Detroit 3 at St. Louis 8
29 Canadiens 2 at Detroit 1
November 1 Atlanta 4 at Detroit 2 (Leiter 19:59 en)
4 Detroit 4 at Canadiens 2
5 Pittsburgh 1 at Detroit 1 (both goals in 3rd)
9 Detroit 3 at Boston 8
12 Detroit 1 at Chicago 5
14 Detroit 3 at Vancouver 3
15 Detroit 4 at California 0 [R. Edwards]
18 Detroit 3 at Los Angeles 8
22 Buffalo 2 at Detroit 6
25 Philadelphia 4 at Detroit 6 (Delvecchio 19:35 en)
26 California 6 at Detroit 4 (J. Johnston 19:21 en)
29 Detroit 3 at Chicago 8
December 2 Detroit 4 at Islanders 1
3 Toronto 3 at Detroit 0 [Plante]
5 Detroit 1 at St. Louis 2
7 Detroit 1 at Buffalo 6
9 Detroit 0 at Minnesota 7 [Maniago]
10 Vancouver 3 at Detroit 3
13 Atlanta 2 at Detroit 0 [Bouchard]
16 Detroit 4 at Toronto 1
17 Minnesota 4 at Detroit 6
20 Los Angeles 1 at Detroit 4
21 Detroit 1 at Boston 8
23 Vancouver 1 at Detroit 5 (afternoon game)
24 Detroit 0 at Rangers 5 [Giacomin] (afternoon game)
26 Pittsburgh 1 at Detroit 1
30 Detroit 2 at Pittsburgh 2
31 Minnesota 4 at Detroit 4
January 4 Buffalo 2 at Detroit 4
6 Detroit 4 at Islanders 0 [R. Edwards]
7 Islanders 0 at Detroit 4 [R. Edwards]
10 Detroit 2 at Pittsburgh 1 (all goals in 2nd)
12 Detroit 7 at Vancouver 1
14 Pittsburgh 2 at Detroit 3
17 Chicago 6 at Detroit 4 (D. Redmond 19:00 en)
20 Buffalo 2 at Detroit 4
21 Minnesota 5 at Detroit 3 (Burns 19:27 en) (afternoon game)
23 Detroit 4 at Philadelphia 4
25 Detroit 4 at Boston 2
27 Rangers 6 at Detroit 3 (afternoon game)
28 Detroit 4 at Canadiens 2 (afternoon game)
February 1 California 4 at Detroit 6
3 Atlanta 0 at Detroit 1 [R. Edwards] (Ecclestone 12:24 2nd)
4 Vancouver 2 at Detroit 8
7 Detroit 5 at Atlanta 3
10 Detroit 1 at Minnesota 3
11 Detroit 5 at Buffalo 2 (Collins 19:05 en)
14 Detroit 2 at Los Angeles 2
16 Detroit 2 at California 2
17 Detroit 2 at Vancouver 2
22 Canadiens 3 at Detroit 3
24 Detroit 2 at Islanders 4 (Dionne (D) tied game at 19:07 with extra attacker / Spencer (I) 19:46 en)
25 St. Louis 0 at Detroit 5 [DeJordy] (afternoon game)
28 Philadelphia 5 at Detroit 6 (Flett (P) 19:54 with extra attacker)
March 3 Rangers 6 at Detroit 3
4 Islanders 1 at Detroit 5
7 Detroit 5 at Atlanta 2
10 Detroit 0 at Canadiens 2 [K. Dryden] (F. Mahovlich 18:42 en)
11 St. Louis 1 at Detroit 3 (Berenson 19:45 en)
14 Canadiens 5 at Detroit 3 (Lemaire 19:24 en)
16 Boston 5 at Detroit 4 (rescheduled from March 17)
17 Boston at Detroit (moved up to March 16)
18 Detroit 2 at Chicago 0 [R. Edwards] (afternoon game)
21 Detroit 3 at St. Louis 6
24 Detroit 3 at Los Angeles 5
25 Detroit 5 at California 8 (afternoon game) (J. Johnston 19:56 en)
27 Detroit 8 at Toronto 1

	29	Toronto 6 at Detroit 4
	31	Chicago 2 at Detroit 4
April	1	Detroit 3 at Rangers 3

1973–1974

October	10	Detroit 1 at Rangers 4
	13	Boston 9 at Detroit 4
	14	Detroit 2 at Philadelphia 5
	16	St. Louis 3 at Detroit 2
	18	Minnesota 4 at Detroit 4 (Libett (D) tied game at 18:46 with extra attacker)
	21	California 2 at Detroit 11
	24	Detroit 3 at California 7
	26	Detroit 3 at Vancouver 8
	27	Detroit 3 at Los Angeles 2
	30	Detroit 0 at Toronto 7 [Johnston]
November	4	Detroit 0 at Atlanta 2 [Bouchard]
	7	Philadelphia 4 at Detroit 1 (all goals in 3rd)
	10	Detroit 4 at Minnesota 2
	11	Toronto 4 at Detroit 5
	14	Islanders 3 at Detroit 4
	17	Detroit 0 at Boston 8 [Gilbert]
	18	Canadiens 4 at Detroit 6 (Collins 19:10 en)
	20	Los Angeles 5 at Detroit 6 (Murdoch (LA) at 19:53 with extra attacker)
	22	Detroit 3 at Islanders 5
	24	Islanders 4 at Detroit 6
	25	California 2 at Detroit 3
	29	Detroit 3 at Atlanta 4
December	1	Buffalo 4 at Detroit 1
	2	Detroit 1 at Buffalo 6
	5	Chicago 8 at Detroit 2
	7	Detroit 1 at St. Louis 1
	8	Detroit 0 at Minnesota 3 [Rivard]
	13	St. Louis 3 at Detroit 7
	15	Detroit 2 at Pittsburgh 0 [Grant]
	16	Vancouver 5 at Detroit 7
	18	Los Angeles 4 at Detroit 4
	20	Detroit 2 at Rangers 5
	22	Boston 2 at Detroit 4
	26	Pittsburgh 2 at Detroit 2
	27	Detroit 1 at Buffalo 3
	30	Atlanta 2 at Detroit 4 (Dionne 19:09 en)
	31	Buffalo 6 at Detroit 5
January	2	Detroit 3 at Toronto 4
	6	Minnesota 6 at Detroit 9 (afternoon game)
	9	Detroit 2 at Minnesota 2
	12	Los Angeles 0 at Detroit 6 [McKenzie]
	13	Detroit 1 at Chicago 4
	16	Rangers 4 at Detroit 4 (MacGregor (R) tied game at 19:37)
	19	Detroit 5 at St. Louis 2 (Boucha 19:59 en)
	20	Canadiens 3 at Detroit 2
	23	California 2 at Detroit 6
	25	Detroit 2 at Atlanta 2
	27	Pittsburgh 5 at Detroit 6
	30	Vancouver 7 at Detroit 3
February	2	Detroit 2 at Philadelphia 12 (afternoon game)
	3	Canadiens 4 at Detroit 1 (afternoon game)
	6	Detroit 2 at Toronto 2
	9	Detroit 4 at Vancouver 5
	13	Detroit 3 at Pittsburgh 5
	15	Detroit 4 at Canadiens 9
	17	Detroit 1 at Buffalo 2
	20	Philadelphia 3 at Detroit 1
	23	St. Louis 3 at Detroit 5
	24	Islanders 3 at Detroit 5 (Redmond 19:38 en)
	26	Toronto 3 at Detroit 7
	28	Detroit 1 at Boston 8
March	2	Boston 4 at Detroit 4 (afternoon game)
	3	Chicago 6 at Detroit 6 (afternoon game)
	7	Detroit 1 at Philadelphia 6
	9	Detroit 3 at Islanders 1
	10	Atlanta 4 at Detroit 0 [Bouchard]
	12	Detroit 2 at Vancouver 1
	13	Detroit 5 at California 2
	16	Detroit 0 at Los Angeles 2 [Vachon] (both goals in 2nd)
	20	Detroit 7 at Canadiens 6
	23	Rangers 3 at Detroit 5
	24	Detroit 0 at Pittsburgh 8 [Brown]
	27	Buffalo 1 at Detroit 3
	30	Chicago 2 at Detroit 1 (afternoon game)

31 Detroit 1 at Boston 6
(afternoon game)

April
3 Detroit 3 at Rangers 5
6 Rangers 3 at Detroit 8
7 Detroit 4 at Chicago 7

1974–1975

October
9 Chicago 1 at Detroit 2
(Charron won game at 19:23)
12 Detroit 2 at Pittsburgh 7
13 California 3 at Detroit 7
16 Atlanta 2 at Detroit 4
(Libett 19:59 en)
19 Washington 4 at Detroit 6
(Redmond 19:49 en)
22 Detroit 3 at Washington 0
[Rutherford]
23 Detroit 1 at Atlanta 10
26 Detroit 2 at Canadiens 4
29 Detroit 0 at Vancouver 7 [Smith]

November
1 Detroit 4 at California 4
2 Detroit 1 at Los Angeles 5
6 Canadiens 4 at Detroit 4
10 Vancouver 4 at Detroit 2
13 Detroit 4 at Minnesota 7
16 Islanders 3 at Detroit 5
17 Boston 5 at Detroit 2
20 Rangers 5 at Detroit 4
23 Detroit 2 at St. Louis 4
(G. Bailey 19:50 en)
24 Los Angeles 4 at Detroit 1
27 Detroit 2 at Philadelphia 6
28 Detroit 2 at Buffalo 5
30 Detroit 1 at Kansas City 0
[Rutherford]
(Dionne 14:25 3rd)

December
1 Toronto at Detroit
(postponed to Feb. 9 because
of weather)
4 Detroit 2 at Rangers 4
5 Detroit 6 at Boston 4
7 Detroit 3 at Toronto 3
8 Vancouver 2 at Detroit 4
12 St. Louis 4 at Detroit 3
15 Pittsburgh 3 at Detroit 2
18 Detroit 5 at Chicago 7
(Daigle 19:25 en)
21 Philadelphia 2 at Detroit 2
(afternoon game)
22 Detroit 4 at Boston 5
26 Minnesota 4 at Detroit 4
27 Detroit 1 at Canadiens 7
30 Los Angeles 3 at Detroit 2
31 California 3 at Detroit 4

January
4 Detroit 1 at Kansas City 2
5 Toronto 1 at Detroit 0 [Favell]
(McDonald 10:43 2nd)
8 Canadiens 4 at Detroit 4
11 Buffalo 3 at Detroit 3
12 St. Louis 2 at Detroit 1
16 Kansas City 4 at Detroit 7
18 Detroit 1 at Islanders 5
19 Minnesota 4 at Detroit 4
(Dionne (D) tied game at 19:02)
23 Detroit 1 at Buffalo 5
25 Washington 2 at Detroit 5
26 Detroit 3 at Washington 6
28 Detroit 4 at St. Louis 4
30 Pittsburgh 2 at Detroit 5

February
1 Islanders 4 at Detroit 1
(afternoon game)
2 Detroit 5 at Rangers 5
(afternoon game)
4 Buffalo 6 at Detroit 1
5 Detroit 5 at Canadiens 8
8 Boston 8 at Detroit 5
9 Toronto 3 at Detroit 5
(rescheduled from Dec. 1)
12 Detroit 2 at California 4
(J. Stewart 19:24 en)
14 Detroit 4 at Vancouver 5
15 Detroit 2 at Los Angeles 8
19 Philadelphia 3 at Detroit 4
22 Atlanta 3 at Detroit 4
23 Detroit 3 at Pittsburgh 1
(Hogaboam 19:44 en)
26 Los Angeles 2 at Detroit 1
27 Detroit 4 at Boston 9

March
1 Buffalo 2 at Detroit 3
2 Toronto 5 at Detroit 4
5 Detroit 3 at Toronto 4
(Sittler won game at 19:38)
8 Kansas City 1 at Detroit 5
9 Detroit 5 at Philadelphia 8
11 Detroit 4 at Islanders 2
(Grant 19:27 en)
13 Detroit 5 at Los Angeles 5
14 Detroit 2 at California 4
16 Detroit 3 at Minnesota 4

	20	Chicago 6 at Detroit 2
	22	Rangers 4 at Detroit 7 (Redmond 19:47 en)
	23	Detroit 4 at Chicago 4
	26	Detroit 3 at Atlanta 5
	29	Pittsburgh 4 at Detroit 2 (afternoon game)
	30	Detroit 8 at Washington 5
April	2	Washington 3 at Detroit 8
	5	Detroit 1 at Pittsburgh 7
	6	Canadiens 4 at Detroit 2

1975–1976

October	8	St. Louis 1 at Detroit 1 (both goals in 3rd)
	9	Detroit 0 at Buffalo 4 [Crozier]
	11	California 5 at Detroit 2 (Murdoch 19:43 en)
	15	Detroit 4 at Chicago 4
	16	Boston 2 at Detroit 2
	18	Detroit 1 at Pittsburgh 6
	19	Detroit 1 at Philadelphia 5
	22	Canadiens 4 at Detroit 1
	25	Buffalo 5 at Detroit 3
	26	Detroit 3 at Boston 7
	29	California 4 at Detroit 6 (Redmond 19:04 en)
November	1	Chicago 3 at Detroit 1
	2	Detroit 6 at Rangers 4
	5	Detroit 3 at Toronto 7
	8	Detroit 0 at Canadiens 5 [Larocque]
	9	Atlanta 3 at Detroit 6
	13	Kansas City 3 at Detroit 6 (McKechnie 19:29 en)
	15	Philadelphia 1 at Detroit 3
	16	Detroit 0 at Rangers 3 [Davidson]
	19	Boston 3 at Detroit 3 (Redmond (D) tied game at 19:50 with extra attacker)
	20	Detroit 2 at Buffalo 7
	22	Detroit 1 at St. Louis 5
	23	Los Angeles 1 at Detroit 4 (McKechnie 19:21 en)
	26	Detroit 2 at Pittsburgh 5
	29	Detroit 5 at Kansas City 3 (McKechnie 19:16 en)
December	3	Detroit 1 at Vancouver 9
	5	Detroit 2 at California 3
	6	Detroit 2 at Los Angeles 3
	10	Pittsburgh 2 at Detroit 3
	12	Detroit 5 at Washington 3
	13	Rangers 5 at Detroit 2
	17	Buffalo 1 at Detroit 3
	19	Detroit 1 at Kansas City 4
	20	Detroit 3 at Minnesota 5 (Hicke 19:33 en)
	26	Islanders at Detroit (postponed to February 6 due to snowstorm)
	28	Vancouver 3 at Detroit 2
	31	Washington 0 at Detroit 4 [Rutherford]
January	3	Detroit 1 at Toronto 0 [Rutherford] (McKechnie 17:51 2nd)
	4	Vancouver 4 at Detroit 3
	6	Detroit 3 at Atlanta 4
	8	Minnesota 0 at Detroit 5 [Rutherford]
	10	Detroit 1 at Canadiens 7
	13	Detroit 0 at Islanders 1 [Resch] (Gillies 6:49 1st)
	14	Kansas City 3 at Detroit 8
	17	Toronto 4 at Detroit 4
	18	Los Angeles 8 at Detroit 3
	22	Detroit 1 at Islanders 8
	24	Boston 6 at Detroit 1 (afternoon game)
	25	Canadiens 3 at Detroit 3
	27	Detroit 3 at St. Louis 2
	29	Detroit 3 at Los Angeles 3
	31	Chicago 1 at Detroit 2 (McKechnie won game at 19:38)
February	4	Minnesota 0 at Detroit 5 [Rutherford]
	6	Islanders 3 at Detroit 4 (rescheduled from December 26)
	7	Rangers 5 at Detroit 4
	8	Detroit 0 at Boston 7 [Cheevers]
	11	Detroit 2 at Buffalo 4 (Luce 19:46 en)
	14	Detroit 3 at Minnesota 2
	15	Detroit 5 at Washington 8 (Meehan 19:18 en)
	18	Islanders 5 at Detroit 3 (Trottier 19:46 en)
	21	Washington 5 at Detroit 1
	22	Pittsburgh 2 at Detroit 2 (afternoon game)
	25	Detroit 0 at Toronto 8 [Thomas]

	26	California 1 at Detroit 1
	28	Los Angeles 3 at Detroit 1
March	3	Detroit 3 at Atlanta 2
	6	Detroit 1 at Philadelphia 6 (afternoon game)
	7	Canadiens 6 at Detroit 1
	10	Detroit 3 at California 4
	13	Detroit 4 at Los Angeles 1
	16	Detroit 2 at Vancouver 4
	18	St. Louis 3 at Detroit 6
	20	Philadelphia 2 at Detroit 4
	21	Detroit 6 at Chicago 0 [Giacomin]
	24	Washington 3 at Detroit 7
	27	Atlanta 0 at Detroit 8 [Giacomin]
	28	Detroit 0 at Pittsburgh 3 [Plasse]
	30	Detroit 3 at Washington 5
	31	Toronto 4 at Detroit 4
April	3	Detroit 3 at Canadiens 6
	4	Pittsburgh 6 at Detroit 5 (Apps won game at 19:57)

1976–1977

October	7	Washington 3 at Detroit 3
	9	Buffalo 0 at Detroit 4 [Giacomin]
	12	Canadiens 4 at Detroit 2
	16	Detroit 3 at Pittsburgh 4
	17	Detroit 4 at Philadelphia 7
	22	Islanders 0 at Detroit 5 [Giacomin]
	23	Detroit 2 at St. Louis 4 (P. Plante 19:52 en)
	26	Detroit 2 at Los Angeles 3 (Williams won game at 19:49)
	28	Toronto 3 at Detroit 1
	30	Chicago 4 at Detroit 1
	31	Detroit 6 at Rangers 5 (Leblanc won game at 19:40)
November	4	Philadelphia 2 at Detroit 3
	7	Atlanta 0 at Detroit 0 [Myre (A) / Giacomin (D)]
	9	Detroit 1 at Islanders 8
	10	Boston 6 at Detroit 4 (Cashman 19:16 en)
	13	Los Angeles 3 at Detroit 3
	16	Detroit 0 at Philadelphia 2 [Parent] (Bridgman 19:53 en) (both goals in 3rd)
	17	St. Louis 5 at Detroit 5
	19	Cleveland 2 at Detroit 5
	21	Detroit 2 at Boston 4
	24	Toronto 3 at Detroit 4
	25	Detroit 3 at Islanders 1
	27	Rangers 5 at Detroit 0 [Davidson]
	28	Detroit 1 at Buffalo 3
December	1	Detroit 5 at Vancouver 2
	4	Detroit 1 at Los Angeles 4
	11	Detroit 0 at Canadiens 5
	12	Detroit 5 at Boston 3 (Dan Maloney 18:55 en)
	15	Detroit 3 at Cleveland 7
	16	Vancouver 3 at Detroit 7
	18	Atlanta 3 at Detroit 6
	19	Detroit 1 at Buffalo 6
	22	Detroit 1 at Atlanta 2
	23	Pittsburgh 2 at Detroit 5 (Nahrgang 19:00 en / R. Wilson 19:43 en)
	27	Los Angeles 7 at Detroit 4 (afternoon game)
	29	Detroit 3 at Chicago 6
	31	Cleveland 2 at Detroit 4
January	2	Colorado 6 at Detroit 4 (afternoon game)
	4	Detroit 2 at Washington 2
	6	Minnesota 7 at Detroit 2
	9	Washington at Detroit (rescheduled to Jan. 10)
	10	Washington 2 at Detroit 0 [Wolfe] (rescheduled from Jan. 9)
	12	Detroit 1 at Cleveland 3
	13	Detroit 2 at Colorado 4
	15	Detroit 0 at St. Louis 4 [Grant]
	20	Colorado 3 at Detroit 1
	22	Chicago 3 at Detroit 0 [Esposito]
	23	Detroit 2 at Canadiens 2
	27	Detroit 1 at Washington 4
	29	Cleveland 3 at Detroit 4
February	2	Detroit 1 at Toronto 9
	5	Detroit 1 at Pittsburgh 3
	6	Vancouver 2 at Detroit 3 (Nahrgang won game at 19:24)
	10	Rangers 5 at Detroit 4
	12	Detroit 2 at Minnesota 2
	13	Canadiens 5 at Detroit 3
	15	Detroit 2 at Colorado 6
	17	Toronto 2 at Detroit 2
	19	Buffalo 2 at Detroit 1
	20	Detroit 2 at Rangers 3
	23	Detroit 2 at Chicago 5

	24	Pittsburgh 2 at Detroit 3
	26	Los Angeles 4 at Detroit 3
March	1	Detroit 3 at Boston 8
	3	Islanders 4 at Detroit 2
	5	Philadelphia 4 at Detroit 1
	9	Detroit 3 at Buffalo 6
	10	St. Louis 4 at Detroit 2 (Berenson 19:21 en)
	12	Detroit 0 at Toronto 6 [Palmateer]
	13	Washington 3 at Detroit 3
	15	Detroit 1 at Vancouver 7
	17	Detroit 2 at Los Angeles 3 (all goals in 2nd)
	20	Detroit 1 at Minnesota 2 (afternoon game)
	23	Boston 6 at Detroit 0 [Cheevers]
	24	Detroit 1 at Atlanta 3
	26	Detroit 0 at Canadiens 4 [K. Dryden] (all goals in 3rd)
	27	Canadiens 6 at Detroit 0 [Larocque] (rescheduled from Mar. 28)
	28	Canadiens at Detroit (moved up to March 27)
	29	Detroit 1 at Washington 6
	31	Minnesota 3 at Detroit 1
April	2	Pittsburgh 4 at Detroit 3
	3	Detroit 2 at Pittsburgh 4

1977–1978

October	13	Toronto 3 at Detroit 3
	15	Detroit 2 at Los Angeles 4
	18	Detroit 2 at Vancouver 3
	20	Canadiens 2 at Detroit 2 (Robinson (C) tied game at 19:44 with extra attacker)
	22	Detroit 4 at Minnesota 2
	26	Detroit 4 at Pittsburgh 3
	27	Minnesota 1 at Detroit 3
	29	Detroit 4 at Toronto 7
November	2	Pittsburgh 1 at Detroit 3
	5	Cleveland 4 at Detroit 3
	6	Detroit 4 at Cleveland 1 (Lochead 19:58 en)
	9	Washington 1 at Detroit 1
	12	Rangers 1 at Detroit 3
	13	Detroit 0 at Philadelphia 3 [Stephenson]
	16	St. Louis 1 at Detroit 10
	18	Detroit 3 at Atlanta 5
	19	Detroit 2 at St. Louis 1 (Libett won game at 19:44)
	23	Philadelphia 1 at Detroit 4
	26	Detroit 1 at Canadiens 3
	27	Islanders 4 at Detroit 1
	30	Detroit 4 at Pittsburgh 6
December	3	Detroit 2 at Toronto 4
	4	Detroit 1 at Buffalo 6
	6	Chicago 2 at Detroit 1
	8	Detroit 4 at Boston 6
	10	Detroit 4 at Islanders 7
	15	Rangers 5 at Detroit 5
	17	Detroit 3 at St. Louis 2
	18	Detroit 2 at Rangers 6
	21	Buffalo 5 at Detroit 3
	23	Detroit 2 at Washington 3
	27	Colorado 2 at Detroit 5 (afternoon game)
	29	Detroit 3 at Buffalo 3
	31	Boston 7 at Detroit 0 [Grahame]
January	5	Toronto 1 at Detroit 2
	7	Detroit at Canadiens (postponed to Feb. 28)
	8	Los Angeles 3 at Detroit 4
	11	Detroit 6 at Washington 3
	12	Canadiens 6 at Detroit 1
	14	Buffalo 2 at Detroit 6
	18	Detroit 4 at Colorado 4
	19	Chicago 2 at Detroit 4
	21	Detroit 1 at Boston 7 (afternoon game)
	22	Washington 3 at Detroit 6 (Joly 19:31 en / McCourt 19:50 en)
	26	Pittsburgh at Detroit (postponed to Jan. 31)
	28	Detroit 1 at Chicago 6
	29	Philadelphia 3 at Detroit 3
	31	Pittsburgh 5 at Detroit 3 (rescheduled from Jan. 26) (Pronovost 19:19 en)
February	1	Detroit 0 at Cleveland 2 [Meloche]
	4	Detroit 2 at Toronto 2
	5	Cleveland 3 at Detroit 4
	7	Detroit 2 at Los Angeles 1
	9	Boston 5 at Detroit 3
	11	Detroit 5 at Islanders 8
	12	Vancouver 3 at Detroit 8
	16	Atlanta 3 at Detroit 5

18 Detroit 2 at Philadelphia 4 (afternoon game)
19 Los Angeles 1 at Detroit 5
23 Washington 1 at Detroit 4
25 Detroit 2 at Atlanta 2
26 St. Louis 3 at Detroit 1 (Currie 19:33 en)
28 Detroit 3 at Canadiens 9 (rescheduled from Jan. 7)

March 1 Detroit 2 at Rangers 3
4 Detroit 3 at Minnesota 1
5 Minnesota 3 at Detroit 4
9 Boston 2 at Detroit 2
11 Colorado 4 at Detroit 5
12 Vancouver 4 at Detroit 4
16 Detroit 3 at Los Angeles 3
18 Detroit 5 at Vancouver 4
19 Detroit 4 at Colorado 6
22 Atlanta 1 at Detroit 4
24 Detroit at Washington (postponed to March 26)
25 Detroit 2 at Pittsburgh 2
26 Detroit 4 at Washington 1 (St. Laurent 19:23 en) (rescheduled from Mar. 24)
28 Buffalo 0 at Detroit 7 [Low]
30 Los Angeles 4 at Detroit 0 [Vachon]

April 1 Detroit 0 at Chicago 2 [Esposito] (Bordeleau 19:09 en) (both goals in 3rd)
2 Islanders 5 at Detroit 2
5 Detroit 5 at Cleveland 5
6 Pittsburgh 4 at Detroit 6 (St. Laurent 19:32 en)
8 Detroit 1 at Canadiens 5
9 Canadiens 0 at Detroit 4 [Rutherford]

1978–1979

October 11 St. Louis 5 at Detroit 4
14 Philadelphia 3 at Detroit 1 (B. Wilson 19:33 en)
15 Detroit 3 at Buffalo 2
18 Detroit 3 at Rangers 3
19 Rangers 2 at Detroit 2
21 Minnesota 4 at Detroit 4
25 Colorado 4 at Detroit 5
27 Detroit 5 at Colorado 2
28 Chicago 2 at Detroit 7

November 1 Canadiens 4 at Detroit 1
4 Detroit 3 at Pittsburgh 7
5 Detroit 3 at Washington 3
8 Vancouver 6 at Detroit 4
9 Detroit 3 at Canadiens 8
11 Boston 1 at Detroit 7
15 Detroit 3 at Atlanta 5
18 Buffalo 3 at Detroit 1 (Korab 19:35 en) (afternoon game)
19 Detroit 3 at Philadelphia 4
22 Detroit 3 at Los Angeles 3
25 Detroit 0 at St. Louis 4 [Myre]
26 Los Angeles 2 at Detroit 4
29 Detroit 2 at Colorado 2

December 1 Detroit 1 at Vancouver 2
2 Detroit 2 at Los Angeles 5
6 Canadiens 2 at Detroit 2
7 Detroit 5 at Boston 6
9 Rangers 4 at Detroit 5
10 Detroit 3 at Chicago 3 (Bulley (C) tied game at 19:00)
13 Atlanta 5 at Detroit 5 (Chouinard (A) tied game at 19:59 with extra attacker)
14 Detroit 1 at Islanders 4
16 Detroit 2 at Toronto 4
17 Islanders 3 at Detroit 0 [B. Smith]
20 Vancouver 2 at Detroit 7
22 Detroit 2 at Rangers 4 (Esposito 19:21 en)
23 Washington 2 at Detroit 2
26 Philadelphia 2 at Detroit 2 (afternoon game) (Bridgman (P) scored at 18:35 with extra attacker / Clarke (P) tied game at 18:51 with extra attacker)
27 Canadiens 5 at Detroit 2
30 Detroit 1 at Pittsburgh 3
31 Pittsburgh 5 at Detroit 4 (Carlyle won game at 19:53)

January 6 Washington 4 at Detroit 1
7 Detroit 3 at Buffalo 4
10 Islanders 5 at Detroit 5
11 Detroit 3 at Philadelphia 3 (Libett (D) tied game at 19:31 with extra attacker)
13 Los Angeles 7 at Detroit 3 (afternoon game)

17 Pittsburgh 1 at Detroit 4
19 Detroit 1 at Washington 5
20 Atlanta 4 at Detroit 3
25 Detroit 6 at Los Angeles 6
27 Buffalo 6 at Detroit 3 (afternoon game)
28 Detroit 2 at Atlanta 7 (afternoon game)
30 Washington 4 at Detroit 7 (Libett 18:53 en)

February 1 Detroit 1 at Minnesota 6
3 Detroit 2 at Pittsburgh 4
4 Pittsburgh 3 at Detroit 8
14 Los Angeles 3 at Detroit 2
18 Pittsburgh 2 at Detroit 6 (afternoon game)
19 Toronto 6 at Detroit 2
21 Detroit 4 at Washington 3
24 Detroit 1 at Islanders 3 (afternoon game)
25 Colorado 1 at Detroit 8
28 St. Louis 6 at Detroit 5

March 3 Detroit 5 at Canadiens 3
4 Boston 6 at Detroit 4
7 Detroit 1 at Minnesota 5
11 Washington 3 at Detroit 3 (afternoon game)
12 Detroit 3 at Canadiens 3
14 Detroit 4 at Washington 1
17 Detroit 3 at St. Louis 1 (afternoon game)
18 Detroit 4 at Chicago 2 (Larson 19:53 en)
20 Chicago 3 at Detroit 5 (Larson 19:01 en)
21 Detroit 4 at Toronto 2
24 Detroit 2 at Boston 5 (afternoon game)
25 Toronto 1 at Detroit 2 (afternoon game)
27 Detroit 2 at Vancouver 5
28 Detroit 1 at Los Angeles 8
31 Los Angeles 5 at Detroit 4 (Murphy won game at 19:45)

April 1 Minnesota 1 at Detroit 3
4 Detroit 1 at Canadiens 4
7 Detroit 3 at Pittsburgh 4
8 Canadiens 0 at Detroit 1 [Rutherford] (McCourt 14:34 3rd)

1979–1980

October 10 Detroit 4 at Los Angeles 4 (P. Mahovlich (D) tied game at 19:36)
12 Detroit 1 at Vancouver 3
13 Detroit 3 at Edmonton 3
17 Detroit 5 at Winnipeg 1
20 Philadelphia 7 at Detroit 3
25 Buffalo 0 at Detroit 4 [Rutherford]
27 Detroit 2 at Canadiens 3
28 Detroit 4 at Philadelphia 5 (Leach won game at 19:00)
31 Minnesota 5 at Detroit 3

November 3 Chicago 0 at Detroit 2 [Vachon]
4 Detroit 1 at Quebec 5
7 Edmonton 3 at Detroit 5
10 Vancouver 2 at Detroit 1
14 Detroit 2 at Rangers 3
16 Detroit 4 at Washington 2
17 Detroit 5 at Islanders 4
21 Detroit 1 at Atlanta 4
23 Detroit 2 at Colorado 5 (Robert 19:43 en)
24 Detroit 3 at Minnesota 3
27 Canadiens 5 at Detroit 5

December 1 Boston 3 at Detroit 6
2 Detroit 4 at Philadelphia 4
5 Winnipeg 4 at Detroit 6
8 Vancouver 1 at Detroit 5
10 Detroit 0 at Buffalo 4 [Edwards]
11 Rangers 2 at Detroit 1
13 Detroit 6 at Boston 6
15 Quebec 4 at Detroit 4
16 Detroit 3 at Chicago 7
19 Detroit 6 at Edmonton 4 (Foligno 19:53 en)
22 Detroit 1 at Toronto 2
26 Detroit 4 at Pittsburgh 6
27 St. Louis 3 at Detroit 2 (first game at Joe Louis Arena)
30 Islanders 2 at Detroit 4
31 Colorado 5 at Detroit 3

January 2 Los Angeles 4 at Detroit 2
4 Detroit 6 at Atlanta 3
6 Detroit 2 at Hartford 1
9 Rangers 0 at Detroit 4 [Vachon]
12 Hartford 6 at Detroit 4
13 Detroit 2 at Chicago 3
16 Colorado 1 at Detroit 5
18 Detroit 5 at Winnipeg 0 [Vachon]

19 Detroit 5 at Minnesota 4
23 Islanders 5 at Detroit 3
26 Atlanta 4 at Detroit 3
27 Detroit 7 at Quebec 6
30 Detroit 4 at Toronto 6
31 Pittsburgh 3 at Detroit 4

February 2 Detroit 3 at St. Louis 0 [Vachon]
3 St. Louis 4 at Detroit 2 (Monahan 19:52 en)
6 Washington 2 at Detroit 2
9 Philadelphia 6 at Detroit 5
10 Toronto 4 at Detroit 1
13 Atlanta 2 at Detroit 2
16 Buffalo 4 at Detroit 3
18 Los Angeles 4 at Detroit 2 (Dionne 19:51 en)
20 Detroit 5 at Pittsburgh 7
23 Detroit 1 at Canadiens 5
24 Minnesota 5 at Detroit 7
28 Washington 1 at Detroit 4 (Bergman 19:23 en)

March 1 Detroit 4 at Islanders 3
2 Toronto 6 at Detroit 3 (Sittler 19:42 en)
5 Boston 5 at Detroit 3
8 Detroit 2 at St. Louis 2 (Sutter (St. L) tied game at 19:34 with extra attacker)
9 Pittsburgh 2 at Detroit 6
12 Hartford 4 at Detroit 4
13 Detroit 2 at Boston 4
15 Detroit 2 at Washington 5
16 Winnipeg 6 at Detroit 2
19 Detroit 3 at Los Angeles 4
21 Detroit 5 at Vancouver 2
22 Detroit 1 at Colorado 5
26 Edmonton 5 at Detroit 2
27 Detroit 1 at Buffalo 10
29 Quebec 7 at Detroit 9 (Korn 19:00 en)
31 Detroit 5 at Rangers 7

April 2 Canadiens 7 at Detroit 2
5 Chicago 3 at Detroit 1
6 Detroit 3 at Hartford 5 (Boutette 19:54 en)

1980–1981

October 10 Detroit 3 at Vancouver 5
11 Detroit 1 at Los Angeles 8
15 Detroit 4 at Toronto 6
16 Islanders 6 at Detroit 4
18 Detroit 2 at Hartford 4
23 Colorado 1 at Detroit 5
25 Rangers 2 at Detroit 4
26 Detroit 6 at Rangers 7 (Hedberg won game at 19:19)
28 Chicago 2 at Detroit 2
29 Detroit 3 at Hartford 5

November 1 Buffalo 4 at Detroit 2 (Gare 19:30 en)
4 Detroit 4 at Islanders 6
6 Canadiens 2 at Detroit 3
8 Detroit 3 at Pittsburgh 5
11 Boston 4 at Detroit 4
12 Detroit 4 at Buffalo 4
15 Detroit 2 at Philadelphia 5 (afternoon game)
19 Detroit 1 at Quebec 2
20 Detroit 3 at Canadiens 7
22 Detroit 2 at St. Louis 6
26 Washington 7 at Detroit 7
29 Detroit 1 at Islanders 5

December 2 Detroit 3 at Boston 5 (Jonathan 19:13 en)
4 Quebec 4 at Detroit 1
6 Philadelphia 2 at Detroit 4 (afternoon game) (McCourt 19:11 en)
7 Detroit 1 at Minnesota 1
11 Los Angeles 2 at Detroit 1
13 Chicago 3 at Detroit 7 (afternoon game)
14 Detroit 5 at Washington 4
16 Edmonton 3 at Detroit 4 (Murdoch 19:59 en)
18 Toronto 3 at Detroit 5 (Foligno 19:48 en)
20 Detroit 3 at Colorado 3
23 Minnesota 6 at Detroit 2 (Christoff 19:30 en)
27 Detroit 4 at Edmonton 4
28 Detroit 4 at Winnipeg 3
31 Pittsburgh 1 at Detroit 3

January 2 Vancouver 2 at Detroit 2
3 Detroit 4 at Pittsburgh 6
6 Canadiens 6 at Detroit 2
8 Detroit 4 at Boston 7
10 Calgary 1 at Detroit 4 (Ogrodnick 19:08 en)
13 Boston 3 at Detroit 3

15 Detroit 0 at Calgary 10 [Lemelin]
16 Detroit 1 at Vancouver 3
20 Detroit 4 at Los Angeles 11
22 Islanders 3 at Detroit 0 [B. Smith] (Gillies 19:56 en)
24 Colorado 2 at Detroit 6
26 Detroit 4 at Toronto 2
28 Detroit 2 at Quebec 2
29 Minnesota 3 at Detroit 3

February
1 St. Louis 4 at Detroit 1 (Sutter 19:21 en)
3 Toronto 3 at Detroit 5
5 Los Angeles 4 at Detroit 6
6 Detroit 3 at Buffalo 7
8 Vancouver 2 at Detroit 3
12 Hartford 2 at Detroit 2 (all goals in 3rd) (Foligno (D) tied game at 19:41)
14 Philadelphia 3 at Detroit 1
17 Winnipeg 4 at Detroit 6 (Kirton 19:58 en)
19 Rangers 3 at Detroit 7
21 Detroit 1 at Canadiens 4
25 St. Louis 3 at Detroit 2
27 Detroit 2 at Edmonton 5 (Gretzky 18:31 en)

March
1 Detroit 4 at Winnipeg 4 (afternoon game)
4 Detroit 3 at Chicago 3
8 Detroit 4 at Rangers 4
10 Hartford 4 at Detroit 4
12 Detroit 4 at Philadelphia 9
14 Detroit 3 at St. Louis 5
17 Quebec 4 at Detroit 3
19 Calgary 6 at Detroit 3
21 Winnipeg 4 at Detroit 5 (afternoon game)
22 Detroit 3 at Minnesota 9 (afternoon game)
24 Detroit 4 at Colorado 7
26 Washington 2 at Detroit 0 [Palmateer]
28 Edmonton 4 at Detroit 2 (afternoon game)
29 Detroit 3 at Chicago 4
31 Detroit 5 at Calgary 5

April
2 Pittsburgh 1 at Detroit 1
4 Buffalo 5 at Detroit 4 (afternoon game)
5 Detroit 2 at Washington 7

1981–1982

October
6 Detroit 5 at Rangers 2
9 Detroit 2 at Philadelphia 2
10 Detroit 3 at Washington 6 (Duchesne 18:24 en)
15 St. Louis 3 at Detroit 6
17 Detroit 1 at Hartford 8
18 Pittsburgh 2 at Detroit 3
22 Boston 2 at Detroit 2
24 Detroit 3 at Quebec 8
25 Philadelphia 4 at Detroit 1
29 Calgary 4 at Detroit 12
31 Detroit 4 at Minnesota 5

November
1 Vancouver 1 at Detroit 3
5 Los Angeles 2 at Detroit 10
7 Detroit 2 at Canadiens 4
9 Detroit 3 at Quebec 5
11 Detroit 5 at Chicago 5
13 Detroit 3 at Washington 3
14 Chicago 3 at Detroit 6
18 Detroit 1 at Los Angeles 8
19 Detroit 3 at Vancouver 8
21 Detroit 4 at Calgary 4
23 Detroit 4 at Edmonton 8
25 Buffalo 3 at Detroit 1 (Perreault 19:36 en)
28 Detroit 3 at Pittsburgh 5
29 Toronto 6 at Detroit 3

December
1 Detroit 5 at St. Louis 7 (Turnbull 19:58 en)
3 Canadiens 3 at Detroit 4
5 Philadelphia 5 at Detroit 2
10 Minnesota 1 at Detroit 4
12 Buffalo 4 at Detroit 2
13 Detroit 2 at Winnipeg 1
17 Quebec 3 at Detroit 2
19 Detroit 1 at Islanders 5
20 Islanders 5 at Detroit 3 (Trottier 19:20 en)
22 Hartford 3 at Detroit 2
26 Detroit 3 at Toronto 8
27 Detroit 2 at Winnipeg 2 (all goals in 3rd) (Ogrodnick (D) tied game at 19:41)
31 Toronto 5 at Detroit 2

January
2 Detroit 3 at Colorado 1 (all goals in 2nd)
3 Detroit 3 at Chicago 4 (D. Savard won game at 19:57)

6 Detroit 2 at Buffalo 5
7 Pittsburgh 4 at Detroit 5
9 Winnipeg 4 at Detroit 2 (Babych 19:53 en)
14 Colorado 1 at Detroit 3 (McKechnie 19:29 en)
16 Washington 5 at Detroit 5
17 Edmonton 4 at Detroit 4
20 Detroit 5 at Chicago 4
21 Calgary 7 at Detroit 4
23 Hartford 2 at Detroit 2 (all goals in 3rd) (Stoughton (H) tied game at 19:07)
26 Winnipeg 3 at Detroit 3
27 Detroit 6 at Minnesota 8 (Broten 19:21 en)
30 Detroit 3 at Canadiens 5 (Gainey 19:27 en)

February 4 Chicago 4 at Detroit 6 (Gare 19:58 en)
6 Detroit 2 at Islanders 6
7 St. Louis 5 at Detroit 8
11 Vancouver 4 at Detroit 4 (Hlinka (V) tied game at 19:30 on a penalty shot)
13 Detroit 1 at Minnesota 6
17 Detroit 3 at Toronto 3
18 Toronto 3 at Detroit 4
20 Boston 7 at Detroit 5
21 Edmonton 7 at Detroit 3
23 Detroit 6 at Colorado 3
24 Detroit 3 at Los Angeles 5
27 Detroit 2 at St. Louis 6
28 Minnesota 5 at Detroit 4 (Ciccarelli won game at 19:49)

March 3 Detroit 4 at Minnesota 6
5 Detroit 0 at Winnipeg 2 [Soetaert] (both goals in 3rd) (Lukowich 19:52 en)
6 Detroit 1 at St. Louis 5
8 Detroit 3 at Rangers 6
11 Rangers 4 at Detroit 1
13 Detroit 3 at Boston 5
18 St. Louis 7 at Detroit 4
20 Chicago 4 at Detroit 3
21 Detroit 2 at Winnipeg 8
24 Detroit 4 at Chicago 6
25 Minnesota 4 at Detroit 3
27 Detroit 2 at Toronto 1 (all goals in 2nd)
28 Toronto 4 at Detroit 6
31 Winnipeg 2 at Detroit 4 (McKechnie 19:29 en)

April 4 St. Louis 3 at Detroit 2

1982–1983

October 6 Detroit 1 at St. Louis 2
8 Minnesota 3 at Detroit 3
9 Detroit 0 at Winnipeg 8 [Staniowski]
14 Calgary 6 at Detroit 4
16 St. Louis 6 at Detroit 0 [Liut]
17 Chicago 6 at Detroit 4
20 Detroit 3 at Quebec 5 (M. Stastny 19:34 en)
23 Detroit 6 at Buffalo 2
24 Philadelphia 7 at Detroit 4 (Sittler 19:53 en)
27 Detroit 5 at St. Louis 4
28 Minnesota 7 at Detroit 3
30 Hartford 2 at Detroit 4

November 2 St. Louis 4 at Detroit 2
3 Detroit 3 at Islanders 3
6 Detroit 1 at New Jersey 1
7 Boston 7 at Detroit 0 [Peeters]
10 Toronto 8 at Detroit 2
13 Detroit 2 at Chicago 3
16 Vancouver 4 at Detroit 4
18 Los Angeles 4 at Detroit 1
20 St. Louis 2 at Detroit 2 (Ogrodnick (D) tied game at 19:07)
21 Chicago 3 at Detroit 0 [Bannerman] (Crossman 19:13 en)
24 Detroit 2 at Canadiens 4 (Napier 19:33 en)
27 Canadiens 5 at Detroit 5
28 Detroit 5 at Edmonton 7

December 1 Detroit 1 at Minnesota 4 (McCarthy 19:39 en)
4 Detroit 6 at New Jersey 2
8 Detroit 2 at Islanders 0 [Micalef] (both goals in 2nd)
11 Toronto 2 at Detroit 6
12 Detroit 7 at Calgary 3
15 Pittsburgh 4 at Detroit 4
16 Philadelphia 7 at Detroit 2
18 Detroit 3 at Rangers 3
21 Detroit 5 at St. Louis 5
23 Detroit 6 at Pittsburgh 4

26 Buffalo 2 at Detroit 2
27 Detroit 4 at Philadelphia 8
29 Minnesota 5 at Detroit 5
31 Detroit 4 at Chicago 1 (Gare 19:26 en)

January
2 Toronto 6 at Detroit 3
3 Rangers 6 at Detroit 2
5 Detroit 2 at Washington 5
8 Calgary 5 at Detroit 2
9 Edmonton 3 at Detroit 4
13 Detroit 4 at Los Angeles 4 (Huber (D) tied game at 19:26)
15 Detroit 4 at Toronto 3
16 Chicago 4 at Detroit 2
19 Minnesota 3 at Detroit 2
22 Detroit 1 at Boston 3
25 Detroit 6 at Vancouver 2
29 Boston 7 at Detroit 3

February
1 Washington 5 at Detroit 2
2 Detroit 3 at St. Louis 4
5 Detroit 3 at Chicago 4
6 Detroit 3 at Toronto 0 [Micalef]
9 Hartford 5 at Detroit 6
12 Detroit 2 at Winnipeg 4
15 Pittsburgh 3 at Detroit 7
17 Detroit 5 at Los Angeles 5
20 Detroit 7 at Hartford 2
22 Detroit 2 at Minnesota 3
24 New Jersey 4 at Detroit 1
26 Islanders 3 at Detroit 5 (Gare 19:47 en)
27 Detroit 4 at Canadiens 4

March
1 Quebec 5 at Detroit 5
3 Detroit 5 at Quebec 3
5 Detroit 1 at Minnesota 4
6 Buffalo 6 at Detroit 4
10 Detroit 4 at Chicago 2 (Osborne 19:41 en)
12 St. Louis 2 at Detroit 1
13 Detroit 2 at Toronto 5
16 Toronto 3 a Detroit 4 (Gare won game at 19:30)
19 Edmonton 9 at Detroit 7 (Messier 19:33 en)
20 Vancouver 6 at Detroit 3
23 Detroit 1 at Rangers 7
26 Detroit 5 at Minnesota 7 (T. Young 19:47 en)
27 Chicago 6 at Detroit 0 [Esposito]
30 Detroit 2 at Toronto 4

April
1 Detroit 8 at Washington 7 (Rowe won game at 19:29)
3 Winnipeg 8 at Detroit 3

1983–1984

October
5 Detroit 6 at Winnipeg 6 (5:00 OT)
8 New Jersey 6 at Detroit 3 (Broten 19:28 en)
9 Detroit 4 at Chicago 6 (Secord 19:55 en)
12 Detroit 3 at Edmonton 8
15 Detroit 3 at Los Angeles 3 (5:00 OT)
19 St. Louis 2 at Detroit 4 (Ogrodnick 19:22 en)
22 Calgary 1 at Detroit 4
26 Buffalo 5 at Detroit 6 (Yzerman 4:38 OT)
29 Quebec 3 at Detroit 4 (Manno :21 OT)

November
1 Detroit 3 at St. Louis 2
3 Chicago 4 at Detroit 7
5 Vancouver 3 at Detroit 2
6 Detroit 2 at Washington 3
9 Minnesota 5 at Detroit 3 (Ciccarelli 19:25 en)
12 Edmonton 7 at Detroit 3
13 Detroit 3 at Rangers 6
15 Detroit 3 at Quebec 1
17 Detroit 2 at Canadiens 4
19 Detroit 4 at Toronto 5
23 St. Louis 0 at Detroit 3 [Mio] (Ogrodnick 19:24 en)
25 Pittsburgh 2 at Detroit 5 (Kisio 19:56 en)
26 Detroit 7 at Pittsburgh 4
30 Toronto 5 at Detroit 3

December
3 Rangers 4 at Detroit 2 (Pavelich 19:36 en)
4 Detroit 0 at New Jersey 6 (Low and Resch share shutout)
7 Detroit 2 at Minnesota 7
10 Detroit 3 at St. Louis 8
11 Detroit 2 at Chicago 4
13 Los Angeles 7 at Detroit 5 (Nicholls 19:58 en)
15 Detroit 2 at Islanders 4 (Trottier 19:29 en)
17 Philadelphia 3 at Detroit 3 (5:00 OT)

18 Detroit 3 at Philadelphia 3 (5:00 OT)
(Yzerman (D) tied game at 19:59)
21 Vancouver 9 at Detroit 5
23 Toronto 2 at Detroit 9
26 Detroit 2 at Toronto 6
28 Detroit 3 at Washington 2
(Ogrodnick 3:55 OT)
29 Detroit 6 at New Jersey 1
31 Chicago 3 at Detroit 4

January 3 Hartford 1 at Detroit 7
5 Detroit 1 at Canadiens 5
7 Philadelphia 8 at Detroit 4
9 Edmonton 7 at Detroit 3
11 Boston 7 at Detroit 2
14 Buffalo 2 at Detroit 1
16 Detroit 5 at Rangers 8
(Larouche 19:49 en)
18 Calgary 4 at Detroit 2
20 Minnesota 8 at Detroit 5
21 Detroit 1 at Minnesota 5
24 Islanders 0 at Detroit 4 [Stefan]
27 Detroit 2 at Buffalo 2 (5:00 OT)
28 Detroit 4 at Islanders 3

February 1 Hartford 6 at Detroit 6 (5:00 OT)
4 Toronto 6 at Detroit 3
(afternoon game)
(Derlago 19:09 en / Derlago 19:52 en)
5 Detroit 6 at Boston 5
7 Detroit 1 at Hartford 4
(Francis 19:36 en)
9 Pittsburgh 3 at Detroit 9
11 Detroit 6 at Minnesota 4
(Foster 19:37 en)
12 Detroit 2 at Winnipeg 2 (5:00 OT)
(all goals in 2nd)
15 St. Louis 4 at Detroit 3
18 Chicago 0 at Detroit 6 [Stefan]
(afternoon game)
19 Detroit 6 at Toronto 2
22 Minnesota 2 at Detroit 5
25 Washington 1 at Detroit 4
(afternoon game)
26 Detroit 4 at Chicago 2
28 Detroit 2 at Quebec 6

March 1 Canadiens 3 at Detroit 1
3 Winnipeg 1 at Detroit 6
(afternoon game)
5 Detroit 1 at Minnesota 5
6 Detroit 3 at St. Louis 1
8 St. Louis 3 at Detroit 6
10 Detroit 3 at Toronto 4
(Gavin :29 OT)
14 Boston 4 at Detroit 2
(Krushelnyski 19:10 en)
15 Detroit 3 at St. Louis 5
(Bothwell 19:49 en)
17 Minnesota 4 at Detroit 3
(afternoon game)
20 Detroit 6 at Vancouver 3
(Dunlop 18:43 en)
22 Detroit 6 at Calgary 4
(Larson 19:32 en)
24 Detroit 7 at Los Angeles 9
(Harris 19:29 en)
28 Toronto 2 at Detroit 4
(Gare 19:14 en)
31 Chicago 4 at Detroit 2
(afternoon game)
(Sutter 19:52 en)

April 1 Detroit 3 at Chicago 4
(afternoon game)

1984–1985

October 11 Detroit 3 at Chicago 7
13 New Jersey 1 at Detroit 4
14 Detroit 4 at Buffalo 6
17 Islanders 6 at Detroit 4
18 Detroit 3 at Hartford 7
20 Chicago 4 at Detroit 7
24 Detroit 1 at Toronto 6
26 Buffalo 3 at Detroit 7
(Manno 19:11 en / Gare 19:16 en / Gare 19:45 en)
30 Detroit 3 at Pittsburgh 4

November 1 Calgary 9 at Detroit 5
2 Winnipeg 3 at Detroit 3 (5:00 OT)
6 Canadiens 2 at Detroit 4
(Manno 19:20 en)
8 Detroit 2 at Boston 5
10 Boston 4 at Detroit 2
13 Detroit 4 at Calgary 5
(Reinhart 4:48 OT)
14 Detroit 2 at Vancouver 3
17 Detroit 3 at Minnesota 3 (5:00 OT)
21 Hartford 2 at Detroit 4
(Lambert 19:32 en)
23 Toronto 5 at Detroit 6
24 Detroit 4 at Canadiens 6
(Naslund 19:56 en)

28 Canadiens 3 at Detroit 3 (5:00 OT)
30 St. Louis 5 at Detroit 3 (Wickenheiser 18:57 en)

December
1 Detroit 5 at St. Louis 10
4 Toronto 6 at Detroit 7 (Ogrodnick won game at 19:11)
5 Detroit 4 at Toronto 2
7 Chicago 4 at Detroit 5
9 Detroit 0 at Washington 4 [Mason] (afternoon game)
10 Detroit 4 at Minnesota 3
12 Detroit 1 at Chicago 5
14 Detroit 4 at Buffalo 4 (5:00 OT)
16 Detroit 2 at Winnipeg 5
20 Quebec 4 at Detroit 5
22 Minnesota 5 at Detroit 4
26 Rangers 2 at Detroit 5 (Gare 19:55 en)
28 Detroit 4 at Calgary 3
29 Detroit 3 at Edmonton 6
31 Pittsburgh 4 at Detroit 4 (5:00 OT)

January
2 Islanders 7 at Detroit 2
3 Detroit 2 at Hartford 6
5 Los Angeles 5 at Detroit 3
8 Washington 4 at Detroit 2 (Jarvis 19:15 en)
12 Detroit 3 at Boston 4 (afternoon game)
13 Detroit 2 at Quebec 5 (P. Stastny 19:43 en)
16 Philadelphia 1 at Detroit 1 (5:00 OT)
17 Detroit 5 at Philadelphia 7
19 Winnipeg 8 at Detroit 5
21 St. Louis 6 at Detroit 3
22 Detroit 5 at Islanders 4
24 Detroit 1 at Rangers 3
26 Detroit 4 at Minnesota 4 (5:00 OT)
29 Washington 3 at Detroit 4
31 Detroit 2 at St. Louis 3

February
2 Quebec 3 at Detroit 6 (afternoon game)
3 Detroit 5 at New Jersey 5 (5:00 OT)
7 St. Louis 5 at Detroit 5 (5:00 OT)
9 Edmonton 6 at Detroit 5
14 Minnesota 5 at Detroit 5 (5:00 OT)
16 Chicago 4 at Detroit 7 (afternoon game) (Foster 19:43 en)
17 Detroit 4 at Chicago 4 (5:00 OT) (afternoon game)
20 St. Louis 2 at Detroit 3
23 Toronto 4 at Detroit 2 (afternoon game)
24 Detroit 2 at Chicago 3 (afternoon game)
27 Vancouver 5 at Detroit 11

March
1 Minnesota 2 at Detroit 6
2 Detroit 2 at Minnesota 5
6 Detroit 5 at Toronto 3 (Foster 19:14 en)
9 New Jersey 8 at Detroit 5 (afternoon game)
10 Detroit 2 at St. Louis 6
13 Detroit 6 at Edmonton 7
15 Detroit 6 at Vancouver 5
16 Detroit 3 at Los Angeles 8
20 Los Angeles 6 at Detroit 8 (Foster 18:42 en)
22 Rangers 3 at Detroit 5
24 Toronto 5 at Detroit 3
26 Minnesota 1 at Detroit 5
28 Detroit 1 at Philadelphia 3
30 Detroit 9 at Toronto 3

April
3 Detroit 3 at Pittsburgh 2
6 Chicago 2 at Detroit 2 (5:00 OT) (afternoon game) (Duguay (D) tied game at 19:49)
7 Detroit 5 at St. Louis 6 (Mullen 1:35 OT)

1985–1986

October
10 Minnesota 6 at Detroit 6 (5:00 OT)
12 Boston 9 at Detroit 2
14 Detroit 1 at Buffalo 6
16 Winnipeg 4 at Detroit 3
17 Detroit 1 at Minnesota 10
19 Chicago 6 at Detroit 2
23 Vancouver 5 at Detroit 0 [Brodeur]
26 Detroit 4 at Calgary 7
27 Detroit 3 at Winnipeg 5
30 Pittsburgh 3 at Detroit 6 (Duguay 19:11 en)
31 Detroit 2 at New Jersey 2 (5:00 OT) (Sulliman (NJ) tied game at 19:32)

November
2 Detroit 5 at St. Louis 5 (5:00 OT)
6 St. Louis 2 at Detroit 4
8 Toronto 3 at Detroit 3 (5:00 OT)
11 Detroit 0 at Vancouver 5 [Brodeur]
13 Detroit 7 at Los Angeles 2

16 Detroit 4 at Minnesota 2
19 Vancouver 7 at Detroit 5 (Gradin 19:05 en)
21 Los Angeles 5 at Detroit 4 (Sykes 3:59 OT)
23 Detroit 3 at Toronto 9
27 Buffalo 1 at Detroit 4 (Gallant 19:59 en)
29 St. Louis 3 at Detroit 5
30 Detroit 1 at Canadiens 10

December 3 Philadelphia 1 at Detroit 4
4 Detroit 2 at Pittsburgh 5
7 Detroit 4 at St. Louis 5
11 Minnesota 10 at Detroit 2
14 Philadelphia 6 at Detroit 4 (Craven 19:53 en)
15 Detroit 4 at Chicago 6
17 Detroit 3 at Minnesota 6 (Acton 19:12 en)
21 Chicago 6 at Detroit 3
23 Detroit 2 at Rangers 10
26 Toronto 5 at Detroit 4 (Ihnacak won game at 19:57)
28 Detroit 5 at Quebec 4
29 Detroit 2 at Hartford 5
31 Islanders 5 at Detroit 4 (Makela :53 OT)

January 2 Buffalo 2 at Detroit 2 (5:00 OT)
4 Quebec 7 at Detroit 2
5 Detroit 6 at Toronto 5
7 Detroit 3 at Washington 4
10 Chicago 9 at Detroit 4
11 Detroit 2 at Islanders 8
13 Detroit 4 at Toronto 7
15 New Jersey 4 at Detroit 3 (Ogrodnick (D) tied game at 19:07) (Higgins 1:23 OT)
18 Calgary 7 at Detroit 4 (afternoon game)
19 Detroit 4 at Chicago 6 (T. Murray 19:35 en)
22 Boston 5 at Detroit 6 (Young 1:32 OT)
23 Detroit 2 at Philadelphia 5
25 Detroit 3 at Boston 6 (afternoon game)
28 Washington 0 at Detroit 7 [Laforest]
31 St. Louis 6 at Detroit 4

February 1 Detroit 3 at St. Louis 4
6 Hartford 3 at Detroit 4 (Loiselle 2:22 OT)
8 Canadiens 5 at Detroit 3 (Nilan 19:21 en)
11 Edmonton 3 at Detroit 2
14 Rangers 7 at Detroit 5 (Maloney 19:17 en)
16 Detroit 1 at Rangers 3
18 Detroit 0 at St. Louis 5 [Wamsley]
21 Pittsburgh 7 at Detroit 3
22 Detroit 2 at Islanders 5
25 Detroit 3 at Washington 4 (Anderson :36 OT)
28 Toronto 7 at Detroit 3

March 1 Detroit 6 at Toronto 4
3 Minnesota 8 at Detroit 5 (Plett 19:49 en)
5 Detroit 8 at Chicago 3
6 Detroit 2 at New Jersey 7
9 Calgary 3 at Detroit 3 (5:00 OT) (afternoon game)
12 Detroit 3 at Los Angeles 0 [Stefan]
14 Detroit 3 at Edmonton 12
16 Detroit 0 at Winnipeg 6 [Bouchard] (afternoon game)
18 Hartford 6 at Detroit 4 (Anderson 18:56 en)
20 St. Louis 3 at Detroit 2 (Norwood 2:49 OT)
22 Chicago 4 at Detroit 8 (afternoon game)
25 Edmonton 7 at Detroit 2
26 Detroit 3 at Chicago 5
29 Minnesota 5 at Detroit 4 (afternoon game)

April 1 Detroit 0 at Quebec 4 [Malarchuk]
2 Detroit 3 at Canadiens 6
5 Detroit 3 at Minnesota 5
6 Toronto 2 at Detroit 4

1986–1987

October 9 Detroit 1 at Quebec 6
11 Chicago 3 at Detroit 4
15 Los Angeles 4 at Detroit 3 (Nicholls 4:41 OT)
17 Detroit 3 at Edmonton 4
18 Detroit 5 at Calgary 3 (Yzerman 19:49 en)
22 Canadiens 4 at Detroit 3
24 St. Louis 1 at Detroit 1 (5:00 OT) (both goals in 1st)

	25	Detroit 3 at St. Louis 1
	29	Chicago 2 at Detroit 5
	30	Detroit 3 at Minnesota 1 (Burr 19:02 en)
November	1	Detroit 0 at Toronto 2 [Bester] (both goals in 1st)
	5	Rangers 4 at Detroit 5 (Shedden 2:21 OT)
	8	Detroit 1 at Islanders 2 (Flatley 4:11 OT)
	9	Pittsburgh 1 at Detroit 2
	12	Detroit 3 at New Jersey 5
	13	Detroit 5 at Philadelphia 7
	15	Detroit 0 at Toronto 6 [Bester]
	19	New Jersey 4 at Detroit 3
	21	Washington 3 at Detroit 3 (5:00 OT)
	22	Detroit 4 at Canadiens 3
	26	Toronto 3 at Detroit 1
	28	St. Louis 2 at Detroit 1 (Hunter 4:10 OT)
	29	Detroit 4 at St. Louis 2
December	2	Detroit 4 at Los Angeles 5
	5	Canadiens 3 at Detroit 3 (5:00 OT)
	6	Detroit 4 at Hartford 1 (McRae 19:39 en)
	9	Buffalo 5 at Detroit 5 (5:00 OT)
	11	Minnesota 6 at Detroit 6 (5:00 OT)
	16	Detroit 3 at Calgary 8
	17	Detroit 5 at Vancouver 4 (Carroll 19:10 en)
	20	Hartford 2 at Detroit 2 (5:00 OT) (Sid Abel Night)
	21	Detroit 4 at Chicago 7
	23	Chicago 1 at Detroit 3
	26	Toronto 2 at Detroit 4
	27	Detroit 5 at Toronto 5 (5:00 OT)
	31	Calgary 4 at Detroit 6 (Higgins 19:28 en)
January	2	Minnesota 1 at Detroit 2
	3	Detroit 3 at Minnesota 2
	6	Toronto 3 at Detroit 1 (M. Ihnacak 19:48 en)
	8	Detroit 4 at Boston 4 (5:00 OT) (Bourque (B) tied game at 19:57)
	10	Winnipeg 5 at Detroit 2 (MacLean 18:59 en)
	11	Detroit 3 at Chicago 5 (B. Murray 19:25 en)
	13	Edmonton 5 at Detroit 3 (Kurri 19:39 en)
	15	Toronto 3 at Detroit 1 (Frycer 19:35 en)
	17	Quebec 2 at Detroit 3
	18	Detroit 1 at Pittsburgh 0 [Hanlon] (Barr 9:55 3rd)
	21	Islanders 5 at Detroit 8
	23	St. Louis 3 at Detroit 4
	24	Detroit 3 at St. Louis 5
	28	Washington 2 at Detroit 1
	31	Detroit 4 at Toronto 2
February	1	Detroit 1 at Buffalo 6
	4	Detroit 4 at Chicago 5
	6	Minnesota 4 at Detroit 6
	7	Detroit 5 at Minnesota 3
	14	New Jersey 1 at Detroit 5 (afternoon game)
	17	Detroit 2 at Rangers 6
	18	Winnipeg 2 at Detroit 5
	20	Quebec 3 at Detroit 6
	22	Detroit 2 at Chicago 2 (5:00 OT)
	24	Detroit 2 at Washington 8
	26	Vancouver 4 at Detroit 5
	28	Rangers 1 at Detroit 4 (afternoon game)
March	2	Detroit 4 at Boston 3 (Klima 4:52 OT)
	3	Detroit 3 at Hartford 5
	5	Minnesota 3 at Detroit 9
	7	Detroit 3 at St. Louis 5 (Cavallini 19:16 en)
	10	Detroit 4 at Vancouver 7 (Sutter 19:37 en)
	11	Detroit 3 at Edmonton 6
	14	Detroit 4 at Minnesota 3 (afternoon game)
	15	Detroit 1 at Winnipeg 1 (5:00 OT) (afternoon game) (both goals in 2nd)
	17	Boston 1 at Detroit 3
	19	Islanders 3 at Detroit 2 (Lafontaine won game at 19:56)
	21	Chicago 0 at Detroit 3 [Stefan] (Burr 19:59 en) (all goals in 3rd)
	22	Detroit 2 at Buffalo 3
	25	Los Angeles 6 at Detroit 1
	28	Detroit 5 at Philadelphia 1 (afternoon game)
April	1	Philadelphia 2 at Detroit 1
	4	Detroit 3 at Pittsburgh 4 (Lemieux 1:26 OT)

5 St. Louis 3 at Detroit 2
(Ramage 3:49 OT)

1987–1988

October 8 Detroit 1 at Calgary 5
9 Detroit 4 at Edmonton 1
(Chabot 19:10 en)
12 Detroit 3 at Vancouver 2
(all goals in 3rd)
16 Toronto 2 at Detroit 3
17 Detroit 4 at Toronto 7
21 Chicago 5 at Detroit 1
23 Pittsburgh 2 at Detroit 5
(Gallant 19:52 en)
28 Detroit 5 at Winnipeg 1
30 Canadiens 5 at Detroit 4
31 Detroit 3 at St. Louis 3 (5:00 OT)

November 3 Minnesota 2 at Detroit 2 (5:00 OT)
4 Detroit 4 at Minnesota 7
(Gagner 19:30 en / Ciccarelli 19:42 en)
6 Hartford 1 at Detroit 3
7 Detroit 3 at Islanders 4
(Kromm 1:46 OT)
(Yzerman (D) tied game at 19:28)
11 Detroit 3 at Chicago 6
14 Detroit 6 at New Jersey 4
17 Detroit 1 at Washington 0 [Hanlon]
(Yzerman 6:33 1st)
19 Vancouver 4 at Detroit 1
(Lanthier 19:16 en)
22 Boston 1 at Detroit 0 [Keans]
(O'Dwyer 16:13 2nd)
25 Winnipeg 8 at Detroit 10
27 St. Louis 0 at Detroit 6 [Stefan]
28 Detroit 3 at Boston 2
(Probert 2:46 OT)

December 2 Edmonton 4 at Detroit 7
4 Chicago 0 at Detroit 12 [Stefan]
7 Detroit 4 at Toronto 5
(Courtnall 2:21 OT)
9 St. Louis 4 at Detroit 4 (5:00 OT)
11 Philadelphia 3 at Detroit 3 (5:00 OT)
12 Detroit 3 at Canadiens 5
14 Detroit 3 at Rangers 4
16 Washington 1 at Detroit 6
18 Minnesota 3 at Detroit 8
20 Detroit 2 at Quebec 4
(P. Stastny 19:55 en)
23 Buffalo 5 at Detroit 2
26 Detroit 3 at Pittsburgh 6
27 Detroit 4 at Minnesota 5
30 Detroit 3 at St. Louis 2
31 St. Louis 2 at Detroit 7

January 3 Detroit 4 at Winnipeg 4
(5:00 OT)
6 St. Louis 2 at Detroit 4
8 Los Angeles 3 at Detroit 5
10 Pittsburgh 5 at Detroit 7
13 Detroit 7 at Rangers 4
15 Minnesota 1 at Detroit 2
16 Detroit 2 at Minnesota 4
18 Toronto 3 at Detroit 4
21 Detroit 3 at New Jersey 2
(Ashton 3:37 OT)
(Shanahan (NJ) tied game at 19:47)
23 Calgary 4 at Detroit 4 (5:00 OT)
24 Detroit 1 at Hartford 2
(Ferraro 2:21 OT)
26 Chicago 6 at Detroit 4
(T. Murray 19:58 en)
29 Toronto 3 at Detroit 3 (5:00 OT)
(Olczyk (T) tied game at 19:57)
30 Detroit 5 at Toronto 5 (5:00 OT)

February 3 Detroit 6 at Chicago 4
5 Calgary 1 at Detroit 5
6 Detroit 5 at Canadiens 4
12 New Jersey 3 at Detroit 4
13 Detroit 3 at St. Louis 5
15 Detroit 6 at Los Angeles 1
17 Detroit 4 at Chicago 3
20 Chicago 1 at Detroit 6
21 Detroit 3 at Philadelphia 5
(afternoon game)
(Tocchet 19:31 en)
23 Philadelphia 11 at Detroit 6
26 Quebec 3 at Detroit 2
27 Detroit 4 at Quebec 5

March 1 Buffalo 0 at Detroit 4 [Hanlon]
3 Minnesota 3 at Detroit 6
5 Detroit 4 at St. Louis 4 (5:00 OT)
6 Detroit 4 at Chicago 3
8 Boston 0 at Detroit 2 [Hanlon]
(both goals in 1st)
10 Vancouver 2 at Detroit 5
12 Detroit 4 at Islanders 3
13 Islanders 1 at Detroit 5
16 Detroit 2 at Minnesota 1
19 Detroit 4 at Los Angeles 7

22 Edmonton 6 at Detroit 4 (Simpson 19:46 en)
24 Hartford 3 at Detroit 2
26 Rangers 4 at Detroit 4 (5:00 OT) (afternoon game)
27 Detroit 5 at Buffalo 3
29 Detroit 2 at Washington 2 (5:00 OT)

April
1 Toronto 3 at Detroit 7
2 Detroit 3 at Toronto 5

1988–1989

October
6 Detroit 2 at Los Angeles 8
8 Detroit 3 at Vancouver 3 (5:00 OT)
10 Detroit 2 at Calgary 5
14 St. Louis 8 at Detroit 8 (5:00 OT) (MacLean (D) tied game at 19:30)
15 Detroit 5 at Toronto 3 (Yzerman 19:37 en)
18 Chicago 3 at Detroit 4 (Yzerman 4:59 OT)
21 Toronto 4 at Detroit 2
23 New Jersey 3 at Detroit 3 (5:00 OT)
26 Canadiens 2 at Detroit 4 (Yzerman 19:11 en)
28 Minnesota 1 at Detroit 4 (Chabot 18:53 en)
29 Detroit 2 at Minnesota 3

November
1 Washington 3 at Detroit 3 (5:00 OT) (Gartner (W) tied game at 19:02 with extra attacker)
4 Philadelphia 4 at Detroit 3
6 Edmonton 2 at Detroit 5
9 Detroit 6 a Minnesota 3 (Nill 19:34 en)
12 Detroit 5 at Philadelphia 4 (afternoon game)
13 Detroit 5 at Rangers 3
16 Detroit 4 at Hartford 3
18 Boston 2 at Detroit 5
20 Detroit 5 at Boston 4 (Yzerman 4:13 OT)
23 Los Angeles 8 at Detroit 3
25 Winnipeg 3 at Detroit 6
27 Washington 4 at Detroit 3
29 Islanders 3 at Detroit 5 (Gallant 19:35 en)

December
1 Quebec 3 at Detroit 7
3 Detroit 4 at Quebec 6 (Fortier 19:02 en)
5 Detroit 2 at Canadiens 7
9 Toronto 3 at Detroit 4
10 Detroit 8 at Toronto 2
13 Minnesota 4 at Detroit 5
16 Los Angeles 6 at Detroit 4 (Gretzky 19:59 en)
17 Detroit 2 at Pittsburgh 3
20 St. Louis 3 at Detroit 6
22 Detroit 4 at St. Louis 4 (5:00 OT)
23 Detroit 2 at Chicago 7
28 Detroit 1 at Buffalo 4
30 Detroit 3 at Hartford 4
31 Hartford 3 at Detroit 2

January
4 St. Louis 2 at Detroit 4
6 Vancouver 2 at Detroit 2 (5:00 OT)
7 Detroit 2 at New Jersey 5
9 Canadiens 2 at Detroit 3
11 Detroit 2 at Chicago 2 (5:00 OT)
14 Detroit 5 at Boston 5 (5:00 OT) (afternoon game)
15 Detroit 8 at Philadelphia 4
17 Calgary 7 at Detroit 1
20 Chicago 3 at Detroit 2 (Graham won game at 19:59)
22 Detroit 4 at Washington 3 (afternoon game)
25 Buffalo 6 at Detroit 3 (Vaive 19:00 en)
27 Toronto 1 at Detroit 8
28 Detroit 5 at Pittsburgh 10
30 Quebec 4 at Detroit 3

February
2 Detroit 2 at Calgary 3 (Nieuwendyk 1:45 OT)
3 Detroit 5 at Edmonton 8
5 Detroit 6 at Winnipeg 2 (afternoon game)
9 New Jersey 6 at Detroit 3
11 Detroit 5 at Minnesota 1
13 Winnipeg 2 at Detroit 2 (5:00 OT)
15 Minnesota 2 at Detroit 4
17 Chicago 5 at Detroit 3 (Manson 18:50 en)
19 Detroit 4 at Buffalo 8 (afternoon game)
21 Detroit 6 at Islanders 5
23 Pittsburgh 6 at Detroit 6 (5:00 OT) (Penguins scored first six goals, Detroit the next six)
25 Chicago 0 at Detroit 5 [Hanlon] (afternoon game)

26 Detroit 4 at Chicago 4 (5:00 OT) (afternoon game)

March 1 Islanders 5 at Detroit 6

4 Detroit 5 at St. Louis 4

7 Detroit 3 at Minnesota 5

9 Rangers 2 at Detroit 3

11 Detroit 3 at Toronto 5 (Osborne 19:43 en)

14 Detroit 2 at Vancouver 2 (5:00 OT)

15 Detroit 8 at Edmonton 6 (Yzerman 19:39 en)

18 Detroit 2 at St. Louis 3

19 Detroit 3 at Chicago 5 (T. Murray 19:04 en)

24 Toronto 2 at Detroit 6

25 Detroit 5 at Toronto 6 (Olczyk 19:19 en)

27 St. Louis 3 at Detroit 2

29 Rangers 3 at Detroit 4

31 Minnesota 5 at Detroit 1

April 2 Detroit 2 at St. Louis 4

1989–1990

October 5 Detroit 7 at Calgary 10

7 Detroit 3 at Vancouver 5 (Krutov 19:59 en)

8 Detroit 0 at Los Angeles 5 [Hrudey]

12 Winnipeg 4 at Detroit 5

14 Buffalo 2 at Detroit 6

15 Detroit 0 at Chicago 3 [Cloutier] (Savard 18:48 en)

18 Minnesota 3 at Detroit 4

19 Detroit 4 at St. Louis 3

21 Detroit 3 at Hartford 3 (5:00 OT)

24 Chicago 5 at Detroit 3

26 Pittsburgh 3 at Detroit 3 (5:00 OT)

28 Detroit 4 at Toronto 6

November 1 Philadelphia 5 at Detroit 5 (5:00 OT)

3 Hartford 4 at Detroit 3

4 Detroit 2 at Islanders 3

6 Detroit 1 at Rangers 6

9 Detroit 1 at Minnesota 5

11 Detroit 2 at Toronto 4

14 Hartford 3 at Detroit 0 [Liut]

16 St. Louis 7 at Detroit 2

18 Detroit 8 at Quebec 1

21 Boston 2 at Detroit 1 (Sweeney 2:09 OT)

24 Calgary 2 at Detroit 3 (Gallant won game at 19:22)

27 Edmonton 6 at Detroit 2

29 Washington 5 at Detroit 3 (May 19:09 en)

December 1 Detroit 3 at Winnipeg 3 (5:00 OT)

3 Detroit 4 at Chicago 3

5 St. Louis 2 at Detroit 2 (5:00 OT)

8 Minnesota 1 at Detroit 2

9 Detroit 3 at Minnesota 1 (Chabot 19:07 en)

13 Toronto 4 at Detroit 2

15 Chicago 4 at Detroit 8

16 Detroit 1 at Canadiens 3

20 Toronto 2 at Detroit 4

23 Detroit 5 at Boston 6 (afternoon game)

26 Detroit 3 at Buffalo 6 (Hogue 18:51 en)

27 Detroit 7 at Toronto 7 (5:00 OT)

29 Detroit 1 at Washington 2

31 New Jersey 4 at Detroit 6

January 2 Vancouver 1 at Detroit 4

4 Quebec 1 at Detroit 4

6 Detroit 3 at Minnesota 4

9 Minnesota 0 at Detroit 9 [Hanlon]

12 Detroit 5 at Winnipeg 7

13 Detroit 4 at Minnesota 6

16 Detroit 6 at Edmonton 4 (Chiasson 19:35 en)

18 Detroit 4 at Los Angeles 9

23 St. Louis 6 at Detroit 3

25 Pittsburgh 5 at Detroit 3

27 Detroit 8 at Quebec 6

31 Edmonton 5 at Detroit 7 (Yzerman 19:10 en)

February 2 Toronto 2 at Detroit 5 (Yzerman 19:33 en)

3 Detroit 2 at St. Louis 4

6 Boston 2 at Detroit 0 [Moog]

8 Chicago 8 at Detroit 6 (Creighton 19:10 en)

10 Calgary 5 at Detroit 7 (afternoon game) (Yzerman 19:13 en)

12 Detroit 1 at New Jersey 1 (5:00 OT)

14 Los Angeles 5 at Detroit 6

16 Philadelphia 6 at Detroit 9 (Adams 18:39 en)

17 Detroit 1 at St. Louis 6

	19	Canadiens 5 at Detroit 5 (5:00 OT)
	21	Rangers 4 at Detroit 4 (5:00 OT)
	24	Detroit 3 at Islanders 3 (5:00 OT) (afternoon game)
	25	Detroit 4 at Washington 9 (afternoon game)
	28	Islanders 3 at Detroit 4
March	2	Toronto 2 at Detroit 3 (Yzerman 3:44 OT)
	3	Detroit 5 at Toronto 2
	5	Detroit 2 at Rangers 3
	8	St. Louis 2 at Detroit 3
	10	Detroit 3 at Canadiens 3 (5:00 OT) (McPhee (C) tied game at 19:25)
	13	Detroit 3 at Chicago 3 (5:00 OT)
	15	Detroit 1 at Pittsburgh 6
	17	Detroit 4 at St. Louis 3 (Kocur 3:47 OT)
	20	Vancouver 4 at Detroit 4 (5:00 OT)
	22	Minnesota 5 at Detroit 1 (Bellows 17:35 en)
	24	Chicago 3 at Detroit 5 (afternoon game) (Yzerman 19:35 en)
	25	Detroit 2 at Chicago 3 (afternoon game)
	27	Buffalo 6 at Detroit 5
	31	Detroit 1 at New Jersey 5 (afternoon game)
April	1	Detroit 3 at Philadelphia 3 (5:00 OT)

1990–1991

October	4	Detroit 3 at New Jersey 3 (5:00 OT)
	6	Detroit 4 at Washington 6
	7	Detroit 2 at Philadelphia 7
	10	Calgary 5 at Detroit 6 (OT) (Probert 4:06 OT)
	12	Hartford 2 at Detroit 4
	13	Detroit 3 at Toronto 3 (5:00 OT)
	16	Chicago 2 at Detroit 3
	18	Canadiens 2 at Detroit 5
	20	Detroit 3 at Quebec 5 (afternoon game)
	23	Vancouver 0 at Detroit 6 [Cheveldae]
	26	Minnesota 6 at Detroit 8 (Carson 19:05 en)
	27	Detroit 2 at Minnesota 2 (5:00 OT)
	30	St. Louis 5 at Detroit 2
November	1	Toronto 4 at Detroit 5
	3	Detroit 2 at Canadiens 5 (Richer 19:08 en)
	6	Detroit 3 at Vancouver 6 (Bozek 19:09 en)
	8	Detroit 1 at Los Angeles 5
	10	Detroit 1 at St. Louis 6
	14	Chicago 3 at Detroit 2 (Probert scored at 19:05 with extra attacker)
	17	Detroit 8 at Toronto 4
	19	Washington 3 at Detroit 2 (Druce 2:31 OT)
	21	Minnesota 3 at Detroit 4
	23	St. Louis 3 at Detroit 5
	27	Los Angeles 3 at Detroit 4
	29	Detroit 5 at Chicago 1
December	1	Chicago 3 at Detroit 4 (afternoon game)
	2	Detroit 3 at Buffalo 3 (5:00 OT) (Andreychuk (B) tied game at 19:39)
	4	Boston 5 at Detroit 4 (Burridge 1:03 OT)
	7	St. Louis 6 at Detroit 3
	8	Detroit 1 at St. Louis 2
	11	Buffalo 3 at Detroit 8
	13	Quebec 2 at Detroit 5
	15	Detroit 3 at Philadelphia 1 (afternoon game) (Fedorov 19:34 en)
	16	Detroit 1 at Pittsburgh 4
	18	Philadelphia 1 at Detroit 3 (Yzerman 19:47 en)
	20	Winnipeg 1 at Detroit 3
	22	Detroit 5 at Winnipeg 2
	23	Detroit 2 at Chicago 3
	28	Detroit 0 at Pittsburgh 5 [Barrasso]
	31	Chicago 4 at Detroit 0 [Belfour]
January	2	Minnesota 2 at Detroit 6
	4	Detroit 2 at Edmonton 3
	5	Detroit 0 at Calgary 7 [Vernon]
	9	Edmonton 3 at Detroit 5 (Barr 19:38 en)
	11	Rangers 3 at Detroit 6
	12	Detroit 2 at Islanders 2 (5:00 OT)
	14	Detroit 1 at Boston 6
	16	Detroit 3 at Buffalo 5
	22	Washington 2 at Detroit 1
	25	St. Louis 9 at Detroit 4

26 Detroit 4 at St. Louis 5
28 New Jersey 6 at Detroit 2
30 Detroit 2 at Minnesota 5
February 1 Toronto 1 at Detroit 4 (Ysebaert 19:55 en)
2 Detroit 5 at Toronto 2
4 Los Angeles 6 at Detroit 4
8 Islanders 4 at Detroit 8
9 Detroit 5 at Minnesota 6
12 Winnipeg 1 at Detroit 6
13 Hartford 6 at Detroit 2
16 Minnesota 3 at Detroit 0 [Casey] (afternoon game)
17 Detroit 3 at Chicago 3 (5:00 OT) (afternoon game)
19 Detroit 4 at Calgary 4 (5:00 OT)
22 Detroit 5 at Edmonton 5 (5:00 OT)
23 Detroit 2 at Vancouver 5 (Linden 19:11 en)
25 Toronto 4 at Detroit 5 (Racine 1:26 OT)
27 Canadiens 3 at Detroit 5
March 1 New Jersey 6 at Detroit 1
5 Quebec 3 at Detroit 6
7 Islanders 0 at Detroit 2 [Cheveldae] (both goals in 2nd)
9 Detroit 2 at Minnesota 6 (afternoon game)
10 Detroit 4 at St. Louis 1 (Yzerman 19:42 en)
13 Detroit 4 at Rangers 1
14 Detroit 2 at Hartford 4
16 Detroit 5 at Boston 3 (afternoon game)
22 Toronto 3 at Detroit 1 (Damphousse 19:33 en)
23 Detroit 1 at Toronto 4 (Gill 19:47 en)
27 Pittsburgh 7 at Detroit 4
30 Rangers 5 at Detroit 6 (afternoon game)
31 Detroit 1 at Chicago 5

1991–1992

October 3 Detroit 3 at Chicago 3 (5:00 OT)
5 Detroit 5 at Toronto 8
10 Canadiens 4 at Detroit 1
12 Detroit 2 at Minnesota 3
15 Edmonton 1 at Detroit 3
17 St. Louis 3 at Detroit 6
19 Detroit 6 at Quebec 1
23 Winnipeg 3 at Detroit 2
25 Toronto 0 at Detroit 4 [Cheveldae]
26 Detroit 1 at Toronto 6
28 Los Angeles 4 at Detroit 3
30 Buffalo 1 at Detroit 3
November 1 Hartford 5 at Detroit 8
2 Detroit 1 at Boston 4
5 Minnesota 3 at Detroit 2
7 St. Louis 3 at Detroit 10
8 Detroit 5 at Washington 4
12 Detroit 5 at Calgary 4 (Sheppard (D) tied game at 19:24) (Sheppard 3:36 OT)
14 San Jose 3 at Detroit 3 (5:00 OT)
16 Detroit 5 at Los Angeles 3
19 Chicago 1 at Detroit 4
22 Minnesota 3 at Detroit 4
23 Detroit 2 at Minnesota 2 (5:00 OT) (Lidstrom (D) tied game at 19:36)
25 Washington 4 at Detroit 5
27 St. Louis 4 at Detroit 6
30 Detroit 3 at St. Louis 7
December 3 Calgary 2 at Detroit 5
6 Rangers 5 at Detroit 6 (Fedyk 4:23 OT)
7 Detroit 2 at New Jersey 2 (5:00 OT) (all goals in 2nd)
10 Chicago 3 at Detroit 5
12 Quebec 1 at Detroit 4
14 Detroit 4 at Calgary 3 (Fedorov 2:10 OT)
15 Detroit 4 at Edmonton 1
17 Detroit 1 at Vancouver 2 (all goals in 2nd)
21 Detroit 5 at Los Angeles 2
28 Detroit 5 at Toronto 4
29 Detroit 6 at Chicago 4
31 Boston 5 at Detroit 3
January 3 Toronto 4 at Detroit 6 (Ysebaert 19:24 en)
4 Detroit 6 at St. Louis 2
7 Islanders 5 at Detroit 2
9 Minnesota 4 at Detroit 9
11 Edmonton 5 at Detroit 5 (5:00 OT)
14 Detroit 2 at Islanders 6
16 Pittsburgh 3 at Detroit 3 (5:00 OT)
21 Philadelphia 3 at Detroit 7

23 Vancouver 3 at Detroit 1 (Bure 19:56 en)
25 Detroit 7 at New Jersey 0 [Cheveldae]
29 Buffalo 4 at Detroit 4 (5:00 OT) (Ysebaert (D) tied game at 19:30)
31 New Jersey 6 at Detroit 3 (Chorske 19:48 en)

February
1 Detroit 3 at Canadiens 4 (Muller 2:14 OT)
3 Detroit 4 at Pittsburgh 4 (5:00 OT)
5 Washington 1 at Detroit 4 (Yzerman 19:58 en)
7 Toronto 4 at Detroit 3
9 Detroit 5 at Rangers 5 (5:00 OT)
11 Detroit 3 at Toronto 4 (Bradley won game at 19:58)
12 Detroit 9 at Buffalo 4
15 San Jose 1 at Detroit 11
17 St. Louis 3 at Detroit 5 (Sheppard 19:15 en)
20 Toronto 2 at Detroit 3
22 Chicago 1 at Detroit 2 (afternoon game)
23 Detroit 4 at Hartford 0 [Cheveldae] (afternoon game)
27 Detroit 2 at Chicago 4
29 Detroit 3 at St. Louis 2

March
3 Winnipeg 4 at Detroit 3
5 Minnesota 4 at Detroit 2
7 Detroit 4 at Quebec 4 (5:00 OT)
8 Detroit 1 at Canadiens 4
12 Detroit 5 at St. Louis 4
14 Detroit 1 at Minnesota 4 (afternoon game) (Gagner 18:46 en)
15 Detroit 1 at Winnipeg 1 (5:00 OT) (both goals in 3rd)
17 Detroit 5 at San Jose 4
20 Rangers 4 at Detroit 2
22 Detroit 3 at Philadelphia 4
24 Pittsburgh 3 at Detroit 4
28 Vancouver 1 at Detroit 3 (afternoon game)
29 Detroit 6 at Islanders 2
31 Chicago 3 at Detroit 3 (5:00 OT)

April
12 Detroit 2 at Chicago 1
14 Detroit 7 at Minnesota 4 (Yzerman 19:19 en)

1992–1993

October
6 Detroit 1 at Winnipeg 4
8 Detroit 5 at Los Angeles 3 (Yzerman 18:57 en)
10 Detroit 6 at San Jose 3
15 Quebec 4 at Detroit 2
17 Edmonton 2 at Detroit 4
20 Winnipeg 3 at Detroit 5
22 Detroit 6 at Pittsburgh 9
24 Detroit 6 at St. Louis 1
25 Detroit 2 at Chicago 8
28 San Jose 3 at Detroit 4
30 Toronto 1 at Detroit 7
31 Detroit 1 at Toronto 3

November
4 Canadiens 4 at Detroit 3
6 Hartford 2 at Detroit 5
7 Detroit 1 at Canadiens 5
11 Detroit 4 at Tampa Bay 6 (Creighton 19:59 en)
13 Pittsburgh 0 at Detroit 8 [Cheveldae]
14 Detroit 2 at Hartford 0 [Cheveldae] (both goals in 3rd)
17 Chicago 4 at Detroit 5
19 Winnipeg 5 at Detroit 3
20 Detroit 7 at Washington 5 (Burr 19:18 en)
23 Tampa Bay 5 at Detroit 10
25 St. Louis 6 at Detroit 11
27 Los Angeles 5 at Detroit 3
28 Detroit 2 at St. Louis 2 (5:00 OT)
30 Washington 4 at Detroit 1

December
2 Detroit 3 at Rangers 5 (Turcotte 19:06 en)
3 Minnesota 4 at Detroit 2
5 Detroit 9 at Tampa Bay 7
8 Chicago 3 at Detroit 2
9 Detroit 3 at Toronto 5
11 Philadelphia 2 at Detroit 4
14 Calgary 3 at Detroit 0 [Vernon] (Stern 19:22 en)
15 Detroit 3 at Ottawa 2 (Fedorov 2:10 OT)
18 Boston 1 at Detroit 6
19 Detroit 3 at Minnesota 3 (5:00 OT)
22 Toronto 4 at Detroit 4 (5:00 OT)
26 Detroit 5 at Toronto 1
27 Detroit 4 at Chicago 0 [Cheveldae]

29 Chicago 6 at Detroit 3
31 Ottawa 4 at Detroit 5
(Kennedy :28 OT)

January
2 Detroit 6 at Quebec 2
4 Toronto 4 at Detroit 2
(Osborne 19:57 en)
8 Vancouver 3 at Detroit 6
11 St. Louis 1 at Detroit 0 [Hébert]
(Butcher 7:46 1st)
13 Tampa Bay 3 at Detroit 5
15 San Jose 3 at Detroit 6
17 Detroit 7 at Philadelphia 4
19 Rangers 2 at Detroit 2 (5:00 OT)
21 St. Louis 3 at Detroit 5
(Konstantinov 19:53 en)
23 Detroit 3 at St. Louis 4
26 Detroit 9 at Calgary 1
27 Detroit 2 at Edmonton 2 (5:00 OT)
30 Detroit 4 at Vancouver 4 (5:00 OT)

February
3 Chicago 0 at Detroit 5 [Cheveldae]
9 New Jersey 5 at Detroit 8
11 Detroit 6 at Los Angeles 6
(5:00 OT)
13 Detroit 3 at St. Louis 4
14 Detroit 5 at Chicago 3
17 Tampa Bay 1 at Detroit 3
(Yzerman 19:13 en)
19 Calgary 3 at Detroit 3 (5:00 OT)
21 Detroit 4 at Minnesota 1
(afternoon game)
(Racine 19:02 en)
22 Detroit 5 at Philadelphia 5 (5:00 OT)
(at Cleveland)
(Fedyk (P) tied game at 19:59)
24 Detroit 7 at Buffalo 10
27 Chicago 2 at Detroit 1
(afternoon game) (all goals in 1st)
28 Detroit 3 at New Jersey 6
(MacLean 19:00 en)

March
2 Detroit 2 at Islanders 3
5 Toronto 1 at Detroit 5
7 Detroit 7 at Minnesota 1
10 Detroit 6 at Edmonton 3
11 Detroit 3 at Calgary 6
14 Detroit 4 at San Jose 1
(afternoon game)
16 Washington 4 at Detroit 2
(Krygier 19:25 en)
18 Minnesota 1 at Detroit 5
20 Detroit 7 at Boston 4
(afternoon game)
21 Detroit 6 at Minnesota 2
23 Islanders 2 at Detroit 3
27 Detroit 8 at Tampa Bay 3
29 Los Angeles 9 at Detroit 3

April
1 Detroit 3 at Chicago 1
3 Vancouver 1 at Detroit 5
(afternoon game)
8 Detroit 9 at Tampa Bay 1
10 Buffalo 5 at Detroit 6
(afternoon game)
15 Minnesota 3 at Detroit 5

1993–1994

October
5 Detroit 4 at Dallas 6
8 Detroit 7 at Anaheim 2
9 Detroit 3 at Los Angeles 10
13 St. Louis 5 at Detroit 2
15 Detroit 3 at Toronto 6
(Gilmour 18:18 en)
16 Toronto 2 at Detroit 1
18 Detroit 6 at Buffalo 4
21 Winnipeg 2 at Detroit 6
23 Detroit 2 at Chicago 4
25 Dallas 5 at Detroit 3
27 Los Angeles 3 at Detroit 8
30 Detroit 5 at Quebec 3
(Drake 19:01 en)

November
2 Boston 1 at Detroit 6
(Coffey 3:30 2nd en — with the Boston goalie John Blue on the bench in favour of an extra attacker on a delayed penalty call, the Bruins' Josef Stumpel took the puck near the Detroit goal and passed back to the point. No one was there, and the puck went into the Bruins' net. Coffey, the nearest Wing, got credit for the goal)
4 Toronto 3 at Detroit 3 (5:00 OT)
9 Edmonton 4 at Detroit 2
13 Detroit 7 at Pittsburgh 3
17 Detroit 1 at Winnipeg 2
20 Detroit 4 at New Jersey 3
(Kozlov :29 OT)
21 Detroit 2 at St. Louis 2 (5:00 OT)
23 Detroit 4 at San Jose 6
(Ozolinsh 19:12 en)
24 Detroit 5 at Vancouver 4 (OT)
(Fedorov 1:18 OT)
27 Dallas 4 at Detroit 10

	28	Detroit 4 at Islanders 1 (Burr 18:42 en)
December	1	Detroit 3 at Hartford 5
	3	Ottawa 1 at Detroit 8
	5	Detroit 4 at Winnipeg 6 (Tkachuk 19:42 en)
	6	Winnipeg 2 at Detroit 6
	9	St. Louis 2 at Detroit 3
	11	San Jose 3 at Detroit 5
	14	Anaheim 2 at Detroit 5
	17	Rangers 4 at Detroit 6 (Sheppard 19:35 en)
	18	Detroit 1 at Canadiens 8
	21	Chicago 1 at Detroit 5 (all goals in 1st)
	23	Detroit 3 at Philadelphia 1 (Sillinger 19:40 en)
	27	Detroit 6 at Dallas 0 [Cheveldae]
	31	Los Angeles 4 at Detroit 4 (5:00 OT)
January	4	Detroit 4 at St. Louis 4 (5:00 OT)
	6	Detroit 10 at San Jose 3
	8	Detroit 6 at Los Angeles 3
	10	Detroit 6 at Anaheim 4 (Williams 19:50 en)
	12	Tampa Bay 4 at Detroit 2 (Savard 18:59 en)
	14	Dallas 3 at Detroit 9
	15	Detroit 3 at Boston 2
	17	Detroit 6 at Tampa Bay 3
	19	Anaheim 4 at Detroit 4 (5:00 OT)
	25	Chicago 5 at Detroit 0 [Belfour]
	27	Detroit 4 at Chicago 3 (Sheppard :51 OT)
	29	Winnipeg 1 at Detroit 7
	30	Detroit 3 at Washington 6
February	2	Detroit 3 at Tampa Bay 1
	4	Pittsburgh 6 at Detroit 3
	5	Detroit 4 at Toronto 3
	8	Vancouver 6 at Detroit 3
	11	Philadelphia 3 at Detroit 6
	12	Detroit 5 at St. Louis 4 (McCarty 3:16 OT)
	15	Detroit 4 at Toronto 5 (Yzerman (D) tied game at 19:52) (Clark 2:55 OT)
	16	Florida 3 at Detroit 7
	18	Edmonton 1 at Detroit 5
	20	Detroit 4 at Florida 3 (Fedorov 4:27 OT)
	23	New Jersey 7 at Detroit 2
	24	Hartford 0 at Detroit 3 [Osgood]
	26	San Jose 0 at Detroit 2 [Osgood]
March	1	Calgary 2 at Detroit 5
	4	Toronto 6 at Detroit 5 (Clark :53 OT)
	6	Buffalo 3 at Detroit 2
	7	Detroit 6 at Rangers 3
	9	Detroit 5 at Calgary 1
	11	Detroit 2 at Edmonton 4 (Olausson 19:55 en)
	15	Vancouver 2 at Detroit 5 (Fedorov 18:50 en / Sheppard 19:12 en)
	17	Islanders 3 at Detroit 1 (King 18:56 en)
	19	Detroit 2 at Winnipeg 4
	22	Chicago 1 at Detroit 3
	23	Detroit 4 at Ottawa 5
	25	Washington 2 at Detroit 2 (5:00 OT)
	27	Detroit 3 at Chicago 1
	29	Hartford 2 at Detroit 6
	31	Quebec 4 at Detroit 2 (Sakic 19:55 en) (all goals in 3rd)
April	2	Calgary 3 at Detroit 3 (5:00 OT)
	3	St. Louis 3 at Detroit 3 (5:00 OT)
	5	Detroit 8 at Vancouver 3
	9	Detroit 2 at Calgary 4
	10	Detroit 3 at Edmonton 4
	13	Canadiens 0 at Detroit 9 [Essensa]
	14	Detroit 3 at Dallas 4

1994–1995

January	20	Chicago 1 at Detroit 4
	22	Calgary 4 at Detroit 1
	24	Vancouver 3 at Detroit 6
	26	Calgary 1 at Detroit 5
	28	Edmonton 2 at Detroit 5 (Yzerman 19:15 en)
	30	Detroit 4 at Edmonton 2
February	1	Detroit 1 at Calgary 2
	3	Detroit 5 at Anaheim 2
	4	Detroit 3 at Los Angeles 4
	7	San Jose 0 at Detroit 6 [Osgood]
	10	Toronto 2 at Detroit 1
	12	Los Angeles 4 at Detroit 4 (5:00 OT)
	15	Detroit 5 at Winnipeg 1
	17	Edmonton 2 at Detroit 4
	20	Detroit 4 at Toronto 2 (Ciccarelli 19:20 en)

22 Toronto 1 at Detroit 4 (Johnson 19:38 en)
23 Detroit 4 at Chicago 2 (Ciccarelli 19:47 en)
25 St. Louis 3 at Detroit 2

March
2 Winnipeg 1 at Detroit 6
5 Detroit 2 at Edmonton 4
6 Detroit 5 at Vancouver 2 (Yzerman 19:30 en)
9 Detroit 4 at Anaheim 4 (5:00 OT)
12 Detroit 2 at St. Louis 1
14 Los Angeles 2 at Detroit 5
16 Dallas 4 at Detroit 5
17 Vancouver 1 at Detroit 3
22 Winnipeg 3 at Detroit 6 (Primeau 19:29 en)
24 Detroit 2 at Calgary 3
25 Detroit 2 at Vancouver 1
28 Anaheim 4 at Detroit 6
30 Dallas 2 at Detroit 3

April
1 Detroit 3 at Dallas 2
2 St. Louis 3 at Detroit 3 (5:00 OT)
5 Detroit 5 at San Jose 3 (Errey 19:42 en)
7 Detroit 4 at Toronto 2
9 Detroit 4 at Chicago 1
11 Detroit 4 at Dallas 1
13 San Jose 0 at Detroit 3 [Vernon]
14 Detroit 3 at Chicago 1 (Sheppard 19:10 en)
16 Detroit 5 at St. Louis 6
19 Winnipeg 5 at Detroit 5 (5:00 OT)
21 Anaheim 5 at Detroit 6
23 Detroit 5 at San Jose 1
25 Detroit 1 at Los Angeles 5
27 Detroit 3 at Winnipeg 4
29 Dallas 2 at Detroit 4 (Ciccarelli 19:26 en)
30 Chicago 4 at Detroit 0 [Belfour]

May
3 Detroit 3 at St. Louis 2

1995–1996

October
6 Detroit 2 at Colorado 3
8 Detroit 3 at Edmonton 1
9 Detroit 5 at Vancouver 3
13 Edmonton 0 at Detroit 9 [Osgood]
15 Detroit 5 at Winnipeg 5 (5:00 OT)
17 Calgary 3 at Detroit 3 (5:00 OT)
19 Detroit 2 at New Jersey 4
21 Boston 2 at Detroit 4 (Primeau 19:23 en) (afternoon game)
24 Ottawa 2 at Detroit 1
27 Detroit 3 at Calgary 0 [Osgood]
30 Detroit 2 at Winnipeg 3

November
1 Detroit 1 at Buffalo 2
2 Detroit 6 at Boston 5 (Yzerman 1:50 OT)
4 Dallas 1 at Detroit 5 (afternoon game)
7 Edmonton 2 at Detroit 4 (Yzerman 19:08 en)
11 Detroit 5 at San Jose 2
14 Detroit 6 at Los Angeles 5
17 Detroit 5 at Edmonton 4 (Yzerman won game at 19:47)
22 San Jose 2 at Detroit 5
24 Detroit 1 at Flyers 4 (Lindros 19:33 en) (afternoon game)
25 Rangers 0 at Detroit 2 [Osgood] (both goals in 1st)
28 Canadiens 2 at Detroit 3

December
1 Anaheim 2 at Detroit 5
2 Detroit 11 at Canadiens 1 (Roy's last game in Montreal)
5 Flyers 3 at Detroit 5 (Fedorov 18:52 en)
7 Dallas 1 at Detroit 3 (Fedorov 18:58 en)
8 Detroit 1 at Rangers 2 (Verbeek :27 OT)
12 Detroit 5 at St. Louis 2
13 Chicago 1 at Detroit 3
15 New Jersey 1 at Detroit 3 (Errey 19:56 en)
20 Detroit 6 at Anaheim 1
22 Detroit 5 at Calgary 1
23 Detroit 1 at Vancouver 0 [Vernon] (Fedorov 2:45 3rd)
26 St. Louis 2 at Detroit 3
29 Detroit 2 at Dallas 1 (Taylor won game at 19:33)
31 Hartford 2 at Detroit 3

January
3 Dallas 3 at Detroit 3 (5:00 OT)
5 Detroit 2 at Pittsburgh 5
6 Chicago 0 at Detroit 3 [Hodson]
8 Winnipeg 6 at Detroit 4
10 Detroit 4 at Dallas 0 [Osgood]
12 Los Angeles 2 at Detroit 3

13 Detroit 4 at Washington 2
17 Colorado 2 at Detroit 3
24 San Jose 2 at Detroit 4
25 Detroit 4 at Ottawa 2
27 Detroit 5 at Chicago 5 (5:00 OT) (Lidstrom (d) ties game at 19:43) (afternoon game)
30 Toronto 2 at Detroit 4 (Yzerman 18:59 en)

February
3 Pittsburgh 0 at Detroit 3 [Osgood] (Fetisov 19:10 en) (afternoon game)
6 Florida 2 at Detroit 4
8 Detroit 1 at Florida 3
10 Detroit 3 at Tampa Bay 2 (Fedorov :52 OT)
13 Los Angeles 4 at Detroit 9
15 Washington 3 at Detroit 4
16 Detroit 3 at St. Louis 4 (Matteau won game at 19:04)
18 Detroit 3 at Toronto 2 (afternoon game)
19 Vancouver 3 at Detroit 4
22 Toronto 3 at Detroit 5
24 Tampa Bay 0 at Detroit 2 [Vernon] (Errey 19:21 en) (both goals in 3rd)
27 Detroit 6 at Islanders 2
29 Islanders 1 at Detroit 5

March
2 Vancouver 3 at Detroit 2 (afternoon game)
3 Detroit 6 at Chicago 2
6 Detroit 4 at Hartford 2 (Osgood 19:49 en)
8 Detroit 4 at Colorado 2 (Ciccarelli 19:42 en)
10 Detroit 5 at Winnipeg 2
12 Winnipeg 2 at Detroit 5
17 Calgary 2 at Detroit 4 (afternoon game)
19 Toronto 5 at Detroit 6
20 Detroit 4 at Toronto 3 (McCarty 2:41 OT)
22 Colorado 0 at Detroit 7 [Vernon]
24 Detroit 2 at St. Louis 2 (5:00 OT)
25 Anaheim 1 at Detroit 5
27 Buffalo 2 at Detroit 4
31 St. Louis 1 at Detroit 8 (afternoon game)

April
2 Detroit 3 at San Jose 6 (Baker 19:37 en)
3 Detroit 2 at Los Angeles 2 (5:00 OT)
5 Detroit 2 at Anaheim 2 (5:00 OT)
7 Detroit 4 at Chicago 1 (afternoon game)
10 Winnipeg 2 at Detroit 5 (Brown 19:09 en)
12 Chicago 3 at Detroit 5 (Draper 19:15 en)
14 Detroit 5 at Dallas 1 (afternoon game)

1995-1996 SUMMARY
REGULAR SEASON

MOST GAMES PLAYED
(full season)

Vyacheslav Kozlov 82

GOALS

Player	Goals
Fedorov	39
Kozlov	36
Yzerman	36
Primeau	27
Ciccarelli	22
Larionov	21
G. Johnson	18
Lidstrom	17
McCarty	15
Coffey	14
Konstantinov	14
D. Brown	12
Errey	11
T. Taylor	11
Draper	7
Fetisov	7
Lapointe	6
Dandenault	5
Ramsey	2
Sheppard	2
Bergevin	1
Maltby	1
Osgood	1
Total	325

ASSISTS

Player	Assists
Fedorov	68
Coffey	60
Yzerman	59
Larionov	50
Lidstrom	50
Kozlov	37
Fetisov	35
Primeau	25
G. Johnson	22
Ciccarelli	21
Errey	21
Konstantinov	20
D. Brown	15
McCarty	14
T. Taylor	14
Bergevin	9
Draper	9
Dandenault	7
Rouse	6
Ramsey	4
Lapointe	3
Osgood	2
Sheppard	2
Grimson	1
Pushor	1

POINTS

Player	Points
Fedorov	107
Yzerman	95
Coffey	74
Kozlov	73
Larionov	71
Lidstrom	67
Primeau	52
Ciccarelli	43
Fetisov	42
G. Johnson	40
Konstantinov	34
Errey	32
McCarty	29
D. Brown	27
T. Taylor	25
Draper	16
Dandenault	12
Bergevin	10
Lapointe	9
Ramsey	6
Rouse	6
Sheppard	4
Osgood	3
Grimson	1
Maltby	1
Pushor	1

PIMS

Player	PIMs
Primeau	168
McCarty	158
Konstantinov	139
Grimson	128
Ciccarelli	99
Fetisov	96
Lapointe	93
Coffey	90
Kozlov	70
Errey	66
Yzerman	64
Fedorov	48
Rouse	48
T. Taylor	39
Ramsey	35
Larionov	34
Bergevin	33
Draper	32
G. Johnson	30
Lidstrom	20
Pushor	17
Dandenault	6
Maltby	6
D. Brown	4
Osgood	4
Eriksson	2
Sheppard	2
Vernon	2
bench minors	18
Total	1551

POWER-PLAY GOALS

Player	Goals
Yzerman	16
Ciccarelli	13
Fedorov	11
Kozlov	9
Larionov	9
Lidstrom	8
McCarty	8
Primeau	6
G. Johnson	5
Coffey	3
Konstantinov	3
Errey	2
Dandenault	1
Fetisov	1
Lapointe	1
T. Taylor	1

SHORT-HANDED GOALS

Player	Goals
Fedorov	3
Errey	2
Primeau	2
Yzerman	2
D. Brown	1
Coffey	1
Draper	1
Fetisov	1
Konstantinov	1
Larionov	1
Lidstrom	1
T. Taylor	1
Fetisov	1
Lidstrom	1
Sheppard	1
McCarty	1

GAME-WINNING GOALS

Player	Goals
Fedorov	11
Yzerman	8
Kozlov	7
Primeau	7
Ciccarelli	5
Larionov	5
T. Taylor	4
Coffey	3
Konstantinov	3
Errey	2
G. Johnson	2
D. Brown	1

Total goals: 97
Total chances: 455
Power-play efficiency: 21.3 % (3rd)

Power-play goals allowed: 44
Power-play chances against: 375
Penalty-killing efficiency: 88.3 % (1st)

GOALIES

	G	W-L-T	MINS	GA	SO	AVG
Kevin Hodson	4	2–0–0	163	3	1	1.10
Chris Osgood	50	39–6–5	2933	106	5	2.17
Mike Vernon	32	21–7–2	1855	70	3	2.26

GOALIE NOTES:

1. Osgood replaced Vernon (no goals) at :43 of 2nd, December 29, 1995
2. Hodson replaced Osgood (4 goals) at 11:58 of 2nd, January 5, 1996
3. Osgood replaced Hodson (no goals) at 15:14 of 1st, January 24, 1996
4. Osgood replaced Vernon (3 goals) at 8:25 of 2nd, April 12, 1996

PLAYOFFS

GOALS	
Yzerman	8
Ciccarelli	6
Larionov	6
Coffey	5
Kozlov	5
Lidstrom	5
Draper	4
Konstantinov	4
D. Brown	3
G. Johnson	3
McCarty	3
Fedorov	2
Bergevin	1
Fetisov	1
Lapointe	1
Primeau	1

ASSISTS	
Fedorov	18
Yzerman	12
Coffey	9
Lidstrom	9
Kozlov	7
Larionov	7
Konstantinov	5
Errey	4
Fetisov	4
Primeau	4
Ramsey	4
T. Taylor	4
D. Brown	3
Ciccarelli	2
Draper	2
Lapointe	2
McCarty	2
G. Johnson	1
Maltby	1
Rouse	1

POINTS	
Yzerman	20
Fedorov	20
Coffey	14
Lidstrom	14
Larionov	13
Kozlov	12
Konstantinov	9
Ciccarelli	8
Draper	6
D. Brown	6
McCarty	5
Primeau	5
Fetisov	5
G. Johnson	4
Errey	4
Ramsey	4
T. Taylor	4
Lapointe	3
Bergevin	1
Rouse	1
Maltby	1

PIMS	
Fetisov	34
Coffey	30
Konstantinov	28
Primeau	28
Ciccarelli	26
McCarty	20
Draper	18
Bergevin	14
Lapointe	12
Fedorov	10
Kozlov	10
Lidstrom	10
Ramsey	10
Errey	8
G. Johnson	8
Larionov	6
D. Brown	4
Maltby	4
Osgood	4
Rouse	4
T. Taylor	4
Yzerman	4
Vernon	2

POWER-PLAY GOALS	
Ciccarelli	6
Yzerman	4
Coffey	3
Larionov	3
Kozlov	2
Bergevin	1
Lidstrom	1

SHORT-HANDED GOALS	
Coffey	2
D. Brown	1
Draper	1
Konstantinov	1
Coffey	1
Kozlov	1
McCarty	1

GAME-WINNING GOALS	
Fedorov	2
Larionov	2
Ciccarelli	1
Fetisov	1
Yzerman	1

Total goals: 20
Total chances: 112
Power-play efficiency: 17.9 % (7th)

Power-play goals allowed: 13
Power-play chances against: 89
Penalty-killing efficiency: 85.4 % (4th)

GOALIES

	G	W-L	MINS	GA	SO	AVG
Chris Osgood	15	8–7	936	33	2	2.12
Mike Vernon	4	2–2	243	11	0	2.72

ON THE FARM — THE ADIRONDACK RED WINGS: 1995–1996 FINAL STATISTICS

NAME	GP	G	A	P	PIM
Dave Chyzowski	80	44	39	83	160
Wes Walz*	38	20	35	55	58
Stacy Roest	76	16	39	55	40
Ben Hankinson	75	25	21	46	210
Mike Knuble	80	22	23	45	59
Anders Eriksson*	75	6	36	42	64
Kurt Miller	73	26	13	39	46
Jeff Bloemberg	72	10	28	38	32
Scott Hollis	55	18	19	37	111
Ryan Duthie	52	16	21	37	36
Mark Ouimet	59	16	16	32	20
Mark Major	78	10	19	29	234
Sylvain Cloutier	65	11	17	28	118
Jason MacDonald	43	9	13	22	99
Yan Golubovsky	71	5	16	21	97
Jamie Pushor*	65	2	16	18	126
Brandon Smith	48	4	13	17	22
Mike Needham	16	5	10	15	12
Aaron Ward	74	5	10	15	133
Kerry Toporowski	53	1	5	6	283
Bob Essensa	3	0	1	1	0
Kevin Hodson*	32	0	1	1	21
Paul Koch	3	0	1	1	0
Norm Maracle	54	0	1	1	4
Todd Wetzel	3	0	1	1	2
Mathieu Dandenault*	4	0	0	0	0
Curt Bowen	3	0	0	0	0
Bob Bell	1	0	0	0	0
Rob Laurie	1	0	0	0	0

* also played with Detroit

GOALTENDERS

	G	W-L	MINS	GA	SO	AVG
Bob Bell	1	0–0–0	30	1	0	2.00
Rob Laurie	1	0–1–0	23	1	0	2.64
Norm Maracle	54	24–18–6	2949	135	2	2.75
Kevin Hodson	32	13–13–2	1654	87	0	3.16
Bob Essensa	3	1–2–0	179	11	0	3.69

PLAYOFFS

NAME	GP	G	A	P	PIM
Ryan Duthie	3	1	0	1	2
Mike Knuble	3	1	0	1	0
Jeff Bloemberg	3	0	1	1	4
Scott Hollis	3	0	1	1	4
Brandon Smith	3	0	1	1	2
Mark Major	3	0	0	0	21
Ben Hankinson	3	0	0	0	8
Dave Chyzowski	3	0	0	0	6
Aaron Ward	3	0	0	0	6
Sylvain Cloutier	3	0	0	0	4
Jamie Pushor	3	0	0	0	5
Yan Golubovsky	3	0	0	0	2
Mark Ouimet	3	0	0	0	2
Stacy Roest	3	0	0	0	2
Anders Eriksson	3	0	0	0	0
Kurt Miller	3	0	0	0	0
Kevin Hodson	3	0	0	0	0
Norm Maracle	1	0	0	0	0

GOALTENDERS

	G	W-L	MINS	GA	SO	AVG
Kevin Hodson	3	0–2	150	8	0	3.21
Norm Maracle	1	0–1	30	4	0	8.00

1996–1997 SCHEDULE

October	5	at New Jersey
	9	vs. Edmonton
	11	vs. Calgary
	12	at Buffalo
	15	at Dallas
	17	at Chicago
	19	vs. Islanders
	21	vs. Los Angeles
	23	vs. Dallas
	25	vs. Chicago
	26	at Boston
	30	vs. Montreal
November	1	at Ottawa
	2	at Toronto
	4	vs. Hartford
	6	vs. New Jersey
	8	at Hartford
	10	vs. Tampa Bay
	13	vs. Colorado
	15	vs. San Jose
	18	at Phoenix
	21	at San Jose
	23	at Los Angeles
	24	at Anaheim
	27	vs. Toronto
December	1	vs. Florida
	3	vs. Vancouver
	4	at Washington
	10	vs. Edmonton
	12	vs. Chicago
	15	vs. Toronto
	17	at Colorado
	18	at Calgary
	20	at Vancouver
	22	at Edmonton
	26	vs. Washington
	28	at Islanders
	30	vs. Phoenix
January	3	vs. Dallas
	5	at Chicago
	8	at Dallas
	9	at Phoenix
	11	vs. Chicago
	14	vs. Los Angeles
	20	at Montreal
	22	vs. Flyers
	25	at Flyers
	29	vs. Phoenix
February	1	at St. Louis
	2	vs. Dallas
	4	vs. St. Louis
	6	vs. Vancouver
	8	at Pittsburgh
	12	vs. San Jose
	14	vs. Dallas
	16	at Florida
	17	at Tampa Bay
	19	vs. Calgary
	22	at St. Louis
	24	at Phoenix
	27	vs. Pittsburgh
March	1	vs. Rangers
	2	vs. Anaheim
	5	at Toronto
	8	at Vancouver
	10	at Los Angeles
	12	at Anaheim
	15	at San Jose
	16	at Colorado
	19	vs. Boston
	21	at Rangers
	23	at Chicago
	26	vs. Colorado
	28	vs. Buffalo
	30	vs. Anaheim
April	1	vs. St. Louis
	3	vs. Toronto
	5	at Toronto
	8	at Calgary
	9	at Edmonton
	11	vs. Ottawa
	13	vs. St. Louis

APPROACHING MILESTONES

AS A RED WING

1000 games	Steve Yzerman (942)
500 games	Sergei Fedorov (432)
400 games	Vladimir Konstantinov (369) Nicklas Lidstrom (372)
1300 points	Steve Yzerman (1255)
600 points	Sergei Fedorov (529)
300 points	Nicklas Lidstrom (250)
250 goals	Sergei Fedorov (212)
100 goals	Vyacheslav Kozlov (87)
800 assists	Steve Yzerman (738)
100 assists	Vladimir Konstantinov (95) Vyacheslav Kozlov (99)
115 wins	Chris Osgood (76 — to tie with Stefan for 6th on All-Time Red Wings list)

CAREER

900 games	Bob Rouse (824)
800 games	Bob Errey (758)
700 games	Brendan Shanahan (632)
500 games	Viacheslav Fetisov (424)
400 games	Igor Larionov (376)
600 points	Brendan Shanahan (598)
200 points	Viacheslav Fetisov (186)
300 goals	Brendan Shanahan (288)
300 wins	Mike Vernon (288)

Sectional Plan *of* Olympia

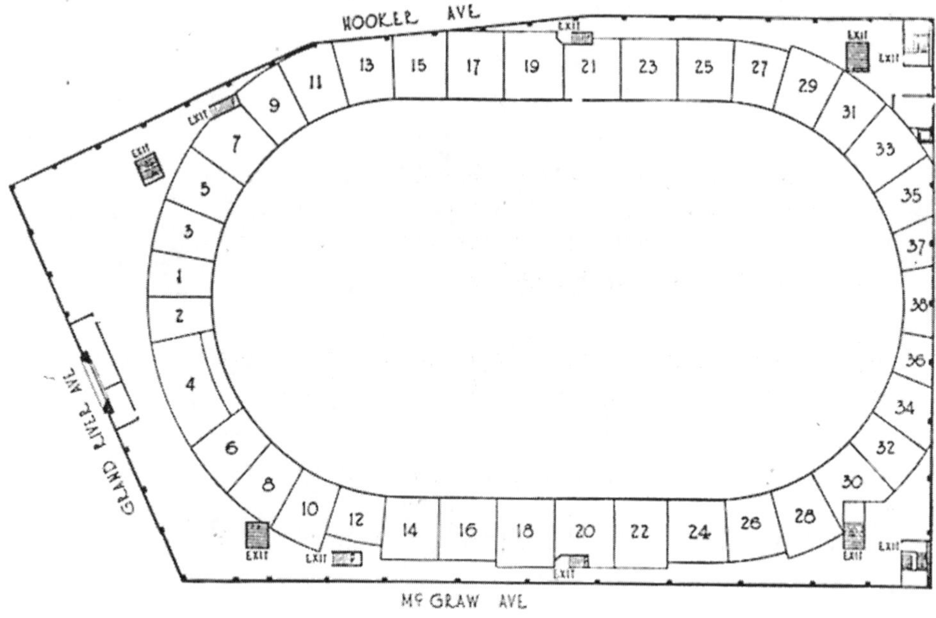

BALCONY

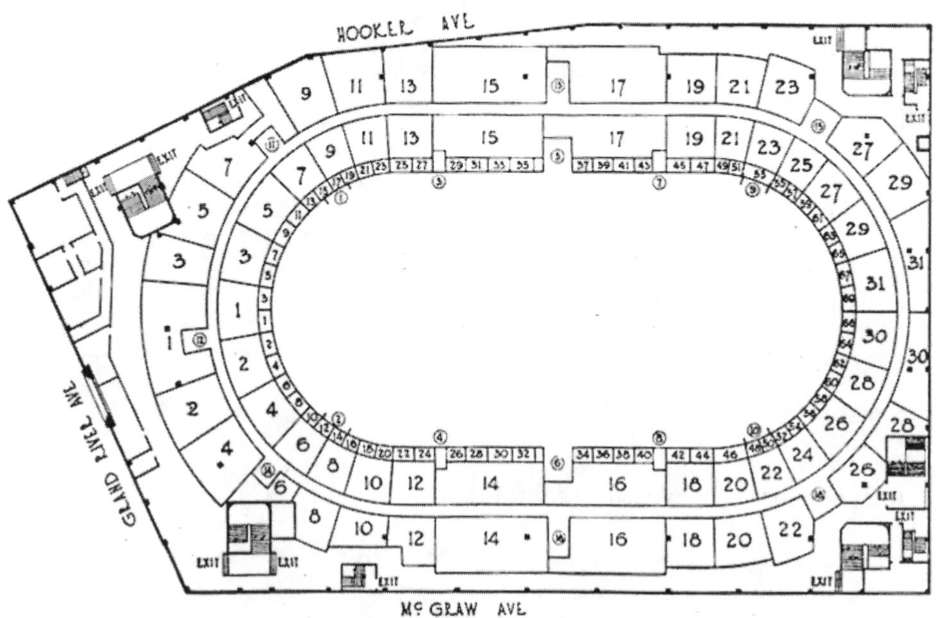

MAIN FLOOR